DICTIONARY OF

Developmental Disabilities Terminology

DICTIONARY OF

Developmental Disabilities Terminology

3rd EDITION

edited by

Pasquale J. Accardo, M.D.

and

Barbara Y. Whitman, M.S.W., Ph.D.

with

Jennifer A. Accardo, M.D.
Joann N. Bodurtha, M.D., M.P.H.
Anne Farrell, Ph.D.
Toni Goelz, PT
Jill Morrow-Gorton, M.D.
Gale B. Rice, Ph.D.
Ginger Smith, M.Ed.

Illustrations by Tony Stubblefield

·P A U L·H·
BROOKES
PUBLISHING C°®

Baltimore • London • Sydney

·P A U L·H·
BROOKES
PUBLISHING Cᵒ.®

Paul H. Brookes Publishing Co.
Post Office Box 10624
Baltimore, Maryland 21285-0624
USA

www.brookespublishing.com

Typeset by Aptara, Inc., Falls Church, Virginia.
Manufactured in the United States of America by
Versa Press, Inc., East Peoria, Illinois.

Library of Congress Cataloging-in-Publication Data

Dictionary of developmental disabilities terminology / edited by Pasquale J. Accardo and Barbara Y. Whitman ; with Jennifer A. Accardo . . . [et al.] ; illustrations by Tony Stubblefield. — 3rd ed.
   p. ;   cm.
   Includes bibliographical references.
   ISBN-13: 978-1-59857-070-0 (pbk.)
   ISBN-10: 1-59857-070-6 (pbk.)
   1. Child development deviations—Dictionaries. 2. Developmental disabilities—Dictionaries.
  I. Accardo, Pasquale J. II. Whitman, Barbara Y. III. Title.
  [DNLM: 1. Developmental Disabilities—Dictionary—English. WS 13]
RJ135.A26 2011
618.92'85889003—dc22
                    2010043389

British Library Cataloguing in Publication data are available from the British Library.

2015   2014   2013   2012   2011
10   9   8   7   6   5   4   3   2   1

Contents

Illustrations

Illustrations are listed according to the term they accompany, followed by their page location in the text.

About the Editors

Pasquale J. Accardo, M.D., Director, Children's Hospital of Richmond Child Development Clinic, 3600 West Broad Street, Suite 229, Richmond, Virginia 23230

Dr. Accardo is James H. Franklin Professor of Developmental Research in Pediatrics at Virginia Commonwealth University and directs the Children's Hospital of Richmond Child Development Clinic in Richmond, Virginia. He completed his pediatric residency at the James Whitcomb Riley Hospital for Children in Indianapolis, Indiana, and his neurodevelopmental disabilities fellowship at the John F. Kennedy Institute (now the Kennedy Krieger Institute) at the Johns Hopkins University School of Medicine in Baltimore, Maryland. He is specialized in pediatrics and has subspecialty certifications in both developmental and behavioral pediatrics and neurodevelopmental disabilities in pediatrics. He previously served as Medical Director of the Knights of Columbus Developmental Center in St. Louis, Missouri, and as Director of Maternal and Child Health Bureau for Leadership Education in Neurodevelopmental Disabilities (LEND) at the Westchester Institute for Human Development in Valhalla, New York. Dr. Accardo is the author or editor of more than 200 publications in the field of neurodevelopmental disabilities. His recent books include *Neurogenetic Syndromes: Behavioral Issues and Their Treatment* (Paul H. Brookes Publishing Co., 2009); *Autism Frontiers: Clinical Issues and Innovations* (Paul H. Brookes Publishing Co., 2008); and *Capute & Accardo's Neurodevelopmental Disabilities in Infancy and Childhood, Third Edition* (Paul H. Brookes Publishing Co., 2008).

Barbara Y. Whitman, M.S.W., Ph.D., Professor of Pediatrics, St. Louis University School of Medicine, 1465 South Grand Street, St. Louis, Missouri 63104

Dr. Whitman is Professor of Pediatrics at St. Louis University School of Medicine. She obtained her master of social work and doctoral degrees at Washington University in St. Louis and completed a postdoctoral fellowship in psychiatric epidemiology at Washington University School of Medicine. She completed additional postdoctoral training in family therapy at the Menninger Clinic, Topeka, Kansas. Dr. Whitman has published extensively in the areas of parents with intellectual disabilities, Prader-Willi syndrome, and attention-deficit/hyperactivity disorders. Her publications include *Management of Prader-Willi Syndrome, Third Edition* (Springer, 2006, with Butler and Lee); *Attention Deficits and Hyperactivity in Children and Adults: Diagnosis, Treatment, Management, Second Edition, Revised and Expanded* (Marcel Dekker, 1999); *Child Maltreatment: A Clinical Guide and Reference, Second Edition* (G.W. Medical Publishing, 1998); *Recognition of Child Abuse for the Mandated Reporter, Second Edition* (G.W. Medical Publishing, 1996); and *When a Parent Is Mentally Retarded* (Paul H. Brookes Publishing Co., 1990).

WITH

Jennifer A. Accardo, M.D., Assistant Professor of Neurology and Psychiatry at the Johns Hopkins University School of Medicine, Director, Kennedy Krieger Institute Sleep Disorders Clinic and Laboratory, 801 North Broadway, Baltimore, Maryland 21205

Dr. Accardo is a member of the faculty at the Kennedy Krieger Institute in Baltimore, Maryland. She received her medical degree from St. Louis University School of Medicine in St. Louis, Missouri. She obtained initial pediatrics training at Cook County Children's Hospital in Chicago; completed neurodevelopmental disabilities training at the Kennedy Krieger Institute; and went on to sleep medicine fellowship training at the Children's Hospital of Philadelphia and the University of Pennsylvania in Philadelphia, Pennsylvania. Dr. Accardo's research and clinical interests focus on sleep problems in children with developmental disabilities.

Joannn N. Bodurtha, M.D., M.P.H., Professor of Human and Molecular Genetics, Pediatrics, Obstetrics-Gynecology, and Epidemiology and Community Health, Virginia Commonwealth University, Box 980033, Richmond, Virginia 23298

Dr. Bodurtha has worked with children and families with genetic conditions for more than 25 years. She directs the Interdisciplinary Leadership Program in Neurodevelopmental Disabilities at Virginia Commonwealth University and is medical director of the genetic counseling program. She received the Genetic Alliance Art of Listening Award in 2008 and the Association of University Centers on Disabilities professional achievement award in 2010. She has authored more than 100 papers, received grant funding from National Institutes of Heath, Maternal Child Health Bureau, Centers for Disease Control and Prevention, March of Dimes, and other organizations, and has mentored more than 100 graduate trainees.

Anne Farrell, Ph.D., Associate Professor, Human Development and Family Studies, University of Connecticut, One University Place, Stamford, Connecticut 06901

Dr. Farrell is a Clinical and School Psychologist and Associate Professor of Human Development and Family Studies (HDFS) at the University of Connecticut. She obtained her B.A. in psychology at Fairfield University in Connecticut and her M.A. and doctoral degrees at Hofstra University in New York. In her former position at the Westchester Institute for Human Development, University Centers for Excellence in Developmental Disabilities Education, Research, and Service (UCEDD), she directed assessment and intervention teams for children with special health care needs. She currently serves as core faculty for the A.J. Pappanikou Center, the Connecticut UCEDD. Dr. Farrell's research is translational in focus and addresses family-centered practices, positive behavioral interventions and supports (PBISs), and interventions for vulnerable populations. She serves as a consulting editor for *Early Childhood Research Quarterly,* coauthored *Positive Strategies for Students with Behavior Problems* (a book on individualized PBIS in schools; Paul H. Brookes Publishing Co., 2007), and provides program evaluation, community training, and technical assistance on disability policies and practices, child welfare, and PBIS. She teaches in the undergraduate and graduate HDFS programs at the University of Connecticut.

Toni Goelz, PT, St. Louis Children's Hospital, #1 Children's Place, St. Louis, Missouri 63110

Toni Goelz graduated from St. Louis University's physical therapy program in 1978. She worked at Cardinal Glennon Children's Hospital for 28 years. She is currently employed at St. Louis Children's Hospital as a member of the neurorehabilitation team.

Jill Morrow-Gorton, M.D., Medical Director, Office of Developmental Programs, Commonwealth of Pennsylvania, Harrisburg, Pennsylvania 17120

Dr. Morrow-Gorton is the Medical Director for the Office of Developmental Programs for the Commonwealth of Pennsylvania. She completed medical school at the University of Pennsylvania and pediatric training at Tufts New England Medical Center, Boston. She completed a fellowship in developmental pediatrics at St. Louis University and M.B.A. training at Lebanon Valley College. She holds board certification in pediatrics and developmental and behavioral pediatrics. Her experience includes providing developmental and rehabilitative services teaching in an academic medical center, consultation to early intervention programs, and managing a developmental evaluation center. She participates in many national-level committees related to health and quality issues for people with developmental disabilities and has authored articles and chapters related to the health and public health of this population.

Gale B. Rice, Ph.D., Professor and Chair, Department of Communication Disorders and Deaf Education, Fontbonne University, 6800 Wydown Boulevard, St. Louis, Missouri 63105

Dr. Rice is professor and chair of the Department of Communication Disorders and Deaf Education at Fontbonne University in St. Louis. Her bachelor's and master's degrees were in speech-language pathology and her doctoral work was in education with an emphasis in language and literacy. Dr. Rice's additional research and clinical interests include augmentative and alternative communication and craniofacial anomalies.

Ginger Smith, M.Ed., Educational Consultant, Children's Hospital of Richmond Child Development Clinic, 3600 West Broad Street, Suite 229, Richmond, Virginia 23230

Ginger Smith is Educational Consultant in the Children's Hospital of Richmond Child Development Clinic in Richmond, Virginia. As a former general and special education teacher, diagnostician, and educational specialist in a large school system, she has provided training for teachers and parents on various topics related to special education. She has conducted workshops on parenting the child with attention-deficit/hyperactivity disorder; special education rules and regulations; administration, scoring, and interpretation of educational assessments; collaborative teaching; homework; individualized education programs (IEPs); and educational strategies. Smith coauthored the article "Tips for a Successful IEP Meeting: Parents Bring a Plan" (ACEI, 2007). She has worked as an educational consultant with Dr. Pasquale Accardo since 2004.

Preface

*DICTIONARY, n. A malevolent literary device for cramping the growth of a language and making it hard and inelastic. This **dictionary**, however, is a most useful work.*
—Ambrose Bierce

***Words**—so innocent and powerless as they are, as standing in a **dictionary**, how potent for good and evil they become in the hands of one who knows how to combine them.*
—Nathaniel Hawthorne

*He has never been known to use a word that might send a reader to the **dictionary**.*
—William Faulkner

Two previous editions of this dictionary established the tradition of framing the Preface with a series of quotes. This third edition continues that tradition. It has been 9 years since the second edition of this dictionary was published. In those 9 years we have added many new words or new word meanings to our daily lexicon: *texting, Twitter, Facebook, blogging, wiki,* and a historical benchmark that is verbally denoted as *nine-eleven*. Few reading this paragraph would need to scurry to a dictionary to determine the meaning of these terms. And, most would accept that the meaning of each goes far beyond the descriptive definition; that is, the term *texting* implies far more than the simple act of sending a verbal text message via cell phone technology. Similarly, *nine-eleven* connotes far more than the fact that four planes perpetrated terrorist acts on September 11, 2001.

So too, does our daily "disabilities" lexicon grow, shift, and alter, necessitating this third edition. In this edition, we have added many new terms, strengthened and perhaps clarified many others, and even eliminated a few. The Human Genome Project has spawned many of the newer terms. And, as with our standard lexicon, these new words imply far more than the descriptive definition. *Microarray* is a term newly included in this edition. In its simplest definition, it is a technique for examining and characterizing an individual's entire chromosomal, genetic makeup. In practice, it implies that we know there is something wrong with this youngster and we are going to survey his chromosomal/genetic structure to search for the causal abnormalities. And, with rare exception when needed for explanation, this edition bans the use of the terms *mentally retarded* and *mental retardation*. Thus we hope to appropriately heed the criticisms implied in the Bierce and Hawthorne quotes.

This work is intended to be of use to professionals, students, and family members involved directly or indirectly in the transdisciplinary diagnosis and management of people with developmental challenges. The terminology herein spans the fields of pediatrics, anatomy, genetics, orthopedics, neurology, neurosurgery, pathology, pharmacology, physiology, psychiatry, psychology, education, social work, family therapy, law, speech-language pathology, linguistics, audiology, physical therapy, occupational therapy, and nutrition. These terms represent signs, symptoms, syndromes, diagnoses, intervention modalities, theories, medications, eponyms, acronyms, organizations, tests, instruments, and even lay descriptors. Unlike the reader mentioned in the Faulkner quote, anyone entering this field will encounter many terms that will send them scurrying to the dictionary. It is our intention that this dictionary meet Bierce's criteria as "a most useful work."

We appreciate the work of those who worked on the first and second editions who, for various reasons, have gone on to different endeavors. We could not be here, had we not been there, and you were there with us. So thanks to Shirley Behr, Carol A. Haake, Claudia Hilton, Carla Laszewski, Ellen Magenis, Pat Miller, Debra Rybski, and Elaine Wilder.

Some of our editors and contributors have been with us from the beginning, and some have joined us for the first time in this edition. To Jill Morrow-Gorton, who has been with us from the beginning, and Anne Farrell, who joined us for the second edition, your meaning to us is far more than "editor and contributor." To Jennifer A. Accardo, Joann N. Bodurtha, Toni Goelz, Gale B. Rice, and Ginger Smith, thanks for joining us in this third effort. And a special thanks to David Kullman, Assistant Professor of Legal Research at Saint Louis University School of Law, who spent many duty hours searching and verifying the legal history and present status of the many disability related laws included herein.

For both senior editors, Pasquale J. Accardo and Barbara Y. Whitman, the addition of Jennifer Accardo as a contributing editor carries special meaning. She is, quite literally, the next generation. Pasquale Accardo claims her biologically as a daughter and as a second generation developmental pediatrician. Barbara Whitman claims her first as a daughter via (unofficial) adoptive rights, following which she became a former student, as well. She has made us both proud, and to you, Jennifer, we pass the baton for the next edition. May your work surpass what we, so far, have attained.

Barbara Y. Whitman, M.S.W., Ph.D.   *Pasquale J. Accardo, M.D.*

Guide to
the Dictionary

The following sample entries from this volume are provided to highlight the various features of the *Dictionary of Developmental Disabilities Terminology, Third Edition;* many of these features are elaborated on the pages that follow.

acronym as
headword

cross-reference to
full name of acronym

AAC *See* augmentative and alternative communication; *see also* augmentative communication.

athetosis Literally, "without position." When used to describe motor disabilities, a pattern of movement disorder characterized by involuntary, slow, writhing, and undulating movements of flexion, extension, pronation, and supination that are more peripheral than central and are sometimes called *vermicular* or *wormlike*. More purely athetoid movements are slower and more sustained than choreiform (involuntary twitching) movements. *See also* choreoathetosis.

head-
words

parenthetical
clarification

specific cross-reference

life dates

basic trust In psychoanalyst Erik Erikson's (1902–1994) version of psychosexual development, basic trust is the major achievement of the first developmental stage (basic trust versus mistrust) in the first year of life; repeated interactions with a caregiver (typically the mother) provide a foundation of positive predictability, safety, and trust, thus instilling in the infant a positive orientation toward the world.

PL Public law. *See specific PL entries.*

nonspecific cross-reference

synonym

port-wine stain *nevus flammeus.* A purple, sometimes raised, irregular vascular (composed of blood vessels) skin lesion; can be a component of Sturge-Weber syndrome.

ENTRY SELECTION

The first, and the major, criterion for the inclusion of an entry in this volume was the likely occurrence of the term in a discipline evaluation or multidisciplinary team report on a person with a developmental disability. The second criterion for entry selection was the probability that the term might not make immediate sense to a reader of such a report whose training was in a different discipline from that of the author of a given section of the report. The goal in defining the selected entries was to provide sufficient information for the term to be intelligible in context. Exactly how much information would then be needed was the subject of continuing discussion among all of the authors of the dictionary. Unlike most dictionaries, this volume does not attempt to define exhaustively all terms in the field of developmental disabilities; those that would be considered obvious to everyone (even if they are the subject of much debate [e.g., intelligence]) have received less attention. Textbooks remain the major source for the student or novice to locate extensive information. Expanding on these original selection criteria, other terms were added to the volume that might not readily appear in a patient/client report but that would help in the understanding of terms that do. Thus, this volume is not intended to be a combined glossary for a variety of disciplines; rather it is a working clinical tool.

MULTIPLE DEFINITIONS

When a single term has different connotations, it may be described continuously, as part of the same entry (e.g., percussion). When, however, meanings or uses of a term are sufficiently distinct and originate from different disciplines with little or no relationship, two separate contiguous definition entries are provided (e.g., accommodation, discipline).

EPONYMS

Eponymous terms ending in syndrome, disease, or sign are presented without the possessive *s* (e.g., Down syndrome, Hirschsprung disease, Macewen sign).

ACRONYMS

Entries are provided for the most commonly used acronyms. Such acronyms are especially likely to appear in professional reports. This alphabet soup includes both formally recognized acronyms (e.g., WISC-IV, NIH) as well as ones that could be considered jargon (e.g., BK, KUB).

SYNONYMS

Synonyms are indicated by italics after applicable terms and before definitions. Each synonym is separated by a comma, and each list of synonyms is followed by a period. Synonyms include alternate names of terms and gene sites (e.g., Bassen-Kornzweig disease for abetalipoproteinemia) and are either capitalized or lowercase per their actual spelling. Not all synonyms appear as cross-references as they are only meant to inform the reader of alternate names of terms. An attempt has been made to include with entries every possible synonym or related usage.

ALPHABETICAL ORDER

The entries are alphabetized in telephone-book style: word by word, including spaces and hyphens.

> day care
> day hospital
> daydream
> Education of the Handicapped Act (EHA) of 1970 (PL 91-230)
> educational sign systems

The alphabetization is alphanumeric: Numbers are positioned as if they were spelled-out numerals. Headwords are given in their most common usage form; this is indicated by cross-references, when appropriate.

CROSS-REFERENCING

Throughout this volume, cross-referencing has been used to assist readers in locating the full name of a word or term that has come to be known by its acronym (e.g., **IEP** to **individualized education program**), in identifying the full and correct name of a public law (e.g., **PL 94-142** to **Education for All Handicapped Children Act of 1975**), and in finding entries that provide significantly fuller information in a place where the reader might be unlikely to look for it (e.g., under **emotion**, *see also* **affect**).

TYPES OF ENTRIES

Medical syndrome and disease entries give synonyms, major diagnostic findings, associated findings, incidence, and genetics or other etiology (if known). Medical syndromes were selected as entries specifically because of the presence of associated neurodevelopmental findings, such as intellectual disabilities, learning disabilities, autism, communication disorders, and impairments of vision and hearing. Occasionally, a syndrome without any associated neurodevelopmental association is included because the condition is frequently mistaken to have such an associated disability. An entry's length generally otherwise tends to vary in direct proportion with its frequency and importance. Also included occasionally are very rare conditions about which it is difficult to find information in standard general textbooks; these conditions have been given more detailed consideration herein.

Information provided with test entries usually includes the type of test (e.g., group or individual, oral or written), the purpose of the test (e.g., to assess cognitive, language, or writing skills), and sometimes the age group (e.g., 11;6 years of age indicates 11 years, 6 months). For the more widely used instruments, details on scoring, subscore breakdown, and interpretation are given. Administration format is sometimes noted. For less widely used tests, less information is provided.

Individual people are listed as entries when their names are synonymous with a theory, an approach, or other major development in the field of neurodevelopmental disabilities. The rule of thumb here has been to be quite restrictive.

INTELLECTUAL DISABILITIES TERMINOLOGY

While we have in all instances attempted to use people-first language, we align our classification of the levels of cognitive handicap with the 1983 system for classification of mental retardation (Grossman, 1983) rather than a newer one (Schalock et al., 2010). The decision to use the older system was based on the fact that the bulk of the scientific literature in print and the majority of patient/client records extant utilize the 1983 terminology. A dictionary's purpose is to explain the meanings of words that may be unfamiliar to a person encountering them. Nonetheless, one may still encounter the records of an adult client with cognitive limitations/handicaps that use the term *mental retardation;* to read a report that characterizes this person as being "moderately mentally retarded" in childhood, it would be helpful to know what was meant by "moderately mentally retarded" even if one currently uses a different terminology and classification schema. Many older (antiquated and sometimes even objectionable) terms for developmental disabilities have been included for a similar reason. One does not change history by rewriting the past à la George Orwell but by writing the future.

PARENTHETICAL CLARIFICATION

Brief parenthetical definitions are provided within entries as short reminders for the reader. For most of the terms so parenthetically defined, fuller and more technically accurate definitions are provided under the entry corresponding with that term.

REFERENCES

Grossman, H.J. (Ed.). (1983). *Classification in mental retardation.* Washington, DC: American Association on Mental Deficiency.

Schalock, R.L., Borthwick-Duffy, S.A., Bradley, V.J., Buntinx, W.H.E., Coulter, D.L., Craig, E.M., et al. (2010). *Intellectual disability: Definition, classification, and systems of supports* (11th ed.). Washington, DC: American Association on Intellectual and Developmental Disabilities.

This book is dedicated to families: those who trusted us with the care of their children, those who supported us through the many editions of this effort, and those who are the future, most especially Jennifer, Matt, Claire, Amanda, and Ryan.

Aa

A not B error Searching for a hidden object where it was last found rather than in its demonstrated new hiding place; this perseveration is typical in infants 8–12 months of age.

AAA *See* American Academy of Audiology.

AABT Association for the Advancement of Behavior Therapy. *See* Association for Behavioral and Cognitive Therapies (ABCT).

AAC *See* achievement ability comparison.

AAC *See* augmentative and alternative communication. *See also* augmentative communication.

AACPDM *See* American Academy for Cerebral Palsy and Developmental Medicine.

AACS *See* augmentative and alternative communication system.

AACTE *See* American Association of Colleges for Teacher Education.

AAFP *See* American Academy of Family Physicians.

AAIDD *See* American Association on Intellectual and Developmental Disabilities.

AAMFT *See* American Association for Marriage and Family Therapy.

AAMR American Association on Mental Retardation. *See* American Association on Intellectual and Developmental Disabilities (AAIDD).

AAMR Adaptive Behavior Scales–Residential and Community: Second Edition (ABS-RC:2) A behavior rating scale for adaptive behavior for ages 18–80. The test items discriminate people with intellectual disability living in institutions from those in community settings.

AAMR Adaptive Behavior Scales–School: Second Edition (ABS-S:2) A behavior rating scale that evaluates the adaptive potential of children between 3;0 and 18;11 years with behavior disorders by examining coping skills in nine behavioral domains and social maladaptations in seven domains. The test items help differentiate those children who require special educational assistance from those who can manage in a general classroom.

AAP *See* American Academy of Pediatrics.

AAPEP *See* Adolescent and Adult Psychoeducational Profile.

Aarskog-Scott syndrome A rare genetic syndrome of faciogenital dysplasia more apparent in males. The syndrome encompasses ocular hypertelorism (widely spaced eyes), a widow's peak, brachydactyly (short fingers), shawl scrotum (with a fold around the penis), cryptorchidism (undescended testes), and growth retardation leading to short stature. Most children with Aarskog-Scott syndrome have typical intelligence, but mild intellectual disability and learning disabilities can occur. Inheritance is X-linked. Alterations in the *FGD1* gene at Xp11.21 are responsible in a minority of individuals. There is symptomatic treatment for the growth retardation and cryptorchidism as well as genetic counseling.

ABA   *See* applied behavior analysis.

ABAS-II   *See* Adaptive Behavior Assessment System–Second Edition.

abasia   The inability to walk. *See also* astasia–abasia.

ABC   *See* Autism Behavior Checklist.

ABC Inventory   A brief screening test for children between 3;6 and 6;6 years that assesses fine motor, academic, and language skills. The ABC Inventory takes 15 minutes to administer.

abducent nerve   The sixth cranial nerve that abducts the eye (turns it outward); damage to this nerve can cause diplopia (double vision) and strabismus (crossed eyes).

abducent palsy   Paralysis of the sixth cranial nerve that causes an internal strabismus (esotropia) that turns the affected eye inward; occurs with fever, increased pressure within the skull, or brainstem tumors.

abduction   Sideways movement away from the mid-line of the body.

ABCT   *See* Association for Behavioral and Cognitive Therapies.

Abecedarian Project   A model North Carolina preschool and school-age educational program; also refers to a controlled scientific study of the benefits of the project to the early childhood education of poor children.

Cohorts of individuals born between 1972 and 1977 were randomly assigned as infants to either the early educational intervention group or the control group. Mothers whose children were in the intervention group achieved higher educational and employment statuses than mothers whose children were in the control group. These results were more pronounced for teen mothers.

aberrant behavior   Behavior that deviates markedly from what is considered typical.

Aberrant Behavior Checklist   A 58-item behavior scale originally developed to measure the effect of drugs and other therapeutic interventions on individuals with moderate to profound intellectual disability. Its five subscales are Irritability, Lethargy/Withdrawal, Stereotypic Behavior, Hyperactivity/Noncompliance, and Inappropriate Speech.

abetalipoproteinemia   *Bassen-Kornzweig disease.* A genetic disorder that combines intestinal malabsorption, progressive ataxia (unsteady gait), intellectual disability, acanthocytes (burr-shaped red blood cells) in the blood, and retinitis pigmentosa (night blindness and a progressively restricted visual field). High doses of vitamin E halt the progression of this neurological syndrome. Inheritance is autosomal recessive.

Abilify   *See* aripiprazole.

ability   A quality that enables an individual to perform an act, solve a problem, or make an adjustment. This term refers to potential performance or whether an individual can act in a specified manner or demonstrate certain skills or knowledge at a given time. Ability can originate from inherited traits, previous learning, or a combination of both. Intelligence tests are assumed to be tests of ability.

ability grouping   An outmoded practice of grouping students based on similar ability for instruction to allow each student to receive the level of instruction most appropriate to the needs of the group.

ablation   Removal; eradication.

AbleData   An Internet database (http://www.abledata.com) with information about products for individuals with disabilities.

above elbow (AE)   An anatomical term used to describe the location of an amputation, either congenital or acquired.

above knee (AK)   An anatomical term used to describe the location of an amputation, either congenital or acquired.

ABR   Auditory brainstem response. *See* brainstem auditory evoked response (BAER).

abruptio placenta   *placental abruption.* The premature detachment (abruption or tearing away) of the placenta (which, among other functions, supplies a fetus with oxygen before the infant is born and can breathe independently). Abruption is accompanied by severe bleeding and represents a significant risk to both the mother and infant. In the typical delivery process, after the infant has been born, the placenta separates spontaneously and a hormonally mediated process prevents severe maternal hemorrhage (bleeding).

absence seizure   Transient loss of consciousness lasting up to 30 seconds accompanied by a typical and highly specific diagnostic electroencephalogram (EEG) pattern of three-per-second spike waves. Such seizures are most common after the age of 5 years and often disappear at puberty. Formerly known as *petit mal seizure.*

ABS-RC:2   *See* AAMR Adaptive Behavior Scales–Residential and Community: Second Edition.

ABS-S:2   *See* AAMR Adaptive Behavior Scales–School: Second Edition.

abulia   Profound apathy due to severe bilateral prefrontal lobe disease.

academic intervention   Instruction based on the use of specific techniques and materials to teach a given subject.

Academy of Certified Social Workers (ACSW)   A certification of practice competence conferred by the National Association of Social Workers (NASW) to social workers who meet several academic and practice standards. These include a master's of social work degree or better, 2 years or more of supervised practice, and successful completion of a competency examination. According to the professional standards of the NASW, a social worker cannot practice independently prior to reaching this level of certification.

ACC   *See* agenesis of the corpus callosum.

ACC   Aplasia cutis congenita. *See* cutis congenita aplasia.

acceleration vocabulary   Words or messages that occur so frequently and are so lengthy that the use of an encoding strategy to retrieve them results in substantial keystroke savings for the user of an augmentative and alternative communication system.

accent   The relative stress or prominence assigned to a particular syllable of a word or group of words. This emphasis is demonstrated through greater intensity (stress accent) or by variation or modulation of pitch or tone (pitch accent). Placement of accent on a word or group of words can be determined by the regional, social, or developmental background of the speaker. Individuals with congenital hearing loss typically have difficulty with standard or expected placement of accent in spoken language and tend to speak in a monotone.

access   Specific equipment or techniques that enable those with disabilities to gain knowledge and information about community integration opportunities as well as physical entry into such opportunities. Examples include the use of braille or enlarged print for reading and writing, sound-supplemented elevators, specially marked household appliances, and voice-supplemented clocks and watches for those with visual impairments.

access barriers Barriers present primarily because of limitations in the capabilities of an individual or his or her communication system.

accessibility Modification of buildings, curbs, and other physical structures to allow unrestricted movement and admittance to people whose mobility may be limited by motor or sensory impairments and who may use a wheelchair. This might include ramps and additional elevators for those with motor impairments and braille and sound adaptations for those with visual impairments. Accessibility also requires modification of services for people who speak a language other than English, those who have a hearing impairment, or those who have other cognitive or learning problems. Accessibility of all public and private facilities is mandated by the Americans with Disabilities Act (ADA) of 1990 (PL 101-336), which was amended by the ADA Amendments Act of 2008 (PL 110-325).

accident prone Describing someone with an unusually high susceptibility to unintentional injury. Although accident proneness can be an emotional symptom in children, it more likely reflects the inattention and impulsivity of attention-deficit/hyperactivity disorder (ADHD), the cognitive impairment of intellectual disability, or the motor impairment of developmental coordination disorder or developmental dyspraxia.

accommodation The ability of the eye to change the shape of its lens to produce a clear image. Problems with accommodation can produce fatigue, visual discomfort, eyestrain, headaches, and blurred vision.

accommodation An adaptation made to an environment, facility, or task to enhance the performance of an individual with a disability. *See* Americans with Disabilities Act (ADA) of 1990.

accommodation A Piagetian learning process that applies a general cognitive structure to understanding a particular situation, which then changes the cognitive structure. Accommodation focuses on the change in the learning organism.

accommodations *IEP accommodations.* Changes made to the learning environment and written into the individualized education program to ensure that the general education curriculum is accessible for students with disabilities.

acetabulum The cup-shaped cavity in the hip bone that holds the head of the femur (thigh bone); impairments of the acetabulum contribute to hip pain, instability at the hip joint, dislocation of the hip, and limping.

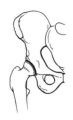

acetabulum

acetaminophen Trade name, Tylenol. A drug used to reduce fever (antipyretic) and pain (analgesic).

acetylcholine (Ach) A neurotransmitter important for memory and peripheral neuromuscular function.

acetylcholinesterase inhibitor A drug that interferes with the breakdown of acetylcholine. This drug class includes donepezil, which is commonly used by older adults with Alzheimer's disease but is also being tested in people with Down syndrome.

aCGH *See* array comparative genomic hybridization.

Ach *See* acetylcholine.

achalasia Difficulty swallowing (dysphagia) due to failure of the lower esophageal sphincter (LES) to relax. Presenting symptoms can include vomiting, difficulty swallowing, and weight loss. Achalasia, the physiological opposite of chalasia, is rare in children.

Achenbach Teacher Report Form *See* Teacher Report Form (TRF).

achievement ability comparison (AAC) A rating that describes a student's achievement in relation to the achievement of other students with the same measured ability.

achievement battery A group of tests that measure the amount and degree of attainment of information, knowledge, and skills in specified areas.

achievement test A test designed to document what a person has learned, usually in specific academic areas such as reading, mathematics, or written language. Such tests are different from intelligence tests, which are designed to reflect an individual's intellectual potential (what could be learned).

Achilles tendon The heel cord; named for Achilles, a hero in Greek mythology whose only weakness was his heel. Shortening or tightening of the Achilles tendon gives rise to toe walking (a gait with obligatory foot extension, also called *plantarflexion*).

Achilles tendon

achondroplasia A genetic condition that combines short stature (commonly known as *dwarfism*) with short proximal limbs, bowed legs, and macrocephaly (large head), usually without hydrocephalus (excess fluid in the brain) or accompanying developmental disorders. Obstructive apnea (temporary cessation of breathing) and neurological complications secondary to bone or disk compression are major medical concerns. Intelligence is usually typical. Inheritance follows an autosomal dominant pattern with a recurrence risk of 50%. *FGFR3* mutations account for >99% of individuals. Incidence is estimated at 1 in 25,000, with 80% of cases representing new mutations. Treatment is generally symptomatic for orthopedic or neurological complications. Formerly referred to as *achondroplastic dwarfism.*

achromatopsia Color blindness.

ACLC *See* Assessment of Children's Language Comprehension.

ACLD Association for Children and Adults with Learning Disabilities. *See* Learning Disabilities Association of America (LDA).

ACMG *See* American College of Medical Genetics.

acoupedic An approach to learning speech among children with hearing impairments that relies on hearing alone.

acoustic Pertaining to sound, the sense of hearing, and the science of sound.

acoustic impedance audiometry Measurement of the sound reflected by the eardrum, performed by emitting a test tone into the ear and measuring three components: 1) static acoustic impedance, which relates to the compliancy or flexibility of the eardrum; 2) acoustic reflex, which measures the contraction of the muscles in the middle ear; and 3) tympanometry, which measures the movement of the tympanic membrane during various pressure changes. These three components measure middle ear functioning in relation to turning sound waves into electrical activity in the cochlea and eighth nerve.

acoustic nerve *See* auditory nerve.

acquired Postnatal; not caused by significant innate, genetic, or prenatal factors. In describing the etiology of developmental disabilities, an acquired condition is contrasted with a congenital one, with *acquired* implying that the person was neurodevelopmentally typical until something happened (e.g., brain injury, brain infection).

acquired epileptic aphasia *See* Landau-Kleffner syndrome (LKS).

acquired hypothyroidism Decreased production of thyroid hormone with a variety of etiologies (causes), leading to a syndrome displaying many of the following features: decreased height growth, obesity, myxedema (dry, swollen skin), goiter (neck swelling), cold intolerance, constipation, thin hair, lethargy, and sluggish deep-tendon reflexes.

acquired immunodeficiency syndrome (AIDS) A chronic disease resulting from infection with the retrovirus HIV-1 (human immunodeficiency virus type 1). The most severe manifestation is suppression or deficiency of the cellular immune system. Other body organs may be infected. Suppression of the immune response system predisposes the virally infected person to other (secondary) infections and malignancies. Transmission is by body fluid (blood or semen); many cases in children result from contact in utero, with an infected mother transmitting the virus across the placental barrier to her fetus or infant. The course of pediatric AIDS is typically prolonged, with neurodevelopmental complications in many affected children. These range from mild delays in attaining developmental milestones to developmental regressions. Therapy includes treatment of the secondary infections and malignancies coupled with administration of drugs specifically targeted to delay the progression of the HIV infection.

acrocentric chromosome A chromosome with the centromere much nearer one end;

in humans the acrocentric chromosomes (13, 14, 15, 21, and 22) have satellited short arms and stalks that carry genes for ribosomal ribonucleic acid (rRNA).

acrocephalopolysyndactyly *See* Carpenter syndrome.

acrocephalosyndactyly type I *See* Apert syndrome.

acrocephalosyndactyly type III *See* Saethre-Chotzen syndrome.

acrocephaly A tower-shaped skull secondary to craniosynostosis (premature fusion of skull sutures). Acrocephaly is found in a number of genetic syndromes, including turribrachycephaly, turricephaly, hypsicephaly, and oxycephaly.

acrocephaly

acrodysostosis A congenital disorder characterized by prenatal growth retardation, intellectual disability, a strikingly small nose, short hands with stubby fingers, and involvement of other bone structures. Inheritance is autosomal dominant in most family pedigrees, but autosomal recessive patterns have been observed. *See also* pseudohypoparathyroidism.

acrofacial dysostosis type 1 *See* Nager syndrome.

acrolect Any dialect that closely resembles the accepted standard usage of a language. For example, in Black Vernacular English (BVE), "he be saying" is the equivalent, or acrolect, of "he is saying." *See also* basilect.

acromelic Affecting the distal (far end) segment of a limb (e.g., the hand, foot).

acronym A word (abbreviation) used to identify a syndrome or other condition in which each letter or syllable is the first letter or syllable of one of the components of the syndrome; the acronym serves as a mnemonic (memory) device (e.g., LEOPARD syndrome, which connotes *l*entigines [benign brown pigmented spots], *E*CG conduction abnormalities, *o*cular hypertelorism [widely spaced eyes], *p*ulmonic stenosis [restriction of blood flow from the right lower chamber of the heart], *a*bnormal genitalia, *r*etardation of growth, and sensorineural *d*eafness).

ACSW *See* Academy of Certified Social Workers.

ACTH *See* adrenocorticotropic hormone.

actigraph *See* actometer.

actigraphy The use of an actometer to measure activity over time. Actigraphy is frequently used to objectively document sleep/wake schedules, in which case an actometer is worn for a number of days, and then the data are downloaded and processed by a computer program that sorts time periods into probable sleep and waking according to how much activity was measured in each period.

actimeter *See* actometer.

acting out A psychoanalytic term that refers to expressing feelings, unconscious drives, or impulses through external behavior rather verbally articulating them. This acting out of feelings is usually expressed in annoying, disruptive, or antisocial ways. Acting out behaviors are similar to conduct disorder misbehaviors or undesirable behaviors but are typically less severe and are not so fixed in the personality. Typical acting out behaviors include fighting, stealing, crying, pouting, hyperactivity, temper tantrums, and verbal threats.

activating A term used to describe medication effects; can include the adverse effect of activation or the effect of promoting alertness and wakefulness as opposed to inducing sleep or causing drowsiness.

activation An adverse effect of certain medications that induces mood changes, irritability, and hyperactivity.

active learning An approach to educating children with visual impairments and multiple disabilities by encouraging active play; it was developed by Dr. Lilli Nielsen.

active range of motion (AROM) Movement at a joint that can be done actively by the person without stretching or help.

active reading process A set of reading strategies articulated by Neil Anderson and based on the assumption that reading is an active meaning-building process. This philosophy is represented with the mnemonic ACTIVE, which identifies six of the eight elements of this approach: A (activate prior knowledge), C (cultivate vocabulary), T (teach for comprehension), I (increase reading rate), V (verify reading strategies), E (evaluate progress). Consider the role of motivation and select appropriate materials are the other two elements. Initially articulated as a set of strategies for teaching a second language, the active reading process has been incorporated into teaching strategies across the life span and in multiple curricula.

activities of daily living (ADLs) Self-help activities such as bathing, toileting, eating, cooking, being mobile, performing simple health care procedures, and keeping house. Performing ADLs is a major goal of habilitation and rehabilitation. *See also* basic activities of daily living (BADLs).

activity-based intervention An early intervention approach that capitalizes on daily caregiver–child transactions. It relies on child-initiated transactions, embeds goals in daily activities, uses logically and naturally occurring antecedents and consequences, and develops functional skills that transfer readily to other contexts.

activity grid display A type of augmentative and alternative communication grid display that involves organizing vocabulary according to event schemes, routines, or activities.

actometer *actigraph, actimeter.* A mechanical device used to measure activity levels; example: a pedometer (an instrument that records the number of steps taken).

acuity The degree of clarity; the sharpness, clearness, and distinctness of stimuli with respect to the reception of sensory data. Visual acuity is measured against a standard of 20/20 (which measures the accuracy with which people with impairments can visually discriminate objects, shapes, or letters at 20 feet against that demonstrated by a person without impairments at 20 feet). (In the metric system, 6/6 is the standard.) A visual acuity of 20/40 indicates that an individual with an impairment discriminates at 20 feet what an individual without impairments can discriminate at 40 feet. Visual acuities better than 20/40 are not typically disabling, whereas those worse than 20/40 may indicate myopia, or nearsightedness. Auditory acuity refers to the sensitivity of the ear to sound.

acuity The degree of urgency or significance. An illness is of high acuity if it is severe and requires immediate, intensive intervention.

acute Sharp or sudden; of short duration (the opposite of chronic). An illness is acute when it comes on suddenly and unexpectedly.

acute dystonic reaction Uncontrolled muscle activity with stiffness or twisting of extremities and other body parts (e.g., facial grimacing, torticollis, oculogyric crisis, opisthotonos [severe arching of the back]). This type of reaction can be a side effect of antipsychotic drugs.

acute infantile spinal muscular atrophy (AISMA) A type of atrophy synonymous with Werdnig-Hoffmann disease.

acute life-threatening event (ALTE) An event in which an infant appears to be lifeless or near death but subsequently survives. ALTE is a descriptor but not a diagnosis, and the lengthy list of potential causes of ALTEs includes epileptic seizure, metabolic disorder, and child abuse. ALTE is sometimes referred to as *near-miss sudden infant death syndrome* (SIDS), but the connection between ALTE and SIDS is unclear.

ADA Americans with Disabilities Act of 1990 (PL 101-336). *See also* ADA Amendments Act of 2008 (PL 110-325).

ADA Amendments Act of 2008 (PL 110-325) *See* Americans with Disabilities Act of 1990 (PL 101-336).

ADAAA *See* Americans with Disabilities Act Amendments Act of 2008 (PL 110-325).

adaptation A biology term indicating an equilibration (balance) between assimilation (the organism changing the new content) and accommodation (the new content changing the organism).

adaptation The extent to which an individual, group, or community copes with the fluctuating demands of daily life.

adapted physical education Physical education is the development of fundamental physical and motor skills and patterns (e.g., throwing, catching, walking, running). Adapted physical education is physical education that has been adapted or modified so that it is appropriate for people with disabilities or delays in motor development or perceptual motor skills. Federal law mandates that adapted physical education be provided to students with disabilities.

Adapted Sequenced Inventory of Communication Development (A-SICD) for Adolescents and Adults with Severe Handicaps An extension of the Sequenced Inventory of

Communication Development–Revised (SICD-R) for adolescents and adults with disabilities, including those with severe hearing loss, legal blindness, epilepsy, spastic quadriplegia, and nonambulation.

adaptive behavior A set of skills and behavior, including feeding, dressing, toileting, and higher level social interaction skills, used by individuals with disabilities to cope with the natural and social demands of the environment. Adaptive behavioral deficits was added as one of two diagnostic criteria for intellectual disability in 1963. Subsequent modifications of the diagnostic criteria have continued to stress both intelligence quotient (IQ) score and adaptive behavioral deficits as dual criteria that must be present to make a diagnosis of intellectual disability.

Adaptive Behavior Assessment System– Second Edition (ABAS-II) A norm-referenced test of adaptive behavior for people from birth through 89 years designed to correspond with 10 areas of adaptive functioning in the definition of intellectual disability. Administration time is 15–20 minutes.

adaptive behavior scale The general name for a number of commercially available standardized instruments for measuring levels of adaptive behavior.

adaptive cuing technique Manual cues that are used to reflect the shape of the oral cavity, the articulatory placement and movement pattern, and the manner in which the sound is produced.

adaptive education A general term referring to education that incorporates modified instructional methods, materials, or expectations to address students' individual differences. *See also* remedial education.

adaptive equipment A wide array of devices that provide proper positioning to facilitate motor performance and independence; adaptive equipment includes seating inserts and positioning devices such as side-lyers and prone standers.

Adaptive Learning Environment Model (ALEM) An older mainstream program for integrating students with mild disabilities into the general classroom on a full-time basis.

ADD *See* Administration on Developmental Disabilities.

ADD Attention deficit disorder. *See* attention-deficit/hyperactivity disorder

Adderall Mixed amphetamine salts; trade name of a stimulant medication made of amphetamine and dextroamphetamine. Adderall is used to treat symptoms of attention-deficit/hyperactivity disorder while improving attention span. Side effects are similar to those of other stimulants. Adderall is available in short-acting, long-acting (XR), and very long-acting prodrug (Vyvanse) forms.

ADDES *See* Attention Deficit Disorders Evaluation Scale.

addiction Lay term that indicates a habit of compulsive drug use and drug-seeking behavior that is associated with physical and/or psychological dependence. The term *addiction* has been replaced in the medical literature and professional practice by the more specific terms substance *tolerance, substance dependence,* and *substance abuse.*

adduction Sideways movement of an extremity toward the mid-line of the body.

adductor tenotomy An orthopedic surgical procedure in which the tendons of several of the hip adductor muscles are cut; this procedure is used to treat severe hip adduction (scissoring), hip dislocation/dysplasia, and related problems in spastic cerebral palsy.

adenoid One of two paired masses of lymphoid tissue located at the back of the nose in the upper part of the throat (pharynx) that can obstruct normal breathing and, when swollen, make speech difficult.

adenoidal facies A characteristic appearance with the mouth hanging open, mouth breathing, and a generally dull and apathetic expression; it usually involves a history of snoring. Adenoidal facies is frequently secondary to hypertrophied (enlarged) adenoids and may accompany recurrent tonsillitis and otitis (inflammation in the ear). Hearing loss is possible, and a more detailed inquiry about allergy symptoms and obstructive sleep apnea should be made.

adenoidal facies

adenoidectomy The surgical removal of the adenoids; often performed simultaneously with tonsillectomy and ear (pressure equalizing [PE] or ventilation) tube placement.

adenoma sebaceum A skin lesion found in tuberous sclerosis. *See* tuberous sclerosis (TS) syndrome.

adenovirus A deoxyribonucleic acid (DNA) virus that can be associated with respiratory infections and diarrhea.

adequate yearly progress (AYP) Under the accountability provisions in the federal No Child Left Behind Act (NCLB) of 2001 (PL 107-110), all public schools, school districts, and states need to meet annual targets for the percentage of students (including students who are poor, speak limited English, are members of racial or ethnic minorities, or have disabilities) who score at least at the proficient level on state tests. AYP criteria are measured on three dimensions: reading/language arts, mathematics, and either graduation rate (for high schools and districts) or attendance rate (for ele-mentary and middle/junior high schools). Many schools seek to have their special education students classified as needing alternative achievement standards. Students who participate in an alternative assessment based on alternative achievement standards can be counted as proficient for accountability purposes, but only up to 1% of the total student population may count as proficient in this way. Schools, districts, or states that receive Title I, Part A, funds and who fail to meet AYP for two consecutive years are subject to certain requirements, such as offering supplemental education services, offering school choice, and/or taking corrective actions.

ADHD *See* attention-deficit/hyperactivity disorder.

ADI-R *See* Autism Diagnostic Interview–Revised.

adjudication A court decision rendered as a result of a hearing or trial. Adults with developmental disabilities may be adjudicated for the purpose of determining the need for a guardian.

adjusted age *corrected age*. The expected developmental age after a correction is made for prematurity. Thus, a 12-month-old infant who was born at 32 weeks' gestation (2 months early) would have an adjusted age of 10 months. The extent to which such corrections should be used remains unresolved.

adjustment disorder A maladaptive reaction to an identifiable stressful event. The hallmarks of this response include onset within 3 months of the stressor; duration of less than 6 months; and impairment in school, social, or interpersonal functioning not due to a previously diagnosed psychiatric disorder.

ADLs *See* activities of daily living.

ADM *See* Autism Dysmorphology Measure.

Administration on Developmental Disabilities (ADD) The federal agency mandated to carry out and monitor programs for people with developmental disabilities. This administrative office was authorized under the Developmental Disabilities Assistance and Bill of Rights Act Amendments of 1990 (PL 101-496) and is part of the U.S. Department of Health and Human Services.

adolescence The transition period between latency (late childhood) and young adulthood, typically between ages 13 and 17 years, although physical changes can occur as early as 10 years of age. Adolescence is characterized by physical changes such as the growth spurt; puberty; and, in girls, thelarche (breast development) and menarche (onset of menstruation). Complex psychosocial changes also occur.

Adolescent/Adult Sensory Profile A 60-item self-report that profiles sensory events in everyday life.

Adolescent and Adult Psychoeducational Profile (AAPEP) A criterion-referenced task performance test that assesses the learning styles and strengths of adolescents and adults with autism and other communication disorders. Test results constitute a profile that can be translated into individualized goals and objectives to serve as a foundation for instructional planning and community placement. A sequel to the Psychoeducational Profile (PEP).

Adolescent Language Screening Test (ALST) A screening test of speech and language for 11- to 17-year-olds. Includes seven subtests: Pragmatics, Receptive Vocabulary, Concepts, Expressive Vocabulary, Sentence Formulation, Morphology, and Phonology.

ADOS-R *See* Autism Diagnostic Observation Schedule–Revised.

adrenergic Mediated by adrenaline, as in the sympathetic nervous system.

adrenocorticotropic hormone (ACTH) A compound secreted by the pituitary gland that stimulates the adrenal gland's cortex (outer part) to make cortisol (a steroid hormone). The side effects of excess cortisol include truncal obesity, striae (stretch marks), stomach ulcers, osteoporosis (thinning of the bones), and an increased susceptibility to infection. ACTH is used therapeutically in infantile spasms. It is given intramuscularly (in the muscle; IM) and used until the spasms and hypsarrhythmia (a chaotic high-voltage electroencephalographic pattern) disappear. The dosage is then decreased until the minimal amount for seizure control is reached, at which point its use may be discontinued. Although ACTH does not alter the outcome in infantile spasms, it can improve both seizures and the electroencephalogram (EEG) pattern. It has also been used to treat children with Landau-Kleffner syndrome (who experience a type of temporal lobe seizure that can precipitate aphasia) and is available in a synthetic form.

adrenoleukodystrophy (ALD) A syndrome that combines a disorder of brain white matter with atrophy (wasting) of the adrenal glands. It is one of several hereditary neurodegenerative disorders that are characterized by progressive intellectual and visual deterioration, spasticity (increased muscle tone), and seizures. It is marked by an insufficiency of the adrenal cortex, which makes cortisol (a steroid hormone). The clinical course is variable, with onset generally between 5 and 8 years of age. The progression begins with disturbances in walking and mild intellectual deterioration, followed by seizures, screaming attacks, spasticity, and ataxia (unsteady gait). It is most commonly an X-linked trait associated with impairments in the *ABCD1* gene.

adrenomyeloneuropathy (AMN) A syndrome affecting spinal cord white matter and associated with atrophy (wasting) of the adrenal glands. This disorder affects adolescent or adult males older than those who typically present with adrenoleukodystrophy, and it progresses more slowly. Males in the same family may have the same gene mutations, with some developing adrenoleukodystrophy and others adrenomyelodystrophy.

ADT-2 *See* Wepman's Auditory Discrimination Test–Second Edition.

adult day care A continuum of services including sheltered work, day hospital, socialization groups, or custodial services provided to adults who are unable to care for themselves. These adults often have developmental disabilities from birth, but they may also be older adults who are no longer able to care for themselves when left alone but who do not need a full-time caregiving placement such as a nursing home.

adult foster care (AFC) Placement in the home of a nonrelated family for adults who are unable to care for themselves because of disabilities or health problems and whose biological families are unable to provide the care they need.

adult protective services Social, medical, legal, residential, or custodial services provided to adults who are unable to gain access to such services for themselves. These adults may have developmental disabilities or aging or disease processes that have rendered them incapable of caring for themselves. In the event that there is no guardian or significant other, or in cases of a guardian or significant other being abusive to the adult with the disability, a public or private agency may provide adult protective and service coordination services.

advance directive *living will.* A legal document that specifies a person's wishes regarding health and end-of-life care in the event of an end-stage condition or terminal illness.

In most states, advance directives must be written by a competent person; therefore, people with intellectual disabilities who are not able to write such documents may not have an advance directive. Some states allow people with intellectual disabilities to name a health care proxy to make those decisions for and with them.

adventitious Acquired; blindness and deafness are divided by origin into two types: congenital (existing at or dating from birth) and adventitious.

adventitious breath sounds Abnormal breath sounds such as crackles, rubs, rhonchi, stridor, expiratory grunting, and wheezing.

adverse effect (AE) A harmful side effect.

adverse event (AE) Term used in research in clinical trials to refer to an episode that may represent a negative side effect of the intervention being tested. Such events are divided into adverse events and serious adverse events (SAEs), which usually involve hospitalization or death.

advocacy The process of speaking for, writing in favor of, supporting, and/or acting on behalf of oneself, another person, or a cause. For example, *parent advocacy* can be defined as action or intervention in the service system on behalf of a child to ensure or obtain the best possible services for that child.

AE *See* above elbow.

AE *See* adverse effect; adverse event.

AE scores *See* age-equivalent scores.

AED Antiepileptic drug. *See* anticonvulsant.

AEP assessment *See* auditory evoked potential assessment.

AEPS® *See* Assessment, Evaluation, and Programming System for Infants and Children–Second Edition.

aerobic exercise Exercise that produces energy from the metabolism of oxygen.

aerophagia The swallowing of air, which can lead to abdominal distension and discomfort. In many infants aerophagia reflects a mild feeding disorder, but children with developmental disabilities may engage in aerophagia as a self-stimulatory behavior; aerophagia may predispose these children to aspiration.

AFB *See* American Foundation for the Blind.

AFC *See* adult foster care.

affect A term used to refer to both subjectively experienced inner feeling states and their external manifestations. Usage separates these two phenomena into 1) mood, to signify inner feeling states; and 2) affect, to refer to the external manifestation of feeling states. Thus, what were once affective disorders have become mood disorders. Although mood and affect are both considered psychological phenomena, each has physiological components that are usually expressed through somatic manifestations such as blushing, crying, excessive heart rate, sweating, or shaking. Changes in facial expression, voice tone, activity level, posture, and gait may occur as well. Disorders of affect and mood occur when the intensity of, duration of, appropriateness of, or ability to cope with one's own inner feeling state becomes impaired. *See also* emotion, mood.

affective disorder *See* mood disorder.

affricates Speech sounds produced by the quick release of an obstructed air stream.

affrication The phonological process that occurs when an affricate is substituted for a nonaffricate sound.

AFLP *See* amplified fragment length polymorphism.

AFO Ankle–foot orthosis. *See* orthosis.

AFP *See* alpha-fetoprotein.

aftercare Continued treatment and support services to formerly hospitalized or institutionalized people after their transition into the community.

AGA *See* appropriate for gestational age.

aganglionic megacolon *See* Hirschsprung disease.

age-equivalent (AE) scores Ratings derived by determining the average raw score obtained on a test taken by children of various ages. For example, if the average score for 8-year-old children on a test is 15 correct out of 25, any child who obtains a score of 15 receives an age-equivalent score of 8.

age ratio The chronological age of a child at one testing date divided by that child's chronological age at a later testing date. This ratio can be used as a crude measure of a test's predictive power, which depends on the age at which the test is given and the length of time between administrations. The younger the child, the poorer the predictive power of a test. The longer the interval between tests, the poorer the prediction from one testing to the next. Thus, prediction would most likely be better from ages 7 to 8 (7/8) than from ages 5 to 6 (5/6).

agenesis Literally, "not born"; failure of a structure to develop. A specific etiology for the absence of the structure as opposed to its later removal or destruction. Agenesis may occur because of genetic factors or because of a vascular accident during fetal development.

agenesis of the corpus callosum (ACC) Congenital complete or partial absence of the corpus callosum, the bundle of nerve fibers that connects the two hemispheres of the brain and allows learned information to pass back and forth between both sides. Rarely an isolated finding, ACC usually accompanies other brain anomalies as well as other birth defects, sometimes as a component of a genetic syndrome (e.g., Aicardi syndrome). Isolated ACC may be associated with only subtle neuropsychological (learning) impairments.

Ages & Stages Questionnaires®, Third Edition (ASQ-3™): A Parent-Completed Child-Monitoring System　The ASQ-3 is a child-monitoring and developmental screening system consisting of 21 questionnaires for children from 1 to 66 months of age to be completed by a parent or caregiver. Each questionnaire covers five developmental areas: communication, gross motor, fine motor, problem solving, and personal-social. Questionnaires are scored by a clinician or online; children who score below the cutoff are recommended for in-depth assessment.

Ages & Stages Questionnaires®: Social-Emotional (ASQ:SE): A Parent-Completed, Child-Monitoring System for Social-Emotional Behaviors　A child-monitoring and developmental screening system consisting of eight questionnaires for children from 3 months to 5 years of age to be completed by a parent or caregiver. Each questionnaire covers seven behavioral areas: self-regulation, compliance, communication, adaptive functioning, autonomy, affect, and interaction with people. Questionnaires are scored by a clinician in 1–3 minutes; children who score above the cutoff are recommended for in-depth assessment.

Aggregate Neurobehavioral Student Health and Educational Review (ANSER)　A series of questionnaires for parents, teachers, and students to assess all aspects of a child's behavior. The ANSER system is not a standardized test but a method of systematically collecting information from parent(s), school personnel, and the child. The Parent Questionnaire (ANSER-PQ; or sections thereof) is the most commonly used component of the test.

aggression　A poorly defined set of human behaviors interpreted from physical or verbal behavior directed at others. The impulsive actions (both verbal and physical) of the child with attention-deficit/hyperactivity disorder (ADHD) can easily be mistaken for aggression and can lead to physical fights.

agitation　Extreme motor restlessness and an increased activity level associated with anxiety and tension; a sign of mental distress.

agnosia　The inability to recognize a stimulus, with particular reference to sensory stimuli, such as visual agnosia, auditory agnosia, color agnosia, and finger agnosia (inability to name the finger touched with eyes closed).

agonist　A muscle that, while contracting to move a body part, is opposed by another muscle, which is termed the *antagonist.* Every muscle in the body is both an agonist and an antagonist to the opposite number that is needed to reverse its movement.

agonist　A substance (i.e., drug or neurotransmitter) that acts on a receptor to produce a biological response.

AGR triad　*See* aniridia–Wilms tumor association.

agrammatism　The inability to produce words in their correct sequence, resulting in marked difficulty with grammar and syntax; speech that is nonfluent, oddly inflected or not inflected at all, slow, and hesitant; speech with initial words stressed and frequent omission of important connectives. Agrammatism can be acquired as a component of Broca's or syntactical aphasia.

agraphia   An acquired condition (usually as a result of brain damage such as follows a stroke in adults) of impaired or absent ability to write or draw (graphomotor skill); the typically milder congenital form seen in children is usually referred to as *dysgraphia* and may be part of a learning disability syndrome.

agyria   *See* Miller-Dieker syndrome.

AHA   *See* American Hospital Association.

AHIP   *See* America's Health Insurance Plans.

Aicardi syndrome   The combination of generalized seizures, severe intellectual disability, agenesis of the corpus callosum (failure of part of the brain that is the major connection between the two hemispheres to grow), and retinal and vertebral defects. Inheritance is X-linked dominant only in females and is lethal in XY males.

aided augmentative communication technique   An augmentative and alternative communication (AAC) method that uses external support devices or procedures (e.g., communication boards, output devices).

AIDS   *See* acquired immunodeficiency syndrome.

AIMS   *See* Alberta Infant Motor Scale.

air–bone gap   The difference between a bone-conduction hearing threshold and an air-conduction threshold for the same sound frequency during an audiogram. Differences of 10 dB (decibels) or more are considered significant.

airplane splint   A shoulder abduction splint. A positioning device designed to maintain or increase the range of motion in shoulder abduction.

AISMA   *See* acute infantile spinal muscular atrophy.

AIT   *See* auditory integration training.

AK   *See* above knee.

akathisia   A disorder with objective motor restlessness accompanied by subjective anxiety; akathisia is not usually described in children but is considered in the differential diagnosis of hyperactivity in adults.

akathisia   One of the motor complications of antipsychotic drugs used to treat severe maladaptive behavior in people with developmental disorders.

akinesia   A state of diminished or absent motor activity.

akinetic mutism   A state of muteness, general unresponsiveness, and reluctance to perform even simple motor activities in spite of preservation of alertness, basic motor and sensory abilities, and fundamental cognitive abilities.

akinetic seizure   *astatic seizure, atonic seizure.* A type of seizure with head-nodding spells and loss of movement without atonia (loss of tone). The term *akinetic seizure* refers inconsistently to the seizure type associated with Lennox-Gastaut syndrome.

ala nasi   The flaring cartilaginous area that forms the outer side of each nostril.

Albers-Schönberg disease   *marble bone disease.* A genetic disease with increased density of all bones or mild osteopetrosis, facial palsy, visual impairment, and conductive (involving the middle and outer ear) hearing loss. The severe variant is lethal by adolescence. Inheritance follows an autosomal recessive pattern.

Alberta Infant Motor Scale (AIMS)   Norm-referenced observational scale of spontaneously occurring gross motor milestones from infancy through independent walking. The 58 items include prone, supine, sitting, and standing positions. Administration time is 10–20 minutes.

albinism The genetic absence of pigment of the skin, hair, and eyes or of the eyes only. Visual impairment, nystagmus (involuntary eye movements), and photosensitivity are common and commonly co-occur. Multiple loci are found on a number of different chromosomes that have been shown to cause albinism. Late-onset sensorineural hearing loss may also occur.

alcohol (EtOH) A chemical compound composed of varying parts carbon, hydrogen, and water. The number of parts of each of these chemical elements determines the type of alcohol. Drinking (ethyl) alcohol consists of C_2H_5OH. All alcohols are, to varying degrees, toxic (poisonous) to humans. Alcohol challenges the body to quickly break it down into its nontoxic elements of carbon, hydrogen, and oxygen. The slower the body's ability to break it down (e.g., in the presence of liver damage), the more toxic the effect of the alcohol. Alcohol is also teratogenic (i.e., it causes malformations in the developing fetus); a child with fetal alcohol syndrome (FAS) may have multiple organ system defects that can include blindness, deafness, and severe intellectual disability.

alcoholic family A characteristic set of family dynamics first identified in families in which one spouse was an alcohol abuser. Similar patterns have since been identified in families with other types of substance abuse. The dynamic interaction between the dependent spouse and the codependent spouse in maintaining the substance abuse has been identified, along with characteristic roles assumed by each child according to his or her birth order in the family. The long-term emotional consequences to the children and the characteristic behaviors they exhibit as they move into their own adult relationships have also been identified.

alcoholism The excessive use of alcoholic beverages motivated by either a psychological or a physiological dependence on the chemical effect and mood impact produced by such beverages. Diagnostic criteria assume this underlying dependence and include 1) quantity of use, 2) failed efforts to stop using, 3) impaired life functioning in social areas such as family and occupation and legal difficulties, 4) inability to stop using despite knowledge of having a persistent problem in one of these life areas due to excess use, 5) increased and driven efforts to obtain alcohol, and 6) increased tolerance for alcohol leading to greater intake before achieving the desired effect.

alcohol-related birth defects (ARBD) *See* alcohol-related neurodevelopmental disorders (ARND). *See also* fetal alcohol syndrome (FAS).

alcohol-related neurodevelopmental disorders (ARND) Term used to describe fetal alcohol effects (FAE). A partial expression of fetal alcohol syndrome (FAS) in which maternal alcohol consumption during gestation has at least two of the following effects on the developing fetus: 1) pre- or postnatal growth retardation, 2) neurodevelopmental impairment, or 3) craniofacial impairments.

ALD *See* adrenoleukodystrophy.

ALEM *See* Adaptive Learning Environment Model.

alertness An attentive, awake learning state.

Alexander technique A form of movement therapy that emphasizes correct posture and the proper positioning of the head with regard to the body.

alexia An acquired condition, usually as a result of brain damage (such as follows a stroke in adults), of impaired or absent ability to read; the typically milder congenital

algorithm 17 alphabet

form seen in children is usually referred to as *dyslexia.*

algorithm A rule used to solve a certain class of problems, especially a formula that automatically generates a solution; loosely, a rule of thumb.

Alice in Wonderland syndrome A symptom complex characterized by metamorphosia (hyper- and hyposchematia [visual distortions of size, shape, and spatial relations]). This symptom can occur with migraine, seizure disorders, drug-induced hallucinations, and infectious mononucleosis.

alimentation Feeding.

ALL *See* Analysis of the Language of Learning.

allele One of a series of two or more different forms of the same gene that may occupy the same position on a given chromosome.

Allen cards A preschool vision screening test for children as young as 2;6 years of age; the child identifies pictures of common items at a distance of 20 feet. The test can be used until children are ready to convert to a letter-based screening chart.

allergen Any substance—food, chemical, drug, or inhalant (e.g., pollen, mold, dust)—that, upon repeated exposure, produces allergic symptoms in a person.

allergic tension fatigue syndrome *cerebral allergy.* The concept that unsuspected (subclinical or otherwise asymptomatic) food allergies can produce central nervous system (CNS) irritability and fatigability and thus mimic or cause attention-deficit/hyperactivity disorder (ADHD) and learning disabilities. The dual symptoms of tension and fatigue are seen in people with classically defined allergic disorders and may exacerbate existing disorders of learning and attention.

allergy Altered reactivity. The production of symptoms in a person by substances (allergens) that do not produce symptoms in most other people. The presence of a family history of atopy (allergy) can help in the interpretation of many nonspecific signs of allergy in children: nasal speech, adenoidal facies, allergic salute (rubbing the nose upward with the heel of the palm), fatigue, nasal polyps, allergic (transverse nasal) crease, allergic shiners (dark circles under the eyes), and a variety of skin conditions (e.g., hives, eczema). Despite high prevalence rates for allergy, the role of allergies in developmental disabilities is often exaggerated. The contribution of poorly defined subclinical allergies to the etiology of developmental disabilities remains unproven and controversial.

allied health professional A person with special training who works under the supervision of a health professional to provide direct patient care; a member of the same discipline may function as an allied health professional in a medical setting and as an independent professional in another setting.

alopecia Hair loss; frequently patchy (alopecia areata) in children. This condition is secondary to a variety of conditions, including trauma, drug use, endocrine disorders, and ringworm.

alpha rhythm An electroencephalographic wave frequency of 8–13 per second (slower in children). This rhythm characterizes a relaxed, awake, but mentally inactive state. It is most prominent when the eyes are closed. It is blocked by attention and mental effort and replaced by slower frequency rhythms with drowsiness.

ALPHA Test *See* Assessment Link Between Phonology and Articulation Test.

alphabet The letters or symbols of a given language arranged sequentially in the order determined by custom.

alphabet knowledge Emerging knowledge of the alphabet. Alphabet knowledge is observed during the first 3 years when a child may name a letter in his or her name or begin to write letters in his or her name.

alpha-fetoprotein (AFP) A normal protein found in the serum (liquid part of blood) that is present in large amounts in a developing fetus. Measurements of maternal blood levels of AFP are used as a screening test for potential problems with the developing fetus. An elevated AFP is found with anencephaly (no brain or absent top of the skull) and open neural tube and abdominal wall defects (spina bifida). The open defect leaks AFP into the amniotic fluid, which then passes it into the maternal bloodstream, thus elevating the maternal AFP level. Maternal serum levels that are 2 or more times normal levels detect 79% of open neural tube defects. Amniotic fluid AFP levels detect 98% of these defects. Low levels of maternal serum AFP may be associated with Down syndrome and chromosome 18 defects in the fetus.

Alport syndrome A genetic syndrome with progressive bilateral sensorineural (involving the inner ear or the auditory nerve) hearing loss (starting by about age 10) and progressive chronic nephritis (starting by age 6). Of those affected, 10% also have ocular/visual impairments. Inheritance is X-linked, resulting from mutations of the type IV collagen gene (*COL4A5*) located at Xq13.

ALST *See* Adolescent Language Screening Test.

Alström syndrome A genetic syndrome characterized by progressive central and peripheral impairment of vision, retinitis pigmentosa (night blindness and progressively restricted visual fields), progressive sensorineural deafness, early transient truncal obesity, and juvenile-onset diabetes mellitus. The syndrome is extremely rare, with all known cases being of Swedish extraction. Inheritance is autosomal recessive.

ALTE *See* acute life-threatening event.

alternative assessment The educational assessment process used for students with significant intellectual disability who are unable to participate meaningfully in general state and district assessments, even with accommodations. It focuses on life and functional skills to demonstrate appropriate outcomes and establishes assessment and accountability requirements that target the same academic content and curriculum standards as for age- and grade-level peers without disability.

alternative communication Any procedure or device that substitutes a nonspeech mode of communication for spoken language. Such alternative communication may be aided (e.g., communication board) or unaided (e.g., sign language). *See also* augmentative and alternative communication (AAC).

alternative dispute resolution (ADR) A variety of methods used to resolve conflicts without resorting to legal processes. These methods include mediation, arbitration, neutral evaluation, and collaborative law. ADR usually involves a neutral third party who uses these processes to achieve a mutually satisfactory resolution rather than focusing on determining who has the stronger position.

alternative medicine *See* complementary and alternative medicine, optometric training.

alveolorization The phonological process in which there is a substitution of an alveolar sound for a labial or linguadental phoneme.

Alzheimer's disease A late-onset, degenerative disease of brain tissue that results in amnesia (impaired memory), apraxia (the inability to perform purposeful movements), agnosia (the inability to recognize objects or familiar people [many people with Alzheimer's disease fail to recognize their spouses]), aphasia (the loss of language skills), impaired thinking and judgment, disorientation, marked personality and behavior deterioration, and loss of adaptive abilities. Among people with developmental disabilities, people with Down syndrome have an incidence rate of Alzheimer's disease greater than that of the general population (33%–40% of people with Down syndrome older than age 50 are affected), and the disease manifests itself at a much younger age. The disorder is named after German neuropathologist Alois Alzheimer (1864–1915).

AMA   *See* American Medical Association.

amanuensis   Someone who takes dictation, transcribes written material, or assists in some other way with written or hand-performed work. For example, in an academic setting, an amanuensis might take notes for a student with disabilities or assist him or her with papers, examinations, and similar tasks.

amaurosis   Blindness specifically due to disease of the optic nerve, with the rest of the eye remaining intact; a component of a number of hereditary neurodegenerative diseases.

ambidextrous   Equally skilled with both hands; not yet exhibiting handedness or hand preference. Ambidexterity can be familial or can reflect global or specific cognitive delay or dysfunction.

ambient noise   All surrounding, background sounds in a particular listening environment.

amblyopia   Decreased vision or visual acuity in one eye. There are two major types of amblyopia: 1) Obstructive amblyopia is the loss of vision resulting from blockage of the retinal path so that images cannot reach the retina (e.g., cataracts, ptosis [drooping eyelid that cannot be raised], corneal opacity [clouding]); and 2) amblyopia ex anopsia is caused by either a refractive error (correctable by glasses) or strabismus (a crossed eye secondary to a weak eye muscle that can be surgically treated). In amblyopia without intervention, the image from the weaker eye is suppressed by the brain, and that eye gradually loses its vision; thus, monocular vision results. If diagnosed early, many of the causes of amblyopia can be treated or managed in such a way that binocular vision is preserved. Treatment can involve patching, glasses, or surgery.

ambulation   Walking (a gross motor skill). Most children walk independently between 12 and 13 months of age; the range for typical walking is 7–24 months.

ambulatory   Able to walk or ambulate (a gross motor skill). A young child or a child with a disability may only be ambulatory while holding someone's hand or using an assistive device such as a walker.

AMCHP   *See* Association of Maternal and Child Health Programs.

amenorrhea   Absence of menstrual periods; this can occur because of pregnancy, endocrine dysfunction, general debilitation associated with poor diet or health, or as part of a genetic syndrome.

America's Health Insurance Plans (AHIP) A national association of 1,300 companies providing health/medical, long-term care, disability income, dental, supplemental, stop-loss, and reinsurance to consumers, employers, and public purchasers. AHIP's stated mission is to provide a unified voice for the community of health insurance plans. A stated policy goal includes supporting its membership to expand access to high quality, affordable coverage to all Americans and to make health care services more affordable. AHIP, formed in 2003, merged the Health Insurance Association of America (HIAA) and the American Association of Health Plans (AAHP). The AHIP Center for Policy and Research, the research arm for the association, publishes research on a variety of forms of private health insurance and provides supports for the association's political advocacy efforts.

American Academy for Cerebral Palsy and Developmental Medicine (AACPDM) A multidisciplinary organization of physicians and other professionals in the fields of cerebral palsy, intellectual disability, and learning and language disorders. Members include orthopedic surgeons, developmental pediatricians, neurologists, physiatrists, and professionals from associated disciplines. Founded in 1947, the AACPDM sponsors an annual national meeting as well as several regional courses; it publishes a newsletter and an official journal, *Developmental Medicine and Child Neurology.*

American Academy of Audiology (AAA) A professional organization of audiologists dedicated to education, research, and increasing public awareness of both hearing disorders and audiologic services. Founded in 1988, the AAA publishes a newsletter and a number of research and practice journals.

American Academy of Family Physicians (AAFP) A national professional organization of family physicians, family medicine residents, and medical students. Founded in 1947, its mission is to ensure high-quality, cost-effective health care for people of all ages; to improve the health of people, families, and communities by serving the needs of members with professionalism and creativity; and to preserve and promote the science and art of family medicine. With more than 94,000 members, the AAFP is one of the largest national medical organizations.

American Academy of Pediatrics (AAP) A professional organization of physicians with board-certified specialty training in the diseases of childhood. It has a Council on Children with Disabilities (COCD).

American Association for Marriage and Family Therapy (AAMFT) A professional organization that certifies and regulates the practice of marital and family therapists. Membership is achieved through demonstrated competence and acceptance of the code of ethics.

American Association of Colleges for Teacher Education (AACTE) A national organization composed of public and private colleges and universities that provide educator training and development. The AACTE is dedicated to the development of teachers and school leaders in order to enhance student learning from prekindergarten through Grade 12. The goals of AACTE are to unify and support its membership by developing clear statements, based on evidence and professional consensus, about educator preparation in five areas: standards, curriculum, assessment, accountability, and who belongs in the profession.

American Association of Speech-Language Pathology and Audiology *See* American Speech-Language-Hearing Association (ASHA).

American Association on Intellectual and Developmental Disabilities (AAIDD) An interdisciplinary association of professionals, parents, individuals with disabilities, and others interested in intellectual disability. The AAIDD publishes the *American Journal on Intellectual and Developmental Disabilities, Intellectual and Developmental Disabilities,* and guidelines for the diagnosis of intellectual disability. The AAIDD is active in advocacy and conducts both national- and state-level professional meetings. Formerly known as the American Association on Mental Retardation (AAMR).

American Association on Mental Retardation (AAMR) *See* American Association on Intellectual and Developmental Disabilities (AAIDD).

American College of Medical Genetics (ACMG) An organization that provides resources to promote, develop, and implement medical genetics information to help better diagnose, treat, and prevent genetic disorders.

American Foundation for the Blind (AFB) An independent nonprofit organization founded in 1921 to function as the national association of local services for people who are blind and have visual impairments. The AFB has national consultants, provides direct consumer resources and services, and conducts research.

American Hospital Association (AHA) An independent nonprofit organization founded in 1898 to serve the dual functions of acting as a trade organization and serving the public interest. The AHA has the mission of "advancing the health of individuals and communities." In so doing, the AHA leads, represents, and serves hospitals, health systems, and related organizations that are accountable to the community and committed to health improvement.

American Manual Alphabet Specific positioning of the hands and fingers to symbolize the various letters of the alphabet. The manual alphabet supplements the use of sign language by enabling communicants to spell out words.

American Medical Association (AMA) Founded in 1847, the AMA is a national association of physicians and medical students whose mission is to promote the art and science of medicine and the betterment of public health. The AMA engages in the activities of professional education, development, and support for physicians and medical students while advocating for physicians and patients to improve the American health care system.

American Nurses Association (ANA) A national professional organization of registered nurses, nurses associations, and organizational affiliates founded in 1896. The ANA seeks to advance and support the nursing profession by fostering high standards of nursing practice, promoting the rights of nurses in the workplace, projecting a positive and realistic view of nursing, and lobbying legislative bodies and regulatory agencies around health care issues that affect both nurses and the public.

American Occupational Therapy Association (AOTA) A national professional association for occupational therapists, occupational therapy assistants, and occupational therapy students. The AOTA advances the quality, availability, use, and support of occupational therapy through standards, advocacy, education, and research. *See also* American Occupational Therapy Foundation (AOTF).

American Occupational Therapy Foundation (AOTF) Founded in 1965, the AOTF raises funds and distributes resources across three program areas: scholarships, publication, and research associated with the profession and practice of occupational therapy. *See also* American Occupational Therapy Association (AOTA).

American Orthopsychiatric Association (AOA) A multidisciplinary organization of mental health professionals founded in 1924 to support knowledge development and professional practice and to advocate for social justice and appropriate public policy in the areas of mental health and human development. The organization is unique in that it was one of the first to seek multiprofessional cooperation in all areas of human development and mental health. It publishes two quarterly journals, the *American Journal of Orthopsychiatry* and the *Ortho Bulletin. See also* orthopsychiatry.

American Physical Therapy Association (APTA) A professional organization for physical therapists and physical therapy assistants, the APTA accredits academic programs in physical therapy, assists in designing certification examinations, and offers continuing education courses. The association publishes a monthly journal, *Physical Therapy,* as well as *PT in Motion* and an online newsletter. It also provides a referral service for individuals who need physical therapy.

American Psychiatric Association (APA) An organization founded in 1844 as the Association of Medical Superintendents of American Institutions for the Insane; the current name was adopted in 1921. The APA's objectives include improving the treatment and rehabilitation of people with mental illness, intellectual disability, and emotional disturbances. The organization promotes professional research and education, provides information to the public, and fosters cooperation among professionals concerned with mental health. Its membership includes psychiatrists, other physicians, mental health professionals, lawyers, and members of various other professions. The APA's official journal is the *American Journal of Psychiatry.* In addition, the APA publishes the *Diagnostic and Statistical Manual of Mental Disorders, Fourth Edition, Text Revision (DSM-IV-TR),* and several newsletters.

American Psychological Association (APA) A professional organization of psychologists with the goals of advancing psychology as a science and profession and as a means of promoting human welfare by the promotion of research; improving the qualifications and usefulness of psychologists through high standards of ethics, conduct, education, and achievement; and increasing and diffusing psychological knowledge through meetings, professional contacts, reports, papers, discussions, and publications. The 56 different divisions of the APA reflect the diverse nature of psychological practice. The APA publishes *American Psychologist* and more than 25 other professional journals.

American Psychological Association (APA) style A commonly used manuscript style detailed in the *Publication Manual of the American Psychological Association, Sixth Edition* (American Psychological Association, 2009), a reference book with guidelines on how to write research papers and manuscripts. The manual details the ethics of authorship, language bias, editorial style, references, and how to get a manuscript accepted, among other things.

American Public Health Association (APHA) A national organization of public health professionals founded in 1872. The APHA's mission is to strive to protect all citizens and communities from preventable, serious health threats and to ensure that community-based health promotion, disease prevention, and preventive health services are universally accessible in the United States. APHA publishes the *American Journal of Public Health; The Nation's Health;* and an e-newsletter, *Inside Public Health.*

American School Health Association (ASHA) A national organization of administrators, counselors, health educators, physical educators, psychologists, school health coordinators, school nurses, school physicians, and social workers dedicated to helping its members to plan, develop, coordinate, implement, evaluate, and advocate for effective school health strategies that contribute to optimal health and academic outcomes for all children and youth. Originally founded as the American Association of School Physicians on October 27, 1927, by 325 physicians at the annual meeting of the American Public Health Association in Cincinnati, its membership was opened in 1936 to all professionals interested in promoting school health and it was renamed the American School Health Association.

American Sign Language (ASL) *Ameslan.* A formal method of communication used by people with hearing impairments in which manual sign symbols function as words. Each sign consists of four basic parameters: hand shape, location or place of articulation, movement in a particular direction, and the palm orientation that occurs with various hand shapes. Recognized as a natural language, ASL has its own structure, semantics (the meaning of words), and syntax (grammar). Manual aspects of ASL include sign formation and placement, whereas nonmanual aspects include facial expression, movements, postures, and other nonmanual signs that enhance and emphasize the meaning of signs.

American Society of Human Genetics (ASHG) An organization founded in 1948 to encourage, expand, and disseminate research in all areas of human genetics. The ASHG publishes the *American Journal of Human Genetics.*

American Speech-Language-Hearing Association (ASHA) The national professional, scientific, and credentialing organization for speech-language pathologists and audiologists. Its mission is for all people with speech, language, and hearing disorders to have access to quality services to help them communicate more effectively. Its activities include setting academic standards and accrediting educational training programs, supporting public and professional advocacy, certifying professional competence, providing continuing education, disseminating knowledge, and ensuring quality clinical and ethical practice. ASHA publishes the *American Journal of Audiology;* the *American Journal of Speech Language Pathology;* the *Journal of Speech, Language and Hearing Research;* and *Language, Speech, and Hearing Services in Schools.*

Americans with Disabilities Act (ADA) of 1990 (PL 101-336) Originally enacted in 1990, PL 101-336 is a joint antidiscrimination and affirmative action federal legislative mandate enacted 1) to protect people with disabilities against discrimination while 2) jointly expanding social role valorization and the inclusion for such people in all aspects of society. The law broadly defines *disability* as a physical or mental impairment that substantially limits one or more major life activities. Titles I–V of the act systematically address employment, public and private services, public and private architectural accommodations, transportation, and telecommunications.

Americans with Disabilities Act Amendments Act (ADAAA) of 2008 (PL 110-325) U.S. Supreme Court decisions resulted in significant departures from the intent of the Americans with Disabilities Act (ADA) of 1990 (PL 101-336), limiting the definition of disability, narrowing the protections available to citizens, and making it difficult for people with disabilities to receive the protection the law intended. PL 110-325 was passed to construe the ADA more broadly in favor of the individual and to reaffirm its commitment to full inclusion and to protecting against discrimination. PL 110-325 is no longer limited by many mitigating circumstances, substantially expands the concept of limits, covers impairments that are episodic in nature or that are in remission, revises the definition of "major life activities," and expands coverage for employees designated as "regarded as disabled." PL 110-325 also provides a basis for more students to be considered eligible for services under Section 504. In addition, the clear and concise language regarding mitigating measures and the expansive list of measures included in PL 110-325 provide a different framework for eligibility decisions. There is also increased demand on employers to accommodate a broader range of conditions, with increased penalty for failure to comply.

Amer-Ind A comprehensive gestural system based on Native American hand talk used for fundamental intertribal communication. *See also* gesture.

Ameslan *See* American Sign Language (ASL).

amitriptyline Trade name, Elavil. A tricyclic antidepressant.

Ammons Quick Test *See* Quick Test (QT).

AMN *See* adrenomyeloneuropathy.

amnesia Loss of memory. Amnesia can be retrograde (affecting memories of events before the injury) or anterograde (affecting memories of events after the injury).

amniocentesis A prenatal diagnosis procedure in which amniotic fluid is removed transabdominally by needle. The cells in the fluid are mostly fetal and can be used for genetic and other tests, including prenatal diagnosis of chromosomal impairments. The fluid can also be used to measure alpha-fetoprotein levels. The procedure can only be performed after 14 weeks' gestation.

amniotic fluid Derived from *liquor amnii,* meaning "water." The fluid in which the developing fetus floats during pregnancy. Sampling such fluid for medical tests is known as *amniocentesis.* Too much (polyhydramnios) or too little (oligohydramnios) amniotic fluid may negatively affect the fetus.

amphetamine A central nervous system (CNS) stimulant drug; street names include *speed* and *upper.* Because of their abuse potential (including addiction), drugs in this group have been placed in the Class II (nonnarcotic) schedule by the U.S. Drug Enforcement Administration and can be prescribed only by a licensed physician in compliance with federal and state regulations. Amphetamines are used to treat attention-deficit/hyperactivity disorder and narcolepsy; their anorectic (appetite-suppressing) side effects must be monitored.

amplification The process of increasing the magnitude of an impulse or signal. For example, an amplifier that increases the strength of electrical impulses is a component of hearing aids.

amplified fragment length polymorphism (AFLP) A deoxyribonucleic acid (DNA) marker found by splitting sections (fragments) of DNA and linking them to specific sequences.

amplitude The magnitude of measured activity or response; intensity.

amputation The absence or removal of a limb or appendage.

amygdala A part of the limbic system of the left temporal lobe of the brain that plays a major role in the processing of social and emotional information. Structural and functional impairments of the amygdala may be associated with the presence of autism spectrum disorders.

AN/AD *See* auditory neuropathy/auditory dyssynchrony.

ANA *See* American Nurses Association.

anaclitic depression A behavioral syndrome of weepiness, apprehension, withdrawal, refusal to eat, sleep disturbances, and eventually stupor, all secondary to a lack of nurturance or mothering in an infant late in the first year of life. Originally thought to be an infantile depression, anaclitic depression is now interpreted as the behavioral correlate of the more severe degrees of failure to thrive or reactive attachment disorder of infancy. When the primary caregiver is suddenly lost, the infant turns inward and becomes extremely passive. *See also* hospitalism, institutionalism.

anacusis *See* anakusis.

Anafranil *See* clomipramine.

anakusis *anacusis.* Total hearing loss; deafness.

anal wink Stimulation of the rectum that produces anal contractions. This reflex may be absent when either sensory or motor pathways to the anal area are interrupted, as occurs in spina bifida or myelomeningocele (protuberance of both the spinal cord and its lining).

Analysis of Sensory Behavior Inventory– Revised Edition (ASBI-R) The ASBI-R rates six sensory modalities as sensory seeking or sensory avoidant to help therapists design a treatment plan.

Analysis of the Language of Learning (ALL) A standardized test of metalinguistic knowledge of words, syllables, and sentences and of understanding directions. The ALL is appropriate for use with 5- to 9-year-old children, even nonreaders.

Analysis of Verbal Behavior (AVB) An applied behavior analysis (ABA) approach to teaching communication that uses a functional rather than a developmental approach to language.

anamnesis Patient history.

anaphylactic shock A life-threatening state of shock caused by a serious allergic response.

anarithmetria *anarithmia.* Difficulty with carrying out arithmetic operations.

anarthria A loss of speech due to severe loss of neuromuscular control of the speech musculature.

anatomical age *See* bone age.

anemia Literally, "low blood." Anemia is reflected in decreases in red blood cell number and size (MCV) or hemoglobin content (MCH). Tiredness and pallor are two of the primary findings in mild anemia.

anencephaly A birth defect in neural tube closure during the first 28 days of embryogenesis that leads to an absent forebrain, an incompletely developed skull, and a variety of facial impairments. Anencephaly is incompatible with survival. The recurrence risk with no other family history is ~4%. Alpha-fetoprotein (AFP) levels, sonography, and x rays allow for prenatal detection.

aneuploidy The deviation of the chromosomal number of a cell by a whole number from the norm of 46 (in humans), as in individuals with Down syndrome who have a single extra chromosome 21.

aneurysm Weakening with resulting bulging or ballooning of the wall of a blood vessel that renders the vessel liable to rupture (break). If an intracerebral (within the brain) aneurysm ruptures, the result is an intracerebral (into the subarachnoid space) bleed and likely a stroke (brain attack).

angel dust *See* phencyclidine.

Angelman syndrome (AS) A genetic syndrome caused by deletion 15q; del(15) (q11–q13). Features include widely spaced teeth, severe intellectual disability, absent speech, paroxysmal laughter, an ataxic marionette-like gait, seizures, and characteristic facies (large mouth, protruding jaw, and mid-face hypoplasia [underdevelopment]). AS results from parent-specific methylation impairments of chromosome 15 in 78% of cases, including those with a deletion, uniparental disomy (UPD), or an imprinting defect (ID); fewer than 1% of individuals have a cytogenetically visible chromosome rearrangement (i.e., translocation or inversion). *UBE3A* sequence analysis detects mutations in an additional approximately 11% of individuals. The deletion is in the same region of chromosome 15 as in

Prader-Willi syndrome (PWS). Formerly known as *happy puppet syndrome*. *See also* Prader-Willi syndrome (PWS).

angiography A radiographic (x ray) study that injects a contrast medium (usually radiopaque iodine) to make the blood vessels visible on x ray. The procedure is helpful in identifying cerebral aneurysms or arteriovenous malformations with their risk of stroke (brain attack).

anhedonia The state of being unable to experience pleasure.

anhidrosis A reduction in or complete loss of perspiration, usually as a side effect of a drug.

aniridia The absence of the iris.

aniridia–Wilms tumor association *AGR triad, aniridia type IV, aniridia–Wilms tumor–genitourinary impairments–retardation, Miller syndrome.* A rare chromosomal disorder that can include intellectual disability; an atypical facies, including microcephaly (small head), prominent forehead, cranial asymmetry, long narrow face, high nasal root, ptosis (drooping) of the eyelids, and low set ears; aniridia (absent irises); and Wilms tumor (a malignancy of the kidney). This association is frequently caused by a deletion of part of the short arm of chromosome 11. *See* WAGR syndrome.

aniseikonia An optometric disorder in which the visual images from the two eyes arrive at the brain having different sizes or shapes. This rare condition is diagnosed with an instrument called an *eikonometer* and is treated with special lenses. The theory that aniseikonia contributes to reading disorders is controversial.

anisometropia An optometric disorder in which the visual acuity in one eye is significantly different from the visual acuity in the other eye.

ankle–foot orthosis (AFO) *See* orthosis.

ankylo A Greek combining form that relates to abnormal fusion, usually of a joint.

ankyloglossia Condition in which the lingual frenulum is abnormally short and restricts the mobility of the tongue. *See* tongue-tie.

anlage An initial or elementary structure that embryologically develops into a more complex structure. The term is used analogously for any primordium (early stage).

anodontia The absence of teeth.

anomalad *See* sequence anomalad.

anomaly A deviation of structure or function. The term *birth anomaly* is preferred to *birth defect.*

anomia An acquired condition (usually because of brain damage such as follows a stroke in adults) of impaired or absent ability to name objects or find the correct words; the typically milder congenital form seen in children is usually referred to as *dysnomia* and may be part of a learning or language disorder pattern.

anonychia The absence of nails.

anophthalmia The congenital absence or hypoplasia (underdevelopment) of one or both eyes.

anorexia Loss of appetite; a common side effect of certain drugs (amphetamines), a symptom of psychiatric disorders (e.g., depression, eating disorders), and a nonspecific sign of acute or chronic illness.

anorexia nervosa An eating disorder that usually occurs in females between the ages of 10 and 30. Anorexia nervosa is characterized by secretive, self-imposed dietary restrictions, often combined with the (over)use of laxatives and extreme amounts of vigorous exercise resulting in a body weight less than 85% of that expected for height and build. The woman sees herself as overweight, even at as much as 25% below the expected weight for her age. Anorexia nervosa often requires hospitalization and carries the highest mortality rate of any psychological disorder.

anoxia   A lack of oxygen delivered to tissue; prolonged anoxia leads to cell death. Anoxia is dangerous to brain tissue because the surviving brain cells cannot replace lost neurons.

ANSER   *See* Aggregate Neurobehavioral Student Health and Educational Review.

antagonist   A muscle that opposes or resists the action of another muscle (the agonist).

antecedent   A preceding event, condition, or cause. A functional analysis of behavior looks for antecedents to maladaptive behaviors so that interventions can be designed.

anterior cingulate cortex   An area of the brain associated with attention.

anteroposterior view (AP)   An x ray taken so that the beam goes from front to back.

anteversion   The degree to which an anatomical structure is rotated forward (toward the front of the body). Some structures change the angle of rotation with maturation. For example, the angle between the head/neck and the shaft of the femur changes from approximately 25–30 degrees in a newborn to 10–15 degrees in an adult. When this evolution is altered or incomplete, the infant or child will often compensate by medially rotating the femur to produce stability.

anthropometry   The science and study of the comparative measurement of the human body.

anticipation   A characteristic of certain genetic disorders in which the age of onset is earlier and/or the condition more severe with each generation.

anticipatory guidance   Parent education about child development that is included as part of the well-child visit with a primary health care provider. Parents are taught how to recognize, respond to, and facilitate age-appropriate behaviors; discipline and developmental stimulation are major concerns. Medical problems that are age related (e.g., bow legs in the toddler) and variations in development in the presence of chronic disease are also covered.

anticonvulsant   Any of a broad class of drugs used to reduce the frequency or severity of seizures (convulsions). The drug chosen is based on the type of seizures. The most common side effects of anticonvulsant medications include blood and liver problems, rashes, and drowsiness. Many of these drugs have subtle effects on attention and cognition, and several are known to be teratogenic (i.e., to cause fetal malformations). Seizure medication must be taken every day and continued for a period of time adequate to treat the type of seizure. The goal is to control the seizures without inducing debilitating side effects.

anticonvulsant embryopathy   *See* fetal phenytoin syndrome.

antidepressant   *See* heterocyclic antidepressants.

antiepileptic drug (AED)   *See* anticonvulsant.

antihistamine   A broad group of drugs used to treat allergic symptoms by blocking the effects of histamine (a naturally occurring chemical in the body that produces allergic symptoms such as pruritus [itching] and urticaria [hives]). A common side effect of most drugs in this class is drowsiness;

however, children with attention disorders may paradoxically become more hyperactive when given such drugs.

antimongoloid slant A term for downslanting (going from the nose laterally) palpebral fissures. This feature is a component of the facies of a variety of genetic syndromes and sometimes an isolated finding of no clinical significance. The name derives from the contrasting mongoloid slant in trisomy 21. The antimongoloid slant may be more common in syndromes with mid-facial hypoplasia (underdevelopment).

antipsychotic A medication used to treat symptoms of psychoses (e.g., hallucinations, delusions).

antisocial personality (ASP) disorder A chronic pattern of irresponsible behavior with poor social relationships and nonconformity with accepted social standards; the person must be at least 18 years of age with a diagnosis of conduct disorder prior to age 15. Failure to parent, pay bills, hold a job, and plan ahead, as well as criminal antisocial actions, are common features, along with substance abuse, spousal and child abuse, and sexual promiscuity. ASP disorder is more common in males with a family history of similar disorders.

antiyeast therapy A proposed but unproven treatment for autism that relates yeast overgrowth to increased intestinal permeability to the opioid peptides in gluten and dairy products. These peptides in turn either directly affect brain function or precipitate an antibody reaction against brain tissues. Treatment components include gluten- and dairy-free diets, antifungal medications, and probiotics.

anxiety An internal state of fear in response to actual or perceived danger. Anxiety may be distinguished from fear, however, in that fear is a response to a real and present external threat or danger, whereas anxiety often exists in anticipation of a future event. Anxiety may be mild (in the form of apprehension) or severe and functionally debilitating (in the form of panic attacks or phobias). It may occur in discrete periods of sudden onset or may become chronic and unfocused (free-floating). Anxiety is an unpleasant emotional state accompanied by physiological arousal and the cognitive elements of apprehension, guilt, and sometimes a sense of impending disaster. Low to moderate levels of anxiety produce physiological arousal and a psychological state of preparedness that may be adaptive (e.g., a student experiences anxiety about an upcoming test and thus prepares for it); however, high levels of anxiety are counterproductive and interfere with performance.

anxiety disorder A generic term for a group of disorders characterized by an internal state of extreme, disabling anxiety and an avoidance behavior pattern. Some anxiety disorders are episodic in nature, such as panic disorder, whereas others are more chronic, such as generalized anxiety disorder. The person is affected by the internal state itself, a subsequent recursive fear of experiencing this internal state in response to certain external stimuli, and a progressive limiting of life experiences due to the need to avoid those stimuli that provoke the anxiety.

anxiolytic A medication for modifying the intensity or impact of mental tension and anxiety without interfering with typical mental activity.

AOA *See* American Orthopsychiatric Association.

A1 *See* primary auditory cortex.

AOS *See* apraxia of speech.

AOSI *See* Autism Observation Schedule for Infants.

AOTA   *See* American Occupational Therapy Association.

AOTF   *See* American Occupational Therapy Foundation.

AP   *See* anteroposterior view.

APA   *See* American Psychiatric Association; American Psychological Association.

apathico-akineticoabulic syndrome   *See* frontal lobe syndrome.

apathy   Lack of feeling or affect that can be seen in severe depression, schizophrenia, and brain injury.

APBS   *See* Association for Positive Behavior Support.

Apert syndrome   *acrocephalosyndactyly type I.* A genetic syndrome characterized by craniosynostosis (premature fusion of skull sutures), turribrachycephaly (an oddly shaped skull), and syndactyly (webbing of the fingers or toes). Conductive hearing loss and speech problems secondary to oropalatal structural defects are common. Because all people with Apert syndrome have some cognitive impairments (regardless of early craniectomy), it is important to distinguish intellectual disability from hearing impairments, speech-language disorders, and other learning disabilities. The true prevalence of intellectual disability in Apert syndrome is unknown; incidence is estimated at 1 in 160,000, with the majority of cases representing fresh mutations, although an autosomal dominant pattern has also been demonstrated. When the latter is true, the recurrence risk is 50%. The condition is associated with *FGFR2* alterations on chromosome 10q26. The disorder is named after French pediatrician Eugene Apert (1868–1940).

Apgar score   A score of 0–2 assigned to a newborn infant at 1 and 5 minutes of age for each of five descriptors using the following mnemonic: A (appearance [color]), P (pulse [heart rate]), G (grimace [response to stimulation]), A (activity [muscle tone]), and R (respiration [breathing effort]). Named after Virginia Apgar (1909–1974), the Apgar score is an acceptable measure of the acute status of the infant; however, it is a poor predictor of later developmental outcome. The best possible score is 10; however, because most infants have blue extremities (arms or legs) for several hours after birth, a score of 9 is usually the highest obtained.

APHA   *See* American Public Health Association.

aphagia   The inability to swallow.

aphakia   The absence of the lens from the eye.

aphasia   A diminished ability to correctly use and comprehend language. In developmental pediatrics, *aphasia* describes a profound lack of language, whereas a language disorder is diagnosed in children with a less severe impairment. Aphasia may be due to damage to the cortex (outer part) of the left hemisphere of the brain.

aphemia   An obsolete and vague term for *aphasia. See* aphasia.

aphonia   Literally, "loss of voice." Aphonia is usually due to a congenital or acquired laryngeal impairment.

APIB   *See* Assessment of Preterm Infant Behavior.

aplasia cutis congenita (ACC)   *See* cutis congenita aplasia.

apnea   Literally, "not breathing." Respiratory arrest, either transient or prolonged, that can lead to cyanosis (blue color), decreased heart rate, hypotonia (decreased muscle tone), and, eventually, brain damage and death.

True apnea is defined as a period of at least 15 seconds without breathing. The origin can be obstructive (mechanical) or central (physiological central nervous system [CNS] response). Apnea is common in premature infants as a result of the developmental immaturity of the regulatory mechanisms of the respiratory system.

apnea monitor A device that sounds an alarm when an infant stops breathing; home apnea monitors are used for some infants at high risk for respiratory arrest, such as premature infants with frequent apneas and bradycardias (accompanying decreases in heart rate) and infants who previously have had acute life-threatening events (ALTEs).

apolipoprotein E (APOE) A brain protein involved in the maintenance and repair of neurons after injury. The presence of different APOE alleles (especially APOE $\varepsilon4$) is a risk factor for the development of Alzheimer's disease and may be a protective factor for the development of cerebral palsy after brain injury.

apoptosis Genetically programmed cell death.

appendicular Relating to an appendage; with regard to the body, the reference is to the peripheral arms and legs rather than to the central head and trunk.

apperception The perception of stimuli combined with additional mental abilities, including interpretation, classification, and recognition. The process of understanding how newly observed qualities of an object, picture, or situation are related to past experience. Apperception is assessed through projective techniques in psychological testing. *See also* Children's Apperception Test (CAT), Thematic Apperception Test (TAT).

applied behavior analysis (ABA) Coined by B.F. Skinner, the term *applied behavior*

analysis refers to the systematic study of behavior and the application of learning principles to alter behavior. Applied behavior analysts use operant conditioning procedures and tend to focus on overt (observable) behavior. As a specific approach to the treatment of autism, ABA targets 10 developmental delays (language, attention, motivation, imitation, toy play, peer play, social interaction, emotional expression, self-help skills, and cognitive functioning) and 2 behavior excesses (aggression [including self-injury] and self-stimulatory behavior [repetitive or ritualistic behavior]). ABA is sometimes referred to as the *Lovaas method* after its developer, O. Ivar Lovaas. It is sometimes used synonymously with intensive behavioral intervention (IBI) or early intensive behavioral intervention (EIBI). *See also* Lovaas, O. Ivar (1927–2010).

APP-R *See* Assessment of Phonological Processes–Revised.

appropriate for gestational age (AGA) A range of weights and lengths compatible with length of pregnancy.

apraxia An impairment in the ability to accomplish previously learned and performed complex motor actions that is not explainable by ataxia, reduced selective motor control, weakness, or involuntary motor activity.

apraxia of speech (AOS) *developmental apraxia of speech (DAS)*. Severe impairment in planning the speech act. A disorder of higher cortical function without a motor component.

aprosody The loss or absence of prosody (melody or rhythm of speech), leading to a monotone delivery. Aprosody can be a component of a communication disorder; milder versions are referred to as *dysprosody.*

APTA *See* American Physical Therapy Association.

aptitude An individual's potential for learning a certain skill or developing a particular type of knowledge. Aptitude differs from ability in that the latter is restricted to a specific skill or area of knowledge. Ideally, aptitude is measured prior to any specific training. Aptitude may result from a combination of hereditary and environmental factors. Aptitudes are usually measured by specifically devised tests; for example, the Scholastic Aptitude Tests (SATs) are designed to measure potential for success in the first year of college.

aptitude test A test that measures specific types of mental competence, often aimed at predicting achievement in certain areas. In practice, descriptions of these tests often use the terms *aptitude, ability,* and *intelligence* interchangeably.

arachidonic acid A long chain polyunsaturated fatty acid (LCPUFA) with a high concentration in the brain. Because its concentration may effect subtle cognitive or behavioral differences in developing children, it is used as a supplement to infant feeding.

arachnodactyly Literally, "spider fingers." Long and slender fingers and toes; can be part of a syndrome such as Marfan syndrome.

arachnodactyly

ARBD *See* alcohol-related birth defects.

arbovirus A member of the ribonucleic virus group which includes the most common causes of epidemic encephalitis (brain inflammation).

ARC of the United States A national network of state and locally based parent–professional cooperatives that provide a range of services to individuals with intellectual disability. The association defines its mission as that of conducting programs that promote the general welfare of people with intellectual disability. Available services depend on local funding. Formerly known as the Association for Retarded Citizens of the United States (ARC-US).

arching The tendency of an infant to bend the head, neck, and back in a concave curve backward as if withdrawing or pulling away from a frontal stimulus. Arching can be a manifestation of an exaggerated tonic labyrinthine reflex (TLR) and may then suggest

arching

an underlying motor diagnosis. It may also be observed in children with autism, pervasive developmental disorder, and other atypical patterns of development, or it may be a response to the discomfort of gastroesophageal reflux.

architectural barrier A structural impediment to the approach, mobility, and functional use of an interior or exterior environment.

ARC-US *See* ARC of the United States.

area *See* domain.

arena assessment An approach to assessment that involves a team of professionals who work within an inter- or transdisciplinary model. In this approach, selected individuals (including the parent) interact with the child while other clinicians observe. Arena assessment teams often vary in terms of composition, location of the assessment, instruments used, and the number of individuals who interact directly with the child.

arginase deficiency A metabolic disorder of the urea cycle. Because the associated hyperammonemia is mild, acute presentation in infancy is less likely to occur. Toe walking and progressive spastic diplegia (paralysis that involves the legs more than the arms) may accompany intellectual disability and recurrent episodes of vomiting, headache, and irritability. Dietary restriction can prevent the progression of symptoms.

argininosuccinicaciduria A urea cycle defect caused by a block in the enzyme argininosuccinate lyase, the gene for which is found on chromosome 9. The condition is characterized by intellectual disability and poor hair growth. It is diagnosed by an elevation in argininosuccinic acid on amino acid screens. Protein loading (giving a protein meal) is often required to identify affected people and carriers.

aripiprazole Trade name, Abilify. An atypical antipsychotic used to treat schizophrenia, bipolar disorder, depression, irritability, and challenging behaviors in autism.

Arithmetic A Wechsler (intelligence test) subtest that measures mental manipulation, concentration, short- and long-term memory, and numerical reasoning ability.

Arizona Articulation Proficiency Scale– Third Edition (Arizona-3) A measure of articulation proficiency for children from 1.5 to 18 years of age; it requires naming responses to picture cards.

ARND Alcohol-related neurodevelopmental disorders. *See* alcohol-related birth defects (ARBD).

Arnold-Chiari malformation A malformation of the brain in which the base (cerebellum, medulla, pons) is elongated and protrudes into the foramen magnum (the opening in the skull from which the spinal cord exits). The four types of malformation are numbered I–IV, indicating increasing severity. Type I is the mildest and is often of unclear clinical significance. Type II is often found in association with a lumbar or sacral myelomeningocele (protuberance of both the spinal cord and its lining). Type III is more commonly associated with a cervical

myelomeningocele. Chiari Type IV with cerebellar malformation is usually not included in the classification. Diagnosis is made by either computed tomography (CT) scan or magnetic resonance imaging (MRI). Hydrocephalus (excess fluid in the brain) is common with Arnold-Chiari malformation, often requires shunting, and generally occurs earlier in life with the more severe types.

AROM *See* active range of motion.

arousal A state of alertness.

array comparative genomic hybridization (aCGH) A method of genetic testing with higher resolution for the detection of copy number variants (CNVs). aCGH can be targeted or can address the whole genome.

arrhinencephaly The congenital absence of the rhinencephalon (section of the brain directly related to the sense of smell). This is seen frequently in individuals with trisomy 13.

arrhythmia Abnormal heart rhythm.

ART *See* assisted reproductive technology.

arthritis Inflammation of a joint; symptoms can include pain, limited motion, warmth, redness, and swelling.

arthro A Greek prefix meaning "relating to the joint."

arthrodesis An orthopedic surgical procedure that immobilizes or fixes a joint by fusion.

arthrogryposis multiplex congenita A genetically heterogeneous condition of multiple congenital joint contractures characterized by a usual pattern of symmetrical involvement of all four limbs. There are generally no associated neurodevelopmental impairments. This is a pure motor impairment syndrome to be treated by physical therapy, casting, and orthopedic surgery. Oligohydramnios (too little amniotic fluid) is suspected to contribute to causation. Recurrence risk varies, depending on whether a specific impairment such as alternation in the survival motor neuron gene is found. There is a higher than expected incidence in identical twins; however, typically only one twin is affected.

articulation The juncture between bones.

articulation The way in which speech sounds are formed. Proper formation requires correct placement; timing; direction; pressure; speed; and integration of the movement of the lips, tongue, palate, and pharynx.

articulation disorder *developmental articulation disorder, difficulty with pronunciation, phonological disorder, speech defect.* A disorder characterized by consistent failure to use developmentally expected speech sounds.

articulators The lower jaw, lips, tongue, soft palate, and pharynx, which are involved in the production of meaningful sounds by shaping the flow of air.

artificial larynx An external mechanical sound source that is substituted for the larynx.

AS *See* Angelman syndrome.

AS *See* Asperger syndrome.

ASA *See* Autism Society of America.

ASBI-R *See* Analysis of Sensory Behavior Inventory–Revised Edition.

ASD *See* autism spectrum disorder.

ASDS *See* Asperger Syndrome Diagnostic Scale.

ash leaf spot A hypopigmented skin lesion found in tuberous sclerosis.

ASHA *See* American School Health Association.

ASHA *See* American Speech-Language-Hearing Association.

ASHG *See* American Society of Human Geneticists.

Ashworth scale A scale for grading the degree of spasticity (increased tone in individual muscle groups) with resistance to passive range of motion. Scores are 1 for no tone, 2 for marked increase in tone but limb easily flexed, 3 for considerable increase in tone such that passive movement is difficult, and 4 for rigidity in flexion and extension.

A-SICD *See* Adapted Sequenced Inventory of Communication Development for Adolescents and Adults with Severe Handicaps.

ASIEP-2 *See* Autism Screening Instrument for Educational Planning–Second Edition.

ASL *See* American Sign Language.

ASP disorder *See* antisocial personality disorder.

Asperger syndrome (AS) A behavioral syndrome characterized by eccentric and obsessive interests, impaired social interactions, average to above-average intelligence, attention-deficit/hyperactivity disorder, gross motor clumsiness, and pragmatic language difficulties. Incidence is estimated at 2 per 1,000 with a 7-to-1 male predominance.

Asperger Syndrome Diagnostic Scale (ASDS) A 50-item yes/no scale used to screen for Asperger syndrome.

asphyxia Suffocation; lack of oxygenation. When asphyxia is mentioned as a possible cause of developmental disability, it must be of sufficient duration and severity to produce the death of nerve cells. For perinatal asphyxia to be seriously considered as a cause of brain damage, the Apgar score should be 0–3 at 10 minutes, and there should also be severe hypotonia (decreased muscle tone) and seizures in the newborn period.

Aspie Informal term for a person with Asperger syndrome. This term originated with people with Asperger syndrome and is sometimes used by people with Asperger syndrome and their families to describe their own condition.

aspiration Literally, "breathing or inhalation." This medical procedure is the removal of a substance from the body by suction.

aspiration pneumonia Aspiration pneumonia is a lung infection caused by breathing (aspirating) an irritating substance such as food, liquid, or secretions into the lungs. Aspiration pneumonias are common with tracheoesophageal fistulas and neuromotor disorders causing swallowing difficulty. Meconium aspiration is common with fetal stress and postmature deliveries. Foreign body (e.g., a peanut) aspiration can produce severe lung disease.

aspirin sensitivity The combination of allergic asthma, nasal polyps, and severe intolerance to aspirin is a widely recognized syndrome in adults. The widespread presence of salicylates (the active ingredient in aspirin) in foods has contributed to salicylates being included on the list of substances to be avoided in almost all of the dietary regimens that claim to treat disorders of attention and learning. Evidence supporting this association remains anecdotal.

ASQ-3™ *See* Ages & Stages Questionnaires®, Third Edition: A Parent-Completed Child-Monitoring System.

ASQ:SE *See* Ages & Stages Questionnaires®: Social-Emotional: A Parent-Completed, Child-Monitoring System for Social-Emotional Behaviors.

Assessing Prelinguistic and Early Linguistic Behaviors in Developmentally Young Children A measure of five early language skills that assesses cognitive antecedents to word meaning, play, communication intention, language comprehension, and language production in children 9–24 months of age.

Assessing Semantic Skills Through Everyday Themes (ASSET) A test of receptive and expressive vocabulary for children 3;0–9;11 years in 10 areas: understanding labels, identifying categories, identifying attributes, identifying functions, understanding definitions, expressing labels, expressing categories, expressing attributes, expressing functions, and expressing definitions.

assessment Information gathering aimed at 1) evaluating previous performance, 2) describing current behavior, and 3) predicting future behaviors. A comprehensive assessment synthesizes past records, evaluations, interviews with significant people, observations of current behavior, results of standardized tests, and other special procedures. Assessment differs from testing in that testing reflects performance at a particular time, whereas assessment requires clinical judgment to give meaning to the overall pattern and interrelationships among the various results. Assessment is further distinguished from evaluation, which may involve a similar set of procedures but whose primary aim may be restricted to determining eligibility for programs.

Assessment, Evaluation, and Programming System for Infants and Children (AEPS®), Second Edition A curriculum-based assessment for children from birth to 6 years old. Linked volumes are designed to easily connect assessment and intervention under the Individuals with Disabilities Education Act (IDEA) of 1990 (PL 101-476). Assessment results are linked to specific instructional activities and goals across six developmental areas: cognitive, adaptive, social–communication, social, fine motor, and gross motor.

Assessment Link Between Phonology and Articulation (ALPHA) Test   A 15-minute test designed to relate articulation assessment results to phonological analysis.

Assessment of Children's Language Comprehension (ACLC)   A test that uses a picture-pointing task to relate single-word vocabulary to the comprehension of two-, three-, and four-word phrases.

Assessment of Phonological Processes–Revised (APP-R)   A 20-minute assessment of phonological processes that can be used for intervention planning.

Assessment of Preterm Infant Behavior (APIB)   An adaptation of the Brazelton Neonatal Behavioral Assessment Scale for use with newborns younger than 37 weeks' gestational age. The APIB rates behaviors in visual, auditory, tactile, organization, and reflex categories. It is used with medically stable premature infants until they react to the environment in a manner similar to full-term infants.

ASSET   *See* Assessing Semantic Skills Through Everyday Themes.

assimilation   A learning process that applies a general cognitive structure to particular environmental data and modifies the data to suit that internal cognitive structure.

assimilation   The phonological process that occurs when a phoneme is altered because it is influenced by, and becomes more like, a surrounding phoneme.

assimilative nasality   A disorder of resonance that occurs when the oral sounds surrounding nasal sounds become nasalized.

assisted reproductive technology (ART)   Procedures to assist infertile couples, including artificial insemination, in vitro fertilization (IVF), zygote intrafallopian transfer (ZIFT), gamete intrafallopian transfer (GIFT), and intracytoplasmic sperm injection (ICSI). Such procedures may be associated with an increased risk of neurodevelopmental disorders in children.

assistive listening device   An electronic device that amplifies the acoustic signal to improve the listener's perception.

assistive mobile device   An orthopedic appliance or device that improves mobility (e.g., cane, crutches, walker, wheelchair).

Assistive Technology Act ("Tech Act") of 1998 (PL 105-394)   Legislation that provides funds to states to support three types of programs: 1) the establishment of assistive technology (AT) demonstration centers, information centers, equipment loan facilities, referral services, and device utilization programs to provide for the exchange, repair, recycling, or other reutilization of assistive technology devices, which may include redistribution through device sales, loans, rentals, donations, and other consumer-oriented programs; 2) protection and advocacy services to help people with disabilities and their families as they attempt to access the services for which they are eligible; and 3) authorized federal and state programs to provide low interest loans and other alternative financing options to help people with disabilities purchase needed assistive technology.

Assistive Technology Act Amendments of 2004 (PL 108-364)   Amendments to the Assistive Technology Act ("Tech Act") of 1998 (PL 105-394) to, among other things, support programs of grants to states to address the assistive technology (AT) needs of individuals with disabilities. PL 108-364 is intended to promote people's awareness of and access to AT devices and services, so that individuals with disabilities can more fully participate in education, employment, and daily activities on a level playing field with other members of their communities. PL 108-364 covers people with disabilities of all ages, with all disabilities, in all environments.

assistive technology device An item, piece of (re)habilitation equipment, or product system used to increase, maintain, or improve the functional capabilities of individuals with disabilities. The Technology-Related Assistance for Individuals with Disabilities Act Amendments of 1994 (PL 103-218) encourages and assists states in developing programs of technology-related assistance and extending the availability of assistive technology to individuals with disabilities and their families.

assistive technology evaluation An evaluation conducted by a technology specialist(s) to assess and make recommendations regarding technology devices that may be helpful to a child with a disability.

assistive technology services Any service that directly assists a child with a disability in the selection and/or acquisition of an assistive technology device.

associated deficits Neurobehavioral findings that do not derive directly from the primary developmental diagnosis but rather indicate more diffuse brain involvement and suggest the possibility of other developmental diagnoses. Associated deficits may be more disabling than the primary diagnosis. Their impact on functioning is more than additive, and they reflect the underlying continuum of developmental disabilities.

associated movements Overflow movements; extraneous or adventitious movements that occur in the performance of a motor act, such as tongue protrusion when

writing. Mirror movements are contralateral (on the opposite side) associated movements; synkinesis refers to ipsilateral (on the same side) associated movements. Associated movements decrease with age and increase with many developmental disabilities; they are inversely correlated with intelligence level. Soft neurological signs or signs of minor neurological dysfunction include associated movements. *See also* motor overflow.

associated reactions Movements seen on the affected side of a hemiplegia (paralysis of half the body) or hemisyndrome in response to voluntary forceful movements in other parts of the body.

association A nonrandom occurrence of multiple anomalies (malformation, deformation, disruption, or dysplasia) in more than two individuals. There is a purely statistical relationship between the anomalies. Understanding of the relationship between anomalies in an association is weaker than in a syndrome, although associations such as VATER or VACTERL may occur as part of a syndrome, such as trisomy 18.

association area The primary visual, auditory, sensory, and motor areas of the cerebral cortex (Brodmann areas 1, 2, 3, 4, 17, and 41) are bounded by association areas (e.g., 5, 6, 7, 18, 42) in which the incoming sensations and outgoing motor actions are interpreted or initiated by the person. Problems with higher order thinking (such as those that occur with learning disabilities) are often localized to the association areas.

Association for Behavioral and Cognitive Therapies (ABCT) An interdisciplinary organization committed to the advancement of a scientific approach to the understanding and amelioration of problems of the human condition through the investigation and application of behavioral, cognitive, and other evidence-based principles to assessment, prevention, and treatment. ABCT publishes two journals and has approximately 25 special interest groups, several of which are relevant to the field of disability.

Association for Children and Adults with Learning Disabilities (ACLD) *See* Learning Disabilities Association of America (LDA).

Association for the Advancement of Behavior Therapy (AABT) *See* Association for Behavioral and Cognitive Therapies (ABCT).

Association for Positive Behavior Support (APBS) An international organization dedicated to promoting research-based strategies that combine applied behavior analysis and biomedical science with person-centered values and systems change to increase quality of life and decrease problem behaviors. The APBS is made up of professionals, family members, trainers, consumers, researchers, and administrators who are involved and interested in positive behavior support. The APBS publishes a journal and a newsletter and holds an annual conference.

Association of Maternal and Child Health Programs (AMCHP) A national nonprofit organization founded in 1944 that represents state public health leaders and others working to improve the health and well-being of families, women, children, and youth, including those with special health care needs. The AMCHP is principally made up of the directors and staff of state public health agency programs for maternal and child health and children with special health care needs in all 50 states, the District of Columbia, and eight additional jurisdictions.

Association of State and Territorial Health Officers (ASTHO) A national nonprofit organization representing the public health agencies of the United States, the U.S. Territories, and the District of Columbia, as well as the 120,000 public health professionals these agencies employ.

Association of University Centers on Disabilities (AUCD) A network of federally funded programs that foster graduate training in 10 core disciplines that serve people with developmental disabilities. *See* University Centers for Excellence in Developmental Disabilities Education, Research, and Service (UCEDD).

associationism A theory of learning that suggests that once two stimuli are presented together, one of them will remind the learner of the other. Basic principles of associationism are that 1) contiguous (occurring close together) stimuli are more likely to be associated than those that occur far apart; and 2) the more frequently the paired stimuli are repeated, the more strongly they will be associated.

assortative mating The tendency of individuals with similarities such as cognitive and emotional disorders to form relationships with one another. Although the majority of pairing occurs between like types (e.g., between people with schizophrenia), there are also pairings of people with complementary or nonrelated disorders. In some cases, assortative mating is enhanced by prolonged association with a particular social reference group (e.g., mental health facility, group therapy, sheltered workshop); however, this phenomenon can occur independent of prolonged affiliation.

ASSQ *See* Autism Spectrum Screening Questionnaire.

astasia An inability to stand due to motor incoordination; this neurological finding can manifest itself in episodes of sudden collapse, with loss of support of the weight of the body. Astasia can be observed in typically developing infants at 4–5 months of age; physiologically speaking, astasia precedes abasia.

astasia–abasia An inability to walk despite the presence of typical motor strength and coordination. This neurological finding can be observed in typically developing infants from 4 to 6 months of age. Prior to that time, the infant may go through the motions of (supported) walking on a reflex basis; after that time, independent walking begins to emerge. Physiologically speaking, abasia (the inability to walk) follows astasia. *See also* abasia.

astatic seizure　*See* akinetic seizure, atonic seizure.

astereognosis　Congenital or acquired difficulty with stereognosis (solid form recognition by touch, such as the ability to identify a key placed in the hand with eyes closed).

asthenic body type　A long, slender habitus (appearance). *See also* ectomorph.

asthma　A disorder characterized by recurrent episodes of wheezing and shortness of breath (dyspnea) precipitated by allergy, infection, and physical or emotional stress. As a chronic disease in childhood, asthma accounts for a significant percentage of school absence.

ASTHO　*See* Association of State and Territorial Health Officers.

astigmatism　Blurring of vision due to a refractive defect in the lens or cornea, which has an elliptical shape in individuals with this condition.

asymmetrical tonic neck reflex (ATNR)　A primitive reflex in which turning the infant's head to one side causes the arm and leg on that side to extend while the opposite arm and leg flex, producing a "fencing posture." This is a physiological (normal) response in newborn infants that gradually disappears during the first 6 months of life; how-

asymmetrical tonic neck reflex (ATNR)

ever, even late in the first year when the reflex is no longer visible it can influence tone and other reflex responses, facilitating extension on the face side and flexion on the occiput side. Any examination of the neuromotor system in infancy should therefore be performed with the infant's head in mid-line. With an obligatory response, the child would be unable to break out of the ATNR pattern so long as the head remained turned to the side; such a response should be considered pathological.

asymptomatic　Not showing symptoms; appearing healthy and without disabilities when in reality there is a disease condition present. Some carriers of infectious diseases remain asymptomatic while spreading the disease; others become symptomatic. Genetic carriers of autosomal recessive conditions may have no symptoms or only mild symptoms compared with homozygotes. Many diseases of various etiologies have quiet phases or asymptomatic stages. Screening tests often attempt to diagnose asymptomatic disorders.

at risk　*Risk* is the likelihood that an individual will develop a given condition in a given time period. *At risk* implies the presence of specific intrinsic or extrinsic individual characteristics (e.g., intrinsic—genetic susceptibility, age, sex, and weight; extrinsic—environmental exposures such as nutrition, housing, or toxic exposure) that are associated with an increased probability of developing a condition or disease. To have risk factors (i.e., to be at risk) does not necessarily imply a diagnosis or etiology. Children at risk either have, or are considered to be likely to develop, a problem (e.g., physical, mental, developmental) that requires monitoring, evaluation, and/or intervention to prevent or lessen future difficulties or developmental delays.

ataxia　Literally, "lack of order." An inability to generate a normal or expected voluntary movement trajectory that cannot be attributed to weakness or involuntary motor activity. An absence or loss of muscular coordination leading to clumsy and uncertain standing, walking, and reaching. Significant ataxia is usually associated with disorders of the cerebellum and can often follow traumatic brain injury (TBI) in children and adults.

ataxia telangiectasia *Louis-Bar syndrome.* A progressive, ultimately fatal genetic disorder characterized by marked coordination problems (ataxia); dilation of the small vessels (telangiectasia) of the eyes, nose, and ears; frequent infections (secondary to immune system involvement); and, in approximately half of the cases, intellectual disability in the later stages of the disease. Incidence is rare, with inheritance following an autosomal recessive pattern. Alterations of the *ATM* gene are found in >95% of individuals.

ataxic cerebral palsy One of the physiological subtypes of cerebral palsy in which the prominent motor signs are early hypotonia (decreased muscle tone) and later ataxia (unsteady gait). When ataxia is the prevailing motor symptom, it exhibits improvement with age. Congenital cerebellar involvement is typical, with some degree of cerebellar hypoplasia or agenesis (small or absent cerebellum). Mild cognitive limitation, tremor, and articulation disorders are also common.

ataxic dysarthria A motor speech disorder characterized by damage to the cerebellum that causes incoordination of skilled movement, disturbances of stance and gait, and a rhythmic tremor of the head and/or body.

atelectasis A collapse of a segment of the lung. The presence of atelectasis is usually associated with preexisting or underlying lung disease, and its occurrence is usually marked by increased respiratory distress.

athetoid cerebral palsy *See* athetosis.

athetoid posturing An atypical movement pattern of the hand and fingers (and sometimes of the foot and toes) that involves splaying of the digits, spooning, and an "almost withdrawal" or "avoidance" posture when attempting to grasp an object and sometimes

athetoid posturing

spontaneously. Athetoid posturing of the feet contributes to the "spontaneous Babinski" of extrapyramidal cerebral palsy.

athetosis Literally, "without position." When used to describe motor disabilities, a pattern of movement disorder characterized by involuntary, slow, writhing, and undulating movements of flexion, extension, pronation, and supination that are more peripheral than central and are sometimes called *vermicular* or *worm-like.* More purely athetoid movements are slower and more sustained than choreiform (involuntary twitching) movements. *See also* choreoathetosis.

Ativan *See* lorazepam.

atlantoaxial instability An enlargement of the distance between the first two cervical (neck) vertebrae that leaves the individual susceptible to spinal cord compression, neurological involvement (transient or permanent weakness or paralysis), and death. Children with Down syndrome are at increased risk for atlantoaxial instability. Radiologic screening (cervical spine x rays), close neurological monitoring, and caution with regard to contact sports and other activities that might precipitate cord compression are indicated.

ATNR *See* asymmetrical tonic neck reflex.

atomoxetine Trade name, Strattera. A selective norepinephrine (brain chemical) inhibitor that is used to treat the symptoms of attention-deficit/hyperactivity disorder (ADHD). Strattera's advantages over traditional stimulant therapy include the fact that it is not a controlled drug and that it may also address accompanying anxiety symptoms.

atonia   Absence of tone.

atonic cerebral palsy   *See* hypotonic cerebral palsy.

atonic seizure   *akinetic seizure, astatic seizure.* A seizure characterized by the sudden loss of posture and tone. In infants who do not stand independently, these seizures are manifested in the "salaam seizures" during which the infant suddenly drops his or her head and neck forward. In older children, the loss of postural tone results in a sudden fall to the ground ("drop attack"). Although there is only a brief loss of consciousness, brain injuries can occur. Atonic spells are most common in the morning shortly after waking but can occur during the day. Atonic seizures are part of Lennox-Gastaut syndrome, which has a poor prognosis for seizure control and cognitive development. *See also* Lennox-Gastaut syndrome.

atonic-astatic epilepsy   *See* Lennox-Gastaut syndrome.

atopy   Literally, "strangeness." A group of allergic diseases with common features. Atopic diseases include hay fever, allergic asthma, certain cases of eczema, and some cases of urticaria (hives). These have a definite familial or genetic tendency but not to specific diseases or allergens.

atresia   The congenital absence of or failure to develop a normally present body cavity or canal.

atrophy   Shrinkage; wasting away. A decrease in the size of an anatomical structure (body part or organ).

attachment   The emotional connection between child and caregiver that prevents an infant from straying too far from a care-giver in an unfamiliar world and that initiates the infant's search when the caregiver is absent.

attachment parenting   A philosophy of parenting that prioritizes strong connections between parents and children and espouses breast feeding, co-sleeping, and positive discipline.

attention   Selective, goal-directed perception. Neuropsychological theories and (neuro)physiological correlates of arousal and attention continue to be studied. The length of time a child can attend to a stimulus (attention span) increases with age, interest, and intelligence level.

attention deficit disorder (ADD)   *See* attention-deficit/hyperactivity disorder.

Attention Deficit Disorders Evaluation Scale (ADDES)   A norm-referenced evaluation tool for the diagnosis of attention deficit disorder (ADD) with or without hyperactivity in children ages 4–18. The ADDES corresponds with the *Diagnostic and Statistical Manual of Mental Disorders, Fourth Edition, Text Revision (DSM-IV-TR)*, criteria and has versions for home (46 items completed by the parent in approximately 12 minutes) and school (60 items completed by school personnel in approximately 15 minutes). The test yields subtest scores for inattention, impulsivity, and/or hyperactivity and has a pre-referral checklist and intervention manual.

attention-deficit/hyperactivity disorder (ADHD)   A neurobehavioral syndrome characterized by short attention span, distractibility, impulsivity, and sometimes hyperactivity. Diagnosis is by interview, observation, and behavior questionnaires. The child or adult should, over a prolonged period of time, demonstrate a behavior pattern that includes the following: fidgeting, difficulty remaining seated, distractibility, difficulty waiting turns, blurting out answers, failure to complete assignments, poorly sustained attention, excessive shifting, noisiness, excessive talking ("motor mouth"), intrusiveness, failure to listen, frequently losing things, and physically dangerous behavior. Motor clumsiness and visual perceptual motor disorders are also common. Prevalence is estimated at 5%–10% of children. Although ADHD is familial in occurrence, genetic transmission patterns have not been fully delineated. ADHD has three types: inattentive type; hyperactive, impulsive type; and combined type. Frequently, children with ADHD also have learning disabilities. *See also* hyperactivity, hyperkinetic syndrome of childhood, minimal brain damage/dysfunction (MBD).

attribution retraining   Programs based on attribution theory are designed to teach children how to change their performance by changing their perception of the cause of success or failure from an uncontrollable factor, such as ability, to a controllable factor, such as effort. Students are given feedback regarding their effort on tasks, such as "You were trying hard" or "We usually fail because we don't try hard enough." It is important that the tasks undertaken be consistent with the students' abilities.

attribution theory   A social psychology theory that explores the rules typically used by individuals to explain observed social behavior. People develop a repertoire of *causal schemata,* defined as a general conception of how certain causes interact. A major division separates those who blame themselves (internal causation) from those who blame others or their environment (external causation). A person's explanations for feelings, successes, failures, or other outcomes may be enhanced or inhibited by his or her position on an internal versus external causal axis.

atypical behavior   Unusual behavior that is cause for concern; the persistence or intensity of a behavior inappropriate for age.

There is nothing inherently abnormal in such behaviors—many simply reflect individual "quirks"—although they can be associated with developmental disorders. Sometimes referred to as *developmental deviance.*

atypical neuroleptics   A newer class of neuroleptics used to treat psychotic disorders but thought to hold less risk for developing tardive dyskinesia. Significant weight gain remains a problem. Examples include risperidone (trade name, Risperdal) and olanzapine (trade name, Zyprexa). Also referred to as *second generation antipsychotics (SGAs).*

AUCD   *See* Association of University Centers on Disabilities.

audiogram   A record showing hearing level by sound frequency. A clinical audiogram should show hearing thresholds measured by both air conduction and bone conduction. Better hearing by bone conduction than air conduction indicates an air–bone gap, a sign of conductive hearing loss.

audiologic screening   A pass/fail procedure used to identify individuals who require further audiological assessment for possible hearing impairments or hearing loss.

audiologist   An individual who holds a degree and/or a certification in audiology and who is concerned with the identification, assessment, and rehabilitation of hearing impairments.

audiology   The study of hearing and hearing disorders; specifically, the assessment of the nature and degree of hearing loss and of hearing conservation, and the rehabilitation of individuals with hearing impairments.

audiometer   An electronic instrument used to measure hearing sensitivity and to quantitate hearing loss.

auditory Relating to hearing or audition.

auditory brainstem response (ABR) *See* brainstem auditory evoked response (BAER).

auditory discovery One component of a teaching approach known as *guided discovery teaching*. Guided discovery teaching seeks to ensure that students learn sound–symbol correspondences and other patterns of language.

auditory discrimination The brain's ability to tell the difference between very similar sounds. People with problems in auditory discrimination have difficulty distinguishing between words that sound alike or that differ in a single phoneme. An impairment in auditory discrimination can interfere with verbal comprehension and the development of functional reading skills.

auditory evoked potential (AEP) assessment An electrophysiological procedure that describes the clinical status of the auditory neural pathway and associated sensory elements. It can help locate the cause of the hearing impairment in the cochlea, cranial nerve VII, or brainstem.

auditory feedback loop A system that is used to monitor one's own productions as they are vocalized and that impels one to go back and correct or modify when something does not sound quite right.

auditory integration training (AIT) A treatment method that attributes behavior, learning, and psychiatric problems (including autism) to atypical sound sensitivity. Treatment uses a desensitization analog that uses modified sound exposure (e.g., filtered and distorted music) to reeducate the brain. AIT includes the Berard method, Tomatis sound therapy, and Samonas sound therapy.

auditory memory The ability to store and retrieve information presented verbally as sounds or in the form of sound symbols.

Auditory memory relates to the acquisition and use of both expressive and receptive language vocabulary.

auditory nerve *acoustic nerve.* The eighth cranial nerve, which has two major branches: the cochlear nerve for hearing and the vestibular nerve for balance.

auditory neuropathy/auditory dyssynchrony (AN/AD) A paradoxical set of audiological findings with normal otoacoustic emission (OAE) results and auditory brainstem response (ABR) impairment.

auditory orienting Turning toward a sound stimulus; localizing the general direction of a sound source, if not its exact location, by the use of hearing unsupported by visual cues. Orienting is a receptive language milestone that has cognitive content; failure to orient does not necessarily reflect a hearing deficiency. Orienting is one of the few language milestones readily open to direct observation in the clinical setting.

auditory perception The ability of the brain to interpret information that enters the body through the ears. Auditory perception is directly related not to auditory acuity or sharpness but to the process by which the brain discriminates sounds from one another and identifies meaningful units of sound.

Auditory Projective Test *See* Braverman-Chevigny Auditory Projective Test.

auditory processing disorder *See* central auditory processing disorder (CAPD).

auditory sequential memory The ability to retain verbally presented information in a particular order. Auditory sequential memory is measured by tests such as digit span and memory for sentences and nonsense syllables. People with auditory sequential memory problems may also have difficulty following a series of instructions.

auditory trainer (FM) A classroom assistive device that transmits from a microphone worn by the teacher to the student's frequency-modulated (FM) receiver (headphones). It is used for children with central auditory processing impairments.

auditory training The process of teaching a person with a hearing impairment how to make the best use of residual acoustic cues (i.e., how to listen, localize, and discriminate). Auditory training is not to be confused with auditory process training, a method of ameliorating learning disabilities that was prevalent in the 1960s.

augmentative and alternative communication (AAC) Temporary or permanent compensation techniques used by individuals with severe expressive communication disorders. AAC interventions utilize an integrated group of components, including the symbols, aids, techniques, and strategies used by individuals to enhance communication. *Symbols* refers to the methods used to facilitate communication by representing conventional concepts (e.g., gestures, photographs, manual sign systems, printed words, spoken words); *aids* refers to physical objects or devices used to assist with the communication process (e.g., boards, charts, devices, computers); *techniques* refers to the way in which the messages are transmitted (e.g., scanning, encoding, signing, natural gestures, role playing, classroom learning); *strategies* are the specific ways in which AAC aids. *See also* alternative communication.

augmentative and alternative communication (AAC) symbol A symbol used in various communication devices; these may belong to one of several symbol systems such as Picture Communication Symbols, Blissymbols, or Widgit Rebus.

augmentative and alternative communication system (AACS) The aggregate communication process for an individual with verbal communication difficulty.

augmentative communication Any procedure or device that facilitates speech or spoken language. *See also* augmentative and alternative communication (AAC).

aura A sensation that may precede a seizure or migraine headache. This may be caused by vasodilation (an increase in diameter) of the blood vessels of the brain in migraines. Symptoms of auras preceding seizures—generally complex partial seizures—are often olfactory (related to smell) or produce a gastric "rising" sensation, fear, visual hallucinations, or, rarely, rage reactions. The frequency of auras appears to increase with age; however, this may reflect the improved ability of a child to describe the phenomenon.

aural Pertaining to the ear or hearing.

aural rehabilitation Educational procedures used with individuals with hearing impairments to improve their overall ability to communicate. Rehabilitation includes developing, utilizing, and integrating existing receptive and expressive modalities such as auditory, tactile, visual, and kinesthetic channels. These techniques use two methodologies: 1) the analytic method, which is a sequential approach that stresses mastery of the parts of the technique for assimilating information into a comprehensive picture; and 2) the synthetic method, which promotes the use of language in spontaneous, simultaneous situations through speech, reading, and writing before the language is presented formally.

auricle The external ear, or pinna. The term is also an antiquated synonym, rarely used, for the heart chamber now called the *atrium*.

auropalpebral reflex A reflex in which the stimulus of a sudden sound near the ear elicits an eye wink or twitch as a response.

auscultation Listening; a diagnostic procedure used to listen to the body's internal sounds. Examples include the use of a stethoscope to auscultate heart sounds and breath sounds or a fetoscope to auscultate an unborn infant's heart rate. *See also* fetoscope.

authentic assessment   A type of assessment, conducted in real-life situations, in which individuals are expected to demonstrate skills that represent realistic demands encountered when learning.

autism   *autistic disorder, early infantile autism, Kanner syndrome.* A pervasive developmental disorder characterized by a pattern of impaired (delayed and deviant) communication skills; failure to develop social relationships; and restricted, repetitive, and stereotypical behaviors. Although approximately half of children with autism also have some degree of intellectual disability, this may be difficult to determine in early childhood. First described by Leo Kanner (1894–1981) in 1943, autism is now recognized as a neurological organic brain disorder with different etiologies that occurs in nearly 1% of the population. There has been a dramatic increase in the prevalence of autism secondary to heightened awareness, redefinition, and diagnostic substitution.

Autism Behavior Checklist (ABC)   A 57-item questionnaire designed to screen for autism. The ABC is part of the Autism Screening Instrument for Educational Planning–Second Edition and is completed by a caregiver, teacher, or parent. Scored and interpreted by a professional, the ABC is designed for use with school-age children but can be used with children as young as 3 years old.

Autism Diagnostic Interview–Revised (ADI-R)   A standardized, semistructured interview for a clinician to use with a child's parent or principal caregiver when assessing autism in children and adults with mental ages of 18 months and older. The interview contains 111 items that tap behaviors in three content areas: reciprocal social interaction; communication and language; and repetitive, restricted, and stereotyped interests and behavior. Items are scored from 0 (*criteria are not fully met*) to 3 (*extreme severity*), with scores generated for each domain. Autism is diagnosed in a child if scores are elevated in each of the three content areas and if at least one content area is atypical prior to 36 months of age. Extensive training in both administration and scoring is required for validity.

Autism Diagnostic Observation Schedule–Revised (ADOS-R)   An instrument that consists of structured and semistructured activities to measure social, communicative, and play behavior in children suspected of having a diagnosis of autism spectrum disorder. There are four modules: Module 1 is designed for nonverbal young children, Module 2 for children with some phrase language, Module 3 for children with age-appropriate play behavior and language at a 4-year level or above, and Module 4 for verbally fluent adults. Use of the ADOS-R requires a trained clinician to record observations and code them to formulate a diagnosis based on cutoff scores for autism and pervasive developmental disorder–not otherwise specified (PDD-NOS). In order to participate in the ADOS-R a child must function at least at an 18-month level cognitively and must be walking. The ADOS-R cannot be used with children who have hearing, visual, or motor impairments. *See also* Prelinguistic Autism Diagnostic Observation Schedule (PL-ADOS).

Autism Diagnostic Observation Schedule–Toddler (ADOS-Toddler)   A new module of the ADOS for use in the diagnosis of autism and pervasive developmental disorders (PDDs) in children younger than 30 months of age.

Autism Diagnostic Observation Schedule–Second Edition (ADOS-2)   An updated version of the ADOS due to be released in 2010. It contains improvements in Modules 1–3 and a module for toddlers.

Autism Dysmorphology Measure (ADM) A structured examination of 12 body parts for dysmorphic features that can be used to subtype children with autism. The utility of this classification approach has not been demonstrated.

Autism Observation Schedule for Infants (AOSI) A 16-item checklist of behaviors in children as young as 6 months that may indicate the later development of autism.

Autism Screening Instrument for Educational Planning–Second Edition (ASIEP-2) A classroom assessment and educational planning system for people with autism, severe disabilities, and developmental disabilities who are between 18 months of age and adulthood and who have low language abilities. The ASIEP-2 includes five components: 1) Autism Behavior Checklist (ABC), 2) sample of vocal behavior, 3) interaction assessment (including self-stimulation, crying, laughing, gesturing, manipulation of toys, conversation, and tantrums), 4) communication, and 5) learning rate.

Autism Society of America (ASA) Parent and professional organization that supports and disseminates information, education, research, and advocacy about autism.

autism spectrum disorder (ASD) Referring to the heterogeneous family of disorders that includes autism, pervasive developmental disorder-not otherwise specified (PDD-NOS), and Asperger syndrome (AS).

Autism Spectrum Screening Questionnaire (ASSQ) A 27-item checklist for Asperger syndrome and high-functioning autism. Parent cutoffs are from 13 to 19; teacher cutoffs are from 11 to 19, with the lower cutoff being less specific.

autism-like Relating to the presence of features of autism in people who do not have autism but who may have severe cognitive impairment, attention-deficit/hyperactivity disorder, or language disorders. *See* extended autism phenotype.

autistic disorder *See* autism.

autistic features Behavioral deviance frequently seen in children with autism, hearing impairment, or other developmental disorders with somewhat atypical presentations. These features can include language delay, noncommunicative language, reference to self in the third person, pronominal reversal, neologisms (the introduction of new words or new senses of words), echolalia (the repetition of what is heard), poor eye contact, lack of cuddliness as an infant, lack of response to auditory input, good rote memory, acting as though one is in one's own world, climbing on or over people like furniture, laughing for no reason, odd play, no peer interactions, water play, toe walking (equinus gait), rocking, twirling, spinning, perseveration (the inability to move to another thought or idea), unusual object attachment, hand regard, hand flapping, stereotypies, and preservation of sameness.

autistic regression A fairly rapid loss of language and social skills that usually occurs between 18 and 24 months of age in children who then develop autism spectrum disorder. Autistic regression occurs in one half to two thirds of children with autism.

autoinflammatory disease One of a series of conditions caused by recurrent attacks of systemic inflammation that can cause neurological involvement. Some of these disorders are genetic or familial, such as familial Mediterranean fever (FMF) or cryopyrin-associated periodic syndromes (CAPS), each of which is characterized by fever, skin lesions, and musculoskeletal involvement. These conditions can result in seizures, meningitis, or developmental delay leading to intellectual disabilities. They may also cause hearing impairment and arthritis, both of which may lead to disability.

automatic processing Behavioral sequences that, after prolonged practice, no longer require attention. Some processes are susceptible to this type of learning, whereas others may be intrinsically incapable of such automatization. Although automatic processes are rapid and efficient, once learned they are inflexible and difficult to change. In a learning situation, automatization failure and deficiency refer to the fact that a person must still devote conscious attention to learning tasks that have become automatic for others. For example, having to consciously decode words hinders reading comprehension, and having to consciously compute math facts decreases the amount of attention available for processing new concepts.

automaticity Habitual response to an expected stimulus. Education attempts to reduce as many learned processes to automaticity as possible. The more reading, decoding, and mathematics facts become automatic or rote, the quicker and more efficient the associated thinking and learning processes will be.

automatisms Semi-purposeful movements or activities that occur frequently with complex partial seizures. These are generally stereotypic movements that may be related to the activity in progress before the onset of the seizure or that may begin after onset. Automatisms occur in five groups: 1) gestural (picking at clothing), 2) alimentary (chewing or lip smacking), 3) mimicking (facial grimaces), 4) verbal occurrences (yelling, laughing, or repetitive speech), and 5) ambulatory (walking or running). In general, automatisms occur after consciousness has been lost, and children do not remember them.

autonomic nervous system The involuntary nervous system that controls the unconscious functioning of the cardiovascular, respiratory, digestive, and reproductive systems; sometimes referred to as *brainstem, vegetative,* or *life-sustaining functions.* There are two major subdivisions to the autonomic nervous system: 1) the sympathetic (adrenergic) and 2) the parasympathetic (cholinergic) nervous systems.

autosomal dominant The inheritance pattern for a trait that appears in every generation and is transmitted by an affected person (one parent) but never by an unaffected person. Transmission and occurrence are not affected by sex. New autosomal dominant mutations can occur in individual sperm or eggs and may not be present in other body tissues.

autosomal recessive The inheritance pattern for a trait that is inherited when a child receives two genes for the trait, one from each parent, both of whom must carry the gene for that trait although they may not be affected by it. A specific harmful recessive gene may be present in a particular population at a higher rate than in the general population. For example, although Tay-Sachs disease is present in all populations, it occurs at a greater rate in the Ashkenazic Jewish population. Consanguinity among ethnically, religiously, or geographically isolated populations can result in an increased number of individuals with rare recessive disorders. *See also* consanguinity.

autosome Any chromosome other than a sex chromosome. Humans have 22 pairs of autosomal chromosomes.

auxology The study or science of (human) growth.

AVB *See* Analysis of Verbal Behavior.

aversive responses Behavioral responses seen during infant feeding that may include crying, grimacing, arching away, and even gagging. These responses may occur in response to touch, taste, temperature, texture, or odor.

aversive stimulus   A noxious stimulus that, applied to a response, decreases the tendency of that response to recur.

avoidant behavior   Behaviors used to avoid stressful situations. Individuals who stutter will avoid certain speaking situations, certain kinds of conversational partners, and specific words.

avoidant disorder of childhood   This term formerly referred to an anxiety disorder in which the feared situation was social contact with others. Avoidant children were observed to be chronically, painfully shy; to shrink from strangers even after long exposure; and to blush, fall silent, and cling to parents in the presence of other adults. The term *avoidant disorder* has been replaced by *social anxiety disorder.*

axial   Central in the body; along the axis of the head and trunk. Axial tone (especially hypotonia [decreased muscle tone]) is often distinguished from appendicular tone.

axilla   The armpit.

AYP   *See* adequate yearly progress.

Bb

babbling   The second stage of infant vocalization following cooing and preceding first words. Consonant and vowel combinations are used repetitively to produce such sequences as "ga-ga-ga" and "da-da-da." Babbling is a maturational phenomenon that starts at 6–7 months, even in children who are hearing impaired, but it is delayed in children with developmental disabilities such as intellectual disability and language disorders.

Babinski sign   A Babinski sign (sometimes termed a *positive Babinski*) is an upgoing movement of the toes (dorsiflexion) and spreading of the toes in response to attempts to provoke a plantar (foot) reflex by stimulating the lateral (outside) border of the sole of the foot. This response

Babinski sign

is not uncommon in the first year of life. A typical response (sometimes termed a *negative Babinski*) occurs later when the toes flex (bend downward). The first movement of the hallux (big toe) and the presence of flaring of the toes are important points in equivocal or uncertain Babinski responses. Positive Babinski responses are signs of pyramidal tract involvement in spastic cerebral palsy, and spontaneous (unstimulated) upgoing Babinski responses can be observed in extrapyramidal cerebral palsy. Joseph François Felix Babinski (1857–1932) first described this reflex.

Babkin reflex   A newborn reflex pattern in which squeezing the infant's palms produces mouth opening, eye closing, and turning and flexing of the head. This palmomandibular sign weakens in the first month and is absent after 4 months of age.

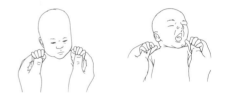

Babkin reflex

Baby Doe   A case that highlighted the issue of denying life-sustaining treatment to newborn infants with permanent disabilities and life-threatening but surgically correctible abnormalities. Baby Doe contrasted the rights of parents to make decisions for their child with the state's power (via federal regulations incorporated into each state's child abuse laws) to protect children from medical abuse or neglect.

babygram   Slang term for an x ray of an infant who is small enough for the single x-ray image to capture the infant's whole body.

BACB   *See* Behavior Analyst Certification Board.

backing   The phonological process whereby consonants are produced near the back of the mouth when they should be produced near the front of the mouth. Example: saying /g/ for /d/. Backing is commonly seen in children with clefting issues.

backward chaining A teaching method in which the components of a task ("chain") are acquired in reverse order (i.e., the last component is taught first and the prior ones are added following mastery of the final one). For example, an instructor first asks a learner to insert the final piece of a puzzle and then teaches and reinforces placement of the other pieces. *See also* chaining, forward chaining.

baclofen A centrally acting muscle-relaxant drug that can be used to treat spasticity in severe cases of cerebral palsy. The preferred method of administration is by continuous intrathecal baclofen infusion (CIBI) via a surgically implanted pump that delivers the drug directly into the spinal fluid. Baclofen can be administered orally and has also been used to treat self-injurious behavior.

BADLs *See* basic activities of daily living.

BAER brainstem auditory evoked response. *See* brainstem auditory evoked potentials.

balance and equilibrium responses Compensatory automatic movements (reflexes) to regain mid-line stability, to maintain and reestablish one's center of gravity.

balance board Adaptive equipment used to promote normal balance responses in children and adults. People can sit, kneel, or stand on the device.

Baller-Gerold syndrome A rare genetic syndrome with craniosynostosis (premature fusion of skull sutures); growth deficiency; abnormalities of the forearm and anus; and, in approximately half of the cases, intellectual disability. Inheritance follows an autosomal recessive pattern. Gene changes in *RECQL4* are thought to be responsible for this condition.

ballismus Rotary flailing; irregular, violent flinging; hurling; large rapid movements at the shoulder or hip. The condition is typically unilateral (hemiballismus) and represents a rare variant of choreiform (involuntary twitching) extrapyramidal cerebral palsy. Ballismus is typically caused by abnormalities in deep brain structures called the *basal ganglia.*

Balthazar Scales of Adaptive Behavior I: Scales of Functional Independence (BSAB-I) Rating scales for adaptive behaviors (eating, dressing, and toileting) in children and adults with severe to profound intellectual disability.

banding A technique of staining chromosomes that produces characteristic but different patterns of cross-bands. G-banding uses Giemsa staining; Q-banding uses quinacrine fluorescence.

Bankson Language Test–Second Edition (BLT-2) A test of language for children from 3 to 7 years of age with results organized into three general categories: semantic (meaning systems) knowledge, morphological/syntactic (language structure) rules, and pragmatics.

Bankson-Bernthal Test of Phonology (BBTOP) An assessment of articulation and phonological processes for children 3–9 years of age.

Bannayan-Riley-Ruvalcaba syndrome *See* Smith-Riley syndrome.

Bannayan-Zonana syndrome *See* Smith-Riley syndrome.

barbiturate A group of drugs that act as central nervous system (CNS) depressants; barbiturates can be used for sedation and seizure control.

Bardet-Biedl syndrome A genetic syndrome characterized by polydactyly (extra fingers or toes), syndactyly (webbing of fingers or toes), obesity, retinitis pigmentosa (night blindness in childhood progressing to complete blindness by age 20), and mild to moderate intellectual disability. Cardiac, renal, and ophthalmological follow-up is indicated. Inheritance is generally autosomal recessive with a recurrence risk of 25% and alterations in more than a dozen associated genes. The original individuals reported by Laurence and Moon had spastic diplegia (paralysis involving the legs more than the arms) and lacked polydactyly. Laurence-Moon-Biedl syndrome, Laurence-Moon syndrome, and Bardet-Biedl syndrome are now known to be separate syndromes.

Barkley's School Situations Questionnaire (SSQ)　A questionnaire designed to evaluate a variety of situations in which children may display problem behaviors. Teachers are asked to rate a child's behavior in both classroom and other school settings. For all positive situations, the severity of the problem behavior is rated on a scale from 1 (*mild*) to 9 (*severe*). Thus, scores are obtained for both the number of situations in which problem behaviors occur and the mean severity rating of those behaviors. Normative data are available for children ages 4–11 years.

Barkley's School Situations Questionnaire–Revised (SSQ-R)　A revision of the original Barkley's School Situations Questionnaire (SSQ) designed to assess specific problems with attention and concentration in a variety of school situations and settings. Scoring is similar to that for the SSQ. Norms are available for children ages 6–12 years.

Barlow maneuver　A test of hip stability used to screen for congenital hip dislocation in infants; medial (inside) to lateral (outside) pressure is applied to the proximal femur (thigh bone). Testing for hip dislocation is a routine component of the pediatric examination in early infancy.

Barr body　The condensed X chromosome in female cells. Each cell in the body of a typical human female has two X chromosomes, but only one X chromosome remains active. The other condenses into a Barr body.

barrel-chested　Describing the appearance of the chest of a child with cystic fibrosis or long-standing back hypertonia whose trunk is rounded in appearance with an increased anterior–posterior (front to back) diameter.

Barrett's esophagus　Tissue damage in the lower esophagus caused by chronic acid reflux; symptoms include dysphagia (difficulty swallowing) and heartburn.

barrier-free　Describing a building, facility, or area that is accessible to people with mobility impairments. Barrier-free access is through ramps or elevators to supplement steps or stairs; doorways are wide enough to accommodate wheelchairs, and bathrooms are equipped to accommodate transfers. The term is also used to refer to the removal of barriers that limit access for people with other disabilities. *See also* universal design.

basal　The point below which test items are assumed to be correct. To shorten test administration time, particularly when the test covers a wide age range, administration procedures often indicate an item at which to begin, based on age or grade. Basals are described specifically for each test or subtest and are often a set number of consecutive items answered correctly.

basal ganglia　A group of nuclei (control centers) in the brain that regulate voluntary motor activity through the extrapyramidal motor system. These nuclei include the striatum (caudate nucleus and putamen), globus pallidus, and substantia nigra. They are very susceptible to damage by hyperbilirubinemia (high levels of bilirubin in the blood) associated with neonatal jaundice (yellowing of the skin). Immediate pathological effects might include opisthotonos (arching of the back) with kernicterus (yellow staining of these brain nuclei); long-term effects include choreoathetoid cerebral palsy.

basal reader series   A series of books containing a collection of stories in which vocabulary is controlled. Such books are typically used with groups of children and represent different reading levels. Series also include teacher's manuals, workbooks, placement and achievement tests, and various audiovisual and duplicating materials.

BASC-2   *See* Behavior Assessment System for Children, Second Edition.

base pair   *See* deoxyribonucleic acid (DNA).

baseline   A record of the frequency, duration, or intensity with which a behavior occurs over a period of time before an attempt to change the behavior is initiated. Comparing the postintervention data with the baseline data indicates the effectiveness of the intervention. This method can also be used to assess the effectiveness of an academic intervention.

baseline exaggeration   A phenomenon in which acute psychiatric symptoms are an exaggeration of preexisting behavior problems in people with intellectual disability.

Basic Achievement Skills Individual Screener (BASIS)   A test that assesses a student's basic skills in mathematics, reading, spelling, and writing. Skills are assessed at first-through eighth-grade levels, and administration time is approximately 1 hour. People with disabilities are included in the standardization sample.

basic activities of daily living (BADLs)   Basic activities of daily living include bathing, toileting, grooming, dressing, feeding, and mobility. *See also* activities of daily living (ADLs).

Basic School Skills Inventory–Diagnostic (BSSI-D)   A norm- and criterion-referenced test for children ages 4;0 to 7;5 years. The BSSI-D uses 110 items to measure six areas of school performance: 1) daily living skills, 2) spoken language, 3) reading readiness, 4) writing readiness, 5) math readiness, and 6) classroom behavior.

basic skill   A fundamental ability. Basic skills are considered to be the activities necessary for functioning on a daily basis, including basic activities of daily living (BADLs). The mastery of basic skills is necessary to progress to higher levels of achievement. Academically speaking, basic skills include speaking, spelling, reading, writing, and doing arithmetic.

basic trust   In psychoanalyst Erik Erikson's (1902–1994) version of psychosexual development, basic trust is the major achievement of the first developmental stage (basic trust versus mistrust) in the first year of life; repeated interactions with a caregiver (typically the mother) provide a foundation of positive predictability, safety, and trust, thus instilling in the infant a positive orientation toward the world.

basilect   A dialect that varies considerably from standard English; common in cultural groups that are not frequently exposed or readily inclined to adopt standard English (e.g., ethnic communities). *See also* acrolect.

BASIS   *See* Basic Achievement Skills Individual Screener.

B-ASQ   Behavior-Ages & Stages Questionnaires®. *See* Ages & Stages Questionnaires®: Social-Emotional (ASQ:SE): A Parent-Completed, Child-Monitoring System for Social-Emotional Behaviors.

Bassen-Kornzweig disease   *See* abetalipoproteinemia.

Battelle Developmental Inventory–Second Edition (BDI-2)   A comprehensive, standardized assessment of the personal–social, adaptive, motor, communication, and cognitive domains of children from birth to 8 years of age. Administration and scoring time is 1–2 hours. A Spanish-language version is available.

Battelle Developmental Inventory Screening Test (BDIST) A 96-item developmental screening test for children from birth to 8 years of age that yields a total test score and seven subtest scores in the personal–social, adaptive, gross motor, fine motor, receptive language, expressive language, and cognitive domains. Derived from the Battelle Developmental Inventory (BDI), the test allows the use of alternative screening cutoffs. Administration time is approximately a half hour. A Spanish-language version is available.

Batten disease A juvenile form of neuronal ceroid lipofuscinosis (NCL). The NCLs are a group of inherited neurodegenerative, lysosomal storage disorders characterized by progressive mental and motor deterioration, seizures, and early death. Visual loss is a feature of most forms; inheritance for juvenile NCL is autosomal recessive.

battered child syndrome *Caffey syndrome, Caffey-Kempe syndrome.* Referring to a specific pattern of bone lesions found on x-ray examination that indicates that a child is being criminally beaten. These radiographic findings may be accompanied by bruises, burns, black eyes, cuts, and abrasions, adding to suspicion of the etiology.

battery A specific group of diagnostic tests used in evaluating an individual for a variety of conditions and in a number of situations. Psychological, educational, neurological, and developmental evaluations include test batteries. Individual tests in a battery focus on different but related skills or on particular aspects of a given skill, providing the examiner with a significant amount of data. Those data, in combination with history, behavioral observation, and clinical judgment, are used to formulate a diagnosis and, subsequently, to suggest directions for intervention.

Bayesian analysis *Bayes theorem.* A probabilistic approach to assessing the effectiveness of a screening test or diagnostic procedure; the approach attempts to allow for how common the condition being tested for is in the population in which the test or procedure is being used. The prevalence of the screened condition is combined with both the specificity and sensitivity of the test being used to yield a conditional probability.

Bayley Infant Neurodevelopmental Screener (BINS) A short form of the Bayley Scales of Infant Development–Second Edition (BSID-II) used to identify children 1–42 months old who may have or be at risk for developmental delays. Children who fall below a cutoff are recommended for further assessment. Administration time is approximately 10 minutes.

Bayley Scales of Infant and Toddler Development–Third Edition (Bayley-III) A measure of cognitive and motor development for children from 1 to 42 months of age, originally developed by Nancy Bayley. It yields scores in cognition (Cog), receptive communication (RC), expressive communication (EC), fine motor skills (FM), gross motor skills (GM), social-emotional skills (SE), and 10 adaptive behavior areas: communication (Com), functional pre-academics (FA), self-direction (SD), leisure (LS), social (Soc), community use (CU), home living (HL), health and safety (HS), self-care (SC), and motor (MO).

BBCS-3 *See* Bracken Basic Concept Scale–Third Edition.

BBRS-2 *See* Burks Behavior Rating Scales–Second Edition.

BBTOP *See* Bankson-Bernthal Test of Phonology.

BCaBA *See* Board Certified Assistant Behavior Analyst.

BCBA *See* Board Certified Behavior Analyst.

BCNS Nevoid basal cell carcinoma syndrome. *See* Gorlin syndrome.

BD *See* behavior disorder.

BDI-2 *See* Battelle Developmental Inventory–Second Edition.

BDI-II *See* Beck Depression Inventory–Second Edition.

BDIED-II *See* Brigance Diagnostic Inventory of Early Development–II.

BDIST *See* Battelle Developmental Inventory Screening Test.

BE *See* below elbow.

BEAM *See* brain electrical activity mapping.

Beck Depression Inventory–Second Edition (BDI-II) A widely used self-administered questionnaire used to screen for the presence and intensity of depressive symptoms in people 13 years of age and older. The BDI-II consists of 21 items rated on a 4-point scale.

Becker muscular dystrophy The mildest of the X-linked progressive dystrophies. *See also* muscular dystrophy.

Beckwith-Wiedemann syndrome *Beckwith syndrome.* A growth disorder characterized by macrosomia (large body size), macroglossia (large tongue), visceromegaly, embryonal tumors (e.g., Wilms tumor, hepatoblastoma, neuroblastoma, rhabdomyosarcoma), omphalocele, neonatal hypoglycemia, ear creases/pits, adrenocortical cytomegaly, and renal abnormalities. Intellectual disability occasionally occurs. There is a characteristic facies with a birthmark on the forehead and

a linear groove in the lobule of the ear. Neonatal hypoglycemia (low blood sugar) and Wilms tumor (a malignancy of the kidney) are among the potential complications. Cytogenetically detectable abnormalities involving 11p15 are found in 1% or less of cases. Clinically available molecular genetic testing can identify several different types of 11p15 abnormalities, including imprinting, uniparental disomy, and specific mutations. Most cases are usually sporadic.

BECTS *See* benign childhood epilepsy with centrotemporal spikes.

bed-wetting *See* enuresis.

Beery and Buktenica Developmental Test of Visual-Motor Integration–Fifth Edition (Beery VMI) A visual-perceptual motor test for people 2–100 years of age that requires the examinee to copy increasingly complex geometric figures without any erasures and without rotating the booklet in any direction. This test identifies problems with visual perception, motor coordination, and visual-motor integration, such as hand–eye coordination.

BEH *See* Bureau of Education for the Handicapped.

behavior analysis *See* applied behavior analysis.

Behavior Analyst Certification Board (BACB) A professional organization that credentials Board Certified Behavior Analysts and Board Certified Assistant Behavior Analysts. *See also* Board Certified Assistant Behavior Analyst, Board Certified Behavior Analyst.

Behavior Assessment System for Children–Second Edition (BASC-2) An assessment tool used to evaluate behavior and emotion in children from 2;6 to 18 years of age. It has five components: self-report, parent rating, teacher rating, structured developmental history, and a structured classroom observation form. The Teacher and Parent Rating Scales require 10–20 minutes for completion and produce scores for internalizing problems, externalizing problems, school problems, and adaptive skills and a composite score, the behavioral symptom index. Behaviors categorized under aggression, anxiety, atypicality, conduct problems, attitude problems, depression, somatization, and withdrawal are rated as typical, at risk, or clinically significant. Self-reports for ages 8–11 years and 12–18 years produce composite and subscale scores for clinical maladjustment, school maladjustment, and personal adjustment.

behavior coach   A one-to-one caregiver for an individual with intellectual or developmental disabilities. The concept of behavior coaching has been expanded so that people of all abilities and situations who wish to improve their success in life or work may seek a behavior coach.

behavior disorder (BD)   A disorder characterized by the presence of problem behaviors over a defined period of time (i.e., behaviors that deviate significantly from socially acceptable norms for the context and the individual's age). Children with behavior disorders are often isolated from others either because they withdraw from social contact or because they behave in an aggressive, hostile manner. Behavior disorders generally consist of four clusters of traits: conduct disorders, anxiety withdrawal, immaturity, and socialized aggression. In an educational setting, children are classified as having behavior disorders if they exhibit one of these clusters of behavior over an extended period of time and to such a marked degree that learning is negatively affected.

Behavior Education Program (BEP)   A set of schoolwide positive behavior supports (SWPBS) targeted at students deemed "at risk" for significant behavior problems. At-risk status is often designated following two

or more discipline referrals for behaviors such as disrupting class, tardiness, noncompliance, aggression, or verbal abuse. BEPs entail defined behavioral goals for individual students and frequently involve check in/check out (beginning and end-of-school-day) procedures, family involvement, and skills training. *See also* positive behavioral interventions and supports (PBIS).

Behavior Evaluation Scale (BES)   A checklist of six developmental areas and one problem area used to help plan educational interventions for children with autism.

Behavior Evaluation Scale–Third Edition (BES-3)   A behavior assessment for children in kindergarten through Grade 12. The BES-3 measures five dimensions corresponding to the five characteristics of behavior disorders or emotional disturbance in the Individuals with Disabilities Education Act (IDEA) of 1990 (PL 101-476): learning problems, interpersonal difficulties, inappropriate behavior, unhappiness/depression, and physical symptoms/fears. There are home (HV) and school (SV) versions. A 7-point scale is used to rate 52 (HV) or 54 (SV) items according to the frequency with which indicated behaviors are observed. Scores for each of the five subscales as well as an overall behavior quotient can be obtained.

Behavior Function Inventory (BFI)   A 55-item inventory of behavior disorder symptoms in people with autism; a 2-day observation period is required to collect the data.

behavior intervention plan (BIP)   The Individuals with Disabilities Education Act (IDEA) of 1990 (PL 101-476) requires the development of a BIP when school personnel seek to change the educational placement of a student with disabilities, for example as a consequence of problem behavior. The BIP emerges from a functional behavioral assessment (FBA) designed to determine the triggers or causes of the problem behavior. The FBA establishes a functional relationship among the environment, the behavior, and its consequences. The BIP is a corresponding concrete plan of action for preventing and managing the problem behavior. Although IDEA does not specify the exact components of a BIP, recommended practices include ways to change the environment to prevent the problem behavior; means to avoid reinforcement of nonpreferred behaviors should they occur; methods to teach and provide reinforcement for alternative behaviors; and systems of observation, tracking, and data collection. School personnel are legally obligated to follow the written BIP; the FBA and BIP can be the subject of due process. *See also* functional behavioral assessment (FBA), manifestation determination.

behavior management An approach to child rearing or parent training that moves the focus of behavior intervention from a reactive stimulus–response approach to a proactive prevention–management approach. Such an approach eliminates environmental support for inappropriate or negative behaviors and provides environmental support for positive behaviors. For children with neurodevelopmental problems, ordinary parenting techniques are usually ineffective. Behavior management has been subsumed by positive behavior supports and related models that aim to teach and reinforce replacement behaviors for maladaptive behaviors that are the focus of intervention.

behavior modeling A training intervention popularized by social learning theory. A practitioner demonstrates (models) the appropriate behavior or uses a visual representation, and the learner is reinforced for accurate replication of the behavior. *See also* modeling.

behavior modification Referring to a set of techniques based on the systematic applica-

tion of learning theory, this term emerged around the 1970s. The approach has been largely replaced by applied behavior analysis and positive behavior supports.

Behavior Observation Scale for Autism (BOS) A 67-item direct observation scale used to diagnose autism.

behavior phenotype A profile of behavior, cognition, or personality that represents a component of the overall pattern seen in many or most individuals with a particular condition or genetic syndrome. Although the profile may not be specific, it is consistent in the syndromal pattern. The existence of behavior phenotypes requires two assumptions: 1) Individuals with the same genetic abnormality have a characteristic behavior pattern that is atypical for the nonaffected population and different from the characteristic behavior patterns associated with other genetic disorders, and 2) there is an assumed causal relationship between the genetic abnormality and the characteristic behavior pattern via a specific effect of the genetic abnormality on brain development and functioning.

Behavior Rating Instrument for Autistic and Atypical Children–Second Edition (BRIAAC) A behavior rating scale that yields seven subscales: Relationship to an Adult, Communication, Drive for Mastery, Vocalization and Expressive Speech, Sound and Speech Reception, Social Responsiveness, and Psychobiological Development. The resulting profile is used for diagnosis, prognosis, and intervention planning in children with autism spectrum disorders.

Behavior Rating Inventory of Executive Function (BRIEF) An 86-item questionnaire completed by parents and teachers of children ages 5–18 years designed to tap functions underlying goal-directed problem solving (executive function). The BRIEF generates eight clinical scales, two indexes (Behavior Regulation and Metacognition), and an overall score (Global Executive Composite).

Behavior Rating Inventory of Executive Function–Preschool Version (BRIEF-P) A measure of executive function in children ages 2–5; a downward extension of the Behavior Rating Inventory of Executive Function (BRIEF).

Behavior Rating Profile–Second Edition (BRP-2) A set of six questionnaires that includes student, teacher, and parent rating scales. The instrument assesses children's behavior in a variety of settings and from different points of view.

behavior regulation Self-regulation skills and abilities in the areas of emotional and behavioral expression, especially with respect to aggressive, noncompliant, destructive, impulsive, and task-focused behaviors. There is an identifiable developmental progression in the acquisition of self-regulatory skills and abilities. By the time a child has reached the end of the toddler period, he or she is expected to be capable of emotional, behavioral, and physiological regulation that supports an emergent independent identity and self-sufficient behavior. Children with neurodevelopmental disorders often demonstrate difficulty with behavioral regulation. When behavioral dysregulation affects a child's ability to learn, the individualized education program (IEP) must include a positive behavior support plan to help him or her develop appropriate regulatory skills.

Behavior-Ages & Stages Questionnaires® **(B-ASQ)** *See* Ages & Stages Questionnaires®: Social-Emotional (ASQ:SE): A Parent-Completed, Child-Monitoring System for Social-Emotional Behaviors.

behavioral support A proactive plan and process for improving behavior regulation, academic achievement, and social competence.

behavioral genetics A field of study concerned with the effects of genes on the expression of behavior. Behavioral genetics reflects the convergence of the following factors: 1) an availability of adequate family pedigrees in countries that have standardized national health records, 2) standardized diagnostic criteria, 3) molecular genetic technology, and 4) computer modeling. For many genetic disorders, the term *behavior phenotype* indicates a specific behavior profile associated with a genetic disorder and implies that the phenotype results from the underlying genetic alteration.

behavioral observation audiometry (BOA) *conditioned play audiometry, play audiometry.* A hearing assessment procedure used primarily with infants and young children. The child is behaviorally conditioned to perform a certain task in response to sound in order to obtain hearing thresholds. Reflex responses are elicited and used to test infants; the following three types are typically used: 1) the hear–turn technique, 2) the high-amplitude sucking technique, and 3) the starter technique. The infant's response is used to determine speech–sound discrimination. Play conditioning for 3- to 4-year-olds pairs a fun activity with the presentation of sound produced by a pure tone audiometer.

behavioral toxicity Negative behavioral side effects of drugs, including parasomnias (undesirable activity during sleep), depression, mania, anxiety, irritability, apathy, and cognitive problems.

behaviorism A theoretical approach to explaining human behavior. Behaviorism assumes that all human behavior is learned. Learning occurs when the consequences of behavior are pleasant (i.e., responses are repeated when they are reinforced). Reinforcement increases the future likelihood of behavior occurring, and punishment reduces that likelihood.

behind-the-ear (BTE) hearing aid   A hearing aid that hangs behind the ear and usually attaches to a tube leading into the ear canal.

Behr disease   A rare hereditary degenerative disease characterized by spastic paraplegia, ataxia (unsteady gait), intellectual disability, optic atrophy, nystagmus (involuntary eye movements), and peripheral neuropathy that begins in infancy. Inheritance follows an autosomal recessive pattern.

Bell palsy   Paralysis (usually temporary) of the facial (seventh cranial) nerve leading to sagging of the face on the involved side with a smoothing out of the usual facial lines, such as the crease between the nose and the mouth (nasolabial fold).

below elbow (BE)   An anatomical term used to describe the location of an amputation, either congenital or acquired.

below knee (BK)   An anatomical term used to describe the location of an amputation, either congenital or acquired.

Benadryl   *See* diphenhydramine.

Bender Face Hand Test   An examination procedure to test for extinction (failure to perceive). The individual is lightly touched on one or both cheeks and/or hands and on the ipsilateral (on the same side)/contralateral (opposite) cheek and/or hand. With eyes closed, the individual is asked to identify the body parts touched. The most common failure involves the extinction of the distal stimulus (hand) when the ipsilateral hand and cheek are touched.

Bender Gestalt   *See* Bender Visual Motor Gestalt Test (BVMGT).

Bender Getsalt–II   *See* Bender Visual Motor Gestalt Test–Second Edition.

Bender Visual Motor Gestalt Test (BVMGT)   *Bender Gestalt.* A measure of visual-motor ability adapted in 1938 by Dr. Lauretta Bender (1897–1987) from drawings used by Dr. Max Wertheimer (1880–1943) in his studies of the gestalt concepts involved in visual perception. The BVMGT is a nonverbal test with a range of applications to all age groups and to populations with diverse cultural and experiential backgrounds. The person is asked to copy on a blank piece of paper nine figures of varying complexity that are presented one at a time. The person is subsequently asked to reproduce the figures from memory, which adds a visual retention component to the test. A significant relationship exists between intelligence and the accuracy of BVMGT reproductions. The individual supplies clues to his or her learning approach, to the ease with which psychomotor skills are acquired, and to how well he or she organizes written work on a page. The BVMGT drawings provide important information about developmental delays, neurological impairment, intellectual disability, and emotional disorders.

Bender Visual Motor Gestalt Test–Second Edition (Bender Gestalt–II)   A measurement of visual-motor integration in people ages 4–85; this second edition has added seven designs to the original nine; four are used exclusively with children ages 4–7;11 years and three with people ages 8–85.

benign   Harmless, not pathological; a typical variant.

benign cerebral hypotonia   Hypotonia (floppiness) in infancy and early childhood that may be associated with mild motor delay but not with more serious motor disorders such as cerebral palsy; it may later evolve into developmental coordination disorder (DCD).

benign childhood epilepsy with centrotemporal spikes (BECTS)   *benign rolandic epilepsy, mid-temporal epilepsy, sylvian epilepsy.* A seizure disorder with infrequent seizures beginning between ages 5 and 10 years. Typically, the seizure is preceded by a sensory aura in the mouth (tongue, cheek, or gums), followed by salivation, speech arrest, and tonic (increased muscle tone) or tonic-clonic (stiffening and jerking) movements of the face. Consciousness is preserved in more than half of the cases. Seizures occur frequently during sleep. Electroencephalogram (EEG) manifestation of seizure activity is spikes (sharp, pointed deviations) most prominent over the central and temporal regions of the brain. Prognosis for this type of seizure disorder has been described as good, as most children respond to anticonvulsants and are generally seizure-free after middle childhood by the onset of puberty. However, learning and behavioral issues are increasingly being recognized in affected children.

benign enlargement of the subarachnoid space in infants (BESSI)　Fluid collection in the subarachnoid (between the brain and the skull) space that gives rise to rapidly increasing head circumference in infants and can be mistaken for hydrocephalus. BESSI is contrasted from hydrocephalus by typical behavior and development and a benign course.

benign rolandic epilepsy　*See* benign childhood epilepsy with centrotemporal spikes (BECTS).

Benton Right-Left Discrimination Test　A 20-item test in which children who are 6 years old are expected to identify the right and left sides of their bodies, children who are 7 years old are expected to touch right-sided or left-sided body parts with the ipsilateral (on the same side) hand, children who are 9 years old are expected to perform the same motion with the contralateral (opposite) hand, children who are 11 years old are expected to identify the examiner's right and left hands, and children who are 12 years old are expected to identify the examiner's right and left with the children's own right or left hands.

Benton Visual Retention Test–Fifth Edition　A test of visual-motor coordination and visual memory with direct copying and delayed memory administrations. The number of correct reproductions and the error score can be compared with age norms for children as young as 6 years, with expected scores being given for different intelligence quotient (IQ) score levels. The results obtained with this instrument do not discriminate among the impact of visual attention, visual memory, and visual-perceptual motor skill areas.

benzodiazepines　A class of antianxiety and anticonvulsant drugs that includes diazepam (trade name, Valium), lorazepam (trade name, Ativan), clonazepam (trade name, Klonopin), clorazepate, and nitrazepam. In general, side effects of the benzodiazepines include sedation, ataxia (unsteady gait), and respiratory depression. Effects can last from several hours to days depending on the drug, and benzodiazepines can lose their antianxiety effectiveness over time.

benztropine　Trade name, Cogentin. Similar in structure to both atropine (an anticholinergic) and diphenhydramine (an antihistamine), benztropine is used to control the movement problems (except tardive dyskinesia) caused by the neuroleptics. It can also be used as adjunctive therapy in parkinsonism.

BEP　*See* Behavior Education Program.

Berard method　*See* auditory integration training (AIT).

Bernoulli effect　A theory of phonation in which molecules flow through a tube while pressures in the tube are constant. At the point of constriction in the tube, the speed of the molecules increases and the pressure decreases.

Bernstein's theorem　According to Bernstein's theorem, because movement coordination depends on the mastery of many redundant degrees of freedom, voluntary control can be facilitated by reducing the amount of freedom; in its simplest application, Bernstein's theorem explains how immobilization of other body parts in people with cerebral palsy can facilitate voluntary movement control of that body part not immobilized. *See* constraint-induced (CI) movement therapy.

BES *See* Behavior Evaluation Scale.

BES-3 *See* Behavior Evaluation Scale–Third Edition.

BESSI *See* benign enlargement of the subarachnoid space in infants.

best practice Accepted procedures based on current research and knowledge. Best practices may be formulated by professional groups into clinical practice guidelines.

best practice guidelines *See* clinical practice guidelines.

beta rhythm An electroencephalographic (EEG) wave frequency greater than 13 per second, usually of low amplitude, often seen during wakefulness.

beta-blocker A drug such as propranolol (trade name, Inderal) that works by blocking beta-adrenergic receptors. Blocking these receptors prevents increases in heart rate and blood pressure related to the constriction of vessels and to the stimulation of the heart muscle. Propranolol is used to prevent migraine headaches and to reduce rage attacks. Side effects include a slow heart rate, low blood pressure, sometimes depression, and occasionally worsened symptoms of asthma.

bethanechol Trade name, Urecholine. A cholinergic agonist drug that stimulates the parasympathetic nervous system. It can be used in the treatment of gastroesophageal reflux and urinary retention.

bezoar A stomach mass of ingested non-food items that may cause symptoms of gastrointestinal obstruction and, rarely, perforation. *See also* trichobezoar.

BFI *See* Behavior Function Inventory.

BHS *See* breathholding spell.

bias Expectations on the part of an observer or with a research sampling process that influence the outcome and ultimately the reliability and relevance of observations.

BIDS syndrome IBIDS syndrome without ichthyosis (very dry skin). *See also* IBIDS syndrome.

BIE *See* Bureau of Indian Education.

bilabial Referring to those sounds made with both lips: /b/, /m/, and /p/. The place of articulation where there is mutual contact of the upper and lower lips.

bilateral Pertaining to both sides of the body.

bilateral cleft A cleft that affects both the right and left sides of the primary palate; all clefts of the secondary palate are bilateral.

bilateral coordination The ability of the two sides of the body to work together to accomplish tasks.

bilateral integration dysfunction *See* vestibular-bilateral disorder.

bilevel positive airway pressure (BiPAP or BPAP) A type of assisted ventilation that may be used in children with obstructive or central sleep apnea. A device propels pressurized air through a tube, and the air is then delivered to the child via an interface (mask). Bilevel pressure refers to there being a higher pressure delivered when the child breathes in and a lower pressure when the child breathes out. The pressurized air effectively stents open the child's airway, preventing collapse, and breathing out against a lower pressure may be more comfortable. The higher pressure can be delivered in a timed fashion (regardless of the child's own breathing pattern) or can be triggered by the child's efforts to inhale.

bilingual Describing fluency of verbal communication processes in two or more languages. The younger the person, the easier it appears to be for him or her to learn multiple languages.

bilingual support model In English as a second language (ESL), an instructional model in which monolingual English special education teachers provide ESL instruction and are teamed with native language tutors or paraprofessionals to provide special education services.

Bilingual Syntax Measure (BSM) I and II A criterion-referenced measure of oral syntactic (language) structures for bilingual (English and Spanish) children in kindergarten through Grade 2 (BSM I) and Grades 3–12 (BSM II).

bilirubin-induced neurological dysfunction (BIND) High levels of bilirubin can damage the immature brain. In addition to the motor (choreoathetosis) and hearing impairments associated with high bilirubin levels in newborns, auditory processing and associated learning disorders may also occur.

binaural Describing the use of both ears in hearing so as to produce stereophonic effects.

BIND *See* bilirubin-induced neurological dysfunction.

Binder syndrome *See* maxillonasal dysplasia.

binocularity The use of both eyes to focus on an object and allow the brain to form a three-dimensional picture of the object.

BINS *See* Bayley Infant Neurodevelopmental Screener.

biofeedback Denotes both the process and the outcome of the application of operant conditioning methods, such that a person acquires the ability to shift autonomic physiological functions to the control of higher cortical processes. Training brings autonomic activities into awareness by electronic monitors that inform the person about ("feed back" information on) such body processes as skin temperature and heart rate. The person learns to change the rate or degree of these body processes as reflected in the electronic indicators by conscious monitoring and body feedback. Biofeedback has been used to facilitate continence in people with spinal cord lesions.

biopsychosocial An approach to understanding and treating human problems that presupposes biological (genetic and organic), psychological (individual cognitive, emotional, and behavioral), and social (cultural) influences together.

biosocial Pertaining to both biological and social phenomena, especially the interrelationship between the two and usually with an emphasis on the social.

biotinidase deficiency A hereditary metabolic condition in which clinical signs and symptoms are extremely variable but can include myoclonic seizures, developmental delay, ataxia (unsteady gait), sensorineural hearing loss, hypotonia (decreased muscle tone), dermatitis (rash), alopecia (hair loss), and optic atrophy. Partial biotinidase deficiency, which tends to produce milder symptoms than profound biotinidase deficiency, is sometimes called *late-onset* or *juvenile multiple carboxylase deficiency.* The incidence of this autosomal recessive syndrome is approximately 1 in 75,000. *See also* multiple carboxylase deficiency.

BIP *See* behavior intervention plan.

BiPAP *See* bilevel positive airway pressure.

biparietal diameter A measurement of the width of the fetal skull made by ultrasound; this length can be used to estimate gestational age.

bipolar disorder A psychiatric disorder characterized by extremes of mood (happiness and sadness) and behaviors that reflect the mood. In the depressive phase, the affected person may reach a complete vegetative depression and see life as hopeless. While in this "pole," the person may stop eating, stay in bed, or attempt suicide. As the depression remits, the person often swings to the opposite pole, where happiness and enthusiasm give way to unrealistic euphoria, untempered enthusiasm and optimism, and behavioral excesses. The affected person may not sleep for days or weeks, may talk for hours (or days) on end, may go on spending sprees, and may engage in sexual excesses. People with bipolar disorder have a failure of the emotional modulating system combined with abnormal thought processes and behavior components that reflect the unrealistic polar extremes of the disorder. Thought to be genetic in origin, the illness is familial. Furthermore, many developmental and learning disorders, such as autism and reading problems, appear in excess in families with bipolar disorder. Bipolar disorder was previously termed *manic-depressive disorder.*

bird-headed dwarfism *See* Seckel syndrome.

birth defect *congenital disability.* The term *birth defect* is discouraged because it implies that the person is damaged and may have contributed to the condition by the process of being born. *See also* congenital.

Birth to Three Developmental Scales A developmental profile for children from birth to 3 years of age that uses observation, direction following, motor and verbal imitation, object and picture naming, and pointing.

birthmark An alteration of skin color caused by abnormal blood vessels or pigment.

bisatellited 15 *See* tetrasomy 15 pter-q12.

bite reflex An oral reflex in which tactile (touch) stimulation to the gums, teeth, or tongue produces a rhythmic opening and closing of the mouth; a primitive reflex apparent between birth and 6 months of age, after which it is replaced by rotary chewing. This primitive infantile reflex may return after brain injury and interfere with feeding.

bivalve cast A cast in two pieces connected at their margins like a bivalve or clam shell; such a cast allows ready access to the casted body part.

BK *See* below knee.

BLAT *See* Blind Learning Aptitude Test.

blended family A nuclear family formed by the joining of two previously unrelated families. For example, a woman and her two biological children may join (usually by marriage) with a man and his two biological children to form a blended family with four children.

blended practices Practices that combine instructional modalities and methods. When used to describe education for those with developmental disabilities, the term usually refers to the blending of special and general education techniques.

blepharoclonus Excessive blinking; often precedes blepharospasm.

blepharospasm Persistent or intermittent closure of the eyelids due to muscle spasm. Uncomfortable, excessive, or uncontrollable blinking.

Blind Learning Aptitude Test (BLAT) A 61-item verbal–touch test of tactile (touch) discrimination for children ages 6–16 years who are blind. The examiner guides the child's hands over pages of patterned dots and lines, and the child is asked to describe what is felt. Learning aptitude is assessed through the recognition of differences and similarities, the identification of progressions and missing elements, and the ability to complete a figure. Administration time is approximately 45 minutes. The BLAT norms are more than 30 years old and are inflated by today's standards.

blindism A self-stimulatory behavior typically exhibited in people who are blind, such as eye gouging or eye rubbing. Other such socially inappropriate behaviors include rocking, hand movements, smelling, and autistic stereotypies (constantly repeated meaningless gestures or movements). *See also* digito-ocular sign of Franceschetti.

blindness A person is termed *blind* when his or her corrected visual acuity is worse than 20/200 in the better eye. It has been recommended that the definition of the term *blind* be restricted to the absence of light perception and that the terms *visual impairment* and *low vision* be extended to describe people with vision worse than 20/200 but who retain light perception.

Blissymbolics A graphic symbol system created by Charles Bliss (1897–1985) in 1942. In this system, symbols are combined in a logical manner to depict aspects of human experience. Blissymbolics uses pictographs (symbols that look like what they represent), ideographs (symbols that represent ideas), and symbols that depict characteristics of the word (e.g., plural, action) to construct compound symbols, providing for a large vocabulary. Blissymbolics is particularly useful to those who are unable to use traditional written language but who can learn and use a large vocabulary. The system is an aided augmentative communication approach for nonvocal individuals with physical disabilities; it has also been used successfully with individuals with intellectual disability or hearing impairments and adults with aphasia (loss of language skills).

Blitz-Nick-Salaam Krämpfe syndrome *See* West syndrome.

Bloch-Sulzberger syndrome *See* incontinentia pigmenti syndrome.

Block Design A Wechsler (intelligence test) subtest that measures a person's ability to analyze and synthesize abstract stimuli; it also involves visual perception, organization, and visual-motor coordination.

blood–brain barrier The relative impermeability of the adult brain that provides protection from certain metabolites and the sudden fluctuations in the levels of these metabolites that occur in the bloodstream. The brains of premature and very young infants are more susceptible to such changes.

blood oxygen level dependent (BOLD) BOLD refers to the differences in blood flow and oxygenation to the brain measured in functional magnetic resonance imaging (fMRI) to identify patterns of greater and lesser brain activation during specific conditions such as being asked to perform a picture-naming task. Primarily used in neuroscience research rather than on a clinical basis.

Bloom syndrome A genetic syndrome characterized by short stature, facial erythema (reddening) with a butterfly distribution (exaggerated by sunlight), mid-face hypoplasia (flattening), and occasionally mild intellectual disability. There is a high incidence of immune defects and cancer. Inheritance follows an autosomal recessive pattern. Risks for this disorder are increased among Ashkenazic Jewish populations, among whom 1 in 100 is thought to be a carrier of the gene. The gene has been localized to chromosome 15q26.1 and is involved in deoxyribonucleic acid (DNA) repair. Sister chromatid exchanges are increased in cells exposed to bromodeoxyuridine (BrdU) and are diagnostic; Bloom syndrome is the only disorder in which such evidence of hyper-recombination is known to occur.

Blount disease Genu varum (bow legs) from an abnormality of the tibia (calf bone).

BLT-2 *See* Bankson Language Test–Second Edition.

blue sclera A bluish tinge to the whites of the eyes that occurs in premature infants and individuals with glaucoma (increased pressure in the eye, often hereditary); it is also found in osteogenesis imperfecta (brittle bone disease), Marfan syndrome, Hallermann-Streiff syndrome, Crouzon syndrome, and Turner syndrome.

BMI *See* body mass index.

BNBAS *See* Brazelton Neonatal Behavioral Assessment Scale.

BNT *See* Boston Naming Test.

BOA *See* behavioral observation audiometry.

board certified Describing a professional who has completed all training and examination requirements in a specified field or subfield of expertise as testified to by the appropriate certifying board.

Board Certified Assistant Behavior Analyst (BCaBA) A person trained and certified by the Behavior Analyst Certification Board to conduct functional behavioral assessments, interpret the results, and design and supervise behavior treatment programs. BCaBA certification requires at least a bachelor's degree, coursework in applied behavior analysis, and relevant experience. The BCaBA often works under the supervision of a Board Certified Behavior Analyst (BCBA). *See also* Behavior Analyst Certification Board (BACB).

Board Certified Behavior Analyst (BCBA) An independent professional who is certified by the Behavior Analyst Certification Board to conduct functional behavioral assessments, interpret the results, and design and supervise behavioral intervention programs. BCBA certification requires at least a master's degree, coursework in applied behavior analysis, and relevant experience. BCBAs supervise the work of Board Certified Assistant Behavior Analysts (BCaBAs) and others who implement behavior plans. *See also* Behavior Analyst Certification Board (BACB).

board eligible Describing a professional who has completed all classroom and practical experiences necessary to be board certified in an area except for the last step of passing a certifying examination administered by the supervising board.

Bobath *See* neurodevelopmental therapy (NDT).

bobble-head doll syndrome A peculiar head-bobbing behavior (two to four times per second) associated with a third ventricle cyst (hydrocephalus or excess fluid in the brain); it may be the presenting sign for this latter condition. Bobble-head doll syndrome is distinguishable from nodding spasms (convulsions that, if occurring in children, result in the head dropping to the chest because of loss of tone in the neck muscles).

Boder Test of Reading-Spelling Patterns A criterion-referenced diagnostic test used to identify the following three subtypes of reading disability originally described by Elena Boder: 1) a dysphonetic pattern (an inability to sound out and blend component letters and syllables of a word), 2) a dyseidetic pattern (limitations in visual memory and visual discrimination), and 3) a mixed pattern (which incorporates both types of errors). The Boder Test of Reading-Spelling Patterns was designed for screening and clinical use and is not standardized.

body concept   The ability to name body parts and their function.

body image   The perception of one's body size, weight, and height.

body mass index (BMI)   A measure of body fat based on height and weight that applies to both adult men and women. BMI results are classified into four weight categories: underweight, <18.5; normal weight, 18.5–24.9; overweight, 25–29.9; and obese ≥30. BMI as a measure of "fat" in children who are still growing in height is not a reliable guide to the need for intervention except if it falls in the upper ranges. In children with abnormal body composition, such as those with Prader-Willi syndrome, BMI frequently underestimates the true percentage of body fat.

body righting reaction   A normal developmental response that occurs when the infant initiates movement around the longitudinal axis through hip flexion, adduction, and medial rotation. The body rolls over segmentally, initially by pelvic rotation.

body righting reflex   A primitive reflexive behavior present in the newborn infant and integrated at 5–6 months of age as the body righting reaction. Log rolling occurs when the examiner rotates the pelvis.

body scheme   An internal representation of the body; the brain's "map" of body parts and how they interrelate.

bodywork therapies   A group of therapies that use hands-on massage and manipulation and positioning of the body to improve

function and outlook. Bodywork therapies include the Alexander technique, Rolfing, Hellerwork, Tragerwork, the Feldenkrais method, trigger point therapy, shiatsu, and cranial sacral therapy.

Boehm Test of Basic Concepts–Third Edition (Boehm-3)   A norm-referenced test used to assess the acquisition of concepts related to academic success in kindergarten through second grade. The Boehm-3 taps 50 basic concepts considered important for school success. It has alternative forms, requires 30–45 minutes to administer, and produces percentile scores.

Boehm Test of Basic Concepts–Third Edition: Preschool (Boehm-3 Preschool)   A norm-referenced, individually administered assessment of concept acquisition for children ages 3–5 years. The Boehm-3 Preschool taps 50 basic concepts considered important for school success. It requires 20–30 minutes to administer, produces percentile scores, and includes an observation and intervention planning tool.

Boehm-3   *See* Boehm Test of Basic Concepts–Third Edition.

Boehm-3 Preschool   *See* Boehm Test of Basic Concepts–Third Edition: Preschool.

BOLD   *See* blood oxygen level dependent.

bolus   A globular mass; refers to food ready to be swallowed or drugs to be injected intravenously in a single dose or administered over a short period of time. The term *bolus feeding* is often used in reference to the administration of amounts of nutritional formulas over short periods of time via tube feeding as opposed to continuous or drip feeds.

bone age   *anatomical age.* Skeletal growth age as determined by the x-ray appearance of the bones compared with standards for different ages; the most commonly used standards are those of Greulich and Pyle for the hand. In children with short stature, chronological age, bone age, height age, and mid-parental height can be used to predict final adult height.

BOR syndrome *See* Melnick-Fraser syndrome.

borderline intellectual functioning An intelligence quotient (IQ) score between 70 and 85 in the absence of functional or adaptive impairment. Earlier classifications referred to this range as *borderline intellectual disability;* there is no association with borderline personality disorder. Educationally speaking, someone with borderline intellectual functioning is a slow learner.

borderline personality disorder A pervasive pattern of instability in interpersonal relationships, self-image and affect, and marked impulsivity beginning by early adulthood. Characteristics might include fear of abandonment, unstable self-image, chronic feelings of emptiness, inappropriate intense anger or difficulty controlling anger, potentially self-destructive impulsivity, recurrent suicidal behavior, and transient stress-related paranoia or severe dissociative symptoms. Not related to borderline intellectual functioning.

Borg Rating of Perceived Exertion (RPE) Scale A tool that monitors exercise intensity and is useful in the development of an exercise program for children with a variety of disabilities.

Börjeson-Forssman-Lehmann syndrome An X-linked genetic syndrome characterized by severe to profound intellectual disability, hypotonia (decreased muscle tone), hypogonadism (inadequate gonadal function), and microcephaly (abnormally small head) with a coarse facies and large ears. Inheritance follows an X-linked pattern. Mutations in the *PHF6* gene have been described.

BOS *See* Behavior Observation Scale for Autism.

Boston Naming Test (BNT) An aphasia test with 60 stimulus picture cards for use with people older than 5 years.

BOT-2 *See* Bruininks-Oseretsky Test of Motor Proficiency–Second Edition.

Botox *See* botulinum toxin.

bottom shuffling *See* scooting.

bottom-up processing Cognitive processing that is based on a detailed analysis of stimulus information. *See also* top-down (conceptually driven) processing.

botulin *See* botulinum toxin.

botulinum toxin (BTX-A) *botulin.* Trade name, Botox. A purified form of strong neurotoxin (nerve poison) derived from *Clostridium botulinum* (a germ that produces botulism or food poisoning). Injected into muscles in minute amounts, this exotoxin can reduce muscle contraction and treat rigidity and spasticity.

bound morpheme A type of morpheme that cannot convey meaning on its own and is linked to free morphemes.

boundaries Emotional and interactional barriers that protect and enhance the integrity of individuals, relationships, and families. Boundaries are unwritten rules that function as invisible lines defining both closeness and distance in a relationship, authority structures in the family, and the relationship of the family to the outside world. Boundaries can be too rigid to allow growth, they can be appropriately clear and flexible, or they can be too loose to protect the family. When boundaries are too rigid or too loose, family therapy may be used to redefine, loosen, or strengthen them. The term also has applications in the workplace (e.g., professional boundaries respect the bounds of a job description and the lines of authority within an organization).

Bourneville-Pringle syndrome *See* tuberous sclerosis (TS) syndrome.

boutonniere deformity Abnormal positioning of the finger in which the middle (proximal interphalangeal) joint is flexed and the fingertip (distal interphalangeal) joint is hyperextended. Boutonniere deformities can be caused by injuries and are common in individuals with rheumatoid arthritis.

bow legs Mild bowing of the legs is physiological (normal) in late infancy. In this mild form, gross motor development is not affected; hence, significant motor delay should prompt a search for other causal factors. *See also* genu varum.

bow legs

bowing reflex *See* Gamper reflex.

BPAP *See* bilevel positive airway pressure.

BPD *See* bronchopulmonary dysplasia.

braces A variety of devices used to stabilize or splint the trunk or extremities of individuals with a variety of developmental disabilities including cerebral palsy, Down syndrome, muscular dystrophy, and spina bifida. Used properly, these devices promote ambulation and functional independence. *See also* orthosis, splint.

brachial Relating to the arm.

brachial plexus The network of nerves located in the armpit that serve the upper extremities. Temporary or permanent upper extremity paralysis can result from damage to the brachial plexus during a difficult birth.

Brachmann de Lange syndrome *See* Cornelia de Lange syndrome.

brachycephaly Literally, "short head." A disproportionately short head from front to back (high cephalic index). *See also* cephalic index.

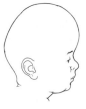

brachycephaly

brachydactyly Short fingers; brachydactyly can be an autosomal dominant trait with or without other developmental or syndromic associations. Short fifth fingers that do not reach the distal interphalangeal (last joint) crease of the fourth finger are a minor dysmorphic feature that may reflect the presence of a neurodevelopmental disorder.

Bracken Basic Concept Scale–Third Edition (BBCS-3) A set of 12 educational diagnostic instruments for use by psychologists, teachers, special needs coordinators, and allied health personnel that measure expressive (BBCS-E) and receptive (BBCS-R) understanding of concepts as well as school readiness (BSRA-3). Administration is by individual or group. Responses may be verbal (stating the number that corresponds with the answer) or nonverbal (pointing to the correct option). Standard scores have a mean of 100 and a standard deviation of 15.

Bracken School Readiness Assessment–Third Edition (BSRA-3) One of the first five subtests of the Bracken Basic Concept Scale–Third Edition (BBCS-3:R) that can be used as a school readiness test for children 3–7 years of age.

bradycardia Slow heart rate. The lower limit of normal in beats per minute varies by age. Younger children tend to have more rapid heart rates and so might be considered to have bradycardia at a rate that would be considered normal in an adult.

braille A system of printing for individuals with visual impairments in which letters are represented by patterns of raised dots that readers discern by moving their fingers over the page. It is named for the inventor Louis Braille (1809–1852).

Brailsford syndrome   *See* Morquio syndrome.

brain   The part of the central nervous system (CNS) contained in the skull or cranium. It performs a multitude of tasks, from control of basic functions (e.g., breathing) to higher cortical functions (e.g., thinking and learning). The brain is divided into four major parts: 1) brainstem, 2) diencephalon, 3) cerebrum, and 4) cerebellum. The brain is also divided into halves, called *hemispheres,* that are connected by a bridge called the *corpus callosum.* For protection, the brain is surrounded by a layer of tissue called the *meninges* and is further protected by a fluid, the cerebrospinal fluid (CSF), that flows through the brain in a system of conduits called *ventricles.* Blockage of these ventricles can cause hydrocephalus (excess fluid in the brain).

brain

brain attack   *See* stroke.

brain bleed   *See* intraventricular hemorrhage (IVH). *See also* stroke.

brain contusion   *See* contusion.

brain electrical activity mapping (BEAM)   A complex computer technology that uses electroencephalographic (EEG) readings to map the electrical activity of the brain. BEAM is a research tool.

brain imaging   *neuroimaging.* A variety of different radiological procedures used to investigate the structure and function of the brain, including x-ray computed tomography (CT) scan, magnetic resonance imaging (MRI), functional magnetic resonance imaging (fMRI), MRI spectroscopy (MRS), regional cerebral blood flow (rCBF), positron emission tomography (PET), single photon emission computed tomography (SPECT), magnetoelectroencephalography (MEG), and brain electrical activity mapping (BEAM). Apart from the CT and MRI scans, most of the applications are experimental. Because fMRI, PET, and SPECT measure cerebral blood flow, they are considered functional imaging techniques.

brain injury   Any external (e.g., blunt trauma) or internal (e.g., stroke) event that ultimately disrupts previous levels of cognitive, language, or motor functioning. Disruption from an injury is different than that from a degenerative process in that the damage often results from mechanical damage to brain tissue rather than deterioration or loss of function of the nerve fibers.

Brain Skills   An online version of the Processing and Cognitive Enhancement Program (PACE), a series of games used to improve memory and attention when practiced for an hour a day, 5 days a week, for 12–15 weeks. *See also* Gibson Cognitive Test Battery.

"brain-damaged child syndrome"   *See* Strauss syndrome.

brainstem auditory evoked potentials (BAEP)   *auditory brainstem response (ABR), brainstem evoked response (BSER).* A test that uses auditory stimuli (sound) to measure the passage of the message along the auditory nerve (cranial nerve VIII) to the brainstem and associated areas of the brain. This gives information about the intactness of the system but not the perception of the sound. Damage to hearing that results in an abnormal BAEP can be caused by meningitis (infection of the spinal cord and brain membranes), hyperbilirubinemia (high levels of bilirubin in the blood), perinatal asphyxia (lack of oxygen), or central nervous system (CNS) disorders such as leukodystrophy. BAEP can be used to assess hearing in children who are too young to cooperate for a behavioral hearing test.

brainstem auditory evoked response (BAER) *See* brainstem auditory evoked potentials (BAEP).

brainstem evoked response (BSER) *See* brainstem auditory evoked potentials (BAEP).

branchio-oto-renal (BOR) syndrome *See* Melnick-Fraser syndrome.

brand name *See* trade name.

Braverman-Chevigny Auditory Projective Test An adaptation of the Thematic Apperception Test (TAT) for people with visual impairments; the stimulus is a conversation with garbled language.

Brazelton Neonatal Behavioral Assessment Scale (NBAS, also BNBAS) A tool used for the assessment of newborn behavior. The 37 items include a careful description of visual and auditory alertness and orientation, tone and posture, cuddliness, and consolability, as well as startle and self-quieting. Elicited responses (primitive reflexes) are scored separately.

breathholding spell (BHS) A paroxysmal behavior observed in preschool children after severe crying following an identifiable emotional upset; it may end in unconsciousness with a brief clonic (rhythmic contraction and relaxation) asphyxic seizure. Breathholding spells are frightening but benign and should be treated behaviorally rather than with anticonvulsant medication. Children with anemia who are treated with iron supplementation may see an improvement in BHS.

breathiness A disorder of vocal quality characterized by excessive audible air leakage during phonation.

Brecht/Gavage feeding A method of feeding in which nourishment is put into a syringe and squirted into the mouth.

breech The delivery of an infant feet first rather than head first. In a frank breech presentation, the infant's pelvis comes out first with the legs flexed (folded) on the body; in footling breech, the feet come out first. The rate of neonatal mortality; incidence of prematurity; and specific genetic syndromes, major organ malformations, and later neurological abnormalities are significantly higher in children born by breech presentation. Breech presentation accounts for approximately 3% of all deliveries. The major obstetrical risk in a breech delivery is that the umbilical cord may be compressed during the relatively prolonged delivery of the largest part of the infant, the head.

BRIAAC *See* Behavior Rating Instrument for Autistic and Atypical Children–Second Edition.

bridge A three-block construction that can be imitated by a child at 3 years of age; a fine motor milestone.

bridge

BRIEF *See* Behavior Rating Inventory of Executive Function.

BRIEF-P *See* Behavior Rating Inventory of Executive Function, Preschool Version.

Brigance Diagnostic Inventory of Early Development–II (BDIED-II) An individually administered curriculum-referenced test used to evaluate children ages birth to 7 years. The BDIED-II covers 46 skills in the five areas of physical development, language development, academic–cognitive development, daily living, and social and emotional development. Test results are expressed as developmental ages. The BDIED-II has a companion curriculum as well as screening tests for kindergarten and the lower grades.

Brigance Screens The Brigance Early Childhood Screens (0–35 months, 3–5 years, and kindergarten–Grade 1 forms), Brigance Head Start Screen (ages 3, 4, and 5), and Brigance Early Head Start Screen (birth to 3 years) are 15-minute screening tests used by teachers to identify learning delays or giftedness in five areas: language, motor, self-help, social-emotional, and cognitive. (All of these screens replace the Brigance Preschool Screen–II.)

Brill Educational Achievement Test for Secondary Age Deaf Students An academic screening test for adolescents 13–20 years of age who are deaf.

Broca's aphasia *expressive aphasia, motor aphasia.* Acquired difficulty with speech production secondary to damage to a specific area of the left frontal lobe (Brodmann area 44, Broca's area, inferior frontal gyrus, anterior speech cortex) of the brain, typically due to a stroke. Understanding of language is preserved. Through increased efforts the speaker can form words that are meaningful but difficult for the listener to understand, which is frustrating for the speaker.

Broderick decision Halderman v. Pennhurst State School and Hospital et al. A 1978 decision rendered by U.S. District Court Judge Raymond Broderick stipulating that keeping individuals with intellectual disability in institutions isolated from the rest of society violates their constitutional rights. This ruling was the result of a class action suit filed in May 1974 by parents of clients at the Pennhurst School for the Mentally Retarded in Pennsylvania. Judge Broderick argued that institutionalization violated the children's rights under the Fourteenth Amendment to the U.S. Constitution.

Brodmann area 17 *See* primary visual cortex (V1).

Brodmann areas Describing a system of numerically mapping the functional areas of the human cortex (covering of the brain), with each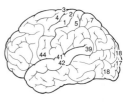

Brodmann areas

number corresponding to an area: sensory reception (areas 1, 2, 3), primary motor (4), sensory association (5, 6, 7), visual reception (17), visual association (18), speech reception (Wernicke; 39), auditory reception (41), auditory association (42), speech motor (Broca; 44).

Brodmann areas 41 and 42 *See* primary auditory cortex.

broken words A type of disfluency in which there is a pause within a word.

bronchial drainage A gravity-assisted positioning technique used to remove secretions from segments of the lungs. Whereas infants are positioned over a therapist's lap, older children are typically positioned over a tilt table or tilting bed. Ten different tilting positions are used.

bronchial hygiene Removal of secretions from a child's airway through a variety of techniques, including gravity-assisted drainage by positioning, manual techniques such as percussion with coughing and suctioning, and newer techniques with positive expiratory pressure and high-frequency chest compression.

bronchopulmonary dysplasia (BPD) Severe chronic lung disease secondary to respiratory distress syndrome and the effects of prolonged high oxygen on the immature lung. Associated developmental problems are twofold: 1) Cardiopulmonary insufficiency has a direct, slowing effect on motor development; and 2) most infants who develop BPD have survived neonatal courses replete with other events potentially traumatic to the central nervous system (CNS). Some infants with BPD develop a movement disorder characterized by chorea and oral motor problems.

BRP-2 *See* Behavior Rating Profile–Second Edition.

Bruininks-Oseretsky Test of Motor Proficiency–Second Edition (BOT-2) An instrument used to differentially assess fine and gross motor skills in people 4–21 years of age; the eight subtests take less than 1 hour to administer.

bruit Literally, "noise." An abnormal sound heard on auscultation (listening with a stethoscope); a cranial (skull) bruit may be heard in the presence of an intracranial vascular (blood vessel in the head) malformation or tumor, hyperthyroidism, heart disease, or fever. Pathological bruits have the quality of "footsteps in an empty church."

Brunnstrom A system of physical therapy for the treatment of cerebral palsy. Developed by Signe Brunnstrom to treat hemiplegia (paralysis of half of the body), this approach induces primitive (fetal) synergistic movement patterns to help teach purposeful movements.

Brushfield spots Mottled, marbled, or elevated speckles (white or light yellow) of the iris observed in 85% of individuals with Down syndrome and 20% of the general population.

brushing *See* Wilbarger protocol.

bruxism *teeth grinding.* Bruxism can reflect a sleep disorder or nervous habit in children. In children with more severe developmental disabilities, this self-stimulatory behavior can lead to severe dental impairment, with teeth being ground flat. Teeth grinding when awake is often associated with intellectual disability.

BSAB-I *See* Balthazar Scales of Adaptive Behavior I: Scales of Functional Independence.

BSER Brainstem evoked response. *See* brainstem auditory evoked response (BAER).

BSM *See* Bilingual Syntax Measure I and II.

BSRA-3 *See* Bracken School Readiness Assessment–Third Edition.

BSSI-D *See* Basic School Skills Inventory–Diagnostic.

BTE *See* behind-the-ear hearing aid.

BTX-A *See* botulinum toxin.

buccal surface The space between the teeth and lips.

bulbar syndrome *See* pseudobulbar palsy.

bulimia nervosa An eating disorder characterized by bouts of binge eating followed by purging in the form of laxative abuse, self-induced vomiting, or excessive exercise. May co-occur with anorexia nervosa.

bupropion Trade name, Wellbutrin. An antidepressant that produces a weak effect on serotonin and norepinephrine and has a stimulant effect on the central nervous system (CNS). It can be used clinically to treat depression and attention disorders. Side effects include sleep problems, agitation, activation of mania, and occasionally seizures.

burden A term used in clinical genetics to describe the total impact of a disorder on an individual, his or her family, and society.

Bureau of Education for the Handicapped (BEH) Former name for the U.S. Department of Education's Office of Special Education and Rehabilitative Services (OSERS). *See also* Office of Special Education and Rehabilitative Services (OSERS).

Bureau of Indian Education (BIE) In coordination with the Indian Health Service

(IHS), the BIE is responsible for the coordination of services, resources, and personnel to facilitate the provision of a free appropriate public education (FAPE) to Indian and Alaska native children who reside on or near reservations. Services are negotiated at a local level and vary depending upon the funding and resources available. Furthermore, the BIE and IHS are charged with providing Child Find, evaluation, diagnosis, remediation, therapeutic, and other coordinated services. Formerly known as the Office of Indian Education.

Burks Behavior Rating Scales, Preschool and Kindergarten Edition   A downward extension of the Burks Behavior Rating Scale for use with children ages 3–6 years. The Preschool and Kindergarten Edition consists of 105 descriptive statements for a parent or teacher to rate on a 5-point frequency scale.

Burks Behavior Rating Scales–Second Edition (BBRS-2)   A 100-item written inventory used to identify patterns of behavior problems in children in kindergarten through 12th grade. A parent or teacher uses a 5-point scale to rate the frequency of the child's observed behaviors. The BBRS-2 can be completed in 10–15 minutes.

buspirone   Trade name, BuSpar. An antianxiety agent that affects the dopamine and serotonin systems. It is typically used to treat anxiety but has also been used in people with autism to treat the target behaviors of aggression, self-injurious behavior, and ritualisms/stereotypies. There is no associated sedation or withdrawal, but side effects may include nausea, headaches, or dizziness.

butyrophenone   A group of antipsychotic medications such as haloperidol (trade name, Haldol).

BVMGT   *See* Bender Visual Motor Gestalt Test.

Cc

CA *See* chronological age (CA).

CAAP *See* Clinical Assessment of Articulation and Phonology.

CACH Childhood ataxia with diffuse central nervous system (CNS) hypomyelination. *See* vanishing white matter disease (VWM).

cachexia Wasting, weakness, or emaciation. In children with unusually severe failure to thrive (poor growth), cachexia suggests the likelihood of an underlying physical disease.

cadence The number of steps per minute; one of the measures taken in a gait analysis.

cadence A rhythmic sequence of sounds in language.

CADeT *See* Communication Abilities Diagnostic Test.

CADL-2 *See* Communicative Activities of Daily Living–Second Edition.

CADRE *See* Consortium for Appropriate Dispute Resolution in Special Education.

CADS Conners' ADHD/*DSM–IV* Scales. *See* Conners' Rating Scales–Revised.

café au lait spot Literally, "coffee with milk spot." Macular (flat) area of skin color greater than 0.5 cm in diameter. More than five café au lait spots of 1.5 cm or greater in diameter can be a sign of neurofibromatosis. A variety of other rarer genetic syndromes

can also be associated with increased numbers of café au lait spots, including McCune-Albright syndrome, tuberous sclerosis, and Fanconi anemia.

caffeine A central nervous system (CNS) stimulant found in coffee, chocolate, and tea.

Caffey syndrome *See* battered child syndrome, shaken baby syndrome.

Caffey-Kempe syndrome *See* battered child syndrome, shaken baby syndrome.

CAI *See* computer-assisted instruction.

Cain-Levine Social Competency Scale A social adaptive scale for use with school-age children with moderate intellectual disability.

calcaneus The heel bone.

calcaneus deformity An orthopedic abnormality in which the forefoot is pulled upward and the heel downward; the resulting appearance resembles a heel-walking stance.

calcaneus deformity

calendar age *See* chronological age (CA).

calipers A highly accurate instrument with two bent or curved arms used to measure the thickness of a solid mass.

Callier-Azusa Scale An adaptive checklist for use with children with hearing and vision impairments, and up to a developmental age of 7 years. The G form assesses overall development; the H form focuses on communication. Administration requires the observation of spontaneous behavior in structured and unstructured situations over a period of 2 weeks.

callosal dysgenesis Varying degrees of failure of development of the corpus callosum (the major connection between the two hemispheres or halves of the brain). This brain lesion (abnormality) can be associated with cognitive impairment, seizures, autism, attention-deficit/hyperactivity disorder (ADHD), and obsessive-compulsive disorders. It is seen frequently in Aicardi syndrome. A child who has his or her corpus callosum surgically cut as part of the treatment for intractable epilepsy experiences relatively few of the neurocognitive symptoms attributed to callosal dysgenesis.

CALP *See* cognitive/academic language proficiency.

calvarium The roof of the skull, or the cranial vault.

CAM *See* complementary and alternative medicine.

campomelic dysplasia (CD) A skeletal dysplasia characterized by a distinctive face, Pierre Robin sequence with cleft palate, shortening and bowing of long bones, and club feet. Other findings include laryngotracheomalacia (airways that collapse easily) with respiratory compromise and ambiguous genitalia or normal female external genitalia in most individuals with a 46,XY (male) karyotype. Many infants die in the newborn period; findings in long-term survivors include short stature, cervical spine instability with spinal cord compression, progressive scoliosis (back curvature), and hearing impairment. *SOX9,* the only gene known to be associated with CD, is altered in ~95% of individuals.

camptodactyly Fixed flexion contracture of a finger; a physical feature found in a number of syndromes.

Camurati-Englemann syndrome A rare genetic syndrome with a progressive bone disorder leading to leg pain; weakness; a waddling gait; an asthenic (slender or slight), malnourished habitus (appearance); and occasionally compromised optic (visual) and auditory (hearing) nerve functions. Inheritance follows an autosomal dominant pattern. Mutations in the *CGF1* gene are found in >90% of individuals.

Cancellation A Wechsler (intelligence test) subtest that measures processing speed, visual selective attention, and vigilance.

cancellation of rapidly recurring target figures A test used to differentiate dyslexia from other learning disabilities and to detect poor concentration. A diamond and the number 592 must be identified in an array of 140 figures and numbers. Visual discrimination problems may affect test scores.

Candida albicans A common yeast or fungus that typically resides on human skin and mucous membranes and that can give rise to thrush (a mouth infection in young infants), candidiasis (a diaper rash), and vaginal yeast infections. Subclinical yeast infections have been alleged to play a role in migraines, depression, fatigue, irritability, attention impairments, hyperactivity, autism, and other neurobehavioral syndromes. A yeast toxin is hypothesized to produce these symptoms; the treatment for this "yeast connection" includes a diet low in sugar and refined carbohydrates and the antifungal drug nystatin. Support for this causal explanation remains anecdotal; the treatment is as yet unproven.

candidate gene A gene proposed to be involved in the determination of a trait or condition because of the known function of one of its products.

candle-drippings A term describing the shape of nodules protruding into the ventricles (fluid-containing spaces) of the brain in tuberous sclerosis.

candling *See* transillumination.

canities Graying of the scalp and beard hair.

Cantelli's sign *See* doll's eye sign.

canthus The corner of the eye slit. Each eye has an inner (nasal or epicanthus) and an outer (lateral or telecanthus) corner. The distance between the inner canthi is used to assess whether eyes are widely spaced (hypertelorism) or narrowly spaced (hypotelorism), which both reflect minor dysmorphic features.

cao gio *See* coining.

CAP *See* Capacity Profile.

CAP *See* Community Alternatives Program.

CAP Inventory *See* Child Abuse Potential Inventory.

Capacity Profile (CAP) A standardized instrument used to measure the need that a child with a disability has for additional care. The instrument, designed to fit within the framework of the International Classification of Functioning, Disability, and Health (ICF), looks at the dependence of the child in five domains: physical health, neuromusculoskeletal and movement-related, sensory, mental, and voice and speech functions. Each level is scored on a scale from 0 to 5, such that 0 means that there is no need for additional care and 5 means that the child needs help in every activity. The goal is to use the child's capabilities to measure his or her need for additional care.

CAPD *See* central auditory processing disorder.

CAPI *See* Child Abuse Potential Inventory.

CAPTA *See* Child Abuse Prevention and Treatment Act of 1974 (PL 93-247).

caput succedaneum Soft-tissue swelling of the scalp that occurs when an infant is born in the vertex presentation (head first); the margins of swelling are not limited by the skull's suture lines; sometimes referred to just as *caput*.

Capute Aptitude Test (CAT) A measure of problem-solving skills in children from birth to 3 years of age. One of two components of the Capute Scales.

Capute Scales A developmental test for children 0–36 months composed of the Capute Aptitude Test (CAT) comprising 58 nonverbal problem-solving items and the Clinical Linguistic and Auditory Milestone Scale (CLAMS) incorporating 42 language items. The instrument can be used for formal developmental assessment and takes about 6 minutes to administer; segments of the test can be used to screen for developmental problems. The complete test or either component can be used with older children who have a developmental age less than 3 years.

carbamazepine Trade names, Carbatrol; Tegretol. An anticonvulsant used to treat partial and generalized tonic-clonic seizures; also effective in treating movement disorders and some psychiatric conditions in people with severe developmental disorders. Unlike some older anticonvulsants such as phenobarbital, carbamazepine has not been reported to produce deleterious effects on cognition and behavior; rather, improvements in memory, mood, perceptual and motor speed, and decision making have been described.

cardiac Relating to the heart.

cardinal points reflex *See* rooting reflex.

cardiomegaly   Enlarged heart.

cardiomyopathy   A wide range of conditions that affect the heart muscle.

cardiopulmonary   Pertaining to the heart and lungs.

cardiorespiratory   Pertaining to the heart and lungs.

cardiovascular   Pertaining to the heart, blood vessels, and circulatory system.

caregiver   Any person with physical or legal responsibility for the care of a child, an older adult, or an adult with developmental disabilities. Examples of caregivers include babysitters, extended family members, child care workers, hospital workers, nurses, and aides.

CARF   *See* Commission on Accreditation of Rehabilitation Facilities.

caries   Tooth decay and death of bone from bacterial action; dental caries are decayed and rotting teeth secondary to poor oral hygiene.

Carl D. Perkins Vocational and Applied Technology Education Act of 1990 (PL 101-392; and PL 105-332 amendments of 1998)   PL 101-392 amends and renames the Carl D. Perkins Vocational Educational Act of 1984 (PL 98-524). The purpose of PL 101-392 is to make the United States more productive and competitive in the world economy by more fully developing the educational and vocational skills of all segments of the population. The definition of "special populations" is expanded to include individuals with disabilities, those who are economically and educationally disadvantaged (including migrant and foster children), individuals with limited English proficiency, those who are in jeopardy of experiencing sex bias, and those in correctional institutions. This law requires that individuals with disabilities, like their counterparts without disabilities, be provided vocational education in the least restrictive environment (LRE) and that they be granted equal access to all aspects of vocational programs and placement activities. PL 105-332 adds the following amendments to PL 101-392: Schools are required to integrate academic, vocational, and technical training; increase the use of technology; provide professional development opportunities to staff, develop, and implement evaluations of program quality; expand and modernize quality programs; and link secondary and postsecondary vocational education. In addition, states must submit an annual report on how special populations engaged in vocational education, including people living with disabilities, are faring relative to the states' performance goals. PL 101-392, and its language as amended in PL 105-332, is closely aligned and interwoven with the Individuals with Disabilities Education Act (IDEA) of 1990 (PL 101-476) and the Individuals with Disabilities Education Act Amendments (IDEA) of 1997 (PL 105-17) to guarantee full vocational education opportunities for youth with disabilities.

carnitine   A chemical found in food and produced in the liver and other tissues that helps in the breakdown of long-chain fatty acids. Carnitine also acts to protect the cell against certain normal breakdown products (acyl-CoA derivatives) that can be toxic to the cell. Carnitine supplementation is used in some metabolic disorders and sometimes valproic acid toxicity. Other postulated uses include as nutritional supplementation in chronic renal (kidney) disease, for premature infants, and in some cases of idiopathic cardiomyopathy (enlarged heart).

carnitine deficiency   Systemic carnitine deficiency is characterized by muscle weakness of varying severity and a progressive presentation. Although carnitine levels are low in the blood, the liver, and muscle, carnitine supplementation has resulted in improvement in only one third of affected people. Muscle carnitine deficiency is an autosomal recessive disorder with normal blood but low muscle carnitine levels. Carnitine supplementation improves weakness in about two thirds of children.

Carolina Curriculum for Infants and Toddlers with Special Needs–Third Edition (CCITSN) A developmentally appropriate curriculum (set of tasks and activities) used for assessment and intervention with children in the birth to 36-month developmental range who have mild to severe delays in development and functioning. A total of 24 teaching sequences address five developmental domains: cognition, communication, social adaptation, fine motor skills, and gross motor skills. Skill levels are assessed by observation and parent report, and the results are used to generate specific teaching interventions, approaches, and materials.

Carolina Curriculum for Preschoolers with Special Needs–Second Edition (CCPSN) An extension of the Carolina Curriculum for Infants and Toddlers with Special Needs (CCITSN), this curriculum-based approach to assessment and intervention is for use with children ages 2–5 years with mild to severe developmental needs. The CCPSN includes 22 teaching sequences across five developmental domains: cognition, communication, social adaptation, fine motor skills, and gross motor skills. Based on an initial assessment, professionals select curriculum items that correspond to individually identified needs. The CCPSN specifies materials needed, teaching procedures, routine integration strategies, sensorimotor adaptations, and intervention activities in group settings.

Carolina Picture Vocabulary Test (CPVT) A norm-referenced test of receptive sign vocabulary for children between 4 and 11;6 years of age who are deaf or have hearing impairments.

carotenemia A yellow tinge to the skin resulting from an excess of carotene in the blood. Carotenemia is secondary to a diet high in yellow/orange (vitamin A–containing) foods. This yellow coloring (i.e., pseudojaundice) may be clinically distinguished from jaundice (a yellowing of the skin) in that it does not involve the whites of the eyes.

carp mouth The combination of down-turned corners of the mouth (relative overgrowth of the upper lip), a thick lower lip, and a short philtrum (indentation in the upper lip below the nose); carp mouth occurs in a number of syndromes.

Carpenter syndrome *acrocephalopolysyndactyly.* A genetic syndrome with a "tower-shaped" skull from craniosynostosis (early fusion of skull sutures), polydactyly (extra fingers or toes), syndactyly (webbing of fingers or toes), and lateral displacement of the inner canthi (i.e., dystopia canthorum) contributing to a "down-thrust" gaze and mild obesity. Occasionally, mild intellectual disability is present. Surgical correction of the craniofacial malformation is indicated, along with audiological monitoring and speech-language therapy. Inheritance is autosomal recessive.

carpus The set of eight small carpal bones arranged in two rows in the wrist.

carrier An individual who is heterozygous for a recessive trait. In reference to a disease or genetic syndrome, *carrier* describes an individual who has a chromosome pair with one normal gene and one abnormal gene for that trait. Carriers appear normal, but the presence of the abnormal gene can sometimes be detected using laboratory methods. Disorders transmitted via carriers are usually recessive and require the mating of two carriers to produce the disease in their offspring.

Carrow Auditory-Visual Abilities Test (CAVAT) A norm-referenced test with 14 subtests that measure auditory, visual-perceptual, motor, and memory skills. The CAVAT is for use with children ages 4–10 years. Test administration time is 1.5 hours.

Carrow Elicited Language Inventory (CELI) A norm-referenced measure of the productive use of grammar for children ages 3;0–7;11 years. The CELI has 52 items ranging from 2-word phrases to 10-word sentences. Children are asked to repeat the items, and their responses are scored and analyzed in terms of grammar, structure, error type, and the production of verb forms. The inventory is used to diagnose expressive language delays and grammatical disorders.

carrying angle The angle of the forearm on the upper arm; the angle at the elbow. Absent sex chromosomes increase the carrying angle; extra sex chromosomes decrease the carrying angle.

CARS *See* Childhood Autism Rating Scale.

CARS2 *See* Childhood Autism Rating Scale–Second Edition.

CAS *See* Cognitive Assessment System.

cascade A series of enzyme activations that amplify a weak chemical signal.

case definition Clinical diagnostic criteria that serve as a template against which to match the presenting signs and symptoms of an individual to determine the nature of his or her illness and the appropriate treatment for epidemiological purposes. Unlike in clinical practice, in which a working diagnosis may be sufficient for initiating clinical management procedures, a case definition must more clearly delineate diagnostic criteria. For epidemiological purposes,

the following questions must be answered: When in the prodromal phase does the person actually become a "case"? When in the clinical course is a "case" cured and therefore no longer a "case"? and Is a subclinical or atypical manifestation of a disease also a "case"? The answers to these questions for any given disease determine who is counted in epidemiological measures of incidence and prevalence.

case history The cumulative medical, psychological, educational, familial, and social record of an individual.

case identification Assignment of a diagnosis to a set of signs and symptoms. Epidemiologists study the occurrence and determinants of diseases in groups of people. Thus, they must count the number of identified cases in any investigation of who contracts a specific disease and where, when, and how. Accurate reporting is also essential in terms of plotting disease patterns. Although accurate case identification is contingent on good case definition, other variables in case identification may impede the accurate counting of a disease in a population. These include 1) the extent to which people in a community use the medical establishment, 2) the extent to which physicians correctly diagnose illnesses, and 3) the extent to which accurately diagnosed cases can be ascertained on a community-wide scale.

case management A procedure for coordinating multiple services to a client or client system. Case management is most effective for clients who need multiple services, long-term service, or both. The case manager coordinates the activities of multiple service providers, thereby helping to eliminate duplication and fragmentation of service. In addition, case management can alleviate the difficulties associated with staff turnover. Case management can occur within a single agency or at the community level, where services are coordinated among agencies. Consistent with person-centered planning and person-first approaches, case management has been supplanted by service coordination within some service systems. *See also* service coordination.

casein A milk protein that is the basis of curd and cheese. An unproven hypothesis claims that casein breakdown products can directly (as a toxin or poison) or indirectly (through an allergic mechanism) affect the brain and cause autism. The proposed treatment is a dairy-free diet.

CASS Conners-Wells' Adolescent Self-Report Scale. *See* Conners' Rating Scales–Revised.

CASS:L Conners-Wells' Adolescent Self-Report Scale, long version. *See* Conners' Rating Scales–Revised.

CASS:S Conners-Wells' Adolescent Self-Report Scale, short version. *See* Conners' Rating Scales–Revised.

CAST *See* Childhood Asperger Syndrome Test.

cast A molded casing composed of plaster of Paris, fiberglass, or plastic that is used to immobilize a body part.

CAT *See* Caputo Aptitude Test.

CAT *See* Children's Apperception Test.

cat eye syndrome *tetrasomy 22 (pter-q11), trisomy.* Chromosomal syndrome characterized by mild to moderate intellectual disability, coloboma (tissue defect) of the irides, the vertical pupils for which the syndrome was named, preauricular (in front of the ears) pits and/or tags, and anal atresia (absence of an anal opening). Among individuals with cat eye syndrome, heart defects are frequent, as is microphthalmia (small eyes).

cat posture *See* symmetric tonic neck reflex.

cat reflex *See* symmetric tonic neck reflex.

CAT scan Computed axial tomography scan. *See* computed tomography (CT) scan.

cataplexy Acute loss of muscle tone lasting from seconds to a few minutes, often provoked by strong emotion and most typically laughter. During an episode of cataplexy, a person typically does not lose consciousness. Cataplexy is often thought of as involving crashing to the floor, but it can be less dramatic, with brief buckling of the knees or even hoarseness of the voice. It is associated with narcolepsy, a neurological disorder of sleep state instability often characterized by excessive daytime sleepiness. It is also a feature of several other rare conditions such as Coffin-Lowry syndrome. *See also* Coffin-Lowry syndrome.

Catapres *See* clonidine.

cataract An opacity of the lens of the eye that blocks normal vision. Cataracts can be congenital or acquired and can be associated with congenital infections (such as congenital rubella syndrome) or metabolic disorders (such as galactosemia). Cataracts may also be inherited and are part of many genetic syndromes. The decrease in vision in the eye associated with a large cataract may produce amblyopia (poorer vision in one eye) and strabismus (squint). Small cataracts may not significantly impair vision. Early diagnosis is critical; in infants, surgery, laser therapy, or other methods of removing the cataract should be performed in the first months of life.

catarrhal otitis *See* serous otitis media.

CATCH *See* Community Access to Child Health.

CATCH An older acronym for the syndromic association of congenital heart disease (conotruncal defect), atypical facies, thymic hypoplasia (decreased tissue development), cleft lip/palate, and hypocalcemia (low blood calcium) that can occur with chromosome 22q11 deletions. *See* velocardiofacial syndrome.

CATCH scale *Chedoke-McMaster Attitudes Towards Children with Handicaps scale.* A scale used to measure the attitudes of peers toward students with disabilities. The scale measures three components of attitudes including the dimensions of affect, behavior, and cognition and has been determined to be both valid and reliable for use in children up to age 16 years. The scale has 12 items in each of the three dimensions, for a total of 36 items. It is available in multiple languages and is widely used in many countries.

catchment school A school that has special education programs not available in all schools. Students who need such programs are bused to the catchment school in order to receive the special education services indicated by their individualized education program (IEP).

cat's cry syndrome *See* cri-du-chat syndrome.

catecholamines A group of chemicals that influences the activity of the nervous system; these chemicals include epinephrine, norepinephrine, and dopamine.

categorical diagnosis An approach to diagnosis (either medical or educational) wherein classification into a diagnostic category is based on an "is or isn't" or "all or nothing" classification. Thus, if a diagnostic category requires an individual to exhibit six symptoms from one set of behaviors and six symptoms from another set of behaviors in order to meet diagnostic criteria, those who have only five symptoms in each of the two sets of behaviors would not be classified into that category. In the educational arena, categorical diagnosis is reflected in the classification of a student into one of four major diagnostic categories of childhood disability: 1) intellectual disability, 2) learning disabilities, 3) behavior disorders, and 4) emotional disorders. The contrast to a categorical diagnosis is one based on a dimensional or continuum approach which, among other things, would suggest a range of severity rather than simply a "is present" or "isn't present" categorical approach. Proponents of a dimensional or continuum approach argue that the person in our example who exhibits only five symptoms from each of two sets of behaviors, is nonetheless impaired (or at least is certainly not "normal") even if one symptom short in each category to be categorized as impaired, and therefore should receive intervention.

categorical trait A complex trait in which each possible phenotype can be classified into one of a number of discrete categories. A meristic trait.

Cattell Developmental and Intelligence Scale A modification of the Gesell schedules for children 3–30 months of age; yields a ratio intelligence quotient (IQ) score.

Cattell-Horn-Carroll (CHC) theory of cognitive abilities The CHC theory is a hierarchical model of intelligence that combines the Cattell-Horn Gf-Gc and the Carroll models of human cognitive abilities. The CHC theory defines 10 broad abilities and more than 70 narrow abilities. The broad abilities are crystallized intelligence (Gc), fluid intelligence (Gf), quantitative reasoning (Gq), reading and writing ability (Grw), short-term memory (Gsm), long-term storage and retrieval (Glr), visual processing (Gv), auditory processing (Ga), processing speed (Gs), and decision/reaction time/speed (Gt). Most of the major tests of intelligence have changed to incorporate CHC theory as their foundation for specifying and operationalizing cognitive abilities and processes. This theory provides the theoretical basis for the construction and interpretation of certain tests such as the Kaufman Assessment Battery for Children–Second Edition (K-ABC-II) and the Woodcock-

Johnson Battery–Third edition: Norms Updated (WJ-III-NU).

caudal regression syndrome A congenital malformation syndrome that involves varying degrees of agenesis (absence of formation) of the lower extremities, pelvis, sacrum, and spinal cord. Gait disorders, incontinence, imperforate (unopened) anus, renal (kidney) agenesis (growth failure), and abnormalities of the external genitalia are also manifestations of this syndrome, which most commonly occurs in infants of mothers with diabetes. In infants who survive, long-term orthopedic, urological, and neurological management is necessary.

CAVAT *See* Carrow Auditory-Visual Abilities Test.

cavernous hemangioma Elevated vascular nevus (skin malformation) or strawberry (having the surface of a berry) nevus of solid red color. Some resolve spontaneously; others require surgical intervention.

cavus foot *pes cavus.* A foot with an extremely high arch (the opposite of a flat foot); this painful foot deformity may be part of a syndrome, such as Friedreich ataxia, or an early sign of a spinal cord tumor.

CBA *See* curriculum-based assessment.

CBC *See* complete blood count.

CBCL *See* Child Behavior Checklist.

CBM *See* curriculum-based measurement.

CBP *See* Child Behavior Profile.

CBT Cognitive-behavioral therapy. *See* cognitive therapy.

CC *See* chief complaint.

CCC *See* Certificate of Clinical Competence.

CCC *See* Children's Communication Checklist.

CCC-A *See* Certificate of Clinical Competence (CCC).

CCC-SLP *See* Certificate of Clinical Competence (CCC).

CCD *See* Consortium for Citizens with Disabilities.

CCI *See* child-centered intervention.

CCITSN *See* Carolina Curriculum for Infants and Toddlers with Special Needs–Third Edition.

CCPSN *See* Carolina Curriculum for Preschoolers with Special Needs–Second Edition.

CCS *See* Crippled Children's Services.

CCSPEA *See* Classroom Communication Screening Procedure for Early Adolescents.

CD *See* campomelic dysplasia.

CD *See* celiac disease.

CDA *See* child development associate.

CDC *See* Centers for Disease Control and Prevention.

CDD *See* childhood disintegrative disorder.

CDF *See* Children's Defense Fund.

CDH Congenital dislocation of the hip. *See* developmental dysplasia of the hip (DDH).

CDI *See* Child Development Inventory.

CDIs Communicative Development Inventories. *See* MacArthur-Bates Communicative Development Inventories–Second Edition.

cebocephaly A form of holoprosencephaly (major brain malformation) with ocular hypotelorism (closely spaced eyes) and an abnormal (or absent) nose with a single blind-ended nostril.

CEC *See* Council for Exceptional Children.

ceiling The point above which test items are assumed to be incorrect. Testing procedures often include a starting point based on age or grade, a basal, and a ceiling. Ceilings are described specifically for each test and are often a set number of consecutive items answered incorrectly; testing is stopped when that criterion is met. In scoring, items above the ceiling, regardless of whether they have been administered or whether they are correct, are scored as incorrect.

CELF-4 *See* Clinical Evaluation of Language Fundamentals–Fourth Edition.

CELI *See* Carrow Elicited Language Inventory.

celiac disease (CD) *celiac sprue, gluten-induced enteropathy, nontropical sprue.* A hereditary intolerance to the protein gluten that typically presents as malabsorption. It is screened for by a panel of antibodies, diagnosed by intestinal biopsy, and treated with a gluten-free diet. A wide variety of neurological complications can occur with CD, and although these are more common in adults, they can occur in children with CD with few of signs of malabsorption.

cell migration A step in the sequence of embryogenesis in which cells move from their original area to their final anatomical location. This process is complex and is subject to damage by teratogens (toxic agents). Failure or irregularities in cell migration in the developing brain can have significant neurodevelopmental impacts.

cell therapy *See* sicca cell therapy.

Center for Social and Emotional Foundation for Early Learning (CSEFEL) A national resource center funded by the Office of Head Start and the Child Care Bureau for disseminating research and evidence-based practices to early childhood programs across the country. CSEFEL is focused on promoting the social-emotional development and school readiness of young children birth to age 5.

Center for Special Education Finance (CSEF) A not-for-profit agency founded in 1992 to study, monitor, and make recommendations on fiscal policy issues related to the delivery and support of special education services throughout the United States. The stated goals include conducting policy-relevant research to improve practices related to funding special education programs and services; providing up-to-date information about federal and state funding systems for special education; producing and disseminating policy-relevant data and reports related to special education finance through an easy-to-navigate web site; and responding quickly to the information needs of stakeholders at the federal, state, and local levels.

Center for Substance Abuse Prevention (CSAP) A division of the U.S. Department of Health and Human Services, CSAP is the federal organization charged with providing national leadership in the federal effort to prevent alcohol, tobacco, and other drug problems.

center-based programs Interventions that focus on exposing children to an educationally stimulating environment outside the home with the aim of facilitating the development of intellectual and social competence. Although *center-based programs* most often refers to early childhood special education (ECSE) programs, the term can also apply to services offered at a centralized location for other populations. The term has evolved to refer to programs that serve students with disabilities, often in a segregated as opposed to an inclusive or natural environment.

Centers for Disease Control and Prevention (CDC) Operating under the umbrella of the U.S. Department of Health and Human Services, the CDC was founded in 1942 as the Office of National Defense Malaria Control Activities, a branch of the U.S. Public Health Service. Its headquarters were located in Atlanta, Georgia, because malaria was endemic in the southern United States. It was renamed the Communicable Disease Center in 1946; became the National Communicable Disease Center (NCDC) effective July 1, 1967; and was again renamed as the Center for Disease Control on June 24, 1970, and as the Centers for Disease Control effective October 14, 1980. An act of the U.S. Congress appended the words "and Prevention" to the name effective October 27, 1992; however, Congress directed that the initials CDC be retained because of their name recognition. The CDC has long focused on matters related to the prevention and control of disease (especially infectious diseases), environmental health, occupational safety and health, health promotion, and education activities. The CDC focus has broadened to include chronic diseases, disabilities, injury control, workplace hazards, environmental health threats, and smallpox and terrorism preparedness.

Centers for Medicare & Medicaid Services (CMS) The federal agency responsible for administering Medicare and Medicaid programs in most states. The CMS determines requirements for services that are organized and paid to provide medical rehabilitation.

central alignment A position for feeding and swallowing, often considered "ideal," that involves neutral head flexion, an elongated neck, a stable and depressed shoulder girdle, an elongated trunk, a stable and symmetrical pelvis, hips at 90 degrees, and feet in a neutral position with slight dorsiflexion.

central auditory processing disorder (CAPD) A language-processing disorder in which an individual has a reduced or impaired ability to discriminate, recognize, or comprehend auditory information despite normal hearing. People with CAPD have difficulty listening to or comprehending auditory information. The problem appears most pronounced when the environment creates distortion, competition, or dampening of sound input. Because many of the behavioral symptoms of CAPD overlap with those of attention-deficit/hyperactivity disorder (ADHD), it is possible that the two conditions may also overlap or even, in many cases, represent the same diagnosis as interpreted by two different professionals, an audiologist (CAPD) and a physician (ADHD). Although CAPD and ADHD can occur independently, children with ADHD often do poorly on tests of central auditory processing, and many of the management steps and intervention techniques are the same for both conditions. *See also* phonological processing disorder.

central axis The mid-line of the body.

central blindness *cortical blindness.* Blindness caused by damage to the visual cortex in the occipital lobe. Visual perception is often more affected than actual vision. People with central blindness are not blind in the sense that they have eyes that do not work but instead have visual impairments because the way they process images is inaccurate and inconsistent.

central deafness *cortical deafness.* A hearing loss resulting from damage to the auditory nerve pathways in the brainstem or cerebral cortex, resulting in the ability to hear pure tones but not necessarily to process or understand sounds or speech.

central nervous system (CNS) The composite system formed by the brain and spinal cord as contrasted with the peripheral nervous system (the system of nerves running throughout the body). The CNS is the center of control for the entire nervous system and has the additional function of controlling voluntary movement and thought. Developmental disorders almost always reflect chronic impairment of the brain but not necessarily of the spinal cord or peripheral nervous system, although impairment of the latter may also be involved. The CNS receives sensory information from the body and sends out nerve impulses that respond to that input by stimulating muscle contractions.

centration Focusing on one aspect of a problem when more than one is important.

cephalic index The ratio of the maximal breadth (horizontal) to the maximal length (vertical) of the skull; a decreasing value suggests scaphocephaly (projected head), whereas an increasing value indicates brachycephaly (irregular, flat head shape). When not associated with craniosynostosis (early fusion of skull sutures) or microcephaly (abnormally small head), many varieties of skull shape are racial or normal variants. *See also* brachycephaly.

cephalocaudal Literally, "head to tail." In describing the human body, *cephalocaudal* means going in a head-to-toe direction. The ability of a child to voluntarily control his or her own body follows a law of cephalocaudal progression, with head control being achieved in the first months of life and independent ambulation occurring late in the first or early in the second year of life.

cephalographs Skull x rays taken in a standardized position and with standardized distance from the person to the film and x-ray source.

cephalohematoma Subperiosteal hemorrhage (bleeding under the periosteum, the tough layer of tissue surrounding the bones) of the skull often associated with a hairline fracture incurred during delivery. So much blood may be lost into the swelling that a blood transfusion may be required. Unlike caput succedaneum, the swelling is limited by the suture lines of the skull (borders of the bones that form the skull). Calcification (hardening) of this swelling can take months to resolve; the hard edge with a soft center may give the misleading impression of a depressed skull fracture.

cephalopelvic disproportion (CPD) A mismatch between the size of an infant's head and his or her mother's pelvis; describing a fetal head that is too large relative to the maternal pelvis to safely allow vaginal delivery. Prolonged labor is one major sign of CPD. The situation is typically addressed by caesarean section delivery.

cerea flexibilitas "Waxy flexibility" sometimes seen in young children with severe environmental deprivation; an arm or leg passively placed in a given position remains there for a long time. This atypical behavior can also be seen in adults with catatonic schizophrenia.

cerebellar cerebral palsy *See* ataxic cerebral palsy.

cerebellar function The coordination and smoothing out of movements by the most posterior part of the brain. Dysfunction is characterized by dysdiadochokinesia (inability to perform rapidly alternating movements of the hands), titubation (staggering gait), intention tremor (trembling with voluntary movement), and ataxia (unsteady gait).

cerebellar stimulation A controversial neurosurgical approach to the treatment of severe movement disorders (e.g., cerebral palsy) that involves implanting electrodes in the cerebellum and subjecting that part of the brain to continuous patterned electrical currents. Claims for the success of this method have been extended to include the treatment of seizures, intellectual disability, and other developmental disorders.

cerebral allergy *See* allergic tension fatigue syndrome.

cerebral gigantism *See* Sotos syndrome.

cerebral palsy (CP) A family of syndromes characterized by disordered movement and posture, delayed motor development, and atypical motor findings on neurological examination. The etiology (cause) of the motor problem is located in the brain rather than in the spinal cord or peripheral nervous system (the system of nerves running throughout the body). Although the causal brain injury is usually prenatal (i.e., occurs before birth), CP is rarely diagnosed in the first year of life. The full clinical picture becomes clear only in the second year of life. CP disorders are all chronic but nonprogressive; with the exception of orthopedic complications, most children with CP do not lose function as they get older. The incidence of associated impairments in CP is high: Intellectual disability (50%–70%), seizures, and visual and auditory impairments are common. Dysarthria (difficulty pronouncing words), strabismus (crossed eyes), feeding disorders, poor physical growth, asymmetrical growth, and asymmetrical neurological findings are also common. The overall incidence of CP is less than 0.5%. The types of CP are grouped under two major headings: 1) the physiological (or neuroanatomical, as defined by the tone and movement pattern) and 2) the topographical (as defined by which parts of the body are more involved). These are outlined as in the table below.

Types of cerebral palsy

Physiological	Topographical
Spastic	Monoplegia
	Hemiplegia
	Diplegia
	Triplegia
	Quadriplegia
Extrapyramidal movement	(Choreo)athetoid
	Ataxic/cerebullar
	Tremor
tone	Rigid
	Hypotonic/atonic

cerebral thumbing *See* cortical thumbing.

cerebrohepatorenal syndrome *Zellweger syndrome.* A rare genetic syndrome involving a peroxisomal (part of a cell that oxidizes toxic substances) enzyme deficiency that leads to hypotonia (low muscle tone), high forehead, flattened face, brain abnormalities, hepatomegaly (liver enlargement), and kidney cysts. Breech presentation, intrauterine and postnatal failure to thrive (poor growth), and death within the first 6 months of life are characteristic. Inheritance is autosomal recessive.

cerebrospinal fluid (CSF) The fluid that fills the ventricles of the brain and the space around the spinal cord and that acts as a shock absorber for these organs. It can be removed from the body for diagnostic testing by a procedure called a *lumbar puncture* (LP). CSF may contain white blood cells, indicating infection (e.g., meningitis [infection of the spinal cord and brain membranes]); red blood cells, indicating a hemorrhage (bleeding); or too much protein, as in neurodegenerative diseases or tumor cells (e.g., leukemia, medulloblastoma).

cerebrovascular accident (CVA) *See* stroke.

Certificate of Clinical Competence (CCC) A post-master's certification in audiology (CCC-A) or speech-language pathology (CCC-SLP) through the American Speech-Language-Hearing Association (ASHA).

certificate of high school equivalency A formal document certifying that an individual has met the state requirements for high school graduation by attaining satisfactory scores on the tests of the general equivalency diploma (GED) or other state-specified examinations. This certificate is often accepted in the same manner as a high school diploma.

certification A recognition of qualification to perform certain professional tasks and duties. Certification is less stringent than licensing and requires only the attainment of specified education or experience standards with no accompanying assessment or monitoring of competence.

cerumen Ear wax.

ceruminosis Impacted cerumen (accumulated ear wax blocking the ear canal). Ceruminosis can contribute to hearing impairment; it is especially common in people with a narrow external ear canal, which occurs in individuals with Down syndrome. Cerumen can be removed by a medical professional using special instruments or irrigation (flushing it out). Drugs can also be used to liquefy the wax.

cervical Relating to 1) the neck, as in cervical vertebrae, which support the head upon the body, or 2) the neck (cervix) of the uterus.

cervical

cervical-thoraco-lumbar-spinal and hip orthosis (CTLSHO) In-chair orthosis for scoliosis (spinal curvature) that provides positional support for the entire spine. *See also* Milwaukee brace.

cervical-thoraco-lumbar-spinal orthosis (CTLSO) *See* cervical-thoraco-lumbar-spinal and hip orthosis (CTLSHO).

cervico-oculo-acoustic syndrome *Wildervanck syndrome.* A genetic syndrome that includes Klippel-Feil syndrome, Duane syndrome (a sixth nerve palsy that limits the outward movement of the eye), and congenital hearing impairment. Inheritance is X-linked dominant or polygenic-multifactorial and is limited to females.

cesarean section The delivery of a fetus by an incision through the abdominal wall into the uterus. A cesarean section is usually performed because of specific indications

such as fetal distress, breech presentation, bleeding, or cephalopelvic disproportion or because a previous child was delivered via cesarean section (no longer considered obligatory).

CF *See* cystic fibrosis.

CFF *See* Cystic Fibrosis Foundation.

C4b protein A plasma protein that is low in the presence of autoimmune disease. This protein may also be low in people with autism, suggesting a possible autoimmune mechanism in the etiology of autism.

CFR *See* Code of Federal Regulations.

Chaddock sign Stimulating the skin in the region of the external (lateral) malleolus causes the big toe to extend; this is considered a sign of pyramidal tract (motor nerve fibers in the spinal cord) involvement and a variation of the Babinski sign.

chaining The linking together of two or more responses into a single complex behavioral sequence by a training program that pairs each successive response into the stimulus for the next response in the sequence. *See also* backward chaining, forward chaining.

chalasia A transient, benign form of gastroesophageal reflux; postprandial regurgitation (spitting up after meals) in early infancy, usually successfully treated by upright positioning, thickened feedings, and smaller feedings.

challenging Problematic or unacceptable, as in "challenging behavior."

CHAMPUS *See* Civilian Health and Medical Program of the Uniformed Services.

Chandler Movement Assessment of Infancy–Screening Test (CMAI-ST) A 10-minute screening version of the Movement Assessment of Infants (MAI).

channeling The continued growth of an infant along any given percentile of the growth curves for length, weight, and head circumference. A failure of channeling involves switching or crossing growth curves to a lower percentile.

chaotic family A family characterized by chronic and severe lack of structure and organization. Individuals in such a family function autonomously with little commitment to or support from the family unit. A child with developmental disabilities in this type of family often experiences understimulation and isolation, owing to the inability of the family to work together to meet the child's constant and special needs.

Chapter 1 of the Education Consolidation and Improvement Act of 1981 (PL 98-211) A mandated program of compensatory education for children with educational disadvantages in schools with concentrations of children from low-income families; formerly known as *Title I of the Elementary and Secondary Education Act*. Federal grants are made through state education departments to local school districts based on the number of children from families in poverty. Services are then provided based on the extent of the student's educational deprivation. The law allows for a range of services, including instructional services, purchase of materials and equipment, teacher training, construction, and social and health services. *See also* Title I of the Elementary and Secondary Education Act (ESEA) of 1965 (PL 89-10).

Charcot-Marie-Tooth syndrome (CMT) An inherited group of genetic conditions that affect the motor nerves (nerves that move muscles) and sometimes the sensory nerves (nerves that transmit sensations), leading to progressive distal muscle atrophy (wasting) and sometimes progressive sensorineural hearing loss. The disorders affect the peripheral nerves but not the central nervous system and so do not affect intellect or behavior. Inheritance can follow an autosomal dominant, autosomal recessive, or X-linked pattern. Lemieux-Neemeh syndrome is CMT syndrome with the addition of chronic nephritis (kidney disease). This syndrome is heterogeneous, with at least 40 different loci involved. One form (Type 1A) involves a duplication of the chromosome 17p1.2–p12 region.

CHARGE syndrome *CHARGE association.* CHARGE is an acronym that represents a recurring group of congenital malformations including coloboma (absence of part of the eye or retina), heart disease, and choanal atresia (nasal blockage) with impaired (slowed) growth and development, occasional intellectual disability, genital anomalies, ear anomalies, and a range of hearing impairments. Visual and auditory problems frequently affect cognitive functioning. *CHD7,* which encodes the chromodomain helicase deoxyribonucleic acid (DNA)–binding protein, is the only gene known to be associated with CHARGE syndrome. Sequence analysis of the *CHD7* coding region has detected mutations in approximately 60%–70% of individuals with CHARGE syndrome.

charter school A nonsectarian public school of choice that operates free of many of the regulations that apply to traditional public schools. The "charter" establishing each such school is a performance contract that details the school's mission, program, goals, students served, methods of assessment, and ways to measure success. The length of time for which charters are granted varies, but most are granted for 3–5 years. At the end of the term, the entity granting the charter may renew the school's contract. Charter schools are accountable to their sponsor—usually a state or local school board—to produce positive academic results and adhere to the charter contract. The basic concept of charter schools is that they exercise increased autonomy in return for this accountability.

CHAT *See* Checklist for Autism in Toddlers.

CHC *See* Cattell-Horn-Carroll theory of cognitive abilities.

check-in/check-out (CICO) procedures In positive behavior interventions and supports, a targeted intervention for youth with emerging problem behaviors. When students arrive at school each day, they check in with a designated adult who reviews expectations and standards and gives them a point card or sheet. At designated intervals during the school day, youth approach teachers for feedback about the extent to which their behavior has adhered to standards. Students "check out" at the end of the day and can use the accumulated points to earn access to desired reinforcers. CICO procedures can reduce problem behavior and increase the use of alternative, more adaptive behaviors.

Checklist for Autism in Toddlers (CHAT) A brief screening instrument for autism in children between 18 and 36 months of age. The CHAT has nine parent questions and five behavioral observations for the clinician. The items that seem to be most sensitive for autism include the absence of pretend play (asking to pour a cup of tea using a toy teapot, cup, and saucer), the lack of protodeclarative pointing as an indication of joint attention (pointing to direct someone else's attention), and the lack of gaze monitoring (turning in the same direction as an adult is looking). Rather than being diagnostic of autism, CHAT scores above a particular cutoff indicate the need for more comprehensive assessment.

Checklist for Autism Spectrum Disorder A 30-item questionnaire based on the symptoms of autism that is designed to identify a diagnosis of autism or pervasive developmental disorder in young children and children with low cognitive ability.

Chédiak-Higashi syndrome (CHS) *Chédiak-Steinbrinck-Higashi syndrome.* A rare genetic syndrome with partial albinism leading to reduced visual acuity; immune defects in the white blood cells contribute to recurrent infections, neuropathy, and, occasionally, intellectual disability. Therapy includes aggressive treatment of the recurrent infections; most affected people do not survive childhood. Inheritance is autosomal recessive with a high rate of consanguinity (intermarriage). Alterations in *LYST*, the only gene known to be associated with CHS, are found in ~70% of affected individuals.

Chedoke-McMaster Attitudes Towards Children with Handicaps (CATCH) scale *See* CATCH scale.

chelation The use of a drug to remove a metal that is harmful to the body. Chelation therapy is used for treating lead poisoning and Wilson disease to bind the lead and copper, respectively, that can cause significant brain impairment.

chelion The corner of the mouth.

chemotherapy Treatment with chemicals or drugs; usually refers to the highly toxic substances used to treat cancer.

cherry-red spot A red patch seen on the retina in children with various neuronal storage diseases, such as Tay-Sachs disease. The lipid compounds that cannot be broken down or excreted are found in the neurons, giving them a grayish color. The red spot is an area that does not contain any nerve cells and therefore is red (the normal color), not gray.

cherry-red spot myoclonus syndrome *See* sialidosis.

cherubism A genetic disorder that causes swelling of the mandible (jaw) along with a "heavenward" glance to produce a cherubic or angelic appearance. Articulation disorders may result from oral structural problems.

Inheritance follows an autosomal dominant pattern with variable expression and incomplete penetrance in females; thus, males with the syndrome are more affected than females. *SH3BP2* gene mutations cause cherubism.

chest physical therapy (CPT) *chest physiotherapy, chest PT.* A group of treatments and maneuvers used to promote more efficient breathing. CPT includes chest percussion, repeated rhythmic blows to the chest wall with a cupped hand or a device specifically to dislodge thick secretions. Other techniques are turning, coughing, postural drainage (changing a person's position to allow gravity to help drain secretions), and incentive spirometry (use of a device that promotes lung expansion by encouraging full inhalation).

Chiari 1 malformation A downward displacement of the cerebellar tonsils below the level of the foramen magnum that produces headache, dizziness, ataxia, tinnitus (ringing in the ears), nystagmus (jerky eye movements), and hearing abnormalities and is associated with other cranial and vertebral abnormalities.

Chiari 2 malformation A downward displacement of the medulla, fourth ventricle, and cerebellum of the brain below the level of the foramen magnum with elongation of other brain structures. Chiari 2 malformation is often associated with myelomeningocele (spina bifida), hydrocephalus, and spine abnormalities.

chickenpox *See* varicella.

chief complaint (CC) The principal symptom or subjective concern leading to a (self-) referral for diagnostic assessment and treatment. The final diagnosis is often associated with the chief complaint, but sometimes the diagnosis is one rarely associated with this symptom.

chignon A temporary edematous (filled with excess fluid) swelling of the scalp often caused by the vacuum-assisted delivery of a newborn.

child abuse The Federal Child Abuse Prevention and Treatment Act Amendments of 1996 (PL 104-235) define *child abuse* as the physical and mental injury, sexual abuse, negligent treatment, or maltreatment of a child under the age of 18 years by a person who is responsible for the child's welfare, under circumstances that indicate that the child's health and welfare is harmed or threatened thereby.

Child Abuse Potential Inventory (CAP Inventory or CAPI) A 160-item screen for physical child abuse that produces three validity indexes, an overall score, six factor scale scores, and two special scale scores. An individual's responses and characteristics are compared with those of known child abusers and combined with clinical data to suggest his or her risk for abusing a child.

Child Abuse Prevention and Treatment Act (CAPTA) of 1974 (PL 93-247) Legislation that sets forth a definition of child abuse and neglect; provides federal funding to states in support of prevention, assessment, investigation, prosecution, and treatment activities; and also provides grants to public agencies and nonprofit organizations for demonstration programs and projects. PL 93-247 also identifies the federal role in supporting research, evaluation, technical assistance, and data collection activities; establishes the Office on Child Abuse and Neglect; and mandates the National Clearinghouse on Child Abuse and Neglect Information. The original law has been amended numerous times, most recently in 2003 by the Keeping Children and Families Safe Act of 2003 (PL 108-36). *See also* guardian ad litem (GAL).

Child Behavior Checklist (CBCL) A norm-referenced assessment of behavior problems and social competence. The CBCL has two versions: for informants ages

18 months to 5 years (CBCL/1½–5; parent form only) and 6–18 years (CBCL/6–18; parent, teacher, and youth self-report forms). It produces *T*-scores for Internalizing, Externalizing, and Total Problems, as well as various subscales. It is widely used in both clinical assessment and research.

Child Behavior Profile (CBP)   A group of standardized and normed questionnaires that includes the Child Behavior Checklist (CBCL), the Teacher Report Form (TRF), the Direct Observation Form (DOF), and the Youth Self-Report Form (YSRF). The CBP can help in the diagnosis of attention disorders, depression, and other childhood behavior problems and psychopathology.

child care   *See* day care.

child development associate (CDA)   Educational and training program leading to certification for Head Start and child care staff.

Child Development Inventory (CDI)   A parent-completed 300-item checklist of developmental skills for children ages 15 months to 6 years. Produces age equivalents and standard deviations for eight domains (social, self-help, gross motor, fine motor, receptive and expressive language, letters, and numbers) and an index of general development.

Child Find   Organized efforts to locate children with developmental disabilities or children who are at risk for developmental disabilities. Two federal enactments have given such efforts increased importance. First, the Education of the Handicapped Act Amendments of 1974 (PL 93-380) requires states to develop and implement systematic procedures for locating all individuals with disabilities from birth to age 21. The mandate particularly focuses on children not enrolled in school programs in order to facilitate an accurate child count for planning intervention programs and to document the need for additional early intervention programs. Second, the Education for All Handicapped Children Act of 1975 (PL 94-142), the Individuals with Disabilities Education Act Amendments (IDEA) of 1997 (PL 105-17), and the Individuals with Disabilities Education Improvement Act (IDEA) of 2004 (PL 108-446) list specific features of a free appropriate public education (FAPE) in the least restrictive environment (LRE), the provision of services to all children with disabilities from birth, and the locating of unserved children.

Child Health Questionnaire (CHQ)   An instrument used to measure health status and well-being in children ages 5–17 years. The scale assesses physical, emotional, and social well-being in a number of areas. These areas include physical functioning, bodily pain or discomfort, general health, change in health, limitations in school work and activities with friends, mental health, behavior, self-esteem, family cohesions, limitations in family activities, and emotional or time impact to the parent. The instrument gathers information from parents or caregivers and from self-reports among older children.

child life specialist   A pediatric health care professional who interacts with hospitalized children with a major focus on providing materials, guidance, and an appropriate environment for play activities; there is an additional emphasis on meeting the child's emotional needs and on ensuring a healthy emotional adjustment to illness and hospitalization.

Child Welfare League of America (CWLA)   A not-for-profit organization formed in 1920 from a coalition of private and public agencies serving children and families. Their aim is to provide expertise, leadership, and innovation on policies, programs, and practices in order to help improve the lives of children across the country. The CWLA publishes *Children's Voice* magazine and *Child Welfare* journal.

child with special health care needs *See* children with special health care needs (CSHCN).

child with special needs *See* children with special health care needs (CSHCN).

child-centered intervention (CCI) An intervention with a flexible sequence that involves exploration and creativity and that is centered on the child's choices and interests. The child is the initiator, and the adult is the facilitator. The organization of the environment is a key element in providing choices that will facilitate development.

Childhood Asperger Syndrome Test (CAST) A 37-item parent questionnaire for children 4–11 years of age to identify Asperger syndrome. This is an epidemiological measure (of prevalence) rather than a clinical diagnostic instrument.

childhood ataxia with diffuse central nervous system (CNS) hypomyelination (CACH) *See* vanishing white matter disease (VWM).

Childhood Autism Rating Scale (CARS) A 15-item diagnostic instrument for autism that rates children's behavior in the presence of an adult and during independent play. Scores 30 and above support a diagnosis of autism. The CARS is widely used with children as young as 2 years; it takes 20–30 minutes to administer.

Childhood Autism Rating Scale–Second Edition (CARS2) A 2010 revision of the CARS that includes the original 15 items on the standard form (CARS2-ST) and an alternative form for assessing individuals with verbal fluency who are considered high functioning (CARS2-HF). Scoring is done by a clinician who rates each item using a 4-point frequency response scale and who notes the intensity, peculiarity, and duration of atypical behaviors following an observation period. The CARS2 also has an unscored parent/caregiver questionnaire.

childhood disintegrative disorder (CDD) *dementia infantilis, disintegrative disorder of childhood, Heller syndrome.* A pervasive developmental disorder (PDD) characterized by a typical course of development until 3–10 years of age (with more cases occurring closer to the lower age cutoff). After a fairly rapid (i.e., within a period of weeks) deterioration involving loss of language, motor, and cognitive skills, the child is left with moderate intellectual disability and a set of qualitative impairments that resemble autism, including impairments in communication and socialization and restricted, repetitive, stereotypical behaviors. Upon detailed neurological investigation, a specific degenerative neurological disorder can be identified in one third to half of cases.

children with special health care needs (CSHCN) Those children who have or are at increased risk for a chronic physical, developmental, behavioral, or emotional condition and who also require health and related services of a type or amount beyond that required by children generally. The CSHCN Program is a programmatic theme of the Bureau of Maternal and Child Health that provides specialized medical care and care coordination services. It seeks to advance the health and well-being of children up to 21 years of age who have certain chronic, debilitating conditions and who meet financial and medical eligibility.

Children's Apperception Test (CAT) Three oral response projective tests that measure the traits, attitudes, and psychodynamics involved in the personality development of children. The measures are used to assess personality in children ages 3–10 years for clinical and diagnostic purposes. The CAT-A consists of 10 pictures of animals in a human social context; the child is asked to tell a story about the pictures. The CAT-H is composed of 10 pictures of human figures in situations of concern to children. The CAT-S is a supplemental form presenting 10 animal figures in family situations that are common but not as universal as those depicted in the two other forms. The picture plates resemble pieces of a jigsaw puzzle so that children who do not relate stories can manipulate the test items in play techniques. Administration of each form of the test takes approximately 30 minutes. As is the case with other projectives, the validity of the CAT with populations of children with disabilities is difficult to establish, and any responses and formulations based on projective data should be verified through other means as well. *See also* apperception.

Children's Coma Scale A variation of the Glasgow Coma Scale. For children ages 3 years and younger, scores range from 3 to 15. A child in a deep coma would score 3.

Children's Communication Checklist (CCC) A 70-item language screening for children 4–16 years old that yields a General Communication Composite (GCC) to identify children with significant communication problems and a Social Interaction Deviance Composite (SIDC) to identify a communication profile characteristic of children with autism.

Children's Defense Fund (CDF) A not-for-profit child advocacy and research group founded in 1973 that works with individuals, communities, and policy makers to enact, fund, and implement public policy and promote successful programs that lift children out of poverty, protect them from abuse and neglect, ensure access to health care and quality education, and provide a moral and spiritual foundation to help them succeed with the support of caring adults and communities.

Children's Version of the Family Environment Scale (CVFES) A downward extension of the Moos Family Environment Scale to elementary school-age children. Children respond to 30 questions by selecting one of three pictures that best represents their family. Scores are generated for cohesion, expressiveness, conflict, independence, achievement orientation, intellectual–cultural orientation, active recreation orientation, moral–religious emphasis, organization, and control. Caution should be used in interpreting these results in children with attention and learning problems.

chi-square A frequently used statistic that is used 1) to test whether observed results are likely to have occurred by chance alone and 2) to test the possibility of a relationship (termed *association*) between two variables.

chloral hydrate A nonbarbiturate, nonbenzodiazepine sedative-hypnotic; a sleep-inducing drug sometimes used to prepare children for surgery or other procedures.

chloride-deficient formulas In 1978 and 1979, two soy-based infant formulas (Neo-Mull-Soy and Cho-Free) lacked adequate dietary chloride and produced serious illness (i.e., metabolic alkalosis) in a small number of children.

chlorpromazine Trade name, Thorazine. An antipsychotic drug used to treat severe behavior disorders. Side effects include tardive dyskinesia (slow, rhythmic automatic movements that may occur after long-term antipsychotic drug use), photosensitivity, and blood and liver chemistry problems.

choice making Occurs when an individual selects a preferred item or activity from two or more options.

chondrodysplasia punctata A clinically and genetically diverse group of rare diseases, first described by Conradi, that share the features of stippled epiphyses (ends of long bones with a speckled appearance on x ray) and skeletal changes. There may be asymmetrical shortening of the limbs, scoliosis (spinal curvature), and facial features characterized by saddle-nose deformity and malar hypoplasia (undergrowth of the mid-face with cheekbones flat or depressed). Growth problems such as failure to thrive and short stature are common. Mild to moderate intellectual disability and cataracts can occur. Incidence is estimated at 2.5 per million. Inheritance follows both autosomal dominant and autosomal recessive patterns. The autosomal recessive form is more severe and usually results in death before 1 year of age; autosomal dominant forms have a milder course. There is also an X-linked form that is lethal in males. *See also* Conradi-Hünermann syndrome.

chondroectodermal dysplasia *Ellis-van Creveld syndrome.* A genetic syndrome that causes short arms and legs, leading to short stature, polydactyly (extra fingers or toes), and nail hypoplasia (failure of fingernails and toenails to develop). Congenital heart disease and abnormalities of the teeth and mouth are frequent. Intellectual disability is sometimes present. Many affected individuals die in early infancy from cardiorespiratory problems. Inheritance follows an autosomal recessive pattern with a 30% rate of consanguinity (inbreeding).

chorda tympani section A surgical procedure that disrupts the course of nerves that serve the salivary glands in order to treat excessive drooling; it is usually performed bilaterally (both sides of the mouth) and combined with a tympanic neurectomy.

chordee Abnormal position of the penis caused by a band of tissue that holds the penis in a ventral (downward) or lateral (sideways) curvature.

chorea Literally, "dance." Chorea is a pattern of movement disorder characterized by spasmodic, irregular, unpredictable, involuntary, and purposeless movements, including large

central twitches or jerking movements. Mild isolated chorea may be seen in individuals with choreiform (involuntary twitching) syndrome. In people with more severe motor delay and chorea, the resulting type of extrapyramidal cerebral palsy is usually described as choreoathetosis. Choreiform movements are quicker and less fluid than athetoid movements.

chorea minor *Sydenham chorea.* A transient chorea that follows rheumatic fever. (*Chorea major* refers to chorea with a psychoemotional etiology.)

choreic hand Choreic hand describes a hand with the arms extended horizontally, the wrists flexed, the wrist and finger joints overextended, and exaggerated spooning (hyperextended).

choreiform syndrome The presence of mild choreiform (involuntary twitching) movements in the outstretched arms of boys standing at attention with their eyes closed. Originally thought to be a marker for juvenile delinquency, it is now considered a nonspecific sign of minor motor dysfunction.

choreoathetosis One of the physiological subtypes of extrapyramidal cerebral palsy in which involvement of the basal ganglia produces a movement disorder with features of both chorea and athetosis (involuntary twisting of the upper extremities). *See also* athetosis.

chorioretinitis An inflammation of the back of the eye or retina characterized by changes in pigmentation (coloration) and scarring in the retina. Chorioretinitis is common in intrauterine infections such as toxoplasmosis, cytomegalovirus (CMV), and congenital rubella. These congenital infections can be associated with intellectual disability, impairments of vision and hearing, and failure to thrive (poor growth).

Chotzen syndrome *See* Saethre-Chotzen syndrome.

CHQ *See* Child Health Questionnaire.

chromatin The complex of proteins and deoxyribonucleic acid (DNA) that compose chromosomes.

chromosomal aberration *chromosomal abnormality.* An abnormal number or structure of chromosomes that may produce an abnormal phenotype.

chromosomal satellite A chromatin attached by a stalk to the tips of the short arms of acrocentric chromosomes.

chromosome deletion The loss of deoxyribonucleic acid (DNA) from a chromosome. The size of the loss may vary from a base pair to an entire arm.

chromosome mapping *gene mapping.* The methods used to assign genes to specific chromosomes or chromosome regions; includes gene linkage, somatic cell hybrids, and *in situ* hybridization.

chromosome translocation The transfer of a piece of one chromosome to another chromosome. If the two chromosomes exchange pieces, the transfer is called *reciprocal.* If no genetic material is lost, the translocation is called *balanced.*

chronic sorrow Chronic grief; parental response to a child's chronic disability or illness. This grief can be quite variable and can progress through stages of helplessness, hopelessness, and dependency. This sorrow or grief tends to be acutely reactivated with each new developmental stage (e.g., entering school, entering adolescence, leaving home) that the child would typically experience were it not for the disability or illness.

chronic subdural hematoma A persistent collection of bloody fluid under the dura (outer layer of the brain) produced by trauma to the head. Clinical presentation includes headaches and changes in personality and alertness. Diagnosis is by magnetic resonance imaging (MRI) or a computed tomography (CT) scan. Treatment involves removing the fluid to relieve the pressure on the brain. Subdural effusions (fluid under one of the meningeal layers) in infants can be acute or chronic and are commonly associated with nonaccidental trauma (abuse). Clinical symptoms in infants are less specific and include failure to gain weight, irritability, lethargy, and vomiting. CT scans often reveal not only a subdural hematoma but also an associated skull fracture.

chronobiology The study of biological temporal rhythms that can be daily (circadian), weekly, monthly (lunar), seasonal, or annual.

chronological age (CA) The actual age of an individual derived from his or her date of birth. Chronological age is expressed in years, months, and days. It is used as a comparison standard for various measures of performance. It is the denominator in the equation for determining a developmental quotient (DQ) by the ratio method: (mental age [MA]/CA) $\times$ 100 = DQ.

CHS *See* Chédiak-Higashi syndrome.

CI movement therapy *See* constraint-induced movement therapy.

CIBI Continuous intrathecal baclofen infusion. *See also* intrathecal baclofen.

cicatrix A scar.

CICO *See* check-in/check-out (CICO) procedures.

ciliary reflex Eyelash reflex. An infant reflex in which touching an eyelash (stimulus) produces bilateral blinking (response).

cimetidine Trade name, Tagamet. An H2-receptor antagonist class medication that blocks the production of gastric (stomach) acid. It is often used in the treatment of gastroesophageal reflux (GER).

CIP *See* Comprehensive Identification Process.

circadian rhythm A biological cycle with an approximate 24-hour period synchronized with the cycle of day and night.

circumduction A circular movement; in a hemiplegic gait, the weaker involved leg, instead of moving directly forward, is held straight and swung out to the side in a semicircle, then dragged ahead.

Civilian Health and Medical Program of the Uniformed Services (CHAMPUS) A federally funded health insurance program for the dependents of active and retired military personnel. CHAMPUS has been reorganized under a managed care program known as TRICARE.

CLAMS *See* Clinical Linguistic and Auditory Milestone Scale.

clanging *clang association.* A type of speech in which sound rather than meaning governs word choice, as in rhyming or punning. The term implies a pathological association (e.g., mania, schizophrenia) rather than typical word play in childhood.

class within a class (CWC) A service delivery model in which students with mild disabilities are educated in the general classroom using a collaborative educational program provided by general and special education teachers. Programs include 1) collaborative curriculum development, in which teachers of students with learning disabilities and general education teachers write the curriculum and plan teaching strategies; 2) a service delivery model that places teachers of students with learning disabilities in the general classroom to promote collaboration between general and special educators; and 3) development of a curriculum to provide students with learning disabilities instruction in learning strategies and study skills.

classical conditioning *Pavlovian conditioning.* A form of learning in which a biological reflex is paired with a neutral stimulus (something that would not usually produce that reflex) to produce a conditioned response. An unconditioned response, such as an eye blink in response to a puff of air, occurs naturally. During conditioning trials, a bell tone (for example) would be heard just before the puff of air to the eye. Over time, the previously neutral bell tone would result in the eye blink even if the puff of air did not follow. As such, the eye blink reflex would become a conditioned response to the bell tone (the conditioned stimulus). Conditioned responses extinguish (stop happening) when the conditioned stimulus (bell tone) is presented repeatedly without the unconditioned stimulus (the puff of air). Unlearned responses, including positive and negative emotions, can be classically conditioned, as when an individual exposed to a traumatic event becomes fearful of elements associated with that event. *See also* conditioned reflex.

classification The process of grouping and defining criteria for inclusion in or exclusion from a group; under federal law, classification into a specific disability category is required for children to be eligible for special education services.

Classroom Communication Screening Procedure for Early Adolescents (CCSPEA) A language screening instrument for use with underachieving upper elementary students prior to entering junior high school. The CCSPEA assesses the ability to scan an assignment for answers, follow oral and multipart written directions, match vocabulary items with definitions and synonyms (words that mean the same thing), and apply abstract thinking skills.

clavicle   Collar bone.

clavicular breathing   A type of breathing characterized by elevation of the shoulders with each breath; may be associated with excessive tension in the shoulders and neck.

claw grasp   Three- or four-finger grasp or jaw chuck (vise grasp); an advance in the radial (thumb and forefinger) rake (use of those fingers to drag or scoop something toward a child) that is not yet a pincer (two-finger) grasp.

CLD   *See* Council for Learning Disabilities.

CLD   *See* culturally-linguistically different.

CLDE student   *See* culturally and linguistically different exceptional student.

cleft   A space or opening; a hollow area or indentation.

cleft lip   An embryonic defect that presents in the newborn with varying degrees of failure of the upper lip to fuse appropriately. It can be associated with cleft palate, hypertelorism (widely spaced eyes), speech disorders, recurrent otitis media (middle ear infection), and conductive (involving the middle and outer ear) hearing loss. Etiology (cause) is genetic with a polygenic (caused by several genes) pattern and varying recurrence risks; about one third of cases of cleft lip are part of another syndrome that may have other associated features and a more definable recurrence rate.

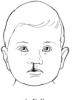

cleft lip

cleft palate   A congenital defect in which the palate (bony roof of the mouth) has not closed or fused in the mid-line during fetal development. Cleft palate is associated with feeding and swallowing problems, failure to thrive (poor growth), aspiration, recurrent ear infections, and speech problems. Cleft palate has multifactorial inheritance; cleft palate with cleft lip also has multifactorial inheritance but is distinct from isolated cleft palate. Clefting can occur as an isolated oral cavity malformation or as part of many genetic and teratogenic (causing malformation in the fetus) syndromes.

cleidocranial dysostosis   *Scheuthauer-Marie-Sainton syndrome.* A genetic syndrome with variable expression of bone defects affecting the clavicle (cleido), delayed eruption of teeth, and late ossification (hardening) of the skull (cranial) sutures. Because they have incomplete clavicles, some people can almost touch their shoulders together in front of their chest. One of the earliest signs of this syndrome may be the late closure of a large anterior (front) fontanel (soft spot). Cognition is typical; hearing and dental monitoring is indicated. Inheritance is autosomal dominant; however, one third of the cases represent spontaneous mutations (new mutations that are not inherited).

client   A social work and human services term denoting an individual, family, group, or community receiving services. In contrast to the medical term *patient,* the term *client* highlights the elements of mutuality, self-determination, and being an informed consumer.

Client Assistance Program   The state agency responsible for providing legal, administrative, and other assistance to individuals seeking and receiving vocational rehabilitation services.

Clinical Assessment of Articulation and Phonology (CAAP)   A formal evaluation of pronunciation for children ages 2;6–8;11 years.

Clinical Evaluation of Language Fundamentals–Fourth Edition (CELF-4)   An individually administered test used to identify individuals ages 5–21 years who lack basic language skills. The CELF-4 consists of 18 subtests organized under four levels of testing.

Clinical Global Impression scales Likert scales used to measure symptom severity (Clinical Global Impression–Severity scale) and treatment response (Clinical Global Impression–Improvement scale).

Clinical Linguistic and Auditory Milestone Scale (CLAMS) A test of early language development in children birth to 2 years of age that uses a parent or caregiver interview and yields an expressive language quotient (ELQ) and a receptive language quotient (RLQ). Although normative data have been published to allow the use of the CLAMS as a standalone screening test, the instrument is intended for use as one component of the Capute Scales.

clinical practice guidelines *best practice guidelines.* The product of a specific methodology used to develop rules (recommendations, not laws) on how to screen, evaluate, diagnose, treat, and monitor outcomes for a complaint, condition, disease, or disorder. Key components to the development of clinical practice guidelines include an extensive literature search, a grading of each publication according to specific research criteria, a rating of each recommendation as to its level of research (evidence) support, and the inclusion of an appropriately representative sample of expertise as well as people or clients in the development of the guidelines. Clinical practice guidelines are the foundation for evidence-based medicine.

clinical psychology A branch of the study of human behavior concerned with assessment, diagnosis, research, and intervention for mental disorders and interpersonal problems.

clinician A professional who is directly involved with the examination, diagnosis, and treatment of individuals or clients.

clinodactyly Lateral (outward) or medial (inward) turning of a finger; a physical feature found in a number of syndromes. Clinodactyly of the fifth finger is a common nonspecific minor dysmorphic (atypical) feature.

CLM *See* Competent Learner Model.

clock training Pseudo toilet training in which the caregiver, rather than the child, is trained. The caregiver places the child on the toilet at regular intervals to catch bowel movements. This reflects more a caregiving refinement than the child's learning to toilet. When successful, clock training decreases the expense for diapers and the caregiver's need to clean the child.

clomipramine Trade name, Anafranil. A tricyclic antidepressant medication with nonselective serotonin reuptake inhibition (meaning that it also inhibits other neurotransmitters such as dopamine and norepinephrine). Anafranil is used to treat obsessive-compulsive disorder (OCD). It may also address certain autistic behaviors, including problems with social interaction and repetitive, stereotypic behaviors.

clonazepam Trade name, Klonopin. An anticonvulsant medication that is also used to treat hypomanic states, self-injurious behavior, and severe maladaptive behavior in people with severe intellectual disability. Side effects include sedation, ataxia (unsteady gait), dysarthria (difficulty pronouncing words), emotional irritability, and weight gain. Clonazepam is used to treat Lennox-Gastaut syndrome.

clone A group of cells that come from one cell and are identical. Deoxyribonucleic acid (DNA) cloning and polymerase chain reaction (PCR) can be used with very small amounts of DNA to identify the presence of a particular kind of DNA. This has potential for use in the identification of genetic disorders.

clonidine Trade name, Catapres. An anti-hypertensive drug (used to treat high blood pressure) that is also used to treat tics, Gilles de la Tourette syndrome, difficulties falling asleep, and impulsivity in attention-deficit/hyperactivity disorder (ADHD). Clonidine can be given in delayed release transdermal (absorbed through skin patches) form. The main side effect is sleepiness.

clonus A rapidly alternating muscle contraction (tensing) and relaxation that leads to repetitive flexion and extension.

closed-captioning An adaptive mechanism for television viewing for people with hearing disorders. Spoken dialogue is printed across the bottom of the screen.

Clostridium tetani The bacterium (germ) that causes tetanus (lockjaw) and against which all children are immunized. It is an unproven hypothesis that chronic diarrhea and overuse of antibiotics allows bowel (gut) colonization with *Clostridium tetani,* whose neurotoxins (poisons) then contribute to the development of autism.

closure A law of gestalt perceptual psychology that asserts that mental processes tend to produce completeness and symmetry; for example, a circle that is missing a few degrees of its circumference is perceived as a circle rather than a long arc.

cloudy cornea Haziness of the normally translucent (clear) cornea (outer covering of the eye). Cloudy cornea can occur in conditions such as congenital syphilis, mucopolysaccharidosis, and mucolipidosis.

cloverleaf skull syndrome *Kleeblattschädel syndrome.* A syndrome of premature synostosis (closure) of the cranial sutures (where the bones of the skull meet) that produces upward and lateral outpouchings of the skull in a three-leaf clover outline; hydrocephalus (excess fluid in the brain),

developmental delay, and early death are associated features.

cloze technique A procedure for teaching and assessing reading comprehension based on the construct of perception and closure as defined in gestalt psychology. In this technique, in a passage of 250 words, every 10th lexical word would be deleted and the reader would be asked to fill it in. This requires various reading skills, including use of context clues, knowledge of linguistic patterns, and general reading comprehension.

clubbing An abnormal curvature of the fingernail and end of the finger sometimes found in individuals with chronic disease, especially pulmonary disease.

clubbing

clubfoot *See* talipes equinovarus.

cluster reduction A phonological process in which there is an omission of one or more segments in a cluster so that the cluster is omitted or reduced to a singleton.

cluttering A fluency disorder in which speech is so excited and rapid that words run together with syllables omitted; the fast rate and irregular clustering of phrases lead to difficulties with intelligibility. Cluttering can occur by itself or be associated with disorders in articulation, language, learning, and attention. *See also* fluency disorder.

CM *See* cochlear microphonic.

CMAI-ST *See* Chandler Movement Assessment of Infancy–Screening Test.

CMMS *See* Columbia Mental Maturity Scale.

CMS *See* Centers for Medicare & Medicaid Services.

CMT *See* Charcot-Marie-Tooth syndrome.

CMV Cytomegalovirus. *See* congenital cytomegalic inclusion disease.

CNS *See* central nervous system.

CNV *See* copy number variation.

coalescence The phonological process that occurs when two adjacent consonants are replaced by one that retains features from both of the original sounds.

coarse facies A facial appearance characterized by swelling of the lips, thickening of the subcutaneous (under the skin) tissue, and broadening of the nose; coarse facies can develop as a side effect of chronic phenytoin (Dilantin) treatment or as a result of a lysosomal storage disease.

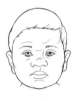

coarse facies

Cobb angle A measure of the degree of curvature in scoliosis (spinal curvature) that uses horizontal lines to vertebral bodies as drawn on x rays. Angles of 20–40 degrees suggest mild scoliosis, angles of 40–60 degrees suggest moderate scoliosis, and angles of greater than 60 degrees suggest severe scoliosis.

cocaine baby Lay term (now considered objectionable) for an infant who has been exposed to crack cocaine in utero and who then exhibits symptoms such as jitteriness, irritability, tremors, overexcitability, sleep difficulties, and possibly more long-term behavior problems because of that exposure. *See also* crack baby, infant of a drug-addicted mother (IDAM), infant of a substance-abusing mother (ISAM).

cochlear implant A device used to treat profound hearing impairment. Surgically implanted in the skull, the

cochlear implant

implant captures sounds in the environment, processes the acoustic signal into highly specialized electrical patterns, and delivers stimulation via an electrode array. Intense aural habilitation is required in order to learn speech after the surgery.

cochlear microphonic (CM) The electrical potentials generated in the hair cells of the organ of Corti in response to acoustic stimulation.

Cockayne syndrome A group of genetic conditions that include failure to thrive (poor growth), premature senility, progressive vision and hearing impairments, intellectual disability, and in some cases skin photosensitivity (unusual sensitivity to light). The lack of subcutaneous (under the skin) fat contributes to a wizened, sunken-eyed appearance. The life span of affected individuals is considerably shortened. Inheritance follows an autosomal recessive pattern. Mutations of the genes *ERCC6* or *ERCC8* cause Cockayne syndrome.

cocontraction Simultaneous contraction of all of the muscles around a joint (agonists and antagonists) to produce stability.

Code of Fair Testing Practices in Education A guide for professionals in fulfilling their obligation to provide and use tests that are fair to all test takers regardless of age, gender, disability, race, ethnicity, national origin, religion, sexual orientation, linguistic background, or other personal characteristics. Fairness, careful standardization of tests and administration conditions, and accurate reporting of results are several of the major areas of concern. This code is directed primarily at professionally developed tests used in formal testing programs and addresses the roles of test developers and test users separately in four areas: 1) developing and selecting appropriate tests, 2) administering and scoring tests, 3) reporting and interpreting test results, and 4) informing test takers.

Code of Federal Regulations (CFR) The codification of the general and permanent rules published in the *Federal Register* by the executive departments and agencies of the federal government. Published by the U.S. Government Printing Office, it is divided into 50 titles that represent broad areas subject to federal regulation. Each volume of the CFR is updated once each calendar year and is issued on a quarterly basis. The CFR is available on the Internet.

code switching The volitional switching of dialects according to situational demands. An example would be changing from Standard American English (SAE) to Black Vernacular English (BVE) in a casual home and family environment.

Coding A Wechsler (intelligence test) subtest that measures processing speed, short-term memory, learning ability, visual perception, visual-motor coordination, visual scanning ability, cognitive flexibility, attention, and motivation.

coenzyme Q10 (CoQ-10) A substance that participates in a cell's generation of energy, particularly in the mitochondria. CoQ-10 is sometimes given as a dietary supplement to people with mitochondrial disorders and other health conditions.

Coffin-Lowry syndrome A genetic syndrome characterized by intellectual disability, unusual facial features (bulbous nose, upslanting eyes or antimongoloid slant, pouting lower lip), tapering fingers, and short stature. Episodes of cataplexy provoked by being startled or stimulus-induced drop episodes (SIDES) are other characteristic features. Inheritance is X-linked with mutations of *RPS6KA3* on chromosome Xp22.2. *See also* cataplexy.

Coffin-Siris syndrome *fifth-digit syndrome.* A syndrome characterized by hypoplastic (short to absent) fingernails on the fifth finger, microcephaly (abnormally small head) with coarse facies but very full lips, intrauterine growth deficiency that continues after birth, intellectual disability, and hirsutism (excessive hair growth) combined with sparse scalp hair growth. Inheritance may be autosomal recessive.

Cogentin *See* benztropine.

cognate A blood relative through the mother's side of the family.

cognitive/academic language proficiency (CALP) The ability to successfully apply second language skills to academic and literacy tasks.

cognitive appraisal An individual's view of a situation. A cognitive appraisal determines whether an event will be perceived as irrelevant, benign, positive, or stressful and threatening. When an event is appraised negatively, then a further appraisal assesses whether the event represents 1) harm: assessment of the damage that the event has already caused, 2) threat: assessment of possible future damage that the event may cause, or 3) challenge: assessment of the potential to overcome and even profit from the event. Although some may stop there and avoid further involvement with the event or situation, others may make secondary appraisals based on an evaluation of their ability to cope with the situation. This further appraisal interacts with the primary appraisal to determine the person's emotional reaction to the event.

Cognitive Assessment System (CAS) *Das Naglieri Cognitive Assessment System.* An intelligence test based on the planning, attention, simultaneous, and successive (PASS) cognitive processing theory; its development is based on the neuropsychological work of Luria and does not include any academic content. Its administration to children 5–18 years takes 40–60 minutes; it is especially helpful in assessing culturally diverse and minority populations.

cognitive sequencing The intake, storage, and retrieval of information requiring a specified order of input and recall (i.e., counting, days of the week, months of the year, words in a sentence). *See also* sequential processing.

cognitive strategies Mental procedures and ordered steps that provide a structure to learning and problem solving. Some common strategies for language learning include repetition, summarizing meaning, guessing meaning from context, and using imagery for memorization. In this example, all of these strategies involve the deliberate manipulation of language to improve learning.

cognitive style An individual's preferred method for approaching a learning or problem-solving situation. Cognitive style can be described in terms of the preferred modality of acquiring (visual, auditory, or kinesthetic) and processing (part to whole, linear, whole to part, simultaneous) information. Although they may indicate a preference, most individuals can use a variety of styles. Cognitive style in an individual with a disability can reflect the underlying neurological profile.

cognitive therapy *cognitive-behavioral therapy (CBT).* A psychological treatment based on a cognitive model of emotional functioning. In contrast to drive-based and conflict-motivated models of emotional functioning, cognitive models assert that emotions and behaviors are mediated by specific thoughts in response to an event. Emotional disorders, such as depression, are seen as the result of learned, habitual, dysfunctional beliefs and patterns of thought that have become so automatic that they are no longer conscious. The automatic filtering of events through these learned, habitual, yet dysfunctional thinking processes leads to a distorted view of events and a distorted emotional response. CBT exposes both the content and process of dysfunctional thinking and removes or replaces them with more adaptive thought processes, leading to less distorted and less toxic emotional outcomes.

Cohen syndrome A genetic syndrome characterized by a peculiar face (e.g., open mouth, short philtrum [the groove between the nose and upper lip], prominent incisor teeth, micrognathia [small jaw]), intellectual disability, hypotonia (low muscle tone), short stature, obesity starting in mid-childhood, and long slender fingers and toes. Inheritance follows an autosomal recessive pattern. *COH1* (also known as *VPS13B*) is the only gene known to be associated with Cohen syndrome.

cohort A subset of a population with a common feature, usually age. The term *cohort* is often used in research to describe a group of people who are followed over time with the goal of describing their outcomes.

coining *cao gio.* An Asian folk medicine practice of rubbing the involved area of the body with a coin. This dermabrasion (causing abrasions of the skin) technique can produce welts and superficial bruises that may be misinterpreted as signs of child abuse.

colic *evening colic, 3 months' colic.* A condition of unknown etiology (cause) that occurs in infants in the first 3 months of life, as a result of which they exhibit restlessness, crying, and apparent pain at a regular part of the day (usually early evening). Symptoms of colic may be treated with drugs, but the condition usually spontaneously resolves in the fourth month; it has no long-term or developmental implications. However, in an infant who cries and refuses to be comforted at all hours of the day after the first 3 months of life, brain involvement may be suspected, especially if the infant cry is shrill and high pitched.

collaboration Interaction among professionals and families as they work toward a common goal. In an educational setting, collaboration is the interaction between special and general education teachers who teach students with disabilities.

collateral A small side branch, for example of a nerve axon (cell) or blood vessel.

Collier sign Eyelid retraction with sclera (white part of the eye) visible above and below the iris (colored part of the eye). Collier sign may contribute to a hyperalert appearance and suggests a problem in the midbrain (as in diencephalic syndrome).

coloboma A cleft, slit, gap, or fissure in any eye structure. Refractive errors (such as nearsightedness or farsightedness) and retinal detachments are potential complications of certain types of coloboma. Iris (the colored ring of the eye) colobomas are readily visible; retinal colobomas (which affect the back of the eye) require ophthalmological examination to be detected. Colobomas are often part of a syndrome, and iris colobomas suggest the need for chromosome analysis.

colon The part of the large intestine that connects the cecum (the last part of the small intestine) to the rectum (the part of the large intestine that stores feces before they are expelled through the anus). The colon is mainly responsible for the absorption of water from fecal material.

color blindness A sex-linked inability to discriminate colors (either between red and green or among all colors) that occurs in 8% of boys and 0.5% of girls. The presence of color blindness does not relate to the occurrence of learning disabilities. *See also* Ishihara test.

colostomy A surgical operation in which an opening is made in the large intestine and a tube inserted to empty into a plastic bag outside the body; the procedure is used to treat cancer, obstruction, and incontinence related to rectal dysfunction that may be caused by spinal cord damage or dysfunction.

Columbia Mental Maturity Scale (CMMS) A multiple choice test that measures global intelligence and requires no verbal and little motor response. CMMS can be used with nonverbal children or with children with physical disabilities who are between 3;6 and 10 years of age. A card of symbols is presented to the child, who must identify which of the pictures is different according to color, shape, use, or symbol. Administration time is less than 20 minutes. The test yields an intelligence quotient (IQ) score with a mean of 100 and a standard deviation of 16.

columella nasi The fleshy outer portion of the nasal septum (the part of the nose that divides the two nostrils). A short columella contributes to an apparent flat nose.

coma A state of decreased consciousness with unresponsiveness even to painful stimuli.

Combined Augmentative Communication Technique A symbol set that incorporates the use of aided and unaided elements.

Commission on Accreditation of Rehabilitation Facilities (CARF) An international private nonprofit organization that accredits programs and services in adult day services, assisted living, behavioral health, employment and community services, and medical rehabilitation. CARF develops and maintains standards of quality for such programs.

common sense Knowledge thought to be widely understood. Generally, common sense is a compilation of cultural traditions or folk knowledge that constitute a body of shared and relatively standardized interpretations of a variety of phenomena—from natural occurrences to social behavior—and contain solutions to everyday problems. As opposed to "book knowledge" or "school smarts," common sense is pragmatic and relies heavily on applying problem-solving skills to real life.

communication The process people use to exchange information and ideas, needs, and desires.

Communication Abilities Diagnostic Test (CADeT) An informal norm-referenced test of language development for children ages 3–9 years that uses stories, board games, and conversational context to assess syntax (grammar), semantics (the meaning of words), and pragmatic (social) language.

Communication and Symbolic Behavior Scales (CSBS) A norm-referenced assessment of language for children whose functional communication age is 6 months to 2 years. A caregiver questionnaire, direct sampling of verbal and nonverbal communicative behaviors, and observation of relatively unstructured play activities generate 18 communicative and 4 symbolic behavior scales. Sometimes referred to as the *Wetherby-Prizant Scale.*

Communication and Symbolic Behavior Scales Developmental Profile (CSBS-DP) A screening and evaluation test of communicative competence of children whose chronological age is between 6 months and 6 years and whose communication skills are typical of children between 6 months and 2 years old.

communication board An apparatus on which letters, numbers, and commonly used words are represented to assist individuals for whom oral expression is difficult or impossible. There are several types of boards, including 1) direct-selection boards, which have a one-to-one correspondence between what the sender wants to express and the elements that the boards provide; 2) encoding boards, whose use requires the acquisition of input techniques; and 3) scanning boards, on which message elements are presented with matching components indicated by a prearranged signal (i.e., an arm, hand, or eye movement), whose use thus requires a minimum amount of physical control by the user.

communication disorder A problem with hearing, language, and/or speech, including with regard to articulation (the ability to form sounds), voice, and fluency (the ability to put sounds together smoothly).

Communicative Activities of Daily Living–Second Edition (CADL-2) A 30-minute test of the functional communication skills of adults with neurogenic communication disorders. Fifty test items are grouped into seven areas.

Communicative Development Inventories (CDIs) *See* MacArthur-Bates Communicative Development Inventories–Second Edition.

communicative intent A behavior that is purposely directed toward another person with intended meaning and that requires dual orientation to both the communication partner and the topic or referent.

communicology Speech-language pathology.

Community Access to Child Health (CATCH) A national program of the American Academy of Pediatrics (AAP) designed to improve access to health care by supporting local pediatricians and communities to ensure that all children have medical homes and access to any other needed health care services.

Community Alternatives Program (CAP) CAP programs involve the use of Medicaid home- and community-based services waivers granted by the Health Care Financing Administration (HCFA). For example, the Community Alternatives Program for Disabled Adults (CAP/DA) allows older adults and adults with disabilities to receive care and services in their home to keep them from having to go into a nursing home. This program is funded through Medicaid.

community of practice (COP) An informal group of people who share an interest, a craft, and/or a profession. The group can evolve naturally because of members' common interest in a particular domain or area, or it can be created specifically with the goal of gaining knowledge related to that field. By sharing information and experiences with the group, members learn from one another.

community supports Activities, services, funding, and other assistance available to people with developmental disabilities, their families, and communities to 1) develop local networks that can provide informal support, 2) make neighborhoods and communities more accessible and responsive to the needs of people with developmental disabilities and their families, and 3) enable these communities to offer their resources and opportunities to such people. Community supports may include community education, personal assistance services, vehicular and home modifications, support at work, and transportation.

comorbidity An overlap of two or more disorders in a single person.

compensation An adjustment or series of adjustments made to counteract or mitigate the effect of some anomaly, impairment, or disability. Both the difficulty and the adjustment can be neural, motoric, psychological, physical, or social in nature, and neither may be readily apparent. Seeking achievement in other areas, working harder than others, and implementing bypass strategies to work around weaknesses are examples of compensatory techniques.

compensation A theory of recovery from brain damage that suggests that the functions of a damaged circuit may be assumed by other circuits and pathways as opposed to recovered by the original damaged circuits.

compensatory education *See* remedial education.

compensatory methodology A methodology that focuses on accomplishing instructional objectives by working around weaknesses and using strengths of the student.

compensatory swallow strategies Maneuvers to eliminate dysphagia (difficulty swallowing) symptoms that do not change the physiology of the swallow; such strategies consist primarily of environmental accommodations (e.g., postural changes, modification of food texture or consistency) and do not require extensive muscular or mental effort.

competency-based training An instructional method in which emphasis is placed on acquiring and maintaining targeted skills.

Competent Learner Model (CLM) An intervention approach to autism that combines applied behavior analysis (ABA) with direct instruction and precision teaching.

complementary and alternative medicine (CAM) Health care practices and products that operate outside of conventional medicine. These include non-Western systems of Chinese medicine and Ayurveda, healing touch therapies, dietary supplements, energy-based therapies such as Reiki, and body manipulations such as chiropractic and massage. Other descriptive synonyms include unorthodox, irrational, controversial, unproven, and fringe therapies.

complete blood count (CBC) A battery of blood tests that include hemoglobin (oxygen-carrying red blood cells), hematocrit (the volume of packed red cells), red and white blood counts, red cell indexes, and a differential white blood cell count.

complete cleft Cleft lip or palate that extends through the nose.

completion test A test that requires the person to fill in blank spaces of test items such as incomplete sentences.

complex partial seizure A type of seizure that includes altered consciousness and often automatisms (robotic behaviors, such as running, fumbling with objects or clothing, or lip smacking). It is often preceded by a simple partial seizure that helps to diagnose the seizure type, warns the person that he or she is about to have a seizure that will alter consciousness, and may help to localize the brain focus of the seizure.

complex sentence A type of sentence with one independent clause and one or more subordinate clauses.

compound sentence A type of sentence with at least two independent clauses joined by a comma and a conjunction or by a semicolon and that does not contain a subordinate clause.

comprehension The process of deriving meaning from text based on linguistic cueing systems and background knowledge. *See* receptive language.

Comprehension A Wechsler (intelligence test) subtest that assesses understanding of the general principles of social situations and the use of social judgment; it measures verbal reasoning, the ability to evaluate and use past experience, and the understanding of conventional standards of behavior.

Comprehensive Identification Process (CIP) A screening test for children ages 2;6–5;6 years who are not participating in an organized preschool program. Motor, cognitive, and speech-language areas are assessed.

Administration time is approximately 1 hour for relatively skilled personnel; 30% of children are subsequently referred for further testing.

Comprehensive Receptive and Expressive Vocabulary Test–Second Edition (CREVT-2) A measure of receptive and expressive vocabulary in people 4–90 years of age.

Comprehensive Test of Nonverbal Intelligence–Second Edition (CTONI-2) An individually administered, norm-referenced test of nonverbal reasoning. Because it requires no oral responses, reading, writing, or object manipulation, the CTONI-2 is appropriate for use with individuals with significant disabilities and limitations in language and physical mobility. Instructions can be pantomimed.

Comprehensive Test of Phonological Processing (CTOPP) A test that assesses phonological (speech sound) awareness, phonological memory, and rapid naming skills in students ages 5–24. People with impairments in one or more of these processing abilities may have more difficulty learning to read than those who do not. There are two versions of the CTOPP: 1) A version for individuals ages 5 and 6 (kindergartners and first graders) contains seven core subtests and one supplemental test, and 2) a version for individuals ages 7–24 years (second grade through college) contains six core subtests and eight supplemental tests. Both versions are individually administered and take about 30 minutes.

Comprehensive Test of Visual Functioning (CTVF) An assessment of visual function in children ages 8–16 years that includes subtests on visual acuity, visual processing/figure–ground, visual tracking, reading word analysis, visual/letter integration, visual/writing integration, nonverbal visual closure, nonverbal visual reasoning/memory, spatial orientation/memory/motor skills, spatial orientation/motor skills, visual design/motor skills, and visual design/memory/motor skills.

Comprehensive Trail Making Test (CTMT) A standardized set of five visual search and sequencing tasks for use with people 8–74 years of age. The score is heavily influenced by attention, distractibility, concentration, and cognitive flexibility and is useful in evaluating brain injury, frontal lobe impairments, and attentional problems.

computed tomography (CT) scan *computed axial tomography (CAT) scan.* A radiological technique in which x rays are passed through the brain (or another body part) to produce a picture that shows that body part in cross-section. Head CT scans are used to delineate the location of brain damage and are particularly helpful in identifying areas of fresh bleeding or bone fracture. A CT scan requires the person to remain still; thus, younger children may need to be sedated.

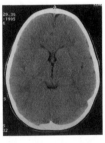

computed tomography
(CT) scan

computer-assisted instruction (CAI) The use of computers and software programs to present a sequence of lessons over an extended period of time while monitoring student progress.

concave A hollowed-out or depressed surface; often used in descriptions of corrective lenses and spinal curvatures.

concentric power The ability to resist force as the muscle is shortened.

concept A commonality in events or objects designated by some label. For example, the concept of *chair* includes easy chairs, desk chairs, straight-backed chairs,

and so forth. The concept of *chair* is itself part of a concept called *furniture.* Concepts may be described as nonverbal or verbal, concrete or abstract. Nonverbal concepts are groups of ideas that go together and are easier to picture than to describe. For example, to understand fractions, it might be easier to picture a pizza being divided than to hear an explanation in words. *Verbal concepts* refers to associated ideas that are readily described through language (e.g., friendship). *Concrete concepts* refers to objects that can be seen or felt (e.g., dog). *Abstract concepts* refers to ideas rather than objects (e.g., democracy, evaporation, creativity). Students with learning disabilities can have difficulty understanding concepts presented by a method not suited to their cognitive strengths. For example, students with language impairments are helped by visual representations of concepts; abstract concepts are often stumbling blocks for them.

Concerta *See* methylphenidate.

concordant Describing the state when both twins have a certain trait. The opposite of discordant.

concrete language Expressive and receptive language that fails to understand language metaphorically; everything is taken literally, and most verbal jokes cannot be understood. The statement "It's raining cats and dogs" produces confusion in the absence of the animals referred to.

concrete operations Piagetian stage in cognitive (thinking) development in which logical thinking emerges but is limited to what is immediately perceived. This approach is prominent from 6 to 12 years of age.

concretism A style of thinking and behavior in which an individual views each situation as new and unique, with a failure or inability to see similarities and relationships between situations that others recognize as similar. In concretism, general knowledge, problem-solving strategies, and comparable components are neither generalized nor assimilated. Concretism is characteristic of individuals with intellectual disability.

concussion Transient neuronal dysfunction that immediately follows head trauma with or without retrograde (before the injury) amnesia (impaired memory); concussion is less severe than contusion. Associated symptoms may include drowsiness, vomiting, seizures, and other neurological findings.

conditioned dysphagia A learned difficulty with food acceptance and feeding that results from an aversion to swallowing.

conditioned play audiometry *See* behavioral observation audiometry (BOA).

conditioned reflex A learned response to a neutral stimulus; the linking of a neutral stimulus to a stimulus that elicits an unconditioned reflex response. For example, individuals blink (the reflex) when posing for a picture because they have come to associate the camera with its bright flash. This response occurs because the sight of the camera has been paired with the flash in the past. *See also* classical conditioning.

conditioning Behavioral training that causes a specific response whenever a specific stimulus is provided. *See also* extinction.

conduct disorder A persistent behavior pattern of violating others' rights and ignoring age-appropriate social standards. Specific behaviors include lying, theft, arson, running away from home, aggression, truancy, burglary, cruelty to animals, and fighting. This disorder is distinguished from oppositional defiant disorder by the increased severity of the behaviors and the fact that they occur even without an occasion for opposition. There is a marked male predominance in incidence.

conductive deafness *See* conductive hearing loss.

conductive education A school of physical therapy for cerebral palsy. *See also* Pëto, Andras (1893–1967).

conductive hearing loss A hearing loss characterized by dysfunction of the outer or middle ear; the inner ear usually functions normally. Hearing loss results from an inability to transmit sound from the air to the tympanic membrane (eardrum) in order to activate the auditory nerve (cranial nerve VIII). Potential causes range from congenital malformations of the outer ear to fluid in the middle ear because of an ear infection.

co-negativity *See* specificity.

confabulation Fabrication; differs from lying in that the person believes what is being said. Confabulation is observed in adults with organic brain syndromes and in children with attention disorders. People who engage in confabulation may respond to questions by trying to fill in the gaps of what they know with stories that seem plausible to them but outlandish to listeners.

"confetti" skin lesions A finding in tuberous sclerosis characterized by small hypopigmented (low pigment) skin areas.

confidence interval *See* error of measurement.

confidentiality A principle of legal and ethical professional practice whereby certain professionals may not disclose or discuss information regarding a client or individual, including the diagnostic and treatment services rendered, without the express written consent of the individual. This restriction includes revealing the identity of the individual, records, opinions, or behaviors. Violation of this principle is considered malpractice. However, confidentiality may be set aside when there is danger of suicide, homicide, or child abuse (i.e., when there is a clear and present danger of harm to self or others).

confined placental mosaicism   A chromosomal abnormality involving the placenta only; the embryo/fetus is unaffected.

confusion reflex   *See* flexor withdrawal reflex.

congenital   Present at birth; either genetic or acquired in utero. *See also* birth defect.

congenital cytomegalic inclusion disease   A syndrome of poor growth, intellectual disability, microcephaly (abnormally small head), periventricular calcifications (deposits of calcium around the ventricles, or fluid filled spaces in the brain, in fewer than 10% of cases), hearing loss (in 50% of cases), and chorioretinitis (inflammation of the choroid [layer of blood vessels in the eye] and the retina [light-sensitive inner back wall of the eye]) that can follow maternal (or fetal) infection. "Blueberry muffin spots" on the skin due to a blood disorder may be noted. Congenital (from before birth) cytomegalovirus (CMV) infection is common, but most cases are asymptomatic (without symptoms). Postnatal (after birth) CMV infection may involve progressive sensorineural (affecting the auditory nerve) hearing loss.

congenital disability   *See* birth defect.

congenital dislocation of the hip (CDH)   *See* developmental dysplasia of the hip (DDH).

congenital hyperammonemia   A group of metabolic disorders that present in infancy with vomiting, lethargy, and coma and progress to severe intellectual disability or death; they are characterized by elevated ammonia levels. Dietary treatment is available. There are five enzymatic subtypes: Four are autosomal recessive, and one is X-linked. Incidence is 1 in 30,000.

congenital hypothyroidism   *cretinism.* A clinical syndrome caused by the absence or hypoplasia of the thyroid gland in newborn infants. Findings include prolonged jaundice (yellowing of the skin), feeding difficulties, sluggishness, somnolence (sleepiness), poor cry, and respiratory difficulties made worse by a large tongue. Cold mottled extremities (arms or legs), a large abdomen, and an umbilical hernia may also be present. A short, thick neck; puffy face; and myxedema (dry, swollen skin) develop. Stunting of physical growth and progressive intellectual disability occur when diagnosis and treatment are delayed.

congenital lacrimal duct stenosis   *dacryostenosis.* Blockage of the tear duct, which can lead to eye irritation and infection.

congenital megacolon   *See* Hirschsprung disease.

congenital pseudohydrocephalic syndrome   *See* Wiedemann-Rautenstrauch syndrome.

congenital retinal blindness   *See* Leber congenital amaurosis (LCA).

congenital retinitis pigmentosa   *See* Leber congenital amaurosis (LCA).

congenital rubella   *See* fetal rubella syndrome.

congenital vertical talus   *rocker-bottom foot.* A rigid, flat foot that has a high association with other congenital anomalies and genetic syndromes, central nervous system (CNS) disorders (especially myelodysplasia), congenital hip dislocation, and arthrogryposis (fixation of the joints).

congenital word blindness.   The most severe form of dyslexia. A person's ability to decode written text is so impaired it is almost as if he or she were "blind" to written words.

Conners' ADHD/*DSM–IV* Scales   *See* Conners' Rating Scales–Revised.

Conners Continuous Performance Task
See continuous performance task (CPT).

Conners' Rating Scales–Revised (CRS-R)
Conners-Wells' Adolescent Self-Report Scale (CASS). A group of normed questionnaires used to assess hyperactivity and inattention. The Scales can be used with children 3–17 years. The Conners' Parent Rating Scale Revised (CPRS-R) and the Conners' Teacher Rating Scale Revised (CTRS-R) are available in both long and short versions for parents (CPRS-R:L, CPRS-R:S) and teachers (CTRS-R:L, CTRS-R:S). There is also the Conners-Wells' Adolescent Self-Report Scale (CASS) for children 12–17 years, which is available in both a long and short version (CASS:L, CASS:S). The parent (CADS-P), teacher (CADS-T), and adolescent (CADS-A) versions of the Conners' ADHD/*DSM–IV* Scales (CADS) are briefer instruments that are focused on the specific symptoms of attention-deficit/ hyperactivity disorder (ADHD).

connexin 26 A gene on chromosome 13 that is responsible for about half of the cases of nonsyndromic recessive hearing loss (NSRHL).

Conradi-Hünermann syndrome A skeletal abnormality whose common feature is punctate (point-like) calcifications (deposits of calcium) at the ends of long bones, which should still be composed of the softer cartilage, during infancy. There are X-linked dominant and X-linked recessive forms. There is also a form caused by the deletion of the distal short arm of an X chromosome. Because of contiguous (adjoining) gene loss in this deletion, ichthyosis (rough, dry, scaly, literally "fish-like" skin) and hypogonadotropic hypogonadism (low levels of sex hormones) may occur in addition to the chondrodysplasia (cartilage abnormality). *See also* chondrodysplasia punctata.

consanguinity The state of having a common ancestor; a blood relationship. Rare recessive disorders are more likely to occur from a consanguineous relationship because the two people involved tend to carry similar genes. Throughout history, laws have prohibited consanguineous marriages because of the increased risk for intellectual disability and genetic abnormalities in the children of such unions. *See also* autosomal recessive.

consecutive bilingualism *See* sequential bilingualism.

consensual light reflex The contraction (becoming smaller) of a shaded (protected from the light) pupil when the pupil of the other eye is stimulated by light.

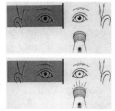

consensual light reflex

consequent stimulus event (CSE) In operant conditioning, the effect produced in the environment by a behavior (operant behavior). The CSE always follows the operant and serves to strengthen, weaken, or maintain the behavior. CSEs that strengthen operant behaviors are called *reinforcers* and may be positive or negative. Positive CSEs strengthen a behavior by immediately following it with a reward (pleasant consequence). During the initial stages of learning, it is important that the CSE immediately follow the operant behavior. A CSE that weakens a behavior is called a *punisher* or *aversive stimulus event* (ASE). Negative reinforcement and punishment are distinct: In punishment, aversive events immediately follow a behavior and therefore reduce that behavior's future likelihood of occurrence. In negative reinforcement, the future likelihood of a behavior increases because it is associated with relief from discomfort. Reinforcers and punishers may be primary (unlearned or unconditioned), such as food or physical pain, or secondary (learned or conditioned). Secondary reinforcers or punishers require pairing with a primary or an established reinforcer or punisher to become effective. *See also* contingency.

conservator A court-appointed person who maintains responsibility for and decision-making authority over the financial affairs of another individual who has been legally judged to be incapacitated. A person who is mentally incapacitated (by illness, accident, or intellectual disability) may have a conservator for financial matters and a guardian to oversee other areas of life decision making. *See also* incompetent.

consolability An infant or child's capacity to quiet following a period of crying or upset. The degree of intervention necessary to help the infant to quiet reflects the infant's ability to regulate state changes.

consonant blend Two or more consonant sounds spoken together, such as /tr/ or /cl/.

Consortium for Appropriate Dispute Resolution in Special Education (CADRE) A project of the Special Education Technical Assistance and Dissemination Network (TA&D), funded by the U.S. Department of Education, Office of Special Education and Rehabilitative Services (OSERS). Although it encourages the use of mediation and other collaborative strategies to resolve disagreements about special education and early intervention programs, CADRE's major thrust is to avoid the need for such drastic measures in the first place by helping parents, teachers, and administrators forge more cooperative relationships. CADRE's web site provides resources on mediation and conflict resolution; training materials; and directories that list trainers, conflict resolution professionals, and state information about mediation.

Consortium for Citizens with Disabilities (CCD) A coalition of approximately 100 national disability organizations that work together to advocate for national public policy to ensure the self-determination, independence, empowerment, integration, and inclusion of all people with disabilities in all aspects of society. Most of the public policy work is carried out through a permanent task force structure. Task forces include Education, Emergency Preparedness, Employment and Training, Fiscal Policy, Health, International, Housing, Long Term Services and Supports, Prevention, Rights, Social Security, TANF (Temporary Assistance for Needy Families)/Welfare to Work, Technology and Telecommunication, Transportation, and Veterans. A number of short-term ad hoc committees advocate in the areas of asset development, tax policy and financial literacy, autism, child abuse prevention, developmental disabilities, and transition.

constipation Infrequent (and often difficult) or absent bowel movements.

constraint-induced (CI) movement therapy The use of restraints (such as casting) on the non-involved upper extremity (arm) to (rein)force the use of the involved extremity in individuals with hemiplegic (one sided) cerebral palsy.

constructional apraxia Difficulty with copying a drawing or inability to copy a drawing.

consultation A system of providing related services in the school system in which the therapist makes recommendations or sets up programs for a child to be carried out by someone else, such as the classroom teacher, teacher's aide, or parent.

contact ulcer *See* granuloma.

contagious Relating to the spread of a disease from one individual to another. Different infectious diseases have greater or lesser degrees of contagiousness; some spread rapidly, whereas others can only be spread through prolonged intimate contact.

contextual clues The relationship of words and word meanings and their uses in phrases, sentences, and paragraphs that can all be used to help decode unknown words. Closure activities (filling in missing words) are often used both to teach and to test the use of contextual clues. For example: "The _____ man shouted and stomped his foot."

contiguous gene syndrome The presence of multiple anomalies due to deletions of genes next to one another on the same chromosome. For example, WAGR syndrome, an acronym for the combination of conditions that includes Wilms tumor (cancer of the kidney), aniridia (absent irises), genitourinary abnormalities, and intellectual disability, is caused by a deletion of multiple adjoining genes on chromosome 11p.

contingency A term from behaviorist learning theory that refers to the conditions in which a consequent stimulus event (CSE) occurs. The contingency is what a child must do before the CSE is presented. For example, a teacher might want a student to write the 3 times table (the operant behavior) with 100% accuracy (the contingency) in order to receive 15 minutes of free time. *See also* consequent stimulus event (CSE).

contingency contracting A specific type of behavior modification program. A teacher makes a contract with a student, who agrees to perform a specific behavior, such as finishing an assignment, in return for an agreed-on reward.

contingency management A behavior modification approach that combines positive reinforcement for desired behaviors with punishment to reduce unwanted behaviors.

continuant A speech sound that can be prolonged or continued, such as /f/.

continuous intrathecal baclofen infusion (CIBI) *intrathecal baclofen (ITB)*. In this procedure, a pump is implanted under the skin and a catheter delivers baclofen (a drug to decrease spasticity) to the intrathecal space of the spinal cord (the fluid-filled area surrounding the cord) at a predetermined rate. This route of drug administration minimizes side effects (sleepiness and decreased muscle tone) and allows for the use of more effective doses than oral administration. The pump needs to be refilled every 2–6 months depending on the dose.

continuous performance task (CPT) A continuous performance test (also CPT) uses a computerized continuous performance task to measure attention span, concentration, and impulsivity by having the person identify a target or target sequence in a rapidly changing stream of targets; error scores and reaction times are calculated electronically. Despite the objectivity of commercially available CPTs, their sensitivity and specificity do not allow them to diagnose attention-deficit/hyperactivity disorder (ADHD) in the absence of a complete diagnostic workup. CPTs include the Conners' Continuous Performance Task, the Gordon Diagnostic System, OPTAx, and the Tests of Variable Attention (TOVA). *See also* OPTAx, Test of Variables of Attention (TOVA).

continuous positive airway pressure (CPAP) A type of assisted ventilation that may be used in newborns with respiratory distress and children with obstructive sleep apnea. A device propels air at a particular pressure through a tube, which is delivered to the child via an interface (mask). The pressurized air effectively stents open the child's airway, preventing collapse.

continuous trait A trait in which the possible phenotypes have a continuous range from one extreme to the other rather than falling into discrete classes (a categorical or meristic trait).

continuum of developmental disabilities An approach to describing the major categories of developmental disabilities that focuses on their similarities (as opposed to their differences). In many cases of a given developmental diagnostic category, associated findings suggest other developmental diagnoses. Thus, children whose primary diagnosis is intellectual disability often exhibit some motor findings common to children with cerebral palsy, children with cerebral palsy often have varying degrees of intellectual disability, and children with severe learning disabilities have a variety of motor and cognitive impairments.

continuum of services The range of services and placements required to be available, as appropriate, for placement of children and adults with disabilities. For school-age children the range may include general classroom, general classroom with itinerant or resource teachers, special classes, home instruction, and instruction in a hospital or residential institution. For adults, a range of living opportunities must be available: family living with appropriate supports, supported living, group home, or institutional care. Vocational choices include sheltered work, supported work, competitive work with supports, and competitive work without supports.

contraction A drawing together, shortening, or shrinkage.

contracture A permanent muscular or other soft-tissue contraction (fixed increased resistance to being stretched) due to tonic spasm or shortening. Contracture at a joint prevents movement through the full range of motion. Contractures arise earlier in spastic cerebral palsy and later, if at all, in extrapyramidal cerebral palsy. Contractures may be prevented by physical therapy, positioning, and bracing; they may be treated by serial casting and surgery. Congenital contractures occur in arthrogryposis (congenital fixation of the joints).

contraindication A reason not to do something; any symptom or special circumstance that makes a treatment or surgical procedure inadvisable. Contraindications may be relative or absolute.

contralateral On the opposite side of the body. Because motor nerve fibers from the brain cross the mid-line (go from one side of the body to the other), the right brain controls motor movements on the left side of the body, and the left brain controls motor movements on the contralateral, or right side, of the body.

contralateral

contrastive analysis An alternative assessment method that is used to analyze language samples of individuals with diverse backgrounds.

contrecoup injury An injury that occurs when the force of a blow to one side of the body causes damage to the other side of the body; such injuries are especially common in brain injuries because when one side of the skull is struck, the brain moves within the skull, where it strikes the other side.

contusion *brain contusion.* A brain injury more severe than a concussion and that results in bleeding into the brain. Associated symptoms may include loss of consciousness, vomiting, skull fracture, seizures, papilledema (swelling of the optic nerve), and neurological residua (symptoms that persist after the injury).

convergence Describing when the eyes move toward each other, turning inward toward the nose in order to focus on nearby objects; opposite of divergence.

convergent assessment An approach that stresses the use of multiple sources, instruments, contexts, and occasions in order to produce the most valid evaluation.

conversation board *See* communication board.

convex Rounded, bulging outward; often used in the description of corrective lenses and spinal curvatures.

convulsion A violent involuntary muscular contraction that can be due to a seizure disorder. Not all convulsions are seizures, and not all seizures are convulsions.

cooing The first stage of infant vocalization consisting of vowel sounds. Cooing may be present near birth in the form of short, squealing sounds and should be easily noticed by 3 months of age. By 6 months of age, cooing evolves into fairly musical play with complex vowel patterns.

cooperative learning An instructional strategy that teaches academic and social skills. Cooperative learning uses small teams, each with students of different levels of ability, and a variety of learning activities to improve student understanding of a subject. Each member of the team is responsible not only for learning what is taught but also for helping teammates learn, thus creating an atmosphere of achievement. Thus, students are taught both subject matter content and interpersonal life skills and develop the ability to work collaboratively.

Cooperative Preschool Inventory–Revised A brief screening test for school readiness in children 3–6 years of age, with an administration time of 15 minutes. The instrument has been used principally to measure the effects of early intervention programs in populations of low socioeconomic status.

Coopersmith Self-Esteem Inventory (CSEI) A self-report measure of an individual's feelings and attitudes about himself or herself. There are two forms of the measure: a School Form for children 8–16 years and an Adult Form for people 16 years and older.

coordinated service model With regard to English as second language (ESL), an instructional model in which a monolingual special education teacher is responsible for providing ESL instruction and implementing individualized education program (IEP) goals in English while a bilingual teacher provides academic instruction in the student's native language.

COP *See* community of practice.

coping skills Skills and strategies that provide an individual with the ability to adjust and accommodate to life stressors without unduly interfering in his or her personal, social, or work life functioning.

co-positivity *See* sensitivity.

copraphagy The eating of fecal matter.

coprolalia The obsessive and compulsive use of obscene words; this symptom can occur occasionally in Tourette syndrome.

copy number variation (CNV) A deleted or duplicated section of the genome that may arise de novo (spontaneously).

CoQ-10 *See* coenzyme Q10.

core vocabulary The words and messages that are commonly used by a variety of individuals and that occur very frequently in written and spoken language.

corectopia A pupil that is not centered in the iris.

cornea The transparent, clear anterior (front) covering of the eye.

Cornelia de Lange syndrome *Brachmann de Lange syndrome, de Lange syndrome, typus degenerativus amstelodamensis.* A syndrome of intellectual disability; hirsutism (excessive hair); microcephaly (small head); short stature of prenatal onset with micromelia (small extremities); a thin, downturning, and long upper lip; and a small nose with anteverted (tilted forward) nares (nostrils). The hirsutism is especially prominent, characterized by bushy eyebrows that tend meet in the middle (synophrys). The intellectual disability tends to be severe, with marked speech and language problems and occasional hearing impairments and autistic features. Recurrence risk is low, but rare cases of autosomal dominant inheritance have been reported. Duplication of part of the long arm of chromosome 3 can produce a phenotype similar to de Lange syndrome. At least two genes have been shown to be altered in more than half of tested individuals. Named after the Dutch pediatrician Cornelia de Lange (1871–1950).

corner chair A seating device for infants and children used to reduce the effects of hypertonia in the upper extremities. Often used with children with spastic quadriplegia from cerebral palsy or head trauma.

coronal plane The anatomical plane that divides the body into an anterior (front) and posterior (back) half.

corporal punishment A form of punishment in which physical (bodily) pain or discomfort is administered. The use of corporal punishment has been demonstrated to produce strong emotional side effects in children, sometimes resulting in behavior that becomes more disruptive instead of less, or is reduced only in the presence of the punisher. Any behavior that provides escape from the punishment (e.g., lying, hiding, cheating) is reinforced and may become part of a child's repertoire. Corporal punishment also provides a model for aggressive behavior.

corpus callosum The portion of the brain that connects the two hemispheres. Agenesis (absence of formation) of this connection or surgical severing to control seizures can affect one's ability to exchange information between the hemispheres. People with such

"split brains" may give different responses to a stimulus depending on which side of the body receives the stimulus. Congenital absence of the corpus callosum can be associated with other abnormalities of the central nervous system (CNS) and cognition. Because there are other connections between the two hemispheres of the brain, absence of the corpus callosum may be relatively asymptomatic (without obvious effect).

correct spelling The pattern of spelling behaviors in which one *regularly* uses the visual features of Standard English.

corrected age *See* adjusted age.

corrective feedback A type of feedback that serves to change behavior that is inappropriate or ineffective, corrective feedback is contrasted with formative feedback (which is designed to build on or continue the development of a behavior). Corrective feedback is staged as follows: 1) Identify the error or behavior in a nonjudgmental way and specifically enough so that the learner understands which behavior needs to be changed; 2) define the correct results; 3) provide, describe, or model the corrective action or lead the participant to provide his or her own correction.

correlation The extent to which two measures vary together. A positive correlation means that as one measure increases or decreases, so does the other; a negative correlation means that as one measure increases, the other decreases, and vice versa.

cortex Gray matter; the outermost, half-inch thick layer of the cerebrum, or largest and topmost portion of the brain. This surface is marked by numerous gyri (hills) and sulci

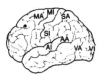

cortex: von Economo lettering

(valleys) resulting in the folded appearance of the brain. Localization of specific functional areas on the cortex can be by

Brodmann area, von Economo lettering, or neuroanatomical nomenclature. Some of the major areas are noted in the table below.

cortical blindness *central blindness.* Visual impairment due to damage to the occipital cortex (area at the back of the brain that processes incoming visual information) in the presence of an intact visual system that includes a working eyeball, lens, retina, and optic nerve pathway. Cortical blindness following head trauma may be transient (temporary).

cortical deafness *See* central deafness.

cortical thumbing *cerebral thumbing.* Fisting with the thumb flexed (bent) inside the clenched palm. Cortical thumbing is often regarded as a sign of abnormal hypertonicity (increased muscle tone); however, it can be cortical thumbing normal in the first 3 months of life, during which time keeping the hands fisted is normal.

co-sleeping An arrangement in which the child sleeps in the parental bed; this behavior exhibits marked cross-cultural variation. Maternal smoking is a strong contraindication to co-sleeping.

cost contingency *response cost.* A behavior intervention procedure in which a reinforcer is removed in an attempt to reduce the frequency of an undesirable behavior. Typically, an individual loses something of value that was previously earned or is usually given.

costa Rib.

co-teaching A service delivery option for special education students in which two or more teachers share responsibility for a group of students for some or all of the school day in order to combine their expertise to meet student needs. Other terms for co-teaching are *collaboration* and *inclusion.*

Cotrel Dubousset procedure A modification of the Harrington rod for the orthopedic surgery treatment of scoliosis (spinal curvature). *See also* Harrington distraction rod.

Council for Exceptional Children (CEC) Founded in 1922, the world's largest professional organization concerned with exceptional children. The organization is divided into 17 special interest groups that focus on such areas as physical and health disabilities, behavior disorders, intellectual disability, communicative disabilities and deafness, learning disabilities, visual impairments, giftedness, early childhood, special education administration, career development and transition, technology and media, culturally and linguistically diverse exceptional learners, and educational diagnostic services. The CEC sponsors national and state conventions and publishes *Exceptional Children, TEACHING Exceptional Children,* and *TEACHING Exceptional Children Plus.*

Council for Learning Disabilities (CLD) Originally formed in 1968 as the Division for Children with Learning Disabilities within the Council for Exceptional

Cortex: heteromodal bifrontal associative areas

MI (motor, idiotypic cortex)	Idiotypic—primary sensory and motor area
SI (sensory, idiotypic cortex)	Idiotypic—primary sensory and motor area
AI (auditory, idiotypic cortex)	Idiotypic—primary sensory and motor area
VI (visual, idiotypic cortex)	Idiotypic—primary sensory and motor area
MA (motor, associative area)	Homotypical isocortex—modal specific unimodal associative area
SA (sensory, associative area)	Homotypical isocortex—modal specific unimodal associative area
AA (auditory, associative area)	Homotypical isocortex—modal specific unimodal associative area
VA (visual, associative area)	Homotypical isocortex—modal specific unimodal associative area

Children (CEC). With the realization in the early 1980s that adults also have learning disabilities, the name was changed to its present form, and the CLD became a separate and independent organization rather than a division of the CEC. The official journal of the CLD is the *Learning Disability Quarterly.*

cover/uncover test *crossed patch test.* A screening test for strabismus (crossed eyes). The person fixates (focuses on) a light or other interesting toy or object, and each eye is alternately covered and uncovered. The inward or outward movement (deviation) of either eye under any of the test conditions yields information useful to the diagnosis of strabismus.

coverage vocabulary Vocabulary that is needed to communicate essential messages, such as an individual's basic communication needs.

cowlick An accessory (extra) hair whorl that produces an unusual upward sweep of a tuft of hair. An example of a minor dysmorphic (atypical) feature.

coxa The hip.

coxsackievirus A group of ribonucleic acid (RNA) viruses associated with a range of disorders, including colds, aseptic meningitis (infection of the spinal cord and brain membranes), and cardiac disease.

CP *See* cerebral palsy.

CPAP *See* continuous positive airway pressure.

CPD *See* cephalopelvic disproportion.

CPK *See* creatine phosphokinase.

CPRS-R:L Conners' Parent Rating Scale Revised, long version. *See* Conners' Rating Scales–Revised.

CPRS-R:S Conners' Parent Rating Scale Revised, short version. *See* Conners' Rating Scales–Revised.

CPT *See* chest physical therapy.

CPT *See* continuous performance test.

CPVT *See* Carolina Picture Vocabulary Test.

crack A street term for an inexpensive form of freebase cocaine. *See also* infant of a substance-abusing mother (ISAM).

crack baby Slang term (now considered objectionable) for an infant who has been exposed to crack cocaine in utero and who then exhibits symptoms such as jitteriness, irritability, tremors, overexcitability, sleep difficulties, and possibly more long-term behavior problems because of that exposure. *See also* cocaine baby, infant of a drug-addicted mother (IDAM), infant of a substance-abusing mother (ISAM).

cracked-pot sound *See* Macewen sign.

Craig Lipreading Inventory A test used to assess the lipreading performance of people with deafness. The inventory may be presented by an examiner or a filmed version with soundtrack can be used, permitting the use of the test for lipreaders alone or for people who have residual hearing. Because many factors, including hearing loss, educational experience, and mental age, contribute to lipreading competency, tests of this skill are best used to compare groups rather than evaluate individual performance.

cranial nerve Any of the set of 12 pairs of nerves that exit from the skull (as opposed to most nerves in the body, which originate from the spinal cord). The cranial nerves are assigned Roman numerals, as indicated in the table on page 116.

craniectomy Excision of a portion of the skull. In the presence of craniosynostosis (premature fusion of skull bones), the sutures can be reopened by a morcellation procedure (bit-by-bit removal of a linear strip of bone and then treatment of the edges so that they do not grow together again).

craniocarpotarsal dysplasia *See* whistling face syndrome.

craniodiaphyseal dysplasia *See* Lenz-Majewski hyperostosis syndrome.

craniofacial dysostosis *See* Crouzon syndrome.

craniometaphyseal dyplasia A disorder characterized by unusual facies (broadened nose, wide space between the eyes, and jerky eye movements). Hearing loss progresses throughout life. This condition may have autosomal dominant or recessive transmission.

craniosacral therapy The chiropractic treatment of developmental (and other) problems in children by massaging the skull along with manipulating the neck.

craniostosis *See* craniosynostosis.

craniosynostosis *craniostosis.* Premature closure (fusion or ossification) of the skull sutures that slows or stops the growth of the skull and possibly inhibits further brain growth, thus contributing to the evolution of developmental disabilities. Because continued brain growth is the major inhibitor of suture closure, most occurrences of craniosynostosis reflect the primary arresting of brain development. When only selected sutures fuse early, total intracranial volume is most likely to be within the normal range.

crawling Locomotion in quadriped (on all fours); regional variations in language use do not clearly distinguish crawling from creeping. Delayed (past the age of walking) crawling, in which the child walks before crawling, is an isolated finding that has no developmental significance.

crawling

creatine phosphokinase (CPK) An enzyme. An elevated CPK level indicates muscle strain or injury and may indicate muscular dystrophy.

Credé maneuver A technique used with paralyzed individuals that involves pressing on the bladder to help push urine out of the body.

credibility The degree to which information provided is reliable, consistent, and

Cranial nerves

Cranial nerve		Function	Dysfunction
I	Olfactory	Sense of smell	Loss may indicate a tumor or Kallmann syndrome
II	Optic	Vision	Blindness
III	Oculomotor	Helps move eye and eyelid	Strabismus, ptosis
IV	Trochlear	Helps move eye	Strabismus
V	Trigeminal	Sensation from lower eyelid to maxilla (upper mouth); chewing	Loss of sensation; dysarthria
VI	Abducent	Helps move eye outward	Strabismus
VII	Facial	Gustatory sense; facial movements	Facial palsy, loss of taste
VIII	Vestibulocochlear	Hearing and balance	Deafness, vertigo (dizzy)
IX	Glossopharyngeal	Swallowing	Dysphonia
X	Vagus	Nerve to larynx and gut	Dysphonia
XI	Accessory	Swallowing	Dysarthria
XII	Hypoglossal	Tongue movements	Dysarthria

believable. Credibility is an especially important consideration when evaluating a child for developmental disabilities because diagnosis is partially based on the child's developmental history as given by parents and other significant caregivers. Individuals are characterized as good or bad historians based on the quality and consistency of the information they provide.

creeping Locomotion in prone (stomach facing down); regional variations in language use do not clearly distinguish creeping from crawling.

cretinism *See* congenital hypothyroidism.

CREVT-2 *See* Comprehensive Receptive and Expressive Vocabulary Test–Second Edition.

cri-du-chat syndrome *cat's cry syndrome, deletion (5)(p15-pter), 5p- syndrome.* A genetic syndrome characterized by poor growth and a mewing cat-like cry in infancy; microcephaly (abnormally small head); a rounded, moon facies with hypertelorism (widely spaced eyes); epicanthal folds; and downslanting palpebral fissures (eye slits). The level of intellectual disability is usually severe to profound. Most cases represent spontaneous partial deletions of the short arm of chromosome 5, but 10%–15% are secondary to a parental balanced translocation with an increased recurrence risk. Incidence is estimated at 1 per 20,000.

CRIL *See* Wiig Criterion Referenced Inventory of Language.

Crippled Children's Services (CCC). The earliest version of direct health care provision (through Crippled Children's Clinics [CCC]) by the Maternal and Child Health Bureau to children with special health care needs. *See also* Maternal Child Health Bureau (MCH or MCHB).

crisis A debilitating mental or emotional state that occurs in response to an event experienced as so threatening that the usual coping skills are insufficient and ineffective. A crisis can be a decisive turning point when it forces a response to a situation that cannot be allowed to continue indefinitely because of its stressful nature. Thus, the possibility of seeking assistance and starting therapy is enhanced.

criterion A predetermined level of performance to be achieved; a targeted standard.

criterion referenced Describing an assessment score developed through comparison of a person's test performance to a preestablished standardized level (an external criterion; e.g., a task within a curriculum, a developmental milestone, or a construct such as the Piagetian concept of object permanence) or specific degree of mastery.

critical period A time period early in the life of an organism when learning essential to later functioning must occur. The concept implies irreversibility: If this window of opportunity is missed, the organism may never be able to achieve that learning. This concept is derived from ethology (the study of animal behavior) and probably does not have a human equivalent. Sensitive periods (when learning is most easily accomplished) and plasticity (the ability to change in response to challenges such as injury) probably better characterize human development. Biologically speaking, there are critical periods in human brain development, but these are mostly prenatal. *See also* sensitive period.

critical region 4p16.3 *See* Wolf-Hirschhorn syndrome.

crossbite A misalignment of the maxillary and mandibular teeth.

cross-categorical Describing the grouping together of students with disabilities without reference to a particular label or category.

Because categories of disabilities are not mutually exclusive, and because children with varying conditions are not always easily differentiated from one another, placement in a common class is advocated by some educators as a viable and practical alternative. Furthermore, assessment and treatment procedures for various categories often overlap, illustrating considerable commonality among some categories.

crossed adductor response When the patellar (knee jerk) reflex is obtained on one side, the other leg adducts (moves inward toward the middle of the body) briefly. This response is normal in young infants but suspicious for increased muscle tone in older children.

crossed extension *crossed extensor reflex.* A primitive reflex in which a noxious (painful) stimulus applied to one foot produces a flexion/extension response in the other foot. Absence or asymmetry of the response is abnormal and indicates damage to the motor system of the side that does not respond. As with other primitive reflexes, this one disappears early in life, usually between the fourth and sixth weeks.

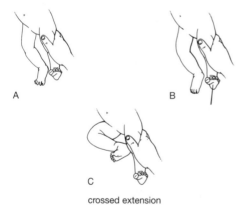

crossed extension

crossed extension pattern The simultaneous forward movement of one arm and the contralateral (opposite) leg in creeping, crawling, and walking.

crossed extensor reflex *See* crossed extension.

cross-eyedness *See* esotropia.

crossed patch test *See* cover/uncover test.

crossing-over The interchange (exchange) of chromosome material in meiosis (a stage of cell reproduction in which there are two copies of each chromosome) between homologous chromosomes. *See* homologous chromosomes.

croup An acute viral respiratory syndrome characterized by a croaky, honking cough; the differential diagnosis includes epiglottitis (inflammation of the epiglottis), laryngotracheobronchitis (inflammation of the wind pipe), and spasmodic laryngitis, with the first of these representing a life-threatening medical emergency. The asphyxia (lack of oxygen) that sometimes occurs with epiglottitis can produce brain damage or death.

Crouzon syndrome *craniofacial dysostosis.* A genetic syndrome characterized by premature craniosynostosis (fusion of skull sutures) leading to brachycephaly (irregular, flat head shape), mid-face hypoplasia (undergrowth), and shallow orbits with exophthalmos or proptosis (a pop-eyed look). The nose is parrot beaked, and there is relative prognathism (prominent jaw). One third to one half of all cases involve a conductive (involving the middle and outer ear) hearing loss. Inheritance follows an autosomal dominant pattern. However, Crouzon syndrome has an extremely variable expression, and about one quarter of cases are spontaneous (new). Alterations in the *FGFR2* or *FGFR3* genes are responsible.

Crowe sign Axillary (armpit) freckling in neurofibromatosis (von Recklinghausen disease).

crown-rump length The distance from the top of the head to the bottom of the buttocks; one of the standard measures of fetal size.

CRS-R *See* Conners' Rating Scales–Revised.

cry A prelinguistic vocalization pattern that can be reflexive (e.g., a birth cry), communicative (e.g., a crying expressing pain, anger, exercise, hunger, fatigue, fretfulness), or pathological (e.g., colic). Tears do not usually accompany crying until 6 weeks of age. Prolonged primitive crying may reflect underlying brain damage or intellectual disability, and certain cry patterns can indicate specific diagnoses: A shrill, high-pitched cry suggests cerebral irritability (e.g., encephalitis, meningitis [brain infections], hydrocephalus [excess fluid in the brain]), a mewing cat cry suggests cri-du-chat syndrome (this cry disappears in older children), a bleating lamb cry suggests Cornelia de Lange syndrome, and a hoarse cry is noted in hypothyroidism.

cryptophthalmus Hidden eye. The absence of a palpebral fissure (eye slits), and, by extension, the absence of eyelashes and eyebrows. Also known as Fraser syndrome.

cryptorchidism Undescended testes; may be unilateral or bilateral. Cryptorchidism can be an isolated finding or a component of a syndrome. Treatment can be medical (with hormones) or surgical. Orchiopexy is the operation to correct cryptorchidism.

crystallized ability A term from the Cattell-Horn-Carroll theory of cognitive abilities. Crystallized ability refers to intellectual functioning or tasks that utilize previous training, education, and acculturation (knowledge acquired through exposure to one's culture). A measure of crystallized ability may represent individual differences in knowledge, including verbal abilities; in the information on which judgment, sophistication, and wisdom are based; and in types of reasoning based on previously learned procedures. *See also* fluid intelligence, Kaufman Assessment Battery for Children–Second Edition (K-ABC-II).

CSAP *See* Center for Substance Abuse Prevention.

CSBS *See* Communication and Symbolic Behavior Scales.

CSBS-DP *See* Communication and Symbolic Behavior Scales Developmental Profile.

CSE *See* consequent stimulus event.

CSEF *See* Center for Special Education Finance.

CSEFEL *See* Center for Social and Emotional Foundation for Early Learning.

CSEI *See* Coopersmith Self-Esteem Inventory.

CSF *See* cerebrospinal fluid.

CSHCN *See* Children with Special Health Care Needs.

CT scan *See* computed tomography scan.

CTLSHO Cervical-thoraco-lumbar-spinal and hip orthosis. *See also* Milwaukee brace.

CTLSO Cervical-thoraco-lumbar-spinal orthosis. *See also* Milwaukee brace.

CTMT *See* Comprehensive Trail Making Test.

CTONI-2 *See* Comprehensive Test of Nonverbal Intelligence–Second Edition.

CTOPP *See* Comprehensive Test of Phonological Processing.

CTRS-R:L Conners' Teacher rating Scale Revised, long version. *See* Conners' Rating Scales–Revised.

CTRS-R:S Conners' Teacher Rating Scale Revised, short version. *See* Conners' Rating Scales–Revised.

CTVF *See* Comprehensive Test of Visual Functioning.

cubitus valgus Increased carrying angle, as seen in Turner syndrome.

cued speech A system of manual cues used in conjunction with speech reading. Cued speech was designed to lessen the ambiguity experienced by individuals with severe and profound hearing impairments when using speech reading to understand spoken language. Because many sounds appear visually similar, cued speech attempts to avoid confusion by providing a visual element to speech reading. Twelve hand signals or cues compose the system: Four cues are hand positions that differentiate between groups of vowel sounds, and eight cues, based on American Sign Language hand shapes, are used to visually discriminate between groups of consonants.

cul de sac resonance Describing phoneme sound that is in the back of the throat and/or mouth instead of in the nasal or oral cavities.

cultural bias The use of material that is familiar to one social or economic group but remote from the experiences of another group.

cultural competence The ability to think, feel, and act in ways that acknowledge, respect, and build upon ethnic, sociocultural, and linguistic diversity.

cultural sensitivity Knowledge of cultural differences and the corresponding use of verbal and nonverbal behavior that optimizes interactions with people from a different cultural background.

culturally and linguistically different exceptional (CLDE) student A non-English learner who has disabilities that affect his or her learning ability and/or social development.

culturally–linguistically different (CLD) Referring to a speaker of a non-mainstream language.

cumulative Enlarging by successive additions, sometimes needing to be added one step at a time.

Cupid's bow The line of the upper lip.

curriculum An organized course of study with defined content, goals and objectives, and learning experiences.

curriculum-based assessment (CBA) *curriculum-based evaluation*. A method of assessment that is linked to an instructional curriculum and that permits assessment of an individual's status with reference to a specified skill sequence. CBA can be used for an initial assessment and to determine progress along instructional objectives. In curriculum-based evaluation, eligibility for services or placement is determined in reference to a child's performance within or along a curriculum.

curriculum-based measurement (CBM) A test that assesses an individual's position with a specific skill sequence; such information can then be used for curriculum and intervention planning.

custodial care Institutional placement with no therapeutic service components as part of the care.

custodian A person who has the custody or care of something; a legal designation for someone who provides long-term care for children, such as a stepparent, someone who is providing long-term foster care, or a relative with whom a child is living permanently.

cutaneous Relating to the skin.

cutaneous facilitation   Skin stimulation as a component of neuromuscular (physical or occupational) therapy; such stimulation includes light-moving touch, fast brushing, and applying ice to the skin.

cutis congenita aplasia   *aplasia cutis congenita (ACC).* The absence of skin in specific areas, commonly the scalp at the top of the head. Seen in certain genetic syndromes such as trisomy 13 or Wolf-Hirschhorn syndrome.

cutis laxa syndrome   A rare congenital disorder that includes loose skin, mild intellectual disability, loose joints, bone abnormalities (e.g., hooked nose, pigeon breast, funnel breast), diarrhea, urinary tract blockages, and deficiencies in lysyl oxidase (an enzyme required to form connective tissue). Because the loose skin is particularly obvious on the face, children with the disorder look sad or mournful. In addition to the X-linked form, there are autosomal dominant and recessive forms.

CVA   Cerebrovascular accident. *See* stroke.

CVFES   *See* Children's Version of the Family Environment Scale.

CWC   *See* class within a class.

CWLA   *See* Child Welfare League of America.

cyanosis   A blue tinge or color to the skin, especially noted peripherally (away from the center of the body) in the lips and fingernails; it can occur with cold, shock, disease of the heart or lungs, and seizures. The blueness results from decreased oxygen that leads to an increase of reduced hemoglobin in oxygen-carrying red blood cells.

cyanotic heart disease   Heart disease of a type that produces some peripheral cyanosis (blue color) of the fingernails or lips. When such heart disease is not associated with a syndrome that also involves the central nervous system (CNS), it does not necessarily affect development. Poor oxygenation leading to cyanosis can, however, slow motor development. In young children, the hypotonia can interfere with speech.

cybernetics   The study of regulating mechanisms in closed systems, particularly the flow of information and feedback loops in those systems.

cyclothymic disorder   An adolescent or adult psychiatric condition involving a chronic, fluctuating mood disturbance with numerous periods of hypomanic symptoms that alternate with numerous periods of depressive symptoms over a period of at least 1 year.

Cylert   *See* pemoline.

cylindrical grasp   The position of the hand for holding an object such as a stick or a pole in which the fingers as a group wrap around the object and the thumb opposes the fingers, wrapping around the object from the other direction.

cynotrichous   Describing straight, curly, or wavy hair as found in Caucasian races.

cyproheptadine   Trade name, Periactin. An anticholinergic, sedative antihistamine that may have antidepressant effects. Cyproheptadine may alleviate anorexia associated with stimulant therapy and is used as an adjunct in the treatment of infant feeding disorders.

cysbolster   Adaptive equipment used to promote normal posture and balance responses in children. Often incorporated into a child's seating system.

cystic encephalomalacia   A brain condition characterized by the formation of cystic cavities (holes) in the white matter of the brain. Generally a result of severe asphyxia (lack of oxygen), cystic encephalomalacia can also be found after viral encephalitis (brain infection). The brainstem nuclei and the thalamus tend to be affected initially, with further damage extending to the basal ganglia and the cerebral cortex. The brain damage can be seen on ultrasound, computed tomography (CT), and magnetic resonance imaging (MRI) scans. The outcome of this type of insult is usually cerebral palsy with intellectual disability. Spastic quadriplegia is the most common type of cerebral palsy associated with cystic encephalomalacia.

cystic fibrosis (CF)　An inherited disorder that affects the exocrine (secreting substances outside the body) glands, respiratory system, and pancreas. Affected children have chronic digestive and pulmonary problems that require medical as well as physical and respiratory therapy management. More than 1,000 alterations in the responsible gene, *CTFR* (cystic fibrosis transmembrane conductance regulator), have been described.

cystic hygroma　A large vascularized mass, swollen with lymphatic fluid, that results from a malformation of a portion of the lymphatic system and is usually found in the neck or on the tongue.

cytogenetics　The study of the relationship of the microscopic appearance of chromosomes and their behavior during cell division to the genotype and phenotype of the individual. More generally, the study of human chromosomes and their abnormalities.

cytomegalovirus (CMV)　*See* congenital cytomegalic inclusion disease.

Dd

DA *See* developmental age.

DA *See* dextroamphetamine sulfate.

DA *See* dopamine.

Daberon Screening for School Readiness–Second Edition (Daberon-2) A standardized measure of school readiness for children 4–6 years of age or children with learning or behavior problems who are functioning at the early elementary school level. The test samples knowledge of body parts, color and number concepts, gross motor development, categorization, and other developmental abilities. It is individually administered in 20–40 minutes.

DAB-3 *See* Diagnostic Achievement Battery–Third Edition.

dacryostenosis *See* congenital lacrimal duct stenosis.

dactyl speech *See* fingerspelling.

dactylology Fingerspelling for the purpose of talking; American one-hand manual alphabet with a configuration for each of the 26 letters.

DAFO *See* dynamic ankle–foot orthosis.

Dallas Preschool Screening Test (DPST) A brief screening test of "primary" learning areas, including speech-language, problem solving, and motor skills. Administration time is 15 minutes.

DAMP *See* dysfunction of attention, motor function, and perception.

Dandy-Walker syndrome A brain malformation characterized by an enlargement of the fourth ventricle that pushes into the cerebellum and prevents the normal formation of the central portion of the cerebellum. This is often associated with hydrocephalus (excess fluid in the brain) and other brain and systemic (body) malformations, such as cleft palate, enlarged kidneys with cysts, agenesis (absence) of the corpus callosum (the part of the brain that links the two hemispheres), or an occipital encephalocele (protrusion of the brain out of the back of the skull).

dantrolene sodium Trade name, Dantrium. A drug that reduces spasticity in cerebral palsy through its peripheral (noncentral) action.

DANVA-2 *See* Receptive Tests of Diagnostic Analysis of Nonverbal Accuracy–Second Edition.

DAP *See* developmentally appropriate practice.

DAS *See* developmental apraxia of speech.

Das Naglieri Cognitive Assessment System *See* Cognitive Assessment System (CAS).

DASE *See* Denver Articulation Screening Exam.

DASG *See* Developmental Assessment of Spanish Grammar.

DASI-II *See* Developmental Activities Screening Inventory–Revised.

data days Days on which targeted behavior is observed and data are recorded. Data days are often used to identify progress toward goals in an individualized education program (IEP) for school system therapy.

DAS-II *See* Differential Ability Scales–Second Edition.

DAT1 *See* dopamine transporter gene.

day care *child care.* Facilities and programs that provide care, stimulation, and socialization to children, older adults, people with developmental disabilities, and other dependents on a nonresidential basis. Care is provided during the day, and the clients return to their homes each evening.

day hospital A facility or program for older adults and people with mental illness; such a program provides health, mental health, and social services during the day and enables individuals to return home at night.

day treatment Intensive, multi-pronged therapeutic services similar to those provided in residential settings, except that in the day treatment setting such services are provided in the local community and the child returns home each evening. Day treatment is the most intensive level of nonresidential service available.

daydream A fantasy that occurs when a person is in a wakeful state, independent of external stimulus, that may gratify wishes not satisfied in real life.

Daytrana *See* methylphenidate.

dB *See* decibel.

DBS *See* deep brain stimulation.

DC:0-3 *See* Diagnostic Classification of Mental Health Disorders of Infancy and Early Childhood.

DCC *See* Developmental Communication Curriculum.

DCD *See* developmental coordination disorder.

DD Waiver *See* Individual and Family Developmental Disabilities Support Waiver.

DDA *See* Developmental Disabilities Administration.

DDAVP *See* desmopressin.

DDH *See* developmental dysplasia of the hip.

de Lange syndrome *See* Cornelia de Lange syndrome.

de Morsier syndrome *See* septo-optic dysplasia (SOD).

de novo *new.* A de novo mutation is a genetic mutation that arises spontaneously; in other words, neither parent had the mutation. De novo mutations occur in the egg, sperm, or fertilized egg.

de Sanctis-Cacchione syndrome A genetic syndrome characterized by xeroderma pigmentosa (extreme sensitivity of the skin to light), intellectual disability, gonadal hypoplasia (small reproductive organs), microcephaly (small head), and neurological complications. Inheritance is autosomal recessive. *See also* xeroderma pigmentosum.

deaf Having nonfunctional hearing, with or without amplification, for the ordinary purposes of daily living. Deafness is characterized by a pure tone loss greater than 90 decibels (units of volume) over the speech range frequency of 500, 1,000, and 2,000 hertz (units of frequency indicating sound pitch). Hearing loss is expressed in a spectrum of degrees ranging from mild to profound. Individuals formerly referred to as *deaf* are now described as having a profound hearing loss.

deaf mute *deaf and dumb.* Antiquated term for an individual who can neither hear nor speak, usually one born with severe to profound hearing loss (i.e., congenital hearing loss). The term is objectionable because it implies intellectual disability.

deaffrication The phonological process that occurs when the substitution of a fricative or a stop is made for an affricate.

deafism A self-stimulating behavior in a person with a hearing impairment; behaviors such as poking at one's ear may produce auditory feedback.

Deaver Describing a system of physical therapy developed by the physiatrist George Deaver for the treatment of cerebral palsy. This approach uses extensive bracing and focuses on the achievement of functional activities of daily living (ADLs). The Deaver system also places a high value on achieving a typical appearance (e.g., working to control grimacing).

deceleration In obstetrics, a decrease in fetal heart rate relative to uterine contractions during delivery. There are three types—early (type I dip), late (type II dip), and variable (type III dip)—according to their timing in relation to uterine contractions. The kind of deceleration may be reassuring (not associated with fetal distress) or nonreassuring (associated with fetal distress). The duration of the contractions and the degree to which the fetal heart rate decreases enable the obstetrician to assess fetal hypoxia (oxygen deficiency).

decerebrate posture A position the body assumes based on brain damage at the brainstem level; decerebrate posture is similar to decorticate posture, except that the upper extremities are extended instead of flexed. *See also* decorticate posture.

decerebrate posture

decibel (dB) A quantitative measure of sound intensity or loudness. In audiology, sound intensity is a ratio of the sound being measured to a standard reference sound level. The relative intensity of sounds is expressed on a decibel scale. Whispering measures about 30 dB, normal conversation is gauged between 50 and 65 dB, and a hairdryer registers 70 dB.

declarative knowledge A term that refers to how certain information is represented in memory. Within this model, knowledge is represented by declarative propositions, which are the basic units of information, each corresponding roughly to one idea. Propositions have varying levels of activity, with most being inactive at any given time and representing a long-term memory store. The few propositions that are active at any one time represent old knowledge that is in conscious awareness. This small part of the network of declarative propositions makes up one part of working memory. *See also* memory, procedural knowledge.

declarative sentence A type of sentence that relates a descriptive statement.

decoding The act of pronouncing written letters and words. Decoding is enabled by an understanding of letters (symbols) and the sounds they represent. Decoding is distinguished from comprehension, which implies an understanding of what is being read.

decorticate posture The posture assumed when the corticospinal tract, the connection between the brain and spinal cord, is extensively damaged; it is similar to the tonic labyrinthine supine posture (extension of all four extremities) and includes flexion of the upper extremities, shoulder adduction/retraction, and extension of the lower extremities. *See also* decerebrate posture.

decorticate posture

decubiti *decubitus ulcers, pressure sores.* Bedsores secondary to pressure and decreased mobility. Decubiti can be prevented by proper hygiene and by frequent repositioning of the individual with limited mobility. Repositioning relieves pressure on bony prominences. Specialized beds, mattresses, pads, and cushions can also be used but cannot substitute for turning and repositioning.

deductive reasoning Drawing a specific conclusion from a general rule, or applying a general rule to a specific situation. *See also* top-down (conceptually driven) processing.

deep brain stimulation (DBS) The use of electrodes surgically implanted in the brain to provide electrical stimulation deep in the brain that alters the brain's own electrical activity.

deep pressure proprioception touch technique *See* Wilbarger protocol.

deep-tendon reflex (DTR) *tendon reflex.* When a tendon is tapped with a reflex hammer, a sudden stretch is applied to the attached muscle; this stimulus produces a reflex muscle contraction that can be observed or felt. A number of different DTRs are routinely elicited on neurological examination: the biceps, triceps, ankles, and knees (the last is sometimes referred to as the

patellar reflex). The response is graded on a 5-point scale from 0 (*pathologically absent*) through 2+ (*physiological/normal response*) to 4+ (*pathologically brisk/exaggerated*). Asymmetries can be significant. Each reflex is associated with one or more spinal nerve roots. The following reflexes are paired with their spinal nerve roots: biceps, C5–C6; triceps, C7–C8; brachioradialis, C5–C6; abdominal, upper, T8, T9, T10; abdominal, lower, T10, T11, T12; cremasteric, L1, L2; knee, L2, L3, L4; ankle, S1, S2.

defect theory *See* difference approach.

defense mechanism A psychoanalytic term for a way in which the ego (self-awareness) avoids awareness of unpleasant and anxiety-provoking stimuli. The ego selectively uses defense mechanisms to ward off conflicts. These conflicts can arise elsewhere in the self (as in the id, or unconscious urges of the mind; or the superego, the conscience) or in external reality. Common defense mechanisms include denial, rationalization, repression, and projection. Defense mechanisms can be healthy responses to stress.

deformation An abnormal form, shape, or position of a part of the body caused by mechanical forces. Prenatal deformations include abnormal foot positions related to oligohydramnios (too little amniotic fluid) or fetal central nervous system (CNS) defects; plagiocephaly (flattened back of the skull in infants who spend too much time lying on their backs) is an example of a postnatal skull (cranial) deformation.

DeGangi-Berk Test of Sensory Integration (TSI) A nonstandardized test of sensory integration for 3- to 5-year-old children suspected of having learning disabilities.

degenerative disorders *heredodegenerative diseases.* A group of neurological diseases that are familial (hereditary) and degenerative in nature. The degeneration is chronic and progressive, resulting in worsening function and often loss of function. These diseases are generally grouped by the area of the brain that is affected and thus determines the functional insult. *See also* neurodegenerative disorders.

deglutition The act of swallowing, which includes the 1) placement of food or liquid in the mouth, 2) oral preparatory phase, 3) oral phase, 4) pharyngeal phase, and 5) esophageal phase.

dehiscence The splitting apart or opening of a closed (surgical) wound.

deinstitutionalization The relocation of people with developmental disabilities and psychiatric illnesses from institutional settings to community placements; one component of normalization. The movement toward deinstitutionalization occurred primarily during the late 1970s and early 1980s.

del(4)(p-) *See* 4p- syndrome.

del(4)(q15-pter) *See* Wolf-Hirschhorn syndrome.

del(7)(q11.23) *See* Williams syndrome.

del(11)(p13p14) *See* WAGR syndrome.

del(22)(q11.21-q11.23) *See* velocardiofacial syndrome.

deletion A missing part of a gene or chromosome. A deletion can be a single base pair (the smallest unit of a gene), a segment of base pairs, or a large part of a chromosome visible under microscopy. The deletion interferes with the proper coding of an enzyme or protein and causes the product to be inactive.

deletion 1p36 A syndrome characterized by microcephaly (small head); characteristic facies; short fingers and feet; cardiac (heart) defects; visual, skeletal, and genital anomalies; developmental delay; hypotonia; and seizures.

deletion (3)(pter–p25) A genetic syndrome that causes poor growth, hypotonia (floppiness), microcephaly (small head), and severe intellectual disability. Epicanthal folds and ptosis (drooping eyelids) contribute to the appearance of small slit-like palpebral fissures (eye openings). Individuals have a prominent nasal bridge, small nose, long upper lip groove, and small jaw. They may have polydactyly (extra fingers or toes), heart defects, cleft palate, and renal (kidney) abnormalities. The deletion is almost always spontaneous.

deletion 4p *See* Wolf-Hirschhorn syndrome.

deletion (5)(p15-pter) *See* cri-du-chat syndrome.

deletion 7q *See* Williams syndrome.

deletion 8(q24),del(8)(q24.13) *See* Landouzy-Dejerine dystrophy.

deletion 11p *See* WAGR syndrome.

deletion 17p *See* Smith-Magenis syndrome (SMS).

deletion 17p (del 17p13.3) *See* Miller-Dieker syndrome.

deletion 22q13 *22q deletion syndrome.* A microdeletion at the end of the long arm of chromosome 22 that can present with hypotonia (floppiness), developmental delay, severe speech and language delay, and autistic-like behaviors.

dementia A marked deterioration of mental processes that is organic in origin. Dementia is characterized by faulty judgment, impaired memory, concrete rigid thinking, and ultimately personality changes. Although some dementias are treatable, such as those due to malnutrition or adverse drug reactions, most indicate ongoing damage to the brain that is not reversible. These processes typically occur in older adults. When such processes are noted in children, they are usually referred to as *degenerative processes* or *developmental regressions.*

dementia infantilis *See* childhood disintegrative disorder (CDD).

denasalization The phonological process that occurs when a stop is substituted for a nasal phoneme.

dendrite A thread-like extension of a nerve cell.

denial In psychoanalysis, a defense mechanism that involves the rejection of elements of reality that would be intolerable if one consciously recognized them. Denial is also the negation of experiences of reality through the refusal to accept them.

Dennyson-Fulford procedure An orthopedic surgery that is a modification of the Grice subtalar arthrodesis (surgical immobilization below the ankle) used to treat valgus deformity of the foot (inturned ankles).

Denver Articulation Screening Exam (DASE) A brief screening test used to assess speech (pronunciation) in children 2;6–6;0 years of age by asking the child to repeat 22 separate words containing 30 sounds. The number of correctly produced sounds is charted on an age graph, and children who score below the 15th percentile for age are referred for more detailed evaluation by a speech-language pathologist (SLP).

Denver Developmental Screening Test– Second Edition (Denver-II) A screening test for developmental delay in children from birth to 6 years of age that divides test items into the Gesell streams of development (gross motor, fine motor, language,

and personal social skills). The test depends heavily on caregiver report. The Denver Prescreening Developmental Questionnaire (PDQ-II) can be used as a first-stage screening and the Denver-II as a second-stage screening.

Denver Eye Screening Test (DEST) A protocol for the assessment of eye functioning in children from birth to 6 years of age. It includes three types of vision tests, each geared toward different age groups, and three tests for strabismus (crossed eyes).

Denver Model Curriculum Checklist *See* Early Start Denver Model Curriculum Checklist for Young Children with Autism (ESDM).

Denver-II *See* Denver Developmental Screening Test–Second Edition.

deoxyribonucleic acid (DNA) The chemical name for the molecule that provides genetic instructions in all living things. The DNA molecule consists of two strands that compose the double helix. Each strand has a backbone made of alternating sugar (deoxyribose) and  deoxyribonucleic acid (DNA) phosphate groups. Attached to each sugar is one of four bases: adenine (A), cytosine (C), guanine (G), or thymine (T). The helix is held together by the bonds between these bases: adenine to thymine, and cytosine to guanine. The sequence of the bases along the backbones serves as instructions for assembling protein and ribonucleic acid (RNA) molecules.

Depacon An injectable form of valproic acid. *See* valproic acid.

Depakene *See* valproic acid.

Depakote *See* valproic acid.

depalatalization The phonological process that occurs when the palatal component is deleted from a palatal phoneme.

Department of Health and Human Services (DHHS) The U.S. federal agency that houses the Office of the Secretary of Health and Human Services (OS), Administration for Children and Families (ACF), Administration on Aging (AOA), Agency for Healthcare Research and Quality (AHRQ), Agency for Toxic Substances and Disease Registry (ATSDR), Centers for Disease Control and Prevention (CDC), Centers for Medicare & Medicaid Services (CMS), Food and Drug Administration (FDA), Health Resources and Services Administration (HRSA), Indian Health Service (IHS), National Institutes of Health (NIH), Program Support Center (PSC), and Substance Abuse and Mental Health Services Administration (SAMHSA). The DHHS was formed in 1979 when the U.S. Department of Education was separated from the U.S. Department of Health, Education and Welfare (HEW) to become an independent agency.

departmentalization The teaching of different subjects by different specialized teachers; this may occur in the same classroom (teachers rotate, pupils remain) or different classrooms (teachers remain, pupils rotate). The onset of departmentalization frequently heightens the difficulties experienced by children with learning disabilities and those with attentional disorders because of their weak organizational skills.

dependency Behavior characterized by overreliance on another person or system. The reliance can be emotional, physical, or financial. The dependent person fails to use his or her own skills and abilities, passively leaning on another person or system to care for his or her needs. The threat of removal or of withdrawal of support is experienced as a psychological threat of loss to the dependent person, who views himself or herself as personally incapable of meeting these needs.

dependent Requiring some degree of assistance to conduct ordinary daily activities.

Depo-Provera *See* progestin.

depression A prolonged mood of sadness, despair, and discouragement. Signs of depression vary and can be culturally specific. Depression may be a symptom of a number of mental and physical disorders, a syndrome of associated symptoms caused by some underlying disorder, or a specific psychiatric disorder. Slowed thinking, a decrease in pleasure, feelings of guilt and hopelessness, decreased physical activity, and disrupted eating and sleeping are common characteristics. Depression is classified by severity, recurrence, and association with mania.

deprivation A state of chronic unmet or incompletely met physical, social, or emotional needs. *See also* maternal deprivation.

depth perception The ability of the visual system to interpret the shape and position of a three-dimensional world while only being provided with two-dimensional sensory input. The use of shadow, size, interference patterns, and other learned visual cues allows for the presence of depth perception even in the absence of binocular (two-eyed) stereoscopic (three-dimensional) vision.

derivational A type of suffix that can be added at the ends of words to change their meaning and grammatical class.

derived score Any score obtained from a statistical treatment or other manipulation of raw scores or raw data.

dermal sinus A mid-line skin pit along the spine that may connect with an underlying sinus (space in the body) and represent a risk for infection. A dermal sinus may reflect an underlying spinal abnormality.

dermatitis Rash; skin irritation or inflammation.

dermatoglyphics Fingerprints and palm prints; surface skin-marking patterns on the fingers, toes, palms, and soles that allow for the unique identification of each individual. Dermatoglyphic abnormalities can be characteristic of specific syndromes. *See also* papillary ridges.

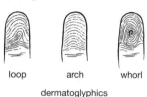

loop   arch   whorl

dermatoglyphics

dermatome The area of the skin enervated (supplied) by a single dorsal nerve root for sensation and motor response.

derotative righting A postural response in which 1) voluntary or passive turning of the head is followed by a segmental or corkscrew (un)rolling of the rest of the body; or 2) voluntary or passive rotation of the pelvis segmentally (one part after the other) rolls the trunk, shoulders, neck, and head. This movement pattern is a prerequisite to voluntary rolling over.

Descriptive Pragmatics Profile A component of the Clinical Evaluation of Language Fundamentals–Preschool (CELF-P-2).

desensitization *systematic desensitization.* An intervention used to help individuals approach feared objects or situations, such as flying or heights. The individual approaches the feared object incrementally (gradually), pausing either at predetermined intervals or when he or she feels overwhelmed by fear. During the pause, relaxation or biofeedback techniques assist the person to deescalate and permit his or her approach. This continues until the person is able to independently reach the feared object or situation. Desensitization procedures are also used to decrease exaggerated

physiological responses that interfere with functioning (e.g., oral motor desensitization for a person with a hyperactive gag reflex).

desipramine Trade name, Norpramin. A tricyclic antidepressant medication that has also been used to treat attention-deficit/hyperactivity disorder (ADHD) and is sometimes used to treat neuropathic pain (pain due to abnormal nerve activity) and as a sedative to help induce sleep.

desmopressin (DDAVP) A synthetic form of the natural pituitary hormone vasopressin that has an antidiuretic (preventing urine formation) effect. It is sometimes used to treat nocturnal enuresis (bed-wetting).

Desoxyn *See* methamphetamine.

DEST *See* Denver Eye Screening Test.

Desyrel *See* trazodone.

detection The response to the presence or absence of sound.

detoxification The removal of purportedly toxic levels of chemicals from the body on the supposition that they can cause or exaggerate the behavioral symptoms of neurodevelopmental disorders such as autism.

Detroit Tests of Learning Aptitude–Fourth Edition (DTLA-4) A criterion-referenced test of specific mental abilities composed of 10 subtests: word opposites, design sequences, sentence imitation, reversed letters, basic information, word sequences, story construction, story sequences, object sequences, and symbolic relations. The subtests are grouped into 16 composites (combinations of other scores) that measure both general intelligence with a general intelligence quotient (GIQ) and discrete (separate) ability areas. The DTLA-4 is designed for use with children 6–17 years of age and takes from 40 minutes to 2 hours to administer. The DTLA-4 also measures the effects of language, attention, and motor abilities on performance.

Developmental Activities Screening Inventory–Revised (DASI-II) A cognitive screening measure for children birth to 5 years of age; it can be adapted for use with preschool children who have visual impairments, hearing impairments, and multiple disabilities.

developmental age (DA) The age (in years and months) that best describes a child's level of performance by equating it to the performance of a typically developing child of that chronological age (CA). For example, a 5-year-old who is just putting two words together and has a vocabulary of 70 words would have an expressive language DA of 2 years, with 2 years being the age at which a typically developing child would exhibit similar language development.

developmental approach The theory that people with mild intellectual disability without evidence of organic (physical) brain damage behave and learn exactly the same as their typically developing peers except for the impact of personality variables. The developmental approach has been referred to as a *motivational* or *social learning theory*. *See also* difference approach.

developmental apraxia of speech (DAS) Severe difficulty with articulation and with volitional or imitative production of speech sounds and sequences.

developmental articulation disorder *See* articulation disorder.

Developmental Assessment of Spanish Grammar (DASG) An adaptation of a developmental sentence-scoring technique for use with Spanish-speaking children.

Developmental Communication Curriculum (DCC) A language curriculum for use with children with developmental ages birth to 5 years. The DCC includes a test called the Developmental Communication Inventory (DCI) that assesses prelinguistic (before the development of spoken language) symbolic relationships and complex symbolic relationships in play contexts.

developmental coordination disorder (DCD) Difficulty performing age-appropriate, skilled motor movements, including both fine and gross motor movements. Mild motor delay may be an early sign of later DCD. Developmental apraxia (the inability to perform purposeful movements) may be synonymous with DCD, but the former usually refers more specifically to problems with fine motor skills. In school-age children, developmental disorders of written language or dysgraphia (impaired writing) are prominent symptoms. DCD is sometimes referred to as *minimal cerebral palsy.* Formerly known as *clumsy child syndrome. See also* gait.

developmental delay A nonspecific term that refers to an individual who is not developing and/or achieving skills according to the expected time frame. Some children with developmental delays may catch up with their typically developing peers, whereas others remain with a developmental disability. The term *developmental delay* is often used in place of *intellectual disability* to describe children younger than 5 years of age. It can also categorize any delay in an individual stream of development.

Developmental Disabilities Administration (DDA) *See* Administration on Developmental Disabilities.

Developmental Disabilities Assistance and Bill of Rights Act of 1975 (PL 94-103) A federal law that extends the definition of developmental disabilities to include autism and selected types of dyslexia; it also set up a task force that in 1977 further broadened the definition of developmental disabilities by using a generic or functional approach (continuum of developmental disabilities) that cuts across specific categories or diagnoses. This act also mandates that each state and territory establish a protection and advocacy (P&A) system as a condition of receiving federal funding under this law. Advocacy agencies are authorized to pursue legal, administrative, and other remedies to protect the rights of individuals with developmental disabilities. Each state's governor designates a program to serve as the P&A system and must ensure that it is independent of any service provider. The Administration on Developmental Disabilities within the U.S. Department of Health and Human Services (DHHS) is responsible for administering a P&A program for people with developmental disabilities at the federal level. *See also* protection and advocacy (P&A).

Developmental Disabilities Assistance and Bill of Rights Act Amendments of 1987 (PL 100-146) Legislation that amends the Mental Retardation Facilities and Community Mental Health Centers Construction Act of 1963 (PL 88-164) and contains a Bill of Rights section for people with developmental disabilities. PL 100-146 expands the definition of developmental disabilities to include intellectual disability, autism, cerebral palsy, and seizure disorders. It also authorizes funding for a wide variety of programs and services for individuals with developmental disabilities.

Developmental Disabilities Assistance and Bill of Rights Act Amendments of 1990 (PL 101-496) A federal law that maintains and further strengthens programs authorized under the Mental Retardation Facilities and Community Mental Health Centers Construction Act of 1963 (PL 88-164) and the Developmental Disabilities Assistance and Bill of Rights Act Amendments of 1987 (PL 100-146) by adding the goals of interdependence, community acceptance, and inclusion for all people with developmental disabilities. PL 101-496 authorizes grants to support the planning, coordination, and delivery of increasingly specialized services to all people with developmental disabilities and expands several programs, including the protection and advocacy (P&A) system and university affiliated programs (UAPs).

Developmental Disabilities Assistance and Bill of Rights Act of 2000 (PL 106-402) A federal law that continues previous efforts set forth in the Mental Retardation Facilities and Community Mental Health Centers Construction Act of 1963 (PL 88-164) and provides for the conversion of university affiliated programs (UAPs) to a National Network of University Centers for Excellence in Developmental Disabilities Education, Research, and Service. PL 106-402 also expands family support services. *See also* developmental disability; University Centers for Excellence in Developmental Disabilities Education, Research, and Service (UCE or UCEDD).

Developmental Disabilities Services and Facilities Construction Act of 1970 (PL 91-517) A federal law that expands the Mental Retardation Facilities and Community Mental Health Centers Construction Act of 1963 (PL 88-164) to include services for people with cerebral palsy and seizure disorders. This law introduces the concept of "developmental disability" and replaces the term *clinical training* with *interdisciplinary training*. PL 91-517 also creates a program of state formula grants to establish councils to plan government activities related to service delivery.

developmental disability A condition in which a static encephalopathy (non-progressive brain damage) or brain injury leads to a serious impairment or limitation of one or more functions controlled by the brain. The "injury" may be structurally programmed in the developing brain. All developmental disabilities bear a "family resemblance" because of their common grounding in brain dysfunction. The Developmental Disabilities Assistance and Bill of Rights Act Amendments of 2000 (PL 106-402) defines *developmental disability* as "a severe, chronic disability of a person 5 years of age or older, which is attributable to a mental or physical impairment or combination of mental and physical impairments; is manifested before the person attains age 22; is likely to continue indefinitely; results in substantial functional limitations in three or more areas of major life activity: 1) self-care, 2) receptive and expressive language, 3) learning, 4) mobility, 5) self-direction, 6) capacity for independent living, and 7) economic self-sufficiency; and reflects the person's need for a combination and sequence of special, interdisciplinary, or generic care, treatment, or other services that are of lifelong or extended duration and are individually planned and coordinated." The term *developmentally disabled* can also be applied to infants and young children from birth to age 5 "who have substantial developmental delay or specific congenital or acquired conditions with a high probability of resulting in developmental disabilities if services are not provided." *See also* Developmental Disabilities Assistance and Bill of Rights Act Amendments of 2000 (PL 106-402).

developmental discontinuity An uneven distribution of skills.

developmental dysplasia of the hip (DDH) *luxatio coxae congenita*. A congenital (present at birth) abnormality of the hip that renders it unstable with regard to keeping the femur (thigh bone) in the joint. This defect leads to a limitation of hip abduction, asymmetry of thigh folds, leg shortening, and persistent adduction of the involved side. It is more common in girls and after breech delivery. Simple tests on physical exam called the Ortolani and Barlow tests are used to routinely screen infants for DDH; later, it will show up as a limp. DDH is often an isolated finding but may occur as part of a more gen-

eralized syndrome. Previously referred to as *congenital dislocation of the hip* (CDH).

developmental dyspraxia The failure to acquire the ability to perform age-appropriate complex motor actions that is not explained by inadequate demonstration/practice, ataxia, reduced selective motor control, weakness, or involuntary motor activity.

developmental hesitation Benign and typical stumblings, repetitions, and prolongations in the speech of a child learning to talk.

Developmental Indicators for Assessment of Learning–Third Edition (DIAL-3) A preschool and prekindergarten developmental screening test for children 3–7 years of age. Its subtest areas include motor, language, self-help, social, and concepts skills. Administration time is approximately 30 minutes. The acronym DIAL-3 also refers to the rotating discs with which visual stimuli for certain test item groups are presented.

Developmental, Individual-Difference, Relationship-Based (DIR) Model *Floortime.* A comprehensive intervention program for children with autism. DIR emphasizes the child's affect and relationships, developmental level, and individual differences (motor, sensory, affective, cognitive, and language functioning). The major intervention strategy used is from six to ten 20- to 30-minute sessions of "floor time" a day during which the parent or therapist sits on the floor to best interact with the child and facilitate interactions that are affective (emotions are expressed) using the child's individual differences and developmental level as a starting point. Also referred to as the *Greenspan approach* after its developer, Stanley I. Greenspan.

developmental language disorders A spectrum of language-based developmental disorders that involve delays or difficulties in understanding, processing, and producing verbal, nonverbal, and written language. The observed behavior associated with a developmental language disorder may vary over time and may range from mild to severe. At the mildest end of the spectrum is the child with delayed verbal (expressive) language who when tested has typical receptive language (can point to concepts and follow commands, indicating normal intake and understanding of language). At this point, assuming a typical level of intelligence, this child would be diagnosed with an expressive language delay. When this same child begins to talk, if many mispronunciations or articulation errors occur, a phonological disorder would be added to the diagnosis. The developmental language disorders increase in severity along the continuum so that receptive language may be delayed or the processing of language may be impaired, affecting understanding. When a child with a developmental language disorder enters school, the disorder may be reflected in difficulty learning to read or write or understanding what is read. These are called *language-based learning disabilities,* but they are caused by the underlying developmental language disorder.

developmental output failure *high output failure.* Describing the case of learning disabilities that do not cause difficulties in school until the demand for specific outputs (the volume of work produced) increases.

Developmental Play Assessment (DPA) Instrument A procedure used to assess the play activities of children with disabilities compared with those of their typically developing peers.

Developmental Profile 3 (DP-3) A 186-item questionnaire for use with children from birth to 11 or 12 years of age that yields developmental ages in five areas (physical, adaptive, social, cognitive, and communication skills) as well as a general development score.

developmental quotient (DQ) Developmental age (DA) divided by chronological age (CA): (DA/CA) = DQ. Use of the DQ is a very approximate way of describing a child's level of performance. Although not statistically accurate or psychometrically acceptable, the DQ may be helpful in counseling families.

Developmental Screening Inventory (DSI) A screening test for developmental disabilities in children 1–18 months of age. The revised form (the Revised Developmental Screening Inventory [R-DSI]) has been extended to an age range of 36 months and has a first-stage prescreening questionnaire, the Revised Parent Developmental Questionnaire (RPDQ; not to be confused with the Denver Prescreening Developmental Questionnaire [PDQ-II]).

developmental surveillance The monitoring of a child's developmental status, usually with the use of informal procedures such as charting achievement milestones during well-child visits to the pediatrician's office. The intensity of the surveillance can be adjusted to the presence of risk factors.

developmental systems model A comprehensive model of early intervention that addresses the diverse range of risks and disabilities in the population, incorporates scientific research on development and intervention, and addresses the practical and individual needs of children and families. This model has three core components: 1) a developmental framework that addresses multiple factors that act in concert to affect child outcomes (e.g., family characteristics, environmental and biologic risk, established disability), 2) integration (i.e., interdisciplinary services provided within integrated support systems and teams), and 3) inclusion (i.e., supports and services in natural environments).

Developmental Test of Visual-Motor Integration (DTVMI or DVMI) A measure used to assess perceptual motor ability in children 4–13 years of age. The child is asked to copy up to 24 geometric figures selected from other developmental tests. The figures are arranged in order of increasing difficulty, beginning with a simple figure such as a circle or square and becoming progressively more complex. Each design is scored on a pass/fail basis, and testing may be discontinued after three consecutive failures. A large number of scoring judgments are subjective. Administration time is 15 minutes.

developmental-difference controversy *See* developmental approach, difference approach, two-group approach.

developmentally appropriate practice (DAP) A set of standards by which the National Association for the Education of Young Children (NAEYC) accredits early childhood programs. The DAP addresses age, individual and cultural appropriateness of environmental arrangements, materials, activities, and teaching methods.

Devereux Behavior Rating Scales *Devereux Behavior Rating Scale–School Form (Devereux–School Form), Devereux Scales of Mental Disorders (DSMD).* Two screening instruments for the presence of emotional or behavior disorders in children: the Devereux Scales of Mental Disorders (DSMD) and the Devereux Behavior Rating Scale–School Form (Devereux–School Form). The DSMD has 110 items and can be completed in 15 minutes; there are forms for children 5–12 and 13–18 years. The Devereux–School Form has 40 items and can be completed in 5 minutes.

deviation intelligence quotient (IQ) score A normalized standard score with a mean (average) of 100 and a standard deviation of 15 or 16, depending on the instrument. The deviation IQ score expresses the deviation of the ratio IQ score from the mean ratio IQ score at each age level. It is not an absolute measure of performance but rather a measure of the relative position of a particular measure of intelligence on a bell (normal) curve.

devoicing The phonological process that occurs when a voiceless sound is substituted for a voiced sound.

dextroamphetamine (DA) sulfate Trade name, Dexedrine. A short-acting stimulant medication that is used in the treatment of attention-deficit/hyperactivity disorder in children and adults. Adderall is a mixture of dextroamphetamine and amphetamine salts. It is manufactured in multiples of 5 mg and is also available in sustained-action (XR) and very-long-acting (Vyvanse) forms. Side effects such as stomachache, headache, anorexia (loss of appetite), poor growth, and sleep problems can usually be managed by adjusting the dosage or timing of administration.

DHA *See* docosahexaenoic acid.

DHHS *See* Department of Health and Human Services.

diadochokinesis Rapid alternating movements (RAM). Rapidly bringing a limb into alternating positions, as of flexing and extending or of pronating and supinating. This facet of motor coordination can be tested in individuals by requesting that they pat their knees with the rapidly alternating palmar and dorsal (knuckle) surfaces of their hands. Performance of the dominant hand (the hand favored for writing and other activities) is usually slightly better than that of the nondominant hand. Difficulty performing this test is referred to as *dysdiadochokinesis. See also* dysdiadochokinesis.

diadochokinetic tasks The assessment of a child's production of rapidly alternating speech sounds.

diagnosis Both a process and an outcome. Diagnosis is the process of compiling and categorizing signs and symptoms (medical, emotional, psychological, or social) exhibited by an individual and reaching a classification based on that compilation. It also involves eliminating other possible categorizations and causes in order to identify a specific condition. The term *diagnosis* tends to be applied to the process engaged in by medical doctors. Social workers, psychologists, nurses, and educators more frequently use the term *assessment.* Diagnosis as the outcome of the process is the classification of the signs and symptoms into a more or less specific condition.

Diagnostic Achievement Battery–Third Edition (DAB-3) An individually administered academic achievement test that provides a profile of abilities in listening, speaking, reading, writing, mathematics, spoken and written language, and total achievement using 14 subtests: Story Comprehension, Characteristics, Synonyms, Grammatic Completion, Alphabet/Word Knowledge, Reading Comprehension, Capitalization, Punctuation, Spelling, Contextual Language, Story Construction, Phonemic Analysis, Math Reasoning, and Calculations. The test takes approximately 1 hour to administer.

***Diagnostic and Statistical Manual for Primary Care* (*DSM-PC*)** A coding manual that includes all of the mental health diagnoses for children and adolescents found in the *Diagnostic and Statistical Manual of Mental Disorders* (*DSM*) but further refines each diagnosis ("disorder") into two categories: 1) a "problem," in which many of the behaviors and symptoms of the disorder are found but in insufficient numbers or severity to qualify for a formal diagnosis of the disorder. Nevertheless, because the symptoms are causing difficulties, the problem can be diagnosed and addressed; and 2) a "variation," in which some of the features of the disorder are found but do not reach diagnostic severity and do not cause the child any problem, so the parent can be reassured that the suspect behaviors are typical variations.

***Diagnostic and Statistical Manual of Mental Disorders* (*DSM*)** The most commonly used classification system for atypical behaviors and mental disorders. Published by the American Psychiatric Association, the *DSM* is the system generally used in the United States for official diagnostic and record-keeping purposes. The first version of the *DSM* was published in 1952 and reflected a view of mental disorders as the reaction of the person to psychological, social, and biological factors. Subsequent editions have classifications compatible with the International Classification of Diseases (ICD) and do not specifically imply any particular theoretical framework for understanding nonorganic (emotionally or psychosocially caused) mental disorders. The *DSM* offers specific diagnostic criteria, a multiaxial classification system (five separate diagnostic dimensions rated), and an increased emphasis on descriptive determinants of mental and physical disorders. Inclusion of specific developmental disorders is considered controversial because many children with these disorders have no other form of mental disorder, and their inclusion suggests that they are psychiatric or emotional conditions. The *Diagnostic and Statistical Manual of Mental Disorders, Fourth Edition, Text Revision* (*DSM-IV-TR*; American Psychiatric Association, 2000), is the most current edition. Publication of the *DSM-V* is anticipated in 2013.

diagnostic assessment An assessment procedure that yields in-depth information about a specific skill.

Diagnostic Classification of Mental Health Disorders of Infancy and Early Childhood (DC:0-3) A functional (based upon the presenting behavior problem) rather than diagnostic classification of developmental problems in infants from birth to 3 years of age. The system focuses on intervention rather than diagnosis. Thus, in the DC:0-3, autism is classified as multisystem developmental disorder (MSDD).

Diagnostic Interview Schedule (DIS) A structured, standardized interview designed to elicit the information required to make certain *Diagnostic and Statistical Manual of Mental Disorders* (*DSM*) diagnoses. Versions of the DIS have been periodically created and contain procedures and probes for use in identifying specific clusters of symptoms not previously included in the schedule. The DIS can be administered by both professional and trained lay interviewers. The most recent DIS-IV and the Diagnostic Interview Schedule for Children (DISC) are available in computerized formats.

Diagnostic Reading Assessment (DRA) An individually administered test that measures a student's reading achievement in areas such as engagement, oral reading fluency, reading comprehension skills and strategies, and oral and written response to reading. It also provides teachers with the information they need to determine students' instructional and independent reading levels, which is critical to effective, differentiated reading instruction. An independent reading level is less than 1 error per 100 words read; an instructional reading level is 2–5 errors per 100 words read.

Diagnostic Reading Scales–Revised Edition (DRS-R) An integrated series of tests that provide a standardized evaluation of a student's silent and oral reading levels (from elementary level for poor readers through high school level for readers of typical ability) and auditory comprehension. The battery measures the nature and extent of word skills and provides an estimate of the student's instructional level. Sometimes referred to as the *Spache Diagnostic Reading Scale.*

diagnostic substitution The extent to which increases in the prevalence of one developmental disorder can be accounted for by corresponding decreases in other diagnostic categories. This often occurs with increasing diagnostic sensitivity. For example, when children who were previously diagnosed with intellectual disability were reclassified as having learning and attention disorders, this diagnostic substitution was incorrectly viewed as an epidemic of learning disabilities and attention-deficit/hyperactivity disorder (ADHD).

diagnostic teaching An informal method of assessing learning abilities when formal diagnostic methods are ineffective or incomplete. "Trial lessons," or "teaching probes," are used to simultaneously test and teach by recording and interpreting the student's reaction to and progress with the material. Diagnostic teaching can be used by therapists in many disciplines involved with people with developmental disabilities.

dial scan An augmentative communication device that looks like a clock face without numbers and with only one hand. Pictures are placed around the perimeter, and selection is made with a switch when the dial points to the desired object.

dialect A distinct form of a language spoken in a specific geographical area that varies uniquely from the official standard of the larger surrounding community in, for example, pronunciation, word usage, or grammar. A dialect is different enough to be regarded as a unique entity but not sufficiently different to be considered a separate language.

DIAL-3 *See* Developmental Indicators for Assessment of Learning–Third Edition.

dictionary *See* lexicon.

diarrhea Rapid movement of digestive material through the intestine, resulting in poor absorption of water, nutritive elements, and electrolytes. Abnormally frequent watery stools are also produced.

diaschisis theory The theory that the return of function following brain damage occurs as the nervous system recovers from a period of shock because the shock had widespread effects on areas of the brain not directly damaged. According to this theory, significant transient brain damage symptoms are attributed to nonspecific shock as opposed to specific brain lesions.

Diastat *See* rectal diazepam. *See also* diazepam, Valium.

diastema A split; a wide space between the upper central incisors (two front teeth).

diastematomyelia A developmental malformation in the spinal cord sometimes found with myelomeningocele. It consists of a splitting of the spinal cord without duplication. A bony spur is often found between the split pieces of cord. *See also* myelomeningocele.

diastrophic dysplasia (DTD) A disorder of cartilage and bone development characterized by short stature, club feet, malformed hands and joints, and often osteoarthritis. The external ears may swell in the newborn and remain deformed. DTD is particularly prevalent in Finland.

diathesis An inherited predisposition or tendency to develop certain diseases or disorders.

diazepam Trade name, Valium. A benzodiazepine used as an antianxiety drug, a muscle relaxant (for spasticity), and an anticonvulsant. It can be administered intravenously or rectally to stop prolonged, uncontrollable seizures. *See also* Diastat, rectal diazepam.

DIBELS *See* Dynamic Indicators of Basic Early Literacy Skills.

Dichotic Listening A test of speech lateralization (distinguishing sidedness) in children in which different stimuli are stereophonically presented to both ears (dichotic); the stimulus that is correctly discriminated indicates the relative efficiency of auditory

processing of the right versus the left cerebral hemispheres (halves of the brain), so that a right-ear advantage is consistent with left-hemisphere language localization.

diencephalic syndrome Progressive failure to thrive in a euphoric (happy), hyperactive, hyperalert infant. Diencephalic syndrome is associated with a brain tumor (usually astrocytoma). It first presents as a disorder of growth, with neurological and neurodevelopmental findings occurring later.

diet therapy The use of special diets (usually elimination diets that exclude specific foods, food groups, or food additives/supplements) to treat neurodevelopmental disorders. Eliminating dairy products and gluten in children with autism (casein-free or gluten-free diets) are the two most popular variants of this approach.

difference approach *defect theory.* The theory that people with moderate to profound intellectual disability as well as those with intellectual disability with evidence of organic (physical) brain damage may not behave and learn in the same way as mental age–matched controls without intellectual disability. This theory argues that there are qualitative as well as quantitative (mental age, intelligence quotient [IQ] score) differences between people with and without mental disabilities. *See also* developmental approach, two-group approach.

Differential Ability Scales–Second Edition (DAS-II) A cognitive abilities battery for use with children and adolescents 2;6–17;11 years. It is composed of 20 cognitive subtests in verbal, nonverbal, and spatial areas as well as diagnostic subtests that yield a profile of strengths and weaknesses. Administration time for the 63 items is 1 hour.

differential diagnosis For any medical symptom or problem, the list of possible causes or diagnoses to be considered. This list is used by clinicians to direct further evaluation, such as testing that will rule in (confirm) or rule out (remove from the list) some possibilities. A condition that is "high on the differential" is one that is considered more likely; a condition that is "low on the differential" is less likely to be the cause.

difficulty with pronunciation *See* articulation disorder.

diffusion tensor imaging (DTI) A magnetic resonance imaging (MRI) method that, when applied to the brain and spinal cord, can identify neural tracts (nerve pathways) based on the ability of water in the body to move only in certain directions in those tracts instead of diffusing (moving) without restriction. DTI typically generates images that show different tracts in different colors. Most often performed on a research basis, DTI has been used with people with cerebral palsy to identify which tracts affecting motor ability have been damaged.

diffusion weighted imaging (DWI) A magnetic resonance imaging (MRI) method that identifies areas of restricted diffusion (movement) of body water, which may indicate injury or edema (swelling). When applied to the brain or spinal cord with apparent diffusion coefficient (ADC) imaging, DWI can be used to localize strokes.

DiGeorge syndrome *See* velocardiofacial syndrome.

digit A finger or toe.

digit A number.

Digit Span A Wechsler (intelligence test) subtest in which the person repeats a series of numbers. Digit span forward, which measures auditory perception of simple stimuli, concentration, and short-term memory, is administered first, followed by digit span backward. Digit span backward

measures the ability to transform information and visuospatial imaging. *See* Visual Aural Digit Span Test.

digito-ocular sign of Franceschetti Poking at the eyes; eye boring or pressing the fists, knuckles, or fingers into the orbits of the eyes. This behavior is an example of a blindism, an activity common in preschool-age children who are severely visually impaired; it can also occur in children with intellectual disability who have no eye pathology. It is probably only mildly specific for visual impairment (as with ear boxing for hearing impairment) and occupies a position on the nonspecific spectrum of self-stimulatory/self-injurious behaviors. *See also* blindism.

diglossia A bifid or forked tongue; a congenital anomaly (malformation) of the tongue.

diglossia The ability of a young child to recognize that two varieties of a language are each to be used in different social settings.

Dilantin *See* phenytoin.

dimethylglycine (DMG) A dietary supplement used to treat autism.

DIP joint *See* distal interphalangeal joint.

diphenhydramine Trade name, Benadryl. An antihistamine that can be used to treat allergy symptoms. Because of its side effect of drowsiness, it has also been used to treat sleep disorders. Paradoxical reactions, side effects consisting of agitation and hyperactivity, are common in young children.

diphenylmethanes A group of minor tranquilizers that includes hydroxyzine hydrochloride (trade name, Atarax) and hydroxyzine pamoate (trade name, Vistaril) and that can be used for the treatment of anxiety.

diphtheria, tetanus, acellular pertussis (DTaP) *See* DPT.

diphthong A speech sound made by blending the production of one vowel sound to that of another. A diphthong may be written as two vowels, as in *coin,* or a single sound, as in *how.*

diplegia *Little disease.* Literally, "two palsy." A topographical (defined by location) subtype of spastic (increased tone) cerebral palsy that involves all four extremities (arms and legs), but the upper extremities less so than the lower extremities. Therefore, sitting is not as delayed as walking. Diplegia is a common sequela (result) to prematurity and can exhibit a relatively benign course. Toe walking, scissoring (crossed legs), strabismus (eyes turning in or out), and typical intelligence are common associated findings. Diplegia is probably the most common subtype of cerebral palsy.

diploid A full set of genetic material consisting of paired chromosomes, with one set of chromosomes from each parent. The human genome is diploid with 46 chromosomes—22 pairs of autosomes (chromosomes that are the same in males and females) and 1 pair of sex chromosomes.

diplomyelia A developmental malformation of the spinal cord sometimes found with myelomeningocele. It is a complete duplication of the cord over several segments. *See also* myelomeningocele.

diplophonia A voice disorder that occurs when two different pitches are produced simultaneously. The true vocal folds and the ventricular folds both vibrate.

diplopia Double vision; a neuro-ophthalmological finding.

DIR *See* Developmental, Individual-Difference, Relationship-Based Model.

Direct Instruction Systems for Teaching Arithmetic and Reading (DISTAR) A reading method that was developed as an outgrowth of a program established primarily as a compensatory effort to prepare disadvantaged African American children for entrance into traditional middle-class, white-oriented school programs. DISTAR is highly structured, fast paced, and directive. The beginning level starts with sound identification, left-to-right sequencing, and oral sound blending. Children learn to read by sounding out words, then by reading groups of words as complete thoughts. The second level expands the beginning level. Reading III, the third level, is described as a regular third-grade level or a remedial reading program. The first and second levels are designed for use in small groups, but much of level III is designed for use with 30 children at a time. A detailed teacher's guide is provided.

direct selection technique A technique in which an individual who uses augmentative and alternative communication (AAC) indicates the desired item directly from the selection set by means of applying physical pressure or depression, applying physical contact, and/or pointing.

direct services A system of providing therapy (e.g., occupational, physical, speech-language) services in the school system in which the therapist sees the child personally in order to provide therapy. The therapist has primary responsibility for providing those services. *See also* related services.

direct swallow therapy Swallow maneuvers that involve the presentation of food and/or liquid.

direction instruction A systematic, scripted form of instruction that emphasizes lessons that are paced, sequenced, and focused. Wilson Reading and Project Read are examples of direct instruction programs.

direction of gaze paradigm Looking at an unfamiliar object to note whether another person will follow the gaze toward that object.

directionality Internal awareness of the right and left sides of the body and the ability to apply this to the outside world. Individuals with directionality problems frequently reverse letters or numbers (*b* for *d* and vice versa) because they cannot consistently determine that the symbol is pointed in a particular direction. Difficulty with directionality is sometimes referred to as *right–left confusion.*

directive Describing intervention approaches in which the professional or parent literally tells the child what to do, in contrast with nondirective (naturalistic) methods, which are generally child directed (i.e., the adult follows the lead of the child and takes advantage of the child's own interests in order to address intervention goals) or client led.

direct-to-consumer (DTC) advertising The advertising and marketing of products (often pharmaceuticals [drugs]) directly to the consumer.

DIS *See* Diagnostic Interview Schedule.

disability Any restriction or lack of ability (resulting from an impairment) to perform an activity in the manner or within the range considered normal for a human being. Disability may be temporary or permanent, reversible or irreversible, and progressive or regressive. Disability may arise as a direct consequence of impairment or as a response (particularly psychological) by the individual to a physical, sensory, or other impairment. The World Health Organization (WHO) defines *disability* as the second level of a continuum: impairment (physical), disability (psychological), and handicap (social).

disability determination A process for determining eligibility for services or financial supports based on a medical or psycho-

logical condition or impairment. The criteria on which the disability determination is based may vary depending on the service or support being sought and the system within which that service is located. For example, the criteria for services for children applying for early childhood special education usually require a minimum level of developmental delay and residence in a circumscribed geographic location; financial criteria are not a part of this eligibility formula. However, if this same child were to be evaluated for receiving a disability income, the medical basis of the delay, the permanence of the condition, and the yearly income of the child's parents would all be part of the eligibility criteria. The criteria for some services and income supplements vary by state, whereas others are based on federal criteria that apply in all states.

disability etiquette Preferred word usage and behavior when writing about, meeting, socializing with, or assisting people with disabilities. General rules include emphasizing abilities, not limitations ("person first"); avoiding words with negative or judgmental connotations; demonstrating patience; and asking whether assistance is desired before giving it. The goal of enlightened language usage and treatment is to more fully integrate people with disabilities into society and to lessen misunderstanding and ignorance among the population without disabilities. *See also* person-first language.

disability, secondary *See* secondary disability.

DISC Diagnostic Interview Schedule for Children. *See* Diagnostic Interview Schedule (DIS).

discharge planning An interdisciplinary process to ease reintegration into the community after a major illness (accident, physical, or mental), usually involving hospitalization or intensive therapy. A discharge plan may include environmental modification (e.g., ramps), adaptive equipment (e.g., a walker), psychological counseling to facilitate adjustment, vocational rehabilitation for work adaptations, visiting nurses for ongoing care, and special transportation arrangements. A discharge plan should be safe and realistic and should allow the person to resume as typical a life as possible.

discipline An area of training and practice. Training, certification, and licensure vary greatly among disciplines, and the degree of independent (self-directed) practice allowed differs among states and clinical settings.

discipline Derived from the Latin *disciplino,* meaning "teaching and learning." In a broader sense, the disciplining of children is the systematic teaching and learning of social rules and norms first in the family setting and continuing in various educational settings. However, common usage of the word connotes limit setting, with rewards for compliance (obedience) and punishment for transgressions (rule breaking). Whereas discipline may include many methods for reaching the goal of self-control, punishment may sometimes be harmful in its long-term effects.

DISCO *See* Dyskinesia Identification System–Coldwater.

discrete trial A behavioral intervention method in which a therapist presents an antecedent or cue, the person responds, and the therapist presents a consequence. The antecedent or consequence can be changed to shape the response. In applied behavior analysis, data on cumulative discrete trials (discrete trials over time) are used to determine whether an individual has acquired a target skill, and the intervention is modified accordingly. Discrete trials are sometimes identified with applied behavior analysis as a whole.

disengagement A pattern of family relationships characterized by extreme emotional distance and detachment, rigid boundaries, and strong individual autonomy (independence) rather than family closeness. Although not necessarily pathological if all members are comfortable with such a style of relating, the pattern can indicate relationship difficulties, including little interaction or exchange of feeling and lack of a sense of belonging. Families with children who have developmental disabilities often develop a style of relating in which one parent (usually the mother) becomes overly close to the affected child to the exclusion of other family members, who may then drift into a pattern of disengagement.

disfluency Speech that is not fluent (i.e., does not have a smooth flow) but is not stuttering. *See also* dysfluency.

disinhibition The inability to resist performing dangerous and socially inappropriate behaviors.

disintegrative disorder of childhood *See* childhood disintegrative disorder.

disk grasp The position of the hand for holding an object such as a disk, in which the fingers are spread and only the pads of the fingers and thumb make contact with the edge of the object.

dislocation Complete and persistent displacement of a bone from its joint; dislocation is accompanied by pain, shortening (as of a leg dislocated from its hip socket), and loss of function. *See also* subluxation.

displaced speech Talk that refers to past or future events and not to the immediate present. In the development of children's language, references to the present develop earliest, followed by references to the past, and finally to the future.

disproportionality A term used in education to refer to the imbalanced number of students of a specific race or gender placed in special education programs relative to the overall number in the school or district.

dissociation The ability to separate two parts of the body in order to perform separate motor tasks with each.

dissociation A discrepancy (gap) between different areas of development. For example, a 5-year-old child with autism can have the language skills of a 2-year-old and the nonverbal problem-solving abilities of a 7-year-old.

dissociative identity disorder A psychiatric disorder characterized by two or more distinct personalities, each with its own identity, characteristics, and memories. The etiology (cause) for such extreme psychological fragmentation is severe physical, sexual, or emotional trauma that occurs under conditions that allow for no physical escape from the source of the trauma—so that the individual can only escape psychologically. The personalities can coexist with no awareness of one another. Previously known as *multiple personality disorder.*

distal Farthest from the center.

distal interphalangeal (DIP) joint The joint that connects the fingertip to the rest of the finger.

distal transverse palmar crease A horizontal flexion crease on the palm of the hand; the "heart line" of palmistry. Specific variations in this crease pattern occur in certain genetic syndromes and nonspecifically in other developmental disabilities.

distal transverse palmar crease

distal trisomy 10q Partial trisomy of the long arm of chromosome 10 (genetic material from three copies of the long arm of 10 instead of the usual two); a chromosomal disorder characterized by growth deficiency, severe intellectual disability, microcephaly (small head), a peculiar facies (facial features), camptodactyly (permanent flexion of the fingers or toes), and heart and kidney malformations.

DISTAR *See* Direct Instruction Systems for Teaching Arithmetic and Reading.

distocclusion *overbite.* A dental alignment in which the mandible (jaw) is too far back in comparison to the maxilla.

distortion product otoacoustic emission (DPOAE) Otoacoustic emissions that are evoked by two continuous sinusoids presented to the ear.

distributed practice A method of interspersing time between practice elements for rest rather than completing all elements in one continuous session.

Ditropan *See* oxybutynin.

divergence Divergence occurs when the eyes move in opposite directions outwardly away from the nose to observe an item that is not near; the opposite of convergence.

dizygotic twins *fraternal twins.* Two individuals born at the same time to the same mother who have different genetic makeups. Dizygotic twins occur when two ova (eggs) are fertilized at the same time. Such twins are no closer to each other genetically than two siblings born to the same parents from different pregnancies. *See also* monozygotic (MZ) twins.

DMD *See* Duchenne muscular dystrophy.

DME *See* durable medical equipment.

DMG *See* dimethylglycine.

DNA *See* deoxyribonucleic acid.

docosahexaenoic acid (DHA)   An omega-3 fatty acid found in high concentrations in the neural membranes of the brain. Variations in its concentration may cause subtle cognitive or behavioral differences in developing children. DHA may be used as a supplement in infant feedings.

Dolch Word List   A list, developed by Edward W. Dolch, of 220 words that constitute more than 65% of all words found in elementary reading materials and 50% of the words found in all reading materials. It includes prepositions, conjunctions, pronouns, adjectives, adverbs, and the most common verbs, but no nouns. Thus, the list comprises structure words that hold language together rather than content words; it is often taught as sight word vocabulary. Many of the words have irregular spellings and cannot be learned by picture clues.

dolichocephaly   A disproportionately long head; a low cephalic (head) index due to early closure of the sagittal (median, dividing the skull into the left and right sides) sutures, producing craniosynostosis (early fusion of skull sutures). A common skull shape in premature infants.

dolichocephaly

doll's eye sign   *Cantelli's sign, negative oculocephalic reflex.* Eye movements normally follow head movements; when the head is rotated and the eyes either do not follow or actually go in the opposite direction, then the "doll's eyes" phenomenon is present. This indicates the absence of the eye-righting (oculocephalic) reflex, reflecting probable brainstem injury in a comatose person.

domain   *area, topic.* The domains of child development typically include expressive language, receptive language, gross motor, fine motor, problem solving (adaptive), personal, and social and emotional.

Doman-Delacato approach   *See* patterning.

Doman-Delacato Developmental Profile   An instrument used to measure improvement during patterning therapy. *See also* patterning.

dominance   The tendency to use one side of the body more than the other, usually reflecting a preferred development of one side of the brain for particular functions. Hand dominance is typically evident by 2 years of age. Delay in the expression of dominance can occur with children who have learning disabilities or intellectual disability.

D1 trisomy syndrome   *See* trisomy 13 syndrome.

Donohoe syndrome   *leprechaunism.* A genetic syndrome characterized by growth deficiency, marked absence of subcutaneous (under the skin) fat, an elfin facies, severe failure to thrive, hypoglycemia (low blood sugar level), and early death. It is due to mutations in the insulin receptor gene. Inheritance is autosomal recessive. The name derives from the dwarf cobblers of Irish folklore.

Doose syndrome   Myoclonic-astatic epilepsy (MAE) of early childhood that is resistant to medication treatment. Attention and executive function are impaired. Outcomes range from complete remission to Lennox-Gastaut syndrome (a severe from of epilepsy).

dopa responsive dystonia (DRD)   *Segawa syndrome.* A movement disorder with autosomal dominant inheritance that produces dystonia. DRD starts in childhood and can be effectively treated by the medication levodopa or dopamine agonists (drugs that produce effects similar to those of dopamine, of which levodopa is a precursor).

dopamine (DA)   A neurotransmitter that plays an active role in motor systems and mood. There are a number of different dopamine receptors. DA is thought to be involved in many developmental disabilities, including attention-deficit/hyperactivity disorder (ADHD; DA insufficiency) and autism (DA excess). The stimulant medications used to treat ADHD increase the amount of DA present.

dopamine transporter gene (*DAT1*) A gene located on chromosome 5p 15.3 (p is the short arm of the chromosome) that is a marker for attention-deficit/hyperactivity disorder (ADHD).

dorsal The back; the opposite of ventral (the front).

dorsum The back; also the posterior or superior surface.

dorsum The middle portion of the tongue.

dosage effect The added effect of gene copies. The more copies of the gene that are present, the higher the levels of enzymes or proteins the gene controls, and the more striking or obvious the phenotype (the appearance of the trait controlled by that gene).

double blind A method of studying treatment outcomes in which neither the person giving and evaluating the treatment nor the person receiving the treatment is aware of whether active or inactive (placebo) treatment is being given.

double hemiplegia A type of spastic (increased muscle tone) cerebral palsy (disorder of movement and posture) in which both arms appear to be more severely involved than both legs. Because the functional and practical implications of this do not always differ significantly from quadriplegia (paralysis of all four extremities), the condition is sometimes described as a quadriplegia.

"dowager's hump" *See* kyphosis.

DO-WATCH-LISTEN-SAY A social and communication assessment and inter-vention curriculum for children with autism.

down regulation The process by which a cell decreases the quantity of a cellular component, such as ribonucleic acid (RNA) or a protein, in response to an external stimulus or decreases sensitivity, receptivity, and reactivity to another agent, such as a hormone or neurotransmitter.

Down syndrome (DS) *47,+21; 46(XX or XY),dter(14)t(14;21); trisomy G; trisomy 21.* A chromosomal condition characterized by hypotonia (low muscle tone), short stature, flat facial profile, epicanthal folds, upslanting palpebral fissures (eye slits), small ears, speckling (Brushfield spots) of the iris (the colored part of the eye), short fingers, single transverse palmar crease, cardiac defects, duodenal atresia (blockage of the small intestine near the stomach), atlantoaxial (neck bone) instability, thyroid disorders, conductive hearing loss, and intellectual disability. Because multiple systems are involved, the person can benefit from ongoing follow-up in an interdisciplinary DS specialty clinical setting. Most people with DS have trisomy 21, an extra chromosome 21, for a total chromosome count of 47 instead of the usual 46. Incidence is approximately 1 in 660 (1 in 1,500 for mothers younger than 30 years of age and 1 in 25 for mothers older than 45 years of age). The recurrence risk of DS is 1%, although it may be higher in the presence of a parental translocation (a rare genetic occurrence in which parts of two chromosomes swap places; this accounts for a very small percentage of infants with DS).

downers A slang term for legal or illegal drugs that depress the central nervous system (CNS). Effects can range from mellowing and causing sleepiness all the way to inducing coma. Such drugs include sedatives, alcohol, and some sleep medications.

DPA *See* Developmental Play Assessment Instrument.

DPOAE *See* distortion product otoacoustic emission.

DP-3 *See* Developmental Profile 3.

DPST *See* Dallas Preschool Screening Test.

DPT *DTaP, DTP.* Combined diphtheria, pertussis (whooping cough), and tetanus immunizations. Often offered in combination with vaccines for other diseases, such as polio.

DQ *See* developmental quotient.

DRA *See* Diagnostic Reading Assessment.

Dravet syndrome Severe myoclonic epilepsy of infancy in which complex febrile seizures progress to severe nonfebrile seizures and previously typical development either plateaus or regresses.

Draw-a-Man Test *See* Goodenough-Harris Drawing Test.

DRD *See* dopa responsive dystonia.

DRS-R *See* Diagnostic Reading Scales–Revised Edition

drug Any nonfood substance that affects living tissue.

drug holiday *drug-free period.* A period of discontinuing the use of a drug in order to reevaluate baseline (before or without treatment) behavior and drug effectiveness. The use of the term *holiday* unfortunately suggests that the drug was bad or unnecessary in the first place. This term sometimes refers to the withdrawal of behavior medication on weekends and during summer vacations.

DS *See* Down syndrome.

DSI *See* Developmental Screening Inventory.

DSM *See Diagnostic and Statistical Manual of Mental Disorders.*

DSMD Devereux Scales of Mental Disorders. *See* Devereux Behavior Rating Scales.

DSM-PC *See Diagnostic and Statistical Manual for Primary Care.*

DTaP Diphtheria, tetanus, acellular pertussis. *See* DPT.

DTC *See* direct-to-consumer advertising.

DTD *See* diastrophic dysplasia.

DTI *See* diffusion tensor imaging.

DTLA-4 *See* Detroit Tests of Learning Aptitude–Fourth Edition.

DTP *See* DPT.

DTR *See* deep-tendon reflex.

DTVMI *See* Developmental Test of Visual-Motor Integration.

Dubowitz Neurological Assessment A brief (10-minute) neurological screening that can be used to monitor the progress of central nervous system (CNS) insults in infants at high risk for brain damage.

Dubowitz Scale An instrument used to determine gestational age (Dubowitz score) by examining 11 physical characteristics and 10 neurological findings.

Dubowitz syndrome A genetic syndrome characterized by microcephaly (small head), eczema (skin rash), short stature, a distinctive facies (somewhat similar to that seen in people with fetal alcohol syndrome [FAS]), and a range of cognitive functioning from average intelligence to severe intellectual disability. Inheritance is autosomal recessive.

Duchenne muscular dystrophy (DMD) An X-linked, progressive, inherited muscle disease caused by mutations in the *DMD* gene, which affects the protein dystrophin. DMD is typically diagnosed only in boys about 4 years of age when they begin to lose motor skills, a process that progresses until death (usually by their early 20s), most often as a result of cardiorespiratory difficulties.

due process *See* impartial due process hearing.

duodenal atresia A congenital (present at birth) malformation of the first portion of the small intestine (nearest the stomach) with complete blockage. Duodenal atresia usually presents with bilious (stained with greenish bile) vomiting starting hours after birth. Unless surgically corrected, duodenal atresia can lead to death. This condition is more common among infants with Down syndrome.

duodenum The first part of the small intestine that connects the pylorus (the lower end of the stomach) to the jejunum (middle of the small intestine).

duplication A deoxyribonucleic acid (DNA) sequence that repeats within a chromosome and can encompass part of a gene, one gene, multiple genes, or a visible piece of chromosome.

duplication 3q dup(3)(q21–qter) A chromosomal disorder in which part of the long arm of chromosome 3 is duplicated three times. Features include craniosynostosis (early closure of skull bones), hypertrichosis (hairiness) and synophrys (eyebrows that meet in the middle), broad nasal root, upslanting palpebral fissures (eye slits), prominent maxilla, long philtrum (upper lip groove), cleft palate, webbed neck, and unusual ears. In addition, there are hypoplastic (underdeveloped) nails, single transverse palmar creases (horizontal hand creases), and clubfoot. Heart defects, urinary tract anomalies, and skeletal anomalies are common. About one third of individu-

als die in the first year. Survivors have severe intellectual disability and growth problems.

duplication 4p dup(4)(p12–pter) Trisomy (extra copy) of the short arm of chromosome 4. A genetic syndrome that causes microcephaly (small head) with a low forehead; marked supraorbital (above the eyes) ridges; synophrys (eyebrows that meet in the midline); a large mouth; large, atypical ears; hypoplastic (underdeveloped) toenails and fingernails; hypospadias (displaced penis opening); and cryptorchidism (undescended testes). There may be small eyes and coloboma (defect of the eye), cleft lip, skin tags, clubfoot, and extra digits. Individuals have severe growth deficiency, severe intellectual disability, severe language impairments, and seizures.

duplication 6q dup(6)(q25–qter) *trisomy 6 long arm.* A genetic syndrome caused by duplication of part of the distal (farthest from the center) long arm of chromosome 6 that includes microcephaly (small head) with a flat occiput (back of the head); a prominent forehead and flat facial features; downslanting, almond-shaped palpebral fissures (eye slits); hypertelorism (widely spaced eyes); carp mouth; thin lips; short philtrum (upper lip groove); low-set ears; short neck; and prominent webbing from the mandible (jaw) to the sternum. Cleft lip and/or cleft palate and contractures of the joints and scoliosis (back curvature) may occur. Intellectual disability is severe.

duplication trisomy 9p *tetrasomy 9p.* A genetic condition usually caused by duplication of part or all of the short arm of chromosome 9. Clinical findings include poor growth, severe intellectual disability, microcephaly (small head), hypertelorism (widely spaced eyes), downslanting palpebral fissures (eye slits), prominent ears, short digits with hypoplastic (underdeveloped) nails, and fifth fingers with a single crease.

durable medical equipment (DME) Medical equipment that is designed for repeated, long-term use; improves function or slows further deterioration of a physical condition; and costs more than $100.

durable power of health attorney A document that appoints a person or organization to make health care decisions for someone who is incapacitated. Powers of attorney can be made "durable" by adding certain text stating that the document will remain in effect or take effect if the individual becomes mentally incompetent.

dwarfism Outdated term with a pejorative (negative) connotation referring to extremely short stature on the basis of endocrinological (hormonal) or genetic etiology (cause). Although poor growth is frequently associated with severe developmental disorders, in general most individuals with syndromes typically referred to under the rubric of dwarfism exhibit typical intelligence and no associated developmental disabilities.

DWI *See* diffusion weighted imaging.

dyad Twosome; pair; a couple treated as a single unit.

Dycem Non-Slip Nonslip material used to cover handles and trays.

Dyggve-Melchior-Clausen syndrome A genetic syndrome characterized by a disproportionately short trunk; short stature; microcephaly (abnormally small head); intellectual disability; and a variety of bone and joint abnormalities, including atlantoaxial (neck bones) instability. Inheritance is autosomal recessive.

Dyke-Davidhoff-Masson syndrome A nongenetic syndrome characterized by facial asymmetry (with x-ray confirmation of the underlying asymmetrical skull), contralateral hemiplegia (paralysis of the opposite half of the body), seizure disorder, and varying degrees of intellectual disability.

dynamic Describing a flexible or nonfixed orthopedic deformity characterized by abnormal positioning of the extremities (arms or legs) that can be corrected by passive repositioning.

dynamic ankle–foot orthosis (DAFO) A flexible brace for the foot, ankle, or lower leg that allows variable flexibility at the joint and provides gait support for people with conditions such as foot drop, hypotonia, and equinus (toe walking).

dynamic assessment An evaluation method that relies on the test–teach–test model to determine how children *learn* during the assessment process and whether they are capable of learning the concepts presented.

dynamic augmentative and alternative communication (AAC) display A computer screen display with electronically produced visual symbols that, when activated, automatically change the selection set on the screen to a new set of programmed symbols.

Dynamic Indicators of Basic Early Literacy Skills (DIBELS) A set of procedures and measures for assessing the acquisition of a variety of reading and literacy skills from kindergarten through sixth grade. The DIBELS provides outcome measures in five areas: Phonological Awareness, Alphabetic Principle, Fluency with Connected Text, Vocabulary, and Comprehension. These are designed to be short (1 minute) measures that can be used regularly for monitoring the development of early reading and literacy skills.

dynamometer An instrument used to measure aspects of grip and pinch strength.

dysarthria Generic name for motor speech problems caused by various impairments of the central or peripheral nervous systems. Faulty speech sound production, characterized by imprecise consonants and irregular articulation, is typical of the disorder.

Respiration, voice, fluency (smooth flow of speech), and prosody (melody of speech) are usually hindered as well. Both volitional and automatic actions, including chewing, swallowing, and other oral motor movements, may also be affected. Children with cerebral palsy can show marked delays in achieving articulation comparable to that of their same-age peers. Most adults with dysarthria acquire it as the result of strokes or degenerative disease after a lifetime of normal speech. *Anarthria,* or the inability to articulate speech sounds at all, is the result of severe neuromuscular involvement.

dysautonomia *See* Riley-Day syndrome.

dyscalculia Mathematics disability. A learning disability in which mathematics is the only or most severely involved subject area. Dyscalculia that begins in the fourth grade (with word problems) may be secondary to a reading disability. Mathematics errors, such as misreading operational signs (addition for subtraction) or reversing numerical order, may reflect a mathematics problem, a reading problem, or attention-deficit/ hyperactivity disorder. Difficulty with mathematics often reflects right-brain impairment. *See also* mathematics disorder.

dyscrasia Blood abnormality, possibly caused by a drug.

dysdiadochokinesis A neurological finding of difficulty performing rapidly alternating movements, such as pronation (turning the palms facing down) and supination (turning the palms facing up) of the arms. *See also* diadochokinesis.

dyseidetic One of the three subtypes of dyslexia (reading disability)—the other two being dysphonetic and mixed—identified by the Boder Test of Reading–Spelling Patterns. These subtypes are based on specific reading–spelling error patterns. Dyseidetic readers show strength in the auditory analytical function and weakness

in the visual gestalt (awareness of the whole) function. In other words, they have poor memory for the way groups of letters and words look and read laboriously, sounding out familiar as well as unfamiliar words. They write good phonetic (representing sounds) equivalents of words that they cannot read. For example, *talk* might be read as "talc" and spelled as "tok." The mixed group exhibits weaknesses in both the visual gestalt and the auditory analytical functions, with resulting disability in developing both sight vocabulary (words recognized on sight without having to be sounded out) and phonic skills (the ability to sound out written words). *See also* dysphonetic.

dyseidetic errors Referring to spelling words phonetically (according to their sounds) yet incorrectly.

dysexecutive syndrome *See* frontal lobe syndrome.

dysfluency Speech characterized by an interruption in the flow of sounds; the speech pattern of people who stutter. Such speech is marked by prolongations, pauses, repetitions, and other rhythmic disturbances. Dysfluency can refer to the developmental hesitation of a child or the dysprosody (loss of melody of speech) of an individual who stutters. *See also* disfluency.

dysfunction Abnormality or malfunctioning of a system.

dysfunction in sensory integration The inability to modulate, discriminate, coordinate, or organize sensation in order to adapt efficiently to the environment. Originally called *sensory integration* by A. Jean Ayres (1920–1988).

dysfunction of attention, motor function, and perception (DAMP) A neurobehavioral syndrome characterized by impairments in attention, motor coordination, and perception; it has also been called minimal brain dysfunction (MBD) with elements of attention deficit disorder (ADD), developmental coordination disorder (DCD), and learning disability (LD). DAMP reflects European usage and is more inclusive than attention-deficit/hyperactivity disorder (ADHD).

dysfunctional family A family that is unable to effectively carry out its tasks or emotional functions. Such families tend to respond to stress situations with rigid, unyielding behavior rather than effectively accommodating the demands of the situation. Frequently, boundaries among individual members are too loose, too rigid, or too distant for cooperation and support to occur. When stress levels reach unmanageable proportions, one member will develop symptoms that force the family to start treatment.

dysgeusia An impairment in taste that ranges from distorted taste to a complete loss of taste.

dysgraphia Poor pencil-and-paper (handwriting and drawing) skills for age. Dysgraphia can be an isolated problem that reflects poor motor planning or execution, or a component of a developmental coordination disorder (DCD) that affects written language. Dysgraphia present only when rushing is characteristic of attention-deficit/hyperactivity disorder.

dyskinesia A term used to describe movement disorders associated with cerebral palsy, including athetosis, dystonia, choreiform movements, ballismus, and tremor.

Dyskinesia Identification System–Coldwater (DISCO) A 34-item movement rating scale used in the diagnosis of dyskinesia.

dyslexia Reading disability. The term *dyslexia* is loosely used to describe any learning disability in which reading, writing, and spelling are more severely involved than other subject areas. In the strictest sense, *dyslexia* refers to a pure reading disorder with no other academic subjects involved and no attentional or other neurological problems. Such pure dyslexia is rare, is often familial, and occurs predominantly among males. There are no diagnostic markers, such as letter reversals, specific to dyslexia. Current research understands the primary underlying deficit in dyslexia to be a phonological processing disorder.

dysmaturity The impact of placental insufficiency (a defect in the placenta such that it does not adequately meet the developing fetus's needs) on a term or preterm infant. This impact may include generalized growth retardation; dry, peeling, cracked skin; meconium staining; and a wide-awake, hyperalert expression.

dysmetria A sign of cerebellar dysfunction assessed using the method of past-pointing, in which a person is unable to accurately determine spatial distance or orientation when reaching for an object.

dysmorphic *See* syndromic.

dysmorphology The study (*-ology*) of abnormalities (*dys-*) of shape, form, or structure (*morph*). In human beings, most disorders of morphogenesis (the development of form and structure) are congenital (present from birth)—either genetic or the result of other prenatal influences. The visual recognition of dysmorphic features is an important component in the identification of genetic and other syndromes (syndromology), sequences, and associations. A cumulative number of mild superficial malformations (minor dysmorphic features) may be of developmental significance even in the absence of an identifiable syndrome.

dysnomia A weakness or inability to name objects (word finding), not as severe as anomia; a frequent component of a language or learning disability.

dysphagia Difficulty swallowing. Dysphagia is one of the signs of oromotor (affecting the muscles of the mouth) dysfunction that is common in cerebral palsy and can contribute to feeding disorders and poor growth.

dysphagia screening A prevention procedure that provides indirect evidence that a swallowing disorder likely exists. This procedure does not inform as to the anatomy and physiology of the disorder, indicate the severity or stage of swallowing impaired, or indicate why the person is aspirating.

dysphasia *See* aphasia.

dysphonetic One of the three subtypes of dyslexia (reading disability)—the other two being dyseidetic and mixed—identified by the Boder Test of Reading–Spelling Patterns. Dysphonetic readers show strengths in the visual gestalt function and weaknesses in the auditory analytical function. In other words, they typically have a functional, although relatively limited, sight word vocabulary but lack phonic word analysis skills (the ability to sound out words). Their most striking error is semantic substitution (i.e., substituting a word similar in meaning to the original word but unlike it phonetically, such as *sweater* for *jacket*). Their misspellings are phonetically inaccurate and include such errors as extraneous letters, omitted syllables, auditory discrimination errors, syllable reversals, letter-order errors, and other auditory sequencing errors. *See also* dyseidetic.

dysphonia A disorder of voice quality characterized by weak or hoarse voice.

dysphoria An acute (sudden), transient (temporary) mood change in the direction of sadness and depression.

dysplasia Abnormal development in shape and size, especially at the cellular level.

dyspraxia Partial loss of or failure to develop voluntary movements, not explainable by intellectual disability.

dysraphism An abnormality of the axial skeleton, including the skull (cranial) and spinal column. Dysraphic states include anencephaly (no brain or absent top of skull), myelomeningocele, and duplications or split spinal cords (diastematomyelia or diplomyelia). These disorders generally involve neurological problems as well as skeletal abnormalities, begin early in fetal life, and have a genetic component. *See also* myelomeningocele.

dysrhythmia Stammering due to incoordination between breathing and speech.

dyssemia A disorder of socialization characterized by problems with respecting boundaries, interpreting gestural language (including facial expressions), and modulating vocal loudness and rhythm.

dysthymic disorder A specific depressive disorder characterized by a constant and chronic disturbance of mood, although less severe than in major depression, involving either sad or irritable mood (particularly in children and adolescents) for at least a year (2 years for adults). Although there may be brief periods of relief, dysthymic depression is present for most of the day more days than not. In addition, there may be other associated symptoms, including appetite disturbances, sleep disturbances, chronic fatigue, concentration and problem-solving difficulties, low self-esteem, and feelings of helplessness and hopelessness.

dystocia Abnormal labor; usually refers to maternal structural abnormalities of the uterus that give rise to premature or prolonged labor.

dystonia (DYT) An abnormality of muscle tone that often leads to unusual posturing (dystonic movements). These involuntary spasms can be painful. A number of transient DYT syndromes have been described in premature infants, and DYT is one of the complications of the antipsychotic drugs used to treat severe maladaptive behaviors in people with developmental disabilities.

dystonia musculorum deformans A disorder, frequently genetic, of movement and posture characterized by progressive, intermittent, or continuous muscle spasms, including torticollis (twisted stiff neck).

dystonic attack *opisthotonic attack.* An intermittent, exaggerated, involuntary total body extension pattern with the head thrown backward in an arching posture. These episodes occur in children with severe motor abnormalities (e.g., cerebral palsy), almost always when the child is supine (lying on the back) or the head has been extended (neck tilted back), so that the episodes can be mistaken for seizures. Modifications in handling usually decrease the incidence of such pseudoseizures.

dystopia canthorum Lateral displacement of the inner canthi (corners) of both eyes.

DYT *See* dystonia. This acronym is often used to name different subtypes of dystonia, which are classified by number (e.g., DYT-1).

E trisomy *See* trisomy 18 syndrome.

EAP *See* employee assistance program.

ear rotation Rotation of the longitudinal axis of the external ear (pinna).

Early and Periodic Screening, Diagnosis, and Treatment (EPSDT) A federal program that funds routine medical and developmental services for Medicaid-eligible people younger than 21 years of age. It is the child health component of Medicaid that covers periodic screening, vision, dental, and hearing services.

Early Childhood Outcomes (ECO) Center Funded through the Office of Special Education Programs (OSEP), the ECO Center is a collaborative effort of SRI International, the University of North Carolina's Frank Porter Graham Child Development Institute, RTI International, and the University of Connecticut. Originally funded in 2003, the ECO Center assists states in designing and implementing outcome measurement systems for early intervention (EI) and early childhood special education (ECSE) programs that meet federally mandated reporting criteria. The center has three goals: knowledge development, technical assistance and dissemination, and leadership and coordination.

Early Coping Inventory (ECI) A 48-item observational measure of coping skills for use with children with a chronological or developmental age of 4–36 months.

Early Detection Inventory (EDI) A screening test for use with children between 3;6 and 7;6 years in the areas of motor, social, behavior, and academic skills.

Early Head Start (EHS) A federal program of the U.S. Department of Health and Human Services, Administration for Children and Families, EHS is a community-based program for pregnant women and for low-income families with infants and toddlers. Its mission is to promote healthy prenatal outcomes for pregnant women, to enhance the development of very young children, and to promote healthy family functioning.

Early Hearing Detection and Intervention Program (EHDI) A program funded by the U.S. Department of Health and Human Services, Centers for Disease Control and Prevention, EHDI has three components: screening (initial infant hearing tests); audiological evaluation (confirmation of hearing loss); and early intervention (including medical treatment, early intervention services, and family support) to enhance the communication, cognitive, and behavior skills children need to achieve academic and social success.

early infantile autism *See* autism.

Early Intensive Behavioral Intervention The gold standard for treating young children with autism; *early* refers to several years prior to age 5 years; *intensive* refers to a significant number of hours per week of one-to-one teaching.

Early Intervention (EI) A program that offers federally mandated specialized health, educational, and therapeutic services to young children (birth through age 2) who have a diagnosed physical or mental condition (with a high probability of resulting in a developmental delay), who have an existing delay, or who are at risk for developing a delay or special need that may affect their development or impede their education. Evaluation and assessments are provided by a multidisciplinary team at no cost to the parent. EI services were reauthorized under under Part C of the Individuals with Disabilities Education Improvement Act (IDEA) of 2004 (PL 108-446). In order for a state to participate in the program, it must ensure that early intervention services will be available to every eligible child and his or her family. All states and eligible territories participate in the program. Because states have some discretion in setting eligibility criteria, eligibility and services vary from state to state. The lead agency responsible for Part C also varies by state. Early intervention services can take place in a variety of settings, with a preference for natural environments (in-home rather than center-based services). Also known as the Program for Infants and Toddlers with Disabilities.

early intervention The philosophy that prompt detection and treatment of delays and disorders is more likely to produce optimal long-term outcomes and reduce the likelihood or degree of disability.

early intervention amendments to the Education of the Handicapped Act (EHA) of 1970 (PL 91-230) The entitlement to a free appropriate public education (FAPE) is extended to children ages 3–5 years via legislation. Children younger than 5 years are not included in special education legislation until the passage of the Education of the Handicapped Act Amendments, which invite states to participate in a coordinated system of services for infants and toddlers under Part H of PL 101-476. *See* Education

of the Handicapped Act Amendments of 1986 (PL 99-457), Education of the Handicapped Act (EHA) of 1970 (PL 91-230), Individuals with Disabilities Education Act Amendments (IDEA) of 1997 (PL 105-17), Individuals with Disabilities Education Improvement Act (IDEA) of 2004 (PL 108-446).

Early Intervention Development Profile (EIDP) A criterion-referenced assessment scale for use with infants from birth to 30 months; its six scales tap perceptual and fine motor, cognitive, language, social and emotional, adaptive, and gross motor skills.

early interventionist A professional trained to assess, plan, and implement a specialized intervention program to meet the developmental needs of a young child (birth to 3 years) and his or her family. This individual may be from a variety of professional backgrounds depending on the needs of the child and the family.

Early Language and Literacy Classroom Observation Tool (ELLCO) A procedure used to assess literacy and language practices in prekindergarten to third-grade classrooms. ELLCO contains three components: the Literacy Environment Checklist (a 15- to 20-minute orientation to the classroom), the Classroom Observation and Teacher Interview (a 20- to 45-minute observation, 10-minute interview), and the Literacy Activities Rating Scale (a 10-minute book reading and writing summary). Administration time is approximately 1–1.5 hours.

Early Language Milestones Scale–Second Edition (ELM-2) A language screening test for children from birth to 3 years of age, as well as older children with developmental delays whose functioning is within this age range. The ELM-2 uses the same format as the Denver Developmental Screening Test (DDST) and divides language into three streams: auditory expressive, auditory receptive, and visual. Administration time is less than 10 minutes.

Early Learning Accomplishment Profile (Early LAP or ELAP) A criterion-referenced assessment tool for children birth to 36 months that measures developmental attainment in the areas of gross motor, fine motor, cognitive, language, self-help, and social-emotional skills. The Early LAP adapts readily for use with children with disabilities and is linked to learning activities.

Early Motor Pattern Profile (EMPP) A motor screening test to be used with infants born prematurely at the corrected ages of 6 and 12 months. The 15 items test both primitive reflexes and other neurological signs. The EMPP has high sensitivity and specificity for the prediction of cerebral palsy.

Early Screening Inventory–Revised (ESI-R) A developmental screening test used to identify children 3–6 years of age who will need special education intervention. There is a preschool version (ESI-P) for children 3;0–4;5 years and a kindergarten version (ESI-K) for children 4;6–5;11 years. The instrument includes a parent questionnaire. Sometimes referred to as the *Meisels* after the test author Samuel J. Meisels.

Early Screening Profile (ESP) A comprehensive screening instrument for use with children ages 2;0–6;11 years. The ESP yields standard scores in cognitive/language, motor, and self-help/social areas to identify children at risk or gifted children.

Early Start Denver Model Curriculum Checklist for Young Children with Autism (ESDM) A comprehensive assessment instrument repeated every 12 weeks to identify intervention goals across multiple developmental skills in toddlers and preschoolers with autism.

ears, nose, and throat (ENT) *See* otolaryngology.

EASIC-3 *See* Evaluating Acquired Skills in Communication–Third Edition.

Easter Seals Society A private service organization that raises funds for children and adults with disabilities. Founded in 1919, this national organization's mission is to help people with disabilities achieve independence through the provision of rehabilitative services, technical assistance, disability prevention, advocacy, and public education. The Easter Seals Society publishes *The Communicator* and other informational materials.

eating disorders A group of problematic eating patterns with accompanying psychological symptoms; the disorders include anorexia nervosa, bulimia nervosa, and binge eating disorders that can result in poor health and even death when continued for an extended period of time. Eating disorders are much more common in girls and women than boys and men and are more prevalent in middle- to upper-class individuals.

EBF *See* electroencephalographic biofeedback.

EBP *See* evidence-based practice.

ECBI *See* Eyberg Child Behavior Inventory & Sutter-Eyberg Student Behavior Inventory–Revised.

eccentric power The ability to resist force as a muscle is lengthened.

ecchymosis A bruise or contusion. The skin discoloration in stages of healing (from red, through blue and brown, to yellow) that suggests the age of the injury. Ecchymosis can be due to accidents, abuse, bleeding disorders, and other disease processes that cause blood to escape from vessels into surrounding tissue.

ECHO *See* Extended Care Health Option.

echolalia *parroting.* Repeating words, phrases, and sentences. Echolalia can be immediate or delayed, with the latter being more problematic. In children without disabilities, this phase of imitation is brief and transitory (temporary), occurring between the ages of 18 and 24 months. In children with intellectual disability, language disorders, and autism, the echolalic phase can be more prominent and prolonged and can be correlated with a mental age closer to 30 months. Echolalia spontaneously observed in clinical situations should give rise to a more detailed assessment of language function.

echopraxia The tendency to mimic the actions of others; sometimes found in Gilles de la Tourette syndrome.

ECI *See* Early Coping Inventory.

eclampsia A condition in pregnancy that requires urgent treatment and delivery of the infant. It is preceded by preeclampsia (high blood pressure, protein in the urine, and edema [swelling]) and characterized by seizures. Eclampsia can affect the oxygen delivered to the brain of the infant and can contribute to later developmental disorders. *See also* preeclampsia.

ECMO therapy *See* extracorporeal membrane oxygenation therapy.

ECO *See* Early Childhood Outcomes Center.

ECochG *See* electrocochleography.

ecogenetic disorder A disease caused by the interaction of a genetic predisposition with one or more environmental factors.

ecological assessment An assessment approach that emphasizes the relationship between the individual and the environment; it generally involves observing the individual in his or her natural contexts (i.e., usual settings, such as home or school). Such an assessment describes and quantifies the environment in terms of the resources (strengths) and difficulties (barriers) facing the child.

ecological curriculum An educational curriculum that focuses on the interactions between the student and his or her environments. An ecological curriculum is often part of transition services that prepare students for adult life.

ectodermal Referring to parts of the body derived from the outermost layer (ectoderm) of embryonic cells. Human ectodermal derivatives include skin, hair, teeth, and the nervous system. Their common origin in the embryo suggests a rationale for the association between minor dysmorphic features (small physical differences) and mild learning, attention, and behavior disorders, as well as more severe developmental problems.

ectodermal dysplasia A group of genetic syndromes characterized by the involvement of ectodermal derivatives (i.e., hair, teeth, and nails). Despite dysmorphic (atypical) facies, neurodevelopmental problems (other than an occasional hearing impairment) are uncommon.

ectomorph Someone with a tall, thin body type or build. *See also* asthenic body type, endomorph, mesomorph.

ectopia lentis Dislocation of the lens of the eye, the tendency to which can be inherited in isolation or as part of several syndromes, such as Marfan syndrome or homocystinuria.

ectrodactyly–ectodermal dysplasia and cleft lip/palate syndrome (EEC1) A syndrome characterized by cleft lip; ectrodactyly (failure of the fingers or toes to develop) involving all four extremities (lobster claw anomaly); absent tear duct openings, keratoconjunctivitis (inflamed eyes), and photophobia (sensitivity to light); hypopigmentation (lack of color) of the skin and hair; and other less frequent anomalies. EEC1 has autosomal dominant inheritance with incomplete penetrance and variable expressivity.

ectropion Eversion (turning out) of the eyelid. Congenital (present from birth) ectropion is seen in one third of individuals with Down syndrome.

eczema A skin disorder characterized by erythema (redness), vesiculation (blisters), flaking or scaling, and pruritus (itching); it sometimes becomes exudative (weeping). Often a sign of atopy (allergy), eczema is also a component of many syndromes.

ED *See* emotional disability.

EDCD *See* Elderly or Disabled with Consumer-Direction Waiver.

edema Fluid accumulation with swelling.

edetate calcium disodium *calcium ethylenediaminetetraacetic acid (EDTA).* Trade name, Versenate. An agent used to treat heavy metal (lead, mercury, zinc, cadmium, manganese, and iron) poisoning by chelating (binding to the metal in the body). The combination of the chelating agent and the heavy metal can then be excreted (expelled from the body).

EDF *See* executive dysfunction.

EDI *See* Early Detection Inventory.

EDPA *See* Erhardt Developmental Prehension Assessment.

EDS *See* Ehlers-Danlos syndrome.

EDTA *See* ethylenediaminetetraacetic acid.

educable mentally handicapped (EMH) *See* educable mentally retarded (EMR).

educable mentally retarded (EMR) *educable mentally handicapped (EMH).* Anti-quated term for people with mild intellectual disability.

Education for All Handicapped Children Act of 1975 (PL 94-142) A federal law that grew out of and strengthened previous acts, including the Education of the Handicapped Act (EHA) of 1970 (PL 91-230), Title VI of the Education of the Handicapped Act Amendments of 1974 (PL 93-380), and similar legislation. PL 94-142 became fully effective in September 1978 and was designed to ensure that all children with disabilities had available to them a free appropriate public education (FAPE). PL 94-142 also provides for impartial and objective decision making, appropriate educational funding, individualized education programming, accountability at all levels of government, and federal financial assistance to state and local school districts. Major provisions of the law include 1) the process for determining that a child has a disability and is in need of special education and related services; 2) the development of an individualized education program (IEP) to meet the unique needs of the child with a disability, for example by providing related services that may be necessary to assist the child in benefiting from special education services; 3) a requirement that students be placed in the least restrictive environment (LRE) that addresses their needs; and 4) creation of safeguards to be used by parents or guardians of children with disabilities. These safeguards allow parents or guardians to examine relevant records on the identification, evaluation, and educational placement of their child and require that parents or guardians be given prior written notice when an educational agency changes or refuses to change the identification, evaluation, or educational placement of the child. PL 94-142 is the core of federal funding for special education. In 1990, PL 94-142 was reauthorized and expanded under PL 101-476 and was renamed the Individuals with Disabilities Education Act (IDEA) of 1990.

The law's name reflected a change in terminology: PL 101-476 uses person-first language, replacing *handicapped children* with *individuals with disabilities*. PL 101-476 was reauthorized as the Individuals with Disabilities Education Act Amendments (IDEA) of 1997 (PL 105-17) and then in 2004 as the Individuals with Disabilities Education Improvement Act (IDEA) of 2004 (PL 108-446). *See also* free appropriate public education (FAPE), learning disability (LD), least restrictive environment (LRE), procedural safeguards, related services, special education.

Education of the Handicapped Act Amendments of 1974 (PL 93-380) Amendments to the Elementary and Secondary Education Act (ESEA) of 1965 (PL 89-10) that include a variety of changes to existing federal education programs and contain two important laws. The first is Title VI of the Education of the Handicapped Act Amendments of 1974 (PL 93-380). This law requires states to establish a timetable for achieving full educational opportunities for all children with disabilities. The act includes procedural safeguards to be used in identifying, evaluating, and placing children with disabilities. It mandates that children be integrated into general classes when feasible and requires that testing and evaluation materials be chosen and used on a nondiscriminatory basis. The second major law, an amendment to the Family Educational Rights and Privacy Act (FERPA) of 1974 (PL 93-380), also called the *Buckley Amendment*, gives parents of students younger than the age of 18, as well as students 18 years of age and older, the right to examine and comment on the records contained in the student's personal file. When a file contains material the parent or eligible student views as inaccurate, misleading, or in violation of the student's rights, provisions are made to challenge and remove the information in question. If school staff and parents disagree about the accuracy or relevance of material, mecha-

nisms for a hearing are stipulated. FERPA applies to all students, including those in postsecondary education. PL 93-380 begins to focus upon and stress the need to fully educate all children with disabilities and to ensure their active participation in the educational process.

Education of the Handicapped Act Amendments of 1983 (PL 98-199) Federal legislation that arranges and reauthorizes discretionary programs for individuals with disabilities by expanding the means for providing transition services from school to work for students with disabilities, establishing and funding parent training and information centers to help parents guarantee their children's rights under the Education for All Handicapped Children Act of 1975 (PL 94-142), and providing financial incentives for increasing research on and implementation of preschool education and early intervention programs. All of these programs fall under the auspices of the Office of Special Education Programs (OSEP), which replaced the Bureau of Education for the Handicapped (BEH).

Education of the Handicapped Act Amendments of 1986 (PL 99-457) Federal legislation that lowers the age of eligibility for special education and related services for all children with disabilities to 3 years of age. This initiative is known as *Section 619 in Part B* and mandated that, in order to receive federal funding, states had to begin providing services to preschool children by October 1991. All states have since complied. This act also includes a Part H, which creates a comprehensive early intervention program for infants, toddlers, and their families. This program is directed to the needs of children from birth to 3 years of age who are identified as needing early intervention services and requires the development and implementation of an individualized family service plan (IFSP) for each participating child and his or her family. State definitions of eligibility under this program may vary, but to receive federal funding a state must have an acceptable service delivery system in place by its fifth year of participation in the program. PL 99-457 reiterates the requirements and stipulations found in the Education of the Handicapped Act (EHA) of 1970 (PL 91-230), its amendments, and the Education for All Handicapped Children Act of 1975 (PL 94-142), including the rights of children and youth with disabilities—regardless of severity—to a free appropriate public education (FAPE) and to an individualized education program (IEP) or IFSP developed and implemented to enumerate the special education, early intervention, and related services that the child, youth, and/or family is to receive. Parents' rights are also delineated, including their rights to participate in all aspects of the identification, evaluation, and placement processes; to give consent for initial evaluation and placement; and to dispute any aspect of the process with specified due process procedures. PL 99-457 also reauthorizes discretionary programming and expands school-to-work transition programs. PL 99-457 was reauthorized as the Individuals with Disabilities Education Act Amendments (IDEA) of 1991 (PL 102-119), later as part of the Individuals with Disabilities Education Act Amendments (IDEA) of 1997 (PL 105-17), and then as the Individuals with Disabilities Education Improvement Act (IDEA) of 2004 (PL 108-446).

Education of the Handicapped Act (EHA) of 1970 (PL 91-230) A federal law that consolidates previous legislation and establishes a new Title VI to replace the one enacted in the Elementary and Secondary Education Act Amendments (ESEA) of 1966 (PL 89-750). This new authorization of Title VI, which has become known as *Part B,* establishes a core grant program for educational agencies at the local level. Part B is the precursor to the Education for All Handicapped Children Act of 1975 (PL 94-142), which significantly expands the educational rights and opportunities for children and youth with disabilities.

education records Records that are directly related to a student and maintained by an educational agency or institution. Such records are covered under the Family Educational Rights and Privacy Act (FERPA) of 1974 (PL 93-380).

Education Resources Information Center (ERIC) A national information system that provides educators, researchers, and the general public with access to a comprehensive, easy-to-use, searchable, Internet-based bibliographic and full-text database of education research and information. ERIC is a programmatic function the U.S. Department of Education. It is the world's largest and most frequently used education digital library, composed of more than 1.2 million bibliographic records dating back to 1966.

educational evaluation A battery of assessments given to determine whether a child has a disability and the nature and extent of the special education and related services the child needs. Federal law requires parental consent for any initial pre-placement evaluation. Under the Individuals with Disabilities Education Improvement Act (IDEA) of 2004 (PL 108-446), all tests and other evaluation materials must be administered in a child's native language, validated for the specific purpose for which they are being used, and administered by trained personnel in accordance with proper instructions. No single test shall be used as the sole basis for determining appropriate educational placement. The evaluation is to be made by a multidisciplinary team and is to include areas appropriate to the individual student. Reevaluation is required at least every 3 years and may be done more often but not more than once per calendar year.

educational sign systems Manual equivalents of spoken English. Seeing Essential English (SEE1) and Signing Exact English (SEE2) are two pedagogical sign systems frequently used with populations of nonvocal people with disabilities. Unlike American Sign Language (ASL), which deviates from oral language, educational sign systems consist of manual translations of spoken English, maintaining its syntax (grammar), structure, and morphology (word structure). These systems can also be part of a total communication system.

Edwards syndrome *See* trisomy 18 syndrome.

EEC syndrome *See* ectrodactyly.

EEC1 *See* ectrodactyly–ectodermal dysplasia and cleft lip/palate syndrome.

EEG *See* electroencephalogram.

effectiveness The probability of benefit under average conditions of use.

efficacy The probability of benefit to individuals in a defined population under ideal conditions of use.

effortful swallow A swallow technique that aims to increase posterior motion of the tongue against the posterior pharyngeal wall by having the person squeeze as hard as he or she can with the tongue and neck muscles while swallowing.

effusion The exuding (oozing) of fluid into the middle ear or other body space.

EFMP *See* Exceptional Family Member Program.

EFT *See* Embedded Figures Test.

egocentrism A young child's inability to understand another's point of view. In Piaget's theory of early development, egocentrism describes a cognitive (thought) limitation without the negative implication that the same behavior would imply in an adult. Egocentrism is a characteristic of children with autism spectrum disorders.

EH Emotionally handicapped. *See* emotional disability (ED).

EHA *See* Education of the Handicapped Act of 1970 (PL 91-230).

EHDI *See* Early Hearing Detection and Intervention Program.

Ehlers-Danlos syndrome (EDS) A group of genetic conditions that involve connective tissue abnormalities and different degrees of joint hypermobility. There may also be skin hyperextensibility, skin fragility, and easy bruisability. Cardiac abnormalities are common and include prolapse of the mitral valve and aortic root dilation.

EHS *See* Early Head Start.

EI *See* Early Intervention.

EIDP *See* Early Intervention Development Profile.

18p- syndrome Deletion of the short arm of chromosome 18; a chromosomal disorder with intellectual disability (with language abilities being more severely impaired), growth deficiency, and a peculiar facies (including jug-handle ears).

18q- syndrome Deletion of the long arm of chromosome 18; a chromosomal disorder with intellectual disability, hearing impairment, growth deficiency, mid-facial hypoplasia (underdevelopment), a prominent antihelix (part of the external ear), occasional behavior abnormalities, and eye defects.

ELAP *See* Early Learning Accomplishment Profile.

elastin deletion *See* Williams syndrome.

Elavil *See* amitriptyline.

ELBW *See* extremely low birth weight.

Elderly or Disabled with Consumer-Direction (EDCD) Waiver A Medicaid program that provides in-home services to older people and people with disabilities as an alternative to nursing facility care. Individuals must meet Medicaid and nursing facility level of care criteria.

elective Optional, non-emergency. Most elective surgery in children is scheduled so that the children miss the least amount of school as possible. Educationally speaking, an elective class is not required for all students but selected as a class the student wishes to take.

elective mutism *See* selective mutism.

electric hair Uncombable or fly-away hair, a minor dysmorphic (atypical) feature. Multiple cowlicks can give a similar appearance.

electric hair

electrocochleography (ECochG) A test that measures the electrical potentials generated in the inner ear in response to stimulation by a sound.

electroencephalogram (EEG) A brain wave test. A clinical tool used to measure electrical activity in the brain between different areas of the scalp and a reference point. An EEG should ideally include measurements made in drowsy, sleep, and awake states and, if possible, with hyperventilation (rapid breathing) and photic (light) stimulation. Combined with the clinical history, an EEG can support the diagnosis of a seizure disorder, help classify the focus (location in the brain) and type of seizure disorder, and contribute to the selection of appropriate anticonvulsant therapy.

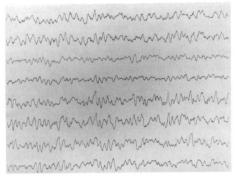

electroencephalogram (EEG)

electroencephalographic biofeedback (EBF) *neurotherapy.* The use of biofeedback techniques to train people with attention-deficit/hyperactivity disorder (ADHD) or emotional problems to increase or decrease certain wavelength frequencies in their electroencephalograms (EEGs) and thus improve their symptoms.

electrolyte A chemical in a fluid such as blood that can conduct an electrical current. *Serum electrolytes* refers to a battery of tests used to determine the levels of these chemicals in the blood. The resulting patterns provide much information on the individual's status and the body's acute (the present) and chronic (over time) response to a variety of disease states. The most important electrolytes are sodium, potassium, calcium, magnesium, chloride, bicarbonate, and phosphate.

electromyography (EMG) A record of the electrical activity in a muscle. EMG is used to identify and help classify the type of myopathy (muscle disorder), neuromuscular disease, or lower motor neuron (the nerve from the spinal cord to muscle) condition present. The pattern of muscle response to the electrical stimulation varies by condition.

electrophoresis A laboratory method that uses an electrical current to separate protein molecules in a gel; it can be used to identify and quantitate (measure) different proteins.

electroretinography (ERG) A measure of retinal (eye) function documented by changes in electrical potentials when light hits the eye. The pattern of electrical changes and the amplitude (degree) of response can be used to diagnose eye diseases that may cause blindness.

Elementary and Secondary Education Act Amendments (ESEA) of 1965 (PL 89-313) Federal legislation that authorizes the first federal grant program targeted specifically to children and youth with disabilities. Grants are awarded to state agencies to educate students with disabilities in state-supported or state-operated schools and facilities.

Elementary and Secondary Education Act Amendments (ESEA) of 1966 (PL 89-750) Legislation that amends Title VI of the Elementary and Secondary Education Act (ESEA) of 1965 (PL 89-10) by authorizing the first federal grant program for the education of children with disabilities at the local school level rather than providing assistance solely to state-operated programs. PL 89-750 establishes the Bureau of Education for the Handicapped (BEH)—now known as the Office of Special Education Programs (OSEP)—to implement, monitor, and evaluate federally funded special education programs. The law also creates the National Advisory Council, now called the Council on Disability.

Elementary and Secondary Education Act Amendments (ESEA) of 1968 (PL 90-247) Federal legislation that establishes a set of "discretionary" programs designed to supplement existing special education services. Among the supportive services are funding for regional resource centers, services for children with sensory impairments, special education research, and the groundwork for continuing education and informational resources.

Elementary and Secondary Education Act Amendments (ESEA) of 1978 (PL 95-561) Part A of Title IX of this federal law is known as the Gifted and Talented Children's Education Act. The statute and its regulations define gifted and talented children and describe the special education services to which they are entitled by virtue of their demonstrated or potential abilities in the arenas of academic, creative, leadership, or visual and performing arts achievement.

Elementary and Secondary Education Act (ESEA) of 1965 (PL 89-10) A federal law designed to strengthen and improve educational quality and opportunity for the nation's elementary and secondary students, particularly economically underprivileged children. This act paves the way for direct federal support for the education of children with disabilities and is the basis upon which early legislation addressing special education is drafted.

elfin facies A triangular facial appearance associated with a number of syndromes, such as Donohoe syndrome and Williams syndrome.

elfin facies syndrome *See* Williams syndrome.

eligibility The ability to receive special education and related supports as a result of meeting federal or state criteria for the presence of a specific qualifying disability. Criteria are specific to each state education agency (SEA) and may vary across state lines. Eligibility is ascertained by a multidisciplinary evaluation (MDE).

elimination diet *See* diet therapy.

ELIP *See* Environmental Language Intervention Program.

Ellis-van Creveld syndrome *See* chondroectodermal dysplasia.

ELLCO *See* Early Language and Literacy Classroom Observation Tool.

ELM-2 *See* Early Language Milestones Scale–Second Edition.

elopement A behavior pattern characterized by frequent attempts to run away. Formerly known as *escape.*

emaciation The wasting away of lean muscle mass and depletion of fat due to starvation.

Embedded Figures Test (EFT) A measure of cognitive style that requires the individual to find simple geometric figures in complex colored designs. Several versions of the EFT exist, including preschool (PEFT), children's (CEFT), and group (GEFT) tests.

emblems Gestural behaviors that can be translated, or defined, by a few words or a phrase and that can be used without speech to convey messages (e.g., nodding the head to indicate yes).

embryo The product of conception from fertilization to 8 weeks of gestation; in the later stages of development, the embryo is referred to as a *fetus.* Sometimes the term *embryo* is restricted to describing development before the fetal stage rather than the entire period of gestation (development in the womb). The major organ systems are formed during this early stage; disturbances in the developmental process at this time contribute to fetal wastage (spontaneous miscarriage) or major organ system malformations.

embryogenesis The process in a fetus in which cells multiply and specialize to form a particular organ or organ system, such as the brain or central nervous system (CNS). This process is a complex progression from induction (in which cells divide) to migration and organization into specialized layers. The critical period of fetal (before birth) development is during embryogenesis, when the cells are particularly vulnerable to damage by a teratogen (toxic agent), which disrupts the typical pattern of events. This leads to CNS malformations that cause a large

number of fetal, neonatal, and infant deaths. It is estimated that 3% of neonates have a significant CNS or other systemic malformation. Genetic abnormalities, maternal infection, drugs, and illness account for 40% of malformations; however, the cause in the remaining 60% is unknown.

emergent literacy The idea that reading and writing skills develop long before children begin to receive formal instruction in these skills in school. Early skills that precede or are presumed to be prerequisites for later developing reading and writing skills include alphabet awareness, print awareness, and phonological awareness.

emesis Vomiting.

EMG *See* electromyography.

EMH Educable mentally handicapped. *See* educable mentally retarded (EMR).

emotion A set of subjective feelings often accompanied by physiological (bodily) changes that can impel one toward action. Examples of emotions include fear, love, surprise, and hate. *See also* affect, mood.

emotional disability (ED) A disability classification in education that includes a wide range of diagnoses, some of which are psychiatric in nature (e.g., depression) and others of which are more neurodevelopmental in nature (e.g., attention-deficit/hyperactivity disorder [ADHD]).

emotional lability Sudden mood changes and/or exaggerated emotional responses to ordinary events.

emotionally handicapped (EH) *See* emotional disability (ED).

empathy The objective or intellectual recognition of the nature and significance of other humans' emotions and behaviors or of their experience of a specific situation. Empathy allows a person to view events from another's perspective. Empathy differs from sympathy, which stems from having a similar personal, cognitive, or affective experience. People with autism seem to lack empathy.

employee assistance program (EAP) Employer-based services that help employees deal with life stresses and problems that negatively affect job performance through such things as accidents, absenteeism, attitude difficulties, emotional problems, or substance abuse. EAP services may include drug treatment, family services (e.g., help with nursing home or group home placement), and marital or family therapy. EAP counseling services can sometimes be used to help a family deal with a child with a developmental disability.

empowerment A means of making families equal partners in the process of obtaining, defining, and participating in all aspects of care and education for their child with a disability.

EMPP *See* Early Motor Pattern Profile.

EMR *See* educable mentally retarded.

enabling Any action by a person or institution that aids the continuation of another person's negative behavior.

enanthem A rash on the mucous membrane (e.g., inside the mouth) usually associated with an exanthem (skin rash) in the presence of systemic (body) disease.

encephalitis An infection or inflammation of the brain that gives rise to altered consciousness, fever, headache, and/or focal (localizing) neurological signs. An episode of encephalitis may be followed by complete recovery, by any degree of permanent brain damage, or by death.

encephalocele A brain herniation (rupture) resulting from the protrusion of brain sub-

stance through a traumatic (due to injury) or congenital (from birth) opening of the skull.

encephalofacial angiomatosis *See* Sturge-Weber syndrome.

encephalopathy Brain abnormality; typically subdivided into static and progressive. Static encephalopathies do not change over time, although additional and differing symptoms may develop as the person ages. Progressive encephalopathies are typically characterized by worsening brain abnormalities and symptoms. The typical outcomes of static encephalopathies include the entire spectrum and continuum of neurodevelopmental disabilities.

encoding system In augmentative communication, the process of assigning codes, abbreviations, or labels to represent a letter, item, or message. The system can be arbitrarily or systematically applied. A common encoding system is Morse code.

encopresis Fecal soiling; fecal incontinence. Lack of or incomplete bowel control can be primary, when the child has never achieved such control; or secondary, when the child previously achieved bowel control but later lost it. Age-appropriate or developmentally appropriate lack of bowel control is not encopresis. Secondary encopresis in otherwise typical children is often "overflow diarrhea," leakage around fecal impaction (a hard mass of feces) associated with prolonged constipation. Secondary encopresis that is more than occasional or transiently (temporarily) associated with emotional stress may be reflective of underlying bowel disease or severe psychopathology.

endemic A disease or disorder that is specific to, or occurs at high rates in, a given population or geographic area (e.g., lead poisoning in inner-city children).

endocarditis An inflammation of the inner layer of the heart, usually bacterial, that is a complication of other types of heart disease. Endocarditis may damage the heart itself or may result in emboli (clots) being passed to other organs.

endogenous Describing a disease or illness that comes from within rather than being caused by external (outside) sources.

endomorph *pyknic body type.* Someone with a rounded body type or build that tends to carry extra weight. *See also* ectomorph, mesomorph.

endorphin An opioid (substance resembling opium) that occurs naturally in the body and is involved in the perception of pleasure and pain. Drugs that affect endorphin levels are used to treat self-injurious behavior.

endoscopy Visual examination of structures inside the body with a tube (endoscope).

endotracheal tube (ETT) A tube that goes from the outside of the body (endo) into the trachea (windpipe) to enable breathing, often attached to a ventilator (breathing machine).

English as a second language (ESL) A pedagogical approach in which students with limited English proficiency receive the majority of their academic instruction in a submersion classroom while receiving some support with English language acquisition.

engram Memory trace; a theoretical physical change in the brain that accounts for the creation of a memory. *Engram* is a research rather than clinical term.

enmeshment A pattern of family relations characterized by strong allegiances and (over)closeness, few or extremely permeable boundaries, and little individual autonomy. Such a pattern of relating often has strong ethnic and cultural origins. When culturally determined, this pattern is less often pathological. When a family is enmeshed to protect itself from psychological pain, that family can become extremely toxic and pathological, as relating outside the family is seen as "traitorous." A family member must often become symptomatic in order to prompt the family to secure help and enable the opportunity to grow. Families who have children with developmental disabilities often develop enmeshed patterns as a way of protecting the child and themselves from hurt.

enrichment Any supplementary activity, intervention, or opportunity added to a child's daily life experiences. The provision of extra social, emotional, and learning stimulation, as well as improved nutrition, sanitary conditions, and regular preventive medical and dental care. Enrichment activities are routinely part of early childhood special education and can include home-based programs that encourage parental involvement and teach parents ways to enhance their child's development. *Enrichment* may also refer to supplementary educational experiences and programming for gifted children.

ENT Ears, nose, and throat. *See* otolaryngology.

enteral feeding *enteral nutrition.* Tube feeding; examples include nasogastric (tube inserted in the nose and extending to the stomach) and gastrostomy (tube inserted through the abdomen directly into the stomach) tube feedings.

entitlement A right, claim, or legal title; qualification. In all states, education and special education services are a legislated entitlement for all children. Adult services, in contrast, may be on a "last resort" basis, with services provided only after all other possibilities have been exhausted.

entropion Inversion (turning in) of the eyelid.

enuresis Urinary incontinence after 5 years of age. Nocturnal enuresis is nighttime bed-wetting; diurnal enuresis is urinary incontinence when one is awake during the day. Primary enuresis describes the child who has never been consistently dry; secondary enuresis is defined as being preceded by at least 1 year of dryness. Most primary nocturnal enuresis runs in families. Secondary enuresis may indicate urinary tract infection or severe emotional stress; it may also be a presenting sign of child sexual abuse.

Environmental Language Intervention Program (ELIP) An assessment/diagnostic remediation program for pre-language and early language skills. The Environmental Pre-Language Battery (EPB) assesses readiness behaviors, such as play in children who have no oral language skills. The Environmental Language Inventory (ELI) assesses language development (two-word or more phrases) in conversation, imitation, and free play.

eosinophilia An excessively high number of a specific type of eosin (red) staining white blood cells; eosinophilia occurs with allergy, parasites (worms), and cancer.

EOWPVT Expressive One-Word Picture Vocabulary Test. *See* One-Word Picture Vocabulary Tests.

EPEC *See* Evaluation and Prescription for Exceptional Children.

epenthesis The phonological process that occurs when a new phoneme is inserted into a word.

ephedrine A drug that increases bladder muscle tone and can be used in the treatment of neurogenic (neurologically dysfunctional) bladder.

epicanthal fold *epicanthus.* A crescent-shaped fold of skin extending downward from the side of the (upper) nose to the lower eyelid and partially covering the inner canthus (eye corner). An epicanthal fold is most commonly an isolated autosomal dominant feature; it is also associated with Down syndrome and other genetic syndromes. It is present in the normal fetus from the third to the sixth months, so its postnatal (after birth) presence may be considered a sign of developmental immaturity. Up to one third of typically developing infants younger than 1 year of age exhibit persistent epicanthus. It is one of a number of minor dysmorphic (mildly atypical) features that, in combination, may have developmental significance and may produce the mistaken impression of strabismus (crossed eyes) by concealing the medial sclera (white of the eye closest to the nose), a condition called *pseudostrabismus.*

epicanthal fold

epicritic Pertaining to the nerves that detect slight differences of pressure, touch, and temperature.

epidemic A disease or disorder with an occurrence rate that significantly exceeds typical rates either in numbers affected or in the rapidity of occurrence.

epidemiology The study of the distribution, determinants, and deterrents of disease. Epidemiologists study disease at the macro level (in large groups of people), whereas pathologists study disease at the micro level (in single individuals). Epidemiologists study groups with a disease and groups without the disease in order to determine the difference between those affected and those spared. For example, to gauge distribution, epidemiologists might study whether the disease is more prevalent in men or women. To isolate its determinants, they might try to find out whether the disease is genetically transmitted or the result of behavior. To identify deterrents, they might ask whether some diets prevent the disease more than others.

epigenetic Referring to changes due to the regulation of the expression of gene activity without change in genetic structure.

epilepsy A neurological condition characterized by recurrent seizures or convulsions of various types often associated with electroencephalographic (EEG; brain wave) abnormalities. Different kinds of seizures can be combined with other findings to form epileptic syndromes.

Epilepsy Foundation A nonprofit volunteer organization dedicated to epilepsy treatment, research, and education. This national foundation and its local chapters provide information regarding epilepsy, its treatment, and related issues, including employment, advocacy, and educational programming. Formerly the Epilepsy Foundation of America.

epileptic Relating to a seizure or seizure disorder.

epileptic myoclonus *See* myoclonus.

epiloia *See* tuberous sclerosis (TS) syndrome.

epinephrine A neurotransmitter associated with the physiological (bodily) changes associated with fear and anxiety.

episodic memory Memory for events and occurrences. Episodic memory has an autobiographical flavor and usually contains spatial–temporal (where and when) information. Repeated exposure to certain kinds of information produces a shift from episodic to semantic (meaning systems) memory.

epispadias Abnormal location of the urethra (opening for urine to exit the body) on the dorsal (upper) surface of the penis.

eponym A syndrome (or sign or symptom) named after the person who first defined, described, or popularized its importance. Use of the possessive is becoming obsolete (e.g., Down syndrome, not Down's syndrome, is preferred). The eponym is an accepted usage before the true etiology (cause) is known. Once the underlying organic basis is discovered, the name should reflect that knowledge (e.g., *Down syndrome* becomes *trisomy 21*).

EPSDT *See* Early and Periodic Screening, Diagnosis, and Treatment.

equilibrium reaction Any of a subgroup of postural reactions that pave the way for voluntary (purposeful) movement to develop late in the first year of life. They let the infant compensate for changes in the body's center of gravity and thus achieve successful head control, sitting, standing, and to maintain an upright posture.

equinovalgus Rocker-bottom foot deformity.

equinovarus *See* congenital vertical talus, talipes equinovarus.

equinus Describing the foot position in toe walking, resembling the posture naturally assumed by a horse's (equus) hoof.

equinus deformity An orthopedic abnormality in which the heel of the foot is pulled upward and the forefoot (front of the foot) downward.

equinus gait *See* toe walking.

equipotentiality A hypothetical explanation for recovery after brain damage that involves undamaged parts assuming control of functions previously performed by damaged areas of the brain.

equivalent score A score that is representative of an average individual for a specific age group or educational grade.

Erb palsy Paralysis of the upper arm due to injury to the upper brachial plexus (nerves to the arm), usually sustained during childbirth. The arm lies limp at the infant's side, with the hand pronated (rotated back) in the "policeman's tip" or "waiter's tip" position. Named after Wilhelm Heinrich Erb (1840–1921).

Erb palsy

ERG *See* electroretinography.

Erhardt Developmental Prehension Assessment (EDPA) A criterion-referenced assessment of hand function development for use with children from birth to 6 years of age that yields age levels for three areas: involuntary hand–arm movements, voluntary movements, and prewriting skills. Administration time is 1 hour.

ERIC *See* Education Resources Information Center.

ERP *See* event-related potential.

error of measurement The standardized difference between the obtained score and the true score. Such a difference is attributed to variability in the test instrument or the examiner. The error of measurement is often expressed in the form of confidence bands. For example, if the mean score on a test is 100, and the standard error of measurement 3, then the confidence interval at the 68% level for a test score of 100 is 100 $\pm$ 3, or 97–103. (That is, there is a 68% chance that the individual's true score lies in the range of scores from 97 to 103.) For the 95% level, the range is defined as the mean $\pm$ 1.96 (standard error), or 100 $\pm$ 6. (That is, there is a 95% chance that the individual's true score falls in the range 94–106.)

erythema Redness of the skin. Erythema is a sign of inflammation and a component of many skin diseases.

erythema infectiosum Fifth disease (so-called relative to an older system of numbering common skin rashes in children); a viral infection in which a usually otherwise well child has red, flushed cheeks ("slapped cheek" appearance).

erythroblastosis fetalis Hemolytic disease of the newborn. A blood group (usually Rh) incompatibility between mother and fetus that causes an anemia (low red blood cell count) in the fetus. Erythroblasts (blood cells that produce red blood cells) then increase in the circulation in which they are typically rare; the increased breakdown of red blood cells contributes to jaundice (yellowing of the skin), liver enlargement, and generalized edema (fluid-filled swelling; hydrops fetalis). With modern preventive treatment of Rh-negative mothers, this condition is disappearing.

erythrocyte sedimentation rate (ESR) A blood test that nonspecifically indicates inflammation or disease.

Escalante syndrome *See* fragile X syndrome.

escape *See* elopement.

ESDM *See* Early Start Denver Model Curriculum Checklist for Young Children with Autism.

ESEA Elementary and Secondary Education Act of 1965 (PL 89-10). *See also* Education of the Handicapped Act Amendments of 1974 (PL 93-380), Elementary and Secondary Education Act Amendments of 1965 (PL 89-313), Elementary and Secondary Education Act Amendments of 1966 (PL 89-750), Elementary and Secondary Education Act Amendments of 1968 (PL 90-247), Elementary and Secondary Education Act Amendments of 1978 (PL 95-561).

ESI-R *See* Early Screening Inventory–Revised.

ESL   *See* English as a second language.

esophageal atresia   A congenital malformation in which the esophagus (the passage from the mouth to the stomach) ends in a blind pouch instead of leading to the stomach.

esophageal phase   The stage of the swallowing process that begins with the relaxation of the upper esophageal sphincter muscle to allow passage of a bolus (a lump of food) into the esophagus, is followed by peristaltic contractions (waves of muscle movements) that move the bolus through the esophagus, and ends when the lower esophageal sphincter relaxes to allow the bolus into the stomach.

esophageal speech   Speech that is produced by insufflation of the esophagus and a controlled release of air that vibrates the pharyngo-esophageal segment for sound production.

esophagus   Throat; gullet. The part of the gastrointestinal tract that connects the pharynx (the back of the throat) with the stomach.

esophoria   An inturning of one eye only after stress. Persistent inturning is esotropia. *See also* esotropia.

esotropia   *cross-eyedness.* Internal or convergent strabismus. The sixth cranial nerve supplies the lateral rectus muscle of the eye, which allows the eye to look in the direction away from the nose; if this nerve is damaged, the unopposed medial rectus muscle pulls the eye inward toward the nose. Increased intracranial (inside the skull) pressure such as occurs in hydrocephalus (excess fluid in the brain) frequently affects this sixth nerve function. *See also* esophoria.

ESP   *See* Early Screening Profile.

ESR   *See* erythrocyte sedimentation rate.

ESY   *See* extended school year.

ethnicity   Descending from a distinct group of people who share a common race, language, customs, and other traditions.

ethnographic assessment   The evaluation of how people interact and communicate from a cultural perspective.

ethosuximide   Trade name, Zarontin. An anticonvulsant used to treat a specific type of seizure called an *absence seizure.* Minor side effects include stomachache, rash, headache, and a reversible blood problem. Unusual side effects at high dosages include hiccups or neurotoxicity with lethargy or hallucinations. Therapeutic blood levels are used to monitor treatment.

ethylenediaminetetraacetic acid (EDTA)   A drug with salts that is injected intramuscularly (IM) to treat lead poisoning. A chelating agent (drug that removes heavy metals).

etiology   Cause. Medically speaking, *etiology* refers to an underlying pathology. Traditional medical etiologies are characterized as belonging to one of the following groups: genetic, infection, trauma, tumor, or toxin (poison).

EtOH   *See* alcohol.

ETT   *See* endotracheal tube.

eugenics   A social engineering philosophy to improve hereditary characteristics. Negative eugenics is concerned with the sterilization of carriers of "undesirable" genetic traits; positive eugenics promotes matings between carriers of "desirable" genetic traits.

eustachian tube   The narrow channel that connects the eardrum with the nasopharynx (back of the nose and mouth). The eustachian tube equalizes pressure on either side of the eardrum. Because children have a wider, shorter tube than adults, they are more prone to infections traveling from the throat to the ear.

euthanasia The permitting or causing of death, usually in a person with a terminal illness or who is in a persistently vegetative state.

Evaluating Acquired Skills in Communication–Third Edition (EASIC-3) A criterion-referenced assessment for use with children with severe impairments who are 3 months to 8 years of age. The EASIC-3 rates the following behaviors: prelinguistic skills, semantics, syntax, and morphology. It is designed for use with children with developmental disabilities, autism, or severe language and cognitive disorders.

Evaluation and Prescription for Exceptional Children (EPEC) An educational planning assessment for use with preschool children.

evaluation, educational *See* educational evaluation.

evening colic *See* colic.

event-related potential (ERP) A wave generated on electrophysiological monitoring of brain response (such as electroencephalogram [EEG]) to a specific sensory stimulus or by activation of the brain during a particular task.

eversion Turning of the sole of the foot outward from the mid-line (middle) of the body; the foot posture used in the indirect Fog test (a gait test that involves walking on the insides of the feet).

evidence-based instruction Instructional programs or methods whose success is based on evidence that, when used in a systematic manner, the programs result in a high rate of achievement. Other terms that convey the same idea are *research-based instruction* and *scientifically based research.*

evidence-based practice (EBP) The integration of research evidence with clinical expertise and client values in order to provide guidelines and recommendations for best practice.

evoked auditory potential An electrical stimulus produced in response to an acoustic stimulus.

exanthem A skin eruption that is a symptom of a more general disease such as roseola (measles) or scarlet fever.

exanthema subitum *See* roseola.

exceptional child A child who is gifted (with superior general intellectual ability) or a child who has a disability.

Exceptional Family Member Program (EFMP) A military program that identifies family members with special needs, documents the services they will require, and considers those needs when making personnel assignments. The application process is specific to each of the uniformed services.

exclusionary discipline The practice of removing a student from the routine school environment for a specified period of time; it includes both supervision and expulsion. When children with disabilities achieve a predefined cumulative total time of exclusion, an individualized education program (IEP) review is mandated.

executive dysfunction (EDF) Difficulties with executive function. *See also* executive function.

executive function The ability of the brain to initiate a set of appropriate responses to the environment and maintain these responses or shift them when necessary. This planning and shifting function is located in the prefrontal cortex (the foremost part of the brain). Executive function may be impaired as a result of disorders of learning and attention, psychiatric disorders (schizophrenia), degenerative changes with age, and drugs. *See also* executive dysfunction (EDF).

exophoria A latent outward turning of one eye after its vision has been blocked. Exophoria can be provoked by the cover–uncover test. This is a milder form of exotropia.

exophthalmos *"pop eyes."* Abnormal protrusion (sticking out) of the eyeballs; bilateral (both eyes) exophthalmos can be a sign of hyperthyroidism, a condition that affects multiple body systems, whereas unilateral (one eye) exophthalmos often reflects localized orbital (eye socket) or neurological disease (e.g., a tumor).

exotropia *wall-eyedness.* External or divergent strabismus. The third cranial nerve controls the medial rectus muscle of the eye, which pulls the eye inward toward the nose; impairment of this nerve often produces some degree of strabismus, sometimes accompanied by ptosis (drooping) of the eyelid.

exotropia

expanded keyboard An augmentative communication keyboard that has keys and spaces between the keys larger than the standard microcomputer keyboard.

expansion A language instruction technique in which the adult takes the child's utterance and repeats it using a higher level language model.

expectant In diagnosis and therapy, describing an approach that involves waiting and watching.

expectorant A medicine that promotes the coughing up of mucus.

explosive personality disorder A rare disorder of impulse control resulting in aggressive and/or destructive outbursts.

exposition Text with the purpose of informing or instructing.

expressive aphasia *See* Broca's aphasia.

expressive interventions A category of therapeutic activities that involve expressive methods, such as role playing, arts and crafts projects, and drama.

expressive language A system for communication with another person or people. Speaking, writing, and signing are expressive language skills.

Expressive One-Word Picture Vocabulary Test (EOWPVT) *See* One-Word Picture Vocabulary Tests.

expressivity The extent to which a gene manifests its effects. *Variable expressivity* means that some individuals may show only mild manifestations of the gene, whereas others show severe manifestations. There are no individuals that do not express some characteristic of a given trait. *See also* penetrance.

extasia The dilation of small blood vessels in the vocal folds.

extended autism phenotype The increased occurrence of certain behaviors associated with autism in the relatives of people with autism who themselves have no specific autism diagnoses. Thus these relatives may exhibit symptoms of disorders associated with autism, such as a language disorder, attention-deficit/hyperactivity disorder, depression, bipolar disorder, problems socializing, and obsessive-compulsive disorder, but do not themselves have autism.

Extended Care Health Option (ECHO) A supplemental TRICARE program that allows eligible participants (Exceptional Family Member Program [EFMP] enrollees) access to an extended set of integrated services (such as therapists, medical equipment, or in-home care or services).

extended family A family unit that includes parents, children, and other relatives, perhaps representing several generations. In some cultures, close or long-term family friends are part of the extended family. A natural support system, extended family members often share the responsibilities for caring for a child with disabilities and, depending on the extent of their involvement, may be included in varying degrees in the child's intervention plan.

extended school year (ESY) Describing the continuation of special education and related support services through the summer vacation so as to maintain skill-level progress and avoid regression (loss of skills). ESY service eligibility is determined by the student's individualized education program (IEP) team.

extension The straightening of a joint.

extensor thrust A sudden extension of the neck, back, hips, and knees so that the body is arched back like a bow; tonic spasm.

external motivation *extrinsic motivation.* Motivation for engaging in a task in order to meet a goal or receive a reward (external or extrinsic motivator) separate from both the task itself and the feeling of accomplishment engendered by successful completion. Pleasing others, getting a good grade, and receiving a reward are examples of external motivators. Attempts should be made to shift attention to intrinsic rewards by making tasks interesting and challenging but achievable, with the value of the skill being made apparent.

external pacing A feeding technique in which the bottle is occasionally tilted down

while still inside the mouth; this temporarily turns the bottle into a pacifier and prevents overfilling the mouth while allowing for an additional swallow to clear the pharynx. With older children, this feeding technique allows for a "dry" swallow between bites or for alternating food consistencies.

external rotation *See* lateral rotation.

externalization Attributing cause for feelings or behaviors to external (outside) sources.

extinction In operant conditioning, the condition in which discontinuing reinforcement produces a diminished level of responding. *See also* conditioning.

extracorporeal membrane oxygenation (ECMO) therapy A method of delivering oxygen to infants with respiratory compromise. ECMO uses a heart–lung bypass system and allows the lungs to rest and heal without the negative effects of high oxygen levels and the complications of ventilator therapy. Often used with extremely premature infants.

extrapyramidal cerebral palsy Any of the physiological (based on tone and movement findings) subtypes of cerebral palsy that do not reflect predominantly pyramidal tract involvement (spastic cerebral palsy). Ataxic/cerebellar, choreoathetoid, hypotonic or atonic (decreased or no muscle tone), rigid, and tremor are the principal members of this group. In general, for similar degrees of motor involvement, the degree of the motor delay is more severe for extrapyramidal than for spastic cerebral palsy. This appears to be because of the more frequent impairment of equilibrium and balance reactions as well as the more variable tone in extrapyramidal cerebral palsy; the variations in tone also contribute to the decreased incidence and later onset of contractures.

extrapyramidal system Voluntary muscle reactions are a result of cooperation between the cortically controlled pyramidal system and three nonpyramidal systems: the vestibular system, the cerebellar system, and the striatal system. This last system, often referred to as the *extrapyramidal system,* includes the caudate nucleus, putamen, globus pallidus, and substantia nigra. Damage to these centers (basal ganglia) produces movement disorders such as Parkinson's disease, Huntington chorea, and choreoathetoid cerebral palsy.

extremely low birth weight (ELBW) A birth weight less than 1,000 g.

extrinsic motivation *See* external motivation.

Eyberg Child Behavior Inventory (ECBI) & Sutter-Eyberg Student Behavior Inventory– Revised Rating scales that assess disruptive behaviors at home and school, as well as the extent to which the behavior is considered troublesome. These parent (ECBI) and teacher (Sutter-Eyberg Student Behavior Inventory–Revised) measures indicate how often each behavior occurs (on a 7-point scale) and whether the behavior is a problem. Administration time is about 5 minutes.

eye contact One of the components of pragmatic language (nonverbal communication) that is often impaired or absent in individuals with autism spectrum disorder (ASD). The person with ASD does not simply look away or down as if shy but rather typically refuses to fix gaze on anyone or anything. In certain cultures it is inappropriate for a child (or a female of any age) to make eye contact with strangers (especially males).

eye exercises *See* optometric training.

eye–hand coordination The direction of fine motor activities of the hand in interaction with the visual system. Activities that require eye–hand coordination include tracing, drawing, writing, tying laces, and using scissors.

Ff

Fabry disease A genetic condition characterized by attacks of burning pain in the hands and feet, dark nodular (lumpy) skin lesions, and progressive renal insufficiency (kidney failure). Symptoms are caused by a deficiency of an enzyme called alpha-galactosidase and can include seizures, hemiplegia (paralysis of one side of the body), and intellectual disability. The gene is located on the long arm of the X chromosome (Xq22).

face validity A test is said to have face validity if its items seem like reasonable ones to measure the areas that the test purports to measure. Face validity alone is not enough to judge the value of the test; it is but one aspect of validity (the extent to which a test item or procedure actually measures what it claims to measure). *See* validity.

FACES-IV *See* Family Adaptability and Cohesion Evaluation Scales–Fourth Edition.

facial gyrus *See* fusiform gyrus.

facial index The ratio of facial height to facial width.

facial nerve The seventh cranial nerve, responsible for facial movement and expression and taste at the front of the tongue.

facies Face, countenance, expression. A facial expression suggestive, diagnostic, or pathognomonic (uniquely indicative) for a specific diagnosis or condition. A leonine (lion-like) facies characterizes craniometaphyseal dysplasia, a pugilistic (boxer's) facies characterizes otopalatodigital syndrome, a triangular facies characterizes multiple lentigines syndrome, and a myopathic (flat, expressionless) facies is seen in myasthenia gravis.

facilitated communication A way of helping someone with communication impairments spell out messages by having another person, called a *facilitator,* put his or her hand over the hand of the person with a disability to point to letters on a board. Research documents that most if not all of the communications come from the facilitator rather than from the person with a disability.

facilitator A person (e.g., social worker, psychologist, counselor) who enables change by helping with communication, linking or strengthening existing systems, starting new systems, channeling or developing resources, and acting as or arranging for an expert consultant. Among other activities, facilitators convene meetings, encourage expression of feelings and opinions, gather and spread information, brainstorm, provide support, and advocate and lobby.

facioauriculovertebral sequence *See* Goldenhar syndrome.

facioauriculovertebral spectrum *See* Goldenhar syndrome.

factitious disorder The reporting of or presence of the symptoms of an actual mental or physical disorder that, on further investigation, are found to be purposely created by the individual. *See also* malingering, Münchausen syndrome by proxy (MSBP).

factor analysis A statistical procedure for analyzing the relationships of a group of test items that have been administered to a large number of individuals. The procedure is based on the assumption that intercorrelation can be accounted for by unobservable facts (factors) fewer in number than the variables themselves. The result of factor analysis is a grid called a *factor matrix* that shows the extent to which each test loads on (is correlated with) one or more of these unobserved factors. Factor loadings are correlations between factors and tests; such loadings indicate how much each factor determines performance on each test. The naming of the factor depends upon the content of the tests that have loaded on that factor. *See also* loading.

fading In operant conditioning, the gradual removal of prompts that occasioned the target behavior. A range of prompts (e.g., hints, rules, verbal instructions, visual cues, physical guidance) and reinforcers might be used to assist an individual in acquiring a new behavior. A prompted response, by definition, does not occur spontaneously, so fading is conducted until the response can be completed without any prompts. Methods for fading prompts include decreasing the amount of verbal or physical assistance provided, delaying the prompt to allow the student to respond, and using least-to-most prompts (starting with a minimal prompt and increasing only if the student does not enact the behavior).

FAE Fetal alcohol effects. *See* alcohol-related neurodevelopmental disorders (ARND).

Fagan Test of Infant Intelligence (FTII) A screening device used to evaluate cognitive function in 6- to 12-month-old infants. Computerized technology is used to measure visual attention to novel stimuli. This nonmotor test is useful in assessing intelligence in infants with severe motor impairments.

failure to thrive (FTT) A presenting symptom (not a diagnosis) in which a child younger than 2 years of age (and usually younger than 1 year of age) exhibits some degree of growth failure in the absence of an obvious cause. The degree of growth failure necessary to raise concern of an underlying illness is not clearly defined. In the past it was common to distinguish organic FTT (in which a physical disease was causing the growth failure) from nonorganic FTT (in which the poor growth was a result of a feeding problem or disorder of parenting).

fall away A test for tone in which an infant is suspended upside down by the feet, and one leg at a time is released while the other is held. The speed of fall of each released leg is compared; the one that falls faster is considered to have relatively decreased tone.

fall away

false belief paradigm A theory of mind (ToM) test used to evaluate whether children understand that what they themselves know might not be known to someone else. Children 3–5 years succeed at this task. Children with autism take longer to do so. *See also* theory of mind (ToM).

false negative An erroneous screening test result that indicates that a disease or condition is not present when it is. One measure of the value of a screening test is the proportion of false negative outcomes (or individuals whose disease is missed by the screening) the test yields. Failure to identify someone with a disease postpones treatment and can, in some conditions, allow for the development of a more serious disease that might have been prevented with an accurate screening test result. In terms of evaluating a screening test, false positive outcomes (erroneous test results that indicate that a condition is present when it is not) are typically considered more acceptable than false negative ones.

false positive An erroneous screening test result that indicates that a disease or condition is present when it is not. One measure of the value of a screening test is the proportion of false positive outcomes the test yields that then require further, more extensive, expensive, and sometimes painful testing procedures.

FAMA *See* Family Apgar.

familial Affecting several members of the same family; not necessarily genetic or hereditary.

familial dysautonomia (FD) *See* Riley-Day syndrome.

family A group of individuals related by blood, adoption, cohabitation, or marriage; a special group of individuals related to one another through reciprocal affections and loyalties. Admission into a family occurs through birth, marriage or domestic partnership, or adoption, and members exit only by death. A family differs from other social groups in three important ways. A family has 1) a shared and relatively predictable cycle of life experiences; 2) permanent membership; and 3) the affectional ties of attachment, loyalty, and positive regard. Thus, even in the absence of biological or legal ties, people may consider them-

selves and be considered a family based on their mutual support for, involvement with, and affection for one another. *See also* nuclear family.

Family Adaptability and Cohesion Evaluation Scales–Fourth Edition (FACES-IV) A 42-item self-report screening questionnaire used to indicate a family member's perception of his or her family's cohesion and adaptability. FACES-IV assesses communication styles, family interactions, and flexibility.

Family Apgar (FAMA) A 5-item self-report questionnaire that elicits a family member's perception of the state of his or her family's functioning. Patterned after the pediatric Apgar, the family Apgar acronym denotes Adaption, Partnership, Growth, Affection, and Resolve, the elements of functioning tapped by the instrument. The reliability and validity of this instrument are adequate for its use as a screening instrument for troubled families. However, an average Apgar score does not rule out family difficulties.

family centered Describing an approach to assessment and intervention that places family concerns, abilities, resources, and priorities at the center of the process and in which the actions of professionals are guided by an understanding of the central role of families in meeting the needs of young children.

family directed Pertaining to an approach to assessment and intervention in which the actions of professionals and other personnel are directed by parent or family concerns, values, and preferences. To some, family-directed assessment is distinct from family-centered assessment; the chief difference is that the guiding emphasis (in family-directed practices) emanates from the parent or family. However, both reference the family as a full partner and expert.

Family Educational Rights and Privacy Act (FERPA) of 1974 (PL 93-380) Federal legislation that protects the privacy of student education records and gives parents certain rights with respect to their children's education records. These rights transfer to the student when he or she reaches the age of 18 or begins to attend a school beyond the high school level. FERPA grants four specific rights: 1) the right to see the information that the institution is keeping on the student; 2) the right to seek amendment (correction) to or to append (add) a statement to those records; 3) the right to consent to the disclosure (release to others) of the records; and 4) the right to file a complaint with the FERPA office in Washington, D.C. The law applies to all schools, including colleges and universities. FERPA has been amended a number of times since its enactment as follows: Buckley/Pell Amendment (PL 93-568), Amendments to Education Amendments of 1978 (PL 96-46), Establishment of Department of Education (PL 96-88), Campus Security Act (PL 101-542), Higher Education Amendments of 1992 (PL 102-325), Improving America's Schools Act (PL 103-382), Higher Education Amendments of 1998 (PL 105-244), Campus Sex Crime Prevention Act (PL 106-386), and USA PATRIOT Act of 2001 (PL 107-56). FERPA regulations were amended in December 2008 to comply with U.S. Supreme Court rulings of provisions of the USA Patriot Act and the Campus Sex Crimes Prevention Act. The amendments add new exceptions, including the disclosure of personally identifiable information from education records without consent of parents; clarified permissible disclosure to parents of eligible students and conditions regarding disclosures of health and safety emergencies, clarified permissible disclosures of student identifiers as *directory information;* allows disclosures to contractors and other outside parties in connection with the outsourcing of institutional services and functions; revises the definitions of *attendance, disclosure, educa-tion records, personally identifiable information,* and other key terms; clarifies permissible redisclosures by State and Federal officials; updates investigation and enforcement provisions, and modifies rights in other circumstances.

Family Inventory of Life Events (FILE) A 71-item self-report instrument designed to assess situations and changes experienced by a family within the preceding year, as well as certain family experiences prior to the past year. The inventory is concerned with the number and length of stressful events that tax a family's resources and that may be sources of distress. Such information is helpful in determining a family's coping abilities and in recognizing the life events that may affect the family's capacity to care for a child with developmental disabilities.

family life cycle The sequence of developmental and transitional changes in family structure and relationships from the time families are joined through the marriage or partnership of adults until the death of the partners, when the process continues with their children. Families of children with intellectual or other developmental disabilities experience a series of crises as the child reaches various developmental stages. Many parents describe life with a child with a disability as a series of ups and progressively greater downs. Demands and stresses are high among parents of preschoolers. These stresses drop off when children enter school programs, and they rise again beyond their original levels when the children become older; entry into both adolescence and young adulthood is particularly stressful. It is important to realize that parents never fully resolve the complexity of feelings about their child's intellectual or other developmental disabilities.

family of origin A family or kinship group related by blood or genetic ties.

family planning Voluntary and deliberate decisions regarding childbearing made prior to conception. The number of children, the timing of the children's births, the origin of the children (biological or adoptive), and any methods of preconception birth control are dimensions of family planning. Although family planning is usually discussed within the context of a couple, many single adults are opting for families independent of their plans for marriage or partnership. Thus, technological reproductive methods may also become part of such adults' family planning strategies.

family therapist A therapist who works with the whole family as the unit of treatment or intervention.

family therapy An intervention in which the family is the unit of treatment or intervention. During the course of therapy, many or all family members may be seen. Sessions may involve one or two members or the whole family. Sessions may focus on individual members or relationship pairs within the family; however, the ultimate goal is a change in interaction patterns at the level of the entire family.

family-centered care Family-centered practices. An approach to ensuring the health and well-being of children and their families through a respectful family–professional partnership that honors the strengths, cultures, traditions, and expertise that everyone brings to the relationship.

Fanconi anemia *Fanconi pancytopenia syndrome.* A genetic condition characterized by growth deficiency, a distinctive facies, microcephaly (small head), mild intellectual disability (in one fourth of people affected), thumb/radial hypoplasia (lack of full development), hyperpigmentation (areas of darker skin color), and a blood disorder. At least eight different genes have been identified in this autosomal recessive condition, all of which involve deoxyribonucleic acid

(DNA) repair. Testing uses clastogens (chemicals that break chromosomes): Chromosomes from people not affected with Fanconi anemia will not be damaged as much as those from people with Fanconi anemia.

Fanconi-Schlesinger syndrome *See* Williams syndrome.

FAPE *See* free appropriate public education.

FAQ *See* Gillette Functional Assessment Questionnaire.

FAQs *See* frequently asked questions.

FAS *See* fetal alcohol syndrome.

fasciculation The visible involuntary twitching of muscles. When accompanied by muscle wasting, it may indicate a spinal cord or neuromuscular disorder.

fascioscapulohumeral muscular dystrophy *Landouzy-Dejerine dystrophy.* A form of muscular dystrophy (an inherited muscle disease that causes weakness) with an autosomal dominant inheritance pattern. This disorder can appear any time from childhood to adulthood. The face and shoulder muscles are primarily affected, but the trunk and pelvis may become involved over time.

fast eating syndrome Rapid food consumption characterized by large bites stored in cheeks; a common cause of dysphagia (difficulty swallowing) and choking incidents. The syndrome is more common in psychiatric inpatients and people with severe intellectual disability.

Fast ForWord A comprehensive remediation program for children ages 4–12 years with learning and language impairments. The program teaches children to distinguish rapidly changing phonetic elements in order to improve their decoding skills. Trained certified professionals use computer-generated artificial speech (e.g., digitized human speech, digital tones and sounds) to teach rapid acoustic processing in trimester units over a period of years.

fast mapping The ability to acquire new words after only a few exposures to the word, often without explicit instruction from an adult.

fatigue Tiredness during prolonged physical or mental activity.

FBA *See* functional behavioral assessment.

FCT *See* functional communication training.

FD Familial dysautonomia. *See* Riley-Day syndrome.

FEAS *See* Functional Emotional Assessment Scale for Infancy and Early Childhood.

febrile seizure A seizure associated with a fever, though sometimes occurring before or after the fever, in the absence of another central nervous system (CNS) disease. In most children, the seizure is precipitated by a rising fever. Most children with febrile seizures do not have other kinds of seizures or cognitive impairments.

Federal Resource Center (FRC) for Special Education A Division of the Office of Special Education Programs (OSEP), FRC strives to improve the educational outcomes for all children, especially those with disabilities, by working with six regional program centers to support state education agencies in the systemic improvement of education, programs, practices, and policies that affect children and youth with disabilities. FRC services include consultation, information services, specially designed technical assistance (including web site development, training, and product devel-

opment), and conferences and institutes to link people and share ideas.

feeble minded Obsolete term used to describe individuals with intellectual disability and an intelligence quotient (IQ) score between 50 and 70; sometimes generically used to categorize all individuals with IQ scores below 70.

feedback Information provided to an individual about his or her behavior, performance, or condition; a variety of modes of feedback (verbal, written, video, role-playing) can be used.

feedback The phenomenon in which sound escapes from the receiver of the hearing aid and cycles back through the microphone.

feeding aversion A self-restriction of type, texture, or amount of food available to a child that can range from mild to severe in nature.

feeding therapy Treatment that seeks to improve 1) the positioning of food in the mouth, 2) the manipulation of food with the tongue, 3) the chewing of boli (masses) of varying consistencies, 4) the recollection of boli into cohesive masses prior to initiating a swallow, and 5) the organization of lingual (tongue) action to propel boli in an anterior–posterior direction.

FEES *See* flexible endoscopic examination of swallowing.

Feingold hypothesis The unproven claim that trace amounts of salicylates (the active ingredient in aspirin), preservatives, food dyes, and food colors can produce behavioral symptoms, attention deficits, hyperactivity, and learning disabilities in children and that many such neurobehavioral problems can be treated or prevented by a diet (the Feingold diet) that strictly avoids the offending additives. *See also* Kaiser-Permanente (K-P) diet.

Feldenkrais method   An educational system based on movement and mind–body integration.

femoral anteversion   An orthopedic deformity in which the femurs (thighbones) turn inward so that the knees and feet both turn in.

femur   Thighbone.

femoral anteversion

fenfluramine   Trade name, Pondimin. An amphetamine-like medication that increases serotonin (a neurotransmitter, or chemical that enables brain cells to signal one another) in the synapses (spaces between the nerve cells) while reducing blood levels of serotonin.

FEP   *See* free erythrocyte protoporphyrin.

feral child   A child, such as a wolf-child, allegedly raised by animals. There are no documented cases of such an occurrence.

Fernald word learning technique   A multisensory approach to reading that incorporates visual, auditory, kinesthetic (related to body movement), and tactile (involving touch; VAKT) components. A word selected by the student is written by the instructor in cursive writing. The child says the word while tracing it with his or her finger on the paper until he or she can write the word without looking at the model. When the child is comfortable with writing and recognizing words, he or she is encouraged to write a story. The story is typed immediately, and the child reads it in typed form while it is fresh in his or her mind. Once the story is complete and a new word has been used in a meaningful way, the word is filed alphabetically in the child's word list. After a period of time, tracing is done mentally, and file words are typed. After the child is able to learn the typed version of new words, the reading approach becomes similar to other methods.

The Fernald procedure also calls for "positive reconditioning" to address the emotional trauma associated with previous school failure. Psychologist Grace Maxwell Fernald (1879–1950) pioneered this approach.

FERPA   *See* Family Educational Rights and Privacy Act of 1974 (PL 93-380).

fertility rate   The number of live births in a given population during a specific time period. Fertility rates are one indicator of the health status of a given population.

fetal alcohol effects (FAE)   *See* alcohol-related neurodevelopmental disorders (ARND).

fetal alcohol syndrome (FAS)   *Smith syndrome.* A syndrome that results from the teratogenic (causing malformations in the developing fetus) effects of maternal alcohol ingestion. Findings include prenatal growth deficiency with microcephaly (small head) and short stature, cognitive impairments, and a characteristic facies with short palpebral fissures (eye slits) and a smooth philtrum (upper lip groove). The entire spectrum of cognitive and neurobehavioral disabilities can be found. Incidence figures may represent children with the full syndrome FAS or alcohol-related birth defects (ARBD), but under-represent those with fetal alcohol effects (FAE) and alcohol-related neurodevelopmental disorders (ARND). More than 10% of mild intellectual disability may be secondary to the impact of alcohol on early brain development. *See also* alcohol-related birth defects (ARBD).

fetal antiepileptic drug syndrome   A constellation of congenital abnormalities associated with maternal use of an antiepileptic (anti-seizure) drug.

fetal cytomegalovirus (CMV) syndrome   *See* congenital cytomegalic inclusion disease.

fetal Dilantin syndrome *See* fetal phenytoin syndrome.

fetal face syndrome *Robinow syndrome, Robinow-Silverman syndrome.* A syndrome characterized by short forearms, hemivertebrae (the absence of half of one or more spine bones), hypoplastic (underdevelopment) genitalia, and a facies that resembles that of a fetus. Intelligence is usually typical, but language disorders have been noted. The syndrome shows both autosomal dominant and recessive inheritance.

fetal phenytoin syndrome *fetal hydantoin syndrome (FHS).* A pattern of fetal malformation caused by the mother's use of phenytoin (trade name, Dilantin; an antiseizure medication) during the first trimester of pregnancy. This pattern includes poor growth, mild cognitive impairments, unusual facies, and digit and nail hypoplasia (the failure of fingers and nails to develop completely). Facial features include hypertelorism (widely spaced eyes); a broad, flat nasal bridge; a short nose; a bow-shaped upper lip; and often a cleft lip and palate. Eye problems, including coloboma (absence of part of the eye or retina), strabismus (crossed eyes), ptosis (drooping eyelid), or slanting of the eyes, may be seen. The fingers are often small at the tip, with small to absent nails. Genetic factors play a role in determining which fetuses are affected by phenytoin exposure and which never show symptoms. Clefting and congenital heart disease are increased in children of mothers with epilepsy regardless of whether the mothers take antiseizure medications during pregnancy.

fetal rubella syndrome *congenital rubella, Gregg syndrome, rubella embryopathy.* When German measles (rubella) is transmitted from the mother to the fetus in the first or second trimester of pregnancy, this produces a syndrome of hearing impairment, cataracts, and cardiac (heart) and central nervous system abnormalities.

Vaccination of women against rubella was begun to prevent cases of fetal rubella syndrome from occurring (primary prevention). Gamma globulin can be administered as secondary prevention when a nonimmune pregnant woman is exposed. Intellectual disability occurs in about one third of children with the syndrome; learning disabilities, language disorders, autism, impulsivity, and behavior disorders are common.

fetal thalidomide syndrome *See* thalidomide embryopathy.

fetal trimethadione syndrome *fetal Tridione syndrome.* A pattern of malformations described in children of mothers who used trimethadione (an anticonvulsant used to treat absence seizures). The syndrome includes growth failure, intellectual disability, and abnormal facial features.

fetal wastage A maternal history of losing previous pregnancies; the cause for high (multiple spontaneous miscarriages) fetal wastage (e.g., genetic risk, congenital malformations) tends to persist.

fetoscope A stethoscope or fiber-optic instrument used in fetal medicine. *See also* auscultation.

fetus The product of conception (embryo) from the eighth week of gestation to the moment of birth.

Feuerstein, Reuven (1921–) An Israeli psychologist who developed the theory of cognitive modifiability (the ability to be changed). This theory asserts that intelligence is not static but is changeable by specific "mediated learning experiences."

fever In children, a body temperature higher than 100°F. Fever is not an illness or a diagnosis but a sign. For diseases of similar severity, children tend to run relatively higher fevers than do adults. High fever in susceptible young children may lead to febrile seizures.

fever of unknown origin (FUO) A prolonged episode of fever without a readily apparent explanation. In infants and young children, this symptom often represents sepsis (infection) and leads to a detailed search for its cause.

FFD *See* freedom from distractibility.

FG syndrome A genetic syndrome whose features can include intellectual disability, hypotonia (decreased muscle tone), seizures, hyperactivity, outgoing personality, short stature, peculiar facies with prominent forehead, and imperforate (closed) anus. Inheritance is X-linked.

fibrillations Invisible, independent, slow, repetitive contractions of each muscle fiber in response to action potentials.

fibrodysplasia ossificans progressiva (FOP) A condition that includes progressive ectopic (in abnormal locations) calcification (hardening) of bone that causes restriction of movement, shortening of fingers and toes, malformation of the big toe, hearing loss, and hair loss. Inheritance is autosomal dominant, though most cases represent spontaneous mutations (gene changes).

fibula One of the calf bones; the smaller of the two lower leg (shin) bones. *See also* tibia.

fidelity of implementation Treatment integrity. The extent to which an actual intervention corresponds with what was intended in the original design of the program.

field theory The application of gestalt (form recognition) psychology to the study of intellectual disability.

fifth disease *See* erythema infectiosum.

fifth-digit syndrome *See* Coffin-Siris syndrome.

figurative language Nonliteral, interpretive language (e.g., idioms, metaphors, jokes, proverbs).

figure–ground discrimination Recognition of the difference between foreground and background in the context of any given set of visual or auditory stimuli. Individuals with visual figure–ground discrimination difficulties may confuse printed words with the paper upon which they are printed or may give undue significance to less relevant sections of the page rather than attending to the most prominent shape or figure. Individuals with auditory figure–ground problems have difficulty discerning the teacher's voice from other noises in the classroom.

FILE *See* Family Inventory of Life Events.

final consonant deletion A phonological process marked by the omission of a single consonant that terminates a word or syllable.

fine motor skills Skills involving the coordination of the small muscles of the body, especially those of the hand. Eye–hand coordination in infancy, problem solving with toys and puzzles in early childhood, and graphomotor (drawing and handwriting) and dressing skills in middle childhood are expressions and indicators of fine motor skills.

fine pincer grasp The position of the hand for holding small objects in which the objects are held between the tips of the index finger and thumb.

fine-finger movements A test of hand coordination in which the thumb is repetitively tapped against the index finger or is tapped against each of the other four fingers of the same hand one at a time in rapid sequence. The task can be given as a timed test of motor coordination, or the degree of clumsiness and presence of inappropriate "spillover" to the opposite side (mirror movements) can be interpreted as signs of minor neurological dysfunction. Asymmetrical performance may indicate unilateral central nervous system (CNS) dysfunction.

finger stick A procedure in which a small sample of blood is obtained for a laboratory test by pricking a finger pad to squeeze out a bead of blood.

fingerspelling *dactyl speech, dactylology.* A form of unaided augmentative (supplemental, in this case to spoken language) communication with finger movements that uses the conventional language system and its vocabulary, spelling, and grammar; the American Manual Alphabet is a fingerspelling system. Fingerspelling is generally used as an adjunct (addition) to sign language in which signs represent whole words or word parts, not letters. Fingerspelling allows users to convey proper names, specialized terms for which no signs exist, and slang.

finger-to-nose test A test in which the tip of the forefinger (index finger or pointer) is rapidly moved from the tip of the person's nose to either the examiner's fingertip or another extended reach position. Dyssynergia (incoordination) or terminal (at the end of the person's reach) tremor can be interpreted as indicating cerebellar disease (involving the part of the brain that helps coordinate complicated movements); however, they may also occur with dysfunction of the cerebral cortex. Asymmetrical performance (worse on one side than the other) should be noted.

first and second branchial arch syndrome *See* Goldenhar syndrome.

First Year Inventory (FYI) A 63-item parent-report questionnaire used to screen for autism and related developmental disorders in 12-month-old children.

first-arch syndrome A group of syndromes that involve derivatives of (structures that come from) the first branchial arch (an embryological neck structure); these include Treacher-Collins syndrome, mandibulofacial dysostosis, Pierre Robin syndrome, cleft lip and palate, and deafness associated with ear deformities.

first-degree relative A person who shares 50% of their genes with a family member (i.e., parent, sibling, child).

first-order change In general systems theories and family therapy based on such theories, first-order change is behavior change without real systemwide change. First-order change is viewed as superficial by many theorists; however, it is often a necessary precursor to more fundamental change in a system (termed *second-order change*).

FirstSTEP: Screening Test for Evaluating Preschoolers A screening test for children 2;9–6;2 years of age with 12 subtests in three areas: cognition, communication, and motor skills. Optional socioemotional and adaptive (functional) behavior scales make up two additional domains or areas. Scores classify performance as within acceptable limits, at risk, or caution (mild to moderate delay). FirstSTEP is designed to address the developmental domains as defined in the Individuals with Disabilities Education Act Amendments (IDEA) of 1997 (PL 105-17).

FISH *See* fluorescent *in situ* hybridization.

Fisher-Logemann Test of Articulation Competence (F-LTOAC) A test of pronunciation used with preschoolers to adults that includes picture and sentence tasks for examining all English phonemes (speech sounds) according to syllabic function.

fisting A hand position with the fingers flexed in a clenched palm. This is the typical posture more than half of the time for the first 3 months of life, after which the hand begins to be open or unfisted at rest most of the time. Persistence of fisting past 3 months is often a sign of hypertonicity or spasticity (increased muscle tone).

fisting

fit *See* seizure.

5-hydroxytryptamine *See* serotonin.

504 plan accommodations Section 504 of the Rehabilitation Act of 1973 (PL 93-112) makes it unlawful for any school that receives federal funds to exclude an individual from participating or deny him or her benefits, services, programs, or activities solely on the basis of a disability. Section 504 accommodations are thus provided in general education settings for children with attention-deficit/hyperactivity disorder (ADHD) or other impairments who do not otherwise qualify for an individualized education program (IEP). Examples of 504 plan accommodations include reduced class size; the provision of a structured learning environment; the repetition and simplification of instructions regarding both classroom and homework assignments; and the use of modified texts and workbooks, modified nonacademic activities (e.g., physical education, recess, lunchtime), multisensory input, behavior management, modified schedules, modified testing procedures, adjunctive and accommodative equipment, classroom aides, and special education consultation and supports as needed. Children whose diagnosis qualifies them for an IEP will have such accommodations included in the IEP. *See also* Rehabilitation Act of 1973 (PL 93-112).

5p- syndrome *See* cri-du-chat syndrome.

fixation The ability of the eyes to maintain focus on one item. Fixation is necessary to be able to read.

fixed Describing an orthopedic deformity (or atypical positioning of the arms or legs) that cannot be passively corrected. The resistance of the deformity prevents the examiner or therapist from moving the limbs to a typical position.

fixed augmentative and alternative communication (AAC) display Any display in which the symbols and items are "fixed" in a particular location.

flaccid Describing floppy, hypotonic (decreased) muscle tone due to neuromuscular dysfunction. Flaccidity may be due to a central or peripheral problem (e.g., cerebral palsy due to central nervous system problems, Erb's palsy due to peripheral or nerve injury).

flaccid dysarthria A motor speech disorder characterized by hypotonia, weakness, and reduced reflexes in the affected muscle(s).

flail To swing freely in large movements, usually inappropriately, due to loss of control.

flaky Informal, nonspecific term describing mild to moderate psychological disorganization demonstrated through such issues as having trouble organizing thoughts, remembering plans, formulating intentions, and carrying out everyday affairs. The term is often used to refer to individuals who may have undiagnosed learning or attention disorders or to characterize an aspect of task performance (e.g., word association).

flat affect Lack of expressed emotion or a fixed emotional state with no or a highly restricted range of variability or emotion. A person with flat affect appears to have no reaction to obvious humor or to hearing good or bad news. Flat affect may be a symptom of autism.

Flesch index   An index of the reading difficulty of a passage. The Flesch index is calculated from formulas that use counts of words per sentence, number of syllables per 100 words, and frequency of personal words (proper nouns and names) to generate reading ease and human interest scores and to calculate grade levels.

flexible endoscopic examination of swallowing (FEES)   An assessment of bolus transport that uses transnasal (through the nose) fiberoptic (video cable) laryngoscopy to view the natural anatomy (e.g., vocal folds) before and after swallowing. FEES involves no exposure to radiation.

flexion   The bending of a joint.

flexion crease   A crease in the skin lying over a joint due to movement at that joint.

flexor   Any muscle that bends a joint. *Flexor tone* refers to the degree to which a person's muscle tone produces a flexor habitus or appearance (keeps the muscles flexed).

flexor withdrawal reflex   A procedure used to trigger active foot dorsiflexion (upgoing movement of the toes). In a sitting position, the individual is asked to flex the hip (lift the thigh) against resistance (downward pressure from the examiner's hand). A positive response is automatic dorsiflexion of the foot at the ankle.

flight of ideas   *tangential speech.* A continuous change of subject and thought content with little apparent connection among the topics and little outside cause for the change. Flight of ideas may be associated with attention-deficit/hyperactivity disorder (ADHD), mania, or schizophrenia.

Floortime   *See* Developmental, Individual-Difference, Relationship-Based (DIR) Model.

floppy infant   An infant with hypotonia (decreased muscle tone) and delayed motor

milestones (such as sitting independently and walking) in the first 1–2 years of life. This condition may be an early presentation for a variety of genetic, cognitive, or

floppy infant

neuromotor disorders. Rarely, the floppy infant is diagnosed as having a congenital myopathy (muscle disease) or neuromuscular disorder via tests called *nerve conduction studies* and *electromyography.* More commonly, severe hypotonia evolves into spastic cerebral palsy by late in the first year of life or extrapyramidal cerebral palsy by late in the second year of life. In the absence of any of these outcomes, the floppy infant most commonly has benign cerebral hypotonia, a motor condition that will be outgrown with regard to motor development (e.g., these children may walk late, but they do walk) but may reveal other developmental disorders. The more severe and prolonged the infantile hypotonia, the greater the likelihood of more pervasive cognitive and motor dysfunction. *See also* hypotonicity.

flora   Bacteria typically residing on or in the body. Gut flora, for example, live in the intestines and are not a sign of infection but of normal colonization.

F-LTOAC   *See* Fisher-Logemann Test of Articulation Competence.

fluency   The ability to do academic tasks with speed and accuracy. Fluency is usually associated with reading but is also a factor in performing other academic subjects such as mathematics and written expression.

fluency disorder   Any condition that results in an interruption in the flow of oral language; this includes, but is not restricted to, stuttering. *See also* cluttering, stuttering.

fluid intelligence   *Cattell-Horn-Carroll theory of cognitive abilities.* The ability to infer relationships and correlations. Fluid intelligence is best measured by tests that are new and unfamiliar to the test taker, particularly when adaptation and flexibility are involved. Tasks intended to measure fluid intelligence should not depend on previously acquired knowledge or earlier learned problem-solving strategies. *See also* cystallized ability, Kaufman Assessment Battery for Children–Second Edition (K-ABC-II), Woodcock-Johnson Tests of Cognitive Ability.

fluorescent *in situ* hybridization (FISH) A genetic mapping approach that uses fluorescent tags to detect the presence or absence of genetic material on a chromosome. FISH tests are usually directed at specific disorders: The laboratory needs to know what disorder is suspected in order to use the tag appropriate to that disorder, and it will not be able to detect other disorders with the same tag. *See also in situ* hybridization.

fluoroscopy An x-ray procedure that makes it possible to see internal organs in motion; this technique uses x rays to produce real-time visual images.

fluoxetine Trade name, Prozac. A selective serotonin reuptake inhibitor (SSRI) used to treat depression, anxiety, obsessive-compulsive disorder (OCD), and similar symptoms in autism. Side effects may include gastrointestinal distress, diarrhea, or increased activity level. Fluoxetine can also cause hypomania (elevated mood). This drug often takes 3–4 weeks to show clinical effects.

fluvoxamine Trade name, Luvox. A selective serotonin reuptake inhibitor (SSRI) used to treat obsessive-compulsive disorder (OCD). It is usually given in a single dose at bedtime. Fluvoxamine can aggravate mania in bipolar disorder (manic depressive disorder) and can trigger seizures in a small percentage of people with known seizure disorders.

FM *See* frequency modulation system.

FMS *See* Functional Mobility Scale.

FO *See* foot orthoses.

focal Having to do with a central point of activity, attraction, or attention. For example, a focal motor seizure can start with twitching in a limited body region, locating the seizure focus (point of origin) in the contralateral motor strip of the brain (the area that controls body movements on the opposite side of the brain from the twitching of the seizure). A focal sign on neurological examination is one that helps locate the part of the brain that is abnormal.

folic acid The B-complex vitamin folic acid, or folate, reduces the risk of neural tube birth defects such as spina bifida when consumed in adequate amounts by women before and during early pregnancy.

folk psychology Folk psychology refers to one's untaught understanding of the social world. The folk psychology/folk physics theory of autism holds that compared with their mental ages, children and adults with autism have typical to superior folk physics abilities with impaired folk psychology abilities.

folk physics Folk physics refers to someone's untaught understanding of the *physical world*. The folk psychology/folk physics theory of autism holds that compared with their mental ages, children and adults with autism have typical to superior folk physics abilities with impaired folk psychology abilities.

fontanel "Soft spots" on an infant's head. There are two palpable (able to be felt) fontanels at birth—the anterior (front) and posterior (back)—but usually only the anterior is followed clinically. Each fontanel represents a soft membranous covering where the cranial bones

fontanel

meet but have not yet fused. The anterior fontanel closes between 8 and 15 months of life; the posterior one by 4 months. Early closure of the fontanel may result from craniosynostosis (early fusion of skull bones); this should be of special concern when associated with either decreasing head growth rate or microcephaly (small head). An enlarging anterior fontanel may reflect hydrocephalus (excess fluid in the brain), especially when accompanied by a rapidly enlarging head circumference. A persistent anterior fontanel may occur in a variety of genetic, metabolic, and bone disorders. In young infants, the anterior fontanel may pulsate with the heartbeat; easily visible pulsations may be seen in increased intracranial pressure and a variety of heart conditions.

food chaining   A therapy technique meant to expand a child's food repertoire (i.e., treat children with feeding aversions). This technique involves taking accepted foods or liquids in the repertoire and modifying or linking them to other specifically selected foods or liquids.

food texture   *See* texture.

foot orthoses (FO)   Orthopedic corrections, including arch supports, braces, shoe inserts, and corrective or orthopedic shoes. Types of FO include AFO (ankle–foot orthoses), KAFO (knee ankle–foot orthoses), and DAFO (dynamic ankle–foot orthoses).

foot-switch system   A component of gait analysis that allows recording of the foot-to-floor contact patterns for each leg.

FOP   *See* fibrodysplasia ossificans progressiva.

Forestown boot   A foot orthosis used to treat equinus (toe walking).

formal assessment   An approach to evaluation that includes the use of published instruments that use standardized protocols to gather information (e.g., tests, observation forms, rating scales).

formal operations   The final stage of cognitive development based on the theories of psychologist Jean Piaget, characterized by achievement of formal logic (induction and deduction) and abstract reasoning (understanding and analyzing relationships, developing theories and hypotheses, applying knowledge in new situations). This stage usually emerges in adolescence (12–15 years of age). People with intellectual disability may not reach the stage of formal operations.

Formal Reading Inventory (FRI)   A method for assessing silent reading comprehension and oral reading miscues in individuals ages 6;6–17;11 years.

formative data collection   A more extensive process of formative evaluation (also known as *developmental evaluation*). Formative evaluation starts in the planning stages, before an intervention program is launched. It continues with frequent data collection throughout the program's implementation. All participants—teachers, principals, coaches, mentors—typically collect formative data. The purpose of formative evaluation is to provide constructive feedback that will improve a plan or program *immediately* so that eventually the data collected will be able to show evidence of the intended long-term results. Formative evaluation and data collection can be done at the level of the individual student and his or her individualized education program (IEP) or can be done at the program level, such as in the evaluation of a new language curriculum.

formboard   A flat board out of which a number of geometric shapes and matching pieces (usually slightly thicker than the board) have been cut; these shapes and pieces can then be inserted into the corresponding holes in the board. The formboard was invented by Edouard Seguin

(1812–1880) to train children's visual-perceptual motor skills and was later incorporated into many intelligence tests.

forme fruste An incomplete form or mild manifestation of a condition or disease.

Forster sign *See* scissoring.

45X *See* Turner syndrome.

45,X/46,XX/47,XXX *See* XXX syndrome.

45,X/46,XX *See* Turner syndrome.

45X/46,XY *See* Turner syndrome.

47,+18 *See* trisomy 18 syndrome.

47,+21 *See* Down syndrome (DS).

47,XX or XY,+8 *See* trisomy 8 mosaicism.

47,XX or XY,+9 *See* trisomy 9 mosaicism.

47,XXX *See* XXX syndrome.

47,XXY *See* Klinefelter syndrome.

47,XYY *See* XYY syndrome.

46,X,del(Xp) *See* Turner syndrome.

46(XX or XY),dter(14)t(14;21) *See* Down syndrome (DS).

46,XX/47,XXX *See* XXX syndrome.

46X,i(Xq) *See* Turner syndrome.

46Xdel(Xq) *See* Turner syndrome.

forward chaining A teaching method grounded in operant conditioning in which the child is taught the first step in a sequence in a task, then each subsequent step in a sequential order until all steps in the task are completed. *See also* backward chaining, chaining.

four finger transverse crease *See* simian crease.

4p- syndrome *del(4)(p-).* Deletion of all or part of the short arm of chromosome 4; a chromosomal disorder characterized by profound intellectual disability, seizures, growth deficiency, and a distinctive facies.

fra (q27) *See* fragile X syndrome (FXS).

fragile X syndrome (FXS) *fra (q27), Martin-Bell syndrome.* A form of X-linked intellectual disability caused by an increased number (more than 200) of repeats of the CGG trinucleotide, leading to altered expression of the FMR protein. Affected males show mild to profound intellectual disability; poor eye contact; cluttered speech; poor pronunciation; hyperactivity; autistic features; macrocephaly (large head); large, prominent ears; prognathism (protruding jaw); nystagmus (jerky eye movements); and (after puberty) large testes. Carrier females tend to be slow learners who may be shy and who are at risk for early menopause. Premutation carrier

fragile X syndrome

males (with an increased number of repeats but below the level seen in young males who are affected) may show a neurological condition associated with tremor and ataxia.

frame An orthopedic device for a bed; the frame is either on or around the bed or is itself a specialized bed. The frame allows for extrinsic support (e.g., a pulley system) for positioning.

frame of reference A guideline for therapy intervention that organizes theoretical material and translates it into practice.

Franceschetti-Klein syndrome *See* Treacher Collins syndrome.

Fraser syndrome   *See* cryptophthalmus.

fraternal twins   *See* dizygotic twins.

FRC   *See* Federal Resource Center for Special Education.

FRDA   *See* Friedreich ataxia.

free appropriate public education (FAPE)   Federal mandates require states to ensure that a FAPE be available to all children with disabilities residing in the state. This means that special education and related services are provided at public expense, under public supervision and direction, and without charge; meet the standards of the state education agency and the requirements of the Individuals with Disabilities Education Act (IDEA) of 1990 (PL 101-476); and take place in the least restrictive (i.e., most natural) environment needed by the child. *See also* Education for All Handicapped Children Act of 1975 (PL 94-142), Individuals with Disabilities Education Act Amendments (IDEA) of 1991 (PL 102-119), Individuals with Disabilities Education Act Amendments (IDEA) of 1997 (PL 105-17), Individuals with Disabilities Education Improvement Act (IDEA) of 2004 (PL 108-446).

free association   A therapeutic technique in which the client is instructed to say whatever thought, feeling, or image comes to mind.

free erythrocyte protoporphyrin (FEP)   A component of hemoglobin (the substance in red blood cells that carries oxygen). When FEP levels are high, lead poisoning or iron deficiency is suspected. The FEP level is not sufficiently sensitive to be used to detect the lowered limits for lead exposure proposed by the Centers for Disease Control and Prevention (CDC).

free morpheme   A type of morpheme (word part) that can stand alone and convey meaning. Free morphemes cannot be broken down into smaller parts.

freedom from distractibility (FFD)   A factor score derived from subtests of either Wechsler or Kaufman batteries that attempts to measure the ability to concentrate and maintain attention.

Freeman-Sheldon syndrome (FSS)   *See* whistling face syndrome.

frenulum linguae   The lingual (tongue) frenulum; a fold of tissue from the floor of the mouth to the middle of the underside of the tongue. A short lingual frenulum is described as tongue-tie and can affect the ability to raise the tongue tip to the palate to produce certain sounds (generally /l/, /t/, /d/), but this is rarely clinically significant.

frequency   A measurement of the pitch of a sound; the number of complete cycles a sound wave makes over a second, expressed in hertz (Hz). Human beings with average hearing can detect frequencies from approximately 20 to 20,000 Hz.

frequency modulation (FM) system   A specialized radio transmission system used by hearing aids and auditory trainers.

frequently asked questions (FAQs)   Describing a strategy that provides answers to the most commonly asked questions about a topic, such as Home- and Community-based Service Waivers. FAQs are generally posted online and made available to the public.

FRI   *See* Formal Reading Inventory.

fricative   A consonant sound produced by restricting most of the air flow as it passes from the mouth, such as in /f/ or /v/.

Friedreich ataxia (FRDA)   A hereditary neurodegenerative disorder characterized by ataxia (unsteady gait), nystagmus (jerking eye movements), kyphoscoliosis (curvature of the spine), and pes cavus (a high-arched foot). Degeneration occurs in nerve cells of the spinal cord (specifically in the axons of the long tracts) and occasionally in other parts of the nervous system (cerebellum, brainstem, and vestibular [balance] and auditory [hearing] systems). Progressive ataxia involves the legs more than the arms. Speech can be affected because of difficulties alternating between breathing and talking. Lateral (side-to-side) nystagmus is present, as is optic atrophy (a dying back of the optic nerve, which carries images from the retina of the eye to the part of the brain that interprets them). Weakness and wasting of the distal (peripheral) muscles are common, as are abnormal sensations such as paresthesias (numbness, tingling, or heightened sensitivity). Intelligence is preserved. Life expectancy is to the 40s or 50s; individuals with advanced cases are often confined to bed and have difficulties swallowing. Mean age of onset (first symptoms) is between 10 and 15 years and usually before 25 years. Approximately two thirds of individuals with FRDA have cardiomyopathy, up to 30% have diabetes mellitus, and approximately 25% have an "atypical" presentation with later onset. The condition is inherited in an autosomal recessive manner. Individuals with FRDA have identifiable mutations in the *FXN* gene. The most common type of mutation is a GAA triplet-repeat expansion in intron 1 of *FXN*.

fringe vocabulary	The vocabulary words and messages that are specific or unique to an individual.

frog posture	A posture that indicates extreme hypotonia (low muscle tone) or floppiness: An

frog posture

infant lies flat with arms out in a surrender posture, hips and knees bent, feet everted (turned outward), and hips abducted (turned outward) so that the knees touch the lateral surface. The infant lies flat in the crib. Bilateral hip abduction deformity is the "frog leg" posture.

frontal lobe	The anterior (front) portion of the brain just behind the forehead; the area of the cerebrum (brain) in front of the central sulcus (fissure of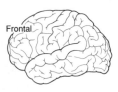

frontal lobe

Rolando, one of the major folds in the brain) that is divided into right and left frontal lobes by the interhemispheric fissure. Loss of the frontal lobes can result in passivity and loss of motivation. The posterior (back) part of the frontal lobe contains the motor cortex, the part of the brain involved in voluntary movement. *See also* frontal lobe syndrome.

frontal lobe syndrome	*apathico-akineticoabulic syndrome.* A syndrome that results from frontal lobe damage due to trauma or neurological disease; it can include loss of executive function skills, olfactory impairment (loss of sense of smell), language and motor impairments (depending on the parts of the frontal lobes involved), mood and motivational disorders, and disinhibition (impulsivity). Many of these symptoms can be observed in a milder form in attention-deficit/hyperactivity disorder (ADHD). *See also* frontal lobe.

fronting	The phonological process in which there is a substitution of a more anteriorly produced phoneme.

frontometaphyseal dysplasia	A condition that includes pronounced bony supraorbital (above the eyes) ridges, generalized skeletal dysplasia (abnormal bone growth), and often hearing loss. This disorder appears to be X-linked, with variable expression in carrier females.

frontonasal dysplasia	*See* median cleft palate face syndrome.

frustration A subjective feeling of discomfort, tension, or disappointment that arises when one's desires or objectives are thwarted.

frustration level In reading, the level at which the text is sufficiently difficult that more than 1 in 10 words presents a challenge and there is a less than 90% success rate. See also independent level, instructional level.

FSS Freeman-Sheldon syndrome. See whistling face syndrome.

FTII See Fagan Test of Infant Intelligence.

FTT See failure to thrive.

fucosidosis A disorder of sugar metabolism (processing by the body) caused by the abnormal accumulation of fucose-containing glycolipids and oligosaccharides inside cells due to lack of the enzyme alpha-L-fucosidase. Fucosidosis has autosomal recessive inheritance and is more common in southern Italians, Hispanic Americans, and Navajo people.

full integration The state in which students are physically present in the same educational settings as their same-age peers during the entire school day.

functional In psychiatry, having an emotional or psychiatric cause; the ability of an individual, entity, or behavior to meet its intended objective or function (e.g., functional language enables a person to communicate his or her wants and needs).

functional analysis See functional behavioral assessment (FBA).

functional aphonia The loss of voice or the inability to produce phonation for speech, although there is no organic pathology.

functional approach An intervention method that identifies skills that children need in order to be successful in their present environment or in one they will soon be entering.

functional behavioral assessment (FBA) The process of determining the cause (function) of problem behavior before developing an intervention, as well as the documents that result from that process. Schools are required to conduct FBAs when students are disciplined for or face removal due to problem behavior. The FBA process entails first identifying and articulating the problem behavior and then gathering detailed information via interviews, direct observation, questionnaires, and other available information. The aim is to identify events that set the stage for and trigger problem behavior, as well as environmental responses that inadvertently serve to maintain it. The hypothesis that identifies the function that a behavior serves for the individual is then tested: The school team manipulates antecedents (triggers) and consequences to see what effect they have on behavior. See also behavior intervention plan (BIP), Individuals with Disabilities Education Improvement Act (IDEA) of 2004 (PL 108-446), manifestation determination, positive behavior support (PBS).

functional communication training (FCT) A procedure to reduce challenging behaviors by replacing them with meaningful or functional communication; a form of a functional behavioral assessment (FBA). The anticipated negative consequences of a challenging behavior are used to encourage a more constructive behavior.

Functional Emotional Assessment Scale for Infancy and Early Childhood (FEAS) A set of 5-point Likert scales used to assess emotional functioning in children 3–48 months of age.

functional imaging The research use of techniques such as single photon emission computed tomography (SPECT), functional magnetic resonance imaging (fMRI), positron emission tomography (PET), and magnetoelectroencephalography (MEG) to localize (locate) a function to a particular part of the brain by measuring blood flow in the brain during the performance of that function.

Functional Independence Measure for Children (WeeFIM) A measure of the severity of disability in children and adults with developmental levels between 6 months and 7 years. Performance on each of 18 items in six domains (self-care, sphincter control [ability to stay dry], mobility, locomotion [ability to get around], communication, and cognition) is assigned to one of seven levels on a scale, with scores ranging from complete independence (Level 7) to complete dependence on a helping person (Level 1). This is a downward extension of a rehabilitation scale for adults, the Functional Independence Measure (FIM).

Functional Mobility Scale (FMS) A scale used to classify the functional mobility of children ages 4–18 years with cerebral palsy. The instrument is designed to measure mobility performance and is scored on the basis of parent/child interview. The FMS measures mobility function over three different distances—5 m (home), 50 m (school), and 500 m (community)—and also takes into account the range of assistive devices that a child with cerebral palsy might use for mobility. The scale can also be used to measure change in function after a surgical procedure.

functional reach test A method used to examine balance in children and adults.

functional skills Those skills that are used in everyday life in a variety of environments and that focus on different areas, such as personal hygiene and health (bathing, brushing teeth, dressing, groom-

ing), home (cooking, cleaning, washing clothes), family, self-help, employment, recreation, and community involvement. Functional skills curricula are usually paired with functional academics. Functional academics is more appropriately termed *applied academics* and focuses on using reading and math skills to negotiate the demands of daily living (e.g., reading skills: reading signs [stop, go, men, women], reading a recipe, reading a medicine bottle; math skills: managing money, going grocery shopping, making change, making and following a budget, telling time; health skills: grooming, practicing oral hygiene, planning healthy meals; employment skills: arriving on time, wearing appropriate dress, communicating with coworkers and bosses). Skills such as communication, cooperation, problem solving, self-initiation, and responsibility have all been shown to be related to job stability. Because learning history, geography, science, and math can be functional and can be in the long-term interests of *all* students, the definition of *functional* has been broadened to include science, art, music, history, English literature, and other subjects.

functional skills training Direct training in the skills and competencies necessary for everyday living, which can include using adaptive equipment, counting change, reading single words, balancing a checkbook, and completing a job application.

fundus The bottom or base of an organ; the part of a hollow organ that is farthest from its opening.

FUO *See* fever of unknown origin.

fusiform gyrus *facial gyrus, fusiform facial area (FFA).* A cortical (surface of the brain) area that includes adjoining parts of the temporal (side) and occipital (back) lobes of the brain, which are used for facial recognition.

futures planning Considering various aspects of people's lives with a special focus on easing the major transitions in life, such as that from adolescence to adulthood.

FXS *See* fragile X syndrome.

FXS Martin-Bell syndrome *See* fragile X syndrome (FXS).

FYI *See* First Year Inventory.

Gg

g factor An index of general mental ability or intelligence that largely represents the reasoning and abstracting aspects of mental ability as opposed to partial aspects of mental ability. Tests with high g loadings (demands for the use of reasoning and abstracting), such as comprehension and hypothesis-testing tasks, require complex mental effort; tests with low g loadings require less complex abilities and involve recall, recognition, and dexterity.

G tube *See* gastrostomy tube.

GABA *See* gamma-aminobutyric acid.

gabapentin Trade names, Neurontin; Gabarone. An anticonvulsant used to treat people with partial seizures, neuropathy (pain caused by nerve damage), postherpetic neuralgia (pain from shingles), and other kinds of pain.

GAD *See* generalized anxiety disorder.

GADS *See* Gilliam Asperger Disorder Scale.

gag reflex A reflex response to a tactile (touch) stimulus to the posterior (back) tongue or pharynx (throat) that produces a gag (i.e., tongue protrusion, head and jaw protrusion, and pharyngeal contractions). This reflex is present by 6 months of gestation, is strong at birth, is hyperactive in neurologically impaired children, and may be hypoactive with ataxia (unsteady gait). Testing this reflex is part of the neurological examination of cranial nerves IX and X.

gait A pattern of walking. Gait tests include walking, running, skipping, hopping (on one foot), heel walking, toe walking, and tandem (heel to toe) walking tests. Disturbances in gait can reflect major motor system involvement (e.g., cerebral palsy) or milder motor system involvement. *See also* developmental coordination disorder.

gait analysis A quantitative description of gait (walk) as performed in a gait analysis laboratory using an optical (visual) recording system and an electrical system comprising a floor pressure sensor and a variety of electromyogram (EMG) components that measure the activity of different muscles. The large amount of data generated is analyzed by specially designed computer programs. Gait analysis is especially useful in predicting the outcome of various orthopedic surgical procedures.

gait cycle The interval between foot contacts of the same leg while walking; the gait cycle is divided into swing (one leg is in motion while the other has its foot in contact with the ground) and stance (vice versa; one leg has its foot in contact with the ground while the other is in motion) phases. One complete gait cycle covers one stride length (two steps).

GAL *See* guardian ad litem.

galactosemia   Hereditary galactose intolerance. An autosomal recessive inborn error of metabolism characterized by hepatomegaly (liver enlargement), splenomegaly (large spleen), and failure to thrive (growth problems). Infants are normal at birth but soon develop jaundice, vomiting, and lethargy. Untreated, they develop cataracts (clouding of the lens of the eye) and intellectual disability. A defect in the activity of the enzyme galactose-1-phosphate uridyl transferase leads to difficulty processing sugar. Diagnosis is suspected by urine tests and confirmed by blood tests. Many states include galactosemia in routine newborn screening. Treatment requires dietary changes to avoid galactose. In general, the earlier treatment is initiated, the better the cognitive outcome.

galactosialidosis   A disorder of sugar metabolism (breakdown and utilization by the body) characterized by growth problems, dysostosis multiplex (bone abnormalities), intellectual disability, cerebellar ataxia (staggering gait), myoclonus (muscle jerks), and seizures. The person exhibits coarse facial features, clouding of the cornea (clear covering of the eye), cherry-red spot on the macula (part of the retina of the eye), and hearing loss. The disorder is autosomal recessive.

Galant reflex   A primitive reflex observed in infants, elicited by holding the infant in prone (stomach down) suspension (held up on the examiner's hand) and stroking the back paravertebrally (along one side of the spine) from top to bottom. The response to this stimulus is an arching or incurving of the trunk toward the stimulated side. An asymmetrical or extremely strong Galant reflex is thought to increase the risk for hip dislocation in children with cerebral palsy.

Galant reflex

Galeazzi sign   Describing the condition in which one knee is lower than the other

when the child is supine (lying on the back) on a flat surface with the knees flexed to 90 degrees. The Galeazzi sign occurs with hip dislocation.

Gallaudet University   A university in Washington, D.C., for people with hearing impairments.

galvanic skin response (GSR)   The measured resistance of the skin to the passage of a weak electrical current, which changes with the amount of moisture (sweat) on the skin. The GSR is an electrophysiological variable used to measure how a person responds to different stimuli.

gamma-aminobutyric acid (GABA)   A neurotransmitter (chemical substance used for transmitting information within the central nervous system) that tends to inhibit (dampen) signaling within the brain and spinal cord.

Gamper reflex   *bowing reflex.* The infant is placed in a supine (lying on the back) position and the thighs are straightened at the hips, causing the infant to come to a sitting "bow" position. This reflex is rare in premature infants but common in infants with galactosemia (difficulty processing sugar) or anencephaly (failure of the brain to develop).

Gamper reflex

gangliosidoses   A group of hereditary disorders characterized by progressive accumulation of gangliosides (brain chemicals) in the gray matter of the brain. The buildup occurs because of problems with the enzyme that should break down the gangliosides but instead is inactive. These disorders present clinically with intellectual deterioration that may also be associated with an enlarged liver. Motor findings include dystonia (erratic muscle tone), hypotonia (low muscle tone), ataxia (unsteady gait), or myoclonus (muscle twitching). Seizures and optic atrophy (a degeneration of the nerve for sight) are frequent. The speed of deterioration and presence of motor and visual problems are specific to the type of enzyme deficiency. Gangliosidoses include the disorders Tay-Sachs disease; Niemann-Pick disease; and types of cerebral sphingolipidosis, lipofuscinoses, lipidoses, and Gaucher disease. Inheritance is generally autosomal recessive.

Gardner Social (Maturity) Development Scale (GSDS)   A brief, 15-minute estimate of how a child 3–13 years old compares socially with chronological-age peers.

GARS-2   *See* Gilliam Autism Rating Scale–Second Edition.

gastrocnemius   One of the calf muscles in the leg.

gastroesophageal reflux (GER or GERD)   The regurgitation of stomach contents back into the esophagus (throat). GER can be an occasional variant of little significance, or it can be a chronic problem that contributes to aspiration (inhalation of food or liquids into the lungs) and failure to thrive (poor growth). GER may be associated with significant neurological impairment or a genetic syndrome and may require surgical treatment with a Nissen fundoplication (a tightening of the top portion of the stomach) and placement of a gastrostomy tube (a feeding tube that leads to the stomach).

gastroschisis   Congenital (from birth) fissure (opening) of the abdominal wall, usually accompanied by protrusion of the small intestine and part of the large intestine. It is caused by a vascular disruption (interruption of blood flow) during fetal development but does not involve the umbilical cord.

gastrostomy   A surgical operation that creates an artificial opening into the stomach, usually for the insertion of a feeding tube.

gastrostomy tube   *G tube, GT.* A tube that goes from the external (outside) abdomen, through the abdominal wall, and into the stomach; it can be used for feeding or for withdrawing gastric (stomach) contents (e.g., for laboratory studies or to remove ingested poisons).

gate   The imitation of a construction using five toy blocks; this serves as a test item that assesses nonverbal (not language-based) problem-solving ability. It can usually be achieved by children 4 years of age.

gate

gate control   A theory of pain that postulates that neural (nerve) mechanisms in the spinal cord act like a gate to modulate (adjust) the flow of nerve impulses from the peripheral (belonging to the body rather than the brain or spinal cord) nerves. The ascending pain signals can be influenced by descending nerve impulses that reflect the brain's past experiences with pain, so that the same degree of pain stimulus may be interpreted quite differently.

Gaucher disease   A progressive condition in which parts of cell membranes called *cerebrosides* are stored in the reticuloendothelial system (organs that control immune function, such as bone marrow or spleen) and sometimes in the nervous system. Chronic Gaucher disease is slowly progressive without neurological involvement until late in life. Infantile Gaucher disease is characterized by marked central nervous system (CNS) involvement and a rapidly progressive downhill course leading to early death. The clinical features include splenomegaly (large spleen), anemia (low red blood cell count), and neurological involvement, with ataxia (unsteady gait), intellectual deterioration, myoclonic seizures, and spasticity (increased muscle tone) presenting in the first decade of life. Diagnosis is made by identifying characteristic types of cells called *Gaucher cells* in bone marrow tissue. Enzyme replacement therapy has largely replaced bone marrow transplant in the treatment of the chronic form of Gaucher disease. Inheritance is autosomal recessive. People of Ashkenazic Jewish ancestry have a higher risk of developing chronic Gaucher disease. Named for the French dermatologist Phillipe C.E. Gaucher (1854–1918).

gavage   Feeding by a tube inserted into the stomach; the tube may be a nasogastric tube (inserted through the nose down the throat), orogastric tube (inserted through the mouth down the throat), or gastrostomy tube (surgically inserted through the abdominal wall). Gavage is used for a variety of reasons usually related to the presence of neurological problems that affect a person's ability to swallow. The orogastric and nasogastric tubes usually represent short-term approaches to treating feeding problems and the gastrostomy tube a long-term approach.

gaze monitoring   Looking in the same direction as another person (following their lead) as a reciprocal (back and forth) social interaction. Gaze monitoring is often impaired in children with autism spectrum disorders.

gaze shift   The ability of the eyes to quickly and accurately change focus from looking at one object to looking at another object, with the eyes moving separately from the head.

GBS infection   *See* group B streptococcal infection.

GCS   *See* Glasgow Coma Scale.

GED   *See* Tests of General Educational Development.

gelastic seizure   An unusual seizure type characterized by paroxysmal (occurring in bursts) laughter. Gelastic seizures have been associated with a kind of central nervous system tumor called a *hypothalamic hamartoma* but can be due to abnormalities in various areas of the brain as well.

gene   The biological unit of heredity that is self-reproducing and located at a definitive position (locus) on a particular chromosome.

gene mapping   *See* chromosome mapping. *See also* genetic mapping.

gene therapy   The treatment of disease by the manipulation of deoxyribonucleic acid (DNA) rather than by the use of drugs, surgery, or other interventions.

general education   A term used to describe classes in school for all students. The term is used in individualized education programs (IEPs) to differentiate from special education.

general intellectual ability (GIA)   The score reported from the Woodcock-Johnson III (WJ-III) Tests of Cognitive Ability as a student's intellectual level rather than academic ability.

generalization   The transfer of learning (i.e., the ability to apply a rule or skill to cases or situations other than those in which it has been learned); also, the continuance of behavior change across people and places without the necessity of continuing intervention. There are two types of generalization. In stimulus generalization, responses occur in circumstances that resemble the original learning situation (e.g., recognizing the word *dog* when it appears in a different font or in all capital letters). In response generalization, change in one behavior results in a similar change in a different (but related) class of behavior (e.g., a child might spontaneously improve organizational skills for reading and social studies tasks).

generalized anxiety disorder (GAD) An anxiety disorder characterized by excessive anxiety and worry about a number of events or activities (such as work or school performance). The person finds it difficult to control the worry. GAD is associated with at least one (in children) or three (in adults) of the following six symptoms: a feeling of restlessness or being keyed up, on edge; a feeling of being easily fatigued; difficulty concentrating or mind going blank; irritability; muscle tension; and sleep disturbance (difficulty falling or staying asleep, or restless unsatisfying sleep). The anxiety and worry themselves cause the person distress and impairment and persist even when the person is not being judged and has always performed well in the past. GAD affects 3%–5% of the population.

generalized glycogenosis *See* Pompe disease.

generalized resistance to thyroid hormone (GRTH) A rare genetic endocrine disorder characterized by tachycardia (rapid heart rate), learning and attention problems, and occasionally a goiter (neck swelling). GRTH represents a very rare presentation for attention-deficit/hyperactivity disorder (ADHD).

generalized seizure A seizure characterized by loss of consciousness and electrical changes that affect the whole brain at once. Such seizures may involve tonic (increased muscle tone) and clonic (rhythmic contraction and relaxation) movements. Seizure types in this category include absence (brief repeated losses of attention and response), tonic, clonic, tonic-clonic (in which tonic movements are followed by clonic jerking), atonic (sudden loss of muscle tone), and myoclonic (lightning-like muscle jerks). The seizures can range in duration from a few seconds to a half hour or more, depending on the type. A postictal (after the seizure) period of disorientation (confusion) and poor coordination is common. Generalized tonic-clonic (GTC) seizures, or major motor seizures (formerly described as *grand mal seizures*), can occur with fever (febrile seizure), with infections such as meningitis (infection of the brain), with certain drugs, or from unknown causes (idiopathic). Diagnosis is generally by a combination of electroencephalogram (EEG; a recording of brain electrical activity) and clinical correlation (a history of relevant symptoms).

generic Describing a chemical formula (e.g., drug) not protected by patent; the official name used to describe the drug regardless of its proprietary name or which pharmaceutical company produces it. *Generic* may also refer to a nontrademarked preparation often sold at a lower cost than a brand name or trade name drug.

generic small talk Small talk that individuals can use with a variety of different conversational partners because it does not refer to specific shared information.

genetic Describing the etiology (cause) of a disorder determined to be in the structure of an individual's genes, which exhibit extra, missing, or rearranged deoxyribonucleic acid (DNA).

genetic counseling The process of helping people understand and adapt to the medical, psychological, and familial implications of genetic contributions to disease. This process integrates the following: interpretation of family and medical histories to assess the chance of disease occurrence or recurrence; education about inheritance, testing, management, prevention, resources and research; and counseling to promote informed choices and adaptation to the risk or condition. Genetic counselors must meet both educational and competency criteria as determined by passing an examination.

genetic mapping A procedure in which variant forms of genes (mutant alleles) or deoxyribonucleic acid (DNA) sequence markers are assigned relative positions along a chromosome. This is done on the basis of their frequency of recombination (how the effects that they are meant to produce appear in people with different alleles).

genetic screening   Testing in a particular population to identify individuals at high risk for carrying or having a specific disorder. Testing for carriers of Tay-Sachs disease among the Ashkenazic (Eastern European) Jews targets a particular subgroup, whereas using the blood test for phenylketonuria (PKU; a condition that results in too much of a protein building block called *phenylalanine* in the blood) occurs in the general population. Other genetic screening tests include newborn screening batteries for a variety of metabolic conditions, hemoglobinopathies (blood disorders), and hearing loss and prenatal screening for chromosome conditions (such as the extra chromosome 21 of Down syndrome) or neural tube defects (e.g., spina bifida, the incomplete closure of the spinal column).

genetics   The branch of medicine concerned with the heredity of disease conditions, the prediction of recurrence risks (how likely another child born into the family would be to have a disease), and the counseling of families about such risks.

genogram   A diagram that shows the family composition and structure for three or more generations. A genogram is used by family therapists to indicate the types of relationships among individuals and by genetic counselors to trace the appearance of traits and inherited diseases; it is also used to track the appearance of behavior disorders, addictions, and psychiatric illness. Biological, legal, and functional family members and the nature of their relationships are shown together with pertinent dates, issues, and information in a one-page format. Once structure is mapped, probing for disorders in each of these family members can be helpful in determining whether

a particular disorder is familial and what its genetic inheritance patterns could be. The genogram can summarize large amounts of information concerning biological and psychological risks, illness, and dysfunction as well as indicate areas of strength and resources. (*See* example on page 200.) *See also* pedigree.

genome   The complete deoxyribonucleic acid (DNA) sequence containing the entire genetic information of a gamete, an individual, a population, or a species.

genome-wide association study (GWAS) A research approach that incorporates the entire genome in order to identify single nucleotide polymorphisms (SNPs; small deoxyribonucleic acid [DNA] changes) uniquely present in people with a disease, disorder, or trait.

genomic imprinting   The different expression of genetic material depending on which parent the genetic material came from. Because chromosomes and genes come in pairs (typically one member of each pair from the father and the other from the mother), it was once assumed that the gene activity or expression of genes was no different in males or females (excluding the X and Y sex chromosome pair, which obviously have different expression). However, genetic studies performed on those with Prader-Willi or Angelman syndrome have revealed that the activity of the genes depends on the parent of origin (e.g., having two normal copies of chromosome 15 from only the father and none from the mother will cause Angelman syndrome; having two normal copies of chromosome 15 from only the mother will produce Prader-Willi syndrome). Therefore, genomic imprinting is the process by which chromosomes of maternal and paternal origin are modified in unique ways via chemical changes that do not affect deoxyribonucleic acid (DNA) sequence but do affect gene expression or results.

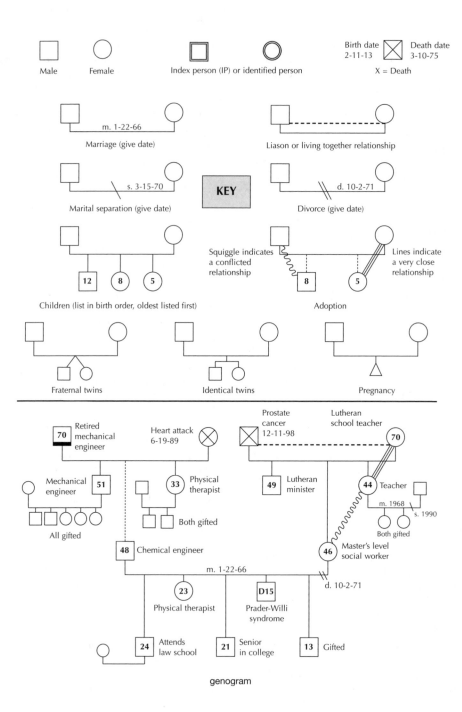

KEY

Male

Female

Index person (IP) or identified person

Birth date 2-11-13 / Death date 3-10-75
X = Death

Marriage (give date) — m. 1-22-66

Liason or living together relationship

Marital separation (give date) — s. 3-15-70

Divorce (give date) — d. 10-2-71

Children (list in birth order, oldest listed first) — 12 8 5

Squiggle indicates a conflicted relationship

Lines indicate a very close relationship

Adoption — 8 5

Fraternal twins

Identical twins

Pregnancy

---

genogram

70 Retired mechanical engineer

Heart attack 6-19-89

Prostate cancer 12-11-98

Lutheran school teacher

70

Mechanical engineer 51

33 Physical therapist

49 Lutheran minister

44 Teacher

m. 1968   s. 1990

All gifted

Both gifted

Both gifted

48 Chemical engineer

46 Master's level social worker

m. 1-22-66

d. 10-2-71

23 Physical therapist

D15 Prader-Willi syndrome

24 Attends law school

21 Senior in college

13 Gifted

genogram

genotype The specific genes that are present on an individual's chromosomes, the expression of which produces the phenotype (appearance).

genu Knee.

genu recurvatum Back-knee; the ability of the knee to bend backward. Secondary to general joint laxity (looseness of joints), genu recurvatum may be a component of a more generalized genetic disorder.

genu valgum Knock-knees; a condition in which the distance between the knees is decreased while the distance between the ankles is increased. The knock-knee appearance is typically seen at about 3 years of age and changes to a more adult-like alignment by 5–6 years of age.

genu valgum

genu varum Bow legs; a condition in which the distance between the knees is increased. Infants and toddlers are typically bowlegged. This posture changes to knock-knees, or genu valgum, at approximately 3 years of age. Legs are in neutral or adult-like alignment by 5–6 years. *See also* bow legs.

geographic tongue Tongue characterized by varying areas of smoothness and roughness on its surface, giving the impression of a map with contours suggesting jagged coastlines. Although geographic tongue does occur as a minor dysmorphic (atypical) feature, it is most often a typical variant. Within a fairly short time period, the map's appearance can change strikingly.

GER *See* gastroesophageal reflux.

GERD *See* gastroesophageal reflux.

germ cells Those embryonic cells destined to become sex cells; those cells that go on to develop into the adult reproductive organs.

German measles *See* rubella.

germline mosaicism The presence of normal cells in most tissues of an individual but with gene or chromosome abnormalities in some or all of the reproductive organs (e.g., ovaries, testes). Germline mosaicism can account for a child having a genetic defect when his or her parents are apparently genetically normal.

Gerstmann syndrome A neurological syndrome that results from damage to the dominant parietal (lateral brain) lobe and leads to the following signs: finger agnosia (the inability to name a finger touched with eyes closed), dysgraphia (impaired writing), dyscalculia (impaired mathematics ability), right–left confusion, and other spatial disorientation. The group of symptoms that occurs in children without obvious brain injury is referred to as *developmental Gerstmann syndrome;* it accounts for a very small percentage of learning disabilities in children.

Gesell, Arnold Lucius (1880–1961) A pediatrician and psychologist whose careful observational studies of infant and child development provided the basis for the maturational theory of development (which states that much of early development depends heavily on the development of brain structures). Gesell originated the description of infant milestones along four major streams, and his infant testing procedures provided the basis for almost all later infant tests. *See also* Gesell Developmental Schedules, infant milestones, maturational theory of development.

Gesell Developmental Schedules A standardized set of tests used to assess development in the areas of motor (gross and fine), adaptive (problem solving), language (expressive and receptive), and personal social (self-help) functioning in children 4 weeks to 6 years of age. The independent assessment of these four areas allows the interpretation of dissociation between streams (differing degrees of maturity in one stream as compared with another; e.g., delayed language milestones but age-appropriate motor milestones) as well as global delay (which affects all streams of development). Almost all existing infant (screening and diagnostic) tests have been adapted from the Gesell schedules. *See also* Gesell, Arnold Lucius (1880–1961).

Gesell Preschool Test   A behavioral assessment of developmental maturity for use with children 2;6–6;0 years of age; it is intended to help in determining school readiness and optimal class setting.

gestalt   Refers to grasping an overall concept without understanding the details relating to that concept.

gestalt   In education, the term may describe recognizing a word as a whole without analyzing it phonetically (sounding it out).

gestalt   A way of seeing or perceiving in which the whole is understood as something more than the sum of its parts. Furthermore, this gestalt may be perceived before the parts that compose it are fully comprehended. The gestalt school of psychology formulated several laws of perceptual organization: 1) the law of proximity: visual elements tend to be grouped together if they are close to each other; 2) the law of similarity: elements will be grouped perceptually if they are similar to each other; 3) the law of good continuation: elements that require the fewest changes, or interruptions—in straight or smooth, curving lines, or contours—will be grouped together; 4) the law of closure: missing parts of a figure are filled in to complete the figure; and 5) the law of Pragnanz: psychological organization will always be as good as prevailing conditions allow, in which *good* describes a figure that is highly predictable from the parts that can be seen. These laws are then applied as a

way of understanding the functioning of human cognition, learning, perception, and emotions.

gestation   Pregnancy; in humans, the 40-week period (plus or minus 2 weeks) from conception to birth. A gestation period shorter than 37 weeks indicates prematurity, whereas one longer than 42 weeks indicates postmaturity.

gestational age   The estimated age of a fetus from conception in weeks. Gestational age can be estimated from birth weight and the evaluation of a variety of physical markers that mature during pregnancy (the Dubowitz Scale is an example of an instrument used to determine gestational age). Typically, the most accurate estimate of gestational age is based on maternal recall of her last menstrual period.

gesture   Movement of any part of the body to 1) communicate, especially when unable to verbally communicate (e.g., an infant waving good-bye); or 2) emphasize or express an idea, emotion, or function. The term does not include formalized symbolic methods of communication, such as fingerspelling, American Sign Language (ASL), or other forms of unaided augmentative communication. Though gestures are relatively easy to learn and use, information communicated solely through gestures is typically limited and constrained. Most often, gestures and facial expressions supplement other augmentative communication systems or are used as a temporary method of communication. *See also* Amer-Ind.

GFCF   *See* gluten-free and casein-free diet.

G-FTA-2   *See* Goldman-Fristoe Test of Articulation–Second Edition.

GFW Battery   *See* Goldman-Fristoe-Woodcock Auditory Skills Test Battery.

G-F-WTAD *See* Goldman-Fristoe-Woodcock Test of Auditory Discrimination.

GIA *See* general intellectual ability.

gibbus humpback Extreme kyphosis (curvature of the spine).

Gibson Cognitive Test Battery A set of screening instruments used to measure processing speed, working memory, auditory memory, visual memory, long-term memory, visual processing, auditory processing, logic and reasoning, and spelling. These results provide a baseline for the use of a specific intensive one-to-one tutoring program, the Processing and Cognitive Enhancement Program (PACE). *See also* Brain Skills.

Giemsa banding A staining technique used on chromosomes that produces characteristic light and dark bands that are unique for each pair.

GIFT *See* Group Intensive Family Training.

gifted Refers to a child with superior ability and/or functioning in at least one specific area. Gifted children give evidence of high performance capabilities in areas such as intellectual, creative, artistic, leadership capacity, or specific academic fields and require services or activities not normally provided by the school in order to fully develop such capabilities. Some definitions separate gifted children (those who have superior general intellectual ability) from talented ones (those who show signs of special aptitude or ability in a specific area of the arts, sciences, or business). Gifted learners occur in nearly every population of students with disabilities. *See also* Omnibus Budget Reconciliation Act (OBRA) of 1981 (PL 97-35).

Gifted and Talented Children's Education Act of 1978 *See* Elementary and Secondary Education Act Amendments (ESEA) of 1978 (PL 95-561).

Gilles de la Tourette syndrome *See* Tourette syndrome.

Gillette Functional Assessment Questionnaire (FAQ) An instrument completed through parent or caregiver interview that assesses the level of ambulation among children with motor disabilities. The 10-point scale uses a range of motor abilities from nonambulatory to independent ambulation to assess where on the continuum an individual child functions. The FAQ can be used to document progress after an orthopedic surgery.

Gilliam Asperger Disorder Scale (GADS) A 40-item parent-administered assessment of behaviors that discriminate Asperger syndrome from autism and other developmental disorders.

Gilliam Autism Rating Scale–Second Edition (GARS-2) A 42-item norm-referenced test designed to assist in diagnosing autism in individuals ages 3–22 years and determining its severity. The 42 items are grouped into 3 subtests that examine Stereotyped Behaviors, Communication, and Social Interaction and yield an Autism Index. Geared to definitions of autism in the *Diagnostic and Statistical Manual of Mental Disorders, Fourth Edition, Text Revision* (*DSM-IV-TR*), and put forward by the Autism Society of America, the GARS-2 is completed by teachers, parents, and professionals and takes approximately 10 minutes for an individual familiar with the child to complete. Respondents rate the frequency with which children engage in behaviors characteristic of the autism spectrum.

Gillingham-Stillman reading method *See* Orton-Gillingham reading method.

gingival fibromatosis–hypertrichosis syndrome A genetic syndrome characterized by generalized hypertrichosis (hairiness) and gingival hyperplasia (overgrowth of gums). Inheritance is usually autosomal dominant; seizure disorders and intellectual disability are more common in the sporadic (probably autosomal recessive) cases.

gingival hyperplasia   Overgrowth of the gums.

glabella   The mid-line point between the eyebrows.

glabellar tap   *glabellar reflex.* A finger tap on the junction between the nose and the forehead (glabella) that causes eyelid blinking even when repeated multiple times. A nonspecific sign of neurological integrity in a newborn that is abnormal in an older person, the glabellar reflex is called a *frontal release sign* (resulting from loss of the frontal lobe's ability to suppress these reflexes in newborns).

Glasgow Coma Scale (GCS)   A standardized quantitative scale used to rate the ability of a person with neurological impairment to open his or her eyes (E, eyes; scored 1–4), talk (V, verbal; scored 1–5), and move (M, motor; scored 1–6). A total score is calculated by adding all of these numbers together. Scores of 13–15 indicate a mild injury; scores below 8 indicate coma. The lower the score, the worse the prognosis (predicted outcome).

glass frustration   An item on infant tests; a toy in which the child shows interest is placed behind a pane of clear glass, and the child's ability to obtain the toy by reaching around the glass is assessed. Success usually occurs by 13 months of age.

glaucoma   A disorder of the eye in which increased pressure within the eye produces pain and varying degrees of loss of vision if left untreated.

glenohumeral joint   Shoulder joint.

glide   A consonant sound that has a gradual change in articulation.

gliding   The phonological process that occurs when a glide sound is substituted for a liquid sound (e.g., /w/ for /r/).

glossectomy   A surgical procedure in which either a portion or all of the tongue is removed.

glossolalia   Literally, "speaking in tongues." Speaking gibberish (nonsense words) or jargoning (imitating speech patterns but [mostly] without recognizable words) in children; in adults, a psychiatric or religious phenomenon.

glossopharyngeal nerve   The ninth cranial nerve; it is responsible for taste at the back of the tongue, the gag reflex, and palatal elevation (raising the soft palate at the back of the throat) on phonation (sound production).

glottal click   *See* glottal stop.

glottal noise   An acoustic measure that indicates miscellaneous noise.

glottal stop   *glottal click.* Use of the glottis (or vocal folds) to make a stop consonant (e.g., /b/, /p/). This phenomenon is commonly seen in children with clefting issues.

glue ear   *See* serous otitis media.

glutamic acid (Glu)   *glutamate.* A neurotransmitter (chemical substance used for signaling within the central nervous system) in the brain. Glutamic acid tends to be excitatory (to activate signaling within the brain instead of dampening it). It is a frequent component in a variety of diets that are claimed to improve intelligence.

gluten-free and casein-free diet (GFCF)   A diet that excludes gluten (the protein found in grains such as wheat and that is associated with celiac disease) and all dairy products (which contain the protein casein) on the hypothesis that these foodstuffs will cause or exacerbate the symptoms of autism.

gluten-induced enteropathy   *See* celiac disease (CD).

gluteus medius gait *See* Trendelenburg gait.

glycogenosis type II *See* Pompe disease.

GMFM *See* Gross Motor Function Measure.

GMQ *See* gross motor quotient.

Goldenhar spectrum *See* Goldenhar syndrome.

Goldenhar syndrome *facioauriculovertebral sequence, facioauriculovertebral spectrum, first and second branchial arch syndrome, Goldenhar spectrum, hemifacial microsomia (HFM).* A syndrome of extremely variable and asymmetric anomalies (abnormalities) of organs that develop from structures in the embryo called the *branchial arches.* Its dysmorphology (atypical features) can include hemifacial microsomia (in which one half of the face is smaller than the other half); microtia (small ear); hypoplasia (undergrowth or narrowing of the ear canal) and preauricular (in front of the ear) skin tags, with conductive hearing loss in 30% of cases; macrosomia (large mouth); cervical (neck) hemivertebra (half of the spinal column bone); and occasional eye abnormalities. Intellectual disability is not common (15% of cases). Cosmetic surgery is indicated in all but the mildest cases. Incidence is 1 in 5,000, with more males than females affected and right-sided involvement predominant. Recurrence risk is 2%.

Goldman-Fristoe Test of Articulation– Second Edition (G-FTA:2) A test of articulation (accurate pronunciation) for use with children 2–21 years of age that uses sounds in words, sounds in sentences, and stimulability (reproducing sounds modeled by the examiner). The G-FTA:2 examines articulation ability by sampling both spontaneous and imitative sound production. Examinees respond to pictures and verbal cues from the examiner with single-word answers that demonstrate common speech sounds. Norms permit the comparison of individual performance to national, gender-differentiated samples.

Goldman-Fristoe-Woodcock Auditory Skills Test Battery (GFW–Battery) Four 15-minute tests of auditory selective attention, diagnostic auditory discrimination, auditory memory, and sound–symbol association for use with people ages 3 years to adult. Useful in the diagnosis of central auditory processing disorder (CAPD).

Goldman-Fristoe-Woodcock Test of Auditory Discrimination (G-F-WTAD) A prerecorded test of auditory discrimination for use with people 3 years of age and older. Includes Quiet Subtest and Noise (competing messages) Subtest.

goniometer A tool used by occupational therapists, physical therapists, and orthopedic surgeons to measure range of motion in terms of the angle in degrees through which a body joint can move or be moved. This measurement is one part of a comprehensive motor assessment of a child or adult. Typical range values are available.

Goodenough-Harris Drawing Test *Harris revision of Goodenough Draw-a-Man test.* A drawing test for use with children ages 3–15 years; the child is asked to draw a person and then to draw himself or herself. The resultant human figure drawing is scored by awarding points for including specific body parts and details; this score is then converted to a mental-age equivalent and a drawing quotient. Higher scores reflect the inclusion of more body parts and details and a higher age equivalent. The drawings can also be interpreted as expressions of the child's emotional state.

Goodman/Smith reading model An approach to reading that views it as a process of deriving meaning directly from print without the intermediary of oral language. Readers make use of syntactic (language structure), semantic (meaning systems), phonological (speech sounds), and morphological (word structure) cues, with errors viewed as a necessary part of learning. This model interprets reading as a process that requires the reader to think on a variety of levels at the same time rather than splintering reading into isolated skills such as phonetic drills, exercises, and games that distract children's attention from actually reading. The model asserts that reading instruction should be meaningful, using a variety of materials to ensure that content is interesting and relevant.

goodness of fit The compatibility of the temperaments of a parent and a child as reflected in their day-to-day interactions. Goodness of fit explains the extent to which parents and other caregivers can encourage or undermine a child's adaptation. For example, a child who reacts intensely to change may develop more optimally if caregivers introduce change gradually and work to contain the child's intense reactions. Caregivers who respond punitively or inconsistently may inadvertently encourage defiance in the child, sustaining an irritable, reactive style.

Gordon Diagnostic System *See* continuous performance task (CPT).

Gordon sign An upgoing movement (dorsiflexion) of the toes in response to squeezing the calf; this reflex is a variant of the Babinski sign (the stroking of the sole of the foot to produce the same response) as an indication of neurological disease.

Gorlin syndrome *nevoid basal cell carcinoma syndrome (BCNS).* A genetic syndrome characterized by basal cell nevi (skin nodules that tend to become cancerous), intellectual disability, broad facies, and rib abnormalities on x ray. Inheritance is autosomal dominant.

GORT-4 *See* Gray Oral Reading Test–Fourth Edition.

Gowers sign Getting up from the floor by climbing up one's own body; straightening the body by pushing one's hands against one's thighs; a finding characteristic of the muscle weakness pattern typical of muscular dystrophy (a progressive muscle disease).

Grace Arthur Performance Scale A nonverbal intelligence test; an adaptation of the Leiter International Performance Scale for children with hearing impairment.

grade-equivalent score A score derived by determining the average score obtained on a test by children in various grades, expressed in tenths of a grade. For example, if the average raw score for children in fourth grade were 30, that would correspond to a grade equivalent of 4.0. The difference in the raw score between 4.0 and 5.0 is arbitrarily divided into tenths, with each tenth corresponding to a grade equivalent of 0.1. If the average raw score for fourth grade were 30 and the average raw score for fifth grade were 50, then a raw score of 32 would equal a grade equivalent of 4.1, 34 would equal 4.2, 36 would equal 4.3, and so forth.

graduated prompting A type of prompting in which the clinician uses a predetermined hierarchy of prompts to facilitate the individual's responses.

grand mal seizure *See* generalized seizure.

granuloma An irregularly shaped mass at the posterior one third of the vocal folds where the arytenoids cartilages are located, commonly caused by intubation.

grapheme The written symbol for a phoneme. Graphemes are composed of the letters of the alphabet and their combinations. For example, the graphemes *t* and *sh* each represent a single phoneme. Approximately 251 graphemes represent approximately 44 phonemes. For example, the grapheme *g* is used in *gate* to represent the hard /g/ and in *gem* to represent the soft /g/.

graphic organizers Displays of information that provide a framework for connecting existing knowledge to new information. Graphic organizers involve text boxes, bubbles, webs, pictures, and other visual representation to organize information for use in learning. Graphic organizers can help younger students organize thoughts for writing and can help older students connect existing knowledge with new information in content classes. Some of the more commonly used graphic organizers are webs, boxes, outlines, and Venn diagrams (graphs that use overlapping circles to show similarities and differences).

graphomotor Having to do with writing or drawing, a set of fine motor skills.

graphomotor production deficit Difficulties or delays in fine motor skills that are reflected in difficulties with developing early academic skills such as writing, drawing simple shapes (e.g., circles, squares), and even using scissors.

graphophonics The knowledge readers and writers have about the marks on the page (e.g., the sound–letter relationships, the white spaces denoting word boundaries).

grasp reflex A reflex in infants in which tactile (touch) stimulus to the palm or sole produces flexion of all of the fingers or toes. Both the palmar (hand) and plantar (foot) grasp reflexes are present at birth. The palmar grasp disappears by around 3 months of age, to be replaced by a voluntary grasp. The plantar grasp persists until 9 or 10 months of age and is one of the last primitive reflexes to disappear before the onset of independent walking. *See also* palmar grasp, plantar grasp.

gravida A pregnant woman. Also the number of pregnancies regardless of duration (gravida 3 describes a woman who has been pregnant three times). Whereas *gravida* refers to the number of pregnancies, *para* (for parity) refers to the number of deliveries; thus, gravida 4, para 3, suggests that a mother is pregnant with her fourth child, whereas gravida 3, para 4, indicates that she has had twins.

gravitational insecurity Atypical anxiety or distress that arises when the gravity receptors of the vestibular (balance) system are stimulated by head position or movement, especially when the child's feet are not on the ground.

gray matter Areas of the central nervous system (CNS; brain and spinal cord) that contain the neurons (nerve cells) that are not insulated with myelin (white matter). The cerebral cortex (outer layer of the brain) has a layer of gray matter. Gray matter diseases, such as Tay-Sachs disease, generally damage or destroy nerve cells.

gray matter diseases A group of degenerative diseases of the central nervous system (CNS; brain and spinal cord) in which cognitive deterioration, seizures, and visual impairment associated with retinal (eye) changes occur early in the course of the disorder; motor findings, such as spasticity (increased muscle tone), are related to white matter involvement and so occur later. Most storage diseases (e.g., Tay-Sachs, Fabry, Niemann-Pick, and other diseases that deposit abnormal cell byproducts into organs of the body) are gray matter diseases.

Gray Oral Reading Test–Fourth Edition (GORT-4) A test that measures oral reading skills in children ages 6–18 years. The GORT-4 is standardized, is individually administered, requires 20–30 minutes to administer, and has two parallel forms. It contains 13 developmentally sequenced reading passages with five comprehension questions that use a multiple choice format. It produces an Oral Reading Comprehension Score, a Fluency Score, and an Oral Reading Quotient. The Fluency Score is derived from the Rate (speed) and Accuracy (number of errors) scores.

Gray Silent Reading Test (GSRT) A companion to the Gray Oral Reading Test (GORT), the GSRT is an individually administered measure of silent reading ability with two parallel forms. Used with people ages 7–25 years, the GSRT can be administered individually or in groups. It requires 15–20 minutes administration time. Like the GORT, it contains 13 developmentally sequenced reading passages with five comprehension questions. The GSRT produces grade equivalents, age equivalents, percentiles, and a Silent Reading Quotient.

Greenspan approach *See* Developmental, Individual-Difference, Relationship-Based (DIR) Model.

Gregg syndrome *See* fetal rubella syndrome.

Greig cephalopolysyndactyly syndrome A genetic syndrome characterized by macrocephaly (large head), high forehead, frontal bossing (prominent forehead), hypertelorism (widely spaced eyes), syndactyly (webbing of fingers or toes), polydactyly (extra fingers or toes), and occasional mild intellectual disability. Inheritance is autosomal dominant. Alterations in the *GLI3* gene on the short arm of chromosome 7 (7p13) are responsible for the condition. Named after the Scottish surgeon David Greig (1864–1936).

Grice procedure *Grice-Green procedure.* The use of a tibial (shin) bone graft to perform a subtalar arthrodesis (surgical immobilization below the ankle) to treat valgus (turning outward) foot deformity.

grief Deep and lingering sadness in response to an important loss. Grief, even when intense, can be a normal reaction with predictable stages and behaviors; presentation varies with individuals and different cultures. Failure to grieve after an important loss is more unhealthy than acute, deep grief. Parents of a child with developmental disabilities experience an initial grief process when first realizing their child has such a disability. Moreover, these parents often face the grief process again with each new developmental stage, such as when their child starts school, reaches adolescence, and makes the transition to adulthood. This recurrent grief process, although unique to parents of children with developmental disabilities, is in no way atypical and should be confronted only when the process gets stuck and prevents the parents from acting in the child's best interest.

Griffiths Mental Development Scales An intelligence test for use with infants and young children. There are two versions: the Griffiths Mental Development Scales Birth to 2 Years (GMDS 0–2) for use with children birth to 2 years, and the Griffiths Mental Development Scales–Extended Revised (GMDS-ER 2–8) for use with children 2–8 years. The tests are based on the Gesell schedules and yield a general quotient and subscores in the following domains: locomotor skills, personal-social skills, hearing and speech, eye and hand coordination, performance, and (for the GMDS-ER 2–8) practical reasoning.

GRIP Growth, Relationships, Independence, and Participation. *See* Individualized Goal Selection (IGS) Curriculum.

Gross Motor Function Classification System A five-level system designed to classify motor function in children with cerebral palsy. Emphasis for the classification system is on sitting or truncal control and ambulation. The distinctions between levels are characterized primarily by functional limitations and the need for assistive technology such as walkers or motorized wheelchairs. Quality of movement is considered but is less important in the categorization. The level chosen for a particular child reflects his or her abilities and functional limitations in the home, school, and community. Level I is typically used to classify a child without cerebral palsy, whereas Level V describes a child who is not ambulatory.

Gross Motor Function Measure (GMFM)
A criterion-referenced motor scale used by physical therapists to examine motor abilities and progress with cerebral palsy. The GMFM looks at changes over a 6-month period in children ages 5 months to 16 years and takes 45–60 minutes to administer.

gross motor quotient (GMQ) Ratio of gross motor age (age of the highest motor milestone achieved) to age in months of the expected motor milestone achievement for chronological age multiplied by 100. It is important to note that 1) neither the numerator nor the denominator is chronological age, and 2) full correction for prematurity is made when estimating the denominator. For example: An infant born 2 months early walks at 18 months; if the typical age for walking is 12 months, this child's GMQ is $[12/(18 - 2)] \times 100 = 75$. GMQs below 45 suggest cerebral palsy, those between 45 and 70 suggest developmental coordination disorder (DCD) or clumsiness, and those above 70 are compatible with typical motor development.

gross motor skills Posture and locomotion skills. Early gross motor skills, such as rolling over, sitting, crawling, walking, and running, seem to be heavily maturational (determined almost exclusively by the development of the central nervous system [CNS]). Later gross motor skills, such as swimming, bicycle riding, and certain other athletic abilities, have an increasingly larger environmental or learned component. Gross motor abilities have little relationship to general intelligence.

group B streptococcal (GBS) infection A severe infection with a specific bacterial strain. In newborns with this infection, there is a 50% mortality rate in the first few days of life; when the onset is after 1 week of age, there is a 25% mortality rate. GBS meningitis (infection of the membranes surrounding the brain) has a high incidence of neurological sequelae (outcomes), such as severe intel-lectual disability, vision and hearing impairment, seizures, and spastic cerebral palsy.

group home A supported living residence licensed by the state for people with intellectual disability, developmental disabilities, and certain mental illnesses. People in group homes use special education, day care, and vocational facilities in the community. Placement in the home may be transitional or permanent. A group home provides its residents with training in independent living skills according to their abilities. The home is supervised by individuals who can live in or nearby the home. The group home environment tries to be like that of a typical home, encouraging shared responsibility and cooperative social interaction. To qualify for federal assistance, group homes must adhere to guidelines established by the Developmental Disabilities Administration of the U.S. Department of Health and Human Services. The structure itself may be owned, leased, or part of a larger facility for individuals with disabilities. *See also* independent living.

Group Intensive Family Training (GIFT)
A program in which parents of preschool children with autism are trained to use early intensive behavioral intervention (EIBI) in the home setting.

growing pains Intermittent mild aches in the leg muscles that occur in approximately 15% of children (girls more frequently than boys).

growth Progressive development toward mature adulthood; this process includes increases in size, changes in proportions, and physiological maturation. Growth rates for individuals and for specific organ systems show variability, accelerations, and plateaus in a complex pattern of interaction. Too much or too little growth can reflect either external (environmental) or internal (genetic and metabolic) factors; depending on the specific cause of a problem in growth, development may also be involved.

Growth, Relationships, Independence, and Participation (GRIP) *See* Individualized Goal Selection (IGS) Curriculum.

GRTH *See* generalized resistance to thyroid hormone.

GSDS *See* Gardner Social (Maturity) Development Scale.

GSR *See* galvanic skin response.

GSRT *See* Gray Silent Reading Test.

GT *See* gastrostomy tube.

guanfacine Trade names, Tenex; Intuniv. An antihypertensive that treats high blood pressure by acting on the central nervous system (CNS) as an alpha-2 agonist. It is also used to treat attention-deficit/hyperactivity disorder (ADHD). Although it is in the same class of drugs as clonidine (trade name, Catapres), guanfacine is less sedating.

guard Position of the upper extremities (arms) during walking. The guard position evolves from arms held high in early walking (high guard) through a middle to low arm position seen in mature walking.

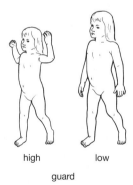

high   low

guard

guardian ad litem (GAL) A legal representative that protects a child's interests in legal proceedings and protects his or her long-range interests. *See also* Child Abuse Prevention and Treatment Act (CAPTA) of 1974 (PL 93-247).

guardianship The care and legal responsibility that a mature adult assumes for a person with a disability with respect to the individual's physical (as in consenting to surgery) and contractual (legal) or fiscal (money) affairs. In individual cases, the level of supervision and decision-making responsibility is specified and tailored to the needs and abilities of the person with a disability. Thus, guardianship can be limited to only certain aspects of an individual's life, or it may cover all aspects. *See also* incompetent.

guessability Relative to language, the degree of similarity in appearance between a symbol and the item it represents.

Guide to Physical Therapist Practice Developed with the support of the American Physical Therapy Association, this document is a reference guide for physical therapists and third-party payers (insurance companies) that describes typical physical therapy practice.

guided oral reading A teaching practice that requires students to read and reread a text or passage aloud until proficiency is reached.

Guillain-Barré syndrome A neurological disorder that affects the peripheral nerves (nerves of the body). An upper respiratory or gastrointestinal viral illness usually precedes a rapidly progressing symmetric (affecting both sides) paralysis that usually begins in the lower extremities (legs) and moves upward until breathing may be affected. Prognosis (outcome) is good for children who receive rehabilitation services, and most children make a full recovery.

gustatory Relating to the sense of taste.

Guthrie test A microbiological inhibition assay (specialized laboratory test) for phenylalanine (an essential amino acid). The amount of phenylalanine present in the blood proportionately inhibits the growth of a specific microorganism (e.g., virus, bacterium, fungus) so that the more phenylalanine, the less growth. The Guthrie test is the basis for newborn screening for phenylketonuria (PKU), one of a number of causes of hyperphenylalaninemia (increased blood phenylalanine).

GWAS *See* genome-wide association study.

gyrus A convolution on the surface of the brain; a "hill" compared with a brain sulcus ("valley"). Gyri are numbered, and many are named for their specific functional associations. *See also* sulcus.

H & P *See* history and physical.

H flu *See* Haemophilus influenzae type B (Hib).

Haberman feeder A specifically designed bottle and nipple compression system used to feed infants with a cleft palate or those with severe hypotonia and an inability to suck sufficiently.

habilitation The provision of medical, psychological, educational, and family services to people with disabilities in order to maximize their vocational, mental, physical, and social abilities and to facilitate their functioning as independently as possible. Whereas the term *adult rehabilitation* refers to the recovery of abilities lost, *pediatric habilitation* connotes the development of abilities not previously mastered. The importance of the distinction lies in the differences in instructional techniques and individual motivation when dealing with an adult who may remember having achieved a particular goal in the past compared with a child who has had no such experience. *See also* rehabilitation.

habitual pitch The average pitch of an individual's speech.

habituation A gradual decrease in the strength of response following repeated stimulation. Humans are prone to respond more strongly to novel stimuli, a tendency that encourages learning. Habituation is adaptive because it permits attention to aspects of the environment that are least known. Increased or decreased habituation may occur in those with intellectual disability and syndromes that involve brain damage. Whether an infant habituates to repeated stimuli and how quickly are components of many infant developmental assessments.

habitus The physical characteristics of a person that may indicate predisposition to (or presence of) disease or personality traits. Habitus can include facies (facial features), somatotype (body shape), gait (pattern of walking), and other movement patterns. Along with dysmorphology (atypical features) and physical signs, habitus is one of the components of visual diagnosis, an approach important in pediatrics because children often cannot otherwise communicate concerns.

Haemophilus influenzae type B (Hib) *H flu.* Once a common cause of bacterial infections (e.g., otitis [ear infections], pneumonia, meningitis [infection of the membranes of the brain]) in children younger than 5 years of age. Routine immunization has markedly decreased the incidence of these infections and their sequelae (complications).

hair analysis A highly questionable quantitative measure of the mineral content of hair to presumably identify mineral deficiencies, mineral imbalances, or heavy metal toxicity.

hair whorl The spiral pattern generated by the hair follicles of the scalp. Variations on the single clockwise posterior (back of the head) hair whorl constitute minor dysmorphic (atypical appearance) features; these include poorly defined, double, and counterclockwise versions.

single   double

hair whorl

Haldeman v. Penhurst State School and Hospital et al.   *See* Broderick decision.

Haldol   *See* haloperidol.

Hall facies   The disproportion of forehead to face, with the size of the forehead increased compared with the size of the face, seen in hydrocephalus (excess fluid in the brain). English physician Marshall Hall (1790–1857) first described this hydrocephalic facies.

Hallermann-Streiff syndrome   *Hallermann-Streiff-François syndrome, oculomandibulodyscephaly.* A distinctive syndrome characterized by ocular (eye) findings (microphthalmia [small eyes] and congenital cataracts [clouding of the lens]), mandibulo (jaw) findings (a small jaw producing a "double" chin with a central dimple or cleft and a long, thin-pointed nose), dyscephaly (a short skull with frontal and side swelling), and hypotrichosis (thin, fine, scant hair). About 1 in 7 cases exhibits intellectual disability. The inheritance pattern remains unclear.

Hallervorden-Spatz syndrome   *See* pantothenate kinase-associated neurodegeneration (PKAN).

hallux   Big toe.

halo effect   According to the halo effect, the perception of a trait is influenced (positively or negatively) by the perception of other traits in the same person. Thus, people who are physically attractive are perceived as good, whereas those who are not attractive may be perceived as bad.

haloperidol   Trade name, Haldol. An antipsychotic neuroleptic (major tranquilizer) drug used to treat Tourette syndrome and severe behavior problems in children. It can cause severe extrapyramidal symptoms (uncontrolled motor movements) and weight gain.

Halstead-Reitan Neuropsychological Test Battery for Older Children   An adaptation of the Halstead-Reitan adult battery for use with children 9–14 years of age. The battery is composed of 45 subtests grouped under such categories as motor, sensory-perceptual, visual-spatial, alertness and concentration, memory, abstract reasoning and logical analysis, and right–left differences. The simultaneous administration of a Wechsler intelligence scale is required to interpret the results and to calculate the Neuropsychological Deficit Scale (NDS) score.

hamstrings   The tendons of the muscles of the posterior thigh (back of the thigh) that act on the hip and knee joints.

hand dominance   *See* handedness.

hand regard   A fairly transient (temporary) behavior observed briefly in children in the first 6 months of life. The infant stares at or through his or her hands. There is minimal movement (mostly slow, stereotyped [the same each time], and rotatory with alternating pronation [palms down] and supination [palms up]). When prolonged, prominent, or occurring at a later age, hand regard is deviant (atypical) and may reflect autism or intellectual disability.

handedness   *hand dominance.* The tendency to prefer using one hand to the other for activities such as writing, eating, and throwing. Predominant use of the left hand is called *sinistrality,* and that of the right hand, *dextrality.* A preference for the right or left hand emerges late in the first year but is not usually fully dominant until close to

2 years of age. Failure to establish handedness by 2 years of age may reflect a developmental disorder. *See also* regard.

handicap A disadvantage for a given individual that results from an impairment or disability that limits or prevents the fulfillment of a role that would otherwise be typical for that individual. The term *handicap* is concerned with the value attached to an individual's situation or experience when it departs from the norm. It is characterized by a discrepancy between the individual's performance or status and his or her personal expectations or the expectations of the group to which he or she belongs. Handicap thus represents the social aspect of an impairment or disability and the consequences for an individual. The term *handicap* is often inaccurately used as a synonym for *disability*. People with or without disabilities may have a societal standard or condition imposed upon them. Except when citing laws or regulations, one should not use the term *handicap* to describe a disability.

Handicapped Children's Protection Act of 1986 (PL 99-372) An amendment to the Education of the Handicapped Act (EHA) of 1970 (PL 91-230) that allows parents who prevail in due process administrative hearings or court actions to be reimbursed for reasonable attorneys fees and other costs of preparing for the proceeding concerning their child's right to a free appropriate public education (FAPE) and related services. The Individuals with Disabilities Education Improvement Act (IDEA) of 2004 (PL 108-446) makes the awarding of attorneys fees to the parents a discretionary decision of the hearing judge.

Hanen Approach A naturalistic approach to training parents as language facilitators to increase and enhance communicative interactions between adults and children.

HapMap *See* International HapMap Project.

HAPP-3 *See* Hodson Assessment of Phonological Patterns–Third Edition.

haptic Tactile; relating to touch.

Haptic Intelligence Scale (HIS) An adaptation of the Wechsler Adult Intelligence Scale for use with people 16 years and older who are visually impaired.

hard neurological sign A neurological finding that can be interpreted as physiological (within the range of normal) or pathological (abnormal) relatively independently of the individual's age. Hard signs help identify the location of a brain injury or abnormality in a person with neurological abnormalities.

hard of hearing Describing a person with a degree of hearing loss that may be significantly improved with amplification (a hearing aid). Although there is reduced hearing activity and sensitivity of the ears to sound, the person's ability to communicate orally is generally maintained.

Harrington distraction rod A metal rod that is implanted into the vertebral column (spinal column) during an orthopedic surgery procedure to correct scoliosis (spinal curvature). *See also* Cotrel Dubousset procedure.

Harrington distraction rod

Harris Infant Motor Test (HIMT) A motor assessment for use with infants 3–12 months of age.

harshness A disorder of vocal quality characterized by an unpleasant, strident, or rough voice because of irregular vocal fold vibration.

Hartford Scale of Clinical Indicators of Cerebral Dysfunction in Child Psychiatric Patients A 30-item measure of cerebral (brain) dysfunction for use with children 2–17 years of age. The scale is divided into three sections: 1) symptoms and signs related to impulsivity or direct aggression, 2) symptoms and signs related to compensatory adjustments against impulsivity or aggression, and 3) items from the individual's early history. Items are rated as present or absent on the basis of clinical interviews with the parents, child, and family as well as medical or school records. The higher the score (more than seven or eight items present), the greater the likelihood that cerebral dysfunction is present in the child.

hatchet face   A facies (facial features) produced by atrophy (wasting) of the facial muscles; a long gaunt face with sharp features. Hatchet face is found in myotonic dystrophy.

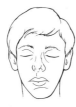
hatchet face

Hawaii Early Learning Profile (HELP)   An assessment instrument for use with children from birth to 3 years (HELP 0–3) and 3–6 years (HELP 3–6) that covers six developmental areas—cognitive (with receptive language), expressive language, fine motor, gross motor, social, and self-help skills—encompassing 685 skills for HELP 0–3 and 621 skills for HELP 3–6. A sequenced checklist can be used to select objectives. The assessment component is keyed to a variety of intervention curricula and approaches.

HCFA   Health Care Financing Administration. *See* Centers for Medicare & Medicaid Services (CMS).

head banging   In infants and young children, striking the head against a hard surface repeatedly for more than a half-hour, usually around bedtime. In children and adults, a more severe stereotypy or self-injurious behavior in which the head is struck against a hard surface with rhythmic and monotonous continuity. The behavior rarely breaks the skin or causes a bruise, but it poses a risk of retinal detachment (dis-

lodging of the inside layer of the eye) and subsequent visual impairment. A form of self-injurious behavior, head banging is more common in children with severe intellectual disability and in those with autism spectrum disorders.

head lag   Inability of the head to keep up with the trunk when the infant is pulled to sitting; some degree of head lag is typical up to 4 months of age.

head lag

Head lag is a frequent finding in the presence of hypotonia (decreased muscle tone) and motor disorders associated with hypotonia.

head retraction   A physical sign in infancy that consists of the head being extended backward. Head retraction occurs 1) as part of a tonic labyrinthine posture (extension of all four extremities [arms or legs]) or 2) with a respiratory disorder.

Head Start   A national program that provides enriched early childhood education for children from low-income families. Established in 1965, Head Start's goals include meeting the developmental and educational needs of young children and increasing their likelihood of later school success. The program also provides a range of additional services designed to help meet health, nutrition, and social needs. In 1972, Head Start legislation was amended to include children with disabilities; 20% of the total Head Start enrollment is reserved for such children. Better grades, fewer grade retentions, limited and more effective use of subsequent special education services, and greater likelihood of completing high school and continuing education are some of the positive effects of such preschool participation.

headwand   A rod that is attached to the head and that has a nonskid covering or writing instrument on the end that enables a person to perform activities such as page turning or writing when it is not possible to do so with the arms.

Health Care Financing Administration (HCFA) *See* Centers for Medicare & Medicaid Services (CMS).

Health Care Proxy *See* durable power of health attorney.

Health Insurance Association of America (HIAA) *See* America's Health Insurance Plans (AHIP).

Health Insurance Portability and Accountability Act (HIPAA) of 1996 (PL 104-191) A set of rules enacted in 1996 to be followed by doctors, hospitals, and other health care providers in regard to patient rights and privacy. HIPAA helps ensure that all medical records, medical billing, and patient accounts meet certain consistent standards with regard to documentation, handling, and privacy. In addition, HIPAA requires that all people be able to access their own medical records, be able to correct errors or omissions, and be informed about how personal information is shared or used. Other provisions involve the notification of privacy procedures to the person. In many cases, HIPAA provisions have led to extensive overhauling with regard to medical records and billing systems.

Health Resources and Services Administration (HRSA) An agency of the U.S. Department of Health and Human Services, HRSA is the primary federal agency responsible for improving access to health care services for the uninsured, isolated, or medically vulnerable. Through its six bureaus and 13 offices, HRSA provides leadership and financial support to health care providers at the state level. HRSA trains health professionals; seeks to improve rural health care; and, through state-level grantees, provides health care to uninsured people, people living with HIV/AIDS, pregnant women, and mothers and children. In addition, HRSA

oversees organ, bone marrow, and cord blood donations; supports programs that prepare against bioterrorism; compensates individuals harmed by vaccination; and maintains databases that protect against health care malpractice and health care waste, fraud, and abuse.

Healthy Mothers, Healthy Babies Coalition (HMHB) A national resource and advocacy force in maternal and child health founded in 1981 through a coalition of six organizations: the American College of Obstetricians and Gynecologists (ACOG), the March of Dimes, the American Academy of Pediatrics (AAP), the American Nurses Association (ANA), the National Congress of Parents and Teachers, and the U.S. Public Health Service. The coalition was formed to improve the quality and reach of public and professional education related to prenatal and infant care.

hearing aid An electronic device that amplifies (makes louder) sound coming into the wearer's ear. The device consists of a microphone, amplifier, and receiver that can route sound for air conduction (to one or both middle ears) or for bone conduction (to the bone of the skull) to augment (increase) the amount of sound stimulating the eighth cranial nerve (which is responsible for hearing). Hearing aids may amplify either all sound or only those frequencies (pitches) that are lost (such as in high-frequency hearing loss). The components of the hearing aid can be placed in a variety of locations to enhance volume, improve the directionality of sound, and balance the sound between the ears.

hearing impairment Loss of auditory ability ranging in degree from slight to profound. Hearing impairments are generally categorized as conductive (involving the middle and outer ears) or sensorineural (involving the inner ear or the auditory [eighth cranial] nerve). Hearing impairment can also be classified as congenital (existing at or dating from birth), prelingual (occurring before the development of speech and language skills), or postlingual (occurring after the development of speech and language skills).

hearing impairment degrees The six categories used to identify the level of auditory loss: slight (unable to hear sounds measuring 16–25 dB [decibels; units of loudness]), mild (26–40 dB), moderate (41–55 dB), moderately severe (56–70 dB), severe (71–90) dB), and profound (91+ dB). Each category has its own characteristics and indicates the disability most likely to result from such a loss. *See also* hearing loss.

hearing loss Any level of auditory impairment ranging from slight difficulty with hearing to profound inability to hear. *See also* hearing impairment degrees.

hearing screening A pass/fail assessment administered to identify individuals who need a full audiological evaluation.

heart rate response audiometry (HRRA) The use of changes in heart rate on an electrocardiogram (EKG) to assess hearing thresholds.

heel cord *See* Achilles tendon.

heel cord lengthening *See* tendo Achilles lengthening (TAL).

HEENT An acronym for head, eyes, ears, nose, and throat; shorthand used in reporting findings on medical examination; a grouping based on anatomical proximity (the organs being located near one another).

Helen Keller International An organization founded in 1915 to assist governments and agencies in developing countries with the prevention and treatment of eye disease and with the education and rehabilitation of people with visual impairment. The organization offers training for teachers and health care workers, with a focus on the prevention of eye diseases. Volunteers are also instructed in counseling families of infants who are blind. Helen Keller International collects and compiles data on blindness throughout the world and publishes a newsletter, fact sheets, and other educational materials.

helicopter parents A colloquial, 21st-century term for parents who pay extremely close attention to their children's experiences and problems. Helicopter parents are so named because they hover closely overhead, rarely out of reach, whether their children need them or not. Helicopter parents try to resolve their children's problems and try to stop them from coming to harm by keeping them out of dangerous situations to such a degree that the children may not learn coping strategies for managing situations. To some extent, the term also references cultural changes that encourage a high degree of parental involvement in a child's life.

helix The shape of a spiral or coil, such as the ridges of the ear or the molecular structure of deoxyribonucleic acid (DNA), which is often described as a *double helix*.

Heller syndrome *See* childhood disintegrative disorder (CDD).

HELP *See* Hawaii Early Learning Profile.

hemangioma A benign (not causing disease) tumor of dilated (enlarged) blood vessels.

hematocrit The volume, expressed as a percentage, of cells (solids) to whole blood (cells and plasma [liquid]). A low hematocrit is one indication of anemia (low red blood cell count).

hemianesthesia Decreased to absent sensation on one side of the body. Hemianesthesia frequently accompanies hemianopsia (blindness in half of the field of vision) and hematrophy (decreased growth and development on one side of the body) in hemiplegic cerebral palsy (paralysis of one side of the body).

hemianopsia Visual field cut; loss of vision for one half of the visual field. In a child with a left hemiplegic cerebral palsy (characterized by weakness and abnormal muscle tone on the left side of the body), the motor control centers in the right brain are damaged. If that injury extends to the right occipital region (the part of the brain responsible for vision), the child may have a cut in the left visual field and not perceive objects that come from the left side. Measuring the visual field (using a process called *perimetry,* which defines the perimeters or outer edges of vision) of young children is difficult, but the possibility of hemianopsia should be suspected in cases of hemiplegic cerebral palsy with hemiatrophy (decreased growth and development on one side of the body) and hemianesthesia (decreased or absent sensation on one side of the body), especially if the child constantly tilts his or her head to one side. The degree of visual impairment is rarely significant but may need to be considered when one is selecting alternative communication devices such as communication boards.

hemiatrophy Undergrowth of the body or a body part on only one side. Although hemiatrophy can be associated with several rare syndromes (e.g., Russell-Silver syndrome), it is more typically found on the involved side in a hemiplegic cerebral palsy (characterized by weakness and abnormal muscle tone on one side of the body). The presence of this unilateral (one-sided) growth disturbance also acts as a marker for such associated impairments as hemianopsia (blindness for half of the field of vision) and hemianesthesia (decreased or absent sensation on one side of the body).

hemiballismus *See* ballismus.

hemifacial microsomia (HFM) *See* Goldenhar syndrome.

hemihypertrophy Enlargement of the limbs on one side of the body. Hemihypertrophy can occur in a number of rare syndromes, such as Russell-Silver, Klippel-Trenaunay-Weber, Beckwith-Wiedemann, chondrodysplasia punctata, as well as in Wilms tumor (a malignancy of the kidney).

hemilaryngectomy A surgical procedure in which half of the larynx is removed.

hemiplegia Literally, "half palsy." A topographical (defined by which parts of the body are involved) type of spastic cerebral palsy in which one side of the body is motorically involved but the other side is spared. On the involved side, the arm is more affected than the leg. The prognosis (outcome) for independent ambulation (walking) is excellent. People with hemiplegia frequently have typical intelligence, and many have learning disabilities, seizures, and hemiatrophy (decreased growth) and hemianesthesia (decreased or absent sensation) on the involved side. Hemianopsia (blindness for half of the field of vision) can be present ipsilaterally to (on the same side as) the motor impairment. Seizure disorders are of such high frequency that they should be closely monitored for the first decade of life. Right hemiplegia is more common than left hemiplegia. *Double hemiplegia* refers to a quadriplegia (cerebral palsy that affects both arms and both legs) in which both arms are more involved than both legs.

hemiplegia, hemiconvulsion, and epilepsy syndrome *See* HHE syndrome.

hemisphere In reference to the brain, one of the two halves (right and left). The left hemisphere is responsible for the comprehension and production of language, whereas the right side controls nonverbal, spatial, and visual tasks. Damage to the left side of the brain may result in aphasia (loss of language skills) or a language problem.

hemisyndrome Any asymmetry of growth, movement, posture, or motor behavior.

hemophilia One of a variety of inherited blood diseases in which the factors that promote clotting are decreased or absent, which thus subjects the person to excessive bleeding.

hemorrhage Bleeding; loss of blood.

hepatic Relating to the hepar (liver).

hepatolenticular degeneration *See* Wilson disease (WD).

hepatosplenomegaly Pathological (abnormal, indicating a disease state) enlargement of the liver and the spleen. Hepatosplenomegaly is a common finding in metabolic storage disorders such as mucopolysaccharidoses and Gaucher disease in which some by-product of faulty metabolism is deposited in organs.

hereditary chorea *See* Huntington disease.

hereditary motor and sensory neuropathy type IV (HMSN-IV) *See* Refsum syndrome.

hereditary sensory and autonomic neuropathy type III (HSAN III) *See* Riley-Day syndrome.

heredodegenerative diseases *See* degenerative disorders.

heredopathia atactica polyneuritiformis *See* Refsum syndrome.

heritability A statistical measure of the degree to which a trait is genetically determined. Heritability is generally used to determine the amount of impact the genes have as compared with environmental factors.

Hermansky-Pudlak syndrome A genetic syndrome characterized by partial albinism (contributing to reduced visual acuity) and a bleeding disorder. Inheritance is autosomal recessive.

hermaphrodite A person who has both testicular and ovarian tissue and, usually, ambiguous external genitalia (sex organs that have a mixture of male and female characteristics).

hernia The abnormal protrusion of part of an organ.

herniorrhaphy The surgical repair (closing) of a hernia.

herpes simplex A deoxyribonucleic acid (DNA) virus group that can produce herpetic skin lesions (typically vesicles, or fluid-filled blisters, on a reddened base of skin), meningoencephalitis (infection of the brain), and congenital (present at birth) infection. Herpes simplex is to be distinguished from herpes zoster (the virus that causes shingles).

hertz (Hz) A unit of frequency; the frequency of 1 cycle per second (CPS), named after the German physicist Heinrich R. Hertz (1857–1894).

Heschl's gyrus *See* primary auditory cortex.

heterochromia irides Eyes of two different colors in the same individual. *See also* Waardenburg syndrome.

heterocyclic antidepressants A class of drugs, including tricyclic and other antidepressants, that share similar chemical structures.

heterogeneity Describing the condition in which multiple genetic causes produce similar effects. The identification of separate genetic causes for the same phenotype (appearance) is the result of a process of testing that includes linkage analysis (a genetic technique for isolating genes that may cause a disorder). *See also* splitting.

heterogeneous grouping In reference to an educational setting, placing students representing a range of characteristics (e.g., ability or age levels) together for instruction.

heterotopia Islands of gray matter in the white matter of the brain. Found commonly with other abnormalities of neuronal (gray matter) migration (movement of brain cells to form the typical layers of the brain), such as lissencephaly (smooth brain surface) or micropolygyria (an increased number of smaller ridgings on the brain surface). Most migration abnormalities result in intellectual disability, motor findings of spasticity (increased muscle tone) or hypotonia (decreased muscle tone), and seizures.

heterotopy Sound displacement during speech, involving the transposition (shifting of position) and reversal of letters and phonemes; a characteristic of cluttered speech (e.g., "filp" for "flip").

heterozygote An individual with different genes for the same trait.

heuristic A "rule of thumb" means for solving problems; a strategy that emerges from observation of prior attempts to solve a problem or reach a conclusion. A heuristic is less formal than an algorithm.

Heyer-Pudenz valve A valve that allows for the unidirectional (one-way) flow of cerebrospinal fluid (the surrounding fluid that cushions the brain and spinal cord) in a tube (shunt) going from the brain to the atrium (heart) or, more commonly, the peritoneum (abdomen) in the treatment of hydrocephalus (excess fluid in the brain).

HFM hemifacial microsomia. *See* Goldenhar syndrome.

HFV *See* high-frequency ventilation.

HGP *See* Human Genome Project.

HGPS Hutchinson-Gilford syndrome. *See* progeria.

HHE syndrome Hemiplegia (paralysis of half of the body), hemiconvulsion (seizures affecting one side of the body), and epilepsy syndrome with a characteristic frontotemporal, spike–slow wave electroencephalographic (EEG; or brain wave) pattern; a complication of acute hemiplegia with febrile (feverish) illness.

HIAA Health Insurance Association of America. *See* America's Health Insurance Plans (AHIP).

hiatal hernia The protrusion of some part of the stomach above the diaphragm. Hiatal hernia contributes to acid reflux and chest pain.

hiatal hernia

Hib *See* Haemophilus influenzae type B.

HIE *See* hypoxic-ischemic encephalopathy.

High Objective Uniform State Standards of Evaluation (HOUSSE) One component of a larger set of requirements established for highly qualified teachers and paraprofessionals. All teachers in core academic areas (English, reading or language arts, mathematics, science, history, civics and government, geography, economics, the arts, and foreign languages) regardless of grade level and all special education teachers must be highly qualified. To be considered highly qualified, teachers must possess the following three highly qualified teacher (HQT) requirements: a bachelor's degree, full state certification or license, and competency in each subject they teach. The Individuals with Disabilities Education Improvement Act (IDEA) of 2004 (PL 108-446) extended the requirements of HOUSSE to special education teachers. *See* Individuals with Disabilities Education Improvement Act (IDEA) of 2004 (PL 108-446), No Child Left Behind Act (NCLB) of 2001 (PL 107-110).

high output failure   *See* developmental output failure.

high state of arousal   *Arousal* is a general physiological and psychological activation of an organism that varies on a continuum from deep sleep to intense excitement. Chronic physiological hyperarousal resulting from a low threshold for sensory input has been associated with autism spectrum disorders. A number of sensory and environmental interventions for use with those with autism spectrum disorders are based on the presumed need for lowering sensory input and abnormal levels of arousal.

high-arched palate   *See* palate.

high-frequency ventilation (HFV)
A type of mechanical ventilation (artificial breathing machine) that uses high rates (e.g., more than 900 breaths per minute) with very low tidal volumes (amounts of air per breath).

high-arched palate

high-technology device   An assistive technology (AT) device that uses electronic or mechanical parts.

highly qualified teacher   A categorization that emerged from the No Child Left Behind Act (NCLB) of 2001 (PL 107-110) that mandates that all public elementary school or secondary school teachers who teach core academic subjects obtain full state certification as a teacher (including alternative certification) or pass the state teacher licensing exam; hold a license to teach in the state; and not have had certification or licensure requirements waived on an emergency, temporary, or provisional basis. Highly qualified teachers are required in all schools that receive federal funds.

HIMT   *See* Harris Infant Motor Test.

hip abduction deformity   *See* frog posture.

hip adduction deformity   Positioning of the thigh closer to (or across) the mid-line. This deformity both leads to and results from hip dislocation. Bilateral (affecting both sides of the body) hip adduction deformity produces scissoring (leg crossing). This deformity is common in spastic cerebral palsy.

HIPAA   *See* Health Insurance Portability and Accountability Act of 1996 (PL 104-191).

hip–knee–ankle–foot orthosis (HKAFO)
An orthosis that both supports and to some degree limits the entire lower extremity (leg). *See also* orthosis.

hippocampus   A part of the limbic system of the brain that plays an important role in long-term memory and spatial navigation.

hippotherapy   Therapeutic horsemanship; the use of horseback riding as a treatment modality to enhance self-esteem and broaden experience in children with disabilities.

hippus   Rhythmic dilation (enlargement) and constriction (shrinking) of the pupils of the eyes.

Hirschberg test   A corneal light reflex test; a screening test for strabismus (crossed eyes) in which the examiner shines a light and observes its reflection in the child's pupils. If the eyes are both straight, the reflection is at the same location in each eye. An inturned eye displaces the light laterally (to the side away from the nose), whereas an outturned eye displaces it medially (to the side toward the nose).

Hirschsprung disease   *aganglionic megacolon, congenital megacolon.* Functional obstruction of the rectum or colon (large intestine). A congenital (present from birth) absence of the nerve supply to the lower colon that causes an absence of peristalsis (wave-like muscular contractions that propel waste along the gastrointestinal tract), which results in an increasing enlargement of the colon, constipation (infrequent, difficult bowel movements), and obstruction (blockage). Treatment is in two stages: 1) a temporary colostomy (surgical opening of the bowel to provide an alternative pathway for the exit of feces) followed by 2) colonic resection (surgical removal) of the involved segment of intestine. Infants with Down syndrome have a tenfold increase in the incidence of Hirschsprung disease. Named after the Danish pediatrician Harold Hirschsprung (1830–1916).

hirsutism   A nonspecific condition of excessive facial or body hair. The cause may be familial, endocrine, or pharmacological.

HIS   *See* Haptic Intelligence Scale.

Hiskey-Nebraska Test of Learning Aptitude (HNTLA)   A nonverbal intelligence test of learning aptitude for use with children ages 3–17 years with severe hearing impairment. The HNTLA has been standardized on both hearing and deaf populations. Although dated, it can enhance a functional evaluation of learning aptitude.

histidinemia   A disorder of amino acid metabolism characterized by high blood levels of histidine; an autosomal recessive condition not associated with any disability.

history and physical (H & P)   The medical format for transcribing a clinical history and physical examination such as may be done in an outpatient clinic or inpatient setting.

history of present illness (HPI)   Part of a medical history and physical examination format. The HPI consists of a description of the person's complaint, including its onset, severity, duration, triggers to symptoms, and treatments that have helped.

HIV   *See* human immunodeficiency virus. *See also* acquired immunodeficiency syndrome (AIDS).

HIV-1   *See* human immunodeficiency virus type 1.

HKAFO   *See* hip–knee–ankle–foot orthosis.

HMD   *See* hyaline membrane disease.

HMHB   *See* Healthy Mothers, Healthy Babies Coalition.

HMSN-IV   Hereditary motor and sensory neuropathy type IV. *See* Refsum syndrome.

HNTLA   *See* Hiskey-Nebraska Test of Learning Aptitude.

hoarseness   A disorder of vocal quality characterized by a combination of harshness and breathiness.

Hodson Assessment of Phonological Patterns–Third Edition (HAPP-3)   A comprehensive evaluation and two screening tests (preschool and school age) used to assess articulation in people 3 years to adult who are highly unintelligible.

Hoffmann sign   The stimulus of sudden extension (straightening) of the middle finger following flicking or snapping the nail of that finger coupled with a flexion response of the thumb and index finger; a sign of pyramidal tract involvement.

holistic learning   An approach to learning in which topics to be learned are not broken down into their component parts but are examined in the context in which they occur. Rather than focusing on a specific and often arbitrary sequence of skills aimed at the remediation of impairments, proponents of the holistic approach advocate providing a language-rich environment in which the fundamental purpose of language (reading, writing, speaking, and listening) is the communication of meaning. Teaching and learning are viewed as an interactive process, with the form of language seen as a tool to be refined in order to enhance meaning rather than as a goal in itself.

holistic medicine A vague catchphrase that indiscriminately connotes either or both of two attitudes toward traditional medicine: 1) a critique of scientific medicine as too exclusively focused on disease, technology, and pathology (origin) rather than on the whole person, health, or prevention; or 2) an espousal of a variety of naturopathic, shamanistic, homeopathic, vitamins and health food, and psychic regimens as self-help approaches to health (especially as part of "New Age" mysticism).

holophrastic speech The use by young children of single words to express complete sentences (e.g., "Cookie" for "I want a cookie" or "Out" for "Let me out of this stroller").

holoprosencephaly (HPE) Impaired midline cleavage of the embryonic forebrain such that to some extent, the resulting brain lacks division into the hemispheres (halves) of the mature brain, resulting in a structure in which the front (-*pros*-) of the brain (-*encephaly*) protrudes as a single (*holo*-) mass. The most extreme form of HPE is cyclopia (a failure to develop two separate eyes); a less severe form is arrhinencephaly (absence from birth of the olfactory lobe of the brain, responsible for the sense of smell).

HOME *See* Home Observation for Measurement of the Environment.

home health Describes the provision of supportive medical services in the recipient's own home. Such services may include dressing care, feeding, intravenous (IV) care, physical therapy, respiratory therapy, nursing, dialysis, bathing, and other health-related services.

Home Observation for Measurement of the Environment (HOME) An observation and rating scale designed to measure the quality and extent of stimulation available to a child in the home environment and to assist in planning interventions. The HOME serves as a screening device for identifying environments that offer limited stimulation and nurturance to children. The HOME has separate inventories for infants and toddlers (birth to 3 years old), early childhood (ages 3–6), and middle childhood (ages 6–10). Through a 45- to 90-minute home visit (with the child present), the observer examines such features as the presence of toys, games, and books; language stimulation; the physical environment; parental responsiveness; academic goals; discipline; and modeling of social maturity as they relate to the age groups covered. The Supplement to the HOME for Impoverished Families (SHIF) assesses the quality of the home environments of young children living in poor urban settings. The 20-item SHIF is conducted in conjunction with the HOME, requires approximately 10 minutes to score, and uses the same scoring procedures.

home schooling The legal option for parents to educate their children at home, typically by themselves but sometimes a tutor, rather than in the formal public or private school setting. Parents cite numerous reasons as motivations to homeschool, including better academic test results, poor public school environment, improved character/morality development, and objections to what is taught locally in public school.

Home Screening Questionnaire (HSQ) A component of the Denver Developmental Screening Test battery that screens children at risk for developmental delay. A parent-report instrument in two forms: blue for birth to 3 years of age and white for 3–6 years of age.

Home Situations Questionnaire A 16-item questionnaire designed to elicit information about the severity of behavior problems experienced in numerous daily home circumstances.

home visitation *home visitation programs.* Programs that offer a variety of family-focused services to pregnant mothers and families with new infants and young children, particularly for families considered to be at risk. These targeted interventions are designed to address issues such as maternal and child health, positive parenting practices, safe home environments, and access to services in order to decrease the likelihood of negative outcomes (e.g., child neglect, chronic illness) and increase the likelihood of good outcomes (prevention of and prompt assessment and intervention for potential health and developmental concerns).

home-based programs A widespread early intervention strategy for children birth to 3 years, home-based intervention was first implemented in the Education of the Handicapped Act Amendments of 1986 (PL 99-457). Because development is so integrally embedded in the family and home environment, the Individuals with Disabilities Education Act (IDEA) of 1990 (PL 101-476) and its amendments require intervention to be conducted in natural environments, including the home, child care center, and so forth. Accordingly, home-based programs capitalize on and enhance the family's own capacity to promote functional skills. Supports in natural environments such as the home are intended not only to put the child and family at ease but to more readily promote functional skill acquisition and family involvement than services in clinical settings. Practitioners from several disciplines (motor therapies, education, special education, nursing, psychology, nutrition, etc.) provide home visits to young children and others who are engaged in home-based intervention. *See also* home visitation.

homebound instruction The provision of educational services for a student in his or her home because of illness, physical injury, or emotional condition. A child is eligible for homebound instruction, which is provided by a visiting or itinerant teacher, when school attendance is made impossible by such conditions. Mandated by the Individuals with Disabilities Education Act Amendments (IDEA) of 1997 (PL 105-17), homebound instruction is categorized as one of the most restrictive alternatives in a continuum of services and is to be considered a temporary measure whenever possible.

homemaker services Social or health services that support and help maintain people with physical or cognitive disabilities in their own homes. Such services may include shopping, budgeting, cleaning, meal planning and preparation, in-home adaptive modifications, and assistance with transportation or communication with other agencies and services. The effort is to provide services in the homes of people with disabilities rather than move these individuals to long-term care facilities.

homeobox A special deoxyribonucleic acid (DNA) sequence found in the coding region of many regulatory genes. These helix-loop-helix structures were briefly considered important in the development of autism.

homeostasis The tendency of biological and other systems to remain internally constant despite interacting with a changing external environment.

homocystinuria A genetic inborn error of metabolism that produces increased homocysteine (an amino acid, a building block of proteins) in the blood and urine. The habitus (physical appearance) is similar to that seen in Marfan syndrome, with a tall, thin stature; a malar (cheekbone) flush; and arachnodactyly (long, thin fingers and toes), except that the ectopia lentis (lens dislocation) is downward in homocystinuria and upward in Marfan syndrome. Osteoporosis (thinning of the bones), intellectual disability (in 50% of cases), and a shuffling ("Charlie Chaplin") gait can be present. Inheritance is autosomal recessive, and it is more common in people of Irish descent. The disorder can be responsive to pyridoxine (vitamin B_6) or a special diet.

homogeneous grouping Students in an educational setting who are grouped together for instruction because they share the same skill level.

homolateral limb synkinesis A mutual dependency such that the movement of the affected upper and lower limbs mirror each other: Arm flexion evokes leg flexion.

homologs *See* homologous chromosomes.

homologous chromosomes *homologs.* A pair of chromosomes, one inherited from each parent, that have the same gene loci in the same order. (For an exception, *see* genomic imprinting, uniparental disomy.)

homozygote An individual with identical alleles at a given locus on a pair of homologous chromosomes.

Horn-Cattell-Carroll theory of cognitive abilities/processing *See* fluid intelligence.

hospitalism *institutionalism.* A behavioral syndrome characterized by delays in mental and physical development, apathy, and waxy immobility that occurs when an infant is separated from the mother or primary caregiver. If the situation is prolonged (institutionalization) or includes frequent and recurrent infections, cachexia (general weight loss) and death may occur. To a milder degree, some form of hospitalism is common in infants and young children admitted to the hospital. Although the effects can be ameliorated (eased) by parents rooming in and other techniques, hospitals are not the most appropriate settings for the cognitive and behavioral development of very young children. Children who exhibit hospitalism often appear to have cognitive impairments that may remit once they are placed in a more stimulating and caregiving environment. *See also* anaclitic depression.

House-Tree-Person Test A projective test that requires children 5 years of age and older to draw and then interpret a house, a tree, and a person (in that order).

HOUSSE *See* High Objective Uniform State Standards of Evaluation.

HPE *See* holoprosencephaly.

HPI *See* history of present illness.

HRRA *See* heart rate response audiometry.

HRSA *See* Health Resources and Services Administration.

HSQ *See* Home Screening Questionnaire.

hug machine *squeeze box. See* squeeze machine.

Human Genome Project (HGP) A long-term research project to identify all of the approximately 25,000 genes in human deoxyribonucleic acid (DNA), their chemical makeup, and their function. The project was officially begun in 1990 as a 15-year project jointly sponsored by the National Institutes of Health (NIH) and the U.S. Department of Energy and was completed in 2003. Information from the HGP has been made available online, at no cost, to aid medical researchers. *See also* International HapMap Project (HapMap).

human immunodeficiency virus (HIV) A human retrovirus (a class of ribonucleic acid [RNA] viruses) that causes acquired immunodeficiency syndrome (AIDS).

human immunodeficiency virus type 1 (HIV-1) *See* acquired immunodeficiency syndrome (AIDS).

humerus Upper arm bone.

Hunter syndrome *mucopolysaccharidosis (MPS) II.* A genetic syndrome characterized by growth deficiency, coarse facies (facial features), stiff joints, and hepatosplenomegaly (enlargement of the liver and spleen). In contrast to Hurler syndrome (MPS IH), MPS II has a more gradual onset with clear corneas. Intellectual disability is variable; hearing loss occurs in half of the cases. In contrast to all of the other types of MPS, MPS II is X-linked, so there are no affected females. Named after the Canadian physician Charles Hunter (1873–1955).

Huntington disease *hereditary chorea.* An adult-onset hereditary neurodegenerative disease that affects the basal ganglia (motor control centers) of the brain and progresses to dementia. There is a rare juvenile-onset rigid (stiff muscles) subtype. Inheritance is autosomal dominant, with an incidence of 1 in 18,000. Named after the American physician George S. Huntington (1850–1916).

Hurler syndrome *mucopolysaccharidosis (MPS) IH, Pfaundler-Hurler syndrome.* A genetic syndrome characterized by growth deficiency, coarse facies (facial features), stiff joints, hepatosplenomegaly (enlargement of the liver and spleen), intellectual disability, and cloudy corneas. Named after the German pediatrician Gertrud Hurler (1889–1965).

Hurler-Scheie syndrome *mucopolysaccharidosis (MPS) I H/S.* A genetic syndrome characterized by symptoms, progression, and severity intermediate between Hurler (MPS IH) and Scheie (MPS I S) syndromes. Inheritance is autosomal recessive.

Hutchinson-Gilford syndrome (HGPS) *See* progeria.

hyaline membrane disease (HMD) *respiratory distress syndrome (RDS), surfactant deficiency.* A lung disease experienced by premature infants because of the immaturity of the lungs and a lack of surfactant, the chemical that helps maintain the lungs' elasticity and allows them to expand and contract easily. Initial treatment can be

with surfactant administered into the lungs via tracheal intubation (insertion of a tube into the airway) at delivery to prevent the development of lung disease. In infants who do not respond to surfactant, the treatment is mechanically supported breathing with a ventilator. Infants treated with such ventilation assistance can develop chronic lung disease, bronchopulmonary dysplasia (BPD).

hybrid augmentative and alternative communication (AAC) display An electronic fixed display with a dynamic component, such as indicator lights, that informs the individual using the device which items in the selection set are available for activation.

hydranencephaly A condition in which the cerebral hemispheres (two halves of the brain) are sacs made of glial (cell and fiber) tissue and filled with cerebrospinal fluid (CSF). Some islands of cortex (brain tissue) are preserved, as are the brainstem, midbrain, and diencephalon (deep brain structures). Clinically speaking, infants may have a normal-size to large head with typical reflexes. However, these infant reflexes persist, and no normal development occurs, leading to cerebral palsy with spastic quadriparesis (paralysis of all four extremities), seizures, and profound intellectual disability. Diagnosis is by neuroimaging, such as computed tomography (CT) scan, magnetic resonance imaging (MRI), or ultrasound. Treatment is supportive.

hydrocephalus *"water on the brain."* A condition in which there is an enlargement of the ventricular system in the brain due to an increase in the amount of cerebrospinal fluid (CSF) present in the ventricles (fluid-containing spaces). It may be caused by decreased absorption or increased production of CSF. Hydrocephalus may be congenital (present from birth) or acquired.

hydrocephalus

Hydrocephalus is divided anatomically into two categories: 1) obstructive and 2) communicating. Obstructive hydrocephalus is caused by a blockage of the circulation of CSF by a tumor, an anatomical narrowing of the outlet (e.g., aqueductal stenosis), or bleeding. Communicating hydrocephalus occurs when the absorption of CSF from the ventricles is blocked. Actively enlarging hydrocephalus that causes increased pressure on brain structures is commonly manifested by ataxia (unsteady gait) and spasticity (high muscle tone) affecting the legs more than the arms. Judgment and reasoning are typically affected, but speech is generally preserved, although often in an atypical manner. Children with hydrocephalus tend to have more expressive than receptive language, resulting in a characteristic talkative speech pattern with little content, often called "cocktail party chatter." Children with hydrocephalus may also experience a decline in mental function, including language use, that may worsen as the hydrocephalus worsens. Hydrocephalus ex vacuo presents with the appearance of enlarged ventricles secondary to atrophy (wasting) of brain tissue with normal to small (microcephaly) head size. (The broken line in the illustration represents normal ventricular space; the solid line represents enlarged ventricular space.)

hydroxyurea   A drug used to prevent recurrent strokes in people with sickle cell disease.

hyperactivity   Spontaneous gross motor activity that is excessive for age. Motor activity increases as age or mental age decreases and in the presence of a variety of medical (e.g., hyperthyroidism), psychological (e.g., anxiety), interactional (e.g., maternal depression), and neurological (e.g., attention-deficit/hyperactivity disorder) conditions. Therefore, hyperactivity is not diagnostic of any particular entity but must be correlated with other findings. *See also* attention-deficit/hyperactivity disorder (ADHD).

hyperacusis   An abnormally acute sense of hearing in which certain or select sounds are experienced as painful or unpleasant.

hyperalimentation   *parenteral nutrition.* The feeding of an individual by total parenteral alimentation or total parenteral nutrition. *See* total parenteral nutrition (TPN).

hyperammonemia, congenital   *See* congenital hyperammonemia.

hyperbilirubinemia   A high level of bilirubin in the blood. Bilirubin is a red pigment produced in the body during the breakdown of hemoglobin (an oxygen-carrying substance in red blood cells); an excessive amount of bilirubin results from either too many red blood cells (e.g., polycythemia, or high red blood cell count), an inappropriate destruction of red blood cells, or a deficit in hemoglobin breakdown (e.g., liver disease). The clinical presentation of hyperbilirubinemia is jaundice (yellowing of the skin). In infants, hyperbilirubinemia is treated with fluorescent lighting (bili lights, bili blankets) and sometimes with partial exchange transfusion (a treatment involving the removal of some of the infant's blood along with the infusion of donor blood) to prevent the bilirubin from damaging the basal ganglia of the brain (centers that help control voluntary movements) and causing choreoathetoid cerebral palsy.

hyperexplexia   *startle syndrome, stiff baby syndrome.* An autosomal dominant syndrome characterized by hypertonia (increased muscle tone) at birth that becomes less pronounced with age. The infant maintains a fetal flexor (rolled up in a ball) habitus with clenched fists and an anxious expression. The fact that the hypertonicity can be suddenly exaggerated by slight stimuli (excessive startling) followed by brief body stiffness and immobility requires careful discrimination from a seizure disorder. Hyperexplexic infants have a high incidence of hernias and respiratory and gastromotility (movement of food and waste through the gastrointestinal tract) disorders but no cognitive impairment.

hyperhidrosis   Excessive or profuse sweating.

hyperkeratosis   Precancerous lesions that appear as irregular, leaf-like overgrowths of cells on the vocal folds.

hyperkinesis   *See* hyperactivity.

hyperkinetic dysarthria   A motor speech disorder characterized by abnormal, involuntary movements that vary between rhythmic or irregular, and rapid or slow.

hyperkinetic syndrome of childhood   A neurobehavioral syndrome characterized by distractibility, short attention span, extreme overactivity, disinhibition (acting without regard to rules), disorganization, impulsivity (acting without regard to consequences), marked mood fluctuation, and aggression. *Hyperkinetic syndrome of childhood* is the preferred term for attention-deficit/hyperactivity disorder (ADHD) in Europe and Great Britain. *See also* attention-deficit/hyperactivity disorder (ADHD).

hyperlexia   Advanced single-word reading skills that exceed grade-level performance in other areas as well as levels expected on the basis of intellectual ability. These accurate word identification skills can be high even in the presence of overall poor reading comprehension. There is no consensus concerning either the etiology (cause) or significance of the condition. Hyperlexia has been reported among children with varying cognitive abilities, including some children with intellectual disability and autism.

hypermetropia   *See* hyperopia.

hypernasality   A disorder of resonance (voice quality) that can be caused by velopharyngeal incompetence (structural or motor incoordination problems with the soft palate).

hyperopia   *hypermetropia.* Farsightedness. A condition in which vision is better at a distance; close vision is not as good. It can be corrected by plus diopter (convex) lenses.

hyperostosis corticalis generalisata   *See* van Buchem syndrome.

hyperpigmentation   Increased pigmentation (color) of the skin. Some birthmarks, such as café au lait spots, are hyperpigmented.

hyperplasia   An increase in the size of an organ through an increase in the number of cells.

hyperpyrexia   A very high fever. Apart from infection, some children with severe brain damage may have poor thermoregulation (body temperature control) and may develop a fever in response to a warm ambient temperature.

hyperresponsivity   A condition in which an individual's nervous system is overwhelmed by ordinary sensory input and reacts defensively to it, often with disproportionately strong negative emotion and activation of the sympathetic nervous system.

hypersomnia   Excessive sleepiness.

hypertelorism   Increased distance between two paired organs. Ocular hypertelorism reflects an increased distance between the eyes (interpupillary distance). Hypertelorism is common in Down syndrome and in a number of other genetic disorders but is also a nonspecific dysmorphic (atypical) feature. As an isolated finding, it may be of no significance.

hyperthyroidism   An endocrine disorder in which an elevated thyroid hormone level gives rise to both physical and behavioral symptoms. The anxiety, emotional overreactivity, agitation, and mania that may occur should not be confused with attention-deficit/hyperactivity disorder (ADHD).

hypertonicity *hypertonia.* Increased muscle tone; typically found in the spastic or rigid types of cerebral palsy. More generally, a neurological sign of motor tract involvement.

hypertrichosis A condition characterized by excessive hair; this can involve scalp, facial, eyebrow, eyelid, and body hair. Hypertrichosis can be genetic (familial or part of a specific syndrome), endocrinological (hormonal), or drug induced. *See also* trichosis.

hypertrophic lingual frenulum *See* tongue-tie.

hypertrophy An increase in the size of an organ through an increase in the size of the cells that compose it.

hyperventilation Rapid, deep breathing that mildly changes blood chemistries by decreasing the carbon dioxide (CO_2) level in the blood. Hyperventilation is used clinically to enhance or induce electroencephalogram (EEG) abnormalities. Hyperventilation is a routine part of the EEG evaluation in a child old enough to cooperate. It can also be a symptom of a panic disorder or panic attack and can result in fainting.

hypocalcemia Low blood calcium levels. Acute symptoms include irritability, a high-pitched cry, tremors, seizures, and tone abnormalities; chronic symptoms relate to delayed skeletal mineralization and rickets (bone disease). Etiologies (causes) include metabolic disorders and deficient calcium or vitamin D intake.

hypochondria *See* somatization disorder.

hypochondroplasia A condition characterized by short stature, limited elbow exten-sion (difficulty fully straightening the arms), mild to moderate brachydactyly (short fingers), and a rectangular-shaped skull with a prominent forehead. This common form of short stature shows an autosomal dominant inheritance. However, most cases are the result of new mutations.

hypoglossal nerve The 12th cranial nerve; responsible for movement of the tongue.

hypoglycemia Low blood sugar. Glucose is the principal fuel for brain activity. Hypoglycemia may be asymptomatic (without symptoms), or it may produce symptoms that range from irritability, seizures, lethargy, fatigue, sweating, or a high-pitched cry to coma. Severe prolonged hypoglycemia can produce brain damage that leads to intellectual disability.

hypokinetic dysarthria A motor speech disorder characterized by the combined effects of reduced range of movement, reduced force, and rigidity in the affected muscles that slows individual movements and creates rapid, repetitive movements.

hypomania A mild form of mania.

hypomanic episode A period of at least 4 days during which there is a constantly elevated, expansive, or irritable mood that is distinctly different from the affected person's usual nondepressed state. The episode must be associated with a change in functioning and must be observable to others.

hypomelanosis of Ito *incontinentia pigmenti achromians.* A condition characterized by streaky, patchy, or lacey areas of hypo- and hyperpigmentation (areas of increased or decreased pigment, or color) of the skin. More than 50% of the cases are associated with mosaicism for abnormal genes, for whole chromosome abnormalities, or for parts of chromosomes. The specific involvement of other systems is dependent on the specific gene or chromosome abnormality.

hypomelia-hypotrichosis-facial hemangioma syndrome *See* tetraphocomelia cleft palate syndrome.

hyponasality A disorder of resonance (voice quality) that occurs with a stuffy nose, allergies, and enlarged adenoids. Hyponasality can affect speech clarity, as speech will sound muffled.

hyponatremia Salt depletion; a marked decrease in the concentration of sodium in the blood. A common cause of hyponatremia in small infants is the ingestion of overly diluted formula. The lowered sodium levels can produce convulsions.

hypopigmentation Decreased pigmentation (color) of the skin. Some birthmarks, such as the ash leaf spots in tuberous sclerosis, are hypopigmented.

hyporesponsivity *underresponsiveness.* A condition in which an individual's nervous system is relatively unaffected by sensory input to which most people respond.

hypospadias A urological malformation in which the urethra opens on the underside of the penis instead of at the distal end (tip). It can be found in different syndromes and may be associated with other urogenital anomalies (malformations).

hypospadias

hypotelorism Decreased distance between two paired organs. Ocular hypotelorism is a decreased distance between the eyes as reflected by a decreased interpupillary distance and usually a decreased inner canthal distance (distance between the inner corners of the eyes). Hypotelorism is often part of syndromes characterized by mid-facial hypoplasia (undergrowth).

hypothalamic midbrain dysregulation syndrome Hypertension (high blood pressure), hyperthermia (fever), hyperventilation (rapid breathing), and decerebration (generalized spasticity) that occurs secondary to a transient disconnection between the midbrain and the brainstem during recovery from coma.

hypothyroidism, acquired *See* acquired hypothyroidism.

hypothyroidism, congenital *See* congenital hypothyroidism.

hypotonic cerebral palsy A physiological subtype of cerebral palsy characterized by severe low muscle tone and pronounced motor delay. Many cases eventually resolve into one of the other subtypes of cerebral palsy. Prolonged or permanent severe hypotonia (atonic cerebral palsy) is rare and is often associated with severe diffuse brain damage and profound intellectual disability. *Flaccid diplegia* is an antiquated term for the transient (temporary) hypotonia that precedes spastic cerebral palsy.

hypotonicity Decreased muscle tone; floppiness, limpness, weakness. *See also* floppy infant.

hypotrichosis A condition characterized by decreased hair. This can include balding; alopecia (hair loss); and decreased eyelid, eyebrow, or body hair. Hypotrichosis can be genetic (familial or part of a specific syndrome), endocrinological (hormonal), or dermatological (skin-related) in cause. *See also* trichosis.

hypovigilance *inattention. See* primary disorder of vigilance (PDV).

hypoxic Describing a low level of oxygen. This state can be due to low ambient oxygen or to respiratory, cardiac, or hematological (blood) disorders.

hypoxic-ischemic encephalopathy (HIE) Nonprogressive brain damage secondary to hypoxia (oxygen deficiency) and ischemia (blood supply deficiency); most perinatal asphyxia (lack of oxygen around the time of birth) occurs in utero (before birth).

hypsarrhythmia The high-amplitude, chaotic electroencephalographic (EEG; or brain wave) pattern diagnostic of infantile spasms.

Hz *See* hertz.

I and R *See* information and referral.

IADLs *See* instrumental activities of daily living.

iatrogenic Resulting from therapy; a cure following an appropriate treatment is most likely iatrogenic. Iatrogenic diseases, however, are often the result of unwanted side effects of therapies. Examples include bronchopulmonary dysplasia from the treatment for respiratory distress syndrome, and hyperactivity or lethargy resulting from medication side effects. A certain degree of iatrogenic disorder may be implicit in a given treatment approach and does not necessarily negate the value of the therapy or the skill of the therapist. Iatrogenic disease represents part of the risk component in the risk–benefit ratio associated with any intervention.

IBI *See* Early Intensive Behavioral Intervention.

IBIDS syndrome A rare neurocutaneous (nervous system and skin) syndrome. The acronym refers to ichthyosis (very dry skin), brittle hair (trichothiodystrophy), infections, dysplastic (malformed) nails, and short stature. Cataracts (clouding of the lens of the eye), microcephaly (small head), hypoplasia (undergrowth) of subcutaneous (under the skin) fatty tissue, hypogonadism (small testicles), and intellectual disability are also found. Inheritance is probably autosomal recessive. At least two different genes have been found to be altered in some individuals with IBIDS syndrome. *See also* BIDS syndrome.

ICCs *See* Interagency Coordinating Councils.

ICD *See* inner canthal distance.

ICD-10-CM *See* International Classification of Diseases, Tenth Revision, Clinical Modification.

ICF *See* intermediate care facility.

ICF *See* International Classification of Functionality.

ICF/DD *See* intermediate care facility for people with intellectual and developmental disabilities.

ICF/ORC *See* intermediate care facility for people with other related conditions.

ICH *See* intracranial hemorrhage.

ichthyosis Dry, scaly skin more severe than that seen in atopic dermatitis (eczema); it is genetically inherited in a variety of modes. Ichthyosis can be found in a number of syndromes, some of which are associated with intellectual disability.

icing The use of a very cold stimulus applied to the skin to facilitate neuromuscular functioning.

ICM   *See* integrated classroom model.

iconicity   Any association that an individual forms between a symbol and its referent.

ICS   *See* individualized curriculum sequencing.

ictal   Pertaining to a seizure. Thus, the aura that may precede a seizure is preictal, and the somnolence (sleepiness) that may follow a seizure is postictal.

icterus   Literally, "yellow." Jaundice.

icterus neonatorum   Jaundice of the newborn. This increased bilirubin (pigment in the blood) can be physiological (part of normal body function) or excessive (hyperbilirubinemia).

IDAM   *See* infant of a drug-addicted mother.

IDDRC   *See* Intellectual and Developmental Disabilities Research Center.

IDEA   Individuals with Disabilities Education Act. *See* Individuals with Disabilities Education Act Amendments of 1997 (PL 105-17), Individuals with Disabilities Education Act of 1990 (PL 101-476), Individuals with Disabilities Education Improvement Act of 2004 (PL 108-446).

ideamotor apraxia   A type of apraxia characterized by an individual's inability to carry out the function of an object (e.g., cannot demonstrate hammering with a hammer).

ideational apraxia   A type of apraxia characterized by an individual's inability to describe the function of an object (e.g., cannot describe that a hammer is used to pound nails into wood).

ideational fluency   A measure of creativity; the number of new or different ideas that can be generated.

identification   Identification occurs when individuals have an affinity for models that possess qualities seen as rewarding. Children with and without disabilities have a number of models with whom they identify, including individuals in their own environments (parents, teachers, coaches), fantasy and fictional characters, and individuals in the media (sports figures, political leaders). In social learning theory, the likelihood of imitating another person is based on the extent to which the model demonstrates a quality that the individual would like to possess or on rewards accrued by the model.

identified patient (IP)   The member of a family or group for whom help is sought. The IP may serve as the entry point for services to other family members.

ideograph   *ideogram.* Graphic symbols used in a system of writing to represent an idea or concept rather than a particular object. Ideographs are typically used in conjunction with pictographs (symbols that look like what they represent) as a form of aided augmentative communication that is particularly useful for use with people who are nonverbal. Such symbols are also used in international road signs to eliminate language barriers.

ideomotor apraxia   A type of apraxia in which an individual has difficulty consciously imitating gestures and consciously carrying out motor commands but has no difficulty performing these same routine activities (e.g., combing hair, tying shoelaces) automatically.

idiopathic   Of unknown origin. From a medical standpoint, a large number of developmental disabilities remain idiopathic.

idiosyncratic   Unique to an individual (e.g., an idiosyncratic drug response is a positive or negative response that is not expected to occur in other people who receive the drug).

idiosyncratic language A pattern of language or word usage that is peculiar to an individual and that makes little to no sense to people unfamiliar with that person's communication style. It can be a symptom of communication impairment.

idiot Obsolete and unacceptable term for a person with intellectual disability and an intelligence quotient (IQ) score below 25. The original Greek term referred to an uneducated private person or layman who did not involve himself in the political life of the city or state.

idiot-savant *See* savant.

IDM *See* infant of a diabetic mother.

IEE *See* independent educational evaluation.

IEP *See* individualized education program.

IEP accommodations *See* accommodations.

IFSP *See* individualized family service plan.

IGDIs *See* Individual Growth and Development Indicators.

IGS *See* Individualized Goal Selection Curriculum.

IHP Individualized habilitation plan. *See* individualized program plan (IPP).

IHS *See* Indian Health Service.

iliac index The sum of the two acetabular angles (the angle at which the hip and the femur [thighbone] meet) and the two iliac angles (the natural angle of the hip bone) divided by 2; this number is smaller in infants with Down syndrome.

iliac index

ilium The largest of the three bones of the pelvis; the hips.

Illinois Test of Psycholinguistic Abilities–Third Edition (ITPA-3) A norm-referenced test used to delineate strengths and weaknesses in the language abilities of children 5; 0–12;11 years of age. The seven oral and five written language subtests tap oral language, reading, writing, and spelling.

illiterate E A vision screening test for use with preschool children 3 years of age and older. Administration is similar to that of the Snellen Test (the familiar eye chart with rows of random letters of decreasing size), except that only one letter, E, is used. The E is placed in different positions, and the child is asked to indicate with his fingers or by rotating an E card (or a model E) which way the legs of the E on a given line of the chart are pointing. The test provides an accurate measure of visual acuity in a child who does not know the alphabet. *See also* Sjogren Hand Test.

illustrator A nonverbal behavior that accompanies speech and illustrates what is being said (e.g., as when a person points emphatically to a chair while saying "Sit down").

imbecile Derived from *imbecillus,* meaning "weak." Obsolete and unacceptable term for a person with intellectual disability and an intelligence quotient (IQ) score between 25 and 50.

imipramine Trade name, Tofranil. A tricyclic antidepressant that has also been used to treat childhood bed-wetting.

imitation Reproduction of the behavior of a model. Various types of imitation emerge at different developmental ages: Newborns can imitate facial gestures, vowel and consonant sequences can be imitated during the first year of life, echolalia (repetition of what is heard) occurs transiently at around 18 months, toileting is imitated at 3 years, and the imitation of hand gestures has been graded for school-age children. Imitation is an important component of language learning. In social learning theory, imitation is learning that occurs when a person observes and emulates the behaviors of others. *See also* modeling.

imitation synkinesis   Mirror movements. When a child is asked to perform a movement with one hand, the other hand may be seen to duplicate (mirror) that movement.

immaturity   A developmental level younger than chronological age; a descriptive rather than explanatory term.

immersion program   An English (or one other language)–only approach in which a child's native language is rarely used in daily lessons at school. The child is mainstreamed into general education English-only classrooms.

immittance audiometry   *impedance audiometry.* An objective measure (hearing test) of the functioning of the peripheral (noncentral, or not involving the brain) auditory mechanism.

immunization   A preventive medical procedure (usually a vaccination or inoculation) performed to reduce susceptibility to certain infectious diseases (e.g., varicella [chickenpox], measles, polio). Such a procedure is used before one has been exposed to the disease. Many of these diseases can cause severe developmental disabilities. Rarely, a reaction to the immunization itself may cause severe disabilities.

immunoglobulins   Serum proteins with antibody activity. There are five major classes: IgA, IgD, IgE, IgG, and IgM.

impairment   Any temporary or permanent loss or abnormality of psychological, physiological, or anatomical structure or function; the inability to perform because of an underlying atypicality. Impairment represents the externalization of a pathological state that, in principle, reflects disturbance at the level of the organ. Examples of impairments include birthmarks, brain lesions, nearsightedness, and incomplete or malformed limbs. From a therapy standpoint, impairment may also affect range of motion (ROM), strength, or tone. A permanent impairment does not automatically imply a "handicap."

impartial due process hearing   A procedure for settling disputes between parents of a child with disabilities and the school system. The hearing is similar to a legal trial in that it includes rules of evidence and other legal procedures, and the decision is based on the evidence presented. The decision of the hearing officer is binding. If parents or the school system disagree with the decision, an appeal may be made for a state-level review of the hearing, or the appeal may go to state or federal court. Either the parents or the school system can request a due process hearing. *See* Individuals with Disabilities Education Act Amendments (IDEA) of 1997 (PL 105-17).

impedance audiometry   *See* immittance audiometry.

imperforate anus   A congenital malformation in which the bowel does not exit through the anus. Imperforate anus is associated with a high incidence of urological, spinal, and other anomalies, often as part of a specific syndrome.

implied consent   An assumption of consent or agreement to action based on failure to protest or resist such action. For example, most states have an implied consent law whereby if one drives an automobile, he or she has implicitly consented to being tested for driving under the influence of alcohol or drugs. Under implied consent laws, refusal to be tested is an automatic revocation of driving privileges, even when one is acquitted of the charges of driving under the influence.

imprinting The differing expression of genetic material, at either a chromosomal or gene level, depending on whether the genetic material has been inherited from the male or female parent.

imprinting A type of animal learning in which a specific environmental stimulus releases a genetically preprogrammed behavior pattern only when the matching of stimulus and response occurs during a critical and sensitive period of development; the resultant behavior is especially resistant to extinction (disappearance).

imprinting, genomic *See* genomic imprinting.

Improving America's Schools Act (IASA) of 1994 (PL 103-382) Legislation that reauthorizes the Elementary and Secondary Education Act of 1965 (PL 89-10). In addition, it includes provisions or reforms for the Title I program, providing extra help to disadvantaged students and holding schools accountable for the results of these students at the same level as other students; charter schools; safe and drug-free schools; professional development; increases in bilingual and immigrant education funding; impact aid; education technology; and other programs.

impulsivity A cognitive style characterized by responding quickly and acting without thinking. In children with attention-deficit/hyperactivity disorder (ADHD), impulsivity occurs because of neurological dysfunction. It is important to understand the neurological basis of the impulsivity rather than attribute it to a personality or motivational impairment in the child.

in situ **hybridization** The mapping (locating and examining) of a gene by the molecular hybridization (bonding) of a cloned deoxyribonucleic acid (DNA) sequence, labeled by radioactivity or fluorescent substances that light up under the microscope, to a chromosome spread on a slide. *See also* fluorescent *in situ* hybridization (FISH).

in utero In the womb (uterus); describing the phase of an individual's life cycle that precedes birth, the usual duration being 9 months. It is during this time that organogenesis (formation of the infant's organs) occurs. During this time, the developing fetus is susceptible to the effects of exposure from the mother's use of harmful substances such as alcohol, drugs, and tobacco. The term *in utero* refers to the entire prenatal period.

inappropriate pitch A voice disorder in which the vocal pitch is inappropriate in relation to the individual's size, age, and/or gender.

inattention *See* hypovigilance.

inborn error(s) of metabolism Neurometabolic diseases or disorders are caused by the absence or relative absence of specific enzymes (body chemicals) due to genetic alterations. An enzyme may be absent entirely or may be present in an inactive form, thereby causing an alteration in normal metabolism (processing of substances for use by the body). Varying degrees of dysfunction and illness can result, most commonly from harmful effects to the central nervous system (CNS), causing progressive deterioration in functioning and loss of skills. These disorders can also cause damage to other organ systems in the body, such as the heart or liver. Examples include neuronal ceroid lipofuscinoses, organic acidurias, amino acidopathies, and urea cycle disorders. Some neurometabolic disorders, such as phenylketonuria (PKU), are treatable, whereas others, such as Batten disease, are not. Some inborn error(s) of metabolism are referred to as *neurogenetic storage diseases*.

inbreeding *See* consanguinity.

incentive *See* reinforcer.

incest Sexual contact (fondling, touching, or intercourse) between blood relatives, especially father–daughter or brother–sister.

Children with developmental disabilities are at increased risk for sexual victimization either by family members or by others. Children subjected to incest may present with apparent learning difficulties due to the trauma of the incest.

incidence   A rate that indicates the number of new cases of a disorder occurring in a given population over a specified time period (usually a calendar year). An increasing incidence of a disorder may reflect a genuine total increase, a newly recognized condition, or increased diagnostic sensitivity (tests or criteria for diagnosis that have changed to enable the identification of more children as having the disorder of interest). Because the overall rate of occurrence and early onset of most developmental disorders is relatively consistent across time compared with more acute medical conditions, the importance of distinguishing between incidence and prevalence is minimal. Because developmental disorders must start during infancy or childhood, their incidence in the adult population should be zero.

incidental teaching   A teaching method (often used with young children with autism) that capitalizes on the child's natural interests. As the adult and child interact, the adult encourages the child to use a desired skill (e.g., requesting an object). In this sense, learning is incidental to the process of interaction. Incidental teaching uses graduated levels of prompting that are offered when the child demonstrates interest in an item or interaction. For example, a child looks at a particular toy (an initiation). The adult first waits for the child to ask for it. If the request does not come, the adult prompts the child to ask for it, then further elaborates the request, models it, and finally prompts the child to provide a simple signal of request if it still does not occur. Once the request is made (even if at the most rudimentary level), the adult reinforces it by providing the desired object.

incision   Surgical cut.

incisive foramen   A major nerve supply located near the incisor teeth.

inclusive education   An educational model in which students with disabilities receive their education in a general education setting among typically developing peers with collaboration between general and special education teachers. *See also* integration, mainstreaming.

incompetent   Incapable; a term used to describe someone who is functionally unable to manage his or her affairs, make informed decisions, or meet responsibilities. People with disabilities that prevent informed decision making may need a guardian to oversee their affairs in one or more areas of their lives (e.g., financial, medical). A legal judgment of incompetency must be rendered through a legal process and a guardian assigned. The judgment of incompetency does not pertain to the person's moral worth; rather, it is a legal means of protecting the person's interests. Usually assignment of guardianship is to a close relative, such as a parent or sibling. *See also* conservator, guardianship.

incomplete cleft   A cleft that does not extend through the nose.

incomplete phrase   A type of disfluency in which speech productions are grammatically and semantically incomplete.

incontinence   Developmentally inappropriate absence or loss of bladder control (i.e., urinary incontinence) or bowel control (i.e., fecal incontinence).

incontinentia pigmenti achromians   *See* hypomelanosis of Ito.

incontinentia pigmenti syndrome   *Bloch-Sulzberger syndrome.* A genetic disorder characterized by depigmented skin lesions (areas of loss of normal skin color), dental abnormalities, alopecia (hair loss), intellectual disability, and seizures. Mutations in the *IKBKG* gene, also called *NEMO,* which maps to Xq28, cause incontinentia pigmenti.

independent educational evaluation (IEE) An evaluation conducted by a qualified examiner who is not employed by the public agency responsible for the education of the child in question. Each public agency must provide to a parent, upon request, information about where an IEE may be obtained and the agency criteria applicable to IEEs. Furthermore, the parent has the right to an IEE at the public's expense if he or she disagrees with an evaluation obtained by the public agency. Once a parent requests an IEE, the public agency must either file a due process complaint to request a hearing to show that its evaluation is appropriate or ensure that an IEE is provided at the public's expense, unless other agency criteria are not met. The right to request an IEE for a child with a disability is one of the most protected parental rights under federal and state special education laws.

independent level A student's functional reading level is often independent if the student can read a text with about 95% accuracy (or misreads only about 1 out of every 20 words). *See also* frustration level, instructional level.

independent living Self-governing and self-sustaining living. For people with developmental disabilities, independent living is often accomplished within a supportive service network that provides protection while maximizing independence. Services provided may be as simple as home health and adaptive equipment for negotiating the environment or life skills supports for people with greater cognitive impairments. Such supports may include transportation, homemakers, budget monitoring, and sheltered or supported work. *See also* group home, supported living.

Inderal *See* propranolol.

index case *See* propositus.

index finger exploration A fine motor milestone that involves poking and feeling objects with the second (or pointer) finger; this tactile (touch) exploration emerges at 10 months and is equivalent to the pincer grasp.

Indian Health Service (IHS) A federal program unit of the U.S. Department of Health and Human Services, the IHS is responsible for providing comprehensive health services to 1.9 million Native Americans and Alaskan Natives who belong to 564 federally recognized tribes. IHS services are administered through 12 area offices and 161 IHS and tribally operated health care services. In addition, there are 34 urban programs ranging from community health to comprehensive primary health care services.

indication A clinical condition or diagnosis for which a given drug is effective. A labeled indication is one that the U.S. Food and Drug Administration allows to be advertised because research data are judged sufficient to support such a claim; an unlabeled indication is one for which the data remain insufficient. Many clinically effective drug therapies, especially for children, remain unlabeled. *See* orphan drug.

indirect swallow therapy Swallow maneuvers that incorporate saliva only (e.g., oral-motor and pharyngeal exercise programs); no food is presented.

Individual and Family Developmental Disabilities Support Waiver (DD Waiver) A Medicaid program that provides eligible individuals with a variety of consumer- and agency-directed services in their homes and communities, helping them to remain at home and avoid placement in an intermediate care facility (ICF). Individuals must be at least 6 years old, have a developmental disability (but not intellectual disability) diagnosis, and meet financial eligibility requirements.

Individual Growth and Development Indicators (IGDIs)　A comprehensive standards-based assessment system for use by early childhood educators to describe individual children's growth and development over time (both current status and rate of development) for the purpose of identifying children at risk, designing and evaluating interventions, and evaluating the effectiveness of interventions. Unlike standardized tests that are administered infrequently, IGDIs are designed to be used repeatedly by practitioners in order to estimate each child's rate of growth over time.

individual plan　The use of preliminary intervention strategies prior to performing an assessment regarding eligibility for services negotiated under an individualized education program (IEP).

individualized curriculum sequencing (ICS)　An instructional model for use with children with multiple or severe disabilities that focuses on skill clusters that cut across content domains in educational programming.

individualized education program (IEP)　A written statement for the education of a child with disabilities that is developed and implemented according to defined federal and state criteria. An education program based upon the child's individual needs is developed at a meeting of the IEP team, whose members should include a representative of the local school system, the child's teacher, one or both parents, a professional who participated in or is knowledgeable about the evaluation, the child (when appropriate), and anyone else the parent would like to have involved. The content of the IEP should include 1) a statement of the child's present level of performance; 2) a statement of long-term goals and short-term objectives; 3) a description of services, including placement, related services, and the

extent to which the child will participate in general programs; 4) a statement regarding the initiation and duration of services; and 5) appropriate objective criteria and evaluation procedures for determining whether goals and objectives are met. The IEP must be reviewed at least once a year. The child's program cannot be changed without another IEP meeting to which parents must be invited. *See* Education for All Handicapped Children Act of 1975 (PL 94-142), Individuals with Disabilities Education Act Amendments (IDEA) of 1997 (PL 105-17), Individuals with Disabilities Education Act (IDEA) of 1990 (PL 101-476), Individuals with Disabilities Education Improvement Act (IDEA) of 2004 (PL 108-446).

individualized family service plan (IFSP)　For children ages birth to 3 years, a statement of child and family needs and outcomes to be achieved and a plan of services necessary to meet these needs, including frequency, intensity, and location of services, method of delivery, and payment arrangements. Family-centered services view the family, rather than only the child with developmental disabilities, as the unit of intervention, incorporating concepts that encourage family decision making and that empower families to participate as full partners in the processes of service planning and intervention. Thus, an IFSP recognizes all family needs and all family members as equally important in devising and implementing an intervention plan. *See also* Education of the Handicapped Act Amendments of 1986 (PL 99-457), Individuals with Disabilities Education Act Amendments (IDEA) of 1991 (PL 102-119), Individuals with Disabilities Education Act Amendments (IDEA) of 1997 (PL 105-17), Individuals with Disabilities Education Improvement Act (IDEA) of 2004 (PL 108-446).

Individualized Goal Selection (IGS) Curriculum　A curriculum with more than 2,000 goals for students with autism. It uses the Growth, Relationships, Independence, and Participation (GRIP) model to select and implement goals and strategies.

individualized habilitation plan (IHP) *See* individualized program plan (IPP).

individualized plan for employment (IPE) A formal statement of vocational goals and the corresponding services needed to pursue those goals for adults eligible for vocational rehabilitation services.

individualized program plan (IPP) A document that contains a statement of present level of functioning for an individual with a disability as well as a listing of goals, objectives, and services with stated completion dates, performance criteria, evaluation procedures, and the plan for service delivery to meet these needs and goals. The IPP is analogous to an individualized education program (IEP). An IPP is also referred to as an *individualized habilitation plan* (IHP). *See also* individualized education program (IEP).

individualized service plan (ISP) A document that contains a statement concerning the total habilitation needs of a person with developmental disabilities, including education, employment, social, emotional, and placement needs, combined with a plan for meeting these needs and that names a responsible service coordinator to oversee the plan's enactment. ISPs are used in adult services.

individualized transition plan (ITP) An individually designed program that outlines a coordinated set of service needs, activities, timelines, agency responsibilities, and outcomes to facilitate the transition of a person either out of early intervention services or from school to adult life. The transition plan must anticipate and provide services that promote movement from one program to another or from school to employment (including supported or integrated employment), postsecondary education, vocational

training, continuing and adult education, adult services, adult living, or community participation. The plan should be comprehensive in scope and longitudinal in nature. It should focus on the specific needs of the individual and should identify who is responsible for initiating and following through on each specified activity. For those transitioning from early intervention services, the ITP should be developed toward the end of the last year of their eligibility for early intervention. For those transitioning into adulthood, the plan should first be developed at least 4 years prior to their graduation and then modified at least once a year until they have successfully adjusted to a postschool vocational placement. The informed participation of parents and guardians, as well as interagency cooperation, is a critical component of the vocational transition process. *See* transition.

Individuals with Disabilities Education Act Amendments (IDEA) of 1991 (PL 102-119) This law amended and reauthorized IDEA, including Part H (birth to age 2 program) and part B (special education for those ages 3–21). Among the amendments included a redefinition of children with disabilities in order to allow states to provide services to 3- to 5-year-olds who are experiencing developmental delays. In so doing, the law required states to plan for transition of children from Part H to preschool programs. This amendment also added vision services, assistive technology and services, and transportation to the definition of early intervention services. The legislation amended language to support early intervention in integrated settings. *See also* free appropriate public education (FAPE).

Individuals with Disabilities Education Act Amendments (IDEA) of 1997 (PL 105-17) Like its predecessor, the Education for All Handicapped Children Act of 1975 (PL 94-142), PL 105-17 mandates that eligible children have available to them special education and related services designed to address their unique educational needs. *See also* free appropriate public education (FAPE), learning disability (LD).

Individuals with Disabilities Education Act (IDEA) of 1990 (PL 101-476)   A federal law that amends and expands the Education for All Handicapped Children Act of 1975 (PL 94-142). The law renames and combines the original act and its amendments. The term *handicapped children* is replaced by *individuals with disabilities*. The definition of *individuals with disabilities* is expanded to include people with autism and traumatic brain injury (TBI) as separate categories. Other major changes include the addition of programs to promote research and the use of technology, transition programs beginning after high school, a program to serve children with emotional disorders, greater emphasis on addressing the needs of culturally and ethnically diverse children with disabilities, and the waiving of states' traditional immunity from private litigation. *See also* learning disability (LD), service coordination.

Individuals with Disabilities Education Improvement Act (IDEA) of 2004 (PL 108-446)   A federal law that improves the Individuals with Disabilities Education Act Amendments (IDEA) of 1997 (PL 105-17). PL 108-446 increases accountability for students with disabilities by requiring their participation in statewide assessments, mandates the presence of highly qualified teachers in special education classroom, expands the methods used to identify learning disabilities, and puts in place procedures to reduce litigation. The law makes changes to individualized education programs (IEPs) by eliminating short-term objectives and including other measures to streamline the IEP process. Other changes from previous legislation include raising the age for transition plans to 16, setting measures that made it easier for schools to discipline students with disabilities, and requiring schools to implement measures to reduce

the overrepresentation of students from diverse backgrounds in special education. *See also* free appropriate public education (FAPE), functional behavioral assessment (FBA), learning disability (LD), natural environment.

inductive reasoning   *See* bottom-up processing.

infant massage   A set of touch or massage techniques that is claimed to promote better infant–parent attachment or bonding and to have other benefits.

infant milestones   Specific skills that are achieved at ages for which norms have been derived for the first several years of life. *See also* Gesell, Arnold Lucius (1880–1961).

infant of a diabetic mother (IDM)   Maternal diabetes is associated with newborn macrosomia (large birth weight and body size) and increased mortality (death) and morbidity (undesirable outcomes) secondary to fetal distress, respiratory distress, central nervous system (CNS) irritability, plethora (elevated hematocrit, or red blood cell volume), and congenital malformations (e.g., cardiac and musculoskeletal abnormalities, including caudal regression syndrome [a major malformation of the lower half of the body]). Meticulous control of maternal diabetes reduces infant mortality and morbidity rates.

infant of a drug-addicted mother (IDAM)   *infant of a substance-abusing mother (ISAM).* Narcotic and nonnarcotic drug use during pregnancy tends to produce premature and/or small-for-gestational-age infants who often have a drug withdrawal syndrome (irritability, fever, breathing difficulties, and gastrointestinal disturbances) in the newborn period. Depending on the drugs used and their contaminants, there may be an increased risk for congenital malformations. Long-term effects on development are not well defined and may be related in part to a chaotic, neglectful, and abusive prenatal, as well as postnatal, environment. Transient (temporary) behavior disturbances are commonly part of a neonatal withdrawal syndrome; long-term problems include hyperactivity, learning disabilities, and behavior disorders. *See also* cocaine baby, crack baby.

infant of a substance-abusing mother (ISAM) *See* infant of a drug-addicted mother (IDAM).

Infant Toddler Sensory Profile A caregiver report, Likert scale questionnaire used to assess sensory seeking, sensory avoiding, sensory sensitivity, and low registration in infants ages birth to 36 months. There are 36 items for infants ages birth to 6 months and 48 items for children ages 7–36 months.

infantile autism *See* autism.

infantile spasms *infantile myoclonic seizures, salaam seizures, West syndrome.* Brief symmetrical contractions of the muscles of the neck, trunk, and extremities (arms or legs) resulting in a head bob or a jackknifing of the body at the waist, depending on the muscles involved. Infantile spasms usually begin between 6 and 8 months of age and rarely persist after 12 months. The seizures generally occur many times a day and often in clusters. They are frequently accompanied by eye movements (e.g., eye deviation [inward or outward], nystagmus [involuntary jerking eye movements]) and a postspasm cry. The classic electroencephalogram (EEG) finding associated with infantile spasms is hypsarrhythmia (a continuous disorganized pattern of high-voltage slow waves [rounded curves] and spikes [sharp points]). Infantile spasms may be associated with brain malformations, genetic disorders, intrauterine infection, brain injury, inborn errors of metabolism, brain infections, and intracranial bleeding. They also may be cryptogenic (with no known etiology). About 85%–90% of infants with infantile spasms have some degree of devel-

opmental delay and intellectual disability. Because of this poor developmental outcome, treatment of infantile spasms is considered urgent. In general, the outcome is more favorable in children with the cryptogenic type.

infantilization Treating a person as much younger than his or her age or abilities would dictate. Children with developmental disabilities may be infantilized by family members and service providers who, with good intentions, may overprotect and under-encourage them. If allowed to continue unchecked, infantilization can become a second, and even more debilitating, impairment.

Infant-Preschool Play Assessment Scale (I-PAS) A criterion-referenced assessment instrument for the systematic observation of children's developmental skills and evaluation of intervention progress.

Infants and Toddlers Coordinators Association (ITCA) The Infant and Toddler Coordinators Association is organized as a not-for-profit corporation to promote mutual assistance, cooperation, and exchange of information and ideas in terms of the administration of Part C (Early Intervention statutes) and to provide support to state and territory Early Intervention (Part C) coordinators. Its mission is to 1) identify and represent the interests of state and territory infant and toddler early intervention programs at the national level; 2) develop and recommend models, standards, policies, and programs that promote quality services to eligible infants and toddlers and their families; and 3) strengthen existing leadership and foster new leadership in early intervention programs at the local, state or territory, and national levels.

Infant-Toddler Checklist (ITC) A 24-item screening test for communication disorders in children 6–24 months of age that can also be used as a screening test for autism; one of the three components of the

Communication and Symbolic Behavior Scales Developmental Profile.

Infant-Toddler Symptom Checklist A criterion-referenced symptom checklist used to screen for sensory and regulatory disorders in children ages 7–30 months old. Completed by the caregiver, it tells whether a child is at risk for sensory or regulatory dysfunction. Given its descriptive nature, it is generally used to supplement clinical observations rather than for diagnostic or classification purposes.

infection Invasion of the body by microorganisms (viruses, bacteria, fungi) that cause disease.

inferior Below, in anatomy.

inflammation A local reaction of the body to insult, injury, or infection that includes redness, heat or warmth, swelling, and pain (the classical rubor, calor, tumor, and dolor).

inflectional A type of suffix that can be added at the end of a word that changes its meaning and grammatic class.

informal assessment The use of nonstandardized, customized measures developed by teachers, speech-language pathologists, and other practitioners to directly evaluate the skills of children with whom they are working.

Informal Reading Inventory (IRI) *See* Quantitative Reading Inventory.

informal supports Families, friends, neighbors, associates, coworkers, and others in the natural environment who provide needed supports to allow someone with a disability to remain in his or her home or the community. Informal support systems are not organized like formal systems are, but they can "get together" to help when people need them, such as by providing

food for several weeks after the death of a loved one or running errands for a young mother with a new infant. Sometimes called *natural helping networks.*

Information A Wechsler (intelligence test) subscale that measures a child's ability to acquire, retain, and retrieve general factual knowledge.

information and referral (I and R) *resource and referral.* An agency or program within an agency whose sole service is to assess individuals' problems and refer them to the appropriate service or entitlement.

information processing A broad framework in which intelligence is studied as a process rather than as a discrete set of abilities. This framework includes an examination of the way in which knowledge is organized and located in the memory system and the mental operations necessary to accomplish intellectual tasks. It is based on mechanical and computer models of information processing. Major elements include encoding (transmitting a message by verbal or nonverbal means), storage (placing information for later retrieval), decoding (giving meaning and understanding to a received verbal or nonverbal message), feedback (commenting on the message received by encoding), kinetic loops (several series of encoding, decoding, and feedback across time), and cybernetics (the unwritten rules defining the boundaries of what communication is and how it occurs).

informative A term used in the analysis of a genetic condition through the use of a pedigree (chart of the family tree) or sophisticated deoxyribonucleic acid (DNA) mapping (locating and describing the DNA sequence of interest). An informative family is one that has enough information about a particular disorder to determine its inheritance pattern.

informed consent A process in which an individual agrees to a procedure, process, or intervention with a reasonably complete understanding of its risks and benefits. A consent for action, it is based on three criteria: 1) adequate information, 2) an ability to understand and process the information, and 3) a lack of coercion (the ability to act freely without being pressured or forced) in the outcome of the decision-making process. Informed consent becomes a more complex issue when one is dealing with adults with intellectual disability. Models stress the importance of offering adults with intellectual disabilities many life decision opportunities previously denied them. *See* self-determination.

inguinal hernia A weakening of the abdominal wall that leads to a bulging and protrusion of abdominal contents outward into the area of the groin. Because of the high risk of incarceration (trapping of a segment of gut) or strangulation (cutting off of circulation to the trapped segment), inguinal hernias are routinely surgically repaired.

in-hand manipulation The process of adjusting objects within one's hand after grasping them. In-hand manipulation includes the ability to change hands, the ability to shift an object one is holding to a more useful position, and the simple and complex rotation both of the hand and of an object in the hand.

inhibition A condition in which one function or circumstance prevents the expression of another function or behavior; an act or process by which the typical or expected response is restrained despite the presence of the eliciting stimulus.

inion Occipital prominence; an anatomical landmark on the back of the skull.

initial consonant deletion A phonological process in which there is an omission of a single consonant that initiates a word.

initiated mutual regulation Child-initiated activities designed to seek support from others or to respond to another's efforts to regulate emotional arousal through sensorimotor and/or cognitive/linguistic strategies in a social interaction.

innate Vague qualifier that suggests a genetic or fixed biological component to an ability or a disability.

inner canthal distance (ICD) A measurement of the distance between the two medial canthi (inner corners of the eyes, closest to the nose). The distance is increased with hypertelorism (widely spaced eyes). Increased ICD is a nonspecific, mild dysmorphic (atypical) feature that may be associated with developmental disabilities.

inner canthal distance (ICD)

insatiable child syndrome Whining, irritable, and demanding behavior that can accompany attention-deficit/hyperactivity disorder (ADHD) and is interpreted as either an inherited or learned persistent dissatisfaction.

insensitivity to pain A neurological finding in dysautonomia (a hereditary disease of the nerves that signal pain) and some developmental disabilities. What is often interpreted as an insensitivity to pain can be a reflection of an altered awareness of sensory input or may be a reflection of the difficulty that people with severe developmental disorders have effectively communicating their awareness of pain.

in-service training Professional training provided to individuals practicing within their profession. Goals include acquiring new skills for immediate application, increasing proficiency of previously learned skills, updating knowledge, and enhancing leadership ability.

insidious Describing an evolution of symptoms or disease that is not easily detectable in part because of a very gradual onset or initially very mild symptoms.

insight In psychology, the ability to be aware of sources, causes, or need for changes in one's behavior and feeling state—a "psychological mindedness" or self-knowledge that enhances a person's understanding of himself or herself and, to some extent, others. Having insight involves interpreting the significance and purposes of one's behaviors and motives and includes having the ability to recognize inappropriateness and irrationality in those behaviors and emotions. An individual's level of insight has implications for the types of treatment approaches that are appropriate for and available to that person. In learning theory, insight is a type of knowledge that facilitates the reorganization of the field of experience to create a new idea or discover a solution to a problem. Three distinct but interdependent psychological processes collectively constitute insight: 1) selective encoding—recognizing recurrent information in a given context, 2) selective combination—integrating relevant information in a new and productive way, and 3) selective comparison—recognizing how new information is related to old information.

insomnia Difficulty initiating or maintaining sleep, or complaints of poor sleep quality. There are several types of insomnia. Insomnia in children is often behavioral, related to sleep onset association (learning to connect conditions such as a parent's presence in the room with falling asleep so that those conditions must be duplicated in order for the child to fall back to sleep) or inadequate limit setting by parents (toleration of repeated requests, stalling, and "certain calls" after bedtime). Psychophysiological insomnia is a common issue in adults who have had sleep disruptions that are then maintained by associations of their bedroom and beds with poor sleep, with these bad

association provoking anxiety and distress that, in a vicious cycle, interfere with falling asleep. Idiopathic (without known cause) or childhood-onset insomnia exists independent of other conditions and may be related to increased physiological hyperarousal, a state of increased body alertness and perhaps mild anxiety that interferes with sleep. Although primary insomnia is commonly diagnosed in adults, its origins are traced back to childhood, and it is possible that some children with disabilities are affected. Comorbid insomnia is that associated with other conditions, including sleep disorders such as obstructive sleep apnea, psychiatric disorders such as anxiety and depression, and substance use or medication side effects.

instinctive avoiding reaction Hyperextension of the fingers in response to forward-upward elevation of the arm. A typical response in an infant or young child but a possible sign of cerebral palsy or traumatic brain injury in older children.

institutional care Care that takes place in a self-contained facility, usually large in size, that provides temporary custodial supervision, evaluation, training, and treatment for individuals with intellectual disability, other developmental disabilities, and certain mental illnesses until appropriate community alternatives are located or become available. In some cases, particularly if the degree of developmental disability is severe to profound or no other form of appropriate placement is available, institutional care can be prolonged and indefinite. The term *institutional care* is also used to refer generically to any residential out-of-home placement that incorporates educational and therapeutic treatment components.

institutional review board (IRB) A committee that is formally designated to oversee, review, approve, and monitor medical and behavioral research with human and animal participants. IRBs were developed in response to abuses of individuals who lacked the social power to object to their own involvement in research, with unethical and inhuman consequences. The U.S. Food and Drug Administration and the U.S. Department of Health and Human Services empower IRBs at medical and research institutions to approve or disapprove research projects based on a review of their risks and potential benefits. IRBs also oversee and approve informed consent procedures and ensure that the rights and needs of vulnerable populations (e.g., children, individuals with disabilities) are protected.

institutionalism A developmental and behavior profile of motor and language (especially expressive) delay, increased visual interest in adults, rocking, and bland indiscriminate amiability with the absence of stranger anxiety in a quiet, sober, noncuddly infant being reared in a nonfamily setting. Institutionalism can be considered a type of maternal deprivation (separation of a child from his or her mother's care) or prolonged hospitalization and can give rise to anaclitic (due to separation) depression and failure to thrive (poor physical growth). Later impairments in forming emotional ties, controlling impulses, thinking abstractly, and being able to enjoy life can become prominent. *See also* anaclitic depression.

instruction, modality-based *See* modality-based instruction.

instructional cloze A procedure in which readers are asked to fill missing words or phrases in passages by using the reading strategies of predicting, confirming, and integrating.

instructional level A student's functional reading level when the text being read is challenging but manageable; no more than 1 in 10 words is difficult, and there is an approximately 90% success rate. *See also* frustration level, independent level.

instrumental activities of daily living (IADLs) Those adaptive behaviors that are necessary for functioning independently in home, school, community, and work environments. Some examples are the ability to independently toilet, dress and groom appropriately, tell time, take public transportation, and read signs (e.g., those needed for choosing the proper restroom in a public place).

insult That which produces injury to an organ.

Integrated Bilingual Special Education Model In English as second language, an instructional model in which a bilingual special educator is responsible for the implementation of the individualized education programs (IEPs); teachers are trained in both bilingual education and special education.

integrated classroom model (ICM) A service delivery model for educating students with mild disabilities and students without disabilities in the same classroom.

Integrated Play Groups (IPG) model An approach to addressing play and peer relations in children with autism that involves play experiences with typical children in natural play environments.

integration The inclusion of individuals with disabilities in the general community; integration may necessitate support in educational, vocational, residential, community, and employment settings. In regard to education, integration is the process of educating all children who have needs and interests to which the schools have previously not responded (e.g., students with disabilities, students who are ethnically or culturally different) in a general, rather than segregated, academic setting. *See also* inclusive education, mainstreaming.

Intellectual and Developmental Disabilities Research Center (IDDRC) The Intellectual and Developmental Disabilities Branch of the Eunice Kennedy Shriver National Institute of Child Health and Human Development (NICHD; an agency of the National Institutes of Health [NIH]) sponsors research and research training aimed at preventing and ameliorating intellectual and related developmental disabilities. The program supports biomedical, biobehavioral, behavioral, and translational research in the etiology, pathophysiology, screening, prevention, treatment, and epidemiology of these disabilities in 14 IDDRCs (formerly known as *Mental Retardation Research Centers* [MRRCs]). These IDDRCs are located at universities and children's hospitals throughout the country. Each IDDRC supports from 40 to more than 100 projects and from 20 to more than 70 principal investigators who receive funding from numerous NIH institutes and centers, other federal agencies, and foundations within the private sector. This allows the IDDRCs to support substantially more projects and affiliates than would be possible using NICHD support alone. Information technology, bioinformatics, and biostatistics services support gene array, proteomics, and behavioral and clinical core services. Translational and clinical research projects make up almost half of all projects for a number of centers. The centers actively pioneer new technologies and instrument development that represent unique, evolving resources.

intellectual disability Cognitive impairment. To meet the criteria for having an intellectual disability under the Individuals with Disabilities Education Act (IDEA) of 1990 (PL 101-476), a student must have an intellectual ability score (IQ) of 70 or below with adaptive and academic skills commensurate with ability. *Intellectual disability* replaces the term *mental retardation* in the United States.

intelligence A hypothetical construct that refers to general cognitive ability. There are many definitions of intelligence, and it has been operationalized (translated into an observable behavior) by different attempts to measure it. Traditional definitions tend to emphasize reasoning, problem solving, and skills underlying traditional learning, whereas contemporary theorists stress interpersonal skills and creativity. Intelligence is assumed to have inherited (genetic) and acquired (environmental) components and reflects the interaction of these components with the sum total of learning experiences in the individual's lifetime. Although there are several popular, reliable tests of intelligence, no single test is thought to measure human learning, problem solving, or adaptability in its entirety, and none measures innate talents such as those for art and music. *See* intelligence test.

intelligence quotient (IQ) A quantitative score that is accepted as reflecting an individual's cognitive abilities. Scores are derived from performance on tests designed to measure verbal and nonverbal aspects of intelligence. IQs are limited by the type of skills they are designed to measure, and they may not provide a comprehensive description of an individual's abilities. IQ ranges vary by instrument but generally have comparable classifications that stem from a mean (average) score of 100: 130 and above, very superior; 120–129, superior; 110–119, high average; 90–109, average; 80–89, low average; 70–79, borderline; and less than 70, intellectual disability.

intelligence test A standardized measure used to establish an intelligence level rating, typically an intelligence quotient (IQ), by measuring an individual's performance on a variety of tasks relating to intelligence. Valid testing considers cultural and linguistic diversity as well as differences in communication and behavioral factors.

intelligibility The adequacy of an acoustic signal to convey information.

intelligibility threshold *See* speech reception threshold (SRT).

IntelliKeys An alternative expanded keyboard that can be adapted for use by a person with limited ability to target keys on a regular keyboard.

intensity The loudness of sound as measured in decibels (dB). To determine a sound's intensity, one compares the sound with a reference level that has been determined to be the faintest sound most humans can detect. The intensity of a whisper from several feet away is 10 dB, whereas a commercial jet taking off nearby produces a sound intensity of about 120 dB.

Interagency Coordinating Councils (ICCs) State councils made up of parents and representatives from local, state, and federal agencies that provide early intervention services. ICCs meet periodically to discuss issues, problem-solve, and set procedures relating to the provision of early intervention in their state.

interalar distance The width of the nose.

interdisciplinary Describing a team approach to the diagnosis and intervention of developmental disabilities. In such an approach, professionals representing two or more disciplines interact so that the final case formulation reflects the conclusions of a process in which convergent (similar) and divergent (differing) findings and conclusions are discussed and resolved in a manner that respects each individual's contribution.

interference *See* transfer.

interjection A type of disfluency in which elements of speech that do not add to the meaning of what is being said are interjected into what is being said.

intermediate care facility (ICF) A facility that serves people with developmental disabilities (not just those with intellectual disabilities) and that assumes a need for some level of medical or custodial care beyond that required in supported living or group home placements but that is less than a full-time intensive medical or custodial need. Although the need for such care arrangements still exists, many people previously supported in ICF environments have moved to more independent supported living arrangements. When appropriate supports can be provided, the latter model is preferred for the long-term care of people with intellectual or developmental disabilities. Formerly *intermediate care facility for people with mental retardation and developmental disabilities* (ICF/MR/DD).

intermediate care facility for people with intellectual and developmental disabilities (ICF/DD) *See* intermediate care facility (ICF).

intermediate care facility for people with other related conditions (ICF/ORC) A facility that serves people with developmental disabilities other than intellectual disabilities, including motor disabilities such as cerebral palsy or spina bifida or health issues such as epilepsy, that significantly affect day-to-day functioning. The designation assumes a need for some level of medical care or support beyond that available in a typical environment. A need for an ICF level of care is used as a basis for determining eligibility for waivers that fund community support services for people with these conditions. *See also* Individual and Family Developmental Disabilities Support Waiver (DD Waiver).

intermittent photic stimulation The use of strobe lights (flashing lights) during an electroencephalogram (EEG) to stimulate brain electrical activity. There are three EEG responses to photic stimulation. One is photic drive, a normal response of rhythmic activity over the posterior (back) regions of the head. Depression (decrease) of this response can be seen with destructive brain lesions, whereas increased amplitude (the height of recorded brain waves) is associated with scarring and an epileptogenic (seizure) focus. The photomyoclonic response is a nonspecific response consisting of fluttering of the eyelids, movements of the eyes, and sometimes jerking of the face. The photoconvulsive or photoparoxysmal response (PCR) is most commonly found in individuals with seizure disorders. It is characterized by a symmetrical spike and wave or multiple spike and wave complexes in response to the light stimulus. This EEG change may be associated with an impairment of consciousness and brisk jerks of the upper body, essentially a seizure that has been triggered by the flashing lights. The PCR response may be familial and may represent a susceptibility to convulsions.

intermittent positive-pressure breathing (IPPB) A type of mechanically assisted ventilation used with infants and children with respiratory distress. With inhalation, positive pressure pushes compressed breathing gases into the airways until a preset pressure is reached. Passive (nonassisted) exhalation takes place through a valve, and the cycle begins again as the flow of gas is triggered by inhalation.

internal rotation The turning of a limb toward the mid-line (middle) of the body clockwise on the left side or counterclockwise on the right side of the body.

internal tibial torsion An orthopedic deformity in which the lower leg is twisted inward so that the feet turn in but the knees face forward. Toeing in is a leg problem and not a foot problem. In children without cerebral palsy, this deformity often resolves spontaneously by 3 years of age if they are walking upright without assistance.

International Classification of Diseases, Tenth Revision, Clinical Modification (ICD-10-CM) A numerical coding system for medical conditions and procedures that is used for billing, research, and statistical purposes.

International Classification of Functionality (ICF) *International Classification of Functioning, Disability and Health.* Developed and endorsed by the World Health Organization (WHO) for measuring health and disability at both the individual and population levels, the ICF is a classification of health and health-related domains that describe body functions and structures, activities, and participation. The domains are classified from body, individual, and societal perspectives by means of two lists: a list of body functions and structure and a list of domains of activity and participation. Because an individual's functioning and disability occurs within a context, the ICF also includes a list of environmental factors. The ICF is useful for understanding and measuring health outcomes. It can be used in clinical settings, health services, or surveys at the individual or population levels.

International Classification of Functioning, Disability and Health *See* International Classification of Functionality (ICF).

International HapMap Project (HapMap) A project funded by the National Human Genome Research Institute at the National Institutes of Health to generate a map of haplotypes in the human genome. *Haplotypes* are common variations in a deoxyribonucleic acid (DNA) sequence that may represent normal variations or may cause or modify disease states. HapMap was started in 2003 as a collaboration among multiple researchers and countries and was completed within 3 years. Information from HapMap is freely available online. *See also* Human Genome Project.

International Phonetic Alphabet (IPA) A system of symbols for writing the speech sounds of all languages. First devised and published in 1888 by a group of French language teachers, its aim was to devise a system for transcribing the sounds of speech that was independent of any particular language and applicable to all languages. The

IPA is used by speech and language therapists, teachers, foreign-language students, translators, linguists, and lexicographers.

international standard manual alphabet A mode of communication in which the speaker strokes block letters with the fingers in a prescribed manner on the palm of the listener; this type of fingerspelling is used predominantly in communicating with individuals who are blind and have profound hearing loss.

International System for Human Cytogenetic Nomenclature (ISCN) The nomenclature system established by the International Standing Committee on Human Cytogenetic Nomenclature to improve worldwide communication among cytogeneticists.

interobserver reliability *interrater reliability.* The consistency of observations or scores recorded by two or more individuals administering the same test to or observing the same individual.

interpersonal supports Planned, person-centered modifications made by teachers, instructional staff, and other social partners in language use, emotional expression, and interactive style. These modifications are effective in helping students with differing abilities process and use language, participate in social interaction, experience social activities as emotionally satisfying, and be available for learning and relating to others. Interpersonal supports also include peer support and training, which provides a child with positive experiences with children who are responsive partners and who act as language and social models, leading to the development of positive relationships and friendships.

interphalangeal (IP) joints The two joints of each finger and the joint of the thumb farthest from the palm.

interpreters for the deaf Hearing individuals who listen to a spoken message and communicate it in some way to an individual with a hearing impairment. In interpreting a spoken message, it is permissible to depart from the speaker's exact words to paraphrase and explain what the speaker is saying. In this way, interpreting is different from translating, which is presenting verbatim another's words. There are various types of interpreters for the deaf, including sign language interpreters, who communicate what has been said through some form of sign language or fingerspelling; oral interpreters, who mouth (enunciate clearly and more slowly) the speaker's message, allowing the individual with a hearing impairment to lipread or speechread; and reverse interpreters, who render sign language or difficult-to-understand speech into clearly spoken English. Specialized interpreters familiar with technical language serve in a variety of settings. Educational interpreters are used to facilitate the inclusion of students who are deaf. In addition to educational applications, interpreters are mandated to be available as a component of vocational rehabilitation services, and most states require that interpreters be available whenever the civil rights of people with hearing impairments are involved. The National Registry of Interpreters for the Deaf promotes training and recruitment, sets standard competencies, and maintains a listing of certified interpreters.

interpupillary distance The distance between the two eyes, using the center of each pupil as the landmark for the measurement.

interpupillary distance

Abnormal interpupillary distances occur with hypertelorism (widely spaced eyes), hypotelorism (decreased distance between the eyes), and strabismus (crossed eyes); normal distances are present in pseudostrabismus (false impression of crossed eyes) and pseudohypertelorism (false impression of widely spaced eyes).

interrater reliability *See* interobserver reliability.

intersensory integration The use of two sensory modalities in accomplishing a task. For example, listening to a series of numbers and writing them requires auditor-motor integration, whereas seeing a list of numbers and saying them requires visual-verbal integration.

interstitial del(17)(p11.2p11.2) *See* Smith-Magenis syndrome (SMS).

interval sample A sampling of behavioral data gathered by monitoring and record-ing behaviors at predetermined times rather than continuously. A teacher may set aside three 5-minute intervals and record a student's behavior only during that time.

intervention Planned strategies and activities that modify a challenging behavior or state of being and facilitate growth and change. Intervention is analogous to the medical term *treatment*. Helping professionals prefer the term *intervention* in order to describe a broader range of activities for the individuals they assist. Thus, intervention may include such activities as engaging in advocacy, undergoing psychotherapy, receiving speech-language therapy, obtaining entitlements, using adaptive equipment, modifying the environment, facilitating resource develop-ment, and networking.

intervocalic singleton consonant deletion A phonological process in which there is an omission of word-medial consonants.

intonation A pattern of pitch and stress that helps differentiate spoken statements, questions, and exclamations and gives a variety of expression to speech.

intracerebral Within the brain, specifically within that portion of the brain called the *cerebrum* (the topmost part of the brain, consisting of two hemispheres).

intracranial Within the skull.

intracranial hemorrhage (ICH) Bleeding within the skull.

intraobserver reliability The consistency of scores the same individual obtains when the same examiner readministers a test.

intrathecal Within or into the sheath (theca), usually referring to the sheath of membranes surrounding the spinal cord.

intrathecal baclofen (ITB) *See* continuous intrathecal baclofen infusion (CIBI).

intrauterine growth retardation (IUGR) A lower birth weight than would be expected for gestational age (or the length of the pregnancy); IUGR is sometimes detected prenatally (before birth). Infants with a weight reduction proportional to their other parameters (small head circumfer-ence, short body length) are more likely to have underlying genetic, metabolic, toxic, or infectious etiologies (causes) that will adversely influence later development. Disproportionate growth parameters (with head circumference approximating normal percentiles) in newborns increase the possi-bility of better developmental outcomes.

intravenous Within a vein; describes the administration of fluids (for replacement, nutrition, medication).

intravenous immunoglobulin (IVIG) A fluid that contains antibodies and that is given through the vein. IVIG is used to treat immune system deficiencies as well as to modulate the immune system in certain neurological conditions such as myasthe-nia gravis, Guillain-Barré syndrome, and Kawasaki disease.

intraventricular hemorrhage (IVH) A bleed-ing into the brain (specifically the subependy-mal [beneath the innermost layer] area), most common in premature infants because their brains and vascular (blood vessel) structures are more delicate than those of infants born at term. When IVH occurs in a term infant, it can be because of a traumatic delivery or, rarely, a bleeding disorder. IVHs are graded 1–4, with Grade 1 being the mildest and involving only the ependymal (innermost) area, Grade 2 involving bleeding into the ventricles (fluid-filled spaces within the brain), Grade 3 involving blood distending the ventricles, and Grade 4 involving bleeding deeper into the brain. Complications of IVH include hydrocephalus (excess fluid in the brain), porencephalic cysts (holes), and leukomalacia (underdeveloped brain matter). The hydrocephalus may be treated with shunts (tubes used to reroute the excess fluid) or medication; however, treatment does not ensure typical development. The developmental outcome can include cerebral palsy and intellectual disability. The severity of outcome is generally worst in bleeds of Grades 3 or 4, although that correlation is not rigid.

intrinsic motivation Motivation for completing a task out of interest and a feeling of personal competence rather than for an external reward. Theories of intrinsic motivation suggest that some tasks are intrinsically motivating because humans have innate tendencies to develop competencies (skills), to be curious about novel events and activities, and to feel that they are autonomous (independent) and engaging in activities of their own volition. An additional assumption is that some children have been socialized (raised and conditioned) to value academic work. Students have been found to be more intrinsically motivated to complete tasks when 1) the tasks are moderately challenging, novel, and relevant to their own lives; 2) the threat of negative external evaluation is not important; 3) their attention is not focused on extrinsic (external, or outside) reasons for completing the tasks; and 4) they can take responsibility for their success by having been given some choice in the tasks.

intubation The placement of a tube through the nose (nasotracheal intubation) or through the mouth (orotracheal intuba-tion) into the trachea (windpipe) to provide artificial ventilation (mechanical help with breathing).

intuition Judgment by perception rather than by reason.

Intuniv *See* guanfacine.

inversion Describing the state when all or part of the sole of the foot is turned inward toward the mid-line of the body.

inversion A rearrangement of material within a chromosome such that a segment of that chromosome is in reverse order or orientation.

inverted duplication 15 *See* tetrasomy 15 pter-q12.

IP *See* identified patient.

IP joints *See* interphalangeal joints.

IPA *See* International Phonetic Alphabet.

I-PAS *See* Infant-Preschool Play Assessment Scale.

IPE *See* individualized plan for employment.

IPG model *See* Integrated Play Groups model.

IPP *See* individualized program plan.

IPPB *See* intermittent positive-pressure breathing.

ipsilateral On the same side. For example, in hemiplegic cerebral palsy, the ipsilateral arm and leg are involved (the right arm and the right leg in a right hemiplegia, and the left arm and left leg in a left hemiplegia). However, because brain control of motor function crosses the mid-line (e.g., the right brain controls movement for the left side of the body), brain injury in a hemiplegia is contralateral (on the opposite side), with a right hemiplegia being secondary to (caused by) an injury to the left brain.

IQ *See* intelligence quotient.

IRB *See* institutional review board.

IRI Informal Reading Inventory. *See* Quantitative Reading Inventory.

iridodenesis Tremor of the iris on movement, usually due to dislocation of the lens.

iris The pigmented area of the eye that surrounds the pupil. The color of the iris is what one describes as the color of the eyes.

Irlen lenses Tinted eyeglasses or lens filters originally used to treat dyslexia; this method has since been applied to the treatment of other developmental disorders. An intervention devised by Helen Irlen, use of Irlen lenses first achieved popularity in Australia. The tinted nonrefractive lenses purportedly treat an underlying disorder known as scotopic sensitivity syndrome; however, both the treatment and the syndrome remain unproven. An inexpensive variant involves the placement of tinted cellophane overlays on top of material to be read. *See also* scotopic sensitivity syndrome.

iron deficiency anemia Anemia secondary to inadequate dietary iron, common from 9 to 24 months of age. Iron deficiency anemia may contribute to apathy, irritability, short attention span, and lowered cognitive performance.

irritability Quick (over)excitability to stimuli; a state of (over)reaction to environmental and interpersonal variables.

ISAM *See* infant of a substance-abusing mother.

ischemia Local anemia (lack of blood) secondary to (caused by) decreased blood flow

associated with hypovolemia (decreased blood volume or shock) or vasoconstriction (narrowing of the blood vessels).

ISCN *See* International System for Human Cytogenetic Nomenclature.

Ishihara test A series of 38 pictures used to screen for color blindness. Each plate depicts a large number of colored dots in which a number (or other design) is embedded that is visible only to a person with intact color vision. The number and types of errors define the presence and type of color blindness (e.g., red–green, total). *See also* color blindness.

isochromosome An abnormal chromosome with arms of equal length caused by the duplication of one arm and the deletion of the other. Chromosomes normally have a short arm, p, and a long arm, q. For example, instead of a p arm and a q arm, an isochromosome might have two p arms. An isochromosome is designated in a chromosome or medical report as an isochromosome number (#), in which the number refers to the number of the affected chromosome. An isochromosome may cause anatomical abnormalities as well as developmental disabilities.

isodisomy A condition in which an individual receives two copies of a chromosome from one parent and none from the other. (A child typically inherits one of a pair of chromosomes from his or her mother and the other from his or her father.) Isodisomy can result in a loss of the effects of imprinting (the differences in chromosomes from different-sex parents) and can cause genetic disorders such as Prader-Willi syndrome.

isometric power The ability to hold a position against the force of gravity or another type of resistance.

isotonic power The ability of a muscle to move through its range of motion with resistance applied throughout.

ISP   *See* individualized service plan.

ITB   Intrathecal baclofen. *See* continuous intrathecal baclofen infusion (CIBI).

ITC   *See* Infant-Toddler Checklist.

ITCA   *See* Infants and Toddlers Coordinators Association.

item   A symptom or behavior being rated or tested on a scale.

item difficulty   The frequency with which any given test item is passed or failed as compared with the other items on the test.

itinerant services   In reference to education, the use of support service personnel who provide instruction to students in the hospital and at home or who travel between schools to supplement instruction typically provided by the classroom teacher. The use of itinerant services differs from a resource room model in that a resource room teacher remains in a specific classroom setting to which students come for instruction.

ITP   *See* individualized transition plan.

ITPA-3   *See* Illinois Test of Psycholinguistic Abilities–Third Edition.

IUGR   *See* intrauterine growth retardation.

IVH   *See* intraventricular hemorrhage.

IVIG   *See* intravenous immunoglobulin.

Jacksonian seizure A focal motor seizure that follows a particular progression (pattern of spread) to other body parts and finally becomes generalized, affecting the whole body. This is rare and is often associated with an identifiable lesion (area of abnormality) in the cerebral cortex of the brain. Named for the English neurologist John Hughlings Jackson (1835–1911).

jargon A body of specialized terms used by various subgroups of a society, especially among professionals in a given discipline, that are not easily understood by those outside the discipline. Meaningful communication is often hindered by the use of such jargon, particularly when individuals from several disciplines are discussing a subject. This is because some words have different meanings according to the discipline in which they are used. When the use of jargon is unavoidable, it should be accompanied by a jargon-free explanation of the meaning of the term.

jargoning A vocalization pattern of infants that has the intonation, inflection, and rhythm of conversational speech but is unintelligible; it sounds as though the infant is talking a foreign language. Immature jargoning is completely unintelligible, whereas mature jargoning contains intelligible words mixed in with the gibberish. Jargoning as an expressive language milestone emerges between 14 months (immature) and 18 months (mature) of age.

jaundice A yellow tinge to the skin that results from hyperbilirubinemia (high levels of bilirubin, a blood breakdown product, in the blood) caused by diseases of the blood or liver. Physiological jaundice occurs in the first week of life in many newborns with bilirubin levels increasing up to 9 mg/dl. Physiological jaundice is due to a transient (temporary) immaturity of the liver enzymes that help the body to remove bilirubin. In some breast-fed infants, this jaundice may be prolonged and somewhat more severe. In older children, jaundice must be distinguished from carotenemia (yellowing of the skin due to excess carotene [a substance contained in some vegetables, such as carrots], rather than bilirubin, in the blood); with carotenemia, the whites of the eyes remain white. In adults, jaundice is most commonly associated with hepatitis (liver inflammation, often viral).

jaw jerk A sharp tap to the chin (stimulus) produces a reflex closure of the jaw (response). The jaw jerk is an abnormal finding consistent with hyperreflexia (overly active reflexes).

jaw stabilization Lack of up-and-down movement of the jaw during drinking.

jaw thrust A strong downward extension of the lower jaw. The mouth appears to be stuck in the open position, and the infant has difficulty closing it to take in food.

JBS *See* Johanson-Blizzard syndrome.

Jebsen Hand Function Test A test used as a broad measure of hand function in adults that has been renormed on children 6–19 years of age. Seven timed subtests address representative hand activities.

Jekyll and Hyde personality Dramatic and sudden emotional lability (mood swings) in the absence of recognizable cause or precipitating (triggering) factors; observed in children with attentional disorders and in Gilles de la Tourette syndrome. This term is derived from Robert Louis Stevenson's (1850–1894) short story *The Strange Case of Dr. Jekyll and Mr. Hyde* (1886).

Jendrassik maneuver A technique in which an individual is asked to pull as hard as possible against hands hooked together by flexed fingers; this enhances the knee jerk, in part by distracting the person's attention and decreasing anxiety over the examination of the lower extremities.

Jervell and Lange-Nielsen syndrome A genetic syndrome of profound congenital hearing impairment associated with syncope (fainting) caused by a heart conduction defect. Distinguishing this specific etiology (cause) for deafness is important, because medication may prevent sudden cardiac death. Incidence is 1.6–6.0 in 1 million, with an autosomal recessive inheritance pattern.

jitteriness Nonspecific irritability in infants; movements can be tremulous and sometimes jerky with clonus (rhythmic oscillations between flexion and extension [bending and straightening a joint]). The absence of abnormal gaze or eye movements helps to distinguish jitteriness from neonatal seizures. The most common causes of jitteriness in newborns include perinatal asphyxia (lack of oxygen around the time of birth), hypocalcemia (low blood calcium), hypoglycemia (low blood sugar levels), and drug withdrawal.

job carving A method of defining a portion of a job for a person with a disability able to perform some, but not all, of a given job's duties.

job coach An individual who accompanies an individual with a disability to a new job to provide direction and assist in job training and related acclimation.

Job Training Partnership Act of 1982 (PL 97-300) The Job Training Partnership Act was enacted to establish programs to prepare youth and unskilled adults for entry into the labor force and to provide job training to economically disadvantaged and other individuals who are in special need of such training and who face serious barriers to employment in order to obtain productive employment. The act includes five titles. Title I mandates and outlines the requirements for the job training partnership; Title II contains the provisions for training services for the disadvantaged, encompassing both adult and youth programs as well as summer youth employment and training programs; Title III provides for identification, training, and employment assistance for dislocated workers; Title IV describes federally administered programs; and Title V contains miscellaneous provisions including some pertaining to the Social Security Act and the Military Selective Service Act. *See also* School Transition to Employment Partnership (STEP).

Johanson-Blizzard syndrome (JBS) Ectodermal dysplasia-exocrine pancreatic insufficiency. A genetic syndrome characterized by hearing impairment, a distinctive facies (facial features) that includes underdeveloped nostrils, growth deficiency due to problems digesting fats because of abnormalities of the pancreas (the source of digestive enzymes), often hypothyroidism, and intellectual disability. Inheritance is autosomal recessive.

joint attention *shared attention.* A prelinguistic communication skill in which a child alternates gaze between a person and an object, literally attending to something conjointly (together) with another person. This both directs the attention of the other person to the object or event and signifies a nonverbal communication. Children typically develop joint attention between 12 and 24 months of age. Children with autism may be delayed in developing this reciprocal (between individuals) social interaction.

Joubert syndrome A genetic syndrome characterized by episodic hyperpnea or apnea (disturbances of respiratory control in the form of overbreathing or pauses in breathing, respectively), opsoclonus (abnormal eye movements), intellectual disability, hypotonia (low muscle tone), ataxia (unsteady gait), and dysplasia (defective development) of the cerebellum (the part of the brain involved in muscle coordination and balance), resulting in partial or complete absence of the cerebellar vermis (the central part of the cerebellum) and other structural abnormalities of the brain. The routine association of this syndrome with severe intellectual disability has been questioned;

severe visual, motor, and articulation problems can contribute to limitations on how well cognition can be assessed. Inheritance follows an autosomal recessive pattern, and at least four different genes have been identified.

joystick A manual device with a movable control lever that can be tilted in different directions to control a computer, wheelchair, or other system.

JRA *See* juvenile rheumatoid arthritis.

jug-handle ear Protruding auricle (pinna, external, ear). In addition to being a minor dysmorphic (atypical) feature, this type of ear protrusion may reflect the presence of neuromuscular disease.

jug-handle ear

juvenile rheumatoid arthritis (JRA) A childhood disease characterized by connective tissue inflammation. Specific diagnostic criteria include age at onset, which is typically younger than 16 years. There are several subtypes.

Kabat *See* proprioceptive neuromuscular facilitation (PNF).

K-ABC-II *See* Kaufman Assessment Battery for Children–Second Edition.

KADI *See* Krug Asperger's Disorder Index.

KAFO Knee–ankle–foot orthosis. *See* orthosis.

Kaiser-Permanente (K-P) diet A modification of the Feingold diet for hyperactivity. *See also* Feingold hypothesis.

kangaroo care The practice of parents holding their diaper-clad premature infant beneath their clothing chest-to-chest and skin-to-skin to reinforce attachment.

Kanner syndrome *See* autism.

karyotype An individual's chromosomes arranged by size and banding pattern (darker stripes in patterns unique to each chromosome) from photomicrographs (photographs taken under the microscope) of the actual chromosomes of a cell. The autosomes (chromosomes that are not sex chromosomes) are paired and then numbered 1–22, with the largest chromosome pair as number 1. The sex chromosomes are heteromorphic (different sizes); the large one is named the X and the small one, the Y. The Y contains genes that are male determining. The X contains genes necessary for fertility in females and many important genes for body form and function. A typical male has both an X and Y chromosome; a typical female has two X chromosomes. *See* page 259.

Katie Beckett Medicaid Waiver A Medicaid waiver that provides funding for medical assistance for children younger than 19 years of age who have long-term disabilities and complex medical needs. This waiver enables the children to continue to live at home instead of in a hospital, nursing home, or intermediate care facility (ICF). Unlike with Medicaid, only the child's income is taken into account for eligibility. Without the waiver, the income of legally liable relatives is counted when the individual is cared for at home.

Kaufman Assessment Battery for Children–Second Edition (K-ABC-II) An individually administered test of intelligence and achievement for use with children 3;1–8;0 years old. The K-ABC-II comprises five global scales: Simultaneous Processing, Sequential Processing, Planning, Learning, and Knowledge. *Simultaneous processing* refers to the mental ability to integrate input simultaneously to solve a problem; it frequently involves spatial or organizational abilities as well as the application of visual imagery. Sequential processing emphasizes the arrangement of stimuli in sequential or serial order for problem solving, wherein each stimulus is linearly or temporally related to the previous one, creating a form of serial dependence. The test can be

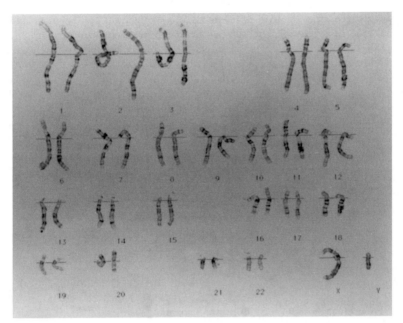

male

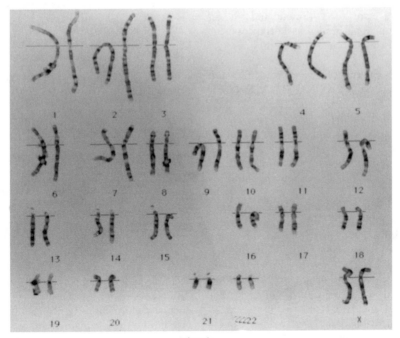

female

karyotype

administered according to two different theoretical models: One (the Cattell-Horn-Carroll) is appropriate for use with mainstream children; the other (the Luria, a neuropsychological model) excludes verbal ability and is more appropriate for use with children from diverse cultural backgrounds. A Spanish-language version of the K-ABC-II is available. Administration time is 25–55 minutes.

Kaufman Brief Intelligence Test–Second Edition (KBIT-2) A brief individual intelligence test for use with people ages 4–90 years that produces age-based standard scores and percentile ranges for both crystallized (verbal) and fluid (nonverbal) intelligence. It requires approximately 20 minutes to administer.

Kaufman Functional Academic Skills Test (K-FAST) A brief, individually administered, norm-referenced test of functional academic skills. The K-FAST produces standard scores for arithmetic and reading and a functional academic skills composite. Administration time is 15–25 minutes.

Kaufman Survey of Early Academic and Language Skills (K-SEALS) A standardized survey of academic and language skills for use with children ages 3–7 years. The K-SEALS produces standard scores for vocabulary and numbers and letters and words, and a descriptive category for articulation (pronunciation of speech sounds) skills.

Kaufman Test of Educational Achievement–Second Edition (KTEA-II) An individually administered, norm-referenced measure of school achievement for use with children in Grades 1–12. It consists of two separate and nonoverlapping forms: 1) a brief screening form (for ages 4–90 years) that provides standard scores in the areas of reading, mathematics, and written expression; and 2) a comprehensive form (for ages 4.5–25 years) that provides scores in the specific domains of reading, mathematics,

and written and oral language and a comprehensive achievement composite. The brief form takes approximately 30 minutes to administer, whereas the comprehensive form may require 1–1.5 hours to complete. The KTEA-II also provides procedures for error analysis as well as a systematic method for determining whether there are significant differences in the subtest results.

Kayser-Fleischer ring Green, yellow, and brown corneal (white of the eye) pigmentation that encircles the periphery of the iris (colored part of the eye) in Wilson disease.

KBIT-2 *See* Kaufman Brief Intelligence Test–Second Edition.

Kent Infant Development Scale–Second Edition (KIDS-2) A norm-referenced parent-report assessment of the overall developmental status of infants birth to 15 months old; it can be used in children up to 6 years of age when their developmental age is less than 15 months.

Keppra *See* levetiracetam.

keratosis A benign abnormal overgrowth of epithelial tissues on the vocal folds.

kernel sentence The basic syntactic structure of English: subject + verb + object.

kernicterus Nuclear yellowing. In newborn infants with severe hyperbilirubinemia (very high levels of bilirubin, a blood breakdown product, in the blood), the basal ganglia and other brain centers (nuclei) are selectively affected to produce a syndrome of supraversion gaze palsy (an upward gaze palsy [inability to look up]), hearing loss, central auditory imperception (difficulty attending to and interpreting sounds), and dental abnormalities (green staining of the teeth from the bile pigment biliverdin). The involvement of the basal ganglia typically produces a choreoathetoid (spontaneous writhing movements) cerebral palsy.

ketogenic diet A diet used to control seizures. The diet restricts protein and carbohydrate consumption by supplying calories through fats. It is usually used after multiple antiepileptic medications and medication combinations have failed to control seizure activity.

ketosis An accumulation of excess ketones (breakdown products of fats) that leads to a metabolic acidosis (a chemical imbalance in the blood). Weakness, malaise (feeling ill), and headache can progress untreated to stupor, coma, and death. Ketosis is common in starvation, kidney (renal) failure, and out-of-control diabetes.

KeyMath 3 Diagnostic Assessment (KeyMath 3 DA) An individual test of mathematics concepts, operations, and applications. The test covers the full spectrum of mathematics concepts and skills that are typically taught in kindergarten through ninth grade. It can be used with individuals ages $4\frac{1}{2}$ through 21 years who are functioning at these instructional levels.

K-FAST *See* Kaufman Functional Academic Skills Test.

KFD *See* kinetic family drawing.

Khan-Lewis Phonological Analysis–Second Edition (KLPA-2) A measure of articulation and phonological processes in people ages 2;0–21;11 years. Phonological processes are pronunciation errors that occur during the process of development. They occur and disappear predictably in children who are typically developing and persist in children with speech and language disorders. The KLPA-2 is designed to be used with the Goldman-Fristoe Test of Articulation–Second Edition (G-FTA:2).

KI mice *See* knockout (KO) and knock-in mice.

KIDS-2 *See* Kent Infant Development Scale–Second Edition.

Killian/Teschler-Nicola syndrome *tetrasomy 12p, Pallister Killian syndrome, Pallister mosaic syndrome.* A genetic syndrome characterized by profound intellectual disability, a peculiar facies (facial features), contractures, seizures, and deafness.

kindling Repeated subthreshold (minimal) electrical or chemical stimuli that progressively increase and finally result in a clinical seizure.

kinesiology *kinesics.* The study of body language, body posture, movement, and facial expression as communication.

kinesthetic Describing a sensory modality for acquiring information through receptors in joints, muscles, tendons, and ligaments that are stimulated by bodily movements and tensions. Examples of kinesthetic learning or memory include being able to get a spoon to the mouth, turn on a light in the dark, and walk up or down stairs. Typing is a more complex example. This modality may also be used in conjunction with visual or auditory modalities, when, for example, patterns of movement such as dialing a touch-tone telephone aid in recalling a number. Although the majority of academic learning activities emphasize visual and auditory channels, the kinesthetic modality has been used by some educators as a method for teaching children who do not learn easily through traditional modalities.

kinetic family drawing (KFD) An assessment procedure in which a child is asked to draw a picture of his or her family with every member doing something. Interpretation parameters cover inclusion and exclusion of family members, specific activities, interactions, and stylistic indicators similar to the Draw-a-Man Test. The KFD is a projective technique devised to assess a child's view of family functioning. It should be used and interpreted with caution, as it is subject to bias, and children with motor impairments may have difficulty executing a drawing.

Kleeblattschädel syndrome *See* cloverleaf skull syndrome.

Klein Bell Activities of Daily Living Scale A nonstandardized behavior rating scale for use with people of all ages to measure independence in activities of daily living (ADLs); 170 items tap areas such as mobility, dressing, toileting, hygiene, eating, and telephone skills.

Klinefelter syndrome *47,XXY.* A genetic syndrome in males characterized by hypogonadism (small testes, small penis, and low testosterone [male sex hormone] production); tall, slim stature with long legs and a later tendency to obesity; and intelligence quotient (IQ) scores about one standard deviation below expected. Shyness in childhood and personality and behavior disorders in adulthood have been described. Incidence is 1 in 1,000. Approximately one fifth of males presenting in infertility clinics have Klinefelter syndrome.

Klonopin *See* clonazepam.

KLPA-2 *See* Khan-Lewis Phonological Analysis–Second Edition.

Klumpke paralysis *Klumpke palsy.* Paralysis of the forearm due to nerve injury usually received at birth that leads to a "claw hand." Klumpke palsy is named after Augusta Marie Déjerine-Klumpke (1859–1927).

Klumpke
paralysis

knee–ankle–foot orthosis (KAFO) *See* orthosis.

Kniest dysplasia A genetic syndrome characterized by disproportionate dwarfism (shortened trunk), flat facies (facial features), joint limitation, conductive (involving the middle and outer ears) hearing impairment, and severe myopia (nearsightedness) with other eye defects. Inheritance is autosomal dominant. Kniest dysplasia is one of a spectrum of skeletal disorders caused by mutations in the *COL2A1* gene.

knockdown mouse *See* knockout (KO) and knock-in (KI) mice.

knockout (KO) and knock-in (KI) mice KO mice have been bred with a specific modification of a gene or set of genes so that the gene(s) in question is rendered inoperative. KO mice are bred in order to study the impact of the nonfunctioning gene on growth, development, physiology, and disease processes. A variety of "knockout" techniques are used to create a KO mouse. KI mice have been bred with a specific modification of a gene or set of genes so that the "normal" gene(s) of interest is replaced with one containing a mutation of interest. The gene-targeting strategy is similar to that used for KO mice, except that an original gene is exchanged for the replacement gene. A knockdown mouse is bred with a conditional knockout gene that enables the deletion of a gene in a specific tissue or for limited and specific times.

Knox Cube Test A performance task in which a person taps a series of four cubes presented in various sequences.

Knox Play Scale A descriptive framework for the analysis of spontaneous play in children from birth to age 6 years; the test is intended to assess the socioemotional maturation of children.

KO mice *See* knockout and knock-in (KI) mice.

Kohlberg, Lawrence (1927–1987) A major theorist of the developmental stages of moral thought and moral reasoning. Kohlberg postulated six stages of moral development: 1) Rules are obeyed to avoid punishment, 2) rules are obeyed to obtain rewards, 3) rules are obeyed to avoid being disliked and to enable the person to be seen as "being good," 4) a conscience develops with an appreciation of society's need for rules, 5) competing and contradictory (yet equally valid) values are recognized as requiring judgment, and 6) the presence and validity of universal moral values and a commitment to them are appreciated. Many children with developmental disabilities who have limited ability to think abstractly develop rigid moral codes with fixed ideas of right and wrong these children may have problems recognizing the need for and behaving flexibly in a given situation.

Kohs Block Design Test   A performance task in which a person must use variously colored cubes to reproduce colored designs from 17 test cards.

Koplik spots   Small white spots inside the buccal cavity (mouth) seen in measles (rubeola).

K-P diet   Kaiser-Permanente diet. *See also* Feingold hypothesis.

Krug Asperger's Disorder Index (KADI)   A 32-item scale used to distinguish individuals with Asperger syndrome from people with other forms of high-functioning autism.

K-SEALS   *See* Kaufman Survey of Early Academic and Language Skills.

KTEA-II   *See* Kaufman Test of Educational Achievement–Second Edition.

KUB   Kidneys, ureters, bladder; an x ray taken to visualize the abdominal contents.

Kübler-Ross Five Stages of Grief   Stages identified by Elisabeth Kübler-Ross as being involved when adolescents and adults cope with death. They are 1) denial, 2) anger, 3) bargaining, 4) depression, and 5)

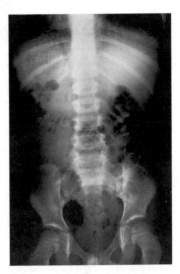

KUB

acceptance. Parents of children with developmental disorders may go through similar emotional stages in learning to deal with their child's disability.

kwashiorkor   *"sugar baby."* Severe protein or calorie deprivation that leads to failure to thrive (FTT; poor growth). Protein is more deficient than calories (high carbohydrate diet), so weight can be more affected than height, and starvation edema (fluid retention) will occur earlier than in marasmus (a type of starvation or malnutrition). The term *kwashiorkor* refers to the dull brown/reddish-yellow, thin, dry, lifeless hair that can be easily pulled out. This type of malnutrition is common in developing countries; its developmental impact on children may be reversible.

kyphosis   *"dowager's hump."* An excessive curvature of the vertebral column (upper spine), convex posteriorly (rounded outward in the back), that produces a round-shouldered appearance.

kyphosis

La Leche League An organization that promotes breast feeding of infants.

labeling The classification and application of a name to a set of symptoms, characteristics, behaviors, or traits. In medicine, such a process is termed *diagnosis*. Although such classification can be necessary for appropriate treatment and planning, such labels—particularly in the area of behavior—eventually become pejorative or a basis for discrimination and perhaps even serve as self-fulfilling prophecies. *See* person-first language, self-fulfilling prophecy.

labile Unstable; fluctuating.

labiodental In articulation, describing the placement of the upper front teeth over the lower lip.

labyrinth Inner ear. The labyrinth is composed of the cochlea (concerned with hearing) and the vestibular and semicircular canals (concerned with balance and equilibrium).

labyrinthine righting response The reflex tendency of the head to move toward an upright vertical position. Head control in this reflex can be assessed in a variety of positions from tilted upright supported sitting to vertical upside-down suspension, as well as many oblique (off absolute vertical or horizontal) positions.

LAC *See* Lindamood Auditory Conceptualization Test.

lacrimal duct stenosis, congenital *See* congenital lacrimal duct stenosis.

lactation specialist A person trained, and in many regions of the country certified, to assist mothers in breast-feeding their infants.

lactic acidosis An imbalance in the body's metabolism (processing of foods) that leads to an increase in the breakdown product(s) lactic and/or pyruvic acid (also called *lactate* and *pyruvate*). Lactic acidosis may be due to a mitochondrial disease or other metabolic disorder.

LAD *See* language acquisition device.

lallation Sound imitation in infancy; primitive echolalia (repetition of what is heard) not necessarily specific to the sounds heard.

Lamictal *See* lamotrigine.

laminectomy *See* spinal laminectomy.

lamotrigine Trade name, Lamictal. An anticonvulsant medication used to treat a wide variety of seizure types, including Lennox-Gastaut syndrome, as well as bipolar disorder. Its most serious side effect is a significant, sometimes life-threatening, rash. It is sometimes used to treat behavioral symptoms in people with developmental disabilities.

Landau reflex A postural response that emerges by 2 months of age in which an infant held in prone (under the body) suspension succeeds in raising his or her head to a vertical position with subsequent trunk, hip, and leg extension (straightening). The Landau reflex is a prerequisite to voluntary rolling over; it is delayed in the presence of hypotonia (low muscle tone).

Landau reflex

Landau 2   *See* Schaltenbrandt reaction.

Landau-Kleffner syndrome (LKS)   *acquired epileptic aphasia.* A rare form of seizure disorder manifested as acquired aphasia (loss of language skills); it may also need to be considered in some presentations of autism. LKS generally begins between the ages of 5 and 7 years, older than the typical age for regression (loss of skills) sometimes seen in children with autism. Affected children usually have clinically apparent seizures. There may be improvement with anticonvulsant therapy.

Landouzy-Dejerine dystrophy   *See* fascioscapulohumeral muscular dystrophy.

Langer-Giedion syndrome   *deletion 8(q24), del(8)(q24.13); tricho-rhinophalangeal syndrome type II.* A syndrome characterized by microcephaly (small head), macrotia (large, protruding ears), a large and bulbous nose, a long philtrum (groove in the upper lip), loose skin, sparse scalp hair, and short hands. Skeletal anomalies include exostoses (bony outgrowths), segmentation defects in the vertebrae associated with scoliosis (curvature of the spine), narrow ribs, and syndactyly (fused digits). The gene deletion is primarily sporadic (random, not inherited).

language   A rule-governed symbol system for communicating meaning through a shared code of verbal, nonverbal, written, or pictorial symbols.

language, expressive   *See* expressive language.

language, receptive   *See* receptive language.

language acquisition   The process of learning to verbally communicate effectively and reciprocally with others. This process includes knowledge of syntax (grammar), semantics (the meaning of words), and pragmatics (the unwritten rules of pacing, intonation, and social exchange).

language acquisition device (LAD)   A hypothesized innate human ability that allows a developing child to understand the language environment in which he or she is being raised by understanding the unwritten set of language processing skills and the rules governing the speech of others and then to use these rules to produce language.

language delay   Describing communication skills that are not developing at the expected rate for chronological age. Language delay is often a symptom in such diagnoses as language disorder, language and learning disability, intellectual disability, and autism.

language disorder   A developmental impairment of comprehension (receptive language) and/or use of spoken, written, gestural, and/or other symbol systems (expressive language) that may involve any combination of 1) the form of language (phonology, morphosyntax), 2) the content of language (semantics), and/or 3) the function of language in communication (pragmatics).

language elicitation task   An activity that is structured in a way that will prompt a certain kind of linguistic response (e.g., imitation).

language experience approach to reading An instructional approach that combines listening, speaking, writing, and reading skills in a single program. This approach assumes that a child learns the following: What I am thinking about, I can talk about; what I can talk about, I can write (or dictate); what is written, I (and others) can read; and I can read what others have written. Instruction begins with a discussion of what is to be written. The teacher then writes what the student dictates, resulting in an individual story or an experience chart that then becomes the basic instructional material used for teaching the student to read. Advocates of this approach suggest that students' level of interest is higher than with other methods because 1) students are reading about something that has actually happened, and 2) they tend to learn material based on their own personal word patterns faster than those contrived by others. There is some concern that students may practice faulty language patterns and may not receive enough encouragement to learn new words. The emphasis on student writing requires students to actually spend more time applying phonics knowledge than is found in traditional programs.

Language Processing Test 3: Elementary (LPT-3) A language test for use with 5- to 11-year-olds; the eight subtests assess labeling, stating functions, associations, categorization, similarities, differences, multiple meanings, and attributes.

language sampling A method for obtaining information about a child's language abilities that consists of collecting and analyzing a sample of his or her language, often in the form of conversational discourse that has been recorded under relatively typical conditions.

Language Use Inventory (LUI) A standardized parent-report inventory used to measure pragmatic language skills in children 18–47 months of age.

lanugo Primary hair; the fine downy hair that covers the entire fetus from mid-gestation to term. Lanugo is replaced by vellus, or secondary hair, at term.

LAP-3 *See* Learning Accomplishment Profile–Third Edition.

large for gestational age (LGA) Describing an infant whose birth weight is above the 90th percentile for age. This condition may be constitutional (the infant comes from physically large parents) or related to conditions such as maternal diabetes or Beckwith-Wiedemann syndrome. Mechanical birth injuries (injuries secondary to the physical difficulty of delivering a large infant) are more common in LGA infants. LGA infants also have a higher rate of birth defects and problems maintaining normal blood sugars.

laryngeal hyperfunction A pervasive pattern of excessive effort and tension that negatively affects the muscles and structures of the larynx.

laryngeal speech Normal speech in which the lungs are used as the power source, the larynx as the sound source, and the vocal tract as the sound modifier.

laryngectomy Surgical treatment in which the entire larynx is removed.

laryngopharyngeal reflux disease The phenomenon in which stomach acid passes through the upper esophageal sphincter and splashes onto laryngeal tissue.

larynx The upper part of the trachea (windpipe) that contains the vocal cords.

larynx

last menstrual period (LMP) *last normal menstrual period (LNMP).* The date of the last menstrual period before a woman becomes pregnant, used in calculating the due date of a pregnancy.

last normal menstrual period (LNMP) *See* last menstrual period (LMP).

latency The elementary school–age period from 4;6 to 11;11 years. This period is named for the latency, or relative inactivity, of the sexual drive between the resolution of the so-called Oedipus complex (which defines the stage when younger children are in love with their parents) and the onset of puberty. During latency, the sexual drive is sublimated (fulfilled by other activities) into social learning.

latency response A term from behavioral learning theory that refers to the time that elapses between a stimulus and response. Put simply, it is the length of time between instructions to perform a task and an individual's response to the request, or the length of time between the individual's response and the delivery of a reinforcer.

lateral pinch The hand position for grasping small objects in which the object is held between the thumb and the thumb side of the index finger.

lateral rotation The turning of a limb away from the mid-line of the body, such as when a leg is turned outward.

laterality Awareness of and ability to use both sides of the body; the recognition of the existence of both the left and right sides of the body. By 5 years of age, most children can tell the difference between their left and right. The ability to perform a task involving both sides on demand (e.g., touching their right knee with their left hand) appears around 7 years of age, whereas the ability to identify the left and right of a person facing them usually occurs by 9 years of age. Children with problems involving laterality may have difficulty with certain learning tasks (e.g., reading) and can display other forms of visuospatial orientation impairments.

late-talking toddler *late talker, slow talker.* A child who has less than a 50-word expressive vocabulary and/or no multiword utterances by age 2 years but who evidences no other communication impairments, developmental delays, or risk factors. The majority of such children appear to be able to

"catch up" in their expressive language with minimal to no special intervention.

latex sensitivity A skin allergy to latex (the traditional "rubber" in hospital gloves) that can develop in individuals such as hospital workers. Because people with spina bifida are extremely prone to this allergy due to frequent exposure to medical interventions and surgeries, all latex products should be avoided.

Laurence-Moon-Biedl syndrome *See* Bardet-Biedl syndrome.

LBW *See* low birth weight.

LCA *See* Leber congenital amaurosis.

LCPUFA *See* long chain polyunsaturated fatty acids.

LCSW *See* licensed clinical social worker.

LD *See* learning disability.

LDA *See* Learning Disabilities Association of America.

lead line On physical examination, a blue line on the gums; on an x ray, a thin line at the growing end of the bone; both lines are indicative of (past) lead poisoning.

lead line

lead poisoning *plumbism.* A type of poisoning from a heavy metal found in interior paint manufactured before 1950 and in exhaust from leaded gasoline that is toxic (poisonous) to the nervous system. Lead poisoning is most commonly found in children 1–6 years of age who live in old, deteriorating inner-city buildings. These children put paint chips, toys, dust, and dirt that often have a high lead content in their mouths. Remodeling old buildings with poor ventilation can dramatically increase the level of airborne lead, and people can develop toxic levels from inhalation alone. The lead is absorbed through the intestine and into all of the tissues in the body. Lead poisoning can contribute to the entire range of developmental disorders. Lead levels of more than 40 μg/dL have been clearly associated with central nervous system (CNS; brain and spinal cord) impairment and a poor developmental outcome. The effects of chronic lower (subclinical) levels of lead exposure are debated. Lead generally causes anemia (low red blood cell count or abnormal red blood cells) by blocking the iron binding, the process that allows the blood cells to manufacture the oxygen-carrying component hemoglobin. Treatment involves 1) prevention through the removal of lead from the environment; 2) a process called chelation, or the use of medications to remove lead from the body; and 3) iron supplementation to treat the anemia.

Léage-Psaume syndrome *See* oral-facial-digital syndrome type I (OFD-I).

leaky gut syndrome The hypothesis (theory) that intestinal diseases that lead to increased permeability (leakiness) of the gut will then leak substances toxic (poisonous) to the brain, resulting in developmental disorders such as autism.

learnability Relative to language, the ease with which a symbol system can be acquired.

learned helplessness Failure to respond appropriately to a negative or stressful situation because of previous experience with uncontrollable outcomes in similar situations. After repeated failures, a person no longer tries. Learned helplessness is characterized by predicable thought, mood, and behavior patterns. It is not merely the perceived lack of control but also a (mis)understanding of why one lacks control that encourages learned helplessness. Thus, students with learning or intellectual disabilities might view their failures as due to their lack

of ability despite the fact that they possess the skills required to accomplish the task. Students may need to be directly taught to reattribute their learning difficulties to factors they can affect or work around.

Learning Accomplishment Profile–Third Edition (LAP-3) A criterion-referenced assessment tool for use with children functioning in the developmental range of 36–72 months. This profile measures developmental attainment in the areas of gross motor, fine motor, cognitive, language, prewriting, self-help, and personal-social skills. It adapts readily for use with children with disabilities and is linked to learning activities.

Learning Disabilities Association of America (LDA) A nonprofit organization whose mission is to advance the education and general welfare of children and adults of typical or potentially typical intelligence who have learning disabilities. The LDA holds annual national and international conventions.

learning disability (LD) A disorder in one or more of the basic psychological processes involved in understanding or using spoken or written language; the disorder may manifest itself as an underdeveloped or complete (in)ability to listen, think, speak, read, write, spell, or do mathematical calculations compared with similar-age peers of equal intelligence. LDs include such conditions as perceptual disabilities (e.g., of visuo-motor integration), brain injury, dyslexia, and developmental aphasia (loss or lack of development of language skills). Children who have learning problems that are primarily the result of visual, hearing, or motor disabilities; intellectual disability; emotional disturbance; or environmental, cultural, or economic disadvantage do not have LD. Because many different tests, standards, and criteria are used to determine whether a child has LD, a student may be classified as having LD in one area of the country but not in another. These disorders are intrinsic to the individual and are presumed to be due to central nervous system (CNS; brain) dysfunction. Even though an LD may occur concomitantly with other disabling conditions (e.g., sensory impairment, intellectual disability, social and emotional disturbance) or environmental influences (e.g., cultural differences, insufficient or inappropriate instruction, psychological [internal, maladaptive feelings and thoughts] factors), it is not the result of those conditions or influences. The Learning Disabilities Association of America (LDA) definition of *learning disability* includes the effect of the disability on self-esteem, education, vocation (job), and activities of daily living (ADLs). The concept of LDs, as it has evolved, reflects a range of neurological dysfunctions that may be manifested in various aspects of life, are innate in the individual, and are life long. People with LD, however, can learn to compensate, attend college and graduate school, and have successful careers. The term *learning disability* was revised to *specific learning disability* with the enactment of the Individuals with Disabilities Education Improvement Act (IDEA) of 2004 (PL 108-446). *See also* Education for All Handicapped Children Act of 1975 (PL 94-142), Individuals with Disabilities Education Act Amendments (IDEA) of 1997 (PL 105-17), Individuals with Disabilities Education Improvement Act (IDEA) of 2004 (PL 108-446), Individuals with Disabilities Education Act (IDEA) of 1990 (PL 101-476), response to intervention (RTI).

Learning Potential Assessment Device (LPAD) Using adaptations from a variety of other tests, the LPAD focuses on the process rather than the product of learning and on the qualitative rather than quantitative aspects of an individual's thinking.

learning style The manner in which an individual learns most efficiently. In addition to a preferred cognitive style (e.g., visual or auditory), learning style also includes environmental variables, such as lighting, noise level, snacking, time of day, and position.

Learning-Style Inventory (LSI) A brief 12-item questionnaire that characterizes how an individual learns and deals with ideas and day-to-day situations. Scores on four learning stages (concrete experience, reflective observation, abstract conceptualization, and active experimentalization) are charted graphically to describe the individual's learning style.

least restrictive environment (LRE) The LRE is one that allows a child to participate in general education programs as much as possible and to benefit from learning with peers who are typically developing while also meeting his or her own special needs. *See also* Education for All Handicapped Children Act of 1975 (PL 94-142).

Leber congenital amaurosis (LCA) *congenital retinal blindness, congenital retinitis pigmentosa.* An autosomal recessive genetic syndrome characterized by progressive blindness, an infant form of retinitis pigmentosa (night blindness and progressively restricted visual field), and, in some cases, intellectual disability. Children with LCA push their fingers up against their eyes and rub their eyes repeatedly. Incidence is 2.5 in 100,000.

legally blind A condition in which an individual has less than 20/200 vision (i.e., cannot see at 20 feet what can typically be seen at 200 feet) in his or her better eye even with corrective lenses or has a very limited field of vision (20 degrees at its widest point, compared with normal ranges of 60 degrees toward the nose [or inward in each eye] and 100 degrees away from the nose [or outward]).

leiotrichous Having straight hair.

Leiter International Performance Scale–Revised (Leiter-R) An untimed, individually administered test of nonverbal cognitive ability for use with individuals ages

2;0–20;11 years. The Leiter-R contains four domains and four behavior rating scales. The test takes approximately 90 minutes to administer, with the actual number of subtests administered depending on the age of the child. Comprehensive administration produces an intelligence quotient (IQ) score, and administration of selected subtests produces a Brief IQ score (for screening purposes) and a Memory Process score (intended to screen for attention-deficit/hyperactivity disorders and learning disabilities).

Lennox-Gastaut syndrome *atonic-astatic epilepsy.* A syndrome characterized by different types of seizures, including absence seizures (frequently repeated brief spells of inattention) along with myoclonic (brief lightning-like jerks), clonic (body jerking), tonic (body stiffening), and atonic (loss of muscle tone) seizures all present in one individual. It is characterized by frequent seizures, including status epilepticus (prolonged, continuous seizure activity), that are difficult to control. The electroencephalogram (EEG) generally shows multifocal (in multiple areas of the brain) abnormalities with abnormal background activity and a spike-and-wave pattern of less than 3 per second. Intellectual disability is common, and the syndrome occurs frequently in children who have had previous encephalopathy (brain damage due to lack of oxygen). *See also* atonic seizure.

lens A transparent material designed to transmit and focus an image. The transparent surface that focuses light rays upon the retina (light-sensitive inner back wall of the eye) is the eye's lens. Artificial lenses are used to correct vision both on (contact lenses) and outside of (glasses) the eye.

Lenz-Majewski hyperostosis syndrome *craniodiaphyseal dysplasia, Lenz-Majewski type; Lenz-Majewski hyperostotic dwarfism.* A syndrome characterized by poor growth; intellectual disability; distinctive facies (facial features); atrophic (thin) skin; sparse

hair; syndactyly (webbing of the fingers or toes); dense, thick bones; and progeroid (prematurely old) appearance. It is thought to be autosomal dominant.

LEOPARD syndrome *See* multiple lentigines syndrome.

leprechaunism *See* Donohoe syndrome.

LES *See* lower esophageal sphincter.

Lesch-Nyhan syndrome *Lesch-Nyhan disease.* A disorder of the metabolism of substances called *purines* that causes a progressive syndrome that can include profound intellectual disability, choreoathetosis (a movement disorder characterized by writhing), and marked self-injurious behavior. Inheritance is X-linked.

lesion Injury; local tissue damage, sometimes with loss of function.

lethargy A state of decreased consciousness from which an individual can be readily aroused, but this aroused state can only be maintained with difficulty.

Let's Talk Inventory for Adolescents (LTI-A) An age-normed (in 2-year intervals) language scale for use with people ages 9 years to young adulthood that helps identify inadequate or delayed social-verbal communication skills. The LTI-A looks at the ability to formulate speech appropriate to pictured situational contexts for the functions of informing, controlling, and feeling. Stimulus pictures present interactions with adolescent peers and with an authority figure.

Let's Talk Inventory for Children (LTI-C) An age-normed language scale for use with preschool and early elementary-age children with inadequate or delayed social-verbal communication skills. Children are asked to formulate speech acts to go with pictured situational contexts.

leukocoria   *See* white pupil.

leukocytosis   A transient increase in the white blood cell count, usually associated with infection.

leukodystrophy   *See* white matter disease.

leukomalacia   Necrosis (tissue death) in the white matter of the brain, generally secondary to anoxia (episodes of oxygen deficiency). In premature infants, leukomalacia is most commonly located around the ventricles (fluid-containing spaces) and is termed *periventricular leukomalacia* (PVL). *See also* periventricular leukomalacia (PVL).

leukoplakia   Precancerous lesions on the vocal folds that appear as flat, white, and plaque-like.

level   Any standard, position, or rank in a graded series of values, often a measure of ability or performance. For example, levels of sensory efficiency, intellectual capacity, or motor development can be determined. Levels are relative, and the cutoffs may be arbitrary.

lever arm dysfunction   A group of neuromuscular or orthopedic abnormalities that adversely affect joint flexibility.

levetiracetam   Trade name, Keppra. An antiepileptic medication used to control partial seizures (seizures that start in one part of the brain).

lexicon   An individual's vocabulary (i.e., the words plus the concepts they represent).

lexicon   *dictionary.* A collection of words, their meanings, and associated information.

Lexington Developmental Scales (Short Form)   A developmental screening test for use with children from birth to 6 years of age. A variety of measures are used to assess motor, personal, social, cognitive-preacademic, language, and articulation (pronunciation of speech sounds) skills. It takes approximately 35 minutes to administer.

LGA   *See* large for gestational age.

LICC   *See* Local Interagency Coordinating Council.

licensed clinical social worker (LCSW)   A person legally sanctioned by state statute to practice clinical social work. Being licensed implies having met minimum standards, which may or may not include academic or professional training and competency-based testing. When seeking a fully qualified social worker, a client should inquire about both licensing and Academy of Certified Social Workers (ACSW) certification.

licensing   A state-legislated and state-maintained competency-based sanction for professional practice. Licensing laws restrict those able to perform certain tasks and duties by virtue of both education and tested competency levels. Thus, a medical doctor may not apply for a license to practice medicine without furnishing documentation of specific competencies and educational attainment. People in other professions, such as social work, psychology, speech-language pathology, nursing, and education, must be similarly licensed. When a profession is regulated by licensing, it is illegal to perform those services without a license.

life skills   A broad group of personal, social, and interpersonal skills that enable successful independent living and functioning. These can include such things as the ability to make change and manage money, make needed health care appointments, travel on public transportation, cook, organize and maintain a clean living situation, make friends, and get to work on time and perform appropriately on the job.

Likert scale   A scaling technique in which a person indicates his or her degree of (dis)agreement with a variety of attitudinal statements, usually on a 3- or 5-point scale (e.g., the person indicates his or her agreement with a statement along a continuum from *strongly agree* to *strongly disagree*).

limb synergy The state in which a group of muscles act as a unit (i.e., all flexing [bending] or all extending [straightening]) in a primitive and stereotyped manner.

limbic system A group of functionally related deep brain structures that regulate emotions and behavior.

Limited Income Subsidy (LIS) A program through Medicare Part D that grants financial assistance to Medicare beneficiaries with low income and resources. This helps them pay for monthly premiums, deductibles, and copayments for medications.

Lincoln-Oseretsky Motor Development Scale A measure of motor dexterity (balance, speed, flexibility, rhythm, and coordination) for use with children between 6 and 14 years of age. *See* Bruininks-Oseretsky Test of Motor Proficiency–Second Edition (BOT-2).

Lindamood Auditory Conceptualization Test (LAC) A 10-minute criterion-referenced test for use with preschool children to adults that measures auditory discrimination and perception (the ability to hear and perceive sounds accurately) of number and order of speech sounds in sequences.

lingua-alveolar In articulation, describing contact of the tip of the tongue against the alveolar (gum) ridge.

linguadental In articulation, describing the placement of the tip of the tongue between the upper and lower front teeth.

lingual frenulum *See* frenulum linguae.

lingual surface The space between the teeth and tongue.

linguapalatal In articulation, describing contact of the tongue against the hard palate.

linguavelar In articulation, describing contact of the tongue dorsum against the velum.

linguistic competence Knowledge of the linguistic code or knowledge as reflected in receptive and expressive skills in one's native language.

linguistic reader An instructional approach that does not emphasize meaning in beginning reading but rather stresses mastery of a limited number of consistent spelling patterns that correspond with syllables heard in oral language. Words are read as wholes, not sounded out letter by letter. Linguistic texts frequently have few pictures in order to avoid distracting the beginning reader.

linguistics The scientific study of the origin, structure, nature, and function of language.

linkage The co-inheritance of two or more traits at a rate greater than one would expect by chance because the originating genes are present side by side on the same chromosome. This linkage helps in the identification of the gene locations for each trait, characteristic, or disorder.

lip closure The ability to seal the lips around a bottle or breast nipple.

lip pit syndrome *See* van der Woude syndrome.

lipidoses A group of progressive neurological disorders characterized by defects in lipid metabolism (fat processing and breakdown by the body). Histochemically speaking (looking at body cells in terms of their chemical processes), the neurons (nerve cells) are filled with lipids (fats), which impedes their ability to function.

lipreading *See* speechreading.

liquids Consonant sounds produced with the soft palate raised (e.g., /r/, /l/).

LIS *See* Limited Income Subsidy.

Lisch nodule Malformations in the iris (the colored part of the eye), usually only visible by a slit lamp (specialized ophthalmological instrument); found in individuals with the genetic syndrome neurofibromatosis-1.

lissencephaly A condition in which there is abnormal migration (movement) of neurons (nerve cells) during early fetal life, resulting in agyria, or a lack of gyri (hills). Lissencephaly is often associated with other abnormalities such as heterotopia (displacement of tissue) involving gray matter (nerve cells), pachygyria (broad, flat cerebral convolutions), or micropolygyria (an increased number of smaller ridgings on the brain surface). Many individuals with lissencephaly have severe intellectual disability and marked hypotonia (decreased muscle tone). Seizures, including infantile spasms and Lennox-Gastaut syndrome, are common. A small number of children with lissencephaly have an accompanying chromosomal abnormality or a known genetic syndrome (e.g., Miller-Dieker syndrome). Lissencephaly can be detected on a computed tomography (CT) scan.

lissencephaly type I *See* Miller-Dieker syndrome.

literacy The ability to identify, understand, interpret, create, communicate, and compute using printed and written materials (in, at least, one's native language) associated with varying contexts.

lithium Medication sometimes used to treat severe behavior disorders in people with developmental disorders. Lithium is believed to normalize receptor site sensitivity in the brain to reduce mood swings. Side effects include drowsiness, tremors, and electrocardiogram (ECG) changes (indicating changes in heart rhythm). Blood levels must be carefully monitored for toxicity (negative side effects on bodily organs such as the liver).

litmus test A test that indicates a solution's degree of acidity or alkalinity. Litmus is a chemical substance (usually in the form of a chemically impregnated [soaked with and dried] paper strip, or litmus paper) that turns red in an acid solution and blue in an alkali, or basic, solution. Metaphorically speaking, a litmus test suggests an easy assignment into one of two clearly distinct groups.

Little disease *See* diplegia.

Little Room A specially constructed play area (large box) with objects suspended so as to allow exploratory play. It is used in Active Learning, a therapeutic approach for children with visual and other developmental impairments.

living will *See* advance directive.

LKS *See* Landau-Kleffner syndrome.

LMP *See* last menstrual period.

LNMP Last normal menstrual period. *See* last menstrual period (LMP).

LNNB-CR *See* Luria-Nebraska Neuropsychological Battery–Children's Revision.

loading A statistical term that refers to the correlations among factors (clusters) and tests in factor matrix (a specific statistical method). Loadings indicate the weight of each element in determining performance on each factor. *See also* factor analysis.

Local Interagency Coordinating Council A local group of families and professionals that focuses on issues related to early intervention for young children with disabilities.

The purpose of such groups is to empower parents and families, increase community awareness, and develop partnerships between families and professionals. *See* State Interagency Coordinating Council.

localization   The determination of a site or place (locus) of any process or lesion (injury or area of abnormality). Localizing a disease involves deciding which organ, organ system, or part thereof is the source of the disease process. In the study of neurological diseases, localization involves identifying which specific component or level within the central (brain and spinal cord) or peripheral nervous system is involved.

locomotion in prone   Movement from one point to another with the body horizontal and the chest and abdomen not raised off the ground; movement is accomplished by coordinated and sometimes alternating pulling with the arms and pushing with the legs. Sometimes a synonym for *creeping*.

locomotion in prone

locomotion in quadruped   Movement from one point to another with the body horizontal and the chest and abdomen raised off the floor so that the child is supported on elbows/hands and knees/feet; movement is accomplished by coordinated and alternating actions of all four extremities (arms and legs). Sometimes a synonym for *crawling*. The child who walks before he or she crawls is not necessarily at increased risk for developmental disabilities.

locomotion in quadruped

locus   The position of a gene in a chromosome. *See also* LOD score.

locus of control   A theory that explains a person's view of most causal mechanisms for feelings, successes, failures, or behavioral outcomes. Two loci of control are postulated:

external and internal. People tend to base most of their causal explanations on either an external cause (e.g., it was God's will) or an internal cause (e.g., I really did a good job). Many educational and psychological interventions are based on a framework that uses a person's predominant locus of control.

LOD score   Acronym for logarithm of the odds. The outcome of a statistical method that tests genetic marker data in families to determine whether two gene loci are linked. The LOD score is the logarithm to base 10 of the odds in favor of linkage; by convention, a LOD score of 3 (odds of 1,000:1 in favor) is taken as proof of linkage and a LOD score of 2 (100:1) as insufficient proof that the loci are unlinked. *See also* locus.

log rolling   *See* neonatal neck righting.

logorrhea   Excessively voluble speech (a characteristic of someone who "talks a lot").

long chain polyunsaturated fatty acids (LCPUFA)   A group of nutrients (substances found in foods and food supplements) that are claimed to have an impact on brain development and functioning.

long leg brace   A brace that extends from the upper thigh to the foot.

long-term care (LTC)   A coordinated set of health, social, personal, and protective services, usually in an out-of-home placement. The underlying long leg brace assumption or connotation of this term is that the affected person has long-term, severe, irremediable impairment (physical or cognitive). Some people with developmental disabilities need some form of LTC. LTC is often obtained through a nursing home or an intermediate care facility. Generally, waiver services require that a person have a need for LTC.

long-term-care insurance A special insurance designed to pay for extended (health) care and support for daily functioning but that does not require hospitalization. Long-term-care insurance usually covers payment for caregivers when needed help with daily activities such as bathing, eating, dressing, or for care in a skilled nursing or rehabilitation center when the individual is no longer able to adequately care for himself or herself because of either injury or age-related cognitive impairment such as Alzheimer's disease. Long-term care and the insurance to pay for it focus on care-oriented conditions, not cure-oriented conditions.

long-term memory The component of conceptual models of memory in which information is stored for later use. In contrast to short-term or working memory, long-term memory has a very large capacity, and information stored there may last a lifetime. The short-term memory encompasses those things held in memory for no more than 30 seconds. Information retained for 1 or 2 minutes may be retained in the same manner as that retained after 1 or 2 days and can be transferred into long-term memory. Memory theorists have divided long-term memory into semantic (meaning systems) memory, episodic memory (memory for specific events and facts), and procedural memory (memory for how to do certain tasks). *See also* memory.

lorazepam Trade name, Ativan. A drug in the class of benzodiazepines (the most widely known of which is diazepam [Valium]) that is used to treat seizures. Lorazepam is a rapidly acting drug that is used in the treatment of status epilepticus (dangerously prolonged seizure activity). It continues to suppress seizure activity for 24–48 hours after administration, and it does not produce much respiratory depression.

lordosis *"sway back."* An excessive curvature of the lower vertebral column (spine), convex anteriorly (curved inward, toward the front of the body), for example, to produce a swayback appearance.

Louis-Bar syndrome *See* ataxia telangiectasia.

Lovaas, O. Ivar (1927–2010) A University of California–Los Angeles psychologist whose research demonstrated the efficacy of intensive behavioral intervention for young children with autism. The Lovaas study is frequently cited in support of intensive early intervention for children with autism. *See also* applied behavior analysis (ABA).

low birth weight (LBW) Describing an infant whose birth weight is less than 2,500 g regardless of gestational age (full term or premature).

low state of arousal Arousal is a general physiological and psychological activation of an organism that varies on a continuum from deep sleep to intense excitement. Chronic physiological hypoarousal is reflected in chronic underresponsiveness to internal or external stimuli.

low vision A severe visual impairment not necessarily limited to distance vision. The term *low vision* applies to all individuals who are unable to read the newspaper at a typical viewing distance, even with the aid of corrective lenses.

Lowe syndrome *oculocerebrorenal syndrome (OCRL).* A genetic syndrome characterized by hypotonia (decreased muscle tone), cataracts (clouding of the lens of the eye), kidney disease, and intellectual disability. Inheritance is X-linked. Lowe syndrome is caused by very reduced activity of the enzyme inositol polyphosphate 5-phosphatase OCRL-1, which is encoded by the *OCRL* gene. The diagnosis is established in affected individuals by demonstrating reduced (<10% of normal) activity of inositol polyphosphate 5-phosphatase OCRL-1 in cultured skin fibroblasts. Molecular genetic testing of the *OCRL* gene detects mutations in approximately 95% of affected males and carrier females.

lower esophageal sphincter (LES)　The circular muscle that closes off the esophagus (throat) from the stomach. It controls the pressure difference between the lower part of the esophagus and the stomach; lowering of this gradient (making the difference less) can contribute to gastroesophageal reflux (when the stomach contents escape back up the esophagus).

lower extremity　Thigh, leg, or foot.

low-set ear　A minor dysmorphic feature in which the upper edge of the external ear (pinna) is lower than an imaginary line drawn straight back from the outer edge of the eye.

low-set ear

low-technology augmentative and alternative communication (AAC) device　An AAC device that does not use electronic instruments (i.e., notepads or message boards).

low-technology device　*light technology device.* Any assistive technology (AT) or augmentative and alternative communication (AAC) device that has no moving parts or electronic components. A pointer is such a "low-tech" device.

LP　Lumbar puncture. *See* spinal tap.

LPAD　*See* Learning Potential Assessment Device.

LPT-3　*See* Language Processing Test 3: Elementary.

LRE　*See* least restrictive environment.

LSI　*See* Learning-Style Inventory.

LTI-A　*See* Let's Talk Inventory for Adolescents.

LTC　*See* long-term care.

LTI-C　*See* Let's Talk Inventory for Children.

LUI　*See* Language Use Inventory.

lumbar　Relating to that part of the back between the ribs and the hips.

lumbar puncture (LP)　*See* spinal tap.

Luminal　*See* phenobarbital.

lumbar

lumping　The tendency to classify together entities that may not at first appear to go together.

Luria-Nebraska Neuropsychological Battery– Children's Revision (LNNB-CR)　A neuropsychological battery for use with children 8–12 years of age.

Luvox　*See* fluvoxamine.

luxatio coxae congenita　*See* developmental dysplasia of the hip (DDH).

Lyme disease　A complex infection caused by the tick-borne spirochete *Borrelia burdorgeri* (a microorganism such as a bacterium) that can produce a low-grade encephalopathy (brain inflammation). The disorder responds to short-term antibiotics, and there is now a vaccine available for people who live in endemic areas (areas with many deer). The name derives from the town where it was first identified.

lymphadenopathy　Swelling of the lymph nodes that produces palpable (able to be felt) masses and sometimes tenderness; it is often a sign of infection but may be associated with other causes of inflammation. When an infection is localized (confined to one area of the body), the lymph nodes nearest the site of the infection are usually more involved (larger). For example, cervical (neck) lymphadenopathy frequently accompanies tonsillitis or pharyngitis (throat infection). Lymph nodes may remain swollen or palpable for some time after an infection has resolved.

lymphangioma Overgrowth of lymphatic vessels (vessels that carry lymph, or the fluid that circulates among the cells of the body).

lymphonodular hyperplasia Increased size and number of lymph nodes in the gut wall hypothesized to be associated with an immune reaction in the etiology (cause) of autism.

Mm

MA *See* mental age.

MABI *See* Mother's Assessment of the Behavior of her Infant.

MAC *See* Manual Ability Classification System.

MacArthur-Bates Communicative Development Inventories (CDIs)–Second Edition A version of the MacArthur Communicative Development Inventory, a caregiver-report instrument used to assess the verbal and gestural communication skills of children 8–37 months (and older children who have developmental delays). The inventories consist of two main forms: one that documents a child's understanding of vocabulary and one that records the child's communicative and symbolic gestures. A third component queries for comprehension, semantics, and syntax. Each form generally takes 20–40 minutes to complete and 10–15 minutes to score. Spanish- and English-language versions are available.

Macewen sign A hollow, "cracked-pot" sound elicited on percussion (tapping) of the skull; present with increased fluid, as in hydrocephalus.

macrocephaly Abnormally large head; *macrocephaly* refers to a head circumference (occipitofrontal circumference) that is larger than 2 standard deviations (a standardized measure of distance from the mean of the 50th percentile) above the mean for age. It can be familial (runs in families); can be associated with a number of dysmorphic (atypical appearance) syndromes, such as Sotos syndrome or fragile X syndrome, as well as several metabolic disorders; and is often an important marker for hydrocephalus (excess fluid in the brain). In the same way that microcephaly (abnormally small head) is not automatically associated with intellectual disability, macrocephaly is not associated with intellectual giftedness. More significant degrees of macrocephaly are likely to indicate the presence of neurodevelopmental disorders. Onset of macrocephaly late in the first year of life may be one of the earliest biological markers for autism.

macrocornea Enlarged cornea (clear covering of the eye) that can occur in glaucoma (increased pressure in the eye, often hereditary) and mucopolysaccharidoses (disorders of the body's processing of certain sugars, which cause neurological and other medical problems).

macroglossia An enlarged tongue, usually as a result of a congenital disorder.

macrogyria *See* pachygyria.

macroorchidism Large testicles. This finding can occur in a number of genetic syndromes (e.g., fragile X syndrome) after puberty.

macropremie A near-term or late-term premature infant; one born between 32 and

36 weeks of gestation, at the upper border of prematurity.

magical thinking   The belief that one's thoughts, wishes, words, or actions can influence events in defiance of the typical laws of cause and effect. Typical in young children, magical thinking can recur in various thought (e.g., psychotic) disorders.

magnesium   A chemical that is normally present in the blood. Low levels may be associated with seizures.

magnetic resonance imaging (MRI)   A scan that uses nuclear magnetic resonances (NMRs; brief bursts of radiofrequency energy) to visualize parts of the body such as the brain. MRI scans do not use radiation but provide important visual information about the structural formation of the brain. They are useful for identifying both major and minor brain abnormalities. MRI scans are used to evaluate anomalies of cortex (the outer layer of the brain) and to evaluate people with refractory (unresponsive to treatment) seizure disorders for an identifiable focus (location where the seizure activity begins). MRI scans provide information about differences in white and gray matter (specific areas of the brain).

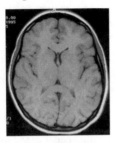

magnetic resonance imaging (MRI)

magnetoencephalography (MEG)   A specialized brain imaging technique that uses a magnetic field to measure the intercellular currents of the neurons in the brain. It then maps these currents structurally so that one can observe and locate real-time brain activity. MEG is noninvasive, uses no radiation, and provides a much higher resolution than previous imaging techniques. At least one application uses MEG to localize the primary somatosensory cortex, sources of focal slow wave activity, sources of interictal (between seizures) epileptogenic activity (brain wave activity indicating seizures), and abnormalities in deeper structures. MEG is primarily used for brain research.

MAI   *See* Movement Assessment of Infants.

mainstreaming   An educational term that indicates placing children with disabilities in general classrooms. Mainstreaming removes stigma, enhances the social status of exceptional children, facilitates modeling of appropriate behavior, provides a more stimulating and competitive environment, and allows for more flexible and cost-efficient service. Simply placing a child in a general education class, however, does not ensure academic achievement or social acceptance. Appropriate modification of classroom expectations and teaching methods based on an analysis of the student's strengths and weaknesses is essential for mainstreaming to be effective and to provide successful experiences for the student. Mainstreaming results in benefits not just for students with disabilities but also for their peers who are typically developing. *See also* inclusive education, integration.

maintenance   A term that refers both to the continuation of a desired response or change over time and the supports provided to promote continuing accomplishment and prevent relapse.

maladaptive behavior   Recurrent, often habitual behaviors and behavior patterns that prevent an individual or a family from attaining a desired goal or meeting the demands of the environment. Examples of such behaviors include temper tantrums, swearing, and theft. It is not necessarily the behaviors themselves but the intensity and frequency of the behaviors that render them maladaptive. There are four types of maladaptive behavior: verbal and physical aggression that cause difficulties in interpersonal relationships; anxious and withdrawn behaviors that hamper interaction and achievement; immaturity or failure to consistently demonstrate age-appropriate behaviors; and socialized aggressive behavior, which is typically manifested as vandalism or group intimidation and violence. Maladaptive behavior is often a symptom rather than the problem per se; the origin and etiology (cause) of the feelings and thought processes that result in the behavior should be explored. Maladaptive behavior can be assessed through behavior checklists, through interviews with teachers and caregivers, and via direct observation of the child's behavior in different settings. Interventions to decrease maladaptive behavior and alleviate its cause include behavior modification, classroom accommodations, psychotherapy, and medication use.

malaise Discomfort; a nonspecific uneasiness and lack of usual level of energy. The feeling of being sick or out of sorts, malaise is a frequent accompaniment of, and prodrome for (prelude to), many illnesses.

male-limited A pattern of inheritance limited from fathers to sons.

malformation A morphological defect (abnormality of structure or shape) of an organ, part of an organ, or larger body region that results from an intrinsically atypical developmental process. *Intrinsic* implies that the primordium (earliest grouping of cells in an embryo) was abnormal from the beginning; if the primordium was normal, the morphological defect is referred to as a *disruption*. If the structural abnormality is at the tissue level rather than the organ level, it is referred to as a *dysplasia*.

malignancy Cancer.

malignant hyperthermia A life-threatening increase in core body temperature that can result from the use of certain drugs (typically those used in general anesthesia) in the setting of underlying genetic susceptibilities.

malingering Literally, "enjoying ill health." Malingering has two forms: 1) refusing to engage in preillness activities on the basis of "still feeling sick" long after a normal recuperative period and with no obvious signs of continued illness and 2) faking illness. Whether conscious or unconscious, malingering serves to enable someone to avoid some undesired obligation or difficult situation through the "legitimate" route of illness when no other legitimate escape seems feasible. Children with developmental disabilities often malinger when school demands become too stressful. *See also* factitious disorder.

malleolus The bony prominence on each side of the ankle. The outside one is the lateral malleolus; the inside one is the medial malleolus.

malnutrition Poor nourishment resulting from inadequate food intake or inadequate utilization by the body of ingested nutrients. The latter can be caused by malabsorption, endocrine disease, or metabolic disease (problems with the body's processing of nutrients once absorbed).

malocclusion Faulty meeting of the upper and lower teeth or jaws. Malocclusion can be part of various genetic syndromes.

mand A prompt for an item; in operant conditioning, a verbal behavior that is equivalent to a request (e.g., it occurs when an individual experiences deprivation [I want] or aversion [no]). A child may say "Cookie" to request one and "Stop" to request cessation of an activity. Mands can be thought of as demands or commands.

mandible Lower jaw; jawbone.

mandibular arch The part of an embryo that becomes the muscles of mastication, anterior of the tongue, some middle ear structures, and mandible.

mandibulofacial dysostosis *See* Treacher Collins syndrome.

mania A state of impulsive, excessive, excited, and uncontrolled behavior coupled with accelerated thought and verbal activity; a lessened physiological need for sleep or food; and an excessive, unrealistic feeling of elation. This state is seen in several mental disorders but is most frequently noted as one phase in bipolar disorder. A transient manic state may also result from the use of certain illegal drugs and some prescribed medications. Other impulse control disorders that may accompany mood disorders include kleptomania (shoplifting), pyromania (fire setting), and compulsive sexual behavior. In these subcategories, the excesses of behavior and activity are limited to a single area of behavioral expression.

manic-depressive disorder *See* bipolar disorder.

manifestation determination A procedure required under the Individuals with Disabilities Education Act (IDEA) of 1990 (PL 101-476) and its amendments, the manifestation determination is conducted to determine whether a student's problem behavior emanates from his or her disability. The manifestation determination may occur during a meeting of the student's individualized education program (IEP) team and is necessary when the school proposes to move the student to a more restrictive educational placement because of an infraction of the school's code of conduct. The meeting must occur within 10 days of the infraction that prompted the removal of the student from placement. All relevant data must be reviewed to determine whether the behavior is a result of the student's disability or the school's failure to implement the IEP. If the team concludes that the problem behavior is related to the child's disability, the team is

obligated to conduct a functional behavioral assessment (FBA) and to develop a behavior intervention plan (BIP), and the student remains in his or her educational placement. If the conduct is not a result of the student's disability, then the student is treated the same as any student without a disability. The FBA determines the triggers that initiate and the consequences that maintain the problem behaviors. The BIP specifies a plan to prevent the triggers and modify the consequences so as to replace the problem behaviors. *See also* behavior intervention plan (BIP), functional behavioral assessment (FBA).

manipulatives *manipulables.* Toys or educational objects that require children to use their hands to play with or manipulate. Some multisensory teaching techniques include manipulatives as an adjunctive teaching tool.

mannerism A stereotyped involuntary or semivoluntary movement that is in keeping with the person's personality. Bizarre and idiosyncratic mannerisms can occur in individuals with autism or schizophrenia.

manometry Pressure measurement; a technique that quantifies the force of contraction of the muscular wall of the gut by the use of pressure transducers. Manometry can be used in the evaluation of swallowing disorders.

Manual Ability Classification System (MAC) An instrument used to classify how children with cerebral palsy typically (not maximally) use both hands together to manipulate objects in daily activities. The resulting five classes range from I (*handles objects easily and successfully*) to V (*does not handle objects and has severely limited ability to perform even simple actions*).

manual dexterity The coordination of the hands and fingers in completing fine motor tasks.

manual English Sign English; a sign system that uses a rapid succession of specific symbols and manual movements, including fingerspelling (signs for each alphabet letter). Unlike American Sign Language (ASL), manual English uses English syntax (grammar) as its foundation.

Manual Muscle Test (MMT)　A tool used to assess and grade the strength of muscles in specific testing positions.

manual sign systems　Referring to three main types of systems: 1) those that are alternatives to the spoken language of a particular country (e.g., American Sign Language), 2) those that parallel the spoken language (e.g., manually coded English), and 3) those that interact with or supplement another means of transmitting a spoken language (e.g., fingerspelling).

manubrium　The upper portion of the sternum (breast bone) that joins with the clavicles and the first two pairs of ribs.

MAP　*See* Miller Assessment for Preschoolers.

MAP　*See* Muma Assessment Program.

maple syrup urine disease (MSUD)　An inborn error of metabolism (an error in the normal processing of body chemicals). An autosomal recessive (inherited) cerebral degenerative disease (brain disease in which symptoms worsen over time) in which problems with the breakdown of branched chain amino acids (certain building blocks of protein) cause the urine to smell sweet like maple syrup. Infants appear typical at birth but then show rapid deterioration. Untreated, MSUD leads to opisthotonos (severe arching of the back), spasticity (increased muscle tone), brain damage, and intellectual disability. With strict adherence to a dietary treatment (i.e., a diet without the branched chain amino acids the body is unable to process) beginning in the first 2 weeks of life, intelligence can be typical. Another intermediate form of the disease, characterized by some residual enzyme

activity in skin cells, presents later on with seizures, intermittent ataxia (unsteady gait), and drowsiness. This form results in mild to moderate intellectual disability.

marasmus　Severe protein–calorie deprivation; infantile atrophy (wasting); malnutrition with a marked deficit in weight for height. Marasmus is marked by failure to thrive (FTT) progressing to an infant's falling below 75% of the expected weight for his or her age; below 65% of the expected weight is considered life threatening. Loss of subcutaneous (under the skin) fat gives the face a lined and aged appearance. Skin folds hang loose, the "sucking pads" protrude in the cheeks, and irritability and anxiety may be replaced by apathy. Hypoproteinemia (loss of protein) may lead to swelling ("starvation edema"). The developmental impact of this state of malnutrition tends to be reversible. Also referred to as *protein energy malnutrition* (PEM).

marble bone disease　*See* Albers-Schönberg disease.

March of Dimes Foundation　An organization founded by President Franklin D. Roosevelt in 1938 as the National Foundation for Infantile Paralysis to combat the nation's polio epidemic. Later that same year, when entertainer Eddie Cantor suggested that people send dimes directly to the White House, the organization became known as the March of Dimes Birth Defects Foundation. With Dr. Jonas Salk's (1914–1995) development of a polio vaccine, the foundation refocused its efforts toward the prevention of birth defects and the overall improvement of pregnancy outcomes. The foundation's mission is to improve the health of infants by preventing birth defects, premature birth, and infant mortality. This mission is carried out through research, community services, education, and advocacy.

Marcus Gunn jaw winking phenomenon　Change in the width of the eyelids during chewing: elevation of the upper lid when the mouth is open and ptosis (drooping) when the mouth is closed.

Marfan habitus *Marfanoid.* A term used to describe the physical appearance of Marfan syndrome in someone who may or may not have that syndrome. The habitus (appearance) includes tall stature, long arms and legs, and arachnodactyly, or spider-like digits (long, thin fingers and toes). It also includes decreased subcutaneous (under the skin) fat. Marfan habitus may represent a familial body pattern or another syndrome such as homocystinuria.

Marfan habitus (Marfanoid)

Marfan syndrome A genetic syndrome that affects the connective tissue (the fibrous supporting framework of the body) to produce a Marfan habitus, hyperextensible (having an increased range of motion) joints, subluxation (partial dislocation) of the lenses of the eyes, and serious cardiovascular abnormalities. The tall stature results from extremities (arms or legs) that are disproportionately long compared with the trunk; the head is dolichocephalic (long), with prominent supraorbital ridges (brows) and a long, thin face. Intelligence is typical, but learning disabilities and attention-deficit/hyperactivity disorder (ADHD) occur in more than a third of people. Incidence is 1 in 5,000. Inheritance is autosomal dominant. Named after the French pediatrician Bernard Marfan (1858–1942).

Marfanoid *See* Marfan habitus.

Marinesco-Sjögren syndrome (MSS) An autosomal recessive genetic syndrome characterized by cataracts (clouding of the lenses of the eyes), intellectual disability, ataxia (unsteady gait), and short stature. MSS is not to be confused with the more common Sjögren syndrome, a condition characterized by very dry mouth and eyes.

maroon spoon A spoon made from an unbreakable material for children and adults with feeding difficulties. The bowl of the spoon is flatter than that of a typical eating spoon and can be either a small, narrow size or a larger, wider size.

Maroteaux-Lamy syndrome *mucopolysaccharidosis (MPS) VI.* An autosomal recessive syndrome characterized by growth deficiency, coarse facies (facial features), stiff joints, cloudy corneas (clear coverings of the eyes), hepatosplenomegaly (enlargement of the liver and spleen), and typical intelligence. Allelic mutations in the structural gene on chromosome 5 encoding the enzyme arylsulfatase B can cause three types of MPS VI.

Marshall syndrome An autosomal dominant syndrome characterized by cataracts (clouding of the lenses of the eyes), sensorineural (involving the auditory nerve) hearing impairment, and a facies (facial features) with a short flat nose; intellectual disability is an occasional finding.

Marshall-Smith syndrome A syndrome characterized by advanced bone age, failure to thrive, respiratory problems, mild to moderate intellectual disability, shallow orbits and prominent eyes, and broad fingers that taper at the ends.

Martin-Bell syndrome *See* fragile X syndrome.

MAS *See* meconium aspiration syndrome.

MAS *See* Motivation Assessment Scale.

Masako maneuver A swallow exercise meant to strengthen the tongue base by having the person hold his or her tongue between the teeth with the tip of tongue protruded during swallow. This stabilizes the tongue so that the contraction is directed to the tongue base.

masking The introduction of a noise to a nontest ear to prevent its participation in the assessment of the test ear.

masking A situation in which intellectual giftedness disguises the impact of an accompanying learning disability by enabling a (relatively) underachieving child to perform at grade level but well below ability level.

Masqutova neurosensory reflex integration (MNRI) A neurophysiological therapy that repatterns reflex movements to treat cerebral palsy and developmental disorders.

mass reflex The response of total body startle or flexion due to the stimulus of a tap on the suprapubic region (the bony prominence just above the bladder).

massed practice Practice sessions in which the amount of practice is greater than the amount of rest time between repetitions. Massed practice tends to have a less positive influence on skill acquisition than practice that is distributed across time.

master of education (M.Ed.) A postgraduate academic master's degree awarded by universities in a large number of countries. This degree in education often includes the following majors: curriculum and instruction, counseling, special education, and administration.

master of public health (M.P.H.) A graduate degree in the epidemiology of disease and the various factors that influence its determinants, distribution, treatment, and prevention at a population level.

master of social work (M.S.W.) A degree granted to a student who completes a 2-year graduate program in social work; the M.S.W. curriculum contains both academic and clinical training. *See also* social work.

mastication The act of grinding, crushing, and chewing solid or semisolid food with or as if with the teeth before initiating swallowing.

mastoid Pertaining to the postauricular (behind the ear) part of the temporal bone (the side of the skull). The mastoid bone can become infected from an otitis media (middle ear infection), a situation called *mastoiditis.* Modern antibiotic therapy of otitis media and mastoiditis has markedly reduced the need for surgical intervention (mastoidectomy).

Matching Familiar Figures Test (MFF or MFFT) A measure of impulsivity and reflectivity for use with children 3–6 years of age. Each item consists of a target picture and four to eight similar pictures, only one of which exactly matches the target figure. Time to respond and number of errors are used to place the child into one of four subgroups: impulsives, reflectives, fast accurates, and slow inaccurates.

MAT-EF Matrix Analogies Test–Expanded Form. *See* Matrix Analogies Test (MAT).

Maternal Child Health Bureau (MCH or MCHB) A bureau within the federal government's Health Resources and Services Administration (HRSA) that focuses on the health of children and mothers. This bureau provides grants to fund initiatives that are designed to promote health and prevent disability in children. Grants promote access to quality health care and family-centered and community-based services.

maternal deprivation Inadequate or absent parenting or nurturance (care and affection) that has immediate and potentially long-term consequences on a child's growth and development. Short-term effects can include failure to thrive (FTT) and developmental and language disorders. The term is so poorly defined that it is better replaced by a more accurate delineation of underlying mechanisms, such as abuse, neglect, feeding disorder, or disorder of parenting. *See also* deprivation.

maternal smoking during pregnancy A risk factor that contributes to fetal distress, low birth weight, prematurity, and intellectual disability.

mathematics disorder *dyscalculia, specific learning disability in mathematics.* A learning disorder in which mathematical ability, as measured by individually administered standardized tests, is substantially below that expected given the person's chronological age, measured intelligence, and age-appropriate education. The disorder significantly interferes with academic achievement and with activities of daily living that require mathematical ability. *See also* dyscalculia.

Matrix Analogies Test (MAT) An individually administered assessment of nonverbal reasoning for use with students ages 5–17 years that requires the student to correctly select from six options a missing element in a set of patterns (an analogical matrix). Because it is nonverbal, the test is considered more "culturally fair" than traditional intelligence and problem-solving tests. There are two versions: Matrix Analogies Test–Expanded Form (MAT-EF) and Matrix Analogies Test–Short Form (MAT-SF).

Matrix Reasoning A Wechsler (intelligence test) subtest that measures fluid intelligence and that is a reliable estimate of general intellectual ability.

MAT-SF Matrix Analogies Test–Short Form. *See* Matrix Analogies Test (MAT).

Matson Evaluation of Social Skills with Youngsters (MESSY) A rating scale used to measure social skills in children 4–8 years of age; it can be used with children who have intellectual disability, visual impairments, or hearing impairments.

maturation Biological or cognitive change as a direct function of increasing age. According to Arnold Gesell's (1880–1961) maturational theory of development, advances in the level of development and behavior are primarily neuroanatomically preprogrammed (determined by the development of the brain).

maturational theory of development Arnold Gesell's (1880–1961) theory of human development that attributes the achievement of different developmental milestones primarily to the genetically preprogrammed maturation of the central nervous system (CNS) through myelination of the nerve pathways (insulation through the laying down of a fatty protective layer). According to this theory, environmental factors play a lesser role in development, providing that these factors remain within certain broadly defined limits (e.g., relating to feeding, clothing, physical contact, and interpersonal interaction). The theory is mostly concerned with development in infancy and early childhood and allows for an increasingly greater impact of environmental and emotional factors in older children. *See also* Gesell, Arnold Lucius (1880–1961).

Maxfield-Buccholz Social Maturity Scale An adaptation of the Vineland Social Maturity Scale used to measure the personal and social development of children with visual impairments up to 6 years of age.

maxilla The bone of the upper jaw.

maxillonasal dysplasia *Binder syndrome.* A distinctive facies (facial features) with flattened nose, hypotelorism (closely spaced eyes), mid-face hypoplasia (flattening), relative prognathism (a prominent jaw) with malocclusion, and typical intelligence without other associated anomalies (malformation, deformation, disruption, or dysplasia). Plastic surgery is indicated.

MBD Minimal brain damage/dysfunction. *See also* attention-deficit/hyperactivity disorder (ADHD).

MBP *See* myelin basic protein.

MBS study *See* modified barium swallow study.

McCarthy reflex Blink reflex. An infant reflex in which tapping on the supraorbital (just above the eye or brow) area produces an ipsilateral (on the same side) blinking response.

McCarthy Scales of Children's Abilities A test of abilities for children ages 2;6–8;6 years. Abilities are assessed in six areas: verbal, quantitative, perceptual performance, general cognitive, memory, and motor development.

McCarthy Screening Test (MST) An assessment of abilities critical to early school success for use with children 4;0–6;6 years; the test items are derived from six scales of the McCarthy Scales of Children's Abilities. The MST classifies children as "at risk" or "not at risk" for later need of special education services. Administration time is 20 minutes.

MCH See Maternal Child Health Bureau.

M-CHAT See Modified Checklist for Autism in Toddlers.

MCHB See Maternal Child Health Bureau.

MCP joint See metacarpophalangeal joint.

MDA See Muscular Dystrophy Association.

mean The arithmetic average of all scores in a set of scores. To obtain the mean, divide the sum of all scores in the set by the total number of scores in the set. This measure is more sensitive to the exact position of each score in a distribution but less sensitive to a few relatively extreme scores. See also measures of central tendency.

mean length of utterance (MLU) A measure of language development (language level) that is calculated by counting the total number of morphemes (smallest units of meaning) in a sample of language (sentences) and then dividing by the number of utterances in the sample.

meaningful Of consequence. In reference to memory, contextual, connected terms are easier to retain than less meaningful, disjointed, or nonsense terms. Meaningfulness is not synonymous with a word's definition or meaning.

means test Financial criteria determine eligibility for certain government-funded health or social services. In a means test, an applicant's income, assets, debts, dependents, and earning status are weighed against preexisting criteria for eligibility. Failure to meet the criteria implies that the applicant already has sufficient means to meet his or her obligations and does not need subsidy.

measles See rubeola.

measures of central tendency Descriptive statistics that measure the central value in a distribution of scores. The three most commonly used measures are mean, median, and mode. See also mean, median, mode. See page 287.

mechanical ventilation The use of a ventilator (breathing machine) to assist an individual with respiratory distress.

meconium The newborn infant's first stool.

meconium aspiration syndrome (MAS) A condition at birth caused by aspiration (inhalation) of meconium into the tracheobronchial tree (the airway, including the branches into the small airways of the lungs).

M.Ed. See master of education.

medial In anatomy, toward the mid-line.

median The midpoint, or the point that divides in half an array of scores or values arranged in numerical order. When the number of scores is odd, the middle score is the median (e.g., 10, 8, 6, 4, 1; median = 6). When the number of scores is even, the median is the mean of the middle pair of scores (e.g., 10, 9, 7, 4, 2, 1; median = [7 + 4]/2 = 5.5). Because the median divides

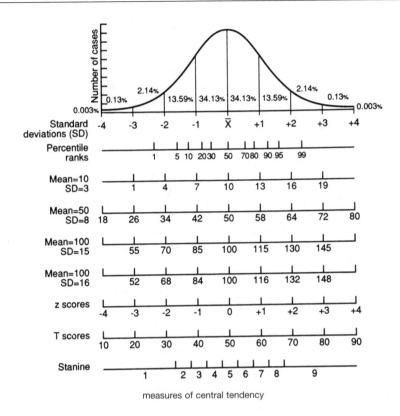

measures of central tendency

a set of scores into equal groups, 50% of the scores fall below the median; thus, the median is always the 50th percentile. *See also* measures of central tendency.

median cleft palate face syndrome *frontonasal dysplasia.* A nongenetic, congenital (present from birth) defect in mid-facial (area around the nose, upper jaw, and cheekbones) development that produces marked hypertelorism (widely spaced eyes); cleft lip, nose, palate; and a widow's peak hairline. Some cases exhibit intellectual disability.

mediastinum A region of the chest that includes all of the contents of the thorax (chest) except the lungs.

mediastinum

Medicaid A federally supplemented, state-administered health insurance program for people with financial needs. Medicaid uses a financial means test to determine eligibility. Administration of the program is usually handled through local offices.

Medicaid Spend-Down A provision in which an individual may be eligible for Medicaid on the basis of having expended (spent) sufficient assets or income on medical expenses.

medical home The source of primary medical care that is comprehensive, continuous, and accessible. For a child this would typically be the pediatrician's office.

Medicare A federally funded comprehensive health insurance program enacted as a supplemental entitlement under Social Security. Medicare has four parts: Part A, Hospital Insurance; Part B, Medical Insurance; Part C,

Medicare Advantage Plans (modeled after health maintenance plans and special population plans); and Part D, Prescription Drug Coverage. Eligible populations include 1) people ages 65 and older, 2) people younger than 65 with certain disabilities, and 3) people of any age with end-stage renal disease. *See also* Social Security Act of 1935 (PL 74-271).

MEG *See* magnetoencephalography.

megalencephaly A large brain (not just a large skull); brain hypertrophy (overgrowth). Megalencephaly is usually associated with neurological problems.

megavitamin therapy The use of very high doses of vitamins to treat schizophrenia, autism, and a range of developmental disorders. The expansion of the therapeutic regimen to include minerals and trace elements (orthomolecular therapy) does not improve its efficacy (effectiveness). Vitamin deficiency can cause developmental symptoms, and some children's metabolism does require higher vitamin intake; however, outside the fairly narrow range of well-defined vitamin deficiency syndromes, (mega)vitamin treatment of developmental disorders is an unproven intervention.

Meisels *See* Early Screening Inventory–Revised (ESI-R).

melatonin (MT) A neurohormone secreted by the pineal gland and involved in the metabolism of serotonin (a neurotransmitter, or chemical used to signal within the brain) and in the maintenance of the body's circadian rhythm (day/night, wake/sleep cycle). MT can treat sleep onset problems and regularize sleep patterns in children with neurodevelopmental disorders. MT is an over-the-counter (nonprescription) drug.

Mellaril *See* thioridazine.

Melnick-Fraser syndrome *branchio-oto-renal (BOR) syndrome.* An autosomal dominant syndrome characterized by hearing loss, kidney abnormalities, and branchial arch anomalies (malformations [e.g., preauricular pits, neck fistulas] involving organs formed from parts of the embryo called branchial arches). Prevalence is 1 in 40,000. *See also* preauricular pit.

melodic intonation therapy (MIT) The unproven use of melodic and rhythmic components to treat adult aphasia and childhood apraxia of speech. Developed on adults with post–brain insult aphasia, the technique is based on the theory that increased use of the right hemisphere through a melodic presentation of speech increases the role of that hemisphere in inter-hemispheric control of language, possibly diminishing or supplementing the language dominance of the damaged left hemisphere.

memory The store of knowledge retained from an organism's activity or experience. Most theoretical models of memory include a sensory register, short-term memory, working memory, and long-term memory. Other conceptualizations of memory include auditory memory, visual memory, motor memory, and recognition memory. *See also* declarative knowledge, long-term memory, motor memory, procedural knowledge, recognition memory, short-term memory.

menarche The onset of menstruation. Menarche tends to occur earlier in physically larger girls and later in physically smaller girls. There is a genetic influence with familial patterns of early or late menarche. Very early (before 8 years of age) menarche may suggest precocious puberty and the need for an endocrinological evaluation. Late menarche is not uncommon in the presence of severe intellectual disability, especially when accompanied by short stature; it is also sometimes associated with sex chromosome anomalies (a number of X chromosomes other than two).

Mendelsohn maneuver A swallow technique that aims to increase the extent and duration of laryngeal elevation and the duration and width of the upper esophageal sphincter opening. The person is asked to swallow and feel his or her Adam's apple rise, then swallow without letting the Adam's apple drop (i.e., hold the squeeze while swallowing).

meninges The layers of tissue covering the brain and spinal cord. There are three layers from outside to inside: the dura mater, the arachnoid mater, and the pia mater. The dura mater is the outermost layer and is thicker and more fibrous than the other layers; the arachnoid mater is thin and transparent, with a space between it and the pia mater, where cerebrospinal fluid (CSF) is found. The pia mater is the layer closest to the brain and spinal cord. Inflammation or infection of these layers is called *meningitis.*

meningitis An infection of the meninges (covering of the brain and spinal cord). The infection is commonly bacterial but may be viral, in which case it is termed *aseptic meningitis.* Other causes (e.g., fungi, protozoa) are less common. Bacterial meningitis can be treated with antibiotics; however, damage to the brain may occur from the inflammation. Complications include brain abscess (pocket of infection), infarction (stroke), hydrocephalus (excess fluid in the brain), subdural effusions (fluid under the dura, one of the meningeal layers), and seizures. Diagnosis is made by examining cerebrospinal fluid (CSF; the fluid that circulates around the brain and spine) obtained by lumbar puncture (spinal tap) for white blood cells, bacteria, and chemical abnormalities. Long-term sequelae (consequences) include intellectual disability, learning disabilities, attention-deficit/hyperactivity disorder (ADHD), cerebral palsy, seizure disorders, and sensorineural (auditory nerve) hearing loss.

meningomyelocele *See* myelomeningocele.

Menkes kinky hair syndrome *kinky hair disease.* An X-linked recessive genetic syndrome characterized by seizures; poor growth and intellectual disability; sparse, lightly colored hair with structural abnormalities visible under a microscope; and a severe neurodegenerative course ending in death. Abnormal copper metabolism has been documented. Mutations in the *ATP7A* gene cause Menkes kinky hair syndrome.

mental age (MA) An age-equivalent score; a measure of mental development as determined by intelligence and achievement tests, expressed as the age for which that level of performance is the average. Intelligence test tasks are arranged in a progressive order of difficulty so that age levels can be assigned to items. MA is determined by the highest age level of the tasks successfully passed. For example, a child with an MA score of 8 is considered to have the general mental ability of an average 8-year-old, regardless of his or her chronological age. MA serves as the numerator in the calculation of a ratio intelligence quotient (IQ) score, whereas chronological age serves as the denominator. MA scores have been largely displaced by standard deviation scores for various reasons; however, MA remains a good "commonsense" concept for helping parents understand the approximate age at which their child functions so that appropriate achievement and behavioral expectations can be used.

mental retardation (MR) *See* intellectual disability.

mental retardation attendant (MRA) *See* behavior coach.

Mental Retardation Facilities and Community Mental Health Centers Construction Act of 1963 (PL 88-164) Federal legislation that creates University Affiliated Facilities (UAFs), now known as University Centers for Excellence in Developmental Disabilities.

Mental Retardation/Intellectual Disability (MR/ID) Waiver   A Medicaid program that provides eligible individuals with a variety of consumer- and agency-directed services in their homes and local communities as an alternative to care in a residential or intermediate care facility (ICF). Eligibility includes a diagnosis of intellectual disability or developmental risk (for individuals younger than 6 years of age) and financial eligibility.

mental status   Cognition, memory, and orientation (awareness of one's environment with regard to people, place, and time). An altered mental state may be relatively permanent (as in intellectual disability) or transient (as in serious, acute illnesses [e.g., diabetic ketoacidosis] that affect the whole body, including the brain).

mentum   The central point of the chin.

mercury   *See* methyl mercury.

Merrill Language Screening Test (MLST)   A brief screening test of receptive and expressive language and articulation for use with kindergarten and first-grade students. Using a storytelling technique, the MLST assesses five areas: production of complete sentences, utterance length, verb tense agreement, elaboration, and communication competence.

Merrill-Palmer Scale of Mental Tests   A timed intelligence test for use with children ages 18 months to 4 years; 19 subtests cover language skills, motor skills, manual dexterity, and matching ability. Some subtests require oral responses while others use tasks that involve a variety of materials. Developed in the 1930s, the original scales were used with children with hearing impairments because the tasks are largely nonverbal, are based heavily on perceptual motor skills, and produce scores even when items are omitted. However, the scales were not normed on children with hearing impairments. The Extended Merrill-Palmer Scale has improved norms and standardization but more verbal demands.

mesiocclusion   A dental alignment in which the mandible (jaw) is too far forward in relation to the maxilla. This type of alignment is common in clefts in which the mid-face is too small, the bottom jaw sticks out, and the lower molar is anterior to the normal position.

mesomelic   Referring to the central part of a limb (forearm or leg).

mesomorph   Someone with a muscular body type. *See also* ectomorph, endomorph.

message feedback   Information sent to an individual using an augmentative and alternative communication (AAC) device as well as his or her communication partner about the symbol or message itself after it has been formulated.

message input   Information that is received from the communication partner of someone using an augmentative and alternative communication (AAC) device.

message output   Information that is sent to the communication partner of someone using an augmentative and alternative communication (AAC) device.

MESSY   *See* Matson Evaluation of Social Skills with Youngsters.

meta-analysis   A synthesis of quantitative research; statistical methods used to integrate data from multiple studies. A meta-analysis is an inductive method that proceeds from particular observations (studies) to general inclusive statements and yields a statistic that represents the magnitude (size) of experimental effects reported in the studies. A meta-analysis converts the findings of several studies into similar measures, allowing for a summary of the effectiveness of a particular intervention (e.g., the average effect size demonstrated).

metabolic disorder   *See* neurometabolic disorders.

metabolic screening A panel of laboratory tests used to search for the presence of atypical metabolites (by-products that result from the body's processing of foods). A metabolic screening is a frequent item in the assessment of a child with significant intellectual disability of unknown etiology (cause).

metabolite A chemical by-product or waste produced in the body by the breakdown or processing of something else. The presence of a metabolite of abnormal quantity or quality in the blood or urine suggests the presence of a metabolic disorder, or a defect in the body's process of chemical processing, often at the level of an enzyme. Untreated metabolic disorders often have significant developmental consequences.

metacarpophalangeal (MCP) joint The knuckle joint of the hand.

metachromatic leukodystrophy (MLD) A progressive and ultimately fatal autosomal recessive disorder of the central nervous system (CNS) due to an enzyme (arylsulfatase A [ARSA]) deficiency. Hyporeflexia and profound intellectual disability are characteristic of MLD. Incidence is 1 in 40,000.

metacognition Knowledge about or awareness of one's thought processes ("thinking about thinking") and how to regulate strategies for thought or learning. Rudimentary metacognition begins in the preschool years as young children realize that they and others have thoughts and feelings that influence behavior. Metacognition develops further through middle childhood as children become aware of and able to apply planning and problem solving, and it becomes more refined in adolescence and adulthood.

Metadate *See* methylphenidate.

metalinguistic awareness The ability to think of language as a system (e.g., the idea that one chooses words, uses them in context, and applies complex rules in order to communicate). Metalinguistic awareness is a skill that develops from about age 6 through elementary school.

metallothionein (MT) A group of proteins that bind heavy metals. MT is purportedly implicated in autism spectrum disorders.

metatarsus adductus An orthopedic deformity of infants in which the feet appear to turn inward from mid-foot forward.

metatarsus adductus

metathesis The phonological process in which there is a transposition of two sounds.

methadone A synthetic narcotic that is used to treat people addicted to opiates such as heroin or morphine. It can also be used for pain control. Like other opiates, methadone is addictive (though it tends to produce more of a steady state than a "high"), and infants of mothers treated with methadone can be born addicted to it.

methyl mercury A chemical fungicide (substance used to kill fungi) that can affect the developing central nervous system (CNS; brain and spinal cord); it can be ingested from contaminated seafood. Prenatal exposure has been linked to cerebral palsy, intellectual disability, and blindness.

Methylin Trade name for methylphenidate (Ritalin) administered in an oral solution or chewable tablets.

methylmalonic aciduria (MMA) *methylmalonic acidemia.* An autosomal recessive metabolic disorder that, if untreated, leads to episodic vomiting, lethargy, and coma as well as intellectual disability. An aggressive treatment regimen includes hydration, a protein-restricted diet, and, for some children, vitamin B_{12}. Incidence is 1 in 50,000 to 100,000.

methylphenidate (MPH) Trade names, Ritalin; Metadate; Concerta; Methylin; Daytrana. One of the most commonly used stimulant medications for the treatment of attention-deficit/hyperactivity disorder (ADHD) and hyperactivity in children and adults. It is manufactured in multiples of 5 mg. The duration of action is 4 hours, although long-acting formulations are available. Because of its addictive potential, the distribution of methylphenidate is regulated as a controlled substance; however, addiction is not typically a problem in people with attentional problems. Side effects include headache, stomachache, anorexia (loss of appetite), poor growth, and sleep problems; these can usually be managed by titrating the dosage or altering the administration schedule.

metoclopramide Trade name, Reglan. A dopamine antagonist (a drug that opposes the actions of dopamine signals) used in the treatment of gastroesophageal reflux (GER). Metoclopramide increases gastric motility (movement through the gastrointestinal tract) and also acts as an antiemetic (i.e., prevents vomiting).

Metropolitan Readiness Tests–Sixth Edition (MRT6) An assessment of skills in reading, mathematics, and language development that contribute to early learning success. The MRT6 is for use with children in prekindergarten through first grade.

MFF or **MFFT** *See* Matching Familiar Figures Test.

MFP *See* Money Follows the Person.

MFP *See* Multidisciplinary Feeding Profile.

MFVPT-III *See* Motor-Free Visual Perception Test–Third Edition.

MI *See* motivational interviewing.

microarray A deoxyribonucleic acid (DNA) technology that looks at gene expression (i.e., what a person's genes produce, and not just the sequence of their information) and that can be used to clinically identify causes of intellectual disabilities as well as to assess gene function in research.

microcephaly An abnormally small head; significantly small head sizes are variously considered to be at least 2.0 or 2.5 standard deviations below the mean (average) for age (i.e., smaller than 97.5% of other children's heads). Small head size automatically implies small brain size, but this in turn does not necessarily indicate intellectual disability. Nevertheless, decreasing head size does correlate with an increasing incidence of intellectual disability. Milder decreases in head size (on the order of 1.5 standard deviations below the mean) have been associated with learning disabilities and language disorders. Proportional microcephaly—a small head size along with short stature—is less strongly correlated with intellectual disability. Microcephaly can result from intrauterine infection and radiation exposure as well as from numerous genetic syndromes. Familial microcephaly can be a marker for familial intellectual disability.

microglossia An abnormally small tongue.

micrognathia A small jaw; micrognathia can be a normal variant, a familial trait, a minor malformation, or part of an identifiable syndrome (e.g., Pierre Robin syndrome).

micrographia Tiny handwriting; it may reflect emotional, neurological (e.g., Parkinson's disease), or pharmacological causes.

micronutrient A dietary element necessary only in small quantities.

microphthalmia *microphthalmos.* An eye that is smaller than normal. Microphthalmia may occur in several genetic syndromes.

micropolygyria An anomaly in the cerebral architecture in which the gyri (ridges of the brain) are too small and too numerous. There are also abnormalities in the number of cortical layers and their orientation. Clinically speaking, individuals with micropolygyria have severe intellectual disability and hypotonia (low muscle tone) or spasticity (increased muscle tone), depending upon the areas of the brain affected. Micropolygyria can be present in syndromes such as Zellweger syndrome (cerebrohepatorenal syndrome, an autosomal recessive disorder); however, most cases are sporadic (random). Magnetic resonance imaging (MRI) can visualize this pattern of gyral architecture.

micropreemies Infants who weigh less than 700–800 g at birth and who are generally born before 26 weeks' gestation.

microswitch A single control used to simplify the operation of electrical equipment from toys to computers. This adaptation increases the accessibility and utility of such items for individuals with severe physical disabilities.

microtia Abnormally small or malformed ears.

MICS *See* Mother/Infant Communication Scale.

micturition Urination.

mid-arm circumference A measure of nutritional status.

mid-line Sagittal plane. An imaginary vertical line dividing the body into the left and right sides. The motor acts of skipping and of drawing a line from the right to the left side of the page involve crossing the mid-line. Difficulty crossing the mid-line or coordinating both sides of the body can be an indication of a perceptual or neurological problem.

mid-line jerk A twitching movement of the eyes at the mid-line during horizontal visual tracking (moving the eyes from one side to another to follow an object).

mid-parental height The arithmetic mean (average) of the heights of both biological parents. This measure is used to project a child's adult height and expected height growth percentile.

mid-range control The ability of specific muscle groups to smoothly perform an action between full extension and full flexion.

mid-temporal epilepsy *See* benign childhood epilepsy with centrotemporal spikes (BECTS).

Mietens syndrome An autosomal recessive genetic syndrome characterized by mild intellectual disability, short stature, corneal (the outer layer of the eye) clouding with visual defect, narrow nose, flexion contractures of the elbows, and short forearms.

Milani-Comparetti Motor Development Screening Test A motoscopic (visual pattern analysis) evaluation procedure for use with children in the first 2 years of life that relates postural control and active movement to primitive reflexes, tilting, righting, and parachute reactions. The protocol sheet provides a graphic record of the child's progress.

mild hearing impairment Hearing loss that ranges in severity from 36 to 40 dBHL (decibels hearing level).

"mild Hurler (MPS IH)" *See* Scheie syndrome.

mild intellectual disability Intellectual disability in which the intelligence quotient (IQ) level is between 50 and 70. Adults with mild intellectual disability typically achieve functional literacy and are able to live independently (or with minimal assistance) in the community.

MILI *See* Multilevel Informal Language Inventory.

milieu teaching A naturalistic language intervention strategy that uses everyday instances of social interaction to teach language. It incorporates many features of incidental teaching but is broader in focus. This model requires teachers to 1) arrange the environment to facilitate a child's use of language, 2) assess the functioning levels of the child, and 3) discover ways in which the child can interact with the environment.

milieu therapy A form of residential treatment that attempts to create and maintain a wholly positive living environment within a residential community by enlisting the efforts of all staff members as providers of therapeutic contact. In an optimal milieu, virtually all interactions promote the well-being of the individuals supported. *See also* residential treatment.

milkmaid grip A grasp that waxes and wanes abruptly (as if squeezing and letting go in milking a cow); it is seen in choreoathetosis.

Miller Assessment for Preschoolers (MAP) A norm-referenced brief assessment instrument used to evaluate children ages 2;9–5;8 years for mild to moderate developmental delays. The MAP produces standard scores on five performance indexes (foundations, coordination, verbal, nonverbal, and complex tasks) and requires 30–40 minutes to administer.

Miller syndrome *See* aniridia–Wilms tumor association.

Miller-Dieker syndrome *agyria, deletion 17p (del 17p13.3), lissencephaly type I.* A specific pattern of malformations that includes a smooth rather than convoluted (ridged) brain surface with other central nervous system (CNS) malformations: brainstem tissue displacement and absent corpus callosum (the bridge between the two halves of the brain). Miller-Dieker syndrome is associated with facial anomalies; microcephaly (small head); high forehead with vertical and central furrowing; small nose with upturned nostrils; and low-set, posteriorly rotated ears. Severe intellectual disability and hypotonia (low muscle tone), opisthotonos (arching of the back), failure to thrive (FTT; poor growth), and seizures are the rule. Individuals usually die within the first 2 years of life. The loss of a particular gene on chromosome 17, *PAFAH1B1,* is responsible for the syndrome's characteristic lissencephaly. The loss of another gene, *YWHAE,* in the same region of chromosome 17 increases the severity of the lissencephaly. Additional genes in the deleted region probably contribute to the varied features of Miller-Dieker syndrome.

Miller-Yoder Language Comprehension Test A picture-format test of language comprehension for use with children between the ages of 4 and 8 years. Comprehension of short sentences with a variety of grammatical structures is assessed.

Milwaukee brace A thoracolumbosacral (including chest, lower back, and pelvis) brace that goes from the chin to the hips and is used to treat scoliosis (spinal curvature). *See also* cervical-thoraco-lumbar-spinal and hip orthosis (CTLSHO), cervical-thoraco-lumbar-spinal orthosis (CTLSO).

Milwaukee brace

Milwaukee Project A controlled, intensive early intervention program for 20 disadvantaged children (and their mothers, who have mild intellectual disability) from early in their first year of life to 6 years of age. The dramatically positive results of this study remain controversial.

minimal brain damage/dysfunction (MBD)
A loosely organized constellation of symptoms that includes short attention span, distractibility, impulsivity, hyperactivity, emotional lability (changeability), motor incoordination, visual-perceptual motor disturbance, and language and learning disorders. MBD is an older term that encompasses attention deficit disorder (with and without hyperactivity), learning disability, developmental language disorder, and developmental coordination disorder (DCD). The utility of the MBD concept is that it stresses comorbidity—the marked overlap among these diagnostic categories. MBD is similar to the European dysfunction of attention, motor function, and perception (DAMP) syndrome. *See also* attention-deficit/hyperactivity disorder (ADHD).

minimal competency score The minimal amount of skill or knowledge an average speaker would demonstrate for a given age and context.

Minneapolis Preschool Screening Instrument (MPSI) A brief screening test for use with 4-year-olds that identifies children who may need special education services.

Minnesota Infant Development Inventory
A parent checklist that measures infant development in five domains: gross motor, fine motor, language, comprehension, and personal-social. The child's development is then compared with age expectations.

Minnesota Percepto-Diagnostic Test (MPD)
A test of visual-perceptual motor skills with separate age norms for children (5–14 years of age) and adults. The test requires the person to copy six designs, with the score based on rotations, separations, and distortions in the copies. The results are one tool to assist in the classification of individuals who may have learning disabilities and emotional disorders. The six stimulus cards are rotations of two Bender Gestalt figures.

minor Slight; inconsequential.

minor dysmorphic features Mild superficial malformations. Singly these dysmorphic characteristics are best considered normal variants or familial traits, but the presence of several of these features together may contribute to an overall appearance that is part of a specific syndrome. When no syndrome is identified, the presence of more than four minor dysmorphic features on the Waldrop scale (a dysmorphology rating scale) is interpreted as suggesting a disturbance occurring during the first trimester of pregnancy, affecting the ectodermal layer of the embryo, and contributing to mild abnormalities of ectodermal derivatives (organs that originate from that layer, such as the hair, skin, and brain). Increased dysmorphology scores are associated with attention problems, hyperactivity, cognitive impairments, and the entire spectrum of neurodevelopmental disabilities. In the presence of a developmental diagnosis, a high minor malformation score provides support for a prenatal etiology (origin). Common minor dysmorphic features include abnormal hair whorl patterns, microcephaly (small head), macrocephaly (large head), epicanthal folds (folds over the inner corners of the eyes), pinna (ear) anomalies (malformations), high-arched or steepled palate, geographic tongue (ridged tongue with areas resembling the landscape of a map), clinodactyly (bent fingers), palmar crease abnormalities (e.g., simian crease, Sydney line), sandal gap deformity (a gap between the great toe and other toes, as if to allow space for a sandal thong), and syndactyly (webbing of the fingers or toes).

minor motor seizures A class of seizures that includes several types: atonic (also called *akinetic;* characterized by brief loss of muscle tone), myoclonic (characterized by lightning-like jerking), and brief tonic (characterized by stiffening). The etiology (cause) of these seizures ranges from infections of the brain (encephalitis and meningitis) to perinatal problems and genetic disorders. Minor motor seizures are generally present throughout an individual's life span. Mental development in children with these types of seizures is slow, and many such children have an intelligence quotient (IQ) score below 75, reflecting the severity of the seizures as well as the underlying brain disease.

minor neurological dysfunction *See* soft neurological sign.

miosis (Excessive) contraction of the pupil. Miosis can result from the use of certain drugs.

mirror movements Associated or overflow movements on the contralateral (opposite) side of the body, such as those that can be observed in one hand when testing fine finger movements on the other hand. Mirror movements are a soft neurological sign or a sign of minor neurological dysfunction.

mirror neurons Specialized cells in the cerebral cortex of the brain that appear to underlie imitative skills. Mirror neurons fire identically when an action is observed and when the organism carries out the behavior on its own. Essentially, they simulate a behavior in the brain while it is being observed.

missing parts test A type of test in which the person must identify the missing part from a picture.

MIT *See* melodic intonation therapy.

mitochondria Organelles (literally, "little organs") of the cells that generate energy and that are most plentiful in cells belonging to organs of the body with high energy demands, such as the brain, heart, and muscles. These organs, therefore, tend to be most affected by disorders of the mitochondria.

mitochondrial myopathy A class of disorders that affect the peripheral (noncentral) muscles and the central nervous system (CNS; brain and spinal cord), often resulting in progressive weakness, seizures, and cognitive deterioration; vision and hearing impairment; and dementia. An example is MERRF, a syndrome characterized by *m*yoclonic *e*pilepsy (seizures consisting of lightning-like muscle jerks) and *r*agged *r*ed *f*ibers in muscle tissue that are visible under the microscope. These disorders are inherited through the mitochondria, the energy generators of the cells, which are found in the cytoplasm (a substance in the body of the cell). Because the embryonic cytoplasm comes only from the egg, these disorders are generally inherited from the mother.

mixed cerebral palsy A case of cerebral palsy that has significant features of more than one subtype, usually a combination of a spastic subtype and an extrapyramidal subtype.

mixed dysarthria A motor speech disorder with the characteristics of one or more of the dysarthrias (pathology in more than one area).

mixed hearing loss Hearing loss characterized by a combination of conductive and sensorineural hearing losses.

MLD *See* metachromatic leukodystrophy.

MLST *See* Merrill Language Screening Test.

MLU *See* mean length of utterance.

MMA *See* methylmalonic aciduria.

MMR Combined live attenuated (with the viruses altered so as not to provoke disease) vaccines against measles, mumps, and rubella; one of the primary routine immunizations (vaccinations) of childhood.

MMT *See* Manual Muscle Test.

mnemonic A device or technique for improving one's memory through aids such as rhymes, rules, phrases, diagrams, or acronyms. An example of a mnemonic device is HOMES for learning the names of the Great Lakes (Huron, Ontario, Michigan, Erie, and Superior).

MNRI   *See* Masqutova neurosensory reflex integration.

mobility   The ability to move with appropriate ease, flexibility, and range. A person with physical or motor disabilities may have impairments in one or more of these respects and may require the use of assistive devices and environmental modifications to facilitate mobility. Thus, an amputee may require a prosthesis; a person with orthopedic disabilities may require special shoes, braces, canes, or crutches; and a person with cerebral palsy or a stroke may require a wheelchair. In addition, ramps, elevators, widened doors, and car and bus lifts may be necessary environmental modifications to ensure complete mobility. For many people, personal mobility may be compromised by a lack of accessible public transportation to allow linkages with needed health and welfare services. The Americans with Disabilities Act (ADA) of 1990 (PL 101-336) mandates the removal of architectural barriers from all public buildings and the alteration of facilities and their amenities to ensure physical accessibility to individuals with disabilities as one aspect of widening the experiences of, and opportunities for, Americans with disabilities.

Möbius syndrome   A congenital and usually bilateral facial (sixth and seventh cranial nerves) paralysis characterized by an expressionless, mask-like facies—"life without a smile." This is a fairly nonspecific syndrome with a variety of associated features (e.g., micrognathia [small jaw] and clubfoot) and diverse etiologies (causes), including sporadic autosomal dominant inheritance. The involvement of other cranial nerves (which can include cranial nerves III, IV, V, IX, X, or XII) can lead to ptosis (drooping eyelids) and feeding and articulation problems.

Möbius syndrome may be part of a broader malformation pattern that includes syndactyly (webbing of the fingers or toes), clubfoot, and limb reduction defects (a missing part of an arm or leg). Only 15% of people with this syndrome have intellectual disability, but the early appearance of the expressionless face, poor speech, feeding disorder, and other impairments may contribute to a misdiagnosis of intellectual disability. Named after the German neurologist Paul Möbius (1853–1907).

modafinil   Trade name, Provigil. A stimulant medication used to treat narcolepsy, a neurological disorder that causes sleep/wake instability that contributes to daytime sleepiness and poor-quality nighttime sleep.

modality   A form of therapy or an apparatus for such therapy.

modality-based instruction   Instruction that presents material in a manner aimed at using visual, auditory, kinesthetic (movement), or tactile (touch) channels (modalities), according to the channel presumed to be strongest in an individual. Multisensory approaches attempt to combine several modalities. Modality-based instruction is often confused with the ineffective process model of educational intervention, in which attempts were made to train auditory and visual-perceptual processes directly in the hope that academic performance would then automatically improve. Modality-based instruction does not attempt to train psychological processes but rather teaches academic material in a manner designed to work around weakness and make use of the learner's strengths. *See* Fernald Word Learning Technique.

mode   The most frequent score in a set of scores (e.g., 3 is the mode for the data 1, 1, 2, 3, 3, 3, 4, 9, 9, 18). When two scores occur more frequently than others and share the same frequency, the distribution is bimodal (e.g., 2 and 7 are the modes for the data 1, 2, 2, 2, 3, 6, 7, 7, 7, 10, 12). When the same is true of more than two scores, the distribution is multimodal (e.g., 4, 5, and 10 are the modes for the data 2, 4, 4, 4, 6, 5, 5, 5, 7, 9, 10, 10, 10, 11). *See also* measures of central tendency.

modeling The enacting of a specific behavior or set of behaviors with the intention of having an observer imitate that behavior. *See also* behavior modeling, imitation, social learning theory.

moderate hearing impairment Hearing loss that ranges in severity between 41 and 70 dBHL (decibels hearing level).

moderate intellectual disability Intellectual disability in which the intelligence quotient (IQ) level is between 35–40 and 50–55. Adults with moderate intellectual disability typically have been trained to perform semiskilled labor and can live in supervised group homes in the community.

modification Any change that improves functioning for people with disabilities in community environments and other settings. Sometimes the strict procedures for administering a test are modified to allow for a person's disability. Classroom and daily living accommodations for various disabilities are also typical modifications.

modified barium swallow (MBS) study *oral-pharyngeal motility study.* An evaluation procedure that involves the use of technical instrumentation (x ray) and offers a dynamic assessment of the oral, pharyngeal, and esophageal phases of swallowing for the purposes of defining abnormalities, identifying treatment options, and evaluating treatment efficacy. During the exam, the person ingests barium-coated boli or liquid barium of varying consistencies to allow visualization of the oral activity during chewing, the oral stage of swallowing, the triggering of the pharyngeal swallow, and the motor aspects of the pharyngeal swallow.

Modified Checklist for Autism in Toddlers (M-CHAT) A 23-item checklist used to screen for autism in children 18–24 months of age. Failure on any three items or on two "critical" items constitutes a positive screening result.

Mohr syndrome *Mohr-Rimoin syndrome, oral-facial-digital syndrome type II (OFD-II).* A genetic syndrome characterized by cleft tongue, peculiar facies (facial features), an abnormality of the big toe, and conductive deafness. Intellectual disability is occasionally an associated feature. *See also* oral-facial-digital syndrome type I (OFD-I).

Money Follows the Person (MFP) A series of grants through the Deficit Reduction Act of 2005 (PL 109-171) that provide an opportunity for people living in institutions such as nursing homes and intermediate care facilities (ICFs) to take their institutional funding and move into community living. The goal is to help states reduce their reliance on institutional care and to create long-term-care opportunities for people in the community. This initiative follows the Real Choice System Change (RCSC) grants, which began to create a foundation for emphasis on community living over institutional care.

mongolian spot *congenital dermal melanocytosis.* (Usually bluish) discoloration of the skin over the back and buttocks, present at birth. It is more common in African American and Asian American infants and tends to fade with time.

mongoloid slant An apparently upward (going from the nose outward) slant to the palpebral fissure (eye slit). A component of the facies (facial features) in Down syndrome and other genetic syndromes, the mongoloid slant

mongoloid slant

can also be a racial and familial characteristic or a sporadic isolated finding of no clinical significance. The mongoloid slant may be more common in conditions with microcephaly (small head) or with malar (cheekbone) hypoplasia (underdevelopment). This characteristic is named after the similar but typical appearance of people who originate from the Asian region of Mongolia.

monitoring ability   The capacity to exercise quality control over one's performance. Someone who has difficulty with monitoring can make careless mistakes but have no perceptual awareness of their having occurred. Children with attention problems often demonstrate poor self-monitoring skills.

monitoring system   A system of providing related services in the school system in which the therapist plans a program that involves specific activities for a student to be carried out with the help of other personnel (e.g., teaching assistant, aide). Regular contact with the therapist is necessary to provide supervision to update the program. Monitored activities could include positioning the student for writing activities; having the student wear a splint; or implementing the use of assistive technology, such as an adapted keyboard.

monopitch   A disorder in which an individual's voice lacks normal pitch variations.

monoplegia   Literally, "one palsy." A topographical (based on the area of the body affected) subtype of spastic (increased muscle tone) cerebral palsy. By the usual mechanisms of brain injury, it is very difficult for the resulting impairment to be localized to a single extremity (arm or leg); thus, pure monoplegic cerebral palsy is rare.

monosomy   A condition in which one of a pair of chromosomes is missing, resulting

in only 45 chromosomes, as found in Turner syndrome (the absence of one X chromosome). No other complete monosomies are compatible with life. Individuals with a partial monosomy are missing part of one chromosome in a pair. Children with partial monosomies of chromosomes other than the sex chromosomes tend to have major anatomical abnormalities (e.g., heart disease), dysmorphic (atypical) features, and intellectual disability. *See* 9p- syndrome.

monosomy of the short arm of chromosome 9   *See* 9p monosomy.

monotherapy   The practice of using a single anticonvulsant in seizure treatment. The selection of the appropriate anticonvulsant is based on the type of seizures and the potential toxicity of the drug. More generally, monotherapy is the use of a single drug to treat a condition. Although monotherapy is the ideal treatment, it is not always successful, and in complicated cases polytherapy (which involves the use of more than one medication) may be needed. Polytherapy increases the risk of drug interactions and side effects.

monozygotic (MZ) twins   Identical twins; two individuals with the same genotype (genetic makeup) who come from a single fertilized egg. MZ twins are contrasted with dizygotic twins, who come from two separate eggs simultaneously fertilized and who do not have the same genotype. In a typical MZ gestation, only one egg is fertilized. MZ twins occur in 1 out of 360 births; incidence is increased when fertilization is by in vitro methods. *See also* dizygotic twins.

Monroe Diagnostic Reading Test   A reading readiness test for use with kindergarten and primary-grade children. It profiles reading skills and yields an arithmetic, spelling, and mental age for comparison.

Montessori method   A physiological approach to educating children. The

Montessori method involves preparing the environment with materials designed to promote children's exploration and self-directed learning. In the first plane or phase of development (birth to 6 years), these materials are organized into categories that include practical life, sensory development, math, language, and culture. The approach was developed by the Italian physician Maria Montessori (1870–1952).

mood A pervasive and sustained emotion that, if extreme, has a marked impact on a person's perception of the world. Examples of moods include depression, anxiety, anger, and elation. *See also* affect, emotion.

mood disorder A class of psychiatric disorders in which mood is altered (e.g., unusually depressed or elevated) beyond a specific time period, accompanied by behavior and cognitive changes uncharacteristic of the person's typical level of functioning. Examples of mood disorders include major depressive disorder, panic states, and bipolar disorder and mania. In children, particularly those with developmental disabilities, mood deviance is more commonly present as anhedonia (the inability to feel happy) or irritability rather than active depression or elation.

Moos Family Environment Scale A 90-item self-report instrument used to measure the social and environmental characteristics of all types of families.

Moral Judgement Inventory A structured interview for use with elementary school–age children to adults, designed to assess stages of moral development as defined by Lawrence Kohlberg. There are two forms of the interview, each consisting of three stories and accompanying questions that address various aspects of the moral issue presented. Examples with answers characteristic of Kohlberg's six developmental stages are provided to facilitate scoring.

morbidity Illness or disease, as opposed to mortality (death).

morbidity rate A count of the number of diseases per number of the population at risk per period of time.

More Than Words: The Hanen Program for Parents of Children with Autism Spectrum Disorder A parent program with strategies that facilitate social and communication skills in children with autism.

Moro reflex A primitive reflex in which sudden extension of the head at the neck (as by allowing the head to suddenly fall backward a short distance) produces extension (straightening) followed by flexion of all four extremities (arms or legs), described as an embrace response. This reflex is present in all newborns and fades in the first several months. Absence, exaggeration, and asymmetry can be significant.

morpheme The smallest meaning-bearing unit in a language. For example, the word *dog* is a morpheme; the -*s* added in the plural form, *dogs,* is an added morpheme. In the sentence "Clean the table," all three words are morphemes because even the two-syllable word *table* cannot be divided without destroying its meaning. The acquisition of grammatical morphemes (e.g., *a, the*) generally occurs in a fixed sequence and is probably controlled by a combination of syntactic (language structure) and semantic (systems of meaning) complexity. *See also* morphology.

morphology The study of meaning units in any particular language; the study of morphemes. *See also* morpheme.

morphology The study of normal biological structure and its development.

Morquio syndrome *Brailsford syndrome, mucopolysaccharidosis (MPS) IV.* An autosomal recessive genetic syndrome characterized by growth deficiency, mildly coarse facies (thickened facial features) with severe kyphosis (curvature of the spine) and knock-knees, cloudy corneas (clear outer coverings of the eyes), and hepatomegaly (liver enlargement); intelligence is usually typical. Named after the Uruguayan pediatrician Luis Morquio (1867–1935).

mortality Death.

mortality rate The number of deaths per number of the population at risk per period of time.

mosaicism A condition in which different cells in an individual have a different genetic makeup. For example, some children with Down syndrome have trisomy 21 in skin cells but not in blood cells. The resulting phenotype may be less severe, or a complete expression of the abnormal cell population may take place.

motherese Baby talk; short, simple, repetitive sentences that adults speak in a high-pitched voice when talking with infants and young children.

Mother/Infant Communication Scale (MICS) A 21-item measure of mother–child interaction that observes and rates language/synchrony, response to distress, feeding, play, and rest.

Mother's Assessment of the Behavior of her Infant (MABI) A modification of the Brazelton Neonatal Behavioral Assessment Scale (NBAS) that can be administered by mothers.

motivation An internal state that activates behavior and gives it direction; desire that energizes and directs goal-oriented behavior. Motivation is a hypothetical construct intended to explain why individuals initiate or persist in efforts to complete a task. There are two main forms of motivation: intrinsic (internal to the person) and extrin-

sic (delivered in the form of reinforcers). The term *unmotivated* is often used pejoratively, as though a student's lack of success is his or her own fault. It fails to consider whether the environment has offered sufficient enticement for a student to produce desired behaviors and whether artificial enticements have been replaced by naturally occurring or intrinsic rewards.

Motivation Assessment Scale (MAS) A 16-item scale designed to assess the factors that motivate problem behavior. Informants estimate the frequency (*never* to *always*) with which an individual is likely to exhibit a specific behavior under specific circumstances. The MAS yields a ranking of four functions that maintain the behavior: sensory reinforcement, escape, attention, tangible. The MAS is used in functional behavioral assessment.

motivational interviewing (MI) A psychological technique that identifies and then uses an individual's personal goals and values to facilitate behavior change by exploring and discussing discrepancies between the individual's goals and the proposed behavior change.

motor aphasia *See* Broca's aphasia.

motor disorders Disorders of movement that involve a delay in the achievement of or a limitation in the performance of gross motor (posture and locomotion) or fine motor (eye–hand) skills.

Motor-Free Visual Perception Test–Third Edition (MFVPT-III) An individual test for visual perception in children and adults in which the tasks avoid motor involvement. It is especially useful for use with those who may have learning, motor, or cognitive disabilities. The test format is a visual multiple choice: The individual is shown a line drawing and is then asked to choose the matching drawing from a set of four on the following plate. Five categories of visual perception are measured: spatial relationship, visual closure, visual discrimination, visual memory, and figure ground. The raw score yields a perceptual age and a perceptual quotient. The MFVPT-III is appropriate for use with people ages 4–70.

motor function Functioning of the voluntary muscles of the body and the nerves that supply them. Important features are muscle mass, tone, and strength. Motor dysfunction is found in many forms of cerebral palsy. For example, in a right hemiplegia (paralysis of half of the body), muscle mass and strength are decreased on the right side compared with the left, but muscle tone is increased. The pattern of dysfunction is used to determine not only into which diagnostic category a person fits but also the location of the lesion (abnormality causing problems in function) in the nervous system. A knowledge of the level of a lesion in a case of myelomeningocele (protuberance of both the spinal cord and its lining) can be used to predict later functional levels in motor skills.

motor impersistence An impaired ability to maintain a motor position for an age-appropriate period of time. A number of tests have standardized norms for tasks such as standing on one foot, but the behavior may be observed spontaneously during the physical examination.

motor learning A set of processes associated with practice and experience that result in permanent changes in producing skilled action. A skilled instrumental musician exhibits very high levels of motor learning, as does a skilled diver.

motor memory The ability to recall distinct motor patterns (e.g., remembering letter formations and playing piano chords). Children with motor memory limitations may have trouble with handwriting. *See also* memory.

motor neuron disease An impairment of voluntary movement caused by the destruction of nerve cells involved in the motor pathway. In upper motor neuron disease, the motor nerve cells that are destroyed are in the brain; in lower motor neuron disease, they are in the spinal cord. Upper and lower motor neuron syndromes have different profiles of signs and symptoms.

motor overflow Involuntary movements that are associated with voluntary movements (e.g., sticking one's tongue out while writing). *See also* associated movements.

motor planning The ability to plan new or nonhabitual movements and then carry them out. *See also* praxis.

motor speech disorders Speech disorders that result from neurological impairments affecting motor planning, programming, neuromuscular control, or the execution of speech.

mouth breathing A behavior commonly secondary to nasal obstruction. When not associated with allergy and nasal obstruction, mouth breathing is sometimes related to intellectual disability.

mouth-opening finger-spreading phenomenon A test of associated movements in which the child's relaxed arms are draped over the examiner's extended forearm and the child is asked to close the eyes, open the mouth, and stick out the tongue. The degrees of extension and spreading of the fingers and spooning (hyperextension) are noted. Excessive response for one's age suggests nervous system immaturity.

mouthstick A piece of assistive technology; a stick that is held in the mouth and that has a nonskid covering or writing implement on the opposite end that enables a person to perform tasks such as writing or turning pages when it is not possible to do so using the arms.

Movement Assessment Battery for Children (Movement ABC) A physical skills assessment and program-planning instrument for use with children ages 4–12 years; it yields both quantitative and qualitative measures of manual dexterity, ball skills, and static (standing) and dynamic (moving) balance and offers guidelines for management.

Movement Assessment of Infants (MAI) A test used to evaluate and describe motor skills in infants from birth to 12 months of age; 65 items comprise four subtests of tone, primitive reflexes (reflexes specific to infants), automatic reactions, and voluntary movement.

movement disorders Conditions characterized by involuntary movements—including chorea (abnormal involuntary movements), athetosis (involuntary writhing), tremor, dystonia (variably abnormal muscle tone and movement), and tics—or a decrease or absence of normal movement. Movement disorders may be associated with neurological or developmental problems, such as cerebral palsy. These can be acute (generally precipitated by an identifiable event, such as an infection or brain injury) or chronic. Chronic disorders may be isolated, associated with progressive neurological deterioration (loss of skills), or found as part of a general disease. Movement disorders caused by medication often resolve after the medication is discontinued. Those caused by diffuse brain damage after brain injury or lack of oxygen to the brain tend to persist. There are many genetic movement disorders: Tourette syndrome, Wilson syndrome, juvenile Huntington disease, and Lesch-Nyhan syndrome. Some movement disorders, such as transient tics, resolve; others, such as the fine tremor of thyrotoxicosis (marked overactivity of the thyroid gland), respond to treatment of the underlying condition; still others do not respond to treatment and may worsen with age.

MPD *See* Minnesota Percepto-Diagnostic Test.

MPD Multiple personality disorder. *See* dissociative identity disorder.

M.P.H. *See* master of public health.

MPH *See* methylphenidate.

MPS *See* mucopolysaccharidoses.

MPS II *See* Hunter syndrome mucopolysaccharidosis II.

MPSI *See* Minneapolis Preschool Screening Instrument.

MR Mental retardation. *See* intellectual disability.

MR scans *See* magnetic resonance imaging.

MRA Mental retardation attendant. *See* behavior coach.

MRI *See* magnetic resonance imaging.

MR/ID Waiver *See* Mental Retardation/Intellectual Disability Waiver.

MRT6 *See* Metropolitan Readiness Tests–Sixth Edition.

MS *See* multiple sclerosis.

MSBP *See* Münchausen syndrome by proxy.

MSDD *See* multisystem developmental disorder.

MSEL *See* Mullen Scales of Early Learning.

MSS *See* Marinesco-Sjögren syndrome.

MST *See* McCarthy Screening Test.

MSUD *See* maple syrup urine disease.

M.S.W. Master of social work. *See also* social work.

MT *See* melatonin.

MT *See* metallothionein.

Muckle-Wells syndrome (MWS) An autosomal dominant genetic syndrome characterized by urticaria (hives), progressive sensorineural (involving the auditory nerve) deafness, and nephritis (kidney disease) due to a pathological process known as *amyloidosis* (accumulation of an abnormal protein called *amyloid* in the body); onset is typically in adolescence. MWS is considered a type of periodic fever syndrome and is caused by a defect in the *CIAS1* gene, which creates the protein cryopyrin. MWS is closely related to two other syndromes: familial cold urticaria and neonatal onset multisystem inflammatory disease.

mucoid ear *See* serous otitis media.

mucolipidoses A group of diseases characterized by physical findings similar to those of the mucopolysaccharidoses (MPS); there is a storage of mucopolysaccharides (complex carbohydrates) and other chemicals in the body tissues with normal levels of metabolites (chemical breakdown products) in the urine. There are four types (mucopolylipidoses I–IV); mucopolylipidosis II is also called I-cell (for inclusion cell) disease. In all of these disorders, an enzyme that enables the breakdown of mucopolysaccharides does not work; therefore, the mucopolysaccharides build up in the cells and cause damage. The resulting physical features include coarsening of the face, poor growth, enlarged liver and spleen, restricted joint mobility, and progressive mental deterioration. These disorders are generally inherited in an autosomal recessive manner and can be diagnosed by testing for enzyme activity or visualizing deposits of mucopolysaccharides and their products under the microscope. The course of the disorder is dependent upon the type of enzyme deficiency and can range from blindness and intellectual disability to death in childhood.

mucopolysaccharidoses (MPS) A group of heterogeneous (varied in expression) genetic syndromes in which excess mucopolysaccharide (a complex sugar) is stored in various body tissues and organs. Depending on the specific enzyme deficit, the severity, the time course, and the organ system involved, a variety of clinical pictures can result. Coarse, thickened facial features, stiff joints leading to a crouched jockey stance, growth deficiency, hepatosplenomegaly (enlargement of the liver and spleen), microcephaly (small head), corneal clouding (clouding of the clear outer coverings of the eyes), and intellectual disability can be present in diverse combinations and with varying degrees of severity depending on the specific type and subtype of enzyme deficiency: IH, Hurler; IS, Scheie; I H/S, Hurler-Scheie compound; II, Hunter; III, Sanfilippo (A, B, C, and D); IV, Morquio (A and B); V, formerly Scheie; VI, Maroteaux-Lamy; VII, Sly; and IX, hyaluronidase deficiency syndrome. Hunter syndrome is X-linked; all of the other MPS syndromes are autosomal recessive.

mucopolysaccharidosis (MPS) I H/S *See* Hurler-Scheie syndrome.

mucopolysaccharidosis (MPS) IH *See* Hurler syndrome.

mucopolysaccharidosis (MPS) III *See* Sanfilippo syndrome.

mucopolysaccharidosis (MPS) I-S *See* Scheie syndrome.

mucopolysaccharidosis (MPS) IV *See* Morquio syndrome.

mucopolysaccharidosis (MPS) VI *See* Maroteaux-Lamy syndrome.

mucopolysaccharidosis (MPS) VII   *See* Sly syndrome.

mucosulfatidosis   A condition with clinical features similar to those found in steroid sulfate sulfatase deficiency (ichthyosis, or severely dry, scaly skin), mucopolysaccharidoses (dysotosis multiplex [bone abnormalities], developmental delay, coarse facial features, hearing loss, and hepatosplenomegaly [enlarged liver and spleen]), and late infantile metachromatic leukodystrophy (motor weakness, developmental delay, demyelinization [loss of myelin, the insulation for nerve tracts in the white matter of the brain], and gliosis [scarring] of the white matter of the brain). Mucosulfatidosis presents during the first 2 years of life, and affected children gradually lapse into a vegetative state and die during the first decade. Inheritance is autosomal recessive.

Mullen Scales of Early Learning (MSEL) An individually administered, norm-referenced developmental assessment tool with five subscales that may be used independently: gross motor, visual reception, fine motor, expressive language, and receptive language. The MSEL is for use with children from birth to 5;9 years. It produces an Early Learning Composite score with a mean of 100 and a standard deviation of 15 and *T*-scores for the subscales.

multiaxial classification system   An approach to diagnosis that uses several different dimensions to compose the final formulation rather than reducing data to a single label or category. A case is characterized in terms of a number of clinically important factors rather than being assigned to a single diagnostic category. The *Diagnostic and Statistical Manual of Mental Disorders, Fourth Edition, Text Revision (DSM-IV-TR)*, has five axes: Axis I, the primary classification or diagnosis of a psychiatric syndrome; Axis II, an individual's developmental and personality disorders of childhood or adolescence that persist into adulthood; Axis III, possible physical or med-

ical disorders; Axis IV, the severity of psychosocial stressors in the recent past that may have contributed to the current clinical problem or may influence the course of treatment; and Axis V, a global assessment of adaptive functioning, with ratings made for both current functioning and the highest level of functioning during the past year.

multicultural education   Teaching that is geared toward a pluralistic (including many diverse groups) society. This concept includes both the impact of various cultures and ethnicities on society at large as well as an awareness of culturally diverse learning and behavior within the educational system.

multidisciplinary   Describing a team approach to the diagnosis and treatment of developmental disabilities; in a multidisciplinary team, the interactions among the professionals representing two or more disciplines are limited to each professional's independent case formulation within that profession's traditional boundaries.

Multidisciplinary Feeding Profile (MFP)   A numerical rating scale used to describe a variety of feeding-related behaviors in dependent individuals with severe disabilities. The scale takes 30–45 minutes to administer.

multidisciplinary team model   A model in which each specialist independently completes his or her portion of an augmentative and alternative communication (AAC) assessment and makes discipline-specific intervention decisions.

multifactorial   Describing a disorder caused by the interaction of multiple factors (e.g., genetic, environmental, psychological). Multifactorial contrasts with polygenic.

multifocal   In many places.

Multilevel Informal Language Inventory (MILI)   An informal language assessment for use with children from kindergarten through Grade 6 that uses survey scenes, survey stories, and other probes to assess critical semantic (meaning systems) relations and syntactic (language structure) constructions.

multiple carboxylase deficiency A family of inherited disorders characterized by enzyme defects that result in problems using the vitamin biotin. *See also* biotinidase deficiency.

multiple disabilities The coexistence of more than one disability in a single individual. The more severe a single disability, the more likely it is that a second disability will be present. The overall impact of multiple disabilities is greater than the impact of the sum of the individual disabilities.

multiple lentigines syndrome *LEOPARD syndrome.* An autosomal dominant genetic syndrome with lentigines (dark freckles), electrocardiographic (EKG) abnormalities (problems with heart rhythm), hypertelorism (widely spaced eyes), pulmonic stenosis (narrowing of the artery that conducts blood to the lungs), genital abnormalities, poor growth, and sensorineural (auditory nerve) hearing impairment. The syndrome is part of a group called Ras/MAPK pathway syndromes, multisystem diseases caused by a mutation in the protein tyrosine phosphatase, nonreceptor type 11 gene (*PTPN11*).

multiple personality disorder (MPD) *See* dissociative identity disorder.

multiple sclerosis (MS) A disease typically thought to affect only adults, MS has been diagnosed in children as young as 2 years. Neurological symptoms usually develop in children between 10 and 15 years of age, with symptoms beginning before age 10 in 20% of cases. MS is more prominent in females, with a sex ratio between 2:1 and 4:1. A progressive neurological disease characterized by demyelinating lesions (loss of white matter on

neuroimaging) and gradual loss of motor functions, MS frequently involves exacerbations (periods of getting worse) and remissions (periods of getting better). Loss of sensation and visual problems can occur. Death usually results from respiratory problems or infection. No cure or preventive measure is available, but treatment to shorten exacerbations of symptoms may be used.

multisystem developmental disorder (MSDD) A group of communicative, social-emotional, and sensory processing behaviors that characterize children under 2 years of age who may later qualify for a diagnosis of a pervasive developmental disorder. The diagnosis of MSDD derives from the *Diagnostic Classification of Mental Health Disorders of Infancy and Early Childhood (DC:0-3)*.

Muma Assessment Program (MAP) A nonstandardized, criterion-referenced "testing for teaching" assessment of cognitive linguistic communication systems for children from preschool through early elementary ages that taps different learning styles; sensorimotor skills; rule- and non–rule-governed learning; and concepts of conservation, quantity, and likeness.

mumps A communicable viral disease that causes inflammation of the salivary glands (parotid) and thus face and neck swelling. The testes may also be involved (which can lead to male sterility), and, rarely, the brain develops a mild encephalitis (inflammation). The disease is preventable through childhood immunization.

Münchausen syndrome by proxy (MSBP) A condition in which a child is presented for medical care with symptoms that are fabricated or produced by the caregiver. Significant maternal psychopathology is usually the cause. The syndrome is at one end of the spectrum of child abuse. Fictitious developmental disability symptoms have been reported. Münchausen syndrome (typically manufactured by the adult who concocts symptoms to obtain repeated and unnecessary surgical and medical procedures) is named after the 18th-century German raconteur Baron Karl Friedrich Hieronymous Münchausen (1720–1797), whose exploits were very exaggerated. *See also* factitious disorder.

murmur A soft sound; usually refers to an unusual heart sound that may be innocent (not indicative of heart disease) or pathological (indicative of heart disease). The presence of a heart murmur does not reflect the severity of any heart disease that may be present. Some childhood heart murmurs resolve spontaneously (are outgrown).

muscular dystrophy A group of genetic disorders that lead to progressive muscular atrophy (wasting) and weakness; the different types exhibit varying distribution, severity, and temporal evolution. When the respiratory muscles become involved, the disorder can become fatal. *See also* Becker muscular dystrophy.

Muscular Dystrophy Association (MDA) An organization that provides financial support, equipment, and other services to children and adults with a variety of neuromuscular disorders.

music therapy A treatment approach that uses music and movement in a variety of forms to modify behavior and to promote mental health, social development, emotional adjustment, and motor coordination. Used as a therapeutic tool in rehabilitation to meet recreational or educational goals, music therapy includes playing instruments, moving to music, creating music, singing, and listening to music. Music therapy is used in a variety of applications in hospitals, schools, institutions, and private settings through both individual and group approaches, often in conjunction with other types of therapy and/or rehabilitation. Both music education and music therapy contribute to special education by promoting learning and self-growth through enjoyable activities.

mutation A change in a gene such that the protein coded for by that gene is manufactured in a nonfunctional or dysfunctional form. Disorders inherited in an autosomal dominant manner are commonly caused by a mutation to a single gene.

mutual regulation Interpersonal interchanges in which the behavior of one person elicits a response from the second, and the response of the second determines the type and quality of another response from the first person; in other words, mutually determined responses based on those of the other.

MVPT-III *See* Motor Free Visual Perception Test–Third Edition.

MWS *See* Muckle-Wells syndrome.

Mycostatin *See* nystatin.

mydriasis Dilatation (expansion) of the pupil of the eye. Drops used by eye doctors to better examine the eye are known as *mydriatics.*

myelin basic protein (MBP) A biochemical marker of brain injury; increased levels of MBP in the cerebrospinal fluid (CSF; the fluid that surrounds the brain and spine) correlate with brain (white matter) damage and demyelinating (myelin-losing) disorders.

myelination The process of covering the axon (part of the nerve cell) with a sheet of myelin (a fatty insulation material), or the condition of having been coated with myelin. The rate of development can be slowed by delays or abnormalities in myelination.

myelomeningocele *meningomyelocele, spina bifida.* A congenital (from birth) defect of the spinal column resulting in the protrusion of the spinal cord and its coverings (meninges) from an infant's back. There

myelomeningocele

are varying levels of functional impairment (motor paralysis and sensory loss) depending on the size and level of the protruding sac along the spine. The condition is also associated with hydrocephalus (excess fluid in the brain) and a variable degree of cognitive impairment. Long-term considerations include ambulation (walking) and bowel/bladder control, which can also be impaired. *See also* diastematomyelia, diplomyelia, dysraphism.

myoclonic-astatic *See* Lennox-Gastaut syndrome.

myoclonus *epileptic myoclonus.* Synchronous, small, recurring twitches that generally occur in the fingers and hands and are associated with chronic seizure disorders such as Lennox-Gastaut syndrome. Myoclonic movements are preceded by abnormalities of the electroencephalogram (EEG). These movements are associated with viral encephalitis (brain inflammation), metabolic disturbances such as uremia (found in kidney disease), and progressive cerebral (brain) degenerative diseases.

myoclonus Rapid and sudden unpredictable motor jerks that are involuntary. These are present in some kinds of seizures but are not always the result of seizure activity. They may occur normally when one is falling asleep or with hiccups (i.e., myoclonus of the diaphragm).

myopathy A disease of the muscle, such as muscular dystrophy.

myopia Nearsightedness, or difficulty seeing far away. Myopia can be corrected by minus diopter (concave) lenses. A child with myopia typically squints and cannot see the blackboard.

myotactic reflex *See* stretch reflex.

myotonic dystrophy *Steinert syndrome.* An extremely variable genetic syndrome that represents a type of muscular dystrophy with mild motor symptoms and cataracts. Apathetic facies, a "hatchet face," or a "lugubrious" appearance have been described in Steinert syndrome in addition to dysarthria (difficulty pronouncing words). Intellectual disability is rare, but learning disabilities are common. Inheritance is autosomal dominant. Myotonic dystrophy-1 (DM1) is caused by a trinucleotide repeat expansion (CTG) in the dystrophia myotonica protein kinase gene on chromosome 19q13. A length exceeding 50 CTG repeats is pathogenic. Myotonic dystrophy-2 is caused by a mutation in the *ZNF9* gene on chromosome 3q. When the syndrome is suspected, prenatal diagnosis is possible. Incidence is approximately 1 in 10,000.

myringotomy A surgical incision in the tympanic membrane (eardrum) to relieve pressure and allow fluid drainage from the middle ear; it is usually accompanied by the insertion of a tube (PE [pressure-equalizing] tube) designed to equalize pressure and prevent fluid buildup.

Mysoline *See* primidone.

myxedema A condition that includes edema (excess fluid retention), puffiness, fatigue, weight gain, apathy, and sluggish tendon reflexes resulting from hypothyroidism.

myxovirus One of a ribonucleic acid (RNA) group of viruses that can produce respiratory disorders but that also includes the viruses for measles and mumps.

MZ twins *See* monozygotic twins.

Nn

NACD *See* The National Academy for Child Development.

NACHRI *See* National Association of Children's Hospitals and Related Institutions.

NAD *See* National Association for the Deaf.

NAEYC *See* National Association for the Education of Young Children.

NAFCC *See* National Association for Family Child Care.

NAGC *See* National Association for Gifted Children.

Nager syndrome *acrofacial dysostosis type 1.* A combination of mandibular hypoplasia (underdeveloped mid-face), molar hypoplasia (underdeveloped molar teeth), radial/ thumb hypoplasia, conductive deafness and articulation (speech pronunciation) problems, cleft lip, cleft palate, typical intelligence, downslanting palpebral fissures, micrognathia (small jaw), partial to total absence of lower eyelashes, and preauricular (in front of the ears) skin tags. Some individuals also have attention-deficit/hyperactivity disorder (ADHD).

naltrexone Trade name, ReVia. An opiate antagonist used to treat addiction to alcohol or opiates. It may help reduce repetitive or self-injurious behaviors in people with developmental disorders.

narcolepsy A neurological disorder characterized by sleep/wake instability that results in both excessive daytime sleepiness and fragmented, poor-quality nighttime sleep. Other features may include cataplexy (temporary loss of muscle tone with strong emotion, especially laughter), sleep paralysis (temporary inability to move on awakening), and hypnogogic and hypnopompic (occurring either when an individual is just falling asleep or just waking up) hallucinations. These other features are the result of sleep characteristics such as the normal loss of muscle tone that occurs during rapid eye movement (REM) sleep (the stage in which the most vivid dreams occur) or dreaming that intrudes into wakefulness. Narcolepsy has been associated with a deficiency of hypocretin (also called *orexin;* a signaling chemical within the central nervous system). Several medication treatments are available, including stimulants to help maintain wakefulness.

nares Openings in the nose, also known as *nostrils.*

narrative A type of text that possesses its own organizational structure and whose purpose is to relate a string of events (i.e., a story).

nasal Describing articulation that is produced by closing the oral cavity to prevent air from escaping through the mouth, lowering the velum (soft palate), and allowing air a free passage through the nose (e.g., /n/, /m/).

nasal   Pertaining to the nose.

nasal bridge   The portion of the nose that lies directly between the eyes. A low (deep-set) nasal bridge contributes to the appearance of a saddle nose; a high nasal bridge leads to a beaked nose.

nasal bridge

nasal cannula   A tube with openings placed in the nostrils to administer oxygen.

nasal emission   Measurable air that escapes through the nose during consonant production.

nasal septum   The bony and cartilaginous partition between the nasal passages.

nasion   The root of the nose, where the nose meets the frontal bone or forehead.

NASN   *See* National Association of School Nurses.

nasoendoscopy   A procedure in which fiberoptic equipment is threaded through the nasal passages in order to examine the nose, the soft palate (the structure at the back of the throat), and the pharynx (the passage connecting the nose and mouth to the esophagus or upper gut). Nasoendoscopy also may be used to evaluate speech and swallowing.

nasogastric tube   *NG tube.* A feeding tube that goes through the nose into the stomach. NG tubes are intended for short-term use; if prolonged tube feeding is anticipated, a gastrostomy (surgical placement of a G tube directly into the stomach through the abdominal wall) should be considered.

nasogastric tube

nasopalpebral reflex   Nose–eyelid reflex. An infant reflex in which a tap on the bridge of the nose (stimulus) produces bilateral blinking (response).

NASW   *See* National Association of Social Workers.

The National Academy for Child Development (NACD)   An organization that promotes the use of patterning; sound stimulation; oral appliances; cranial manipulative techniques; hormonal supplements; nutrition (diets and additives); Fast ForWord; and treatment of food allergies, yeast infection, and environmental toxins to facilitate the development of children, particularly those with Down syndrome and other neurodevelopmental disorders. Many of the techniques advocated lack either a solid scientific base or valid efficacy studies. *See also* patterning.

National Association for Family Child Care (NAFCC)   A nonprofit organization dedicated to promoting quality child care by strengthening the profession of family child care. Its stated goals are to strengthen state and local associations as the primary support systems for individual family child care providers; promote a professional accreditation program that recognizes and encourages quality care for children; represent family child care providers by advocating for their needs and collaborating with other organizations; promote the diversity of the family child care profession through training, state and local associations, public education, and board membership; and deliver effective programs through strong organizational management. NAFCC represents the profession of family child care at the national level as an advocate on issues of public policy. It publishes a quarterly newsletter, *The National Perspective.*

National Association for Gifted Children (NAGC)   An organization that pursues improved education of the gifted (those who have superior general intellectual ability) and sponsors programs to enhance such children's creative potential and capacity for individual thought. The NAGC publishes *Gifted Child Quarterly.*

National Association for the Deaf (NAD) An organization that is open to all adults with profound hearing impairment and other interested individuals. The organization is active in legislative advocacy for the protection of the civil rights of people with profound hearing impairments in such areas as employment, communication, and citizenship. The NAD maintains a speakers bureau and a legal defense fund and also offers educational, therapeutic, and vocational services to its members. It provides training in communication and publishes newsletters and educational materials.

National Association for the Education of Young Children (NAEYC) A national not-for-profit organization founded in 1926 and dedicated to improving the quality of educational and developmental services for children from birth through age 8. NAEYC is committed to becoming an increasingly high-performing and inclusive organization. It is composed of 90,000 members as well as a national network of more than 300 local, state, and regional affiliates and a growing global alliance of like-minded organizations. NAEYC publishes *Young Children,* a peer-reviewed, professional journal; and *Teaching Young Children,* a magazine for preschool educators.

National Association of Children's Hospitals and Related Institutions (NACHRI) A not-for-profit organization of children's hospitals with members in the United States, Canada, Australia, the United Kingdom, Italy, China, Mexico, and Puerto Rico. NACHRI promotes the health and well-being of children and their families through support of children's hospitals and health systems that are committed to excellence in providing health care to children. It does so through advocacy, education, research, and health promotion.

National Association of School Nurses (NASN) A national, not-for-profit specialty nursing organization that represents school nurses exclusively. Its mission is to support the health and educational success of children and youth by developing and providing leadership to advance school nursing practice by specialized registered nurses. NASN publishes *Journal of School Nursing.*

National Association of Social Workers (NASW) The national professional organization of social workers, whose function is to promote the professional development of social work and social workers, establish and maintain professional standards of practice, promulgate and administer professional ethics boards, and certify advanced-level practice competency. NASW publishes *Social Work.*

National Center for Education in Maternal and Child Health (NCEMCH) NCEMCH provides national leadership to the maternal and child health community in three key areas: program development, education, and state-of-the-art knowledge to improve the health and well-being of the nation's children and families. NCEMCH collaborates with a broad range of federal agencies, corporate and philanthropic partners, professional organizations, and academic institutions to 1) launch national health initiatives involving multiple partners; 2) develop and disseminate culturally competent child health and development materials for families and professionals; and 3) provide a virtual maternal and child health library of state-of-the-art knowledge and information services for health professionals, educators, researchers, policy makers, service providers, business leaders, families, and the public.

National Center for Learning Disabilities (NCLD) An organization that promotes public awareness of learning disabilities, neurological disorders, and related impairments that can be a barrier to literacy. The NCLD provides resources and referrals on a national level to volunteers, parents, and professionals. It is active in grant making, legislative advocacy, training seminars, and dissemination of information about learning disabilities to the public. The NCLD publishes several newsletters, a list of recommended readings, various training materials, and other resources for parents and professionals.

National Council on Family Relations (NCFR) A professional organization of family researchers, educators, and practitioners who share in the development and dissemination of knowledge about families and family relationships, establish professional standards, and work to promote family well-being. NCFR sponsors the Certified Family Life Educator (CFLE) program, a national program to provide professionals with coursework and experience in family life education, including formal teaching, community education, curriculum and resource development, health care, military family support, counseling, and ministry. NCFR publishes *Family Relations* and *Journal of Marriage and Family.*

National Down Syndrome Congress (NDSC) A national organization of parents and professionals that disseminates information and assists with referrals. Many local Down syndrome family associations are affiliated with this organization, which publishes *Down Syndrome News.*

National Drug Code (NDC) A unique identifier for human drugs that is used by pharmacy programs such as Medicaid and Medicare Part D to identify particular drugs.

National Dysphagia Diet **(NDD)** A publication that establishes standard terminology and practice applications for dietary needs in dysphagia management.

National Early Childhood Technical Assistance Center (NECTAC) A programmatic unit of the U.S. Department of Education's Office of Special Education Programs (OSEP) whose mission is to provide technical assistance to states in order to strengthen service systems to ensure that children with disabilities ages birth through 5 years and their families receive and benefit from high-quality, culturally appropriate, family-centered supports and services.

National Education Association (NEA) The largest professional organization in the United States for teachers at all levels of education. The primary focus of the NEA is the rights and welfare of teachers; it functions predominantly as a teachers union. The NEA also advocates for improved education for all people, including those with disabilities; maintains a governmental relations unit and a political action network; and endorses candidates for national office.

National Information Center for Children and Youth with Disabilities (NICHCY) A programmatic unit of the U.S. Department of Education's Office of Special Education Programs (OSEP), the NICHCY is a central information center for states and individuals regarding 1) disabilities in children and youth; 2) programs and services for infants, children, and youth with disabilities; 3) the Individuals with Disabilities Education Act (IDEA) of 1990 (PL 101-476), the nation's special education law, and its amendments; 4) the No Child Left Behind Act (NCLB) of 2001 (PL 107-110), the nation's general education law; and 5) research-based information on effective practices for children with disabilities.

National Institute of Child Health and Human Development (NICHD) A division of the National Institutes of Health, the NICHD was initially charged with supporting the world's best minds in investigating human development throughout the life span, focusing on understanding developmental disabilities (including intellectual disability) and illuminating important events that occur during pregnancy. This mission has evolved to ensuring that 1) every person is born healthy and wanted; 2) women suffer no harmful effects from reproductive processes; 3) all children have the chance to achieve their full potential for healthy and productive lives, free from disease or disability; and 4) the health, productivity, independence, and well-being of all people is maximized through optimal rehabilitation. To carry out its mission, the NICHD provides funding for a number of research networks, center programs, career development programs, and research initiatives.

National Institute of Mental Health (NIMH) A division of the National Institutes of Health, NIMH's mission is to transform the understanding and treatment of mental illnesses through basic and clinical research, paving the way for prevention, recovery, and cure. In support of these goals, NIMH seeks to generate research and promote research training to fulfill four objectives: 1) promoting discovery in the brain and behavioral sciences to fuel research on the causes of mental disorders; 2) charting mental illness trajectories to determine when, where, and how to intervene; 3) developing new and better interventions that incorporate the diverse needs and circumstances of people with mental illnesses; and 4) strengthening the public health impact of NIMH-supported research. NIMH also provides technical assistance to state and local mental health agencies. Seven distinct divisions support these efforts: 1) the Division of Neuroscience and Basic Behavioral Science (DNBBS), 2) the Division of Adult Translational Research and Treatment Development (DATR), 3) the Division of Developmental Translational Research, 4) the Division of AIDS and Health and Behavior Research (DAHBR), 5) the Division of Services and Intervention Research (DSIR), 6) the Division of Extramural Activities, and 7) the Division of Intramural Research Programs (DIRP).

National Institute on Disability and Rehabilitation Research (NIDRR) One of three components of the U.S. Department of Education's Office of Special Education and Rehabilitative Services (OSERS), NIDRR operates in concert with the Rehabilitation Services Administration (RSA) and the Office of Special Education Programs (OSEP). Its stated mission is 1) to generate new knowledge and promote its effective use to improve the abilities of people with disabilities to perform activities of their choice in the community and 2) to expand society's capacity to provide full opportunities and accommodations for its citizens with disabilities. To meet these goals, NIDRR conducts comprehensive and coordinated programs of research, training, and related activities in such areas as employment, health and functioning, technology for access and functioning, independent living and community integration, and other associated disability research areas.

National Institutes of Health (NIH) A federal agency that supports and conducts research into the causes and prevalence of diseases and furnishes information to health professionals and the general public. It is composed of 27 institutes, including the Eunice Kennedy Shriver National Institute of Child Health and Human Development (NICHD), the National Institute on Deafness and Other Communication Disorders (NIDCD), and the National Institute of Neurological Disorders and Stroke (NINDS).

National Organization for Rare Disorders (NORD) A federation of 140 nonprofit, volunteer health organizations dedicated to helping people with rare diseases and assisting the organizations that serve them. A rare disease is one that affects fewer than 200,000 people in the United States. Yet all together, more than 6,000 rare disorders affect approximately 25 million Americans. NORD is committed to identifying, treating, and curing rare disorders through programs of education, advocacy, research, and service. NORD is the primary nongovernmental clearinghouse for information on rare disorders. It also provides referrals to additional sources of assistance and ongoing support.

National Professional Development Center on Inclusion (NPDCI) A unit of the National Information Center for Children and Youth with Disabilities (NICHCY) the NPDCI is a project of the Special Education Technical Assistance and Dissemination Network (TA&D) funded by the U.S. Department of Education, Office of Special Education and Rehabilitative Services (OSERS), to work with states to create a system of professional development for early childhood personnel to support inclusion in education.

National Society of Genetic Counselors (NSGC) The professional organization representing genetic counselors. It includes a special interest group on disabilities.

natural environment An environment (e.g., home, child care) in which a child would ordinarily be regardless of a disability. Federal law mandates that early intervention services be provided in natural environments. *See also* Individuals with Disabilities Education Improvement Act (IDEA) of 2004 (PL 108-446).

natural language Children's attempts to produce adult words. These attempts are not random with respect to approximation or error but seem to follow distinct processes. Limitations (physical, mental, and experiential) that prevent correct pronunciation lessen as a child matures and develops increased greater intellectual abilities. The term *natural language* is also used to describe oral communication in the daily life experiences of a child.

natural proportion The element of full inclusion that requires students with disabilities to be placed in general classrooms at a rate consistent with the incidence rate of the disability within the student population. For example, the more students there are with Down syndrome, the more students with Down syndrome should be in general classrooms.

naturalistic approach An instructional approach that uses the immediate, natural environment as the basis for language instruction and intervention.

NBAS Neonatal Behavioral Assessment Scale. *See* Brazelton Neonatal Behavioral Assessment Scale.

NCEMCH *See* National Center for Education in Maternal and Child Health.

NCFR *See* National Council on Family Relations.

NCLB *See* No Child Left Behind Act of 2001 (PL 107-110).

NCLD *See* National Center for Learning Disabilities.

NCS *See* nerve conduction study.

NCV *See* nerve conduction velocity.

NDA *See* neurodevelopmental assessment.

NDC *See* National Drug Code.

NDD *See National Dysphagia Diet.*

NDDs *See* neurodevelopmental disorders.

NDSC *See* National Down Syndrome Congress.

NDT *See* neurodevelopmental therapy.

NE *See* norepinephrine.

NEA *See* National Education Association.

NEC *See* necrotizing enterocolitis.

neck extensor hypertonia Increased muscle resistance in infants younger than 6 months of age based on increasing muscle tone that develops on repeatedly flexing the head. Neck extensor hypertonia may be an early sign of motor disability.

neck righting reaction A normal developmental reaction first noted shortly after birth when the infant, placed in a prone position (lying on the stomach), lifts his or her head off the floor enough to clear the nose and mouth. Normal head righting is seen in the side-lying position and later supine (lying on the back) at approximately 4 months and 5–6 months, respectively. The neonatal neck righting reflex is followed by the neck on body reaction: When the head is turned by an examiner, or when the infant turns his or her head to the side, segmental rotation starts at the head and proceeds in a cephalocaudal (head to toe) direction. By age 5 years head turning no longer stimulates this response. In general, involuntary righting reactions remain throughout life but are modified by voluntary responses in the person.

necrotizing enterocolitis (NEC) A condition that occurs in preterm infants in which parts of the bowel become ischemic (characterized by a decreased blood supply), potentially leading to ileus (bowel paralysis), perforation, and peritonitis (massive infection). Surgical treatment may include colectomy (surgical removal of part of the bowel) and colostomy (creation of a sometimes temporary surgical opening to the bowel through which feces is removed).

NECTAC *See* National Early Childhood Technical Assistance Center.

negative oculocephalic reflex *See* doll's eye sign.

negative practice A form of punishment that requires the individual to perform or engage in a maladaptive behavior so many times that it becomes aversive to him or her. For example, if a child plays with matches, one can have the child light several hundred matches in succession.

negative reinforcement Increasing a behavior when the aversive consequence following it is removed.

negative sentence A type of sentence that rejects or denies an affirmation.

negligence Failure to meet responsibility; omission or forgetfulness.

Nellhaus chart Composite international and interracial head circumference graphs for boys and girls from birth to 18 years of age. The name derives from Gerhard Nellhaus, who pooled data from numerous other studies to produce this chart.

neologism A word substitution or mispronunciation that may indicate underlying language problems. Neologisms may be structural (*coptiheler* for *helicopter*), phonological (*brad* for *bread*), or semantic (*pull on* for *boots*). Structural neologisms usually occur along with other difficulties in organizing semantic relations, semantic neologisms often reflect a problem in understanding perceptual and functional attributes of words, and phonological neologisms occur frequently with auditory misperceptions. Phonological neologisms are not as strong an indication of extensive language difficulties as are structural and semantic neologisms.

neonatal Pertaining to newborns, especially in the first 28 days of life.

Neonatal Behavioral Assessment Scale (NBAS) *See* Brazelton Neonatal Behavioral Assessment Scale.

neonatal intensive care unit (NICU) A designation applied to a range of regionalized hospital-based services used to diagnose and treat perinatal problems. There are three levels of NICU. Level I provides for resuscitation, observation, and stabilization; relatively uncomplicated deliveries and normal newborns are accommodated at such hospitals. Level III centers have the ability to handle complicated deliveries and the pediatric subspecialty staff to support severely premature infants; teaching and research are usually carried out at such centers. Level II hospitals are intermediate between Levels I and III with regard to the services available.

neonatal neck righting *log rolling, nuchal righting.* A primitive (infant) reflex in which turning the head to one side (stimulus) causes the body to follow along as though it were a log or all of one piece (response). This pattern must break up into a segmental rolling response (with the body following one part after another instead of all at once) before voluntary rolling over can emerge. Persistent neck righting can accompany severe hypertonia (increased muscle tone) and related neuromotor disorders.

Neonatal Neurological Examination (NNE) A brief qualitative assessment of habituation (decreasing responsiveness to a repeated stimulus), movement, tone, reflexes, and neurobehavioral items in preterm and full-term newborn infants, with items scored in terms of maturity (what age the infant seems to be on assessment) and normality (absence of negative neurological signs or symptoms).

Neonatal Oral-Motor Assessment Scale (NOMAS) A brief 42-item semiquantitative scale that rates tongue and jaw responses in newborns during nonnutritive (nonfeeding) and nutritive (feeding) sucking.

neonatal seizures Seizures that occur during the neonatal period (the first 28 days of life). Manifestations of seizures in neonates may be subtle and include lip smacking, eye deviation (eyes fixing in a particular direction), or blinking; or they may include more motor involvement, such as pedaling movements ("bicycling") or tonic (increased muscle tone) extension of the extremities (similar to stretching). Tonic seizures have a poorer prognosis, as they are often associated with intraventricular hemorrhage (bleeding into the brain). Neonatal seizures may also be caused by hypoxic-ischemic encephalopathy (brain damage due to lack of oxygen), hypoglycemia (low blood sugar level), hypocalcemia (low blood calcium), infection (e.g., meningitis [infection of the brain]), drug withdrawal, or abnormal formation of the brain. The outcome of neonatal seizures is related to the underlying etiology (cause), with reversible problems such as hypocalcemia having a better developmental outcome than, for example, intraventricular hemorrhage.

neonatal withdrawal syndrome Infants of substance-abusing mothers (ISAMs) may exhibit the following acronymic "withdrawal" syndrome: *w*akefulness, *i*rritability, *t*remulousness, *t*achypnea (rapid breathing), *h*yperactivity, *h*igh-pitched cry, *h*yperreflexia (increased reflexes), *d*iaphoresis (sweating), *d*iarrhea, *r*espiratory distress, *r*hinorrhea (runny nose), *a*pnea (pauses in breathing), *a*utonomic nervous system dysfunction (poor temperature control), *w*eight loss, respiratory *a*lkalosis (alteration of the body's acid–base balance due to a loss of acid from the rapid breathing), *l*acrimation (excess tears), and seizures.

neonate A newborn.

NEPSY–Second Edition (NEPSY-II) A neuropsychological assessment for use with children 3–16 years. The NEPSY-II produces standard scores for attention/executive functions, language, visuospatial processing, sensorimotor functions, and memory and learning. There are forms for children 3–4 and 5–16 years of age. Administration time for these forms are 90 minutes and 2–3 hours, respectively.

nerve block A procedure in which an anesthetic agent is injected into a nerve or the muscle surrounding a nerve to produce local or regional anesthesia (numbness) in the area supplied by the nerve. This technique can be used to predict the orthopedic outcome of surgery in which the nerve is cut.

nerve conduction study (NCS) Measurement of the speed with which a signal travels along a nerve. An NCS is performed by stimulating the nerve and measuring the difference in time between the stimulus and muscle contraction (also known as the *nerve conduction velocity* [NCV]). NCVs are reduced in diseases that damage the myelin (fatty insulation material) sheath; they are normal in muscular diseases. *See also* nerve conduction velocity (NCV).

nerve conduction velocity (NCV) A neurophysiological measure of the speed with which electrical impulses travel along the path of specific nerves; this measure is used to help distinguish muscle problems due to peripheral nerve disorders from those due to disorders of the muscles themselves. *See also* nerve conduction study (NCS).

nerve deafness *See* sensorineural hearing impairment (SNHI).

nervous breakdown A nonmedical, non-specific (lay) term for a sudden-onset mental disorder. When conducting family histories, one can encounter a history of "nerves" or "nervous breakdowns" in extended family members that often span several generations. This anecdotal observation may weakly support the familial transmission of neurological disorders that manifest as both psychological and learning problems, leaving the affected individual more vulnerable to stress and an acute breakdown from an inability to cope with the stress. Many people with developmental disorders are more vulnerable to "breakdowns" from excess stress.

nervous system The body's communication network. It consists of two divisions: 1) the central nervous system (CNS), or brain and spinal cord; and 2) the peripheral nervous system, or the nerves that communicate between the CNS and the rest of the body and that function by responding to the environment outside of the body in a coordinated manner.

NESS *See* Neurological Examination of Subtle Signs.

networking The use of formal and informal linkages of people and resources for the purpose of facilitating access to services, skills, contacts, and knowledge.

neural efficiency In people with cerebral palsy, the difference in muscle response between electronic stimulation of muscles and voluntary stimulation or movement.

neural plasticity The ability of the brain to make changes (usually in terms of repair or recovery after brain injury) that affect the individual's functional capability. The degree of plasticity decreases with age.

neural tube The brain and the spinal cord in early fetal development. Nerve cells migrate to form folds that fuse together and create the neural tube, leading to the development of the brain and spinal cord. Defects in the development of the neural tube occur very early in fetal development and produce a range of neural tube defects (NTDs) such as anencephaly (no brain with absent top of skull) and myelomeningocele (protuberance of both the spinal cord and its lining from the back) in the cephalocaudal (head to tail) direction and holoprosencephaly (fused halves of the brain) and craniospinal rachischisis (congenital spinal column fissure or split) in the caudocephalal (front to back) direction. These result in various forms of developmental disabilities (e.g., intellectual disability, learning disabilities) and medical problems (e.g., paralyzed bladder).

neuroanatomy The study of the structure of the nervous system including not only gross structures (what can be seen with the eye) but also microscopic ones.

neuro-assisted augmentative and alternative communication A type of augmentative and alternative communication (AAC) that uses bioelectrical signals such as muscle-action potentials to activate and display messages on a computer monitor.

neurochemical Having to do with the chemical makeup and function of the nervous system, including the effects of chemicals on the functioning and structure of the nervous system.

neurocutaneous syndromes *See* phakomatoses.

neurodegenerative disorders A broad group of rare disorders in children that are also sometimes referred to as *neurodegenerative diseases.* Typically genetic in nature, these disorders result in the progressive loss of motor or cognitive function. Other neurodegenerative disorders are metabolic in nature and may be called *neurometabolic disorders.* In general there is no known treatment for most of these diseases, and they are irreversible. *See also* degenerative disorders.

neurodevelopmental assessment (NDA) A clinical evaluation by a board-certified developmental pediatrician to diagnose the presence, etiology (cause), and severity of a developmental disability. The assessment battery includes a medical and developmental history, a physical examination (including identification of dysmorphic [atypical physical] features), an expanded neurological examination (including, e.g., primitive [infant] reflexes and signs of minor neurological dysfunction), and an evaluation of developmental levels. The NDA may be the sole battery conducted on a preschool-age child, but with a school-age child it is almost always supplemented by psychological and educational testing.

neurodevelopmental disorders (NDDs) *neurodevelopmental disabilities, static encephalopathies.* A group of disorders that originate from abnormal brain functioning and that are characterized by delayed or impaired development of typical brain functions. They include disorders of cognition (slow learning, intellectual disability), movement (cerebral palsy, developmental coordination disorder), language (speech delay, aphasia, apraxia), attention (attention-deficit/ hyperactivity disorder), and processing (dyslexia, dyscalculia, dysgraphia, and other learning disabilities) and autism spectrum disorders. These disorders originate from sometimes subtle alterations of brain functioning rather than from altered brain structures. NDDs are sometimes grouped separately under the spectrum and the continuum of developmental disabilities.

neurodevelopmental therapy (NDT) A system of physical therapy for the treatment of cerebral palsy. Devised by physical therapist Berta Bobath (1907–1991) and physician Karl Bobath (1906–1991), the NDT approach interprets the abnormal tone, movement, and posture of cerebral palsy as secondary to a failure of primitive reflexive patterns (which are normal in infants) to integrate or due to the presence of abnormal postures or movement. Training and certification are available for physical and occupational therapists, but the approach can be used by parents, teachers, and anyone who works with and interacts with children with motor impairment. Sometimes referred to as the *Bobath method.*

neurofibromatosis (NF) *von Recklinghausen disease.* A genetic syndrome characterized by café au lait spots (more than five "coffee with milk"–colored skin patches of at least 1.5 cm in diameter in older children and at least 0.5 cm in younger children), neurofibromas (tumors of the skin, brain, or optic [vision] or auditory [hearing] nerves), and bone lesions. Axillary (armpit) and groin freckling may occur; the number of café au lait spots, neurofibromas, and secondary symptoms all tend to increase with age. Lisch nodules (pigmented specks) in the iris (the colored part of the eye) visible on ophthalmological examination can help to clarify the diagnosis. Intellectual disability occurs in approximately 10% of cases and seizures in approximately 5% of cases. The orthopedic, visual, and auditory complications of NF suggest that routine follow-up in a multidisciplinary specialty NF clinic may be advisable. Incidence is 1 in 3,000. The gene for NF type 1 is localized to chromosome 17q11.2 and is called *neurofibromin*. Inheritance is autosomal dominant, with a high occurrence of spontaneous mutations (50%); recurrence risk is 50%. NF type 1 has been called *classical NF;* NF type 2 is associated with vestibular schwannomas (tumors of the nerves responsible for hearing and equilibrium) and other nervous system tumors. The gene for NF type 2 encodes neurofibromin-2 (NF2), which is also called *merlin,* on chromosome 22q12.2.

neurogenetic disorders A group of diseases that involve the nervous system and have a genetic cause. Although many neurogenetic disorders are autosomal recessive in nature, they may also be inherited in other ways. Such disorders tend to be rare, and many present in infancy or early childhood. Some are degenerative (having symptoms that worsen over time) in nature. Examples include disorders such as MERRF (myoclonic epilepsy with red ragged fibers), which is a mitochondrial disorder, and Batten disease, an autosomal recessive disorder characterized by a buildup of lipopigments (fat and protein) in the cells that can present at any age.

neurogenic stuttering An acquired disfluency of speech characterized by sound or syllable repetitions, prolongations, hesita-

tions, and/or blocking caused by central nervous system disease or pathology.

neuroimaging *See* brain imaging.

neuroleptic malignant syndrome A possible side effect to neuroleptic drugs (antipsychotic medications) that includes rigidity, fever, sweating, hypertension (high blood pressure), and altered consciousness, with a 20% mortality rate.

neuroleptics Medications typically used to treat psychosis. Neuroleptics block dopamine (a chemical used for signaling within the brain) but also interact with histamine, acetylcholine, and norepinephine (brain chemicals) receptors. They have also been used to treat stereotypy (repetitive movements and behaviors), aggression, and labile affect (changeable moods). Long-term side effects include tardive dyskinesia (a severe movement disorder) and weight gain.

neurolinguistic programming (NLP) A controversial communication model of behavior and therapy based on human channels of perceiving and processing information. NLP assesses the way in which information is received through the five senses, the organization of the data through verbal and nonverbal linguistic channels, and the output of information and its ultimate impact on communication. Although this method is very popular, supporting research is lacking.

neurological assessment Examination of the nervous system of the body, including a systematic evaluation of the function of each component of the central and peripheral nervous systems. The following are assessed: 1) cranial nerves, 2) motor function, 3) sensory function, 4) reflexes, 5) the cerebellum (the part of the brain that contributes to balance and the coordination of complex movements), and 6) mental status (level of alertness and cognitive function) and speech. Abnormalities may indicate an etiology (cause) for a developmental problem and/or suggest necessary additional testing. An evaluation specific to a child with developmental disabilities can be performed by a neurodevelopmental pediatrician or a child neurologist. All children who have or are suspected of having developmental disabilities should undergo a detailed neurological assessment.

Neurological Assessment of the Preterm and Full-Term Newborn Infant A standardized clinical assessment used to document changes in the neurological examination in the newborn period.

Neurological Examination of Subtle Signs (NESS) A battery of soft neurological signs (abnormalities in speed or quality of performance of certain motor tasks that tend to be present in children with neurodevelopmental disabilities) that allows for comparisons of children at different ages.

neurometabolic disorders A group of metabolic disorders (genetically caused disorders of body chemistry) that impact on the function of the brain and can produce central nervous system dysfunction and neurodevelopmental disability. Often progressive, these disorders can lead to death.

neurometrics Computerized mapping and analysis of auditory evoked potentials (increased areas of brain activity corresponding to an auditory stimulus) that can be visually displayed using, for example, brain electrical activity mapping (BEAM). This research approach to brain localization has been applied to a variety of cognitive and psychiatric disorders.

neuromuscular Pertaining to the joint functioning of muscles and nerves; neuromotor.

neuromuscular electrical stimulation (NMES) The use of electrical stimulation to contract and strengthen the muscles of people with cerebral palsy.

neuromuscular reflex therapy *See* patterning.

neuron The nerve cell that comprises a cell body and a "tail" called the *axon*. Within a nerve cell, a message is passed from the cell body to the axon by a change in electrical potential that stimulates the release of the chemicals (neurotransmitters) responsible for passing the message from neuron to neuron across the synapse (gap between the axon of one neuron and the dendrites [branches] of the cell body of another). When killed, nerve cells do not regenerate.

neuronal migration disorders A group of congenital brain abnormalities that arise from defective formation of the central nervous system. During early brain development, neurons follow intricate and complicated pathways to the sites where they need to be in order to function (a process known as *neuronal migration*). Failure to migrate appropriately can produce gross brain malformation or heterotopia (layers of cells in the wrong place in the brain). Most people with neuronal migration disorders exhibit epilepsy and intellectual disability.

neuron-specific enolase (NSE) A biochemical marker for brain injury; increased levels of NSE in the cerebrospinal fluid (CSF) correlate with neuronal (grey matter) damage.

Neurontin *See* gabapentin.

neuropathy Disease of the peripheral nerves (those that communicate between the brain and spinal cord and the rest of the body).

neuropeptide A chemical made up of linked amino acids (the basic building blocks of proteins) that is used for signaling in the nervous system, typically in the brain.

neurophakomatoses *See* phakomatoses.

neurophysiological psychology An approach to treating neurodevelopmental disorders as well as some emotional conditions that examines children for persisting primitive reflexes and then pursues a course of physical education to diminish the reflex patterns and alleviate the developmental and behavioral symptoms.

neurophysiology The study of how the nervous system functions.

neuropsychological battery A group of tests designed to assess specific human abilities and functions, especially to identify specific neuropathology (brain injury) or areas of dysfunction and to suggest approaches to support, rehabilitation, and remediation. Neuropsychological batteries (series of tests) include a range of individual tests selected for their applicability to individual difficulties or presenting problems. Tests of distinct brain processes are used to localize brain damage and dysfunction and discriminate those higher cortical dysfunctions secondary to central nervous system (CNS) damage. The most commonly used batteries are 1) the Halstead-Reitan neuropsychological batteries, which must be administered with the age-appropriate Wechsler intelligence scale and the Wide Range Achievement Test (WRAT), and 2) the Luria-Nebraska Neuropsychological Battery. A psychological battery is concerned with describing cognitive, emotional, and social functioning; a neuropsychological battery has the added goal of localizing to specific regions of the brain the neural substrate for any problems found. A neuropsychological assessment is most useful pre (before) and post (after) brain surgery and post traumatic brain injury (TBI).

neuropsychology An interdisciplinary approach to studying brain–behavior relationships (how the central nervous system affects behavior). Clinical neuropsychology is concerned with applying scientific knowledge to the assessment of and intervention with human problems. Populations typically served by neuropsychologists include individuals with brain injury, dementia, degenerative disease, learning disabilities, or infectious or inflammatory illnesses who may have associated cognitive difficulties and other disabilities.

neurotherapy *See* electroencephalographic biofeedback (EBF).

neurotransmitter A chemical released by the nerve cell axon (the "tail" of the cell) that transmits a message from one nerve cell to another. Many substances (e.g., dopamine, acetylcholine) are clearly neurotransmitters, and others are thought to be. Neurotransmitters are specific to certain areas of the nervous system. They can be inhibitory (decreasing activity) or excitatory (increasing activity) and often work in conjunction with one another to control body movement and function.

neurotypical (NT) A description for people who are typically developing or "normal." This term originated among some in the "autism community" as a way to describe people without autism. A related term, *neurodiversity*, implies that there is a wide spectrum of people in terms of neurological and, in particular, social function, with no one group being superior to any other.

neutrocclusion A type of dental alignment in which the maxilla and mandible are in correct alignment but individual teeth may be misaligned, rotated, or jumbled.

nevoid basal cell carcinoma syndrome (BCNS) *See* Gorlin syndrome.

nevus flammeus *See* port-wine stain.

nevus sebaceus of Jadassohn A skin lesion, usually on the face or scalp, with linear yellow, orange, and tan stripes that become increasingly greasy and verrucous (warty) over time. It is sometimes associated with seizures and intellectual disability and can also become cancerous. *See* *also* Schimmelpenning-Feuerstein-Mims syndrome.

newborn intensive care unit *See* neonatal intensive care unit (NICU).

newborn hearing screening A test of a newborn's ability to hear, usually accomplished through otoacoustic emission and auditory brainstem response, to detect hearing impairments present at birth. Hearing impairment is the most prevalent abnormal condition present at birth. Before newborn hearing screening was instituted, diagnosis of hearing impairments typically did not occur until at least 2.5 years of age. Newborn screening has moved the time of diagnosis to under 4 months and initial intervention to under 7 months, potentially avoiding the delays in language and language functioning commonly experienced in children with hearing impairments. Universal hearing screening is required by law in a majority of U.S. states.

newborn screening A series of tests done on infants at birth to identify various (usually) genetic disorders that are usually rare but often treatable. Which tests are performed depends on the locality in which the infant is born, but most U.S. states include testing for phenylketonuria and congenital hypothyroidism, disorders that can result in intellectual disabilities if not treated early. With the exception of newborn hearing screening, newborn screening is done with a few drops of blood from the newborn's heel.

NF *See* neurofibromatosis.

N400 An event-related potential (ERP; a measure of brain responsivity) that is negative (N) in direction and that occurs approximately 400 ms after the stimulus event; it is significant during neurophysiological monitoring of brain function and activity.

NG tube *See* nasogastric tube.

NICHCY *See* National Information Center for Children and Youth with Disabilities.

NICHD *See* National Institute of Child Health and Human Development.

NICU *See* neonatal intensive care unit.

NIDRR *See* National Institute on Disability and Rehabilitation Research.

Niemann-Pick disease A group of disorders characterized by a deficiency in lysosomal (contained in the lysosomes, or the organelles ["little organs" of cells] that break down cell wastes) enzymes that break down sphingomyelin, a chemical in the body. This results in a buildup or storage of sphingomyelin in the reticuloendothelial system (which is composed of cells that ingest matter). These disorders, termed *lysosomal storage diseases,* are generally inherited in an autosomal recessive manner. Neurological symptoms, including hypotonia (decreased muscle tone), dystonia (variable muscle tone), developmental arrest (failure to acquire new skills), cerebellar ataxia (unsteady gait), or seizures, may be seen in types A, C, or D; type B has no neurological symptoms.

night-waking disorder *night-waking protodyssomia.* Episodes of night awakenings that occur at least 5 times per week for at least 4 weeks in children older than 12 months of age and that require parental intervention.

night-waking protodyssomia *See* night-waking disorder.

NIH *See* National Institutes of Health.

NIMH *See* National Institute of Mental Health.

9p monosomy *monosomy of the short arm of chromosome 9, 9p2.* A chromosomal disorder characterized by intellectual disability, craniosynostosis (premature fusion of skull sutures) with trigonocephaly (a triangularly shaped head), a peculiar facies (facial features), and congenital heart disease.

9p- syndrome *monosomy; 9p,del(9)(p22).* A condition in which craniosynostosis of the forehead is frequent and leads to trigonocephaly (a triangularly shaped head), flat occiput (back of the head), prominent eyes, upslanting palpebral fissures (eye slits) and epicanthal folds, mid-face hypoplasia (undergrowth), arched eyebrows, depressed nasal bridge, a long philtrum (groove in the upper lip), microtia (small ears), and broad neck. Heart defects, primarily ventricular septal defects, are frequent. Other skeletal abnormalities include long middle phalanges of the fingers; short distal phalanges; polydactyly (extra digits); and rib, vertebral (bones of the spine), and clavicular (collarbone) anomalies (abnormalities). Intellectual disability is moderate to severe.

9p,del(9)(p22) *See* 9p- syndrome.

9p2 *See* 9p monosomy.

nipple confusion The difficulty an infant displays when switching between bottle and breast feeding. Nipple confusion is presumed to be the result of the difference in tongue movements required by the two different feeding methods. Mothers of neonates (newborns in the first 28 days of life) are often counseled to breast-feed exclusively to avoid nipple confusion.

NLP *See* neurolinguistic programming.

NMES *See* neuromuscular electrical stimulation.

NNE *See* Neonatal Neurological Examination.

NNS *See* nonnutritive sucking.

No Child Left Behind Act (NCLB) of 2001 (PL 107-110) In part, a January 2002 reauthorization of the Elementary and Secondary Education Act (ESEA) of 1965 (PL 89-10). NCLB is based on the theories of standards-based education reforms, which assert that setting standards and measurable goals will improve individual outcomes in education. NCLB requires states to develop assessments in basic skills for all students in all grades of those schools receiving federal funds. It also requires schools to provide highly qualified teachers (as defined within the law) for all subject areas. The goal is to close the gap between high- and low-performing children, especially the achievement gaps between minority and nonminority children and between disadvantaged children and their more advanced peers.

nociceptive Relating to the perception of pain.

nodule A benign lesion caused by inflammatory degeneration of the superficial layer of the lamina propria (part of the vocal cords). Nodules are generally found at the anterior and middle third junction of the vocal fold (part of the vocal cords) and are caused by vocal abuse.

noise Sound that distorts a signal or message. The level of background, or ambient, noise can affect the ability of a person with (or without) a hearing impairment to successfully discriminate sounds.

NOMAS *See* Neonatal Oral-Motor Assessment Scale.

nomenclature Classification system, glossary, dictionary. The term usually refers to more specialized vocabularies.

nonadherence *See* noncompliance.

noncategorical Describing the grouping together of students with different diagnostic categories of disabilities in the same classroom.

noncompliance *nonadherence.* Lack of cooperation with carrying out recommended steps in a treatment program.

nondisabled Descriptive term for people without disabilities that is often used in speech or writing. Use of the term *nondisabled* avoids the more subjective term *normal,* which implies that people with disabilities are abnormal on the basis of their disabilities. The preferred terms in the disabilities field, however, are *typically developing* or *people without disabilities.*

nondisjunction The failure of two homologous chromosomes (those that are paired and have the same number) to separate during meiosis or in early embryogenesis in mitosis (early phases of fetal cellular development). This can result in two chromosomes from one parent and one chromosome from the other parent being passed on to the child, producing a trisomy (three chromosomes of the same number). This is how Down syndrome commonly occurs.

nondominant The side of the body (usually the left) innervated (supplied with input and output from nerves) by the contralateral (opposite) brain hemisphere (usually the right) that is not specific for language; the nondominant side of the body is usually very slightly weaker, smaller, and less coordinated.

nonepileptic myoclonus Myoclonus (muscle jerks) not associated with seizures, as found in many situations (e.g., in people who are falling asleep). A familial form of myoclonus (probably autosomal dominant) called *paramyoclonus multiplex,* or *essential myoclonus,* combines frequent but nonprogressive myoclonus with low–average intelligence. This condition is also associated with an exaggerated startle, hypertonia (increased muscle tone) in infancy, nocturnal leg jerking, and an unsteady gait. It often responds to the benzodiazepine drug clonazepam (trade name, Klonopin). Myoclonus may originate in the brainstem or the spinal cord and may produce myoclonic jerks not triggered by sensory stimuli that persist in sleep. Cortically mediated myoclonus (that which originates in the brain) is generally precipitated or aggravated by sensory stimuli such as light or noise; these muscle contractions are irregular and disappear in sleep.

nonexclusionary discipline Those disciplinary practices that do not involve removing a student from the school environment and thus allow for continued implementation of individualized education program (IEP) goals. Nonexclusionary discipline includes loss of recess and other privileges, detention, time-out, and in-school suspension. Because some states and many school districts do not prohibit corporal punishment, the IEP should specify accepted disciplinary procedures as part of the behavior management plan.

nonfocal Describing a physical finding that does not contribute to localizing the source of a disorder. For example, fever does not point to any specific body part as the source of a possible infection, and a generalized seizure does not indicate the involvement of any specific part of the brain.

nonnutritive sucking (NNS) The sucking reflex that occurs in the absence of food or liquid. Fast and rhythmic sucking averaging two sucks per second and used by the infant for calming. *See also* nutritive sucking.

nonorganic Describing a symptom or disorder that lacks a physical, biological cause; by implication such a symptom or disorder is due to an emotional or psychiatric cause. *See also* organic.

nonsuppurative otitis media *See* serous otitis media.

nontropical sprue *See* celiac disease (CD).

nonverbal Without spoken language.

nonvocal Describing individuals who have not developed functional oral (spoken) communication skills. Individuals with hearing impairment, intellectual disability, autism, tracheostomy tubes, or severe physical impairments may be nonvocal. The terms *nonvocal* or *nonverbal* are preferred to *mute* or *dumb* because the latter suggest that mental incapacitation accompanies hearing loss or the inability to speak.

Noonan syndrome *Turner-like syndrome.* A syndrome characterized by many features similar to those in Turner syndrome (e.g., short stature, webbed neck, low posterior (back) hairline, shield-like chest, cubitus valgus [lateral deviation of the forearm], and abnormalities of the pinnae [earlobes]), except that it occurs in both sexes and involves normal chromosomes. In Turner syndrome the cardiac defect is left sided (coarctation [critical narrowing] of the aorta, the major artery carrying blood to the body); in Noonan syndrome it is right sided (valvular pulmonic stenosis [narrowing of the valve of the artery that carries blood to the lungs]). Intellectual disability is rare in Turner syndrome but occurs in more than half of people with Noonan syndrome. Menstrual cycles are normal in females with Noonan syndrome. Incidence is 1 in 1,000 severely affected and perhaps as many as 1 in 100 mildly affected. Three quarters of cases are parent-to-child transmission, consistent with autosomal dominance with markedly variable expressivity. The most common form of Noonan syndrome (NS1), which maps to chromosome 12q24.1, is due to mutations in *PTPN11*, a gene encoding the nonreceptor protein tyrosine phosphatase SHP2. Alterations in this gene are found in about 50% of individuals with NS1. Named after the American pediatrician Jacqueline Noonan (1921–).

nootropics A class of psychoactive drugs (drugs that have effects on cognition) that are purported to selectively improve the efficiency of higher cortical functions; an example of such a drug is piracetam, which has been claimed to selectively improve reading ability. No drugs of this class have proven efficacy.

NORD *See* National Organization for Rare Disorders.

norepinephrine (NE) A neurotransmitter concerned with mood, arousal, and memory.

norm The performance measure of a normative group on a tested skill.

normal occlusion A type of dental alignment in which the lower first molar is one half tooth ahead of the upper first molar.

normalization The philosophy and principle of making available to all people with developmental disabilities—regardless of the severity of those disabilities—daily experiences and activities that are culturally normative (as close as possible to the prevailing patterns of mainstream society).

norm-referenced test *norm-based test.* A test on which a score is relative to that of a large group of individuals (i.e., an individual's performance is compared with that of the larger group). Developing a norm-referenced test includes giving that test to a large group of individuals who represent various traits and backgrounds (in terms of gender, age, language, culture, disability status, etc.) in proportion to the entire population. The test is administered under very similar circumstances (i.e., directions and tasks are "standardized"). Scores obtained by this "representative" sample are transformed into norms. The norms then allow reference to a larger group of individuals who took the same test under similar conditions. With an intelligence quotient (IQ) test, for example, this allows the tester to assume that performance derives primarily from an individual's ability rather than extraneous factors. Norm-referenced tests can also be standardized on clearly defined groups (e.g., individuals with specific disabilities).

Norpramin *See* desipramine.

Norrie syndrome *oculoacousticocerebral degeneration.* A genetic syndrome characterized by vision loss that progresses to blindness, progressive intellectual disability, and non-progressive sensorineural (involving the inner ear or the auditory nerve) hearing loss. Inheritance is X-linked recessive. Named after the Danish ophthalmologist Gordon Norrie (1855–1941).

Northwestern Syntax Screening Test (NSST) A language test for use with children 3–8 years of age. A picture-pointing task measures receptive language, and a delayed-imitation task measures expressive language.

nosology The systematic or scientific classification of disease; nosology is especially concerned with the criteria used to define and distinguish subtypes from one another.

NPDCI *See* National Professional Development Center on Inclusion.

NSE *See* neuron-specific enolase.

NSGC *See* National Society of Genetic Counselors.

NSST *See* Northwestern Syntax Screening Test.

NT *See* neurotypical.

nuchal righting *See* neck righting reaction, neonatal neck righting.

nuchal rigidity Stiff neck; a finding on physical examination that raises the suspicion of meningitis (infection of the brain) in young children.

nuclear family An individually housed family unit consisting of parents and their dependent children. *See also* family.

nucleotides The component parts of the nucleic acids (deoxyribonucleic acid [DNA] and ribonucleic acid [RNA]) that form the genetic material of all living cells.

nucleus A spheroid body within a cell that contains the genome (all of the chromosomes and their components). The control center of the cell.

NUK nipple A nipple made in a contoured shape to resemble a mother's nipple. The shape may enhance the infant's ability to compress the nipple and express formula and may promote better suction.

nursemaid elbow Pulled elbow; dislocation of the proximal radial head (forearm bone near the elbow) from excessive traction (the act of drawing or pulling). Nursemaid elbow is a common injury in preschool children as adults pull them (sometimes hard) by their hands.

nutritional supplement Nutritional products used in place of, or as a supplement to, normal nutrition when a child is unable to obtain adequate nutrition by typical means. Nutritional products can be administered as oral, enteral (digested through the stomach even if given via a feeding tube), or parenteral (given intravenously [IV]) formulas.

nutritionist A professional trained to evaluate a person's eating habits and nutritional status. Nutritionists can provide advice about normal and therapeutic nutrition, special feeding equipment, and techniques to increase feeding skills.

nutritive sucking Sucking during feeding. Rhythmic sucking averaging about one suck per second and occurring in patterns known as bursts interrupted by pauses used to breathe and rest between bursts. *See also* nonnutritive sucking (NNS).

nyctalopia   Night blindness.

nystagmus   A jerking movement of the eyes, usually back and forth. Nystagmus in far lateral gaze (with eyes looking all the way to the left or all the way to the right) can be a normal variant. Congenital nystagmus can be inherited and may be associated with decreased vision. Occasionally, nystagmus accompanied by a head tilt and titubation (bobbing and nodding) can be indicative of a central nervous system (CNS) disturbance, such as a tumor or a post-infectious encephalopathy (inflammation due to infection). Nystagmus can be induced by drugs such as antidepressants, anticonvulsants, or tranquilizers. It can also occur during seizures and in some degenerative disorders or ischemic (blood supply deficiency) disorders. Treatment is specific to the underlying cause.

nystatin   Trade name, Mycostatin. An antifungal agent used to treat infections from the yeast *Candida albicans.*

Oo

OAD   *See* overanxious disorder.

OAEs   *See* otoacoustic emissions.

obesity   The state of being markedly overweight for one's height. Overweight, in which there is extra body weight from muscle, bone, fat, and/or water, is distinct from obesity, which involves a high amount of extra body fat. The most useful measure of overweight and obesity is the body mass index (BMI), which distinguishes normal, overweight, and obese based on age, height, and weight. For adults, overweight is defined as a BMI of 25–30; obese, 30–40; and morbidly obese, > 40. For children, the Centers for Disease Control and Prevention (CDC) defines obesity as a BMI ≥ 95th percentile for age and sex. Higher weight and body fat are associated with increased risk for heart disease, high blood pressure, diabetes, gallstones, respiratory problems, and certain cancers. Most obesity is attributable to exogenous (related to overeating) and familial factors rather than endocrine causes. Rarely, obesity is related to a specific syndrome. An obese newborn may have Beckwith-Wiedemann syndrome or Sotos syndrome, or the child's mother may have diabetes; obesity of later onset occurs in Prader-Willi syndrome and Bardet-Biedl syndrome. Exogenous obesity secondary to a combination of overeating and inactivity is common in adolescents and adults with developmental disabilities.

obesity hypoventilation syndrome   *Pickwickian syndrome.* Reversible cardiopulmonary (heart–lung) problems that result from obesity; hypoventilation syndrome with extreme obesity (i.e., underbreathing that leads to inadequate oxygen supply along with retention of carbon dioxide that would normally be exhaled). This syndrome identifies a tendency to sleepiness in people with cardiac (heart) and respiratory (breathing) problems caused by being severely overweight. It is named after the behavior that Charles Dickens (1812–1870) ascribed to "Fat Boy Joe," who falls asleep in any situation, in *The Posthumous Papers of the Pickwick Club* (1837).

object permanence   The realization that objects continue to exist when they can no longer be perceived; for example, when a toy falls and a child can no longer see it, he or she will look to see where it has gone. In contrast, a child without object permanence will act as if the toy has ceased to exist. This developmental milestone emerges late in the first year of life.

objective   Independent of observer bias.

obligatory   Compulsory, necessary, involuntary.

OBRA   *See* Omnibus Budget Reconciliation Act of 1981 (PL 97-35).

Observation of Communicative Interactions (OCI)   An observational measure of 10 categories of caregiver responsiveness to an infant's cues.

observational learning Learning that takes place by observing and remembering how others succeeded or failed. *See* imitation, modeling, social learning theory.

obsessive-compulsive disorder A disorder characterized by persistent, unremitting, unrelenting, and irrational thoughts (obsessions; e.g., worries about germ contamination) and corresponding urges (compulsions; e.g., hand washing) that are expressed in the form of driven or ritualistic behaviors. Behaviors are refractory (unresponsive) to ordinary coping and change methods and result in functional impairment. Treatment usually involves a multimodal (using more than one method) approach that includes behavior therapy, medication, and long-term support. Effective behavioral interventions include response prevention (i.e., not permitting the individual to engage in the compulsive behavior), which serves to disassociate (break the link) between the thoughts and the behavior. Some individuals have cognitive rituals (such as counting) that are particularly difficult to treat.

obstipation Intractable constipation. Obstipation can occur in Hirschsprung disease (in which a segment of the bowel lacks normal nerves); it is also associated with Down syndrome.

obstructive sleep apnea (OSA) A condition characterized by repeated pauses in breathing during sleep due to blockage of the airway, with accompanying symptoms of snoring, labored (difficult) breathing, and gasping for air. OSA often causes oxygen desaturations (decreases in oxygen levels in the blood), hypercarbia (carbon dioxide retention), and sleep fragmentation. Factors that play a role in OSA in children include hyperplasia (enlargement) of the tonsils and adenoids, anatomic differences

such as micrognathia (small jaw) or macroglossia (large tongue), abnormal muscle tone, and obesity. OSA may accompany or complicate a variety of genetic syndromes (notably Down syndrome and Prader-Willi syndrome) and static encephalopathies (brain damage due to lack of oxygen). The disorder is treatable by adenotonsillectomy (removal of the tonsils and adenoids) or continuous positive airway pressure (CPAP; a type of ventilation that provides pressurized air through a mask, thereby keeping the airway open and preventing it from becoming blocked). OSA stands in contrast to central sleep apnea, in which there are repeated pauses in breathing without blockage or increased effort to breathe, and which raises concern for central nervous system (brain and spinal cord) disorders.

obtained score *See* raw score.

obtundation A state of decreased consciousness in which an individual can be aroused with some difficulty (and without painful stimuli), but the aroused state cannot be maintained.

obturator nerve The nerve that supplies sensation to the inner thigh and movement to adduct the thigh (pull it toward the middle of the body).

obturator neurectomy A surgical procedure in which the obturator nerve is cut. In children with spastic (increased muscle tone) cerebral palsy and scissoring (legs pulled so tightly toward the middle of the body that they cross), the adductors (thigh muscles that pull the legs toward the mid-line of the body) are too strong; this operation relieves this extreme adduction.

occipital lobe *occipital cortex.* The back part of the brain that contains the visual centers; the posterior part of the cerebrum (halves or hemispheres of the brain) that contains the optic radiations, pathways that bring messages from the eye. Damage to the occipital cortex can produce cortical blindness (inability to see due to brain dysfunction rather than problems with the eyes).

occipital lobe

occipitofrontal circumference (OFC) Head circumference.

occiput The back of the head.

occult Hidden; not readily observable, such as occult (internal) bleeding.

occult submucous cleft palate A submucous cleft of the palate not detectable on oral examination because of the absence of the typical stigmata of submucous cleft palate.

occupational therapy (OT) The use of adaptive, work, and play activities to increase independent function, enhance development, modulate sensory integration, improve fine motor skills, and prevent disability. The task or the environment may be adapted to achieve maximum independence and to enhance the quality of life. *See also* registered occupational therapist (OTR).

OCI *See* Observation of Communicative Interactions.

OCRL Oculocerebrorenal syndrome. *See* Lowe syndrome.

ocular Relating to the eye.

ocular pursuit The ability of the eyes to smoothly follow a moving object.

oculist A dated term for an optometrist or ophthalmologist.

oculoacousticocerebral degeneration *See* Norrie syndrome.

oculoauriculovertebral dysplasia *See* Goldenhar syndrome.

oculocerebrorenal syndrome (OCRL) *See* Lowe syndrome.

oculogyric crisis The state of the eyes rotating in a fixed circle; this can occur as a side effect of certain antipsychotic drugs.

oculomotor control The ability of the eyes to move smoothly and efficiently to allow the individual to view his or her entire visual field.

oculomotor nerve The third cranial nerve, responsible for constriction of the pupils, elevation of the eyelids, and vertical and medial (toward the nose) gaze.

oculus dexter (OD) The right eye.

oculus sinister (OS) The left eye.

OD *See* oculus dexter.

ODD *See* oppositional defiant disorder.

odor Smell can suggest specific metabolic diagnoses: maple syrup (maple syrup urine disease [MSUD]); musty, mousey, horsey (phenylketonuria [PKU]); yeast or dried celery (methionine malabsorption syndrome, also called *oasthouse urine disease* or *Smith-Strang disease*); sweaty feet (isovaleric acidemia). Strong body odors in children are more often a reflection of hygiene.

odynophagia Pain on swallowing.

OFC *See* occipitofrontal circumference.

OFD-I *See* oral-facial-digital syndrome type I.

OFD-II Oral-facial-digital syndrome type II. *See* Mohr syndrome.

off label Describing the use of a drug to treat a condition not listed on the U.S. Food and Drug Administration (FDA)–approved label. Off-label drug use is common in pediatrics, as many medications have not been FDA approved for use in children.

off task Not paying attention to assigned work or activities, typically defined in schools as looking at materials or the teacher as directed, reading, writing, or otherwise responding to work or instructions (in short, not doing what one should be doing). The opposite of on task, in which there is purposeful involvement with materials or activities.

Office of Special Education and Rehabilitative Services (OSERS) One of 13 federal offices within the U.S. Department of Education charged with overseeing education in the United States. OSERS directs, coordinates, and recommends policy for special education programs and services to address the needs of individuals with disabilities. It supports programs to assist children with special needs, provides for the rehabilitation of youth and adults with disabilities, and supports research that addresses quality-of-life issues for individuals with disabilities. OSERS comprises the Office of Special Education Programs (OSEP), the Rehabilitation Services Administration (RSA), and the National Institute on Disability and Rehabilitation Research (NIDRR). *See also* Bureau of Education for the Handicapped (BEH).

Office of Special Education Programs (OSEP) The component of the Office of Special Education and Rehabilitative Services (OSERS) that administers and oversees all programs related to the free appropriate public education (FAPE) of children, youth, and adults with disabilities.

Ohtahara syndrome Early infantile epileptic encephalopathy. A severe seizure disorder characterized by an onset in early infancy and diffuse cortical (outer layer of the brain) malformation. The seizures are

treatment resistant, and the prognosis is death or severe disability.

OKN *See* optokinetic nystagmus.

OKN drum *See* optokinetic nystagmus.

olfactory Relating to the sense of smell.

olfactory nerve The first cranial nerve, responsible for the sense of smell.

oligohydramnios Decreased volume of amniotic fluid during a pregnancy. Oligohydramnios is a risk factor associated with abnormalities of the infant's urinary tract, postmaturity (birth after a prolonged pregnancy), and intrauterine growth retardation (growth failure before birth).

oligosaccharidosis One of a number of metabolic disorders that cause an inability to break down complex sugars into simple sugars.

Olmstead v. L.C. U.S. Supreme Court decision of 1999 confirming the mandate of the Americans with Disabilities Act (ADA) of 1990 (PL 101-336) that public agencies must provide services for people with disabilities in the least restrictive environment providing that professionals assess that environment as appropriate. The court case came about when the State of Georgia petitioned to keep two women with intellectual disabilities in a state hospital after professionals had recommended that they be moved to community placement. This decision required that people with disabilities be offered community living over institutional placement.

OLSAT *See* Otis-Lennon School Ability Test.

OME Otitis media with effusion. *See* serous otitis media.

omega-3 An essential fatty acid most often found in fish that is important to brain function.

omega-6 An essential fatty acid found in most processed oils that is important to brain function.

OMIM *See* Online Mendelian Inheritance in Man.

omission Failure to act or include.

Omnibus Autism Proceeding In this set of three test cases against the Vaccine Indemnification Program of the U.S. Department of Health and Human Services in 2009, the Office of Special Masters of the U.S. Court of Federal Claims (the "vaccine court"), responsible for oversight of all claims for compensation due to vaccine-related injuries, found no causal relationship between autism and exposure to either thimerosal or vaccines.

Omnibus Budget Reconciliation Act (OBRA) of 1981 (PL 97-35) This act was the first to use the process of "reconciliation" as outlined in the Congressional Budget Act of 1974 (PL 93-344). Budgetary stalemates have triggered the reconciliation process more than 25 times since 1981. The reconciliation process is initiated when Congress passes a concurrent resolution on the budget requiring one or more committees to report changes in law affecting the budget by a certain date. All involved committees send their recommendations to the Budget Committee of the House, and the Budget Committee packages the recommendations into a single omnibus bill. OBRA was the first such omnibus budget bill, consolidating 57 formerly categorical grant programs into nine new or revised block grants, and drastically reducing funding for these programs. The bill reset poverty guidelines, consolidated six programs authorized under Title V of the Social Security Act into a single block grant authority (Maternal and Child Health) to address, among other things, the needs of children with special health care needs; converted the existing Title XX program into a Social Services Block Grant Program; authorized the Secretary of Health and Human Services to grant "home and community-based" waivers to enable states to furnish personal assistance and other services to individuals who, without such services, would require institutional care provided that costs under the waiver do not exceed the cost of providing institutional care to the target population; and encompassed such diverse budgetary targets as Aid to Families with Dependent Children (now called Temporary Assistance to Needy Families), Direct Funding of Indian Tribes, Social Services Block Grants, Low-Income Home Energy Assistance, Community Services, Primary Care Block Grants Substance Abuse Prevention and Treatment Program, Medicaid and Medicare, Social Security, the mentally ill, Head Start, and Adult Education. *See also* gifted.

omphalocele Protrusion, at birth, of part of the abdominal contents through a defect (opening) in the abdominal wall at the umbilicus (belly button). Only a thin transparent membrane covers the protruding bowel.

on task Meeting the criteria of engaging in expected, assigned tasks.

1, 2, 3 Magic A discipline technique to address problem behaviors in children 2–12 years of age that uses counting and time-out in a decidedly unemotional manner for optimal effect.

One-Word Picture Vocabulary Tests A set of tests that include the Receptive One-Word Picture Vocabulary Test (ROWPVT) and the Expressive One-Word Picture Vocabulary Test (EOWPVT), which provide measures of receptive and expressive vocabulary for children ages 2;0–18;11 years. The receptive tests require the examinee to select the picture that matches the word spoken by the examiner, thus assessing receptive vocabulary (what words the child understands). The expressive tests require the examinee to name the picture presented by the examiner.

Online Mendelian Inheritance in Man (OMIM) A web site (http://www.ncbi.nlm.nih.gov/omim) that lists recognized genetic syndromes and gene associations and provides the most current information on syndrome components and gene localization.

onychotillomania Picking at or pulling out one's nails. Onychotillomania may indicate the rare genetic syndrome Smith-Magenis syndrome.

OPD-1 *See* otopalatodigital syndrome type 1.

open bite A dental alignment in which the upper and lower teeth are even and meet in the middle; there is no overlap in teeth.

open classroom A child-centered approach to education that lacks or ignores physical barriers such as walls and allows children to work on different subject material at an individually supervised rate. The open classroom model is based on British infant schools and is also known as *free school, integrated day school,* or *family-centered school.*

open-label study A study of the effectiveness of a treatment in which everyone involved (participants as well as investigators and research staff) knows that participants are receiving the experimental drug or treatment. This type of study is considered less reliable than a double-blind study, in which the treatment status is unknown to participants and researchers until after the results are collected.

operant conditioning Involves the training of an organism's behavior so that a specific stimulus produces a specific and targeted response whenever the stimulus is applied. Operant (voluntary) behavior is shaped (modified or changed) and maintained by its consequences. A consequent stimulus

event (CSE) always follows an operant and may serve to strengthen, weaken, or maintain the current status of the operant. The condition or conditions upon which a CSE occurs is called the *contingency.* CSEs that strengthen the operants they follow are called *reinforcers;* these may be either positive or negative. In positive reinforcement, the addition of a consequence following a behavior increases the future likelihood of the behavior occurring (e.g., a child whines and the parent provides a desired object). In negative reinforcement, the removal of an aversive or irritating stimulus that is contingent upon a behavior increases the behavior's likelihood of occurring (e.g., the parent removes an irritating object [e.g., a food the child doesn't want to eat] and the whining stops). The weakening of an operant by withholding a known reinforcer is referred to as *extinction.* CSEs that serve to weaken behaviors are called *punishers* or *aversive stimulus events* (ASEs). *Satiation* occurs when a reinforcer loses its reinforcing properties over time because of overexposure and loss of reward potential. *Deprivation* refers to a state of need in which the reinforcer becomes more powerful—the opposite of what happens in satiation. Operant conditioning principles provide the theoretical and empirical underpinnings for behavior therapies and applied behavior analysis.

operational competence The technical skills needed to operate an augmentative and alternative communication system accurately and efficiently.

operational definition The specific procedures or steps for putting an idea into practice.

ophthalmologist An eye specialist; a physician who specializes in the diagnosis and treatment of eye disease and performs delicate eye surgery.

ophthalmoscope A medical instrument with lenses and a source of light that is used to look into the eye to visualize the retina (light-sensitive inner back wall of the eye).

opioid *opiate.* A chemical that reduces pain and may induce sleep. Some opioids are endogenous (produced naturally in the body), whereas others are exogenous (synthetic chemicals or drugs). Disorders of naturally occurring opioids can affect pain thresholds and contribute to self-injurious behavior (SIB). Exogenous opioids can be addictive.

opisthotonic attack *See* dystonic attack.

opisthotonos A posture of the body characterized by significantly increased muscle tone and trunk arching such

opisthotonos

that the spine is markedly extended (bowed and stretched) so that if the individual is lying on his or her back, the opisthotonos results in the individual's body resting on its head and heels. This posture can be seen in tetanus but occurs intermittently in severe cerebral palsy. These tonic (characterized by increased tone) spasms may be misinterpreted as seizures. When they are prominent in choreoathetosis (involuntary writhing movements), the term *tension athetosis* may be used. Opisthotonos may be considered the most extreme form of decerebrate posture (stiff and extended extremities and extended head) or tonic labyrinthine position (extension of all four extremities [both arms and both legs]).

Opitz syndrome *Opitz-Frias syndrome.* A genetic syndrome characterized by hypertelorism (widely spaced eyes), hypospadias (abnormal position of the urethral opening of the penis in males), severe swallowing problems, imperforate (no opening) anus, and intellectual disability in two thirds of cases. The syndrome is heterogeneous (varied in how it manifests), with an X-linked locus at chromosome Xp22 and an autosomal dominant locus linked to 22q11.2.

Oppenheim sign Stimulation downward along the medial tibia (inner shin) that produces dorsal extension (upward movement) of the big toe; a variant of the Babinski sign as an indication of motor disorder.

opportunity barriers Barriers that are imposed by people other than the individual with the severe communication disorder and that cannot be eliminated simply by providing an augmentative and alternative communication (AAC) system or intervention. Opportunity barriers include policy, practice, knowledge, and skill barriers.

opposition The position of the hand to hold an object in which the thumb is facing or opposite the fingers.

oppositional defiant disorder (ODD) A pattern of negative and hostile behavior more pronounced than is usually seen in children of similar age. ODD includes such symptoms as anger, argumentativeness, resentment, swearing, deliberate rule breaking, and annoying others. Although ODD is often more a symptom of other disorders than an entity in itself, it can evolve into a conduct disorder.

OPTAx A continuous performance task (CPT) test used to measure a child's ability to pay attention. *See also* continuous performance test.

optic atrophy A paling of the optic disc (nerve ending) as seen on fundoscopic examination of the retina (light-sensitive layer in the back of the eye) due to lack of vital function. A pale optic disc is a sign of damage that can present as loss of visual acuity (leading to overall unclear vision) or a field defect (loss of vision in one part of the visual field, or the area one is able to see).

optic disc The circular tip of the optic nerve (cranial nerve II, which carries visual information from the retina of the eye to the occipital lobe of the brain for interpretation) that can be seen on the retina (light-sensitive inner back wall of the eye) through the pupil. Abnormalities of the optic disc can be hereditary, secondary to toxins (poisons) or infection, or vascular (having to do with the blood vessels).

optic nerve The second cranial nerve. Cranial nerve II is responsible for vision and is the only nerve in the body that can be seen on direct physical examination (i.e., ophthalmoscopy, or looking into the eye using the light of an ophthalmoscope) via the optic disc (the visible tip of the optic nerve) on the retina. Damage to the optic disc can result in blindness in that eye.

optical head pointer A piece of assistive technology; a light attached to the head or to a computer that can be used to indicate choices when hands and arms do not function or verbal skills are not adequate.

optical righting The use of visual clues to maintain the head in a vertical position.

optician A professional who grinds prescriptive lenses and fills eye prescriptions.

opticokinetic nystagmus *See* optokinetic nystagmus (OKN).

optimal arousal A physiologically appropriate level of consciousness; psychologically speaking, *optimal arousal* refers to a complex concept that incorporates levels of anxiety, attention, and vigilance. In order to perform academically (or competitively at sports), one must have an increased level of arousal that sharpens his or her ability to observe, think, and perform but not so much so that it becomes debilitating. This optimal level of arousal may be different for each individual.

optokinetic nystagmus (OKN) *opticokinetic nystagmus.* Flickering involuntary eye movements induced by tracking a kinetic (moving) stimulus. Because the tracking does not need to be voluntary, the response

can be used to test vision in infants. A spinning cylinder covered in large strips called an *OKN drum* can be passed in front of the infant's eyes to provoke these movements. The presence of OKN documents the presence of some vision.

optometric training An intervention for reading disorders based on the observation that children who experience reading difficulties frequently display abnormal saccades (small eye movements) when tracking print across a page. The coincidence of visual-motor and visual-perceptual disturbances in children with reading problems reinforces this theory, as does the phenomenon of reversals. The training is supervised by an optometrist and consists of the daily practice of visual pursuit and tracking exercises. *See also* alternative medicine.

optometrist A professional who measures visual acuity (sharpness of vision) and prescribes corrective lenses (glasses).

OPV *See* oral polio vaccine.

oral apraxia The inability to execute voluntary motor movements of the mouth (e.g., lip puckering, tongue wagging, chewing) despite being able to demonstrate normal muscle function. This inability is not related to a lack of understanding or to any kind of physical paralysis but is caused by a problem in the cortex of the brain.

oral defensiveness Aversion to objects and sensations in and around the mouth.

oral hypersensitivity A condition in which touch to the mouth is unpleasant, painful, or unfamiliar. Previously familiar and even pleasurable tastes, touches, textures, and other stimuli become unfamiliar to the mouth. An oral-motor program to treat this condition is often begun by an occupational therapist (OT) and continued at home by the caregiver.

oral phase The stage of the swallowing process that involves anterior–posterior propulsion of a bolus (wad of food) through the oral cavity; it begins with the posterior tongue action that moves the bolus up and back toward the pharynx and ends as the bolus passes through the anterior faucial arches when the swallowing reflex is initiated.

oral polio vaccine (OPV) One of the primary routine immunizations given to children to protect against polio, an almost extinct viral disease that causes paralysis. OPV is trivalent (effective against all three poliovirus types).

oral preparatory phase The stage of the swallowing process that involves manipulation of food in the oral cavity (e.g., chewing, tasting). Goals of this phase include 1) breaking down food into appropriate consistencies, 2) mixing it with saliva for predigestion, and 3) forming the mixture into a cohesive bolus in the center of the tongue.

oral-facial-digital syndrome type I (OFD-I) *Léage-Psaume syndrome.* A genetic syndrome characterized by multiple frenula (webs) in the mouth; clefts in the tongue, lips, and palate; hypoplasia (undergrowth) of the nasal cartilages; and a variety of digital (finger and toe) abnormalities. Mild intellectual disability occurs in about half of the cases. Inheritance is X-linked dominant. Alterations in *OFD1,* the only gene known to be associated with OFD-I, are found in the majority of individuals with the condition. Type I is one of at least nine different types. *See also* Mohr syndrome.

oral-facial-digital syndrome type II (OFD-II) *See* Mohr syndrome.

oralism A method of educating people who are deaf (i.e., those who have profound hearing loss) that focuses on verbal communication to the exclusion of manual or unaided augmentative communication.

oral-motor apraxia *See* oromotor dysfunction.

Oral-Motor/Feeding Rating Scale An observational tool used to assess oral-motor and feeding functioning in eight areas: breast feeding, bottle feeding, spoon feeding, cup drinking, biting (soft cookie), biting (hard cookie), chewing, and straw drinking. The scale is applicable to people of all ages, and the assessment results can be used for planning interventions.

oral-motor function All aspects of motor and sensory function of the structures in the oral cavity (inside of the mouth) and pharynx (throat) related to swallowing until food enters the esophagus (passageway to the stomach).

oral-pharyngeal motility study *modified barium swallow (MBS) study, videoflouroscopy swallow study (VFSS).* A video-imaging study used to obtain a detailed analysis of the structures and function of the oral (mouth) and pharyngeal (throat) mechanisms during feeding and swallowing. X-ray films record the swallowing of a radio-opaque solution (liquid visible on x ray). The information obtained not only identifies whether aspiration (inappropriate passage of food or liquid into the airway) occurs but also helps to determine the factors causing the aspiration so that appropriate decisions regarding treatment and methods for nutritional intake can be made.

orchiopexy Surgical treatment of cryptorchidism (undescended testes).

Ordinal Scales of Psychological Development *Uzgiris-Hunt Scales.* Based on Piaget's sensorimotor stage of development, these scales are theoretically based, not norm referenced. They provide a description of the infant's progress in eight areas: object permanence, use of objects to solve problems, learning and foresight, development of schemata, understanding of cause and effect, spatial relations, imitation of vocalizations (sounds), and gestures. The scales yield estimates of the child's accomplishment of Piagetian stages. They are useful in planning interventions for young children up to about 1 year of age. *See* object permanence; Piaget, Jean (1896–1980); schema; sensorimotor.

organ of Corti The sensory part of the inner ear that converts pressure waves from sounds into nerve impulses that are then transmitted to the brain by cranial nerve VIII (the auditory nerve).

organic Caused by physical pathology; impairment in an organ or organ system. *See also* nonorganic.

organic aciduria Organic acids are chemicals found in blood and urine that in increased amounts may indicate an enzyme deficiency. Organic acidurias are illnesses characterized by episodes of vomiting, lethargy, and ketosis (an increase in ketones) accompanied by an increase in the amount of a specific organic acid in the urine because of a failure of the enzymes to metabolize it. Treatment can include a low-protein diet, sometimes supplemented with carnitine. Cognitive functioning can be typical in some disorders (e.g., isovalericacidemia) but marked by profound intellectual disability in others (e.g., methylmalonic acidemia).

organic impairment A disability with an organic etiology (physical cause) as compared to a nonphysical (emotional or social) etiology.

organomegaly Enlargement of an organ. The term is typically used in reporting negative abdominal examination findings with regard to the size of the liver and spleen. Thus, "no organomegaly" in describing abdominal palpation (examination by touch) means that neither the liver nor spleen is enlarged.

orientation Awareness of the environment with respect to place, time, and people; in developmental terms, the act of locating and turning toward the source of a stimulus (usually light or sound).

orientation and mobility A set of techniques to aid those with visual impairments in becoming familiarized with their surroundings and to enable them to travel safely and independently. Orientation involves determining where one is positioned in relation to objects in the environment, and mobility involves moving from place to place safely and efficiently.

orientation and mobility specialist An individual who specializes in orientation and mobility training of people with visual impairments.

orienting, auditory *See* auditory orienting.

ornithine transcarbamylase (OTC) deficiency A hereditary urea cycle (metabolic) disorder that leads to hyperammonemia (a high level of ammonia in the blood), intellectual disability, failure to thrive (FTT), headaches, vomiting, and lethargy (sluggishness) in cyclic episodes related to protein intake. OTC is the only urea cycle enzyme that has X-linked inheritance, and it is the only one that is treatable.

orofacial examination An examination designed to assess the structural and functional adequacy of the oral mechanism.

orofaciodigital syndrome An inherited syndrome, of which there are multiple types, characterized by multiple and/or hyperplastic (overdeveloped) frenula (webs or folds) between the buccal mucous membrane (inside of the cheek) and the alveolar ridge (gums); cleft palate; hypoplasia (undergrowth) of the alar cartilages (cartilage supporting the wings of the nostrils); and asymmetric shortening of the digits (fingers and toes) with polydactyly (extra digits), syndactyly (fused digits), and/or brachydactyly (short digits). The syndrome shows

X-linked dominant inheritance and causes death in the majority of affected males.

oromandibular-limb hypogenesis A disorder characterized by small mouth, variable clefting or aberrant (abnormal) attachments of the tongue, mandibular hypodontia (small or fewer lower teeth), hypoglossia (small tongue), varying degrees of limb hypoplasia (underdevelopment), adactyly (absent fingers or toes), syndactyly (fused fingers or toes), and possible nerve defects. There is no known inheritance pattern, and cases are usually sporadic.

oromotor dysfunction *oral-motor apraxia, oromotor apraxia.* Difficulty with the motor (involving movement) control and coordination of the lips, tongue, cheeks, and pharynx (throat), oromotor dysfunction can contribute to and be associated with early feeding problems (which can lead to failure to thrive), drooling and choking, and later articulation (speech pronunciation) disorders. The relationship among oral-motor reflexes, infantile feeding experiences, and mouth sensation (stimulation) is complex.

orotracheal tube A tube that goes from the mouth to the trachea (windpipe) and is used both to clear an airway of obstruction and to assist ventilation (breathing) either through a manually pumped bag or a mechanical ventilator (breathing machine).

orotracheal tube

orphan drug Any drug used to treat diseases in fewer than 200,000 potential people at the time of U.S. Food and Drug Administration (FDA) approval. The Orphan Drug Act of 1983 (PL 97-414) provided financial incentives for pharmaceutical companies to develop and market drugs for such rare diseases.

orthogenetic principle The theory that development proceeds in a directed manner

from a state of less differentiation to a state of greater differentiation, increasing complexity, and hierarchic organization.

orthomolecular treatment Therapy based on a hypothesized vitamin deficiency. The treatment program involves administration of megavitamins (very high doses of vitamins) and often also diverse trace elements (substances present in extremely small amounts in the body).

orthopedist A surgeon who specializes in the treatment of diseases of the bones, joints, and muscles.

orthoplast One of a group of thermoplastic materials used by therapists to make splints for positioning to improve function, protect lax or unstable joints, or reduce the potential for contractures.

orthopsychiatry An interdisciplinary field that emphasizes the development of mental health (rather than illness) from infancy and that supports efforts for the prevention of mental illness. *See also* American Orthopsychiatric Association (AOA).

orthoptics Eye exercises; optometric training.

orthoroentgenogram An x ray that includes a ruler next to the index limb to accurately measure bone length.

orthosis Orthopedic appliance; any device or appliance used to support, align, prevent, or correct orthopedic deformities or otherwise improve motor functioning. Orthoses include braces and splints for either the upper extremities (the arms, including the elbow, wrist, and hand) or the lower extremities (the legs, including the knee, ankle, and foot). *See also* braces, hip–knee–ankle–foot orthosis (HKAFO).

orthotics The science and practice of designing, measuring, fitting, evaluating, and teaching about the use of orthoses (orthopedic devices). The term *orthotics* is sometimes used as a synonym for *splinting*.

Ortolani sign   A maneuver to elicit an audible hip click; when present, such a click is indicative of congenital dislocation of the hip. Testing for hip dislocation is a routine component of the pediatric examination in early infancy.

Orton-Gillingham reading method   A structured multisensory approach to reading, spelling, and writing. This method is based on the rationale that children must be taught through the constant use of association of 1) how a letter or word looks; 2) how it sounds; and 3) how the speech organs and the hand feel when saying, writing, and tracing the letter or word. This method has proven to be highly effective for students with reading problems, particularly dyslexic students. Psychologist Anna Gillingham (1878–1963) based this remedial methodology on neurologist Samuel T. Orton's (1879–1948) theories about dyslexia (a specific reading disability).

OS   *See* oculus sinister.

os calcis   Calcaneus; the heel bone.

OSA   *See* obstructive sleep apnea.

oscillation   The absence of a clear trend toward traversing the sequence of Piagetian (based on the work of psychologist Jean Piaget) stages of development. Children with intellectual disability may fluctuate among the various stages.

OSEP   *See* Office of Special Education Programs.

OSERS   *See* Office of Special Education and Rehabilitative Services.

ossicles   Small bones; the term usually refers to the three small bones of the middle ear (the incus, malleus, and stapes).

ostension   The act of showing by pointing: "That's a(n)…" A technique used to increase young children's vocabulary.

osteogenesis imperfecta   A heterogeneous group of inherited disorders of connective tissues (the cartilage, bones, and other organs that give the body its shape) characterized by bone fragility. Associated features include blue sclera (the outer layer of the eye, which is usually white), opalescent teeth with characteristic radiologic features (appearance on x ray), hearing loss, deformity (abnormal shape) of the long bones and spine, and joint hyperextensibility (ability to be straightened beyond normal limits). The severity of the disorder varies widely among and even within families; some individuals have minimal involvement of the skeleton and may never have a fracture, whereas others have very severe involvement and many fractures. Dominant as well as recessive inheritance has been reported.

osteomyelitis   Bone infection.

osteotomy   An orthopedic surgery procedure that changes the alignment of a bone, usually by removing a wedge-shaped portion of that bone.

OT   *See* occupational therapy.

OTC deficiency   *See* ornithine transcarbamylase deficiency.

other health impairments   An educational classification under the Individuals with Disabilities Education Act (IDEA) of 1990 (PL 101-476) and its amendments used to provide supports, accommodations, and services to children who have medical conditions that affect their learning but who do not otherwise qualify for an individualized education program (IEP).

Otis-Lennon School Ability Test (OLSAT)   A measure of cognitive ability as related to school success for use with children in kindergarten through Grade 12. There are seven levels of the test for the different grades, with clusters of 10–15 items in the five areas of verbal comprehension, verbal reasoning, pictorial reasoning, figural reasoning (pattern recognition), and quantitative reasoning. This test is often used by schools to determine eligibility for gifted and talented programs.

otitis externa *"swimmer's ear."* Inflammation of the external auditory canal (the passage from the outer ear to the eardrum).

otitis media Middle ear infection; inflammation of the middle ear (the organs behind the eardrum that transmit the vibrations of sound from the outside to the inner ear, where they are converted to nerve signals). There are three subtypes: serous (marked by an accumulation of fluid in the middle ear), secretory (an accumulation of thick fluid—"glue ear"), and suppurative (accumulation of pus). Associated ear pain and fever are common.

otitis media with effusion (OME) *See* serous otitis media.

otoacoustic emissions (OAEs) Sounds that are produced by healthy ears in response to acoustic stimulation (outside sounds). They are considered to be by-products of the activity of the outer hair cells in the cochlea. These are spontaneous OAEs, or SOAEs; evoked OAEs are used in screening hearing in children. *See also* transient evoked otoacoustic emissions (TEOAEs).

otolaryngology *ears, nose, and throat (ENT).* The surgical specialty involving the ears, nose, and throat.

otology The science or study of the ear and its functions. Physicians who specialize in otology are otolaryngologists, or ENT (ear, nose, and throat) doctors.

otopalatodigital syndrome type 1 (OPD-1) A genetic syndrome characterized by moderate conductive (involving the middle and outer ears) hearing loss; cleft palate; irregular digits (fingers and toes) with short, broad terminations (tips); mild intellectual disability; a variety of skeletal abnormalities; and a characteristic pugilistic ("boxer-like") facies. Inheritance is X linked. OPD-1 is part of a spectrum of disorders caused by alterations in the *FLNA* gene.

ototoxic Damaging to the eighth cranial nerve (the acoustic nerve, or the one responsible for hearing); drugs that cause nerve deafness are ototoxic.

OTR *See* registered occupational therapist.

OT-SI Occupational therapy (OT) that uses a sensory integrative (SI) approach to treat sensory processing disorders (SPDs), such as disorders of balance that are not due to ear difficulties and disorders of touch such as tactile (touch) defensiveness. *See also* sensory integration.

outer canthal distance The distance between the two lateral canthi (outside corners) of the eyes. Outer canthal distance is not a very sensitive indicator of dysmorphology (abnormal appearance) because it is influenced by the angle of the palpebral fissures (eye slits): Large angles (found in eyes that are very upslanting or downslanting) will influence this distance.

outer canthal distance

outer-directedness A personality characteristic of people with intellectual disability that includes both their tendency to imitate others and their reliance on external (outside) cues, especially from adults, to guide their behavior.

output In the field of augmentative and alternative communication (AAC), the appearance of the display and how it enhances communication with a listener.

overanxious disorder (OAD) A disorder characterized by extreme self-consciousness, excessive and unrealistic worries, and anxiety about competence. Signs may include stomachaches, headaches, and difficulty falling asleep. Once considered a separate disorder, OAD now falls under generalized anxiety disorder in the *Diagnostic and Statistical Manual of Mental Disorders, Fourth Edition, Text Revision (DSM-IV-TR),* suggesting that it is a syndrome (cluster of symptoms) but not a distinct disorder. Unlike with other disorders, meeting diagnostic criteria for OAD is not systematically associated with a clinical referral or significant functional impairment in children.

overbite *See* distocclusion.

overcorrection A mildly aversive (characterized by withdrawal from something perceived as unpleasant or painful) behavioral intervention technique. In restitutional overcorrection, the person being treated is made to restore the environment to a better condition than before the inappropriate behavior (e.g., washing all of the desks in the classroom as punishment for writing on one). Positive practice overcorrection requires the overpracticing of acceptable behaviors incompatible with the behavior to be eliminated or the repeated performance of a behavior until it becomes learned (e.g., correctly writing a missed spelling word 100 times).

overdetermined Having multiple causes, with the implication that one cause would suffice. In developmental disabilities, a disability is often overdetermined by a combination of genetic, environmental, familial, social, and learning factors.

overflow movements *See* associated movements.

overprotection A style of caregiving characterized by 1) an encouragement of dependency on the parent and 2) an exclusion by the parent or family of outside influences on the child. In an attempt to protect the child from perceived danger, the parent intrudes on and controls the child's world. The result is a child with reduced opportunities to learn from experience, diminished capacity to cope with new situations, and a mistrust of his or her own capacities. Thus, the child may develop socialization difficulties, anxiety, depression, and sometimes rebelliousness. In the long term, the child's ability to function and cope independently may be restricted. Anxious parents and parents of children with clear health, social, or developmental vulnerabilities may be more inclined toward overprotection.

overweight *See* obesity.

oxcarbazepine Trade name, Trileptal. An anticonvulsant (anti-seizure) drug similar to carbamazepine and effective against most partial (affecting one part of the brain) and generalized (affecting the whole brain) seizure types, with perhaps milder side effects than carbamazepine. Oxcarbazepine can cause hyponatremia (potentially dangerous low blood sodium level).

oxybutynin Trade name, Ditropan. A spasmolytic (one that decreases muscle spasms) drug that increases bladder capacity and decreases the urgency to urinate. Oxybutynin is used in the treatment of neurogenic bladder (bladder with voiding malfunction due to nerve damage).

oxycephaly *turricephaly.* A small tower-shaped skull produced by craniosynostosis (premature fusion of skull sutures [seams between the bones of the skull]) involving all sutures. There is a high vertical index (height of the skull divided by length of the skull).

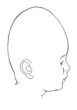

oxycephaly

Pp

PA   *See* posteroanterior view.

P&A   *See* protection and advocacy.

PACE   *See* Processing and Cognitive Enhancement Program.

PACER   *See* Parent Advocacy Coalition for Educational Rights.

pachygyria   *macrogyria.* A condition in which the brain has few (*pachy-*) broad (*-macro-*) ridges (*gyri*) with shallow sulci (grooves). This anomaly is more common than lissencephaly (a smooth, rather than convoluted, brain surface), and the injury producing it can occur later in gestation. Pachygyria causes severe to profound intellectual disability with seizures; many people with pachygyria also have spasticity (increased muscle tone). Pachygyria can be visualized on a magnetic resonance imaging (MRI) scan.

pachyonychia   Thickened nails.

packing therapy   Wrapping the child in damp cloths while leaving the head and face unwrapped and talking to the child about his or her feelings. This technique is used to treat catatonia, anxiety, and autism.

PAIP   *See* Preverbal Assessment Intervention Profile.

paired associate learning (PAL)   *pairing.* A learning task used to measure attention: The person is shown a series of pairs (of words, letters, symbols, or combinations of these) and is then asked to provide the other item when one of the pair is presented. Numerous standardized and nonstandardized test procedures use this task.

palatal fistula   A hole that forms in the palate after a palate repair comes undone.

palatal obturator   *palatal lift.* A prosthetic device that extends the soft palate (the back of the roof of the mouth) to reduce hypernasality (extremely nasal sound).

palatal training appliance (PTA)   A device that assists with velar (palate) function through pressure and tactile input to the soft palate and uvula (structures at the back of the roof of the mouth), resulting in subsequent palatal elevation to facilitate phonation.

palate   The roof of the mouth, composed of an anterior (front) hard palate and a posterior (back) soft palate. Deviations in the shape of the palatal arch, that result in it being variously described as high arched, elevated, or steepled, are minor dysmorphic (atypical) features and can be components of a variety of syndromes. Such deviations are independently associated with both microcephaly (small head) and underdeveloped (hypoplastic) structures of the mid-face.

palatoplasty   Surgical repair of a palatal (roof of the mouth) defect.

palilalia   The tendency to repeat one's own words (as opposed to echolalia, or the tendency to parrot or repeat the words of others), often in the context of increasing rate and decreasing loudness. Palilalia has been described in Tourette syndrome.

palitalization   The phonological process that occurs when a palatal component is added to a nonpalatal component.

Pallister-Killian syndrome   *Killian/Teschler-Nicola syndrome, Pallister mosaic syndrome, tetrasomy 12p.* Infants with this syndrome may be large at birth but grow slowly over time. Intellectual disability is severe; speech may not occur, and hearing impairment is common. The face appears "heavy" and coarse, with upslanting palpebral fissures (eye slits), hypertelorism (widely spaced eyes), strabismus (crossed eyes), a short nose, a long philtrum (upper lip groove), a prominent lower lip, and sparse scalp hair. Streaks of hyper (increased or darker) and hypo (decreased or lighter) skin pigmentation may be seen.

palmar grasp   Reflex closure on or voluntary prehension (grasp) of an object or stimulus with the hand. *See also* grasp reflex.

palmar grasp

palmomental reflex   An infant oral-motor reflex in which the stimulus of stroking the palm of the hand produces the response of a wrinkling of the ipsilateral (on the same side) mentalis muscle (the muscle that lifts the corner of the mouth). An intact palmomental reflex in infants reflects normal facial nerve (cranial nerve VII) function; an easily elicited palmomental reflex in older children is associated with postencephalitic (following a brain infection) syndrome or degenerative disorders.

palpation   Examination by the hands to feel the size, shape, and consistency of various body organs.

palpebral fissure   Eye slit; the opening between the upper and lower eyelids. The corners of the palpebral fissures are canthi; the distance between the canthi of an eye is the palpebral fissure length (PFL). The most common syndrome characterized by decreased PFL is fetal alcohol syndrome (FAS). Upslanting eyes (palpebral fissures that rise going outward from the side by the nose) are associated with Down syndrome and many other genetic syndromes; downslanting (also from the nose outward) palpebral fissures are also associated with a number of genetic syndromes. PFL is usually 80%–90% of the inner canthal distance (ICD) measurement; PFL values less than 80% of the ICD represent shortened PFLs. As with other dysmorphic (atypical) features, isolated findings may be of no significance.

PALS   *See* Program for the Acquisition of Language with the Severely Impaired.

palsy   Paralysis or weakness.

PANDAS   *See* pediatric autoimmune neuropsychiatric disorders associated with streptococcal infections.

pandemic   An epidemic of global magnitude. In actual usage, the term has come to mean physical or mental disorders that affect multiple and often unrelated, although not necessarily global, populations. Thus, acquired immunodeficiency syndrome (AIDS) is a pandemic of an infectious agent. Exposure to cocaine in utero is a pandemic of a toxic agent.

pantothenate kinase–associated neurodegeneration (PKAN)   Formerly known as *Hallervorden-Spatz syndrome,* this progressive neurological condition involves abnormalities of tone and movement (dystonia, chroreoathetosis), speech problems, and abnormalities of the retina (light-sensitive back layer of the eye). Intellectual disability is often present. Life span is variable. On magnetic resonance imaging (MRI) of the brain, iron deposition in motion- and tone-controlling sensors called the *basal ganglia* produce a distinctive appearance called the *eye of the tiger sign*. Inheritance is autosomal recessive.

papilla Bumps on the tongue that contain sensory nerve receptors for taste.

papillary ridges Fingerprints. The three basic patterns of papillary ridges are the loop, the whorl, and the arch. In addition to providing a quantitative means of identifying each individual, gross deviations from the typical patterns of loops, whorls, and arches can be part of specific genetic syndromes. *See also* dermatoglyphics.

papilledema A condition in which the optic disc, the head of the optic nerve (the nerve for vision), is swollen. This can be seen on examination of the optic fundus (the back of the eye or retina) with an ophthalmoscope (a lighted lens instrument used in eye exams). Papilledema may indicate an acute brain swelling (with increased intracranial pressure) such as after head trauma or due to a vascular etiology (cause). Toxic levels of certain drugs and vitamins (e.g., vitamin A) can also produce papilledema. There often is a history of intermittent (on and off) blurring of vision. Treatment is specific to the cause, and the optic discs are generally not permanently damaged.

papilloma A nonmalignant, wart-like cluster of tissue that tends to proliferate on the vocal folds.

papule A small, elevated, solid skin area; a "raised dot."

para *See* parity.

parachute Anterior parachute response; a postural response (a reflex that must develop in order to support the later development of voluntary motor function) in which the stimulus of being suddenly thrown forward toward the floor from a position of horizontal suspension

parachute

(being held prone horizontally) produces the response of rapid protective extension of both upper extremities (throwing out both arms as if to catch oneself). This is one of the last postural responses to emerge before the onset of independent walking. There is also a downward parachute, in which the infant is moved suddenly toward the floor in a position of vertical (upright) suspension; the response involves a transition from "sitting in air" to extension of both lower extremities (straightening the legs as if to support one's weight). The downward parachute emerges by 3 months of age with receding flexor habitus (less time spent in a curled-up posture). *See also* protective extension.

paradigm A constellation of beliefs, values, standards, and techniques shared by members of a (scientific) community.

paradoxic vocal fold dysfunction A respiratory pattern in which the vocal folds adduct during inspiration, resulting in difficulty breathing and stridor.

paradoxical directive A set of psychotherapeutic strategies. Although these strategies have a number of forms, the unifying theme revolves around the therapist overtly advocating the retention of a symptom or dysfunctional behavior with the covert (hidden) intention that the opposite will occur. Thus, the paradox is that the therapist advocates for no change, but the result is that the client does the opposite and makes a positive change in the direction of health—an example of reverse psychology.

paradoxical response An opposite response from that expected. Certain medications worsen rather than alleviate a symptom or behavior. Certain antihistamine medications typically make children drowsy, but a paradoxical response in which some children become wound-up and irritable instead is not uncommon. Reverse effects sometimes can be used therapeutically.

paragraphia The insertion of wrong or unintended words in what one writes.

paralexia A disturbance of reading in which letters, words, or syllables are substituted or transposed (changed in place).

paralinguistics Nonverbal communication through, for example, intonation (tone of voice) or gestures.

parallel play Play that occurs independently beside, but not with, other children. Parallel play may involve incidental use of the same or shared toys, but it is distinct from associative play, in which materials are borrowed, or cooperative play, in which children take part in shared activities and assume cooperative roles.

parallel talk A child-centered technique used to stimulate early language development in which the adult talks about what the child is doing or looking at as they play in an unstructured setting.

paralysis Loss or impairment of voluntary movement; a neurological impairment.

paraphasia A disorder of verbal output that includes transposition of letters in a spoken word and, in semantic paraphasia, the substitution of one word for another in the same class (e.g., "Tom checked the time with the clock on his wrist"). Semantic paraphasia occurs in Wernicke aphasia.

paraphrasing *See* restating.

paraplegia A topographical subtype (classification based on the location of affected body parts) of spastic (increased muscle tone) cerebral palsy in which only the lower extremities (legs) are involved. Theoretically speaking, a pure paraplegia must be caused by a spinal cord injury, transection (severing), or tumor and would not therefore be a cerebral (brain-based) palsy; it would also lack any associated dysfunction secondary to brain involvement. In fact, many childhood nontraumatic cases of paraplegia represent cases of spastic diplegia (involving both sides) in which lower extremity (leg) involvement is more noticeable and upper extremity (arm) involvement is relatively mild but still present. In such mild cases of spastic diplegia, delay in walking and a clumsy gait are observed in the first several years of life, but the upper extremity fine motor difficulties associated with handwriting do not become apparent until school age.

paraprofessional An aide or associate-level staff person who has not completed the educational requirements for licensure or certification as an independent practitioner. Different disciplines have different formal educational requirements for paraprofessional status.

parasomnia A class of abnormal behaviors that occur during or surrounding sleep. Parasomnias include nocturnal enuresis (bedwetting), somnambulism (sleepwalking), nightmares, pavor nocturnus ("night terrors"), and somniloquy (sleeptalking).

parasympathetic nervous system The division of the autonomic nervous system (part of nervous system that works outside of consciousness) that unconsciously controls life-sustaining processes when the individual is not under stress. The vagus nerve is one of the major components of this cholinergic system (characterized by the use of the chemical acetylcholine as a signal).

parent The biological or legal permanent (as in adoption) caregiver of a child or minor.

Parent Advocacy Coalition for Educational Rights (PACER) A funded project of the Office of Special Education Programs (OSEP) that is dedicated to creating opportunities and enhancing the quality of life of children and youth with disabilities and their families. Through more than 30 projects, PACER addresses special needs for all stages of childhood and all disabilities by providing individual assistance, workshops, publications, and other resources to help families make decisions about services and education for their child or young adult with disabilities.

Parent Perception Inventory (PPI) A questionnaire that provides a comprehensive measure of a family's coping with the presence of chronic illness or disability in a child.

parental child *parentified child.* Usually an older child who assumes responsibility for and functions as a parent for younger children. This situation can be adaptive (healthy) in large or single-parent families when supported by clear rules and power boundaries. Such an assumption of responsibility is maladaptive (unhealthy) when it results from a parent abdicating (abandoning) responsibility. In families with a parent with intellectual disability, the parental child frequently assumes parenting functions not only for the other children but also for the parent. In families whose firstborn child has a disability, another child frequently assumes a parental-child role in relation to the child with a developmental disability.

parental rights for parents of special education students The Individuals with Disabilities Education Act (IDEA) of 1990 (PL 101-476) and its amendments require schools to provide parents of a child with a disability with a notice containing a full explanation of the procedural safeguards available under the IDEA and U.S. Department of Education regulations. A copy of this notice must be given to parents only once per school year as well as 1) upon initial referral or parent request for evaluation, 2) upon receipt of the first state complaint and upon receipt of the first due process complaint in a school year, 3) when a decision is made to take a disciplinary action that constitutes a change of placement, and 4) upon parent request.

Parent–Child Interaction Therapy (PCIT) A research-supported intervention for use with children with problem behavior or emerging conduct disorders, PCIT emphasizes improving the quality of the parent–child relationship and changing parent–child interaction patterns. Parents learn specific skills for establishing a nurturing and secure relationship with their child while increasing their child's positive behavior and decreasing negative behavior. Two main strategies are used: 1) child-directed interaction (CDI), in which parents engage their child in a play situation with the goal of strengthening the parent–child relationship and improving the child's behavioral regulation; and 2) parent-directed interaction (PDI), similar to clinical behavior therapy, in which parents apply behavioral intervention techniques with their child.

parenteral Describing nutrition administered via an intravenous (IV) route (i.e., through a needle inserted into a vein).

parenteral nutrition *See* hyperalimentation.

parent-focused therapy Therapy that involves parents in the child's therapy. Parent-focused therapy usually includes teaching the parents to recognize child behaviors that are limiting their child and assigning the parents a significant role in the child's goals. It is based on the belief that parents are crucial to the success of any therapy program and that many children with social and behavior problems have a parent with similar problems.

parentified child *See* parental child.

Parent–Infant Interaction Scale A scale used to assess parents' interaction with their infants who have developmental delays; the scale addresses caregiver interaction behaviors, caregiver and child social referencing (how the caregiver frames new experiences for the child), reciprocity (the give-and-take of the relationship), and caregiver affect (mood).

Parent–Infant Relationship Global Assessment Scale (PIR-GAS) A rating system for categorizing parent–infant problems. Scores range from 1–10 for documented maltreatment to 90–100 for well adapted. Scores less than 40 indicate a relationship disorder. The PIR-GAS is a *Diagnostic Classification of Mental Health and Developmental Disorders of Infancy and Early Childhood–Revised Edition (DC:0-3R)* tool.

Parenting Stress Index (PSI)–Third Edition A self-report instrument for parents of children ages 1 month to 12 years that is designed to identify stressful aspects of parent–child interaction. The PSI has 120 questions that tap child characteristics (seven subscales) and parent personality and situation (eight subscales). It also contains a defensive responding (validity) scale and produces a life stress score. The short form (PSI-SF) has 36 items; it yields total stress, parental distress, parent–child dysfunctional interaction, and difficult child scores along with a validity scale.

Parents' Evaluation of Developmental Status (PEDS) A well-standardized 10-question parent-report survey used to screen for developmental problems in children 4 months through 8 years of age.

paresis A weakness of the affected muscle(s).

parietal lobe An area of the cerebrum (hemispheres, or halves of the brain) between the frontal and occipital lobes. This area contains the somesthetic (sensory) or parietal cortex (the outer surface

of the brain), which receives messages (input) from all sensory neurons except those involved with vision and hearing. Damage to this area can produce impairment in sensation or paresthesias (numbness, tingling, or heightened sensitivity) as well as some more complex perceptual problems (ignoring one side of the body, difficulty dressing oneself, confusing right and left).

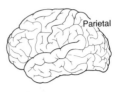

parietal lobe

parity The status of a woman with regard to childbearing; the number of pregnancies that have proceeded to a time of viability (about 24–25 weeks' gestational age) and delivered, with infants live or dead. One parity could result in a single or in multiple (e.g., in the case of twins) newborns. *See also* primipara.

Parkinsonism A motor syndrome similar to Parkinson's disease of older adults (with resting tremors) that can result from and complicate the use of antipsychotic drugs to treat severe maladaptive behavior in people with developmental disorders.

parotid duct ligation Surgical procedure that eliminates salivary flow from the parotid gland employed as treatment for drooling.

parotid duct transposition Surgical procedure that redirects salivary flow from the parotid gland as treatment for drooling.

paroxetine Trade name, Paxil. A selective serotonin reuptake inhibitor (SSRI; a medication that prolongs the action of the neurotransmitter serotonin) used to treat depression, obsessive-compulsive disorder, and panic attacks. Side effects include nausea, headache, and sleepiness.

paroxysm A spasm, seizure, sudden occurrence, or worsening of symptoms.

parroting   *See* echolalia.

PART   *See* Program Assessment Rating Tool.

Part C   *Early Intervention.* A component of the Individuals with Disabilities Education Act (IDEA) of 1990 (PL 101-476) and its amendments that serves children from birth to 36 months who are not developing as expected or who have a medical condition that can delay development. Formerly known as *Part H.*

partial seizures   Seizures that arise from a specific location on the cortex (outer layer of the brain). These may be manifested by a convulsive movement of part of the body or even disorders of thought or sensation (such as a déjà vu sensation). Partial seizures may be simple or complex: Simple seizures do not involve any change in level of consciousness (alertness, awareness, responsiveness to the outside world); complex ones do.

parturition   The birth process.

Passavant's pad   A muscle bundle that develops on the pharyngeal wall due to velopharyngeal insufficiency.

passive   Not active, inert; of deficient vitality.

PAT   *See* Photo Articulation Test.

Patau syndrome   *See* trisomy 13 syndrome.

patella   The kneecap.

patent ductus arteriosus (PDA)   A cardiac defect common in premature infants in which a fetal structure (the ductus arteriosus [DA]) continues to function after birth. The DA in the fetus shunts blood from the pulmonic (serving the lungs) side of the heart to the systemic (left, serving the body) side, bypassing the lungs. In the

patent ductus arteriosus (PDA)

typical newborn, the patent (open) ductus closes around the time of birth. In many premature and some full-term infants, the ductus remains open and must be closed medically with a drug (indomethacin) or surgically.

paternal age   The chronological age of the father; the age of the biological father at the time of the conception of a child. Whereas advanced maternal age is associated with the incidence of Down syndrome, advanced paternal age is associated with dominant mutations, such as achondroplasia, Apert syndrome, and Marfan syndrome.

pathognomonic   A sign, symptom, or behavior that is highly characteristic, almost uniquely so, of a given diagnosis. A truly pathognomonic individual sign or symptom, one that is completely unique to a single disorder, is rare; most signs and symptoms must be interpreted in context, especially the context of other signs and symptoms.

patrician foot   A condition in which each successive toe from the big toe outward is shorter than the one before it—in contrast to the plebian foot, in which the toes are of similar length.

patrician foot

patterning   Neurological reorganization; a system of physical therapy for the treatment of cerebral palsy. Derived from the theory that ontogeny (the development of the individual) repeats phylogeny (the evolution of the species), this approach involves exercises in which the child imitates the movement patterns of fish, amphibians, and reptiles before assuming an anthropoid (literally, "humanoid"; upright) posture. The concept that proficiency at each evolutionary level must be achieved before proceeding to the next level is the source of the myth that it is pathological (abnormal) to walk before one crawls. In an expanded form such as the Doman-Delacato approach, this therapy is used for a wide variety of developmental disorders. *See also* Doman-Delacato Developmental Profile; National Academy for Child Development, The (NACD).

Pavlovian conditioning   *See* classical conditioning.

Paxil   *See* paroxetine.

PBIS   *See* positive behavioral interventions and supports.

PBS   Positive behavior support. *See* positive behavioral interventions and supports (PBIS).

PCA   *See* postconceptional age.

PCIT   *See* Parent–Child Interaction Therapy.

PCS   *See* Picture Communication Symbols.

PDA   *See* patent ductus arteriosus.

PDD   *See* pervasive developmental disorder.

PDD-NOS   *See* pervasive developmental disorder-not otherwise specified.

PDDST-II   *See* Pervasive Developmental Disorder Screening Test–II.

PDMS-2   *See* Peabody Developmental Motor Scales–Second Edition.

PDP   *See* prescription drug plan.

PDQ-I   *See* Psychological Development Questionnaire for Toddlers.

PDQ-II   Prescreening Developmental Questionnaire–II. *See* Denver Developmental Screening Test–Second Edition.

PDSS   *See* Pediatric Daytime Sleepiness Scale.

PDV   *See* primary disorder of vigilance.

PE tubes   *See* pressure equalization tubes.

Peabody Developmental Motor Scales– Second Edition (PDMS-2)   A standardized, norm-referenced test that assesses fine and gross motor skills in children from birth to 5 years. Administration takes less than 1 hour.

Peabody Individual Achievement Test– Revised: Normative Update (PIAT-R/NU) An individually administered test of achievement for use with individuals ages 5–22 years old. Produces age- and grade-based standard scores (what the average child of the same age or grade should achieve) and percentile ranks for subtests (General Information, Reading Recognition, Reading Comprehension, Written Expression, Mathematics, and Spelling) as well as composites and a total test score.

Peabody Picture Vocabulary Test–Fourth Edition (PPVT-IV)   A norm-referenced test of receptive language at the single word level for use with individuals ages 2–90 years of age. Changes from previous editions include full-color, realistic illustrations; a balance of sex and race/ethnicity examples; a larger easel format; and more stimulus words, with better representation of word types across all levels of difficulty. Growth Scale Value (GSV) is a new measure of progress over time.

peak clipping   The phenomenon in which loud portions of an acoustic signal are "clipped off" and redistributed within the signal, creating distortion.

PECS   *See* Picture Exchange Communication System.

pectus   The chest. Pectus carinatum is keel chest, pigeon breast, or chicken breast, in which the sternum (breastbone) projects forward; pectus excavatum is funnel chest, in which the sternum appears caved into the chest. Although these anterior (front) chest wall deformities may be cosmetically problematic, it is rare for cardiac or pulmonary functioning to be impaired enough to indicate surgery. Occasionally, these unusual chest shapes are parts of a larger malformation syndrome.

pectus carinatum

pectus excavatum

PEDI *See* Pediatric Evaluation of Disability Inventory.

pediadontist A general children's dentist.

pediatric autoimmune neuropsychiatric disorders associated with streptococcal infections (PANDAS) Recurrent, acute fulminant tics and/or obsessive-compulsive behaviors that follow an infection with streptococcus.

Pediatric Behavior Scale A checklist that provides information about a number of different behavior and health characteristics of a child. The scale has two versions: one for parents and the other for teachers. It measures characteristics of disorders, including attention, impulsivity, incoordination, eating, sleeping, expressive communication, and social immaturity. Each item in the scale is scored from 0 to 3, with 0 being *absent* and 3 being *present very often/much*. There are separate norms for boys and girls from ages 6 to 12 years.

Pediatric Daytime Sleepiness Scale (PDSS) A self-rated assessment of daytime sleepiness. Eight statements are rated on a Likert scale from 0 to 4; scores above 26 for sixth and seventh graders and scores above 30 for eighth graders are abnormal.

Pediatric Early Elementary Examination 2 (PEEX-2) *See* Pediatric Neurodevelopmental Examinations.

Pediatric Evaluation of Disability Inventory (PEDI) A parent-report instrument used with children ages 6 months to 7 years with chronic illnesses or disabilities. Functional status and functional change are measured in the areas of skill level, caregiver assistance, and adaptive equipment modification. Administration time is 20–30 minutes.

Pediatric Neurodevelopmental Examinations A series of nonstandardized examination procedures intended to generate narrative descriptions of relative strengths, weaknesses, and preferred learning styles in children with learning disabilities. Four separate examinations cover specific age groups: Pediatric Extended Examination at Three (PEET)—age 3; Pediatric Examination for Educational Readiness (PEER)—ages 4–7; Pediatric Early Elementary Examination 2 (PEEX-2)—ages 7–9; and Pediatric Examination of Educational Readiness at Middle Childhood 2 (PEERAMID-2)— ages 9–15. Each examination includes a physical and neurological assessment, an evaluation of the maturation of the nervous system, administration of tasks that tap specific areas of development, and systematic behavioral observations. The developmental functions evaluated include fine and gross motor functions, memory, language, visual/spatial processing, temporal sequential organization, and selective attention. These tests produce neither an overall score nor specific subtest scores; rather, they use a descriptive approach to evaluating and managing developmental dysfunctions. Each takes about 1 hour to administer.

Pediatric Rancho Scale A scale used to measure the cognitive and behavioral functioning of infants and children through 7 years of age following acquired brain injury. Adapted from the Rancho Los Amigos Scale.

Pediatric Symptom Checklist (PSC) A checklist developed to measure a range of emotional and behavioral concerns in a primary care setting. Completed by parents, it measures their impression of their child. The categories parallel those of the Child Behavior Checklist, a test commonly used by child psychologists. The PSC can be used with preschoolers as well as school-age children, although four of the questions are omitted for children ages 2–5 years.

pedigree Family tree. An organized system of presenting the genealogic history of a family. The pedigree visually depicts both individuals and generations, as well as inherited disorders, in a manner that is easily analyzed. The diagram that shows a family pedigree is called a *genogram. See also* genogram.

PEDS *See* Parents' Evaluation of Developmental Status.

PEEP *See* positive end expiratory pressure.

PEER Pediatric Examination for Educational Readiness. *See* Pediatric Neurodevelopmental Examinations.

peer review The process used for the review of articles submitted for publication in some scientific and medical journals in which feedback from scientists with similar expertise is obtained to help the editors judge whether the work merits publication and whether any questions or concerns should be addressed prior to publication. The author's name and affiliation are commonly absent from the submitted work so that peers judge the work on its merits instead of being swayed by reputation or personal relationships.

peer support A one-to-one or group relationship among people who share similar life experiences and who come together to provide knowledge, experience, and emotional or practical help to one another. Peer support is based on the theory that people who have like experiences can better relate and can consequently offer more authentic empathy and validity. Peer supporters are a class of paraprofessionals who are trained to listen nonjudgmentally; offer emotional support; share their experiences of struggling with a disability, disease, or other life-changing event; and discuss community resources and coping mechanisms that worked for them. The term *peer support* also refers to self-help organizations (e.g., Alcoholics Anonymous) in which colleagues and others meet as equals to give one another support on a reciprocal basis. *Peer* in this case implies that no one person has more expertise as a supporter than another, and therefore that the relationship is one of equality.

peer tutoring The practice of students assisting other students who need supplemental instruction. Although the practice may be beneficial to both tutor and tutee, some studies indicate that it is the tutors who learn more and are more satisfied with the experience. This suggests that students should have experience as both tutors and tutees.

PEERAMID-2 Pediatric Examination of Educational Readiness at Middle Childhood 2. *See* Pediatric Neurodevelopmental Examinations.

peers Social equals. In developmental terms, people who are similar in characteristics such as age or developmental level. Peers form peer groups, or close associations, with one another, often in the form of play groups at school or in the neighborhood. Children with developmental disabilities are often described as "immature" and as having "poor social skills," making it difficult for them to associate with their peer groups by age or grade. Often, younger children or others with developmental disabilities compose these children's peer groups because they are more equal on a developmental level. Peer groups are important to all children in forming models for identification.

PEET Pediatric Extended Examination at Three. *See* Pediatric Neurodevelopmental Examinations.

PEEX-2 Pediatric Early Elementary Examination 2. *See* Pediatric Neurodevelopmental Examinations.

PEG *See* percutaneous endoscopic gastrostomy.

pegboard An item used in many infant tests to measure both fine motor coordination and nonverbal problem-solving ability. The most commonly used pegboards are the Wallin A (six round pegs evenly spaced in a straight line along the board) and the Wallin B (six square pegs evenly spaced in a straight line along the board). Successful completion of pegboards typically occurs in the second half of the second year of life.

pellagra A syndrome due to niacin (vitamin B₃) deficiency that includes "the four Ds": dermatitis (skin rash), diarrhea, and dementia (diffuse brain involvement), sometimes progressing to death.

pelvic obliquity Vertical (up and down) movement of the pelvis on the invisible line that divides the body into a front and back. A certain degree of pelvic obliquity is normal during walking and is measured as a component of gait analysis.

pelvic rotation Movement of the pelvis on the invisible line that divides the body into top and bottom; a component of gait analysis. The purpose of pelvic rotation is to swing the leg forward and elongate step length.

pelvic tilt A slanting of the pelvis away from the horizontal in the sagittal (median) plane (which divides the body into a right and a left); a certain degree of pelvic tilt is normal during walking and is measured as a component of gait analysis. The term *pelvic tilt* is sometimes used generically to include pelvic obliquity (up and down movement in the coronal plane, which divides the body into anterior and posterior halves).

pelvis The lower end of the trunk formed by a ring of bones including the hips and tailbone; the pelvic inlet is the bony canal through which infants pass to be born.

pemoline Trade name, Cylert. An older stimulant medication used to treat attention-deficit/hyperactivity disorder; because of potential liver complications it is no longer manufactured.

Pendred syndrome An autosomal recessive genetic syndrome that associates congenital sensorineural (involving the auditory nerve) hearing loss with goiter (swelling of the thyroid gland). This syndrome accounts for approximately 5% of sensorineural hearing loss in children. The deafness is associated with an abnormality of an ear bone that can be diagnosed by computed tomography (CT) examination of the temporal bones (the bones at the side and base of the skull). Vestibular function (internal balance mechanisms equivalent to a gyroscope) is abnormal in the majority of affected people. Mutations in the *SLC26A4* gene are identified in approximately 50% of multiplex families (families with several affected members).

penetrance The proportion of carriers of an autosomal dominant gene (people who have one copy of the particular gene) who show any signs of that gene. A carrier who does not manifest any sign of the gene is said to be *nonpenetrant. See also* expressivity.

penetration A condition in which foods, liquids, or oropharyngeal secretions fall to the level of the true vocal folds.

penicillamine A drug given by mouth to treat individuals with an overload of heavy metals, such as lead poisoning and Wilson disease.

People to People Committee for the Handicapped A self-help mutual aid organization that provides information and referral regarding entitlements, services, and organizations for people with disabilities. A periodically published resource manual is available.

people-first language *See* person-first language.

PEP-3 *See* Psychoeducational Profile–Third Revision.

percentile score A score reflecting an individual's position relative to others taking the same test. It is obtained by converting an individual score to the percentage of observations that fall below that score. Someone who scores at the 35th percentile performs better than 34% of others taking the test. (One cannot score at the 100th percentile because it is impossible to perform better than 100% of the people taking the test.)

perception Awareness of an object or event through the sense organs. Patterns of selection, organization, and interpretation of specific stimuli are partially determined by prior learning, experiences, and interests.

perceptual disorder An impairment in one of the modalities used for assimilating information (usually visual or auditory). A perceptual disorder is not one of acuity (the sharpness or keenness of a sense). The mechanics of hearing and vision are normal; the disorder involves a difference in the way the information is processed or perceived. A child with a visual-perceptual limitation has difficulty making sense of things that he or she sees; a child with an auditory perceptual (more often termed *auditory processing*) impairment has difficulty making sense of information that he or she hears.

perceptual-motor The integration of the modalities used for processing information (usually visual or auditory) with a nonverbal response. For example, auditory motor integration is required for listening and taking notes, whereas visual-motor integration is required for copying forms or words. In practice, *perceptual-motor* is sometimes inaccurately used synonymously with *visual-motor.*

percussion Tapping. Determining the density or solidity of a body part by tapping on its surface (as one taps a barrel to decide if it is full) and listening for sound differences. Also a technique used to remove secretions from the chest (e.g., in a child with cystic fibrosis).

percutaneous endoscopic gastrostomy (PEG) An approach to placing a gastrostomy tube endoscopically (using a fiberoptic instrument) rather than through intraabdominal incision. PEG can be performed under local anesthesia.

Perez reflex A primitive reflex in which pressure applied to the spine (vertebral column) in a caudocephalad direction (from tail to head) causes the infant to flex (bend) his or her arms and legs, elevate his or her head, and urinate/defecate.

performance contract A written agreement used for behavior management of older school-age children that specifies expected behavior, rewards, and consequences. It should be signed by the child and the adult(s) involved and be made public.

performance test A set of tasks in which the role of language is minimized. Overt demonstrations of various motor skills, rather than verbal responses, are required. The Leiter International Performance Scale is an example of a performance test; on the Wechsler Intelligence Scales for Children, performance subtests include Block Design, Picture Concepts, Matrix Reasoning, and Picture Completion (optional).

Periactin *See* cyproheptadine.

perimetry A test procedure used to determine the extent of the visual field (area of sight); this can range from confrontation with a flicking finger at the periphery (edges) of the individual's line of sight to the use of complex instrumentation to map the visual field. Visual field cuts (gaps in the line of sight) can occur in hemiplegic cerebral palsy.

perinatal Pertaining to the period just before, during, and just after birth. Many perinatal problems have no relationship with the quality of obstetrical care. Perinatal death rates are reported for all fetuses or for fetuses past a specified length of gestation (from 20 to 28 weeks) and up to 7–28 days of age.

perineum The structures in the lower pelvic area, or pelvic outlet. A tear may occur here during delivery.

periodicity A regularly recurrent or intermittent cycle, often related to the presence of a biological clock. Premenstrual syndrome (PMS) is the most commonly recognized example of periodicity; however, children with developmental disabilities may exhibit behavior fluctuations in cycles of varying length.

peripheral nervous system The collection of nerves (sensory and motor) that connect the spinal cord and brain to the rest of the body.

peripheral vision Sight that utilizes retinal cells outside the macula. Because the macula is the part of the retina (the light-sensitive inner back wall of the eye), which picks up light stimulation from what one is looking at, the rest of the retina is, to varying degrees, sensitive to visual stimuli outside one's primary focus of attention—the periphery.

peristalsis Waves of alternate contraction and relaxation of tubular structures such as the esophagus and intestines.

periventricular leukomalacia (PVL) A lesion (abnormality) of the white matter near the lateral (outside) ventricles (fluid-containing spaces) of the brain caused by necrosis (tissue death). PVL is most commonly found in premature and low birth weight (LBW) infants and is thought to be related to an asphyxial insult (injury due to lack of oxygen). In premature infants, the brain vasculature (blood vessels) is thought to be immature and fragile and thus more sensitive to changes in blood pressure and oxygen levels, resulting in damage without other complications. The range of developmental outcomes for infants with PVL includes intellectual disability and cerebral palsy. PVL can be diagnosed by ultrasound, computed tomography (CT) scan, or magnetic resonance imaging (MRI). *See also* leukomalacia.

Perkins-Binet Tests of Intelligence for the Blind An intelligence test adapted from the Stanford-Binet Intelligence Scale for use with people with severe visual impairments. There are two versions of the test: Form U, for children with usable vision; and Form N, for children with nonusable vision.

perseveration The continuation or repetition of an action or thought after it has become inappropriate. Such fixation may reflect an associated, but opposite, disorder to a short attention span or focus. When a child has difficulty understanding or executing a given direction, he or she may, like a broken record, repeat an earlier correct but now inappropriate response. At other times, when a child is asked to do something once, he or she will do it (or some component of it) several times. More striking examples of perseveration occur in autism spectrum disorder.

persistent vegetative state (PVS) A condition in which people with severe brain damage exhibit no recognizable mental function, although they may have cycles of wakefulness, when their eyes open and move, and sleep.

Personality Inventory for Youth (PIY) A measure of emotional and behavioral adjustment, family interaction, and academic functioning in children 9–19 years; the first 80 of its 270 items can be used as a screening instrument.

person-centered planning An ongoing, problem-solving, process-oriented approach to empowering a person with disabilities as an approach to determining, planning for, and working toward that person's preferred future or his or her family's plan for the future. It focuses on the person and his or her needs (as opposed to systems that may or may not be available to serve those needs) by putting the focal person in charge of defining the direction for his or her life. A person-centered team meets to identify opportunities for the focal person to develop personal relationships, participate in the community, increase control over his or her own life, and develop the skills and abilities needed to achieve these goals.

person-first language Describing the preferred way of referring to specific disabilities or individuals with disabilities, which typically involves referring to the person first and the disability second (e.g., "individuals with Down syndrome"). Person-first language avoids the use of categorical groupings, substituting "children with intellectual disability" for "intellectual disabled children" or "the intellectually disabled." Person-first language generally uses neutral, descriptive terms, such as "has cerebral palsy" or "uses a wheelchair" rather than "suffers from cerebral palsy" or "is confined to a wheelchair." *See also* disability etiquette.

person-in-environment A view of human behavior that sees both behavior and personality development as functions of environmental variables as well as innate psychological and physiological processes. This perspective encompasses the interactive relationships among an individual; relevant others; and the physical, cultural, and social environments. Thus, for a person with a physical disability, a pervasive sense of helplessness and isolation would be assessed to determine whether this is a personality trait or whether, in fact, the environment denies physical and social access, making isolation and helplessness the only possible reality.

pertussis Whooping cough. A severe bronchitis with an explosive cough. This potentially fatal disease can be prevented by immunization.

pervasive developmental disorder (PDD) A category of developmental disabilities characterized by a pattern of impaired communication and socialization skills in the presence of restricted, repetitive, and stereotypical behaviors (repetitive movements). PDD includes five conditions: Asperger syndrome, autism, childhood disintegrative disorder, pervasive developmental disorder-not otherwise specified, and Rett syndrome.

pervasive developmental disorder-not otherwise specified (PDD-NOS) One of the pervasive developmental disorders (PDDs). A syndrome in which there is severe impairment in the development of reciprocal (characterized by give-and-take) social interaction; impairments in verbal and nonverbal communication; and restricted and stereotypical (repetitive) interests and activities but in which the full criteria for autism are not met. PDD-NOS may coexist with the full range of intelligence levels.

Pervasive Developmental Disorder Screening Test–II (PDDST-II) A parent-report measure that screens for autism in children 18–36 months of age. There are three stages for use in 1) primary care clinics, 2) developmental clinics, and 3) specialty autism clinics.

pes cavus *See* cavus foot.

pes planus Flat foot.

PET *See* positron emission tomography.

petit mal A nonspecific term applied historically to absence seizures (which usually manifest in brief staring spells) but that has been used for other epileptic events as well. Literally, "small illness" (as opposed to *grand mal* ["big illness"]), the term was used historically to describe generalized tonic-clonic seizures. Often *petit mal* refers to simple absence seizures with a diagnostic electroencephalogram (EEG; or brain wave) pattern consisting of a 3-per-second spike (point) and wave (curve). Children with attention-deficit/hyperactivity disorder (ADHD) are often suspected of having petit mal episodes because of their tendency to daydream.

Pëto, Andras (1893–1967) A Hungarian physician who established the Pëto Institute in Budapest, Hungary. Pëto also developed conductive education, a system of using physical and cognitive therapy to treat motor disorders that focuses on the conscious rhythmic practice of activities of daily living (ADLs). *See also* conductive education.

Pfaundler-Hurler syndrome *See* Hurler syndrome.

Pfeiffer syndrome Acrocephalosyndactyly (peaked head and webbed fingers and toes). An autosomal recessive genetic syndrome with craniosynostosis (early fusion of skull) leading to turribrachycephaly (tower-shaped skull), broad thumbs, big toes, and syndactyly (webbing of the fingers or toes). Neurodevelopmental complications are rare. Alterations in the *FGFR2* (fibroblast growth factor receptor 2) gene are associated in more than 95% of individuals.

PGD *See* preimplantation genetic diagnosis.

PHACE syndrome This syndrome includes the following features: posterior fossa brain malfunction; facial hemangioma; and arterial, cardiac, and eye abnormalities. Seizures and developmental delays may occur.

phakomatoses *neurocutaneous syndromes, neurophakomatoses.* An older term that groups syndromes that have both brain disorders and skin lesions, such as neurofibromatosis.

phalanges The small bones in the fingers and toes.

phalanges

pharyngeal manometry A procedure that measures change in intrabolus pressure and times pharyngeal contractile waves.

pharyngeal phase The stage of the swallowing process that consists of reflex actions of the swallow; it involves velopharyngeal closure, laryngeal closure by an elevated larynx to seal the airway, reflexive relaxation of the upper esophageal sphincter for the bolus to enter the esophagus, and reflexive contractions of the pharyngeal constrictors to move the bolus down into the esophagus.

pharyngitis Throat infection that may include sore throat, fever, tender cervical (neck) lymphadenopathy (lymph node swelling), erythema (redness) of the pharynx, and sometimes exudate (white patches). Most pharyngitis is viral in etiology (origin) and unresponsive to antibiotics.

pharynx The throat. This irregular space is capable of considerable change in size and is divided into the nasopharynx (top, back of the mouth), oropharynx (middle, behind the mouth), and laryngopharynx (bottom, near the windpipe). It is involved in breathing and swallowing and acts as the principal resonating organ in speech.

phasic bite reflex The stimulus of pressure on the gums produces the response of rhythmic closing and opening of the jaws. This oral reflex is innervated by cranial nerve V (the trigeminal nerve); it is present by 1 month of gestation and disappears by 1 year of age.

phasic reactions Reflex patterns that coordinate the muscles of the limbs in patterns of either total flexion or total extension.

phencyclidine *angel dust.* Trade name, Semylan. A discontinued veterinary anesthetic with hallucinogenic and neurotoxic effects that has the street name "angel dust."

phenobarbital Trade name, Luminal. An anticonvulsant that is a member of the barbiturate family; it can be used to control generalized tonic-clonic or simple partial (focal) seizures. Side effects of phenobarbital (sometimes familiarly called *phenobarb*) include sedation; hyperactivity; a decrease in attention span; and cognitive impairment, with a lowering of an intelligence quotient (IQ) score by about 5–10 points.

phenotype The external physical characteristics of an individual, including morphology, biochemistry, and physiology, as determined by the interaction of genes with the environment. *Genotype* is the sum of all genes in any given person.

phenylanine An amino acid (basic building block of proteins) that rises to levels harmful to the brain in the inherited metabolic disorder phenylketonuria (PKU).

phenylketonuria (PKU) An inborn error of metabolism in which the enzyme phenylalanine hydroxylase is absent or nonfunctional, resulting in an increase in the level of phenylalanine, an essential amino acid (basic building block of proteins), in the blood. Treatment involves a diet low in phenylalanine. Untreated PKU is associated with intellectual disability, microcephaly (small head), seizures, athetosis (involuntary writhing of the arms), hand posturing, and behavioral stereotypies (repetitive behaviors). The earlier dietary treatment is initiated, the better the developmental outcome. When the diet is started before 3 weeks of age, there are no discernible problems. When it is started between 3 and 6 weeks of age, there are mild

impairments. Treatment shows little positive effect when begun after about 6 months of age. Infants with PKU appear normal at birth, except possibly for some irritability and vomiting. Delayed development is often not noted until 4–9 months of age. Because of the insidious presentation and the importance of early treatment on developmental outcomes, PKU is routinely tested for in newborns. Children with PKU are frequently blue-eyed, blonde, and fair-skinned, with a tendency toward eczema (skin rash). Inheritance is autosomal recessive.

phenytoin Trade name, Dilantin. An anticonvulsant that can be used for a number of seizure types. Elevated levels produce nystagmus (involuntary eye movements) and ataxia (unsteady gait). Other side effects include gingival hyperplasia (gum overgrowth) and hirsutism (excessive hair growth).

philtrum An infranasal (below the nose) upper lip depression; the groove in the middle of the upper lips. The philtrum may be shortened, elongated, or flattened. A flattened philtrum is characteristic of fetal alcohol exposure.

philtrum

phobia An exaggerated and debilitating fear of an object or situation that is based neither on an actual danger nor on an actual threat. Common phobias include claustrophobia (fear of enclosed spaces) and nyctophobia (fear of darkness). Specific phobias (e.g., of bridges, school) can become problematic when the person avoids the feared object or situation, resulting, for example, in the inability to travel or attend school. This places strain on the phobic person's interpersonal relationships and functioning. Phobias can be successfully treated through behavior therapy techniques, including systematic desensitization and exposure and response prevention.

phocomelia The congenital absence of the proximal (nearer to the trunk) segment of a limb. The hand or foot will sometimes be attached almost directly to the trunk, like a flipper. This condition is rare in isolation and can occur as part of a genetic syndrome.

phonation   Voicing. The voluntary production of sound by moving air through the vocal tract. Phonation is a function of the vocal cords in the larynx (larynx).

phoneme   The smallest unit of sound in any particular language. Various languages use phonemes that are not used in any other language. The English language uses approximately 44 different phonemes.

phonemic awareness   A phonological skill that includes the ability to focus on and manipulate phonemes in spoken words.

phonemic spelling   The pattern of spelling behaviors in which one who has discovered the phonetic principles of spelling attempts to capture the sounds of words in writing.

phonemic synthesis   *See* sound blending.

phonetics   A study of the perception and production of all of the speech sounds in language. Phonetics has been applied to the teaching of reading.

phonics   A word attack (attempt to decode or sound out print material) skill that involves the sound of letters, the division of words into syllables, and the blending of sounds together to form words. Some phonics programs are synthetic, in that letters and sounds are blended to form words. Others are analytic, in that they depend on the analysis of previously learned words. The functional use of phonics skills also includes checking the pronunciation in the context from which the word was taken. Many achievement tests have tests that measure how well a student can generalize phonics rules to nonsense words, which tests only applications of phonics skills

without relying on or checking against the pronunciation of known words. The "back to basics" movement sometimes views phonics as the best approach to reading rather than one of a variety of tools for extracting meaning from print. Students with auditory processing problems (difficulty recognizing and interpreting sounds) often have difficulty mastering phonics, especially using synthetic approaches.

phonological disorder   A problem with articulation.

phonological processes   Techniques used by children to simplify speech when attempting to produce adult words.

phonological processing disorder   *See* dyslexia. *See also* central auditory processing disorder (CAPD).

phonology   The study of the linguistic system of speech sounds in a particular language.

phoria   A latent (hidden) tendency for the eyes to deviate from their normal fusion (linked movement when tracking). In the presence of esophoria (tendency toward convergence) or exophoria (tendency toward divergence), optometric tests that stress the eyes' ability to maintain fusion produce esotropia (a visible turning in of the eyes) or exotropia (a visible turning out).

phosphatase and tensin homolog (*PTEN*)   A gene located on chromosome 10 that codes for a tumor suppressor protein, one that, among other things, prevents abnormal cell division that could lead to cancer. Mutations in the *PTEN* gene can lead to conditions such as Cowden syndrome, a cancer syndrome in which individuals are susceptible to a variety of tumors. *PTEN* mutations have also been associated with autism spectrum disorders, specifically in children with macrocephaly (large heads).

photic drive *See* intermittent photic stimulation.

Photo Articulation Test (PAT) A test of pronunciation that uses the naming of color photographs to test the articulation of all consonants, vowels, and diphthongs (combinations of two sounds).

photoconvulsive response *See* intermittent photic stimulation.

photomyoclonic response *See* intermittent photic stimulation.

photoparoxysmal response *See* intermittent photic stimulation.

photophobia Extreme sensitivity to light. Photophobia can be associated with a variety of acute and chronic conditions, such as conjunctivitis (eye inflammation), measles, albinism (lack of pigment in the skin and eyes), migraine, meningitis, and encephalitis (infection of the brain).

photosensory seizure A convulsion induced by a visual stimulus, typically a flickering light such as a strobe light or a television screen. Thus, photic stimulation involving a rapidly flickering light is one of the techniques used when administering an electroencephalogram (EEG; or brain wave test) in order to try to provoke abnormal brain wave activity as a test for susceptibility to seizures.

phototherapy The use of "bililights" (fluorescent light bulbs) to lower the level of bilirubin (a substance that causes jaundice) in a newborn infant. The infant's eyes are protected with eye patches or goggles. This is a fairly common treatment for infants with mild elevations in their bilirubin levels, and its use in the newborn period has no long-term developmental implications.

phrenic nerve A cervical (neck) nerve that innervates the diaphragm; one of the principal respiratory (breathing) muscles.

physiatry *See* physical medicine and rehabilitation (PM&R).

physical disabilities A broad category of disabilities that typically involve the motor system and place some limitation on the person's ability to move about. However, such disabilities can include diseases of any organ system that have a significant impact on functional ability. Although they are distinguished from mental or emotional disabilities, physical disabilities may coexist with these disorders.

physical medicine and rehabilitation (PM&R) *physiatry.* A medical specialty concerned with the management of chronic diseases (some, such as traumatic brain injury, with acute onsets), especially those that are neuromuscular (e.g., stroke, brain injury, arthritis); rehabilitation to return the individual to a pre-disease or pre-injury state is the goal. Diagnostic techniques in PM&R include electromyography and nerve conduction studies (EMG/NCS; tests of muscle activity and how quickly nerves transmit signals). Treatment modalities include heat, ice, physical and occupational therapy, traction, and orthoses (corrective appliances). PM&R specialists are also referred to as *physiatrists.*

physical therapy (PT) A discipline that deals with the examination of gross motor skills and disorders of movement and posture and their treatment through a variety of interventions. These modalities include handling and relaxation techniques, a range of exercises (e.g., strengthening, balancing, and increasing or maintaining range of motion to prevent contractures [permanent contraction of muscle]), and use of adaptive equipment and orthoses (corrective appliances such as braces), all to maximize independent motor functioning.

physiological classification Describes the disorder of tone or movement that characterizes each subtype of cerebral palsy, often with an implication of specific brain area involvement. Spastic and extrapyramidal are the two main subgroups in physiological classification. Physiological classification stands in contrast to topographical classifications of cerebral palsy, which characterize the regions of the body that are most affected. Also known as *neuroanatomical classification.*

phytanic acid storage disease *See* Refsum syndrome.

Piaget, Jean (1896–1980) A Swiss psychologist who researched the cognitive development of children. Concepts integral to his theories include structures (organized patterns for dealing with the environment), adaptation, stages of development, conservation, equilibration, and egocentrism.

PIAT-R/NU *See* Peabody Individual Achievement Test–Revised: Normative Update.

PIBIDS syndrome IBIDS syndrome plus photosensitivity (sensitivity to light). *See* IBIDS syndrome.

pica The eating of dirt or other nonfood objects. Plumbism (lead poisoning) is a major concern with pica, as chips of lead paint or contaminated dirt may be ingested. Pica is seen more frequently in children with autism and intellectual disability who may be at a developmental level at which they tend to explore by putting things in their mouths. When a child pulls out his or her hair and eats it (i.e., trichotillomania), a trichobezoar (hair ball) can form in the stomach. In a developmentally typical child, this behavior should lead to a child psychiatry referral. A reported association between pica and iron deficiency anemia may be coincidental and due to both problems being more common in children of lower socioeconomic background. However, pica may disappear with iron treatment.

Pickwickian syndrome *See* obesity hypoventilation syndrome.

Picsyms A picture symbol system based on easily recognized line drawings of familiar objects.

pictograph *pictogram.* A picture of an item; a graphic symbol that resembles the object it represents. Pictographs were used in some of the earliest systems of written language. Along with ideographs (symbols that represent ideas), pictographs constitute a form of aided augmentative communication used by individuals who are unable to communicate verbally.

Pictorial Test of Intelligence–Second Edition (PTI-2) A battery of instruments used to measure intellectual ability in 3- to 8-year-old children with multiple motor and speech impairments. It requires no verbal and minimal physical responses. Typically, the child is asked to point to the answer. However, the cards are designed so that the examiner may determine a response by observing the eye movements of a child with a physical disability. Testing time is approximately 30 minutes. The PTI-2 is a useful nonverbal measure of learning aptitude for young children with speech and motor disabilities.

Picture Communication Symbols (PCS) A widely used system of more than 7,000 clear, simple, black-and-white or color drawings.

Picture Completion A Wechsler (intelligence test) subtest that measures visual perception, concentration, and visual recognition of essential details of objects.

Picture Concepts A Wechsler (intelligence test) subtest that measures abstract, categorical reasoning.

Picture Exchange Communication System (PECS) A structured behavior program for speech development developed in 1994 for individuals with autism. It uses aided symbols (pictures, photographs, icons, and other visual-graphic symbols) to teach an individual to exchange a symbol for the desired item. For example, a nonverbal child can select a cutout picture of a glass of milk to hand to his or her parent when a glass of milk is desired. The picture allows the child a method of communicating his or her need at that moment in time without using words and without being frustrated at an inability to verbally state his or her needs.

Picture Naming A Wechsler (intelligence test) subscale that measures expressive language ability, word retrieval, and association of visual stimuli with language.

Picture Story Language Test (PSLT) A writing test used in the differential diagnosis of learning disabilities, intellectual disability, emotional disturbance, or reading disability. Children ages 7–17 years are asked to write the best story possible about a picture. Five scores are derived: total words, total sentences, words per sentence, syntax (grammar), and abstract–concrete meaning.

Pidgin Signed English (PSE) *See* Signed English.

piebaldness A depigmentation (absence of color) pattern of skin similar to that of a pinto horse. Piebaldness can be inherited as autosomal dominant or recessive and may be associated with sensorineural (auditory nerve) deafness.

Pierre Robin syndrome A combination of mandibular hypoplasia (micrognathia, or small jaw), soft palate cleft, and glossoptosis (forward displacement of tongue) that produces what is described as a "bird-like" facies. The major medical problem with this syndrome is upper airway obstruction and early failure to thrive (growth difficulties). It occurs in otherwise normal individuals but may also be part such genetic syndromes as Stickler syndrome or trisomy 18. Inheritance is polygenic-multifactorial

(complex with many sources). Recurrence risk is 5%.

Piers-Harris Children's Self Concept Scale–Second Edition *"The Way I Feel About Myself."* A self-report instrument for use with children 7–18 years to quantitate (measure) self-attitude. Sixty statements are scored yes or no; the raw scores yield percentile norms and six factor scores. The scale can be administered individually or to groups of children in 20 minutes.

PIMRA *See* Psychopathology Instrument for Mentally Retarded Adults.

pincer grasp A fine motor milestone in the evolution of infant prehension (the holding of objects in the hand); the grasping overhand of a small object (e.g., pellet, raisin) between the tips of the first two (thumb and index, or pointer) fingers. This mature pincer typically occurs at 10 months of age; an immature pincer or tripod (using the first three fingers) grasp can be observed a month or two earlier.

pincer grasp

pinna The external ear. Pinnal abnormalities are examples of minor dysmorphic (atypical) features that can be normal variants, familial traits, or components of genetic syndromes. Significant ear malformations include folded ("lop-eared"), protuberant ("jug-handle"), posteriorly rotated (tilted backward from the vertical), low set, and excessively rounded ears.

pinna

PIP joint *See* proximal interphalangeal joint.

piracetam A nootropic (substance that improves cognitive abilities); a drug that originally was claimed to treat dyslexia (reading disorder) and that is being researched for effectiveness in treating age-related dementia and Down syndrome.

PIR-GAS *See* Parent–Infant Relationship Global Assessment Scale.

pitch The quality of sound that depends on the frequency of the vibrations producing it. The greater the frequency, the higher or more acute the pitch; the lower the frequency, the lower the pitch and more grave the tone.

pitch break A voice disturbance in which there are unexpected breaks in vocal pitch that cause a deviation in the smooth rate with which the vocal folds normally vibrate.

Pittsburgh Side Effects Rating Scale (PSERS) A clinician-rated scale used to assess the severity of adverse events (AEs; or side effects) associated with medication usage. Such effects include dullness, tiredness, listlessness, headache, stomachache, loss of appetite, and trouble sleeping.

pivotal behavior The acquisition of skill that allows a child to learn many other skills more effectively.

pivotal response training (PRT) A behavioral intervention composed of 1) choice, 2) clear and uninterrupted instructions or opportunities, 3) reinforcement of approximations and attempts, 4) reinforcement has a specific relationship to the desired behavior, 5) presentation of multiple examples or multiple components. Based on the principles of applied behavior analysis (ABA), PRT has been most successful for teaching language, play, and social interaction skills in children with autism.

pivotal response treatment (PRT) PRT was previously called the natural language paradigm (NLP). It is a behavioral intervention model based on the principles of applied behavior analysis (ABA). PRT uses natural learning opportunities to tar-

get and modify key behaviors in children with autism; to teach language; to decrease the occurrence of disruptive/self-stimulatory behaviors; and to increase social, communication, and academic skills by focusing on critical, or "pivotal," behaviors that affect a wide range of behaviors. The primary pivotal behaviors are motivation and the child's initiations of communications with others. Unlike ABA, which targets individual behaviors one at a time, PRT targets pivotal areas of a child's development, such as motivation, responsivity to multiple cues, self-management, and social initiations. The goal of PRT is to produce positive changes in the pivotal behaviors, leading to improvement in communication skills, play skills, social behaviors, and the child's ability to monitor his or her own behavior.

PIY *See* Personality Inventory for Youth.

PKAN *See* pantothenate kinase–associated neurodegeneration.

PKU *See* phenylketonuria.

PL Public law. *See specific PL entries.*

PL 74-271 *See* Social Security Act of 1935.

PL 88-164 *See* Mental Retardation Facilities and Community Mental Health Centers Construction Act of 1963.

PL 89-10 *See* Elementary and Secondary Education Act (ESEA) of 1965.

PL 89-313 *See* Elementary and Secondary Education Act Amendments (ESEA) of 1965.

PL 89-750 *See* Elementary and Secondary Education Act Amendments (ESEA) of 1966.

PL 90-247 *See* Elementary and Secondary Education Act Amendments (ESEA) of 1968.

PL 91-230 *See* Education of the Handicapped Act (EHA) of 1970.

PL 91-517 *See* Developmental Disabilities Services and Facilities Construction Act of 1970.

PL 93-112 *See* Rehabilitation Act of 1973.

PL 93-247 *See* Child Abuse Prevention and Treatment Act (CAPTA) of 1974.

PL 93-380 *See* Education of the Handicapped Act Amendments of 1974.

PL 93-380 *See* Family Educational Rights and Privacy Act (FERPA) of 1974.

PL 94-103 *See* Developmental Disabilities Assistance and Bill of Rights Act of 1975.

PL 94-142 *See* Education for All Handicapped Children Act of 1975.

PL 95-561 *See* Elementary and Secondary Education Act Amendments (ESEA) of 1978.

PL 95-602 *See* Rehabilitation, Comprehensive Services, and Developmental Disabilities Amendments of 1978.

PL 97-35 *See* Omnibus Budget Reconciliation Act (OBRA) of 1981.

PL 97-300 *See* Job Training Partnership Act of 1982.

PL 98-199 *See* Education of the Handicapped Act Amendments of 1983.

PL 98-211 *See* Chapter 1 of the Education Consolidation and Improvement Act of 1981.

PL 98-221 *See* Rehabilitation Act Amendments of 1983.

PL 99-372 *See* Handicapped Children's Protection Act of 1986.

PL 99-401 *See* "Children's Justice and Assistance Act of 1986." *See also* Temporary

Child Care for Handicapped Children and Crises Nurseries Act of 1986.

PL 99-457 *See* Education of the Handicapped Act Amendments of 1986.

PL 99-506 *See* Rehabilitation Act Amendments of 1986.

PL 100-146 *See* Developmental Disabilities Assistance and Bill of Rights Act Amendments of 1987.

PL 100-407 *See* Technology-Related Assistance for Individuals with Disabilities Act of 1988.

PL 101-336 *See* Americans with Disabilities Act (ADA) of 1990.

PL 101-392 *See* Carl D. Perkins Vocational and Applied Technology Education Act of 1990 (PL 101-392; and PL 105-332 amendments of 1998).

PL 101-476 *See* Individuals with Disabilities Education Act (IDEA) of 1990.

PL 101-496 *See* Developmental Disabilities Assistance and Bill of Rights Act Amendments of 1990.

PL 102-119 *See* Individuals with Disabilities Education Act Amendments (IDEA) of 1991.

PL 102-569 *See* Rehabilitation Act Amendments of 1992.

PL 103-218 *See* Technology-Related Assistance for Individuals with Disabilities Act Amendments of 1994.

PL 103-382 *See* Improving America's Schools Act of 1994.

PL 104-191 *See* Health Insurance Portability and Accountability Act (HIPAA) of 1996.

PL 105-17 *See* Individuals with Disabilities Education Act Amendments (IDEA) of 1997.

PL 105-332 amendments of 1998 *See* Carl D. Perkins Vocational and Applied Technology Education Act of 1990 (PL 101-392; and PL 105-332 amendments of 1998).

PL 105-394 *See* Assistive Technology Act ("Tech Act") of 1998.

PL 106-170 *See* Ticket to Work and Work Incentives Improvement Act (TWWIIA) of 1999.

PL 106-402 *See* Developmental Disabilities Assistance and Bill of Rights Act of 2000.

PL 107-110 *See* No Child Left Behind Act (NCLB) of 2001.

PL 108-36 *See* Child Abuse Prevention and Treatment Act (CAPTA) of 1974.

PL 108-364 *See* Assistive Technology Act Amendments of 2004.

PL 108-446 *See* Individuals with Disabilities Education Improvement Act (IDEA) of 2004.

PL 110-325 *See* Americans with Disabilities Act Amendments Act (ADAAA) of 2008.

PL 111-80 *See* Special Supplemental Nutrition Program for Women, Infants, and Children (WIC).

placement An out-of-home living situation for people with long-term-care needs due to physical, cognitive, emotional, or social disabilities. The term may also refer to a classroom, program, and/or therapy that is deemed most appropriate for a student based on diagnostic outcomes and support needs—the educational setting in which a student is "placed." *See* least restrictive environment (LRE).

placenta The afterbirth; an organ that exists during pregnancy and links the mother and the fetus. The placenta assumes many of the functions of the lungs, kidneys, liver, and endocrine system in place of the undeveloped fetal organs. Chronic placental dysfunction can contribute to poor growth of the fetus and low birth weight (LBW).

placenta previa A placenta that is implanted low in the uterus (womb) so that it partially covers the cervical opening (entrance to the uterus). During labor, such a placenta tends to separate (abrupt) and cause bleeding that, if excessive, can threaten the lives of the mother and the infant.

placental abruption *See* abruptio placenta.

placing A primitive reflex in which tactile (touch) stimulation of the dorsum (top) of the foot and/or hand or the anterior (front) aspect of the relevant extremity (arm or leg) results in a complex response of flexion and extension (bending, then straightening in order to "place" the extremity on top of the

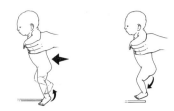

placing—lower extremity

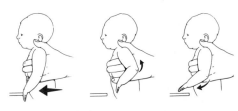

placing—upper extremity

stimulus surface). Lower extremity (leg) placing is present at birth, but upper extremity (arm) placing does not emerge until 3 months of age. Absence or asymmetry of the response is significant.

PL-ADOS *See* Prelinguistic Autism Diagnostic Observation Schedule.

plagiocephaly A positional deformation of the skull (i.e., an abnormal change in shape due to positioning over time) with one side more developed anteriorly (toward the front) and the other side more developed posteriorly (toward the back). This asymmetry can be produced by prolonged lying on one side of the head. Once known as *asynclitism*.

plagiocephaly

PLAI-2 *See* Preschool Language Assessment Instrument–Second Edition.

plantar grasp Reflex (automatic) closure on or voluntary prehension (deliberate grasping) of an object or stimulus with the foot. *See also* grasp reflex.

plantar grasp

plantigrade Describing normal standing/walking posture of the foot in which weight is evenly distributed across the sole and the foot is in a flat position against a surface with the ankle position at 90 degrees. Human gait is a bipedal (involving two feet) plantigrade progression.

plasticity *See* neural plasticity.

plateau A level or leveling off; a period of relative stability and decreased change following a period of normal to increased change.

play A voluntary activity engaged in for pleasure (not work) that can nevertheless serve other social, emotional, and learning functions. Different theories of play generate diverse stages (with overlapping ages) depending on whether the focus is on the type of social interaction, the toys or games used, or the level of imagination and degree of creativity involved. The observation of play can be very informative: An experienced child life worker or preschool teacher can accurately distinguish the evolution from solitary (alone), parallel (side-by-side), and mirror (imitation) play to cooperative play and can reach both quantitatively and qualitatively valid conclusions regarding the child's developmental level. Play is often assessed by occupational therapists both as a means and an end to optimal performance. Factors observed by occupational therapists include 1) what the player does, 2) why the player enjoys the chosen play activities, 3) how the player approaches play, 4) the player's capacity to play, and 5) the relative supportiveness of the environment.

play audiometry *See* behavioral observation audiometry (BOA).

play therapy A psychological method of assessment and treatment used with children. The child is observed as he or she plays freely with a selection of toys designed to help him or her address emotional concerns and traumatic past experiences. Play therapy is often used with children who have been abused and with those who have language disorders. In psychotherapy or speech-language therapy, the strategy is based on the premise that play is the child's natural medium of self-expression, allowing him or her to convey thoughts, feelings, and experiences more easily and directly than would be possible through words.

play-based assessment A naturalistic approach to developmental assessment wherein attainment across developmental domains is assessed through observation of play. This approach can involve a single evaluator working with a child or, as in arena assessment, a facilitator playing with the child while several clinicians observe in order to glean information relevant to their disciplines. *See also* transdisciplinary play-based assessment (TPBA).

pleuritis   Pleurisy; inflammation or infection of the pleura (linings of the lung and chest); symptoms include chest pain, fever, and cough. Treatment is for the underlying cause and is symptomatic.

PLS-3   *See* Preschool Language Scale–3.

plumbism   *See* lead poisoning.

PMA   *See* postmenstrual age.

PMH   Profound mental handicap. *See* profound mental retardation (PMR).

PM&R   *See* physical medicine and rehabilitation.

PMR   *See* profound mental retardation.

pneumonia   Lung infection; symptoms include fever, cough, tachypnea (rapid breathing), and dyspnea (difficulty breathing). The infection is often localized to one side or to one lobe (part) of the lung. *Double pneumonia* is a vague lay term that alludes to the involvement of both lungs. Recurrent right middle lobe pneumonia is often associated with swallowing problems and aspiration (inhalation of food or liquids) in people with neurological impairment.

pneumonitis   Inflammation of the lungs.

PNF   *See* proprioceptive neuromuscular facilitation.

Pohl   A system of physical therapy for the treatment of cerebral palsy; this approach focuses on one joint or muscle action at a time.

pointing   A gesture that can be used to indicate wants (expressive) and identification

(receptive). A receptive language milestone, pointing to pictures and body parts typically begins to emerge at 18 months of age.

Poland anomaly   A unilateral (one-sided) defect of the pectoralis muscle (upper front chest wall) and the ipsilateral (on the same side) hand (i.e., syndactyly [fused or partly fused fingers]). There are no associated developmental disabilities.

POLG   Polymerase (DNA directed), gamma. A gene located on chromosome 15 that is involved in copying mitochondrial deoxyribonucleic acid (DNA). (Mitochondria are cell organelles ["little organs"] that generate energy for cells and have their own DNA [genetic material]). Mutations in the *POLG* gene may result in mitochondrial disorders such as Alpers syndrome, Leigh syndrome, and progressive external ophthalmoplegia (paralysis of the muscles that move the eyes). Children with *POLG* mutations are at increased risk of liver damage if they are given the anticonvulsant (anti-seizure) medication valproate.

poliomyelitis   Polio; infantile paralysis. A viral infection of the central nervous system (CNS; or the brain and spine) that can produce a permanent paralysis that usually affects the lower extremities (legs) more than the upper extremities (arms). The most common source of contagion is respiratory droplets, and most cases are extremely mild. Treatment is supportive (symptomatic) and preventive; immunization (vaccination) of all infants with trivalent oral polio vaccine is recommended. Localized recurrence of muscle weakness can occur decades after initial involvement and is referred to as *postpolio weakness*.

poliosis   Localized depigmentation (loss of color) of hair seen in a variety of syndromes such as tuberous sclerosis. The distinctive white forelock of the genetic syndrome Waardenburg syndrome is a well-known example of this phenomenon.

polydactyly A condition characterized by extra fingers and/or toes (more than five per hand or foot; sometimes very rudimentary). Polydactyly can be an isolated finding, a familial trait, or a component of a genetic syndrome.

polydipsia Excessive consumption of fluids. Polydipsia can be due to diabetes insipidus (nonsugar diabetes), kidney disease, medication effects, or an acquired habit.

polyform One of a group of thermoplastic materials used by therapists to make splints for positioning to improve function, to protect lax or unstable joints, or to reduce the potential for contractures.

polygenic Describing a disorder or trait determined by many genes on different chromosomes or on different parts of the same chromosome. Each gene has a small additive effect.

polyhydramnios Hydramnios; an excessive amount (> 2 L) of amniotic fluid (which surrounds the fetus) during a pregnancy. This condition is associated with a high incidence of fetal abnormalities, especially in relation to the central nervous system (CNS; the brain and spine). These abnormalities can include anencephaly (absent brain) and high alimentary tract obstruction (blockage of the passage from the mouth to the stomach; e.g., esophageal atresia).

polyp A fluid-filled lesion with an active blood supply in the superficial layer of the lamina propria (intestinal wall).

polypharmacology *polypharm.* The use of multiple medications to treat a single condition with the added risk of side effects and negative drug interactions.

polyribosyl ribitol phosphate (PRP-D) *Haemophilus influenzae* type B and diphtheria toxoid conjugate vaccine. The PRP vac- cine is meant to reduce the incidence of *H. influenzae* infections, especially bacterial meningitis (brain infection). Commonly referred to as the Hib (*H. influenzae* type B) vaccine. Other Hib vaccines include Hboc and PRP-OMP.

polysemy A condition in which a single word has two or more meanings. Poetry is often polysemous.

polysomnogram (PSG) An overnight sleep study; a test consisting of recordings of multiple physiological parameters (body activities) obtained during sleep to diagnose sleep disorders, typically sleep-related breathing disorders. Parameters studied can include simultaneous recordings of oral and nasal airflow, electroencephalogram (EEG; or brain wave), electromyogram (muscle activity), electro-oculogram (eye movements), electrocardiogram (ECG; or heart activity), and oxygen saturation. Such studies are usually carried out in a specialized sleep laboratory, although portable devices for limited home studies are becoming available. Not all sleep problems are appropriately evaluated by PSG.

polysomy The presence of more than two chromosomes of the same kind. A trisomy (three chromosomes of the same number) is one sort of polysomy. Polysomies of chromosomes other than the sex chromosomes are generally lethal or cause multiple congenital malformations and intellectual disability. Children with polysomy X, or multiple copies of the X chromosome, may have problems ranging from mild cognitive impairments (such as language disorders) to more severe global cognitive problems with intellectual disability.

polytherapy The use of more than one therapy (usually drugs). This term is generally used in reference to seizure treatment that involves the use of two or more anticonvulsant agents (anti-seizure medications). The goal behind polytherapy is better seizure control; however, it has some disadvantages and is not the preferred treatment for an uncomplicated seizure disorder. Toxicity (side effects) of anticonvulsants is greater with multiple drug therapy. The cumulative effect of multiple agents often includes lethargy and decreased cognitive performance.

Pompe disease *generalized glycogenosis, glycogenosis type II.* A storage disease in which an excess of glycogen, a storage form of sugar, accumulates in the body because of problems with the enzyme that normally breaks it down. Untreated Pompe disease results in progressive hypotonia (low muscle tone), intellectual disability, cardiomegaly (enlarged heart), cardiorespiratory failure, and death. Treatment with enzyme replacement is available.

POMR *See* problem-oriented medical record.

Pondimin *See* fenfluramine.

"pop eyes" *See* exophthalmos.

population A group of people with similar characteristics. Most references to populations indicate specific groups, such as males, females, those with learning disabilities, or those with Down syndrome. Researchers generally study the characteristics of a particular group as compared with the general population, which is a larger, more heterogeneous group. Often the effect of an intervention on a particular population is studied. It is important to clearly define the characteristics of a group in a research protocol in order to be able to generalize the research results to others in that population.

porencephalic cyst A cavity in the brain caused by focal damage to brain tissue. Porencephalic cysts may be caused by vascular (blood vessel) abnormalities such as hemorrhage (bleeding) or infectious insults.

The injury may occur prenatally (before birth) or postnatally (after birth). The cyst can mimic a brain tumor and can cause hydrocephalus (a buildup of fluid in the brain). Neurological impairments are generally asymmetrical and contralateral (on the side opposite the cyst). Typical development can occur even with large porencephalic cysts. Porencephalic cysts can occur in premature infants after an intraventricular hemorrhage (IVH; or bleeding into the fluid-filled spaces in the brain).

Portage Project *Portage Early Education Program.* A home-based early education program for preschool children with disabilities with a focus on parental involvement. The program has its own assessment instrument (i.e., the Developmental Sequence Checklist) that is used to generate an individual curriculum by selecting one of four to seven ways to teach each of the 580 skills contained in the assessment. It is named for Portage, Wisconsin, the site of the original program.

Porteus Maze Test An intelligence test for use with people ages 3 to adult; it is composed entirely of paper-and-pencil mazes and has been used as a measure of attention as well as of visual-perceptual motor ability. Two additional versions, the Maze Test Extension and the Extension Supplement, are used to control for practice effects (an improved score because of familiarity with the test items).

portfolio assessment A curriculum-based approach to assessing language that consists of assessing a collection of work selected by the learner and various professionals (e.g., speech-language pathologist, teacher) that profiles the learner's use of targeted communication behavior(s). Items in the portfolio might include writing samples, journal entries, projects, essay responses, and presentations.

port-wine stain *nevus flammeus.* A purple, sometimes raised, irregular vascular (composed of blood vessels) skin lesion; can be a component of Sturge-Weber syndrome.

position in space perception The awareness of the spatial properties of an object.

positive behavioral interventions and supports (PBIS) *positive behavior support (PBS), schoolwide positive behavior support (SWPBS).* The application of research-supported behavioral science to preventing problem behavior, supporting individuals and groups, and promoting valued outcomes such as lifestyle change and community participation. A proactive alternative to consequence-based (behavior modification) approaches to managing problem behaviors, PBS is based on the assumption that persistent problematic behavior serves some function for the individual. PBS began as a reaction to aversive therapies applied to reduce problem behaviors in individuals. Individualized PBS, mandated under all authorizations of the Individuals with Disabilities Education Improvement Act (IDEA) of 2004 (PL 108-446), involves conducting a functional behavioral assessment (FBA) to understand the function of problem behavior (why it occurs) and then developing a behavior improvement plan (BIP). The BIP indicates short-term interventions designed to prevent the behavior from occurring through environmental adaptations or accommodations and longer term solutions that focus on replacing the problem behavior by teaching socially acceptable alternatives or skills that serve the same function. Contemporary PBS is commonly called PBIS or SWPBS and involves a three-tiered approach: the use of 1) universal or primary prevention strategies for all members of a community or context, 2) secondary or targeted interventions for individuals at risk or with emerging problems, and 3) individualized PBS for individuals with established problems. SWPBS provides an operational framework for achieving outcomes such as improving student academic and behavioral outcomes. SWPBS is a decision-making framework that guides the selection, integration, and implementation of evidence-based academic and behavioral practices to improve important academic and behavioral outcomes for all students. An important component of PBIS and SWPBS is the emphasis on organizational and cultural systems that encourage or discourage adaptive and desirable behavior as well as data-based decision making at all levels. *See also* Behavior Education Program (BEP), functional behavioral assessment (FBA), positive strategies.

positive end expiratory pressure (PEEP) A type of assisted ventilation (breathing support) used with children with respiratory distress. PEEP uses gases (either room air or air with added oxygen) pumped at a certain pressure to keep open the airway in order to avoid collapse at the end of expiration (breathing out).

positive reinforcement *See* consequent stimulus event (CSE).

positive strategies Designed for managing challenging and persistent behaviors that interfere with learning and adjustment, positive strategies seek to replace dangerous, challenging, and problematic behaviors with more functional, adaptive alternatives. Positive strategies are based on three basic elements: understanding the context and reinforcers of the behavior, preventing the behavior in the future, and replacing problematic behaviors with more adaptive alternatives. *See also* positive behavioral interventions and supports (PBIS).

positive support A complex postural response in which pressure on the feet produces varying degrees of lower extremity extension (leg straightening) and body support. A sequence of positive supporting reactions occur from early newborn 1) neonatal supporting ("sitting in air"), through the state of 2) abasia-astasia (ataxic gait), to the mature form of 3) positive support seen at

5–6 months of age. Supporting reactions remain throughout life.

positron emission tomography (PET) A technique used to investigate brain function with radioactively labeled compounds. These compounds are taken up by areas of greater brain activity and can be visualized on imaging. PET scans can localize within the brain areas of abnormal functioning, such as in focal seizure disorders.

postconceptional age (PCA) Chronological age (CA) plus gestational age according to the obstetrical history of the mother's last menstrual period (LMP); thus, a 4-week-old (CA) infant born at 28 weeks' gestation has a PCA of 32 weeks. In extremely premature infants, PCA (which is dependent on maternal history) is often more accurate than an age dependent on physical examination.

postconcussion syndrome Headache, dizziness, irritability, nervousness, poor concentration, and behavioral and cognitive impairment that may follow a concussion (brain injury with transient loss of consciousness). Parents may report that a child's personality changed or that hyperactivity and an attention disorder began after a specific brain injury. Most of the minor brain injuries experienced by toddlers learning to walk have no sequelae (consequences).

posteroanterior view (PA) Describing an x ray taken so that the beam goes from the back of the body to the front.

postictal Occurring after a seizure. During the postictal period, behavior such as somnolence (sleepiness), confusion, ataxia (unsteady gait), and poor coordination may occur. Mild abnormalities are often found in the neurological examination. Occasionally, temporary blindness, aphasia (loss of language skills), or paralysis (i.e., Todd paralysis) may be seen. The postictal period can last several hours.

postmaturity The gestational period of an infant born beyond 42 weeks of pregnancy. Placental insufficiency (loss of placental substance that nourishes the fetus in the uterus) contributes to the infant's looking thin and wasted, with dry, peeling skin, and meconium (fetal stool) staining of the skin and nails; length and head circumference may be increased.

postmenstrual age (PMA) Chronological age (CA) plus gestational age calculated from the mother's last menstrual period (LMP); thus, an 8-week-old (CA) infant born at 28 weeks' gestation has a PMA of 36 weeks.

postnatal Occurring after birth; pertaining to the individual's life cycle after the conclusion of the perinatal period (after 28 days of life).

postpartum The period after the birth of an infant, in reference to the mother.

postprandial After eating.

postterm Describing an infant born after the typical length of gestation (pregnancy)— usually more than 2 weeks after 40 weeks (9 months). Postterm infants are at risk for problems caused by the placenta (the organ connecting the fetus and mother) ceasing to work, thus not providing them with enough oxygen and nutrition.

posttraumatic amnesia Memory loss for the period of "clouded consciousness" that follows a closed brain injury (one in which the skull remains intact); it ends when the individual remembers waking. Also referred to as *anterograde amnesia.*

posttraumatic stress disorder (PTSD) A psychological syndrome that follows an extraordinary stress or trauma. Symptoms of this disorder may include sudden, intrusive vivid visual or auditory memory flashbacks; hyper-alertness; difficulty concentrating; feelings of numbness; and an inability to participate in intimate relationships. Children with PTSD may appear to have developmental delays. Long-term psychotherapy is the indicated treatment.

postural control The ability to maintain body position while upright.

postural drainage Techniques used to help clear mucus from the respiratory tract (airway and lungs). It is used in people with chronic respiratory problems (e.g., asthma, cystic fibrosis, cerebral palsy with limited ability to move that increases vulnerability to recurrent respiratory infections). Postural drainage can be performed or supervised by a physical or respiratory therapist.

postural response A group of reflex patterns that appear after birth, become prominent after 6 months of age, and facilitate the development of voluntary movement. They include the Landau, righting, equilibrium, and propping reactions.

postural-ocular movement disorder *See* vestibular-bilateral disorder.

poverty A chronic low standard of living that undermines the health, morale, and self-respect of an individual or group of individuals. Poverty is relative to the general standard of living in a society, the distribution of wealth, and social expectations. The impact of neurodevelopmental disabilities is intensified by family educational level and limited access to resources.

power grasp The position of the hand for holding objects, such as a knife or a tool, in which the middle, ring, and little fingers and thumb hold the object. The index finger may control the object's movement or assist the other fingers in holding the object.

PPD *See* purified protein derivative.

PPI *See* Parent Perception Inventory.

PPVT-IV *See* Peabody Picture Vocabulary Test–Fourth Edition.

PR *See* primitive reflex.

practice effect An improved performance or score on a test as a result of repeated exposure to the test items, either from practice or drills on such tasks or from a recent administration of the same version of the test. Most test manuals indicate the period of time needed to elapse to minimize practice effects on test readministration.

Prader-Willi syndrome (PWS) *Prader-Labhart-Willi syndrome.* A genetic syndrome with three phases: 1) infancy with hypotonia (floppiness) and failure to thrive (poor growth); 2) childhood with almond-shaped eyes, short palpebral fissures (eye slits), hypogonadism (small testicles), hypoplastic (small to absent) scrotum, hyperphagia (ravenous appetite) with central obesity (extra weight carried mostly in the trunk and abdomen) but small hands and feet, cognitive impairments (two thirds of the cases are marked by intellectual disability, one third by learning disabilities and language impairments); and 3) young adulthood with an increased severity of childhood symptoms coupled with severe behavior and emotional symptomatology and, occasionally, thought disorders. This syndrome reflects a hypothalamic dysfunction (the hypothalamus is an area of the brain) secondary to an alteration of genetic material on chromosome 15. Without adequate dietary management, life expectancy is limited by heart failure and respiratory symptoms secondary to obesity. *See also* Angelman syndrome (AS).

pragmatics The effective use of language appropriate to a given context. For children to achieve communicative competence, they must acquire a repertoire of socially acceptable strategies for controlling or influencing the behavior of their listeners, including informing, requesting information, taking turns in conversations, adjusting what they are saying to their listener's linguistic ability, and responding to requests for clarification. Pragmatics may be described as one more level of rules after phonology (speech sound), syntax (grammar), and semantics (the meaning of words). However, a broader interpretation includes the integration of structural, conversational, and social rules. Thus, a different set of pragmatic strategies would be necessary in the classroom than at home. Assessment may be done informally and may need to be repeated in different settings.

prandial aspiration Aspiration associated with eating.

praxis Skill in planning purposive movements. *Apraxia* is the absence of such skill, such as an inability to write. *See also* motor planning.

preauricular pit A small indentation near the front of the ear; 1 in 200 children with preauricular pits will have a profound hearing loss. *See also* Melnick-Fraser syndrome.

precipitous delivery Abnormally rapid expulsion of the fetus at birth.

predictive validity The degree to which a test predicts future performance on a related task.

preeclampsia The preconvulsive (before seizures) stage of the condition eclampsia (an acute, life-threatening complication of pregnancy). Preeclampsia is primarily seen in primigravidas (first-time mothers). Preeclampsia was formerly called *toxemia of pregnancy*, but the term was changed because no apparent "toxins" were identified. The individual often has high blood pressure, protein in the urine, and pitting edema (swelling due to fluid retention, to the point that pressure on swollen areas leaves an indentation ["pitting"]). *See also* eclampsia.

prefix A type of bound morpheme that can be added at the beginning of a word to change its meaning.

prehension Physical grasp; the manner in which the hand takes an object (e.g., pincer grasp, radial rake).

preimplantation genetic diagnosis (PGD) A procedure performed prior to in vitro fertilization to test cells for the presence or absence of specific genetic defects before the embryo is transferred to the uterus. PGD is offered to high-risk individuals.

Prelinguistic Autism Diagnostic Observation Schedule (PL-ADOS) A version of the Autism Diagnostic Observation Schedule (ADOS) designed to assess autism in children who do not use language. Administration by a trained clinician involves a 30-minute semistructured observation of play and social interaction. The clinician codes observations to formulate a diagnosis based on cutoff scores for autism and pervasive developmental disorders. *See also* Autism Diagnostic Observation Schedule–Revised (ADOS-R).

prelinguistic vocalizations The guttural (harsh and grating) sounds, cooing, and babbling that an infant uses before words. Despite a lack of verbal content, such vocalizations exhibit an orderliness and sequentiality that allow them to be used to monitor early expressive language development. A decrease in such vocalizations—the "quiet baby"—suggests the presence of a developmental disorder.

Premack principle A principle whose premise indicates that if a frequent behavior is made contingent upon an infrequent behavior, the infrequent behavior will increase in frequency. Also known as *Grandma's rule*: "You can't have dessert unless you finish eating your broccoli." In a classroom setting, an example of the Premack principle is allowing a child computer time after his or her mathematics is finished. A broader application of this principle structures a student's academic day so that a difficult task is followed by an easier or more enjoyable one. Named for psychologist David Premack (1925–).

prenatal Preceding birth; pertaining to the gestational period (pregnancy) from conception to birth (the beginning of the perinatal period).

prenatal diagnosis Identification of a fetal problem before birth. Techniques such as ultrasound and amniocentesis (transabdominal sampling of the amniotic fluid) are used to look at the structure of the fetus, the fetal chromosomes, and any fetal or genetic syndrome or disorder that can be identified by a biochemical test.

preoperational stage A Piagetian stage of cognitive development in which the child begins to internalize and manipulate symbols and images in an egocentric fashion. This stage is prominent from 2 to 6 years of age.

prephonemic spelling The pattern of spelling behaviors in which one uses letter or letter-like symbols to represent language, suggesting a lack of understanding between the correspondence of print and oral language.

presbyopia Farsightedness. With advancing age, presbyopia may correct or improve the myopia (nearsightedness) of the preceding years.

Preschool Language Assessment Instrument–Second Edition (PLAI-2) A nonstandardized test used to assess a variety of language skills; six subtests and an overall Discourse Ability Score are generated. It can be used with children 3–6 years of age.

Preschool Language Scale–3 (PLS-3) A language test for use with children from 2 weeks to age 6;11 years that yields total language, auditory comprehension, and expressive communication scores. Administration time is 30 minutes. A normed Spanish-language version is available.

Preschool Screening System A screening test for use with children between 2;6 and 5;6 years of age. Subtests include gross and fine motor, vocabulary, and speech and language skills. Administration time is approximately 20 minutes.

Prescreening Developmental Questionnaire (PDQ-II) *See* Denver Developmental Screening Test–Second Edition.

prescription drug plan (PDP) A plan offered by one of several private companies that provide the prescription drugs for people with Medicare through Medicare Part D. These companies must follow rules regarding the classes and number of choices of drugs in each class. Plans use a formulary that lists the drugs they cover. Everyone with Medicare is eligible for prescription drug coverage through a PDP if he or she does not have equivalent coverage through another source. People with disabilities who are eligible for both Medicare and Medicaid (also referred to as *dually eligible*) must receive their prescription drugs through Medicare unless they are not covered under Part D.

prescriptive approaches Prescriptive education approaches are individually designed curricula based upon thorough diagnostic evaluation of a child's specific learning abilities and disabilities. They include educational programming, presentation methodologies, and task assignment based on the student's needs and abilities rather than instruction aimed at the "average" learner.

presentation The chief complaint (stated main concern), symptoms (reported problems), and signs (objective abnormalities present on physical examination or in other test results) present when an individual first comes to a physician's attention.

presentation The part of the infant that comes out first during delivery. There are three main types of presentation: vertex (head first), face (chin first), and breech (sacrum [tailbone] first). A transverse presentation usually involves the shoulder coming out first. The most common vertex presentation is left occiput anterior (LOA; or left side of the back of the head first).

preservation of sameness The tendency to resist change; a nonspecific sign of brain impairment. In its mildest forms, preservation of sameness is similar to a typical child's need for a bedtime ritual; in its more severe forms, the child may throw prolonged tantrums if a single item is out of place.

preservice training Literally, "before service." Training efforts, often at a university or other educational institution, designed to prepare individuals for entry-level positions within their fields before they serve in a professional role.

Pre-Speech Assessment Scale (PSAS) A nonstandardized rating scale used to measure pre-speech behaviors (e.g., feeding, oral motor, breath sound items) in children from birth to 2 years of age.

pressure equalization (PE) tubes *tympanostomy tubes.* Tubes that are surgically implanted in the ear in order to equalize the pressure on both sides of the eardrum and prevent the accumulation of fluid behind the eardrum. This procedure results in improved hearing and a decreased number of ear infections.

pressure points Points on the body at which an underlying artery can be pressed against a bone to stop distal bleeding; also, an area on the skin that is highly sensitive to the application of pressure. These points are especially vulnerable to the development of "pressure sores," such as bedsores for those confined to bed or sitting sores for those permanently confined to wheelchairs or other sitting supports.

pressure sores *See* decubiti.

pressured speech Speech that is increased in amount and speed, loud and emphatic, and difficult to interrupt. It occurs in mania and other psychiatric disorders.

pretend play Play that involves object substitution; objects are used as if they have other properties or identities (e.g., pouring "tea" from a toy teapot into a toy teacup in the absence of any liquid, or waving a stick as if it were a sword).

preterm Describing a pregnancy that does not go to the expected (due) birth date. Preterm indicates a gestational age less than 37 weeks, very preterm is less than 32 weeks, and extremely preterm is less than 28 weeks. Early preterm is less than 34 weeks, whereas late preterm (not near term) is 34–37 weeks. *Preterm* describes the pregnancy, whereas *premature* describes the infant.

prevalence The number of cases of a disorder that exist in a given population at a specific time (point prevalence) or over a defined period of time (period prevalence). Prevalence is affected by both the rate of occurrence of the disorder as well as the duration of the condition. An increasing prevalence might reflect an actual increase in the rate of occurrence of the condition, or it might also reflect improved medical treatment with longer survival. For example, the availability of better medical care and healthier living conditions should lead to an increase in the total number of people with intellectual disability in the population at any given time.

prevention Measures that decrease the incidence or limit the progression of a disease or its sequelae (consequences). There are varying classifications of the different levels of prevention; because these were originally developed with regard to acute infectious diseases, they do not always translate smoothly to neurodevelopmental disabilities.

Preverbal Assessment Intervention Profile (PAIP) A standardized Piagetian assessment of sensorimotor prelinguistic (occurring before the development of speech and language skills) behavior that can be used with individuals of all ages with severe, profound, and multiple disabilities.

prewriting skills A group of skills necessary for successful writing, including pencil grasp and the ability to copy simple forms.

primary auditory cortex (A1) *Brodmann areas 41 and 42, Heschl's gyrus.* The area of the brain responsible for the reception of sound. Although input from the contralateral (opposite) ear is predominant, the temporal lobe of each hemisphere (area of the brain responsible for hearing in each half of the brain) receives input from both ears. *See also* temporal cortex.

primary disorder of vigilance (PDV) *Weinberg syndrome.* A disorder characterized by decreased alertness, wakefulness with tiredness, inattention, dawdling, disorganization, daydreaming, sleepy-eyed ("glassy-eyed") appearance, and motor restlessness (e.g., fidgeting, moving about [minor busyness], yawning, stretching, and talkativeness). The syndrome resembles attention-deficit/hyperactivity disorder (ADHD).

primary palate The hard palate or the roof of the mouth.

primary prevention Efforts that decrease the likelihood of accidents, violence, or disease. In primary prevention, the aim is to intervene prior to the occurrence of disability to prevent it from happening or to decrease its impact.

primary process A psychoanalytic term that refers to primitive, irrational, wishful thinking or thought dominated by uncon-

scious emotions and instinctual drives. In counseling parents of children with developmental disabilities, too much focus is often placed on the cognitive content (secondary process) of the information communicated, to the exclusion of the emotional impact (primary process).

primary visual cortex (V1) *Brodmann area 17.* The occipital pole (tips of the back portion of the halves of the brain, responsible for vision) and the calcarine fissure (a specific anatomical landmark) of the brain. The striate cortex (part of the outer layer of the brain with a "striped" appearance under the microscope) in each hemisphere (half) receives input from the contralateral (opposite) visual fields of both eyes.

primidone Trade name, Mysoline. An anticonvulsant drug used to treat seizures.

primigravida A woman pregnant for the first time. First pregnancies may need closer observation than later pregnancies and may be associated with slightly increased risks for both mother and child.

primipara A woman with only one (her first) pregnancy, either during or after that pregnancy. *See also* parity.

primitive reflex (PR) A group of reflex patterns present at birth that tend to be suppressed or linked into more functional voluntary movement patterns over time. These patterns originate in the brainstem (the connection between the brain and the spinal cord) and may persist in the presence of cortical (outer layer of the brain) or other brain damage that interferes with the evolution of voluntary movements; they may also reappear in older children and adults after severe brain injury. They play a clinical role in the examination of infants younger than 6 months of age. Most of the patterns involve the overriding impact of head position and head movement on the tone, movement, and posture of the four extremities (arms and legs). PRs include the Moro, Galant, asymmetrical tonic neck, symmetrical tonic neck, tonic labyrinthine (extension of all four extremities), stepping, crossed extension, and placing reflexes.

print awareness A child's interest in printed material, understanding that printed material is organized from left to right, and understanding that printed words and letters have specific names.

prion diseases A group of infectious diseases in which the infectious agent (prion) causes sponge-like holes in the brain. They include kuru (transmitted among the Fore culture in New Guinea by consumption of infected human brains) and bovine spongiform encephalitis (BSE; or "mad cow disease") transmitted from eating infected meat. Prion diseases can be hereditary (e.g., Creutzfeldt-Jakob disease).

PRN *See* pro re nata.

pro re nata (PRN) As needed; whenever necessary; as the occasion arises. Sometimes used as a direction for administration of medications or therapies.

proband *See* propositus.

probe A sample of a child's work used to conduct a curriculum-based assessment.

probe A test for generalization (the ability to take something learned in one context and apply it in another context) in operant language training.

probe In competency-based training (training to a specific level of skills), an opportunity for the student to demonstrate skill acquisition without assistance or feedback.

probiotic A dietary supplement containing live bacteria or yeast that is used to help the intestine (gut) to reestablish its natural flora, especially in the case of presumed yeast overgrowth. The most commonly used probiotic is yogurt.

problem solving Often used to refer to non-verbal cognitive abilities in infants and young children; this stream of development is measured by visual-perceptual-motor items (e.g., playing with toys) on infant tests.

problem-oriented medical record (POMR) The result of an approach to record keeping with a focus on a defined list of problems. Notes are written in a SOAP structure: S—subjective data (what the individual reports), O—objective data (what the evaluator sees), A—assessment (what the evaluator identifies as issues), and P—plan.

procedural knowledge A construct concerned with the way in which certain information is represented in memory. Procedural knowledge is composed of knowing "how" to do something. It is dynamic in that it results not simply in recall but in a transformation of information. Once learned well, procedural knowledge operates in a fast, automatic fashion (e.g., print is decoded by skilled readers with little awareness of the process). *See also* declarative knowledge, memory.

procedural safeguards Those checks and guards that ensure that timely and appropriate services are provided to children with special education needs. For instance, all special education laws require that children with disabilities be served in the least restrictive environment (LRE) appropriate to their educational needs based on the timely provision of nondiscriminatory testing and the use of multiple criteria in the determination of placement. *See also* Education for All Handicapped Children Act of 1975 (PL 94-142).

procedure A surgical operation.

Processing and Cognitive Enhancement Program (PACE) An intensive one-to-one tutoring program that uses games to improve attention, memory, and the processing skills presumed to underlie learning. Brain Skills is the online version of PACE.

prodrome An early symptom of a disease that usually appears before the disease shows sufficient other symptoms to allow it to be diagnosed. The term *prodrome* can also refer to a grouping of symptoms that collectively represent the first stage of a disease before the full-blown syndrome shows itself.

profound hearing impairment Hearing loss that ranges in severity greater than 90 dBHL (decibels hearing level).

profound mental retardation (PMR) *profound mental handicap (PMH).* Antiquated term that describes intellectual disability in which the intelligence quotient (IQ) level is less than 25. The preferred term is *profound intellectual disability.* Adults with profound intellectual disability often need assistance in adaptive skills and may reside in intermediate care facilities.

progeria *Hutchinson-Gilford syndrome (HGPS).* A rare condition characterized by premature aging and shortened life expectancy; cognition is unaffected. A G608G mutation in exon 11 of the *LMNA* gene is present in all individuals with progeria.

progestin A hormone used to treat women who exhibit symptoms associated with menstrual irregularities or premenstrual syndrome (PMS); long-acting injections of progestin (e.g., Depo-Provera) are also used for contraception.

prognathia A protuberant jaw. Prognathia can be a normal variant, a familial trait, a minor malformation, or part of an identifiable syndrome.

prognosis A prediction; a description of the probable course and outcome of a given disease or therapy.

Program Assessment Rating Tool (PART) A program instituted in 2002 by President George W. Bush and administered through the U.S. Office of Management and Budget (OMB) to rate all federal programs on their effectiveness. The PART is also the diagnostic questionnaire designed to help assess the management and performance of federally funded programs and to drive improvements in program performance. Once completed, PART reviews help inform budget decisions and identify actions to improve results. Agencies are held accountable for implementing PART follow-up actions, also known as *improvement plans,* for each of their programs. The PART is designed to provide a consistent approach to assessing and rating programs across the federal government. PART assessments review overall program effectiveness, from how well a program is designed to how well it is implemented and what results it achieves.

Program for the Acquisition of Language with the Severely Impaired (PALS) A functional, environmental, and conversational approach to the assessment of severe language disorders that uses caregiver interviews and environmental observations to identify communication partners, communication content, and communication behaviors. The Diagnostic Interview Survey is then used with nonspeaking or minimally verbal clients. The Developmental Assessment Tool is the more formal third step in this individualized evaluation and treatment program.

programmed learning A self-instruction method that presents subject content in a predetermined sequence that allows students to check their progress, determine what part of the sequence they may not have effectively learned, go back in the sequence as necessary, and proceed at their own pace. Programmed learning is presented in the form of workbooks or computer programs.

progressive encephalopathy Degenerative disease of the central nervous system; refers to progressive deterioration (loss of function over time) or a progressively downhill course.

projectile vomiting Vomiting in which the material is ejected with great force.

projective test A technique that uses vague, ambiguous stimuli to elicit the person's characteristic mode of perceiving the world. The individual "projects" his or her unconscious conflicts, thoughts, and feelings into the unstructured test item, which might be an inkblot (Rorschach test), drawing, or scene (the Thematic Apperception Test [TAT]); individuals may also be asked to draw a person, house, or tree. Projective tests assume that direct questions produce answers that are carefully crafted and filtered by the respondent's conscious mind. The validity of projective tests is difficult to establish within the general population, in part because scoring is subjective (prone to bias). The result is different interpretations of test results, depending on the examiner and the context. Furthermore, individuals with disabilities may be placed at a particular disadvantage on projective tests because disabilities commonly affect visual, motor, and language skills that shape responses.

prolongation A type of disfluency in which the duration of speech or articulatory segments is noticeably longer than expected.

prompt An action that increases the probability of a target behavior occurring by reducing the time the person has to do to complete it. Prompts can range from verbal cues to being physically guided through the motions of the desired response.

Prompts for Restructuring Oral Phonetic Targets (PROMPT) A speech therapy technique that links motor movements of the mouth, face, and jaw to communicative intent.

pronation The turning of an extremity downward. For example, the palm turns downward with pronation of the forearm.

pronation

prone The anatomical position in which the person is lying face downward on his or her abdomen (the opposite of supine, or lying on the back).

prone stander Adaptive equipment used to promote kneeling or full standing posture in infants or children unable to stand. The trunk and extremities are supported on the child's prone side (tilted forward).

prone wedges Foam wedges that support the child and promote upper extremity (arm) weight bearing while in the prone position (lying on the stomach).

pronominal reversal Confusion between first- and second-person pronouns (not the genders of third-person pronouns). Pronominal reversal is probably related in part to echolalia (repetition of what is heard), in part to the phenomenon of referring to the self by name or by third-person pronouns, and in part to egocentrism. Mixing up the case of pronouns—*I/me, he/him, she/her,* and *they/them*—does not count as pronominal reversal. Pronominal reversal can occur in autism and language disorders.

prophylaxis Prevention.

propionic acidemia An autosomal recessive metabolic disorder characterized by recurrent vomiting, lethargy, and coma that can lead to developmental delay and death. Prenatal diagnosis is available, and there is some response to protein restriction and biotin (one of the B vitamins) supplementation.

propositus The index case, or proband. The person in a family who first comes to the attention of professionals with an identified trait (quality), possibly leading to the identification of that trait or others within a family. For example, the child with intellectual disability who is diagnosed with the genetic condition tuberous sclerosis, leading to an evaluation of the family for tuberous sclerosis, is the propositus.

propping Holding weight on an extended (usually upper [the arm]) extremity. *See* protective extension.

propranolol Trade name, Inderal. A beta-adrenergic blocker drug with many cardiovascular applications. It is sometimes used to treat aggression and self-injurious behaviors in people with severe developmental disabilities.

proprietary name Trade name or brand name. *See* trade name.

proprioception Position sense. This sensory function is often evaluated during neurological examinations by having an individual close his or her eyes while the examiner lifts the person's toes up and down and has him or her identify the direction in which the toes have been moved.

proprioceptive facilitation Therapeutic activities that treat neuromuscular dysfunctioning by stimulating the proprioceptive system (position sense). Proprioceptive facilitation techniques include heavy joint compression, stretch, resistance, tapping, and vibration.

proprioceptive neuromuscular facilitation (PNF) A system of physical therapy used to treat cerebral palsy that uses spiral and diagonal mass movement patterns and heavy resistance isotonic exercises.

prosody The pattern of speech as determined by rate, inflection, and rhythm. Prosodic variations include shouting, rising versus falling pitch, angry voice, and wheedling tone. The babbling of infants eventually reflects the prosody of the parent language before actual words are uttered.

prosthesis An artificial body part (e.g., artificial leg, glass eye).

protection and advocacy (P&A) Describing a system of state agencies established through federal legislation to protect and advocate for the rights of people with developmental disabilities. P&A agencies are independent of other governmental agencies or units to ensure that they are able to freely serve the interests of their clientele. Duties and activities of the P&A staff may include negotiation, administrative or legal intervention on behalf of individuals seeking services, or securing and protecting of people's rights and privileges as citizens. Public dissemination of information concerning the rights of individuals with developmental disabilities through publications, presentations, and workshops is a further responsibility of P&A systems. Education, employment, transportation, housing, recreation, facility accessibility, and the entitlement of people with developmental disabilities to these services are of interest to the P&A system. The specific names of such agencies vary from state to state. *See also* Developmental Disabilities Assistance and Bill of Rights Act of 1975 (PL 94-103).

protective extension Propping reactions; a subgroup of upper extremity postural responses concerned with maintaining an upright position. This group of reflexes includes anterior (front), lateral (side), and posterior (back) propping and the anterior parachute response. *See also* parachute.

anterior parachute response

protective reactions Postural reactions that protect a person from a fall by extension of the extremities (arms or legs) in a forward, lateral (sideways), or backward direction.

protective services Services ranging from mandated monitoring to alternative placement for people in danger of harm from themselves or others or who are no longer physically or cognitively able to care for themselves.

protocol A list of rules, often hierarchical or with a decision tree. Research and treatment protocols detail how research or therapy is to be conducted (i.e., the research or treatment methodology).

protodeclarative pointing Pointing at an object or event for the purpose of drawing someone else's attention to it. By the beginning of the second year of life, children will point to something to indicate a want (protoimperative pointing); by the middle of the second year of life they will point to identify something (demonstration of receptive language development). By 2 years of age they will point to an object to draw someone else's attention to it (protodeclarative pointing); this is a reflection of joint attention, a reciprocal (give and take) social interaction that is typically delayed or absent in children with autism spectrum disorder.

protopathic Relating to the indistinct peripheral (noncentral) sensation of pain and temperature.

protrusion Extension beyond the usual limits; sticking out.

Provigil *See* modafinil.

proximal Closest to the center.

proximal interphalangeal (PIP) joint The middle joint of each finger.

proximal transverse palmar crease A flexion crease on the palm of the hand.

proximal transverse palmar crease

Prozac *See* fluoxetine.

PRP-D *See* polyribosyl ribitol phosphate.

PRT *See* pivotal response training.

PRT *See* pivotal response treatment.

pruritus Itching.

PSAS *See* Pre-Speech Assessment Scale.

PSC *See* Pediatric Symptom Checklist.

PSE Pidgin Signed English. *See* Signed English.

PSERS *See* Pittsburgh Side Effects Rating Scale.

pseudarthrosis False joint. This can occur as a complication of surgery after a fracture fails to heal properly or secondary to some other underlying disease (e.g., neurofibromatosis).

pseudobulbar palsy Impaired swallowing, talking, and chewing secondary to brain damage. The oral motor control of the lips, tongue, mouth, larynx (windpipe), and pharynx (throat) by cranial nerves X and XII (the vagus and hypoglossus nerves, respectively) typically resides in the bulba (medulla oblongata, a part of the brainstem). Damage to these centers produces a bulbar palsy (motor neuron disease). When a similar pattern of dysfunction occurs as a result of more diffuse brain involvement, it is referred to as *pseudobulbar palsy* and is sometimes associated with the more severe degrees of cerebral palsy.

pseudohypertelorism The misleading appearance of hypertelorism (widely spaced eyes) when this condition not really present. Epicanthal folds and an increased inner canthal distance (the distance between the inner corners of the eyes) can contribute to this illusion, but a normal interpupillary (between the pupils of the eyes) distance corrects this impression.

pseudohypoparathyroidism A genetic syndrome characterized by short stature, short extremities (arms or legs), short hands and feet, obesity, intellectual disability, and seizures. Albright hereditary osteodystrophy is an inherited form of pseudohypoparathyroidism. *See also* acrodysostosis.

pseudoretardation   The state of acting cognitively limited when one is not; it is often secondary to significant psychiatric stress or emotional disorder.

pseudothalidomide syndrome   *See* tetraphocomelia cleft palate syndrome.

PSG   *See* polysomnogram.

PSI3   *See* Parenting Stress Index–Third Edition.

PSI-SF   Parenting Stress Index–Short Form. *See* Parenting Stress Index–Third Edition.

PSLT   *See* Picture Story Language Test.

psychiatric disorders   Disorders of five separate classes: behavior, affect (mood), cognition (thinking), interpersonal relationships, and somatization. Diagnostic schemas (e.g., the *Diagnostic and Statistical Manual of Mental Disorders, Fourth Edition, Text Revision* [*DSM-IV-TR*]; American Psychiatric Association, 2000) approach diagnosis by classifying disorders on the dimension most symptomatically affected. Classification schemas by symptom groups avoid the issue of etiology (cause), thus giving minimal treatment guidance.

psychoanalysis   A school of psychology based on the work of the Viennese neurologist Sigmund Freud (1856–1939). The approach relies heavily on the use of free association and dream interpretation to reveal and resolve unconscious conflicts between repressed instincts and defense mechanisms. Perhaps one of the major contributions of this approach has been the definition of normal and abnormal "psychological defense mechanisms" such as denial, compartmentalization, and repres-

sion. When family members are struggling with the diagnosis of or care for a child with disabilities, it is helpful to be able to understand their coping and defense mechanisms and any internal conflicts regarding some of their feelings about the situation in order to be supportive.

Psychoeducational Profile–Third Revision (PEP-3)   A norm-referenced assessment instrument used to plan individualized educational interventions for children with autism of chronological ages 1–12 years (developmental ages 0;6–7;0 years). Nine subtests assess communication, motor skills, personal self-care, and maladaptive behaviors.

psychogenic   Describing disorders or conditions that are nonorganic in origin, stemming instead from an individual's mind or psyche.

psychogenic pain   Recurrent severe pain with no evident organic (biologic or bodily) origin, thus assumed to be psychological in origin.

psychogenic water drinking   *psychogenic polydipsia.* Excessive intake of fluid (usually water) that does not result from kidney or other medical disorders but is often due to a psychiatric disorder.

Psychological Development Questionnaire for Toddlers (PDQ-I)   An 11-item parent report of the appearance of developmental features between 12 and 36 months. The PDQ-I is used to screen for autism.

psychometry   Psychological testing; the science and practice of testing and quantifying a variety of psychological parameters. Psychometry is often restricted to intelligence testing.

psychomotor   Pertaining to voluntary (psychically determined) movement; referring to the relationship between the brain and the muscles.

psychomotor retardation Literally, "slowing down of movement." The term is used (sometimes with contradictory meanings) to describe various emotional and/or physical states.

psychopathology Behavioral, emotional, personality, interpersonal, or somatic (body complaint) dysfunction within an individual.

Psychopathology Instrument for Mentally Retarded Adults (PIMRA) A 56-item inventory used to assess symptoms of psychopathology in adults with intellectual disability. Both self-report and informant versions (divided into eight subscales of seven items each) are available for the purposes of diagnosing schizophrenia, anxiety, somatization (body symptoms with a psychological, not physical, cause), personality disorders, adjustment disorders, depression, psychosexual disorders, and poor mental adjustment.

psychosocial deprivation syndrome Reversible hyposomatotropinism (low levels of pituitary growth hormone). Bizarre behavior in the child along with short stature secondary to deficient pituitary growth hormone can be due to severely disordered parenting. Abnormal behaviors include drinking from toilet bowls, eating from garbage cans, polydipsia (excessive drinking), polyphagia (excessive eating) alternating with food refusal and food hoarding, insensitivity to pain, encopresis (fecal incontinence), and an unusual wake–sleep cycle. All of the behaviors are corrected when the child is placed in a warm, nurturing environment, but it may take months for growth hormone levels to return to normal. Transient developmental delay is common. Frequently seen in new adoptees from countries in which orphanage care is mostly warehousing with little social or developmental stimulation.

psychosomatic Describing functional disorders with no detectable organic cause but that are due instead to emotional conflict or stress. The three most common psychosomatic symptoms in children are headaches, stomachaches, and leg pains. These symptoms can be precipitated by problems at home or in school but also typically have strong family histories. The female predominance seen in somatization disorder is less striking in young children. In the presence of similar degrees of stress at school, psychosomatic complaints do not seem to be as frequent in children with intellectual disability or language-based learning disabilities.

psychostimulant *See* stimulant.

psychotropic Describing medications that alter thought, mood, or behavior.

PT *See* physical therapy.

PTA *See* palatal training appliance.

PTEN *See* phosphatase and tensin homolog.

P300 A late component of the auditory evoked response/auditory evoked potential (AER/AEP) that may be absent or reduced in certain developmental disabilities. It represents a positive (P) wave that occurs approximately 300 ms after the stimulus.

PTI-2 *See* Pictorial Test of Intelligence–Second Edition.

ptosis A falling of any organ so that it is located below its normal position. Without further specification of which organ, ptosis often refers to a drooping eyelid. Ptosis can be a congenital minor malformation or an acquired one and is often due to a problem with either the muscle of the eyelid or the oculomotor nerve (cranial nerve III). Ptosis is commonly found in a number of syndromes such as fetal alcohol syndrome (FAS), neurofibromatosis, and Sturge-Weber syndrome.

PTSD *See* posttraumatic stress disorder.

puberty The age period during which secondary sexual characteristics and the ability to reproduce mature; the onset of physical changes that are part of the broader phenomenon of adolescence. Puberty is sometimes early, but more often late, in people with significant intellectual disability, but this varies with the specific etiology (cause) of the disability.

pubis *See* symphysis pubis.

public health The science of preventing disease, promoting health, and prolonging life through organized activities. The public health system consists of a national group called the Centers for Disease Control and Prevention (CDC), state-level departments of health, and departments of health at local levels such as in cities and counties. One of the goals of public health is to assess the impact of disability on health and to identify ways to improve the health of people with disabilities. Public health models typically involve a three-tiered model of prevention that was first proposed by the Commission on Chronic Illness in 1957: primary (universal interventions designed to benefit all members of the population by minimizing the appearance of new problems or cases of disease), secondary (interventions for individuals at risk for specific problems), and tertiary (individualized interventions for individuals with established problems).

public law (PL) *See specific PL entries.*

pull-out therapy The removal of a child from the classroom to provide therapy services outside of the classroom.

punishment The future likelihood of a behavior occurring is decreased when the behavior is met with an unpleasant consequence (punishment); in behavioral (operant conditioning) terms, reducing behavior by following it with something negative—an aversive stimulus event (ASE), or punisher. Punishment is contingent on the appearance of an undesired or inappropriate behavior and is administered immediately following it. Although punishment in the form of discipline is often considered first as a way to eliminate undesirable behavior, it can only be defined as punishment if it effectively serves to reduce the target behavior. For example, a teacher may send a child to the principal's office for disruptive behavior. If that dismissal does not reduce disruptive behavior, it is *not* a punisher; in fact, it may inadvertently reinforce the disruptive behavior because it helps the student escape an unpleasant situation or difficult task. The use of punishment does not teach individuals more appropriate responses, nor does it reinforce them. It can only be delivered effectively if the adult or other responsible agent witnesses the undesirable behavior and applies the punisher promptly. Because of this, punishment can lead to avoidance behavior, such as sneaking, cheating, or lying. In addition to being objectionable to some, aversives such as hitting may be problematic from a social learning perspective (e.g., spanking a child for hitting is modeling the type of behavior it intends to reduce). If punishment occurs too frequently, across enough settings, and without ample access to reinforcement, the individual may experience the entire experience as unpleasant, a situation that is not conducive to learning. Punishment can occur naturally, as when peers reject inappropriate behaviors, when a student finishes an assignment ahead of peers and is immediately assigned additional work, or when a student who has difficulty completing work is required to miss recess. Whether it is intentional or not, the behavior in question is less likely to occur in future. *See* operant conditioning, reinforcer.

Pupil Rating Scale–Revised A teacher questionnaire used to screen for learning disabilities in students 5–14 years of age. A 5-point scale is used to rate items in five separate areas: auditory comprehension and memory, spoken language, orientation, motor coordination, and personal social behavior. Administration time is 10 minutes.

Purdue pegboard A 50-hole pegboard in which pins and pin–collar–washer assemblies are to be placed; the number correctly placed in a fixed time period is a measure of fine motor coordination.

Purdue Perceptual Motor Survey An instrument used to assess the perceptual motor skills required for academic learning in children 6–10 years of age.

pure tone audiometry A method of assessing hearing through earphones using a machine that generates pure tones, calibrated in decibels (units of loudness). Pure tone audiometry can be used to screen for significant hearing loss and to diagnose the degree of hearing loss in either ear for both bone and air conduction (in other words, the hearing loss due to malfunctioning of either the outer and middle ears [in the case of bone conduction] or the inner ear [in the case of air conduction]).

purified protein derivative (PPD) A skin test for tuberculosis that involves the subcutaneous (under the skin) injection of tubercular material that is then observed for an inflammatory response 2–3 days after injection.

push-in therapy Therapy provided inside the classroom. Also referred to as *integrated therapy.*

PVL Periventricular leukomalacia. *See also* leukomalacia.

PVS *See* persistent vegetative state.

PWS *See* Prader-Willi syndrome.

pyknic body type A body type that is round, fat, short. *See* endomorph.

pyknodysostosis A genetic syndrome characterized by short stature, increased bone density, abnormalities of the terminal digits (fingers or toes), and a dolichocephalic skull (long front-to-back diameter) with a peculiar facies (facial features). About one fifth of cases exhibit intellectual disability. Inheritance is autosomal recessive. Pyknodysostosis is caused by mutations in *CTSK,* the gene encoding cathepsin K.

pyrexia Fever. Aspirin is an antipyretic (a drug that reduces fever).

pyridoxine Vitamin B_6. Pyridoxine has been used to treat seizures in those rare infants with pyridoxine-deficient seizures.

pyridoxine deficiency Vitamin B_6 deficiency. Symptoms include seizures and hyperirritability in newborns with a familial pyridoxine dependency.

Qq

QALY *See* quality-adjusted life year.

QNST-II *See* Quick Neurological Screening Test–Second Edition.

QoL *See* quality of life.

QRI *See* Quantitative Reading Inventory.

QT *See* Quick Test.

QTL *See* quantitative trait locus.

quadriceps Quadriceps femoris; a group of four muscles located on the front of the thigh. The quadriceps flexes the thigh (femur; in other words, bends the leg at the hip) and extends (straightens) the knee.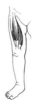

quadriceps

quadriplegia Literally, "four palsy." A topographical (based on body localization) subtype of spastic (characterized by increased muscle tone) cerebral palsy in which all four extremities (arms and legs) are severely involved. Asymmetries are frequently present but not in such a way as to qualify for another topographical classification. Severe intellectual disability usually accompanies quadriplegia.

quadruped On "all fours." A prone (stomach down) position with support by the elbows and knees or the hands and feet.

qualitative research Research that relies on nonnumeric data such as verbal reports,

descriptions, observations, or interpretations of events and issues. Qualitative data are not subject to traditional statistical analysis; rather, they require careful, often lengthy analysis, including identification of themes and unique or idiosyncratic information. The main advantages of qualitative approaches are that they capture the richness and diversity of human experience and can be useful for generating hypotheses (theories) to be examined via quantitative methods. Their limitations include the laborious nature of data collection and analysis and the limited applicability (generalizability) of the findings.

quality-adjusted life year (QALY) A year of life as adjusted for its quality or value, especially as it refers to health. QALY is a measure not only of the burden of disease but also of the impact of a health intervention and is used in public health research to characterize interventions and the impact of disease. For example, if perfect health scores a 1.0, then being in the hospital might drop the score to 0.75.

quality of life (QoL) The general wellbeing of an individual or society. Many QoL measures have been applied to people with various medical conditions and developmental disabilities in an attempt to assess the impact of these conditions on individual satisfaction, "happiness," and other subjective variables. Most definitions and tools propose various dimensions (e.g., physical, material, social, civic) and propose a positive standard or state of wellness that moves beyond the absence of illness or disease. Most professionals rank the perceived QoL for people with disabilities lower than do the people with disabilities themselves, and care should be taken not to make assumptions about QoL in this population.

quantifier An adjective that expresses amount, either specific (*one, two, three,* and so forth) or nonspecific (*all, some, none, most, more, each,* and so forth).

Quantitative Reading Inventory (QRI) A type of literacy assessment based on an Informal Reading Inventory (IRI). The major purpose of an IRI is to enable the teacher to identify a student's functional reading level. Seven functional reading levels can be identified by administering an IRI, which in turn enables the teacher to devise the appropriate reading program based on the student's reading skills.

quantitative research Research that relies on numerical data that are subject to statistical analysis, regardless of their original form (e.g., individual responses are coded numerically). The main advantages of quantitative approaches include the ability to include multiple measures, the ease of summarizing and analyzing data from a large sample of individuals, and the ease of comparing the results of multiple studies that use similar measures. However, the richness of individual responses is sacrificed for an understanding of group or average responses.

quantitative research synthesis *See* meta-analysis.

quantitative trait locus (QTL) Stretches of deoxyribonucleic acid (DNA) on a chromosome that are closely linked to the genes associated with a specific trait under investigation.

quick incidental learning *See* fast mapping.

Quick Neurological Screening Test–Second Edition (QNST-II) A screening tool designed to assess neurological integration as it relates to learning in individuals 5 years and older. Areas addressed include maturation and motor development, gross and fine motor skills, motor planning and sequencing, sense of rate and rhythm, spatial organization, visual and auditory perceptual skills, balance and vestibular function, and attention disorders.

Quick Test (QT) *Ammons Quick Test.* A brief cognitive screening test for use with children ages 2 years and older. Administration time is approximately 15 minutes.

quickening The earliest maternal perception of fetal movement, typically in the fourth or fifth month of pregnancy. Deviations in the time of occurrence of quickening may suggest either problems with the fetus or error in the estimated length of pregnancy. If the infant is felt to be moving earlier than the fourth month, then the pregnancy may be further along than initially estimated; if the infant is not felt to be moving after the fifth month, then the pregnancy may be less far along or the infant may be experiencing difficulties due to placental or embryological abnormalities.

Rr

radial palmar grasp Grasp in which the object is held by the whole hand from the thumb side.

radial rake A stage in the evolution of voluntary grasp in which the hand approaches the object from the radial (thumb and forefinger) side; prominent from 6 to 9 months of age.

radius

radius The thicker of the two bones of the forearm, located on the thumb side. Dislocation of the radial head (the end near the elbow) is a common childhood injury (also known as *nursemaid elbow*) that results from the child being pulled by the forearm. *See also* ulna.

railroad track ear A finding in fetal alcohol syndrome (FAS) in which the pattern displayed by the inner markings of the ear resembles the parallel lines of railroad tracks.

rake A stage in the development of reaching and grasping in which the infant scoops an object with the entire hand. In the ulnar rake, which is prominent around 6 months of age, the hand approaches the object with its pinky side; in the radial rake, which becomes prominent after 6 months of age, the hand approaches the object with its thumb and forefinger side.

Rancho Los Amigos Scale *Rancho Los Amigos Cognitive Scale, Rancho Scale.* A scale used to measure the level of coma and predict the level of cognitive recovery; detailed criteria are provided to describe each of eight levels.

random practice Nonsystematic practice of the same task that leads to suboptimal practice performance but enhanced retention and transfer of learning for the task practiced.

range of motion (ROM) A component of the neuromuscular examination that measures the extent (angle in degrees) of movement at a joint (from full extension to full flexion); ROM also describes active and passive exercise designed to maintain or increase the amount of movement at a joint. ROM exercises may prevent or treat contractures in a variety of neuromuscular disorders.

ranitidine Trade name, Zantac. A drug used in the treatment of gastroesophageal reflux. Ranitidine is an H2-receptor antagonist that suppresses gastric acid production.

rapid eye movement (REM) A phase of sleep that coincides with dreaming.

rapport The relationship established between individuals that allows them to work together in a therapeutic fashion. Ideally, a professional gathering information attempts to create a warm, comfortable, and receptive atmosphere to facilitate positive regard and the free exchange of information.

Rapport is an integral part of the psychological and developmental testing process; it is required to enhance the likelihood of achieving a valid estimate of the testee's abilities. Establishing and maintaining rapport becomes especially difficult when the therapist or tester has unrealistic expectations of the testee's abilities or is unaware of the impact of an organic diagnosis on performance. Professionals can hinder the building of rapport by appearing judgmental, by misunderstanding the level of cognitive impairment, and by confusing impulse control difficulties with willful uncooperativeness or defiance.

RAS   *See* reticular activating system.

Rasch analysis   A statistical technique used to group items in clusters according to level of difficulty.

Rasmussen encephalitis   A rare autoimmune (allergy to self) degenerative disease of the brain that starts in childhood with seizures, progresses to one-sided paralysis (hemiplegia), and later results in blindness in one eye (hemianopsia) and mental deterioration. The disease tends to be resistant to anticonvulsants but may respond to hemispherectomy (surgical removal of the affected side of the brain).

ratio intelligence quotient (IQ)   An intelligence score derived by dividing an individual's mental age (MA) by his or her chronological age (CA) and multiplying the result by 100 to eliminate the decimal. Thus, ratio IQ = (MA/CA) × 100. Because the standard deviation of the ratio IQ distribution does not remain constant with age, IQ scores for different ages are not comparable; the same ratio IQ score at different ages has different meanings. By transforming the raw score (a number that represents actual test performance) to a standard score with a given mean and standard deviation (deviation IQ), one can eliminate this problem. For this reason, the use of the deviation IQ has replaced the use of the ratio IQ in most tests.

Raven's Progressive Matrices   Tests of nonverbal intelligence for people 6 years of age to adult. There are three versions of the test: Standard Progressive Matrices (SPM; ages 6 and older, with 5 sets of 12 items), Colored Progressive Matrices (CPM; 5–11 years of age, with 3 sets of 12 items), and Advanced Progressive Matrices (ages 11 and older). The SPM also comes in a parallel version (SPM Parallel) and an SPM Plus version with more powerful items. Each version presents a series of progressively more complex, incomplete designs that the person must complete by choosing from a number of fragments presented. The results are scored as percentiles. The tests are completely nonverbal and allow children with language disabilities to demonstrate their abstract reasoning ability more effectively than in other tests. Although Raven scores correlate well with performance intelligence quotient (IQ) scores in children younger than 10 years of age, for older children the correlation becomes stronger with verbal IQ scores because of the increasingly sequential character of the more advanced items.

raw score   A record of test performance expressed in original test units; the actual number of items "passed," correct answers given, or tasks successfully completed.

razzing   The raspberry, or "Bronx cheer"; a spluttering sound produced by blowing through vibrating lips. An expressive language milestone of infancy that typically emerges around 5 months of age.

RCBF   *See* regional cerebral blood flow.

RCD   *See* reading comprehension disorder.

RCSC Grants   *See* Real Choice System Change Grants.

RD   Reading disorder. *See* dyslexia.

RDI *See* Relationship Development Intervention.

RDLS-R *See* Reynell Developmental Language Scales–Revised.

RDS *See* respiratory distress syndrome.

reactive airway disease *See* asthma.

reactive attachment disorder of infancy A behavioral syndrome with an onset before 8 months of age in which poor or unresponsive caregiving leads to a lack of social responsiveness, apathy, growth failure (failure to thrive), depressive affect, and developmental delay in an infant.

readiness A condition or state in which it is possible for a person to engage in a given learning activity.

readiness skills In education, those skills that are prerequisite to success in a formal classroom setting. They traditionally include skills related to oral language (speaking in complete sentences, using words adequately to describe), listening (remembering what is heard), perceptual-motor development (knowledge of body parts, direction, and balance), visual-perceptual development (eye–hand coordination; knowledge of size, shape, and spatial concepts), reading readiness (letter recognition, sound–symbol association), social-emotional development (interacting with peers, accepting responsibilities), and number readiness (counting, number values, knowledge of concepts such as more and less).

reading comprehension disorder (RCD) Reading difficulties associated more with oral language disorders and language comprehension difficulties than with decoding problems.

reading conference A meeting between a reader and an interested other in which the reader shares and contemplates what is being read.

reading disorder (RD) *See* dyslexia.

reading epilepsy A convulsive disorder in adolescents with reading disorders in which reading precipitates complex partial seizures. This condition is extremely rare and seems to correlate with, but not cause, the reading disorder.

reading flexibility The ability to adjust reading behaviors (e.g., effort, rate of reading) according to situational factors (e.g., purpose for reading, linguistic density of text).

reading fluency The rapid and smooth processing (reading) of text; an apparently effortless construction of meaning.

reading miscue analysis An assessment practice that involves the intensive examination of a single reading performance. Students are asked to read aloud a text that is challenging but not frustrating. Their miscues (errors) in reading are coded and classified according to a detailed taxonomy (e.g., syntactic acceptability, semantic acceptability, meaning change).

Real Choice System Change (RCSC) Grants A series of grants available through the Centers for Medicare and Medicaid Services (specifically under Medicaid) with the goal of improving services that are integrated into the community. As part of the New Freedom Initiative, these grants help states build infrastructure to assist people with disabilities and their families in making real choices about where and how they receive services to allow them to be an active part of their community.

real estate therapy Colloquial term for the voluntary relocation of a family with a member with a disability across county, state, or national lines to obtain access to more appropriate therapy or other support services through school systems or other agencies or providers.

rebound A medical term for an increase in the severity of symptoms of a disorder being treated when medication is withdrawn.

rebus A graphic puzzle that represents a word, phrase, or sentence. Letters, numbers, and pictures of objects with names that sound similar to the words or syllables they represent are used. A rebus is a form of aided augmentative communication used as an alternative method for teaching reading.

rebus

rebus symbol A picture that visually or nominally represents a word or syllable (i.e., a rebus of a knot could be used to symbolize *knot* or *not*).

receptive language *comprehension.* The ability to understand spoken language and other forms of communication. Many communication disorders are restricted to problems with expressive language and do not involve receptive abilities. Similar degrees of involvement of both expressive and receptive language skills suggest a more severe communication disorder.

Receptive One-Word Picture Vocabulary Test (ROWPVT) *See* One-Word Picture Vocabulary Tests.

Receptive One-Word Picture Vocabulary Test–Upper Extension (ROWPVT-UE) *See* One-Word Picture Vocabulary Tests.

Receptive Tests of Diagnostic Analysis of Nonverbal Accuracy–Second Edition (DANVA-2) A measure of the ability to read nonverbal emotional cues through photographs or taped tone of voice.

Receptive-Expressive Emergent Language Scale–Third Edition (REEL-3) A test of language development for use with children from birth to 3 years of age that uses the child's mother as an informant. Chronological age is compared with an achieved receptive language age and an achieved expressive language age. Although the REEL-3 shares limitations common to all caregiver report scales, in most clinical settings an interview format remains the most effective approach.

reciprocal social interaction Two-way (back-and-forth) communication between two or more people.

reciprocal teaching A group strategy that encourages students to become aware of and take control of their reading and understanding of text. Reciprocal teaching takes the form of a dialogue among teachers and students and uses four strategies: summarizing, question generating, clarifying, and predicting. The teacher and students take turns assuming the role of teacher in leading this dialogue, explaining concepts in reading to the other students in the group.

recognition memory The realization that some stimuli have been previously encountered. Multiple choice testing may allow primarily for the use of recognition skills. *See also* memory.

rectal diazepam Trade name, Diastat. A preparation consisting of a preloaded delivery system for home use in case of prolonged seizures in children with known epilepsy. *See also* diazepam, Valium.

rectum The last 6 inches of the large intestine before the anus.

recurrence risk A public health statistic that indicates the probability that an illness or disorder will recur. More specifically, in the area of developmental disabilities the term usually refers to the probability that a disorder will recur in a family in future offspring.

red herring A misleading clue. The term is used often in medicine to describe a sign or symptom that can be associated with a particular condition unrelated to the diagnosis.

red reflex A physical finding produced by shining a bright light at the eye and looking for its reflection from the retina (inner back wall of the eye), which is red. This red reflex is blocked if there is an abnormality in the cornea (e.g., cloudy cornea found in mucopolysaccharidoses), the lens (e.g., cataract), or the retina itself (e.g., tumor such as retinoblastoma). The red reflex is the cause of the red eyes seen in some photographs.

reduplication The phonological process that occurs when a sound or syllable is repeated in place of all others (e.g., "ba-ba-ba" for *banana*).

REEL-3 *See* Receptive-Expressive Emergent Language Scale–Third Edition.

referential communication A measure of communicative ability in which individuals are evaluated on their ability to explain a task to each other.

reflex hypoxic crisis *See* breathholding spell (BHS).

reflex seizure A seizure precipitated by a specific sensory stimulus. Such stimuli include music, sound, light, reading, and somatosensory stimuli such as tapping or teeth brushing.

reflex standing The ability of a child with severely hypertonic cerebral palsy to stiffen all extensor muscles so as to support weight when balance is maintained from outside. Because such children are usually unable to sit, reflex standing should not be interpreted as a prelude to walking; it is a pathological rigidity that actually inhibits walking.

reflux *See* gastroesophageal reflux (GER or GERD).

refractory Unresponsive to treatment. The term is often used to describe seizures that

cannot be controlled with standard anticonvulsants.

Refsum syndrome *hereditary motor and sensory neuropathy type IV (HMSN-IV), heredopathia atactica polyneuritiformis, phytanic acid storage disease.* A rare autosomal recessive genetic syndrome characterized by retinitis pigmentosa (night blindness and a progressively restricted visual field), cerebellar ataxia (unsteady gait), and progressive sensorineural (involving the auditory nerve) hearing impairment. The syndrome is usually detected by clinical symptoms within the first 20 years of life. Dietary restriction of phytanic acid precursors may slow its progression.

regard To look at, to pay attention to. *See also* hand regard.

region of interest (ROI) In neuroimaging or other imaging studies, the area to be focused upon or looked at more closely.

regional cerebral blood flow (RCBF) A neuroanatomical research procedure used to localize brain abnormalities.

registered occupational therapist (OTR) A professional with a minimum of a master's degree in occupational therapy and an additional 6 months of fieldwork who has passed the American Occupational Therapy Association's (AOTA) certifying examination. *See also* occupational therapy (OT).

Reglan *See* metoclopramide.

regression The loss of previously acquired developmental milestones that occurs with a degenerative disease of the central nervous system (CNS) or sometimes with serious emotional disorders. Such a loss of skills can be associated with a decline in measured intelligence quotient (IQ) scores.

regression toward the mean A statistical phenomenon in which people who achieve very high or very low scores on a given test are more likely to score closer to the mean on a retest. In population genetics, traits controlled by multiple genes may also exhibit this same phenomenon; in each succeeding generation it becomes less likely that a similar combination of multiple genes will come together to produce extreme variations from the mean expression of that trait.

regressive autism A type of autism in which language and social skills are acquired and then lost rather than never developed at all. Between one third and one half of children with autism will demonstrate such a loss between 18 and 24 months of age, but because these children do not differ significantly from those who do not show regression in terms of treatment response or eventual outcome, the validity of a specific subtype remains unclear.

regular education initiative (REI) A movement to restructure education that would require general and special education programs to work more closely together. Proponents maintain that dual systems of education, separate professional organizations, separate personnel preparation programs, and separate funding patterns inhibit the inclusion of students with disabilities and reduce the effectiveness of education. Some have advocated for the merger of special and general education; others, although questioning the "second system" approach, do not advocate the elimination of separate special education services.

regulators Nonverbal behaviors that maintain and regulate conversational speaking and listening between two or more people.

regurgitation In relation to dysphagia, a backward flowing (sloshing) of food.

rehabilitation The return to a previous state of function and well-being. Rehabilitation

after injury or as a remediation of congenital or other acquired impairments is usually accomplished through a multidisciplinary team approach. *See also* habilitation.

Rehabilitation Act Amendments of 1983 (PL 98-221) Federal legislation that authorizes several demonstration projects related to transition services from school to work for youths with disabilities.

Rehabilitation Act Amendments of 1986 (PL 99-506) A federal law that establishes discretionary programs for supportive employment services for individuals with disabilities. Supportive employment services include job coaching for people with severe disabilities (including learning disabilities) that affect employability.

Rehabilitation Act Amendments of 1992 (PL 102-569) A federal law that revises and extends the programs of the Rehabilitation Act of 1973 (PL 93-112). These amendments incorporate the philosophy of the Americans with Disabilities Act (ADA) of 1990 (PL 101-336), including provisions to ensure that the individual's issues and concerns are considered during the process of developing the individualized written rehabilitation program (IWRP) and throughout its implementation. The law also clarifies which services, including personal assistance, transition, and supported employment, constitute components of vocational rehabilitation. Individuals with severe and profound disabilities are eligible for vocational rehabilitation, and intensive services are to be provided based on a maximum amount of services possible, as well as on the person's particular strengths, resources, interests, and concerns.

Rehabilitation Act of 1973 (PL 93-112) A federal law with a civil rights component that prohibits denial of participation in federally funded programs or activities to individuals with disabilities who are otherwise qualified. The intent of this law is to implement a national policy of integrating people with disabilities into society by providing and expanding employment opportunities in public and private sectors. Major components of the law include 1) Title IV, which defines an individual with a "handicapping condition" as anyone who has a physical or mental impairment that substantially limits participation in one or more major life activities, who has a record of such impairment, or who is regarded as such at the time; and 2) Title V, which establishes civil rights protection. Section 503 provides for affirmative action with federal contractors, and Section 504 outlines civil rights aspects. This law permits parents to file complaints with the U.S. Department of Education's Office of Civil Rights if a qualified student with a disability is denied access to an appropriate education. Students with disabilities not listed in the Education for All Handicapped Children Act of 1975 (PL 94-142) and its amendments, such as attention-deficit/hyperactivity disorder (ADHD), have been found to be eligible for services under Section 504. *See also* 504 plan accommodations, Rehabilitation Services Administration (RSA).

Rehabilitation, Comprehensive Services, and Developmental Disabilities Amendments of 1978 (PL 95-602) A federal law that enacts a "functional," rather than categorical, definition of developmental disability. This new definition requires substantial functional limitations in at least three of the following major life activities: self-care, receptive and expressive language, learning, mobility, self-direction, capacity for independent living, or economic self-sufficiency.

Rehabilitation Engineering Society of North America (RESNA) A professional organization dedicated to service, education, and research in the use of assistive technology to support the independence of and improve the quality of life for individuals with disabilities.

Rehabilitation Services Administration (RSA) One of the three program areas of the Office of Special Education and Rehabilitative Services (OSERS), the RSA allocates grants to state vocational rehabilitation agencies to help people with mental and physical disabilities obtain job training, employment, medical and psychological assistance, and other individualized services. Priority is given to individuals with severe disabilities. The RSA also funds training programs for rehabilitation professionals and funds programs that enrich and enhance the lives of individuals with disabilities within their communities. The RSA operates the Client Assistance Rehabilitation Act Rehabilitation Services Program, which informs people with disabilities about government benefits and assists them receiving those benefits for which they are eligible. *See also* Rehabilitation Act of 1973 (PL 93-112).

REI *See* regular education initiative.

reinforcer *reinforcement.* A pleasant event or reward that follows a behavior and that increases the future likelihood of that behavior occurring. Primary reinforcers are physiologically or biologically pleasurable stimuli; secondary reinforcers become pleasurable from being paired with primary reinforcers. Food is an example of a primary reinforcer; socialization and attention are examples of secondary reinforcers. *See* negative reinforcement; consequent stimulus event (CSE).

Reinke's edema The filling of Reinke's space (the nonmuscle part of the vocal fold that is right underneath its surface lining) with viscous fluid as a result of long-standing trauma.

Reiss Scales for Dual Diagnosis in Children A 60-item problem rating scale for use with people with intellectual disability 4–21 years of age. The instrument yields 10 subscale scores for anger, anxiety disorder, attention-deficit/hyperactivity disorder, autism, conduct disorder, depression, poor self-image, psychosis, somatization, and withdrawn behavior, among other significant behaviors.

Reitan-Indiana Neuropsychological Test Battery for Children A neuropsychological battery for use with children 5–8 years of age. The battery was developed as a downward extension from the adult version, with many of the adult tests simply shortened or eliminated for this version. Extensive training is required for both administration and interpretation. Reliability and validity are less than those of the adult tests.

related services Transportation and such developmental, corrective, and other supportive services as may be required to assist a child with a disability to benefit from special education. Among services specifically covered as related services are speech pathology and audiology, psychological services, medical services (for diagnostic and evaluation purposes only), physical therapy, occupational therapy, recreation, and counseling. The precise definition of related services remains a subject of debate. *See also* direct services, Education for All Handicapped Children Act of 1975 (PL 94-142).

Relationship Development Intervention (RDI) A treatment program that exposes people with autism to emotional relationships in a gradual, systematic way.

Relationship Problems Checklist (RPCL) A descriptive checklist used to characterize problems in parent–infant relationships that can be overinvolved, underinvolved, anxious/tense, angry/hostile, and abusive (verbally, physically, or sexually).

relative risk (RR) *risk ratio.* The ratio of the probability of an event (such as a diagnosis) in one group versus in another group.

relaxation The use of psychotherapeutic approaches to reduce muscle tone in young children with cerebral palsy. These approaches may include slow rocking, rhythmic rotation, and gentle shaking. Relaxation therapy is also used to successfully treat anxiety disorders and phobias. These techniques differ from those used to reduce muscle tone in that they require a significant amount of cognitive participation and practice on the part of the individual.

release The action of letting go of an object that has been held in the hand.

reliability The extent to which tests and other instruments consistently yield reproducible results. A test is considered appropriate for use only if it is consistent or reliable and is valid for the intended purpose.

REM *See* rapid eye movement.

remedial education *compensatory education.* Specialized or additional instruction in certain academic areas when deficiencies in these areas are assumed to be a result of environmental factors. The expectation is that the student will master the general curriculum through regular channels. *See also* adaptive education.

remission The lessening or cessation of disease symptoms while the disease remains.

remnant book A book or album made up of "remnants" or scraps saved from past events or activities to communicate those events or activities.

renal Relating to the kidneys.

Renpenning syndrome *X-linked intellectual disability, otherwise undifferentiated.* The clinical manifestations are variable; the most common findings include microcephaly (small head), hypogonadism (small testes), and short stature.

repetition A type of disfluency in which a unit of speech (i.e., a sound or syllable, word, and/or phrase) is repeated.

repetitive motion injuries Overuse injuries. In children, these injuries include stress fractures, tendonitis, and bursitis. The injuries are typically sports related and are usually due to improper training (particularly during different growth phases) or to poor equipment or improper playing surfaces. In adults, they may result from repetitive use of body parts while in the wrong position (e.g., carpal tunnel syndrome results from repetitive typing on a poorly designed keyboard placed at the wrong height and with inadequate support for the wrist and forearm structures).

replicate Duplicate; copy.

RE/PMT *See* Responsive Education and Prelinguistic Milieu Teaching.

requesting A communication interaction between two people that involves an individual who is inclined to provide mediation or assistance if asked to do so and an individual who attempts to gain access to a specific activity or item (and is unable to do so without the assistance or mediation of another person).

Residential Services Indicator (RSI) A standardized protocol used to collect a variety of data to be used in selecting residential and support services for people with developmental disabilities. The residential intake record will include detailed checklists for such domains as personal history; family history; intellectual and adaptive behavior; educational, vocational, and medical needs; dual diagnosis; and support services.

residential treatment A treatment modality in which the person lives away from home in a facility where he or she receives education, psychotherapy, nurturance, structure, safety, and extracurricular and peer interaction opportunities. The need for this intensive, coordinated treatment can be related to significant family issues in addition to the person's problems, which not only render the family unable to cooperate in necessary treatment but also often cause them to undermine the efficacy of existing treatment resources. There is no specific developmental or psychiatric diagnosis for which this level of treatment is indicated; rather, the cumulative effect of several factors leads to its recommendation and utilization. *See also* milieu therapy.

residual Left behind or left over.

resilience An ability to recover from or adjust to illness or trauma.

RESNA *See* Rehabilitation Engineering Society of North America.

resonance The tonal quality imparted to voice sounds by the resonance-chamber action of mouth and pharynx (throat) configurations and, in some cases, of the nostrils. The eventual outflow of sound waves that are recognized as the human voice is the result of filtering of that sound by the resonance system. The source of the voice is the larynx (voice box); impairment of vocal resonance can be any condition in which there is an abnormal acoustical signal due to inappropriate modification of the laryngeal tone. Clinically speaking, hypernasality (excessive nasal resonance) and nasal emission (the escape of air through the nose during the production of pressure consonants) are the most frequently seen vocal resonance problems. Hyponasality (insufficient nasal resonance) is also a disorder of resonance. Hypertrophic (large) tonsils and adenoids, nasal deformities, cleft lip or palate, congenital palatopharyngeal incompetence (CPI), and craniofacial (head and face) malformation syndromes can result in disturbances of normal vocal resonance. There are therapeutic, behavioral, and surgical approaches to improve or correct disorders of resonance.

resource services One set of services in a continuum of educational support and placement alternatives. Assistance is provided to the student for some portion of the school day in a resource room (special education); the rest of the day is spent in the general (regular) education classroom. The resource services provided are listed in terms of goals and objectives in the student's individualized education program (IEP). The ways in which these goals are met varies among schools and teachers. The resource room teacher may act as a consultant to the general education teacher in planning for an individual child or children.

respiration Breathing; breath support for speech.

respiratory distress syndrome (RDS) A condition of newborn infants that includes dyspnea (difficult breathing) and cyanosis (blue color). It is most common in premature infants and infants of diabetic mothers (IDMs). RDS can present with hyaline membrane disease (HMD) or idiopathic (unknown cause) respiratory distress syndrome (IRDS). Long-term effects can include chronic lung disease (bronchopulmonary dysplasia [BPD]) and adverse neurological and developmental outcomes related to poor cerebral blood flow and bleeding into the head that occur during the acute phase of RDS. See hyaline membrane disease (HMD).

respiratory rate The speed and rhythm of breathing.

respite The use of specially trained providers to temporarily care for an individual with disabilities in order to provide a period of relief to the primary caregivers. Respite is used to decrease stress in the homes of people with disabilities, thereby increasing caregivers' overall effectiveness.

respondent behaviors A term from behavioral learning theory that refers to reflexive behaviors controlled by the autonomic nervous system and involuntary muscles. The eye-blink reflex, knee-jerk reflex, and saliva-tion are examples. Respondent behaviors are elicited or caused by a prior stimulus.

response cost *See* cost contingency.

response cost procedure A behavioral intervention technique that involves the withdrawal of a reward or reinforcer when an undesirable behavior occurs. For example, a student may have a token system in which tokens are earned for attention to task. Once the student surpasses a certain threshold, such as remaining on task 90% of the time, a response cost would involve withdrawing some tokens for inattention. Thus, response cost systems sometimes function as punishers for undesirable behaviors. Response cost procedures are recommended only when the student has demonstrated success and has ongoing access to reinforcers.

response to intervention (RTI) A systematic process for providing preventive, supplementary instructional services to students who are not meeting specified benchmark levels of achievement. RTI models compel schools to provide quality interventions matched to student needs, coupled with formative evaluation to obtain data over time, to make critical educational decisions before initiating referral to special education. Schools are no longer required to consider whether a child has a severe discrepancy between achievement and intellectual ability (discrepancy model). Instead, RTI focuses on screening and early intervention for identified problems, along with ongoing monitoring and evidence-based interventions. *See also* learning disability (LD).

responsivity education and prelinguistic milieu teaching (RE/PMT) A play-based incidental teaching method that trains both children with autism and their parents to improve communication.

restating *rewording.* A language instructional technique in which an adult acknowledges what the child has said and provides alternative models for communicating the same information.

restriction fragment length polymorphism (RFLP) Variation between individuals in deoxyribonucleic acid (DNA) fragment sizes cut by specific restriction enzymes, usually caused by a mutation at a cutting site. Polymorphic sequences that result in RFLPs are used as markers on genetic linkage maps.

retention Holding back; requiring a child to repeat a grade in school. Although retention is one of the most commonly used interventions, research has documented its long-term ineffectiveness.

reticular activating system (RAS) An area of the brainstem involved in the control of attention, wakefulness, and sleep.

retina The light-sensitive inner layer of the eyeball. The retina can be examined by looking through the pupil with an ophthalmoscope; it is the only part of the central nervous system (CNS) available for direct visualization.

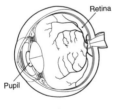

retina

retinitis pigmentosa A disorder of the eye that produces nyctalopia (night blindness) and progressive vision loss. Retinitis pigmentosa can be associated with a variety of conditions: lipidoses (e.g., Gaucher disease), spinocerebellar degeneration (e.g., Friedrich ataxia), hearing loss (e.g., Usher syndrome), mucopolysaccharidoses, myotonic dystrophy, Laurence-Moon-Biedl syndrome, and syndromes with renal (kidney) disease or external ophthalmoplegia (ocular muscle paralysis).

retinopathy of prematurity (ROP) *retrolental fibroplasia (RLF), Terry disease.* An eye disease that is a major cause of blindness.

ROP occurs predominantly in premature infants and is more severe with decreasing birth weight; the concomitant use of high levels of oxygen exacerbates the condition. Both the active (proliferation) and cicatricial (scarring) stages are scored 1–4, with higher numbers reflecting more severe involvement.

retraction Drawing back. Muscle shortening secondary to tone or attempts to stabilize often result in the retraction of a body part, in particular the shoulder or pelvis.

retrognathia Placement of the jaw back from the frontal plane of the forehead; receding jaw.

retrograde amnesia A specific impairment of memory for events experienced immediately before a closed brain injury. The period of time included in the amnesia varies with the severity of the brain injury as reflected in the duration of unconsciousness.

retrolental fibroplasia (RLF) *See* retinopathy of prematurity (ROP).

Rett syndrome A pervasive developmental disorder (PDD). An X-linked (with the involved gene *MECP2* at Xq28) degenerative condition that occurs in girls who develop typically until between 6 and 18 months of life, when they undergo a rapid (in terms of weeks) loss of motor, cognitive, and social skills that subsequently stabilizes at a profound level of impairment. Autistic behaviors include gaze aversion and hand stereotypies (wringing, clapping, tapping, washing, and mouthing). There is also an acquired microcephaly (small head): The head stops growing and thus leads to a progressively more severe microcephaly. Treatment is symptomatic and supportive. Seizures and scoliosis are common late complications.

reverberation time (RT) The degree to which the temporal aspects of the information-carrying components of the speech signal are preserved.

reversals Letters, numbers, or words written or read backward (e.g., *b/d, p/q, 6/9, was/saw*); reversals are often erroneously considered a pathognomonic (diagnostic) sign of dyslexia. Younger children frequently reverse the direction of letters and numbers; some degree of reversal persists in the early elementary grades and should not be considered atypical until 8 years of age or third grade. Marked use of reversals (and mirror writing) can be indicative of learning disabilities when accompanied by other suggestions of academic difficulties. Rotations or inversions of letters or numbers across an axis other than the vertical is usually more serious than the common right–left reversals.

Reversals Frequency Test A three-part instrument that measures the frequency of letter and number reversals in three situations: execution (writing), recognition (reading), and matching (same/different comparison). This test purports to differentiate children with minimal brain dysfunction from typically developing children when used as a screening instrument.

reverse genetics A laboratory procedure that uses gene mapping (identifying the location of a gene on a chromosome) to make copies of a gene found in a particular disease in which the biochemical problem is not known. The goal is to identify the protein that is made from the gene and thus learn more about that particular disease.

reversed tailor *W-sitting.* A sitting posture associated with hypotonia (decreased muscle tone) or hip instability; sometimes referred to as *mermaid sitting,* after the statue of the Little Mermaid in Copenhagen. The opposite of tailor or ring sitting.

reversed tailor

reversible hyposomatotropinism *See* psychosocial deprivation syndrome.

reversible obstructive airway disease (ROAD) *See* asthma.

ReVia *See* naltrexone.

Revised Problem Behavior Checklist (RPBC) A checklist that rates challenging behaviors in children from kindergarten through 12th grade. The RPBC is used as part of a diagnostic battery to screen for behavior disorders and to measure behavior change associated with interventions. Items are organized into four major subscales: Conduct Disorder (22 items), Socialized Aggression (17 items), Attention Problem–Immaturity (16 items), and Anxiety–Withdrawal (11 items). Two minor subscales are also included: Psychotic Behavior (6 items) and Motor Tension–excess (5 items). Using a 3-point rating scale, respondents (parents, teachers, or other professionals) score the degree to which each item characterizes the child's behavior. Items from the subscales are scattered throughout the test. Templates are provided for adding circled numbers (1, 2, and 3) to yield a raw score for each subtest. Raw scores for each subscale are then converted to normalized *T*-scores with a mean of 50 and a standard deviation of 10. The tables have some potentially confusing features, and the user is advised to read the headings carefully.

Revised Token Test (RTT) A measure of language functioning in adults ages 20 through 80 with aphasia, brain damage, and severe language disorders.

revision A type of disfluency in which lexical modifications in speech are made without any significant change in the main idea being expressed. For example, the use of circumlocution.

revisualization A memory task in which the person must recall the configuration (shape of a letter or word) in the absence of visual clues. Phonetic spelling errors are common in children with revisualization impairments.

rewording   *See* restating.

Reye syndrome   An acute, life-threatening, postinfectious (following flu or chickenpox) encephalopathy (brain damage) syndrome with hepatitis. Because salicylate (aspirin) has been implicated in the etiology (cause), the use of aspirin in children has decreased markedly. Mortality is 30%. Morbidity can include the spectrum of neurodevelopmental disorders of varying severity.

Reynell Developmental Language Scales–Revised (RDLS-R)   A test that provides separate measures of expressive language and verbal comprehension for children 1–17 years of age. The RDLS-R is normed and is more commonly used in the United Kingdom.

Reynell-Zinkin Developmental Scale for Visually Impaired Young Children   An assessment instrument for use with infants and preschoolers with visual impairments from birth to 5 years of age. The scale has separate age norms for children who are totally blind, partially sighted, and sighted.

Reynell-Zinkin Scales   An assessment tool used to evaluate the cognitive development of children from birth to 5 years of age with multiple disabilities and visual impairments. The instrument uses parent report, direct observation, and selected item administration and is grouped into five scales: Social Adaptation, Sensorimotor, Environmental Exploration, Response to Sound/Words, and Expressive Language.

Reynolds Intellectual Assessment Scale (RIAS)   A brief (20-minute) individually administered test of intelligence and memory.

RFLP   *See* restriction fragment length polymorphism.

Rh factor   A genetically determined blood antigen, the presence or absence of which is important in the compatibility of blood for transfusion purposes. Repeated maternal–fetal Rh incompatibility, with the mother not having the factor (Rh–) and the infant having the factor (Rh+), can lead to the mother producing antibodies against the infant's red blood cells, with increasingly severe responses with each successive incompatible pregnancy. Treatment with RhoGAM prevents this sequence.

rheumatic fever   A relatively rare acute illness that follows streptococcal infection and may affect the heart. Most commonly, the valves become inflamed and may leak. Later, scarring of the valves may interfere with function.

rhinitis   Inflamed or runny nose.

rhinorrhea   Runny nose.

rhizomelic   Referring to the proximal segment of a limb (e.g., the upper arm or thigh).

rhizotomy   The cutting of a nerve root. *See also* selective posterior rhizotomy.

Rho (D antigen) immune globulin   Trade name, RhoGAM. A gamma globulin given to a mother after an Rh-incompatible pregnancy to prevent the formation of antibodies that can harm the infant in a later pregnancy.

Rhode Island Test of Language Structure (RITLS)   A test of language structure designed for use with children ages 3–20 years with hearing impairments; it can also be used with children ages 3–6 years without hearing impairments but who have intellectual disability or learning disabilities or who are bilingual.

RhoGAM   *See* Rho (D antigen) immune globulin.

rhythmicity Regularity in biological functions such as sleeping, eating, or defecating.

RIAS *See* Reynolds Intellectual Assessment Scale.

rib hump An elevation of one side of the thorax (chest) when an individual with scoliosis (spinal curvature) bends forward 90 degrees at the hips. A rib hump indicates rotation of the thoracic vertebrae to the convex (curved outward) side of a scoliosis.

ribonucleic acid (RNA) A nucleic acid in which the sugar constituent is ribose; RNA is single-stranded and contains the four bases adenine, cytosine, guanine, and uracil.

Richards-Rundel syndrome An autosomal recessive genetic syndrome characterized by progressive severe intellectual disability, nystagmus (involuntary eye movements), ataxia (unsteady gait), muscle wasting, absent secondary sexual characteristics, and sensorineural (auditory nerve) deafness.

rickets Stunting of growth and bone deformities secondary to a failure of normal calcification of bone. This condition can be nutritional or based on a variety of metabolic disorders.

RIDES *See* Rockford Infant Developmental Evaluation Scales.

Rieger syndrome An autosomal dominant genetic syndrome or anomaly (malformation) characterized by abnormalities of the anterior (front) part of the eye (i.e., the iris), glaucoma (increased pressure in the eye), hypodontia (decreased number of teeth), and intellectual disability. The syndrome is detected in the neonatal period or later, depending on the presence of structural eye defects. Treatment is restorative for the teeth, with ongoing ophthalmological care for the eye complications.

righting reaction One of a subgroup of postural reactions concerned with maintaining the position of the head in space.

righting reaction

rigidity A lack of flexibility or sluggishness in thought processes that may interfere with effective problem solving.

rigidity A physiological type of extrapyramidal cerebral palsy characterized by consistently increased tone ("lead pipe" or "cogwheel"), such that there is resistance to passively moving an extremity (arm or leg) throughout the entire range of motion. In many ways, this stiffness or inflexibility is similar to the most severe forms of spastic quadriplegia (paralysis of all four extremities) and is usually associated with severe to profound intellectual disability.

Riley Preschool Developmental Screening Test A 15-minute screening test for use with children 3–6 years of age that includes six graphomotor tests of visual-perceptual and fine motor skills.

Riley-Day syndrome *familial dysautonomia (FD), hereditary sensory and autonomic neuropathy type III (HSAN III).* An autosomal recessive genetic syndrome of insensitivity to pain; lack of tear formation, contributing to corneal ulceration; dysarticulation; poor motor coordination; increased sweating; cutis marmorata (blotching or marbling of the skin); smooth tongue; and typical intelligence. The primary defect is one of the autonomic nervous system, with death often occurring before the age of 20 from respiratory complications. The diagnosis of FD is established by molecular genetic testing of the *IKBKAP* gene. Two gene changes account for more than 99% of mutant alleles in individuals with FD of Ashkenazic Jewish descent. *IVS20(+6T>C),* the major founder mutation, is responsible for virtually all occurrences of FD among the Ashkenazim. Antibiotic treatment for recurrent respiratory infections is indicated.

ring chromosome A structurally abnormal chromosome in which both ends of the chromosome are deleted and the broken ("sticky") ends join to form a ring. The clinical manifestations vary with the amount of genetic material that is missing and the chromosome involved.

ring chromosome

ringworm *See* tinea.

RIPA-2 *See* Ross Information Processing Assessment–Second Edition.

risk ratio *See* relative risk.

risperidone Trade name, Risperdal. An atypical neuroleptic (second-generation antipsychotic [SGA]) used to treat psychotic disorders and as an adjunct therapy with a mood stabilizer to treat bipolar disorder. Risperidone is sometimes used nonspecifically in cases with aggressive and disruptive behavior. It has the potential side effects common to the neuroleptics, including acute dystonia and tardive dyskinesia.

Ritalin *See* methylphenidate.

RITLS *See* Rhode Island Test of Language Structure.

ritodrine hydrochloride Trade name, Yutopar. A beta-sympathomimetic drug used to treat preterm labor and prevent premature birth.

RLF Retrolental fibroplasia. *See* retinopathy of prematurity (ROP).

RNA *See* ribonucleic acid.

R/O *See* rule out.

ROAD Reversible obstructive airway disease. *See* asthma.

Roberts–SC phocomelia syndrome *See* tetraphocomelia cleft palate syndrome.

Robin sequence A disorder characterized by micrognathia (small jaw), glossoptosis (abnormal downward or backward placement of the tongue), and a cleft in the soft palate. Robin sequence generally occurs in otherwise typically developing individuals but can co-occur with disorders such as trisomy 18 and Stickler syndrome.

Robin syndrome *See* Pierre Robin syndrome.

Robinow syndrome *See* fetal face syndrome.

Robinow-Silverman syndrome *See* fetal face syndrome.

rocker-bottom foot *See* congenital vertical talus.

Rockford Infant Developmental Evaluation Scales (RIDES) A developmental behavior checklist for use with children from birth to 4 years of age.

roentgenogram Older term for x ray. Named after Wilhelm Conrad Roentgen (1845–1923), discoverer of the medical usefulness of x rays.

ROI *See* region of interest.

role taking The ability to put oneself in another's place to experience his or her perspective; egocentricity includes immaturity or deficiency of role taking.

rolfing Structural integration. The manipulation of body tissue via deep massage. A form of body-centered psychotherapy that has been applied to the treatment of cerebral palsy. Named after Ida Rolf (1897–1979).

rollator A walker with wheels; an assistive device used to aid ambulation.

rolling over A gross motor milestone of infancy. Children typically roll from prone (front) to supine (back; P→S) at 4 months of age and from supine to prone (S→P) at 5 months of age. Markedly delayed rolling over is considered a sensitive early indicator of cerebral palsy. Rolling S→P before P→S suggests significant hypertonia (increased muscle tone).

ROM   *See* range of motion.

Rood   A system of physical therapy for the treatment of cerebral palsy that uses exaggerated sensory input in the form of stroking, brushing, icing, heating, pounding, squeezing, and pressure to facilitate an awareness of normal movement patterns. Named after Margaret Rood (1834–1895), a physical and occupational therapist.

root   Referring to the tongue, the base of which is attached to the hyoid bone at the back of the throat.

rooting reflex   A primitive oral motor reflex found in infants from 32 weeks' gestation to 6 months of age; a tactile (touch) stimulus to the lips or cheeks causes the infant to respond by turning the head in the direction of the stimulus and reaching the mouth toward the stimulus. Because there are four possible directions (up, down, right, left), the reflex is also referred to as the *four cardinal points reflex*. The reflex persists longer and actually becomes stronger in breast-fed infants. This reflex is innervated by cranial nerves V, VII, XI, and XII.

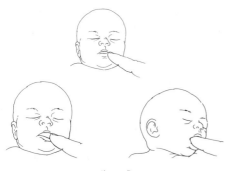

rooting reflex

ROP   *See* retinopathy of prematurity.

Rorschach inkblots   A projective psychological test that consists of 10 symmetrical inkblot cards, half colored and half black and white, with various nuances of shading. The test is administered by showing the cards one at a time in a definite order and asking the individual what he or she sees in them. After the person has responded to the inkblots in an unstructured manner (in the free association or performance proper period), the examiner asks questions about particular responses (in the inquiry period) to clarify ambiguous answers and to elicit latent repressed content. A third period (i.e., testing of limits) may be used to further clarify responses. The first step in interpreting the Rorschach record is numerically tabulating formal scoring categories and percentages. Records are scored for area or location, determinants, content, and popularity of responses. This composite Rorschach picture is based on the reciprocal relationship between formal structure and dynamic content. The use of this or any other projective psychological testing techniques requires specific training and extensive practice, can be subject to bias, and may be inappropriate with individuals with language and cognitive impairments.

roseola   *exanthema subitum.* A viral illness in preschool children in which 3–4 days of very high fever are followed by a transient (subitum) rose pink rash. It has no developmental sequelae.

Ross Information Processing Assessment–Second Edition (RIPA-2)   A test instrument that assesses cognitive-linguistic impairments following acquired brain injuries in adolescents and adults. The RIPA-2 can be used to quantitate cognitive impairments, establish severity ratings, and develop rehabilitation goals and objectives with profiles in 10 areas: immediate memory, recent memory, temporal orientation (recent memory), temporal orientation (remote memory), spatial orientation, orientation to environment, recall of general information, problem solving and abstract reasoning, organization, and auditory processing and retention.

Rossetti Infant-Toddler Language Scale A criterion-referenced assessment scale for use with infants and toddlers from birth to 3 years of age that probes prelinguistic and verbal communication and interaction through direct observation and caregiver report. Areas assessed include interaction–attachment (relationship between the caregiver and the infant), pragmatics (the way in which language is used to communicate and affect others), gesture, individual and social play, language comprehension (understanding), and language expression. This measure is a combination of direct child assessment, observation, and parent report.

rotary chewing Rotating the jaw in order to grind and mash food. This skill develops between 12 and 24 months of age.

rotated ear *See* pinna.

rotation The action of turning or rolling an object with the pads of the fingers using one hand alone.

rotation A turning movement of muscles around an axis, such as the turning of an arm or leg in and out or the turning of the trunk from side to side.

rotator cuff of the shoulder A band-like arrangement of muscle, cartilage, and bone that holds the shoulder joint together. Four muscles (the supraspinatus, infraspinatus, tere minor, and subscapularis) are crucial to the stability of the shoulder joint. Degeneration and tearing of the tendons are common pathologies.

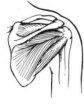

rotator cuff of shoulder

ROWPVT Receptive One-Word Picture Vocabulary Test. *See* One-Word Picture Vocabulary Tests.

ROWPVT-UE Receptive One-Word Picture Vocabulary Test–Upper Extension. *See* One-Word Picture Vocabulary Tests.

RPBC *See* Revised Problem Behavior Checklist.

RPCL *See* Relationship Problems Checklist.

RPE *See* Borg Rating of Perceived Exertion Scale.

RR *See* relative risk.

RSA *See* Rehabilitation Services Administration.

RSI *See* Residential Services Indicator.

RSS *See* Russell-Silver syndrome.

RT *See* reverberation time.

RTI *See* response to intervention.

RTT *See* Revised Token Test.

rubella *German measles.* An acute infectious disease characterized by low-grade fever, exanthem (rash), coryza (nasal inflammation), lymphadenopathy (swelling of the lymph nodes), and arthritis (pain in the joints). The importance of prevention through immunization (vaccination) with live virus stems from the teratogenic (malformation causing) effects of the rubella virus (i.e., fetal rubella syndrome) on the developing fetus. Rubella is also known as *3-day measles* in reference to the typical duration of the rash, in contrast to the 7-day measles (roseola).

rubella embryopathy *See* fetal rubella syndrome.

rubeola *measles.* A highly contagious viral exanthem (rash) with fever, cough, coryza (nasal inflammation), conjunctivitis (eye inflammation), an enanthem (Koplik spots), and photophobia (extreme sensitivity to light). It is also known as *7-day measles* because of the duration of the rash. Unlike German measles (i.e., rubella), rubeola is not teratogenic (i.e., it does not cause malformation). It is, however, a much more severe illness, with a 0.1% incidence of encephalitis (brain inflammation) and a 1 in 100,000 risk of subacute sclerosing panencephalitis (SSPE; a generally fatal "hardening" in the brain).

Rubinstein-Taybi syndrome A dysmorphic (atypical appearance) syndrome that includes broad thumbs and toes; a characteristic facies, including downslanting palpebral fissures (eye slits), maxillary hypoplasia (midfacial undergrowth), and a beaked nose; and intellectual disability. The gene for this syndrome is located on chromosome 16p13.3. The syndrome is the result of a mutation in the gene encoding the transcriptional coactivator CREB binding protein.

rugae Ridges or folds, such as those noted on the scrotal sac and on the roof of the mouth.

rule out (R/O) A term prefixed to a diagnosis or condition to indicate that tests must be or were done to assess the presence of that diagnosis. "R/O appendicitis" as an admission diagnosis suggests that the physician was concerned about that possible diagnosis. "R/O appendicitis" as a discharge diagnosis suggests that the diagnosis was not confirmed.

rumination The regurgitation (spitting up after meals) of food or liquid that is either allowed to run out of the mouth or is rechewed and reswallowed. Originally considered a bizarre psychosomatic disorder of infancy, rumination is more common in people with significant intellectual disability; its frequent occurrence in institutional and deprivational settings suggests that it may be a self-stimulatory behavior. Behavioral intervention is the most effective intervention approach. The behavior can be fatal because of chronic malnutrition.

rumination Chronic, persistent worrying or brooding that accompanies some mental disorders and occurs occasionally in most individuals.

Russell-Silver syndrome (RSS) A syndrome characterized by a distinctive facial appearance, short stature of prenatal onset, skeletal asymmetry, clinodactyly (curved fingers), café au lait spots, and a small triangular facies that contributes to a misleading impression of hydrocephalus (excess fluid in the brain; i.e., pseudohydrocephalus). Cognition is usually typical. RSS is a genetically heterogeneous condition. The diagnosis is typically based upon identification of consistent clinical features, especially prenatal and postnatal growth retardation with normal head circumference. About 10% of individuals have maternal uniparental disomy for chromosome 7. Epigenetic mutations of the imprinted region of chromosome 11p15.5 can occur in some individuals with RSS. An increased incidence of the disorder has been found among children whose parents used assistive reproductive technology to aid conception.

Ruvalcaba syndrome A syndrome characterized by a distinctive facial appearance, macrocephaly (large head), intestinal hamartomatous polyposis (tumor-like growths), lipomas (fatty tumor-like growths), pigmented macules (colored areas) of the glans penis, intellectual disability, "jovial" personality, small mouth, short fingers, and other bone abnormalities. This syndrome is part of the PTEN hamartoma spectrum that also includes Cowden syndrome and Proteus syndrome.

Ruvalcaba-Myre syndrome *See* Smith-Riley syndrome.

Ss

saccade *saccadic movement.* A series of involuntary, rapid, small jerky movements of both eyes together (conjugate) that better enable a person to center the fovea (the area of clearest vision on the retina of the eye) on a changing point of fixation to follow a target.

sacral agenesis A congenital malformation that includes the absence of the sacrum and coccyx (tailbone). If the sacral nerves are involved in the bony abnormality, a neurogenic bladder will result; toileting and gait disorders are the most commonly associated disabilities. Cognitive functioning is usually typical unless associated with a congenital brain malformation that causes intellectual disability. Children with sacral agenesis often have recurrent urinary tract infections leading to hydronephrosis (kidney enlargement) and chronic pyelonephritis (kidney infection). Sacral agenesis occurs in 1% of infants of mothers with insulin-dependent diabetes. The term *sacral agenesis* is often used synonymously with *caudal regression syndrome.*

sacrum The tailbone. The triangular bone at the base of the spine that derives from the fusion of the last five vertebrae.

sacrum

Saethre-Chotzen syndrome *acrocephalosyndactyly type III.* An autosomal dominant genetic syndrome characterized by craniosynostosis (premature fusion of skull bones) that leads to brachycephaly (flat head shape), maxillary hypoplasia (jaw undergrowth), prominent crus (an ear landmark), facial asymmetry, and syndactyly (webbing of the fingers or toes). Mild intellectual disability and hearing loss are occasional findings. The craniosynostosis may lead to optic nerve atrophy. *TWIST1* is the only gene known to be associated with Saethre-Chotzen syndrome. Treatment is primarily correction of cranial-facial abnormalities. *TWIST1* gene changes are identified in more than half of affected individuals using a combination of deletion/duplication analysis and sequence analysis. People with Saethre-Chotzen syndrome occasionally have a chromosome translocation that involves 7p21 or ring chromosome 7.

sagittal plane The anatomical plane that divides the body into a right half and left half.

SAL *See* system for augmenting language.

salaam seizures *See* infantile spasms.

sagittal plane

salicylate *See* aspirin sensitivity.

salmon patch A small, flat, reddish pink, irregularly bordered birthmark sometimes found on the back of the neck (commonly called a "stork bite" or "Unna's mark"), over the eyes, or on the forehead (commonly called an "angel's kiss") of newborns. Such a mark tends to fade with time as subcutaneous (under the skin) tissue increases in thickness and is of no diagnostic significance.

SAMI *See* Sequential Assessment of Mathematics Inventories–Standardized Inventory.

sandal gap deformity An increased space (more than a quarter of an inch) between the first two toes. This minor dysmorphic feature may occur with developmental disabilities either as part of a syndrome or nonspecifically.

sandal gap deformity

Sandifer syndrome The combination of reflux of gastric contents into the mouth accompanied by abnormal head cocking and neck extension/flexion movements, with esophagitis (inflammation of the esophagus) and anemia. Often misinterpreted as the result of disordered parenting or an emotional disorder, Sandifer syndrome is secondary to a hiatal hernia and resolves upon surgical correction of the hernia.

Sanfilippo syndrome *mucopolysaccharidosis (MPS) III.* An autosomal recessive genetic syndrome characterized by the mild physical features of mucopolysaccharidosis but severe intellectual disability and significant behavior management problems. Synophrys (growing together of the eyebrows) is present. Sanfilippo syndrome comprises several forms of lysosomal storage diseases due to impaired degradation of heparan sulfate. There are four enzymatic subtypes (A, B, C, D); type A is the most common.

Santmyer swallow A primitive reflex in which the stimulus of a puff of air blown into an infant's face produces the response of a swallow; this reflex is present in premature infants and disappears by 2 years of age.

SAR *See* socially assistive robotics.

satiety Glut, surfeit.

saturation The phenomenon in which a hearing aid is physically incapable of delivering any louder output no matter how loud the input is. Saturation causes distortion of the acoustic signal.

savant *savant syndrome.* A condition in which a person with a developmental disorder (especially autism) has an astonishing island of ability or talent in contrast to his or her overall disability. Savant abilities are usually restricted to right brain functions such as those involving music, art, mathematics, calendar, mechanics, and memory. Formerly *idiot savant.*

saying "no" The infant's receptive language ability to respond to the verbal command "no" emerges at around 1 year of age. The child's expressive language use of "no" emerges at around 2 years of age and is, from an ego psychology perspective, the child's first word, and from a behavioral perspective, part of the phase known as the "terrible twos."

SB5 *See* Stanford-Binet Intelligence Scale–Fifth Edition.

SC syndrome *See* tetraphocomelia cleft palate syndrome.

SCA *See* sex chromosome abnormalities.

scaffolding Adjusting the level of support provided to a person based on his or her level of function. For example, when introducing new material, an instructor might use ample specific instruction and modeling and then gradually withdraw this support as the learner attains mastery.

scaled score A score on a test that results from the conversion of the raw score to a number or position on a standard reference scale. For example, college aptitude tests are typically reported on a scale of 200–800; according to this scale, a score of 600 is intended to indicate the same level of ability from year to year regardless of the form of the test used or the composition of the candidate group at a particular administration.

SCAN *See* Screening Test for Auditory Processing Disorders.

scan path The field of view perceived by an individual while moving his or her eyes across the visual field.

scanning selection A selection technique in which an individual using an augmentative and alternative communication (AAC) device waits while either a facilitator or an electronic device scans through undesired items before reaching the item of choice. Once the item of choice has been reached, the individual using the AAC device indicates in some way that the desired item has been presented.

scanning speech Speech that is slow, with pauses between each syllable.

scanogram An x ray that includes a ruler on the film so that accurate bone measurements can be made. Scanograms are especially useful for quantifying leg length discrepancies.

scapegoat A family member who is held responsible for all family conflict and who takes the blame for all family distress. Over time, this member is targeted by other family members as the sole cause of all that is wrong with the family. Thus, marital conflicts, sibling rivalry, and even financial problems are described in terms of the scapegoated member's culpability for the problem. Scapegoats evolve when at least two people in a family (usually the parents) cannot openly deal with their own issues. The weakest member of the family is often selected as the scapegoat. Therefore, a child with developmental disabilities is likely to become the family scapegoat.

scaphocephaly A narrow skull (low cephalic index) often with a ridge along the

prematurely closed sagittal suture. Linked with dolichocephaly (prominent forehead), scaphocephaly is a common but transient skull shape in premature infants.

scaphocephaly

scapula The shoulder blade.

scarf sign A technique used to evaluate tone in the newborn; the infant's hand and arm are drawn across the front of the neck as if they were a scarf. In a full-term infant with normal tone, the elbow will not pass the chin and the hand will not pass the shoulder; in a premature or hypotonic (low muscle tone) infant, these landmarks will be passed.

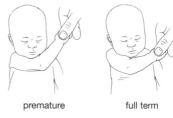
premature   full term

scarf sign

scent *See* odor.

SCERTS® *See* Social Communication, Emotional Regulation, and Transactional Support.

Schaltenbrandt reaction *Landau 2.* A postural reaction that is usually included in the description of the Landau reaction. It is the phase in which head flexion produces a loss of all the extensor tone that composes the Landau 1.

schedule board A device used to lay out the day's schedule, often with picture cards attached by Velcro.

Scheie syndrome *"mild Hurler (MPS IH),"* *mucopolysaccharidosis (MPS) I-S.* A genetic condition characterized by cloudy corneas that can lead to blindness, mild growth impairment, joint contractures, but typical intelligence; frequently, psychotic episodes are present. The disorder is detectable at 10 weeks' gestation by enzymatic assay of chorionic villi. Surgery for joint contractures may be indicated. Inheritance is autosomal recessive; the gene is located on chromosome 4p15.3. Scheie syndrome is caused by mutation in the gene encoding alpha-L-iduronidase.

schema A theoretical structure that organizes familiar experiences and provides a framework for making inferences; a basic concept. A schema is a hierarchically organized description of classes of concepts and their interrelations. At the top of the hierarchy is a general schema that incorporates all aspects of the concept class, including both an abstraction and a conceptual frame of reference for all events within this area. As one moves down the hierarchy, the number of embedded schemata increases at each level, each becoming narrower in scope. At the lowest level are specific perceptual events such as yesterday's lunch at the hot dog stand. In a narrower Piagetian sense, schemata are the sensorimotor equivalents of concepts.

schema theory reading model A construct that envisions the process of reading as requiring the simultaneous coordination of schemata at all levels. Bottom-up processes (visual features) may lead to higher level schemata (letters) and then to even higher level schemata (words), and the process continues upward. At the same time, higher level schemata are evoked by information from the print. These higher level schemata structure readers' expectations and enable them to fill in gaps in specific information in a top-down manner. Reading, like other forms of thinking, does not occur in a fixed sequence. The interaction of top-down and bottom-up processes enables children who have difficulty with decoding to use higher level knowledge to compensate and make guesses about unknown words on the basis of their prior knowledge and context clues.

Scheuthauer-Marie-Sainton syndrome *See* cleidocranial dysostosis.

Schilder Arm Extension Test A test in which a child stands at attention, eyes closed, feet together, with arms stretched out in front for 20 seconds. Spooning, choreiform (involuntary twitching) movements, swaying, or drifting of the arms is noted. The head may be passively turned to one side of the trunk to further assess balance.

Schimmelpenning-Feuerstein-Mims syndrome The association of the mid-facial linear nevus sebaceus of Jadassohn with epilepsy and intellectual disability. Diagnosis is made at birth. Inheritance may be autosomal dominant. Treatment is cosmetic for the nevus, with pharmacological management for the seizures. *See also* nevus sebaceus of Jadassohn.

Schinzel-Giedion syndrome A genetic syndrome characterized by growth deficiency, profound intellectual disability, seizures (hypsarrhythmia—a continuous disorganized slow spike/wave pattern on electroencephalography), spasticity (increased muscle tone), a peculiar facies, vision and hearing impairments, and kidney disorders. Inheritance may be autosomal recessive. Death usually occurs in the first 2 years of life.

schizencephaly An anomaly in cortical architecture (the outermost layer of the brain) characterized by clefts in the brain tissue that run from the surface of the brain to the ventricle. The tissue around the clefts is hypoplastic (underdeveloped) and arranged in a symmetrical fashion. Depending on the location of the clefts, children with schizencephaly may show a variety of neurological abnormalities, including cerebral palsy, intellectual disability, hypotonia (low muscle tone), spasticity (increased muscle tone), hemiparesis (one-sided paralysis), tetraparesis (paralysis of all four extremities), microcephaly (small head), or seizures.

School Function Assessment (SFA) A criterion-referenced instrument for evaluating a child's participation in nonacademic school activities in kindergarten through Grade 6. The SFA uses clinician judgments to determine a child's strengths and needs in two major areas, participation in six school activity settings, and task supports for physical and cognitive-behavioral demands. Each of 10 individual scales can be administered in about 10 minutes and produces a cutoff score.

school phobia Fear of school. The child who exhibits school phobia is usually not afraid of school per se but may instead have a broader social phobia (fear of others' reactions to them) and may occasionally have an idiosyncratic fear (e.g., that something might happen at home while he or she is away at school). Consequently, the child wants to stay home and may demonstrate significant distress and agitation when pressed to attend school. Missing school serves to reinforce the agitation and avoidance. School phobia is treated with behavior therapy, in which the child is taught coping strategies (with family and school involvement) while being required to attend and stay in school. With adherence and support, the child usually tolerates attendance well after a relatively short period of intervention. There is no specific term to describe the anxiety and fear related to school that occurs in a child who is being bullied or is failing academically.

School Transition to Employment Partnership (STEP) Job training for eligible students with disabilities, students with economic or academic disadvantages, dropouts or potential dropouts, and those with demonstrated barriers to employment (e.g., single parents, adjudicated offenders) that includes 1) instruction regarding employability competencies; 2) work experience, on-the-job training, and try-out employment funded through the Job Training Partnership Act of 1982 (PL 97-

300); 3) an employer tax credit for targeted jobs that train eligible youth; and 4) supportive employment training services provided through special or vocational education, vocational rehabilitation, or social services. STEP may also include other cooperative education programs, prevocational training programs, special education assistance, and work experience programs designed specifically for eligible students. Local educational units that wish to participate in the STEP program must be approved by the Office of Vocational and Adult Education (OVAE) and the U.S. Department of Labor's Job Training Partnership Office. *See also* Job Training Partnership Act of 1982 (PL 97-300).

schoolwide positive behavior support (SWPBS) *See* positive behavioral interventions and supports (PBIS).

School-Years Screening Test for the Evaluation of Mental Status (SYSTEMS) A cognitive screening test for use with children 5–12 years of age. The test has 46 questions and can be administered face to face in about 7–12 minutes. The SYSTEMS is the pediatric equivalent of the Mini-Mental State Examination for adults.

scissoring *Forster sign.* A posture of the legs in which the legs tend to assume a crossed position with extension at the knees. This is typically a sign of increased tone in the lower extremities or tight adductor muscles. It is common in spastic cerebral palsy, especially diplegia (paralysis more of the lower extremities). An increasing tendency to scissor will make an ambulatory child trip more frequently over his or her own feet and will contribute to hip instability. An adductor tenotomy (with or without an obturator neurectomy) is an orthopedic surgical procedure that may correct the scissoring.

scissoring

sclera The white of the eye. The sclera will become yellow in the presence of jaundice (yellowing of the skin due to excess bilirubin), remain white with carotenemia (yellowing of the skin due to excess carotene), or develop a bluish tinge in a variety of systemic diseases.

scoliosis An abnormal lateral (to the side) curvature of the spine (vertebral column). Curves may be C-shaped or S-shaped. The etiology (cause) of scoliosis may be idiopathic (unknown), congenital (with strong genetic or familial influences), or neuromuscular. Scoliosis on a neuromuscular basis worsens even after growth is complete; this puts these people at increasing risk for respiratory infection and cardiopulmonary compromise.

scoliosis

scooting Locomotion in sitting; a rare pattern of locomotion that may reflect motor disability, intellectual disability, severe psychopathology, or some combination of these.

scotopic sensitivity syndrome A group of visual distortions that relate to light sensitivity, resolution, attention, and perseverance grouped together on the basis of two arbitrary principles: 1) They are distinct from visual-perceptual processing and peripheral/central visual field problems, and 2) they are susceptible to remediation by the use of tinted lenses or filters. The syndrome is a controversial entity. *See also* Irlen lenses.

SCPNT *See* Southern California Postrotary Nystagmus Test.

SCREEN *See* Screening Children for Related Early Educational Needs.

screening The process of identifying unrecognized disease or problems using tests, examinations, or other procedures that can be applied rapidly, inexpensively, and often by personnel with a lower level of training than that required to make a diagnosis. A first step in diagnosis, screening is a form of secondary prevention. Screening alone is insufficient to make a diagnosis, plan, or intervention. Screening is applied only to asymptomatic (without identified problems) populations. Thus, pediatricians routinely conduct developmental screening as part of well child care, but when a parent expresses explicit concern about a child's development, an assessment is needed.

Screening Children for Related Early Educational Needs (SCREEN) An educational screening test for current or potential school problems in children 3–7 years of age. The four subtests take approximately one half-hour to administer.

Screening Kit of Language Development (SKOLD) A screening assessment for use with children ages 2–5 that assesses preschool language development in six areas: vocabulary, comprehension, story completion, individual and paired sentence repetition without pictures, and comprehension of commands. Administration time is 15 minutes. The test is norm referenced both for children who speak Black Vernacular English (BVE) and for those who speak standard American English.

screening test An instrument that distinguishes people who probably do not have a specific disease or condition from those who probably do have the condition. The validity of a screening test is measured by its sensitivity, specificity, and false positive and false negative rates. In some instances, the dividing line between diagnostic and screening tests is not fixed; a test used as a screening instrument in one context may be diagnostic in another context.

Screening Test for Auditory Processing Disorders (SCAN) A test of auditory processing in children ages 3–11 years. The SCAN yields three subscores: filtered words, auditory figure–ground, and competing words.

Screening Tests for Young Children and Retardates (STYCAR) Tests in which block letters, miniature toys, and graded balls are used to screen vision; and noisemakers, toys, and pictures are used to screen hearing in children as young as 6 months of age. These vision and hearing tests are part of a more comprehensive approach referred to as the STYCAR sequences, which describe children's developmental progress from birth to 5 years.

Screening Tool for Autism (STAT) A 20-item test that is administered to children 2–3 years in a play context to distinguish autism from other developmental disorders.

SD   *See* standard deviation.

SDCT   *See* Slosson Drawing Coordination Test for Children and Adults.

SDR   Selective dorsal rhizotomy. *See* selective posterior rhizotomy.

SDRT-4   *See* Stanford Diagnostic Reading Test–Fourth Edition.

SDT   *See* speech detection threshold.

Seckel syndrome *bird-headed dwarfism.* A group of several genetic conditions characterized by short stature, microcephaly (small head), intellectual disability, and a "bird-like" facies (e.g., protuberant beaked nose, thin face, sloping forehead, and prominent eyes). Inheritance is autosomal recessive. Detectable at birth, the syndrome can be identified prenatally by serial ultrasound. The first identified form of Seckel syndrome (SCKL1) is caused by mutation in the gene encoding ataxia-telangiectasia and RAD3-related protein, which maps to chromosome 3q22.1-q24. Other loci for Seckel syndrome have been mapped to chromosomes 18p11-q11 (SCKL2) and 14q (SCKL3).

second signaling system One of two phylogenetic lines used by Ivan Pavlov (1849–1936) to describe brain function: 1) the first signaling system, which is the animal part of the brain that uses direct sensory perceptions; and 2) the second signaling system, which is the human division that uses intellect with an emphasis on language. These levels are somewhat analogous to Sigmund Freud's (1856–1939) primary and secondary process thinking. *See also* secondary process.

secondary disability A disability or adverse circumstance that does not necessarily follow as a direct consequence of a primary disability but for which the primary condition is a risk factor.

secondary gain The advantages experienced through being ill, such as being pampered and cared for and getting out of school or other responsibilities.

secondary palate The soft palate or velum, located behind the primary (hard) palate in the oral cavity.

secondary prevention A system of prevention that refers to specific interventions, arrangements of care systems, and environmental modifications to prevent the onset of problems or reduce their effects among at-risk populations.

secondary process A term from psychoanalysis that refers to logical, controlled thinking with minimal affective components; conscious intellectualization. Secondary process thinking is also characterized by delay or postponement, unlike the immediate discharge or gratification seen in primary process thinking. The secondary process identifies language as the principal component of rational control. *See also* second signaling system.

secondary school High school; classes at the postelementary and precollege level.

secretin A gastrointestinal hormone that has the function of reducing stomach acidity. It is a matter of debate whether secretin might also function as a neurotransmitter.

secretory otitis media *See* serous otitis media.

SED *See* seriously emotionally disturbed.

sedation A state of allayed irritability or excitement; calm. Sedation drugs depress brain activity and contribute to tiredness.

SEE-1 *See* Seeing Essential English.

SEE-2 *See* Signing Exact English.

SEEC *See* Vineland Social-Emotional Early Childhood Scales.

Seeing Essential English (SEE-1) A manual sign language modification of American Sign Language (ASL) to resemble English; signs stand for English prefixes, roots, suffixes, and verb tenses. English syntax (grammar) is emphasized; words are represented by the American sign word plus affixes (suffixes or prefixes) as needed.

Segawa syndrome *See* dopa responsive dystonia (DRD).

segmental rolling The mature phase of derotative righting in which the infant rolls over with one body segment preceding another in a "corkscrew" fashion. Also known as *neck on body reaction*.

Seguin Formboard A puzzle that requires the correct placement of 10 distinct geometric shapes in the matching holes in the test surface. One of a variety of different formboards designed for training and later used for testing purposes, the Seguin Formboard has been used to assess the presence of higher level visuomotor problem-solving skills in young children with autism.

seizure A convulsion or epileptic attack. Epilepsy is a disease with recurrent chronic seizures. A seizure is characterized by a paroxysmal burst of electrical activity in the brain that is clinically manifested by unconsciousness or impaired consciousness, usually with rhythmic movements of the extremities (arms or legs) or other atypical behaviors. The etiology (cause) of seizures may be idiopathic (unknown). Seizures of known organic etiology are more likely to be associated with abnormalities and specific genetic conditions. Seizures may be classified as partial or generalized, simple or complex. Combinations of seizure types that commonly occur together are termed *epileptic syndromes*. Diagnosis and treatment typically require a clinical history of the event and a corresponding abnormal electroencephalogram (EEG). Treatment with anticonvulsant medication is based on age and seizure type.

selection set The visual, auditory, and tactile presentation of all messages, symbols, and codes that are available at one time to an individual who relies on augmentative and alternative communication (AAC).

selection technique In the field of augmentative and alternative communication (AAC), the method used by an individual to select symbols on his or her communication device (e.g., scanning, direct selection).

selective attention The ability to attend to relevant sensory input while ignoring irrelevant input.

selective dorsal rhizotomy (SDR) *See* selective posterior rhizotomy.

selective integration The spending of part of a student's day in learning environments other than those that are typical for his or her classmates, such as resource rooms and special education classrooms.

selective mutism A manifestation of a shy and inhibited temperament, selective mutism may be a variant of social phobia. The core feature of selective mutism is the individual's failure to speak in specific social situations despite speaking in other situations. The disorder is not due to oppositional behavior or trauma, or to vocal or other physical impairments. Formerly referred to as *elective mutism* because children were assumed to be willfully refusing (a type of oppositional behavior) to talk in response to early trauma and dysfunctional family dynamics.

selective posterior rhizotomy *selective dorsal rhizotomy (SDR).* A neurosurgical ablative procedure used to reduce spasticity (high muscle tone) in severe spastic cerebral palsy in children 4–8 years of age. During the surgical procedure, motor and sensory nerve roots are separated. The sensory nerve roots are tested by electromyography and abnormal rootlets are selectively cut, producing a reduction in the spasticity. The operation is characterized as selective because only nerve rootlets that demonstrate an exaggerated electromyographic response on stimulation are cut. *See also* rhizotomy.

selective serotonin reuptake inhibitor (SSRI) A drug that acts by selectively blocking the reuptake of serotonin by nerve cells in the brain.

self-concept The appraisals that an individual makes and strives to maintain with regard to him- or herself. Self-concept includes the thoughts, attitudes, characteristics, feelings, and behaviors that a person considers vital to who he or she is. It also concerns one's comparison between an ideal "self" and one's observation of one's behavior.

self-contained classroom A special education instructional environment in which students with special needs spend the majority of their academic day in a separate (noninclusive, segregated) classroom. Self-contained classrooms do not permit meaningful interaction among children with and without disabilities, contact that is believed to be beneficial for both groups. Some students remain in self-contained classrooms and are "included" with peers without disabilities during nonacademic classes (music, art, physical education) and on the playground.

self-determination The rights of an individual with a disability to take charge of and responsibility for his or her life, including the right to decide where he or she will live, and with whom; what type of services he or she requires, and who will provide them; how he or she will spend his or her time; and how he or she will relate to the community. Service providers are bound by four basic principles of self-determination: 1) The ability of the individual together with family and friends to plan a life with necessary support; 2) the ability of a person with a disability control a certain sum of dollars in order to purchase services (with appropriate supports as needed); 3) the arranging of formal and informal resources and personnel sufficient to assist an individual to achieve community integration; and 4) the acceptance of a valued role in a person's community through competitive employment, organizational affiliations, spiritual development, and general caring of others in the community, as well as accountability for spending public dollars in ways that are life enhancing for persons with disabilities.

self-esteem An individual's perception and valuation of his or her worth, especially when compared with a particular reference group, and the feelings that emerge from those judgments. Having a disability, requiring special education, and experiencing failure in social situations are examples of events that can negatively affect a child's self-esteem. Self-esteem can be enhanced by the experience of success in any of a range of areas. High self-esteem in children is associated with effective parenting, perseverance on difficult tasks, and high achievement.

self-fulfilling prophecy The impact that a judgment (prediction or prophecy) has on an outcome (fulfillment). The actions of a person can be influenced by the expressed expectations of others. For example, a person with test anxiety maintains that he or she will fail an upcoming exam. The prophecy comes true (is fulfilled) because he or she rehearses this idea and anxiety increases to the point of interfering with his or her performance. This term also refers to the consequences of labeling, in which teachers and others bound their expectations of a student based upon a belief about the child's capabilities (e.g., a child labeled as gifted is believed to be quite capable and does in fact succeed, and a child labeled with a weakness or disability does not). Research has demonstrated that adults invest more (or less) effort based upon such assigned labels. The Rosenthal effect and the Pygmalion effect are positive versions of self-fulfilling prophecies.

Self-Help Assessment–Parent Evaluation (SHAPE) A test that assesses activities of daily living (ADLs), community functioning, self-control, relationships, and interactions. The SHAPE uses a pictorial format for parents to rate the abilities of their own child ages birth to 6 years.

self-help group *See* support group.

self-injurious behavior (SIB) Repetitive and chronic self-inflicted behaviors that can cause physical harm and tissue damage to the person performing these behaviors. The behaviors, which appear dysfunctional and devoid of desirable consequences, can include face slapping, head banging, biting, pinching, scratching, gouging, rumination, pica (eating nonfood items), and coprophagia (eating feces). The behaviors are stereotyped, self-stimulatory, and more common in individuals with severe intellectual disability. They occur more frequently in specific syndromes (e.g., Lesch-Nyhan), but they can also reflect the absence of meaningful ways

for an individual to communicate. Contemporary interventions for SIB include positive behavior supports, which seek to prevent and replace the SIB with alternatives, as well as pharmacological (medications) and protective interventions (e.g., helmets).

self-instruction A range of strategies that learners use to manage themselves and direct their own behavior, including regulating their attention to task, checking their work, monitoring their progress, and responding adaptively to interruptions and distractions.

self-monitoring Recording one's own behavior in order to effect change. The process of self-monitoring first involves recognizing the need to regulate or change a specific behavior (e.g., negative comments, time off task, talking out). The behavior to be changed must be measured against a standard, which is often defined by determining a baseline (data collected on a behavior before any intervention occurs). This phase may require another person to collect the data. The individual then keeps a record of the occurrence of the targeted behavior. Self-monitoring may be combined with self- or external reinforcement; however, in some cases, the act of record keeping alone is effective in producing change, presumably because the individual becomes more aware of the behavior.

self-regulation A range of strategies that individuals use to adjust their emotional and attentional states and behavior in order to accomplish goals. Self-regulation, sometimes called *effortful control,* includes the use of cognitive strategies (e.g., self-talk used to calm down during a stressful situation, organizing oneself to complete homework) and the increasing ability over the course of childhood to manage emotional states.

self-soothing behavior Relaxation techniques, such as thumb sucking, used to reduce stress.

self-stimulatory behavior Persistent, highly repetitive, invariant motor actions, mannerisms, or sequences that have no recognizable purpose (are nonfunctional) and are not injurious to the individual. They include such stereotypies as hand flapping and rocking; if they become harmful to the person, they are reclassified as self-injurious behavior.

self-talk Both one's internal self-statements and a cognitive-behavioral intervention in which an individual learns to monitor and replace maladaptive thoughts. For example, a coping statement for a child with school phobia might be "Even though I feel afraid I can still go to school" rather than "I have to avoid places where I get nervous."

semantic memory The memory component that contains the most knowledge of the world (e.g., word definitions, names of presidents). The most obvious fact about this memory component is that it is highly organized, as shown by the ability to quickly recall one relevant bit of information from the millions stored. The form of this organization is not clear, but a network model with concepts and categories that play key roles seems likely. The organizational structure of semantic memory is similar to that described in declarative knowledge.

semantics The study of the history and meaning of words. Knowledge of semantics involves understanding the way in which meaning is associated with words as well as how meaning is conveyed through sentences. Knowledge of vocabulary refers to a part of semantics that relates to the ability to understand and use the meaning of an independent word. Some aspects of semantics have been associated with simultaneous processing.

semantic-syntactic grid display A type of augmentative and alternative communication (AAC) grid display that organizes vocabulary items according to their part of speech and their relationships within a syntactic framework.

semilingualism The assumption that second language proficiency is partially a function of competence in the primary language; when the second language is introduced before competency in the first language has been achieved, development in both languages may be arrested and the child may not fully develop either language.

semiotics The signs and gestures that accompany verbal language and that may either clarify or contradict verbal communication.

sensation The most fundamental level of receptive behavior. Sensation refers solely to the activation of sensorineural structures. Impairments at this level include deafness, blindness, and other peripheral (noncentral) nervous system impairments. Sensation contrasts with perception, which is the interpretation or processing of sensory information. Mild disorders in sensation can often be compensated for by the perceptual operations of the brain.

sensation avoiding A pattern of sensory processing characterized by low sensory thresholds and active strategies to limit bothersome sensory input. *See* sensory defensiveness.

sensation seeking A pattern of sensory processing characterized by high sensory thresholds accompanied by active strategies to increase sensory input.

sensitive period A period of time in an organism's development when conditions are optimal for the emergence of a specific function. Missing this temporal window of opportunity does not preclude the later evolution of this function but renders it more difficult. *See also* critical period.

sensitivity An epidemiological term that denotes a true positive rate. Sensitivity is a statistic that describes the ability of a screening test to successfully identify those tested who actually have the condition for which they are being screened. Sensitivity is the ratio of true positives (positive test result, condition present) to all positive test results (whether the condition is present or not). The closer this ratio is to 1.0, the better the screening test.

sensorimotor Describing the earliest Piagetian stage of cognitive development; six substages during the first 2 years of life demonstrate increasing structuring of motor responses to immediately perceived objects.

sensorimotor Relating to the use of sensory (including visual, auditory, tactile [touch], olfactory [smell], proprioceptive, and kinesthetic) information to produce an adapted (purposeful, goal-directed) motor response.

sensorineural hearing impairment (SNHI) *sensorineural deafness.* A hearing impairment in which the abnormality is located along the auditory nerve (cranial nerve VIII) from the inner ear to the brainstem. This can be caused by a congenital abnormality in the nerve, by damage to the nerve (e.g., from certain antibiotics), or by disorders such as Friedreich ataxia. Many syndromes are associated with a sensorineural hearing loss that may be static or progressive. Frequent monitoring of hearing acuity is necessary in individuals with progressive hearing loss to keep their hearing aids functioning effectively.

sensory defensiveness An overresponse to sensory input in which the individual's nervous system is overwhelmed by ordinary sensory input and reacts defensively to it, often with strong negative emotion and activation of the sympathetic nervous system. This symptom is one component of the syndrome of dysfunction of sensory integration. This response may be seen from all types of sensory input, or it may be specific to one or a few sensory systems.

sensory deficits Sensory problems in touch, hearing, vision, or visuospatial skills. These impairments are seen with cerebral palsy, acquired brain injury, attention-deficit/hyperactivity disorder (ADHD), and other neurodevelopmental disabilities.

sensory diet A specifically designed combination of sensations at appropriate intensities to be therapeutic for the child who has dysfunction in sensory integration.

sensory discrimination dysfunction A dysfunction of sensory integration in which a person has difficulty interpreting the temporal or spatial characteristics of sensory input, resulting in inefficient responses to the environment.

sensory function Assessment of a sensory modality by appropriate neurological tests. These include pain sensation (a pinprick), light touch, temperature, position sense, vibration, stereognosis (solid form recognition by touch), graphesthesia (recognition of items written on the skin), and two-point discrimination. Sensation requires that both the central and the peripheral nervous systems be intact. Asymmetric brain lesions may result in the loss of sensation on one side only.

sensory integration The neurological process that organizes sensation from one's own body and from the environment and enables one to use the body effectively within the environment. The spatial and temporal aspects of inputs from different sensory modalities are interpreted, associated, and unified. The brain selects, enhances, inhibits, compares, and associates sensory information in a flexible, constantly changing pattern.

Sensory Integration and Praxis Tests (SIPT) A battery of 17 performance (nonverbal) tests used to assess the relationships among tactile (touch) processing, vestibular-proprioceptive processing, visual perception, visual-motor coordination, practicability, and bilateral integration and sequencing in children 4–8 years of age with moderate learning, behavior, or developmental irregularities. Administration time is 1.5 hours, with computer scoring to compare patterns in six different cluster groups: impairment in bilateral integration and sequencing, visuo- and somatodyspraxia, dyspraxia on verbal command, generalized sensory integrative dysfunction, low-average sensory integration and praxis, and high-average sensory integration and praxis.

sensory integration theory   A theory of brain–behavior relationships that attempts to explain impairments in interpreting sensory information from the body and the environment, and impairments in academic or neuromotor learning in people with learning disabilities or clumsiness. The theory includes a specific battery of assessment instruments and a menu of intervention techniques for a wide variety of developmental disorders. A. Jean Ayres (1920–1988) was the founder of sensory integration theory.

sensory modulation dysfunction (SMD)   A syndrome within the dysfunction of sensory integration in which a person is hypo- or hyperresponsive to sensory input from the body or environment. Individuals who are hyporesponsive may show an underresponse or be sensory seeking; may exhibit reduced reactions to pain; may respond slowly or even fail to become dizzy when spun around or during a swinging test; may crave hugs or heavy input or be unaware of their body position in space, resulting in clumsy behavior. Individuals who are hyperresponsive may overrespond or withdraw from input; avoid or exhibit aggressive behavior in response to touch; be afraid of or become sick with movement; and avoid or dislike activities that require gross motor movements, such as jumping and hanging from a bar.

sensory profile   A tool designed to provide a standard method for professionals to measure a child's sensory processing abilities and to profile the effect of sensory processing on functional performance in the daily life of a child. A sensory profile is most appropriate

for use with children 5–10 years of age but can be used with 3- and 4-year-olds.

sensory register   Information from the sensory receptors (rod and cone sensitivity to light, middle-ear bone sensitivity to sound, proprioceptor cell sensitivity to touch, etc.) stored in the central nervous system (CNS). It is usually assumed that there are as many sensory registers as there are sense modalities, each being modality specific. Most stored information fades quickly, with the temporal duration of auditory information (approximately 2 seconds) generally lasting longer than that of visual information (about 0.5 second). From the immediate representation of sensory information, a small fraction is kept for continued representation in short-term memory, whereas the rest is lost from the system.

sentence completion technique   A projective measure that is an extension of the word association test. The person is presented with incomplete sentences and is asked to complete them. Examples include "I worry about . . ." or "I am happy when . . ." The sentences are typically analyzed in terms of the attitudes, concerns, and motivations expressed in the responses. Caution must be exercised when analyzing responses from people with developmental disabilities. The length and quality of responses can be significantly affected by language impairment, processing problems, and attention deficits.

separation anxiety   Childhood anxiety caused by actual or threatened separation from a major attachment figure or place, such as a parent or home; a positive sign of the presence of attachment or bonding. Separation anxiety becomes prominent late in the first year of life around the same time as stranger anxiety, from which it is distinct. Although separation anxiety may recur briefly on the first day of school, it is distinct from school phobia. It becomes undesirable in older children, such as middle school–age children, or when it is so intense that it interferes with normal activities. At that point, it is usually accompanied by morbid fears, preoccupations, and nightmares and is also known as *social phobia* (not school phobia).

sepsis workup   A battery of tests (microbiological, blood, chemical, and others) used to identify the presence and nature of an infection (sepsis); the particular battery of tests varies with the age of the child and the nature of the presenting signs and symptoms. Infections in premature infants and young infants can be nonspecific and so quickly life threatening that sepsis workups are more frequent in this pediatric age group and are often performed simultaneously with the initiation of antibiotic treatment for an as-yet-undiagnosed infection. If cultures and other test results are negative after several days, therapy may be discontinued. The child suspected of having an infection is referred to as "septic" or "ill looking"; sepsis does not require fever but may include lethargy and anorexia (loss of appetite).

septo-optic dysplasia (SOD)   *de Morsier syndrome.* A syndrome that includes abnormal development (i.e., the absence of the septum pellucidum that separates the front portions of the lateral fluid-containing spaces of the brain), optic nerve hypoplasia (undergrowth) resulting in severe visual impairment, and growth hormone deficiency with short stature and sometimes other hypothalamic pituitary endocrine dysfunction. Many people with this syndrome have no associated limitations, but a wide spectrum of neurodevelopmental disabilities can be present. Replacement hormone therapy can be beneficial.

sequela   A morbid condition that follows as a consequence of another disease or condition; the original condition is a cause of the sequela, which is an effect. For example, intellectual disability, hearing impairment, and cardiac disease are possible sequelae to prenatal rubella.

sequence anomalad   A pattern of multiple anomalies (malformation, deformation, disruption, or dysplasia) derived from a single prior anomaly or mechanical factor. The term *sequence* implies greater understanding of the impact of the initial event or subsequent formation than a syndrome.

Sequenced Inventory of Communication Development–Revised (SICD-R)   A scale of expressive and receptive language milestones for use with children 4–48 months. The instrument, which is part parent interview and part child performance, evaluates receptive items of awareness, discrimination, and understanding and expressive items of imitation, initiating, responsiveness, and verbal output. It is grossly scored in 4-month increments; however, standardization figures are available.

Sequential Assessment of Mathematics Inventories–Standardized Inventory (SAMI)   An individual test of mathematics achievement for use with children from kindergarten through eighth grade. The 243 items assess eight curriculum strands: mathematical language, measurement, ordinality, geometric concepts, number and notation, mathematical applications, computation, and word problems.

sequential bilingualism   A type of bilingualism in which the second language is acquired after the individual begins school.

sequential processing   The manipulation or processing of stimuli one at a time, with each idea linearly and temporally related to the preceding stimulus. Both verbal and nonverbal information may be processed sequentially when the order of the stimuli is necessary for extracting meaning or problem solving. Sequential processing is related to a variety of school-oriented tasks, including memorization of number facts, application of stepwise mathematical procedures, phonics, spelling, grammatical relationships and rules, chronology of historical events, and following directions. The Kaufman Assessment Battery for Children (K-ABC) is based on the concept of sequential versus simultaneous information processing. *See also* cognitive sequencing.

serial casting The use of a sequence of casts to progressively correct a deformity; each successive cast positions the body part closer to the desired norm.

seriously emotionally disturbed (SED) An educational label for a condition that includes impaired learning, unsatisfactory interpersonal relationships, inappropriate behaviors, depression, and physical symptoms related to school.

serotonin *5-hydroxytryptamine.* A transmitter that operates both centrally in the brain and peripherally in the gastric system. Serotonin metabolism is involved in aggression, anxiety, impulsivity, mood, pain perception, and sleep.

serous otitis media *catarrhal otitis, glue ear, mucoid ear, nonsuppurative otitis media, otitis media with effusion (OME), secretory otitis media.* A middle ear effusion (fluid collection) as evidenced by visual and tympanometric (eardrum) findings but without the signs and symptoms of infection.

sertraline Trade name, Zoloft. A short-acting selective serotonin reuptake inhibitor (SSRI) used to treat depression, obsessive-compulsive disorder, and panic disorder. Sertraline (Zoloft) usually takes about 2 weeks to show clinical effects. It may have gastrointestinal side effects, such as nausea or diarrhea, and may also cause trouble sleeping.

service coordination A procedure for coordinating multiple services to a client or client system. Effective service coordination includes encouraging the full participation and increasing the empowerment of individuals and families rather than viewing them

as cases to be managed. Previously known as *case management. See also* case management, Individuals with Disabilities Education Act (IDEA) of 1990 (PL 101-476).

SES *See* socioeconomic status.

setting sun sign Deviation of the eyes below the horizontal so that the white of the sclera is visible above the cornea. This finding can be a sign of progressive hydrocephalus (excess fluid in the brain).

setting sun sign

severe and profound intellectual disability *severe and profound mental retardation (SPMR).* Describing a grouping of people with severe intellectual disability (intelligence quotient [IQ] score between 20–25 and 35–40 with concomitant impairments in adaptive behavior and function) and people with profound intellectual disability (IQ score below 20 or 25 with concomitant impairments in adaptive behavior and function) for the purposes of education and habilitation. The term *severe to profound handicap* (SPH) refers to people with similar functional impairments whether or not they have intellectual disability.

severe hearing impairment Hearing loss that ranges in severity between 71 and 90 dBHL (decibels hearing level).

severe intellectual disability *severe mental retardation (SMR).* Intellectual disability in which the intelligence quotient [IQ] score is between 20–25 and 35–40.

severe to profound handicap (SPH) *See* severe and profound intellectual disability.

sex chromosome The chromosome responsible for the determination of sex (XX in females, XY in males).

sex chromosome abnormalities (SCA) A group of chromosomal conditions that involve abnormal numbers of X and Y chromosomes (i.e., the sex chromosomes). This group includes both monosomies (e.g., Turner syndrome [XO]), with only one X chromosome instead of the normal two (XX), and polysomies (e.g., Klinefelter syndrome [XXY]), which involve an extra X or Y chromosome. Other variations are multiple X chromosomes (e.g., trisomy X [XXX or XXXY], tetrasomy X [XXXX or XXXXY]) and multiple Y chromosomes (XYY). In general, abnormal numbers of sex chromosomes are associated with milder cognitive and behavioral effects than are other chromosomal abnormalities. Nonetheless, the trend is that individuals with greater numbers of chromosomes have more impaired cognitive functioning.

sex-influenced   Describing a trait that, although not X-linked in its inheritance, is nonetheless expressed differently (either in the extent or frequency of expression) in males and females.

sex-limited   Describing a trait that is expressed in only one sex, even though the gene may be present in the other sex. Sex-limited genes are not necessarily X-linked.

sex-linked   *See* X-linkage.

SF-12   *See* Short Form-36 (SF-36).

SF-20   *See* Short Form-36 (SF-36).

SF-36   *See* Short Form-36.

SFA   *See* School Function Assessment.

S-FRIT   *See* Slosson Full-Range Intelligence Test.

SGA   *See* small for gestational age.

shagreen patch   A skin lesion found in tuberous sclerosis; a patch of thickened, raised, green/gray/brown skin usually found in the lumbosacral region (lower back).

shaken baby syndrome   *Caffey syndrome, Caffey-Kempe syndrome.* A type of child maltreatment characterized by intracranial injury and long bone fractures that represents an important masked presentation of child abuse. When an infant is violently shaken, flailing of the limbs causes metaphyseal lesions (irregularities at the growing ends of long bones visible on x ray) and shaking of the head causes subdural bleeding and retinal (eye) hemorrhages (bleeding).

sham oral feeding   Feeding in which intake does not enter the stomach but is collected as it exits the stoma (opening). The process may be used in infants with tracheoesophageal fistula/esophageal atresia to mirror the oral and feeding experiences of a typically developing child.

SHAPE   *See* Self-Help Assessment–Parent Evaluation.

shaping   A term from behavioral learning theory (operant conditioning) that refers to the process of gradually changing a person's behavior by reinforcing progressively closer approximations of the desired behavior. For example, a student who is seldom in his or her seat more than 3 minutes at a time might be reinforced for progressively closer approximations of the target behavior of staying in his or her seat for 20 minutes. First, the student would be reinforced for staying in his or her seat for 3 minutes, then 4, then 5, and so forth until the student reaches the target of 20 minutes.

shared attention   *See* joint attention.

sharp frequency tuning   The frequency at which each auditory nerve fiber optimally responds.

sheltered employment   *sheltered workshop.* A protected, monitored work environment for people with developmental disabilities and other cognitive or physical impairments.

Work programs are based on an individual's capacity to produce rather than on an external production standard. Thus, one worker may produce 5 units per hour and another 25 units per hour, yet each is producing at his or her maximum capacity. Once the mainstay of "employment" for adults with developmental difficulties, sheltered employment settings are criticized for their "protective" (e.g., paternalistic) stance, segregation (the fact that they are not located in the community and that participation is limited to individuals with disabilities), and failure to meaningfully prepare some individuals for employment in competitive (typical) work environments.

sheltered immersion   A type of program for second language learning that provides instruction almost entirely in the second language but in a self-contained classroom consisting only of second language learners.

sheltered workshop   *See* sheltered employment.

shifting   The action of moving an object in a linear direction on the finger surface using one hand alone, such as scooting a pencil from holding it by the eraser end to positioning it for writing.

shimmer   An acoustic measure that indicates fluctuations in amplitude.

short bowel syndrome   Any malabsorption condition that results from loss or resection of significant lengths of the small intestine; symptoms can include diarrhea, poor growth and nutrition, and fatty stools.

Short Form-36 (SF-36)   A health survey used to research the impact of particular disease conditions and treatments on a group of people. It is available in at least 121 languages and measures both physical and mental health through 36 questions in eight different scales. It measures health functioning as well as well-being. The SF-

36 is used in both research and clinical practice to assess the health status of a person or group of people. The SF-36 was originally developed by the RAND Corporation for use in the Medical Outcomes Study. Shorter versions of quality-of-life measurements like this one are also available through the RAND Health group; these include the SF-12 and SF-20.

short leg brace   A brace that extends from just below the knee to the foot.

short leg brace

short stature   Height below –2.5 standard deviations for age and sex.

shortness of breath (SOB)   The state of gasping for air, being unable to fill the lungs with air automatically, or getting "winded."

short-term memory   The memory that receives information from a sensory register and corresponds roughly with awareness. Short-term memory is also called *working memory*. The term *short-term memory* emphasizes the duration of information, whereas the term *working memory* emphasizes the function. Two key characteristics usually associated with short-term memory are the fragility of storage and its extremely limited capacity. Unless it is rehearsed, information passes out of short-term memory in about 10 seconds. A slight distraction will cause the information to be lost sooner. Approximately seven chunks of information can be held in short-term memory at one time. A chunk may be described as the highest level integration of stimulus material available to an individual. For example, 346 represents one chunk, whereas 3-4-6 represents three chunks. Discriminating between deficits in attention and impairments in short-term memory in students with learning difficulties may be difficult, as either can appear as a lack of ability to accurately retain information for immediate recall. The typically limited capacity also plays a part in reading and mathematics disabilities. If decoding skills or mathematics facts are not learned automatically, they "take up space" in working memory that would otherwise be used for comprehension or problem solving. Thus, providing an aid to working memory (e.g., a number chart, number line) can allow some students to better use their intact conceptual skills. *See also* memory.

Shprintzen syndrome   *See* velocardiofacial syndrome.

shunt   A surgical anastomosis, or artificial passage. *See also* ventriculoperitoneal (VP) shunt.

SI   *See* social intelligence.

sialidosis   *cherry-red spot myoclonus syndrome.* The sialidoses are a group of disorders of sugar metabolism. One form, juvenile or adult normosomatic (normal body) sialidosis, exhibits macular cherry-red spots with visual loss and myoclonus. The facies are normal, and there is no dysostosis multiplex. There are three forms characterized by dysmorphic phenotype and coarse (thickened features) facies: 1) a congenital lethal variety that presents with hydrops fetalis, 2) an infantile form (nephrosialidosis) that presents initially from birth to 1 year of age, and 3) a childhood form (Spranger syndrome) that usually has an onset between 8 and 15 years and that becomes progressively worse. All types have autosomal recessive inheritance. The gene is located at 6p21.3.

sialorrhea   Excessive drooling; unintentional loss of saliva and other oral contents from the mouth. Some normal drooling can persist until 18 months of age.

SIB   *See* self-injurious behavior.

sibling   A brother or sister; one of two or more children with the same mother or father. When a family includes a child with a disability, siblings often feel left out owing

to the attention and "special treatment" the child with a disability requires and receives. Research suggests that parents of children with developmental disabilities often place increased demands on their other children. Siblings may be expected to help care for the child with a disability and to subordinate their needs and feelings to those of their sibling. These children may feel guilty about their lack of a disability and may be pressured to excel and to be "perfect" in order to compensate for their sibling with a disability. Young siblings of children with disabilities may mistakenly think they are at risk of developing the same disability. Sibling support groups are available to help address many of these issues.

sibling rivalry   Competition among children of the same generation in a family for parental attention, approval, recognition, and affection. The quality of sibling relationships helps to determine the degree to which individuals will have successful interpersonal relationships later in life. A weakness, special need, or disability can complicate and alter this typical developmental process, making the competition one-sided, cruel, unfulfilling, or ineffective, and can create negative feelings (e.g., guilt, shame, anger) that hinder growth. Siblings of children with developmental disabilities have a unique perspective on, and experience of, themselves as well as their families. This perspective must be identified and addressed to facilitate optimal individual development and family functioning. Groups and organizations for siblings exist for these purposes.

sibship   A group that includes all of the brothers and sisters (siblings) in a family. This is an important grouping for determining the mechanism of transmission of a genetic disorder. For example, a disorder in a family with typical parents but two affected siblings is probably recessive.

sicca cell therapy   Injection of fetal sheep brain cells to promote brain growth and improve intelligence in individuals with Down syndrome and intellectual disability; an unproven and hazardous intervention.

SICD-R *See* Sequenced Inventory of Communication Development–Revised.

sickle cell (SS) anemia *sickle cell disease.* An autosomal recessive disorder common in African American and Mediterranean populations. It is caused by a gene base pair substitution that produces a type of hemoglobin (in oxygen-carrying red blood cells) that does not bind oxygen well. The red blood cells assume a sickle shape that can cause a stroke by blocking blood flow through the vessels. Such brain damage can produce loss of function in the form of hemiparesis (one-sided paralysis), aphasia (loss of language skills), or even intellectual disability. The sickling can also cause pain (called a *sickle crisis*) and swelling of the hands or feet. Children with sickle cell anemia are prone to infections.

side effect An unintended consequence of a drug or other treatment, usually but not always adverse.

sidelyer A firm device that helps a child maintain a position of lying on one side.

sidelying A posture in which a person lies on his or her right or left side with his or her legs slightly bent; a variety of cushions or pads are sometimes used to help maintain this posture.

sight word A whole word that is recognized based on the memory of the whole word. This is in contrast to a word is that recognized as a result of phonetic (representing sounds) sequential analysis.

Siglish *See* Signed English.

sign An objective, physical marker of a condition or disease; a finding that is objectively measurable or localizable (e.g., fever

can be a sign of infection or other disease). Signs are usually detected on the physical examination of the individual, but some signs are found on laboratory or radiological examination. Signs are objective; symptoms are subjective.

sign systems Manual communication systems used by people with severe and profound hearing loss. A sign system may have its own structure and syntax (grammar) or may use that of another language. Signs can be either phonetic (representing sounds), idiographic (representing ideas), or pictographic (representing objects). Sign systems in use include American Sign Language (ASL), manual English, signed English, Seeing Essential English (SEE-1), and Signing Exact English (SEE-2).

Signed English *Siglish, Pidgin Signed English (PSE).* A sign system that shares some of the characteristics of American Sign Language (ASL) and some of English, effectively reducing the grammar used from each.

Signing Exact English (SEE-2) A sign language system in which signs represent words instead of word roots, as in Seeing Essential English (SEE-1). Prefixes and suffixes are added when necessary.

silent pauses A type of disfluency in which there are inappropriate breaks in speech and vocalization is stopped.

Silver syndrome *See* Russell-Silver syndrome (RSS).

Silverskiold test An orthopedic examination to differentiate whether limited dorsiflexion (upgoing movement of the toes) at the ankle is due to gastrocnemius (a muscle in the lower leg) contracture or to gastrocnemius and soleus (a muscle in the calf) contractures. If foot dorsiflexion is greater with the knee flexed than with the knee extended, the gastrocnemius is the main site of the contracture. In the latter condition, orthopedic surgical treatment of equinus (an involuntary foot extension) deformity of the foot involves a transplantation of the heads of the gastrocnemius muscle; if the equinus deformity persists regardless of the position of the knee, then a tendon lengthening is in order.

simian crease *four finger transverse crease.* A single transverse palmar crease instead of the more common pattern of two incomplete palmar creases. This is a minor dysmorphic (atypical) feature that occurs (at least unilaterally) in approximately 50%–55% of people with Down syndrome, in approximately 0.4%–10% of people without disabilities, and with variable frequency in a variety of other syndromes and throughout the spectrum of neurodevelopmental disorders. The term *simian crease* is no longer preferred by genetic practitioners.

simian crease

simian grasp *See* ulnar grasp.

similar sequence hypothesis A theory that people with intellectual disability and those without intellectual disability traverse the same stages of cognitive development but at different rates and with final attainment of different stages.

similar structure hypothesis A theory that, when matched on mental age, people with intellectual disability and those without intellectual disability solve problems in the same way (with regard to the underlying formal cognitive structures).

Similarities A Wechsler (intelligence test) subtest that measures verbal reasoning and concept formation. It involves auditory comprehension, memory, and verbal expression.

simple partial seizure A seizure type with unilateral hemispheric involvement resulting in focal or localized symptoms, including

motor, sensation, or psychic characteristics. Consciousness is unimpaired during a simple partial seizure. Simple partial seizures may evolve into generalized seizures or complex partial seizures. Partial seizures arise from a specific locus (area) in the brain, and the symptoms manifested are related to that location. For example, abnormal electrical seizure activity in the motor cortex for the arm may produce a twitching of that arm.

simple sentence A type of sentence with an independent clause without a subordinate clause.

Simpson-Golabi-Behmel pre- and postnatal overgrowth syndrome A condition that includes coarse (thickened features) facies with mandibular (jaw) overgrowth, cleft palate, heart defects, hernias, supernumerary (extra) nipples, and renal and skeletal abnormalities. Wilms tumor and/or neuroblastoma (childhood cancers) may occur during early childhood. Etiology is X-linked, with most cases mapped to Xq26; another form, a lethal form with multiple anomalies and hydrops fetalis, has been located at Xp22. Death usually occurs within the first 8 weeks of life.

simultaneous bilingualism A type of bilingualism in which two languages are spoken to a child beginning in early infancy so that he or she develops skills in both languages at the same time and with competence in each language equal to that of monolingual speakers.

simultaneous processing The manipulating or processing of many stimuli or aspects of stimuli at the same time in a holistic fashion. Both verbal and nonverbal stimuli may be processed simultaneously when the meaning or solution requires the input to be integrated and synthesized at once, rather than one step at a time. Simultaneous problem-solving skills are related to a variety of academic skills, including deriving meaning from pictures and other visual stimuli, number shapes, basic arithmetic concepts, and more complex mathematical principles; shapes of letters and configuration of words; understanding main ideas, diagrams, and flow charts; and creative problem solving. The Kaufman Assessment Battery for Children (K-ABC) is based on the concept of simultaneous versus sequential information processing.

single photon emission computed tomography (SPECT) A procedure that uses gamma-ray emission isotopes to measure regional blood flow in an area of the brain or other organ.

single umbilical artery The umbilical cord typically has two arteries and one vein (three vessels); when there are only two vessels (and one umbilical artery), there is a significant association with a variety of major organ malformations. The presence of three vessels is ascertained when the cord is cut at delivery.

single-gene disorder A disorder produced by a single mutant (changed) gene with a large effect on phenotype (appearance).

sinus A recess, cavity, or channel; often used to refer to a collection of skull cavities (paranasal sinuses: frontal, ethmoidal, sphenoidal, and maxillary) that are subject to allergic inflammation and secondary infection (i.e., sinusitis) and that contribute to sinus headaches.

sip and puff switch A switch used for people who have little functional use of their hands. The switch usually resembles a straw and is controlled by air being sucked (sipped) out of or blown (puffed) into the straw.

SIPT *See* Sensory Integration and Praxis Tests.

SIS *See* Supports Intensity Scale.

sit A gross motor milestone of infancy. There are three distinct phases in the

achievement of sitting: 1) tripod sitting with anterior (front) propping at 5 months, 2) unsupported sitting with lateral (outside) propping at 7 months, and 3) mature sitting with posterior (back) propping at 9 months. Failure to achieve sitting by 1 year of age suggests the presence of cerebral palsy or another motor disability; failure to achieve sitting by 2 years of age suggests that the child may not walk independently. Long sitting is sitting with the legs straight out in front. Cross-legged sitting is sitting with the knees flexed and the legs crossed in front. Side sitting is sitting with the legs and thighs flexed to the same side. Between-heel sitting is the reversed tailor position.

tripod sitting

unsupported sitting

mature sitting

SIT-R3 *See* Slosson Intelligence Test–Revised.

sitting in air A descriptive phrase applied to the posture assumed by a very young infant when one attempts to elicit a positive support response.

sitting in air

69 *See* triploidy.

Sjogren Hand Test A vision screening test for use with children 3 years and older. A variant of the illiterate E test that uses a hand rather than an E as the directional stimulus. *See also* illiterate E.

Sjögren-Larsson syndrome A genetic syndrome characterized by ichthyosis (very dry skin), short stature, spasticity (increased muscle tone), and intellectual disability. Chorioretinal (eye) lesions are noted in approximately 50% of affected individuals. The syndrome is usually detected in the neonatal period. Treatment is symptomatic for the skin lesions, with special education modifications for the cognitive limitations. Inheritance follows an autosomal recessive pattern. Sjögren-Larsson syndrome can be caused by mutation in the gene encoding fatty aldehyde dehydrogenase.

Skeels and Dye study A follow-up study conducted in 1939 of 25 infants who had exhibited variable developmental delays in an institutional setting; those children who received mothering from women with intellectual disability while living in institutions made dramatic cognitive gains, qualified for adoption, and continued to exhibit significantly better outcomes three decades later.

skiascopy Measurement of the refractive error of an eye by focusing on the retina (light-sensitive inner back wall of the eye).

skin grafting The transferring of a section of intact skin on a person's body to cover an area with damaged (e.g., burned) skin.

skinfold thickness Measurement of the compressed double fold of fat plus skin at normed sites of the body to estimate the size of subcutaneous (under the skin) fat stores. Skinfold thickness is measured using a caliper.

Skinner, Burrhus F. (1904–1990) The originator of operant conditioning, a psychologist who distinguished between two types of behavior—respondent and operant—and clarified how various reinforcement contingencies could control or modify behavior.

SKOLD *See* Screening Kit of Language Development.

skull fracture A break in one of the bones of the head. A history of head trauma that includes a skull fracture diagnosed by x ray is unlikely to adequately explain the presence of a significant developmental disability. A depressed skull fracture with neurological impairments, seizures, and coma may, how-

ever, contribute to a later developmental disorder.

SLD Specific learning disability. *See* learning disability (LD).

sleep apnea Stoppage of breathing during sleeping. Sleep studies are conducted to investigate the cause and plan appropriate intervention.

sleep onset disorder / *sleep-onset protodyssomnia.* Problems getting to sleep in children older than 12 moths of age that last longer than 4 weeks.

SLES *See* Speech and Language Evaluation Scale.

SLI *See* specific language impairment, speech-language impairment.

slight hearing impairment Hearing loss that ranges in severity between 16 and 25 dBHL (decibels hearing level).

Slingerland Multisensory Approach An approach to reading and writing that teaches patterns for the automatic association of the auditory, visual, and kinesthetic modalities. The letters of the alphabet are taught first. Strategies are then taught for thinking through what is not simply memorized. This integrated language arts approach incorporates the teaching of reading, spelling, handwriting, and oral and written expression.

Slingerland Screening Tests for Identifying Children with Specific Language Disability A group-administered test designed to identify children with specific language disabilities. This instrument actually tests perceptual-motor functions thought to affect receptive and expressive language skills. The basic tasks required for all grades are the same and differ mainly in the difficulty of vocabulary involved. Subtests in each form include copying from a sample; visual perception and memory of words, letters, and numbers; visual discrimination to perceive similarities and differences; visual perception and memory linked with kinesthetic motor performance; brief exploration of groups of words, phrases, letters, and numbers; auditory perception and memory linked with visual-kinesthetic-motor association—groups of letters, numbers, and words are to be written; auditory-visual kinesthetic linkage—adding the requirement of making auditory discrimination of single sounds within whole words; auditory-visual linkage without the kinesthetic motor requirement of writing from dictation—a word, letter, or number is located from a group; and an echolalia (repetition of what is heard) test (individually administered to selected pupils), which permits more careful evaluation of auditory perception and memory than can be made from verbal responses alone. Forms include A (Grade 1 and beginning Grade 2), B (Grade 2 and beginning Grade 3), C (Grades 3 and 4), and D (Grades 5 and 6).

SLOS *See* Smith-Lemli-Opitz syndrome.

Slosson Drawing Coordination Test for Children and Adults (SDCT) A figure-copying test for use with children 1–12 years of age; accuracy scores below 85 warrant further evaluation. Age norms for accuracy are reported in the manual.

Slosson Full-Range Intelligence Test (S-FRIT) A brief verbal, performance, and memory screen for the purpose of tentatively diagnosing intellectual strengths and weaknesses in individuals 5;0–21;11 years of age. The instrument yields standard scores (with a mean of 100 and a standard deviation of 16) for general cognitive measures of Full-Range Intelligence Quotient (FRIQ), Rapid Cognitive Index (RCI), and Best g Index (BgI). Standard scores (with a mean of 50 and a standard deviation of 8) are provided for cognitive subdomains by a Verbal Index (VI), Abstract Index (AI), Quantitative Index (QI), Memory Index

(MI), and a combined abstract and quantitative Performance Index (PI).

Slosson Intelligence Test–Revised (SIT-R3) An individually administered screening test used to measure general verbal intelligence in individuals 4 years old to adult. The SIT-R3 generates a mental age equivalent (MAE) that can be converted to a total standard score (TSS) with a mean of 100 and a standard deviation of 16.

Slosson Oral Reading Test–Revised Preschool–Adult (SORT-R3) A reading screening test for use with children from first grade through high school. The test stimuli are 10 lists of 20 single words of graded difficulty. The test yields a grade score.

slow learner An imprecise educational term sometimes used to refer to children with borderline intellectual functioning (intelligence quotient [IQ] score of 70–85) or mild intellectual disability (IQ score of 50–70) or both.

slow talker *See* late-talking toddler.

SLP *See* speech-language pathologist.

Sly syndrome *mucopolysaccharidosis (MPS) VII.* A genetic syndrome characterized by growth deficiency, coarse (thickened features) facies, cloudy corneas, and intellectual disability. Affected individuals can have dislocated hips and be subject to frequent respiratory illness. Inheritance patterns are autosomal recessive; detection at 10 weeks' gestation is possible through chorionic villus sampling. Treatment is symptomatic.

SMA *See* spinal muscular atrophy.

SMA1 Spinal muscular atrophy type 1. *See* Werdnig-Hoffmann syndrome.

small for gestational age (SGA) Small for date; dysmature; describing a low birth weight (less than 2,500 g) infant whose weight is also below the 10th percentile for gestational age. Thus, there are SGA term and SGA premature infants.

SMD *See* sensory modulation dysfunction.

Smith syndrome Fetal alcohol syndrome (FAS) phenotype (appearance) without a known history of prenatal alcohol exposure. The term is also used as a nonculpatory synonym for FAS.

Smith-Johnson Nonverbal Performance Scale A performance intelligence test for use with children 2–4 years of age; instructions are in pantomime, and hearing impairment norms are provided.

Smith-Lemli-Opitz syndrome (SLOS) A genetic syndrome characterized by poor growth, anteverted nostrils, eyelid ptosis (drooping), syndactyly (webbing) of the second and third toes, genital abnormalities in boys (e.g., hypospadias [lower placed urethral opening], cryptorchidism [undescended testes]), and moderate to severe intellectual disability. Inheritance is autosomal recessive. SLOS is caused by mutations in the gene encoding sterol delta-7-reductase (*DHCR7*; 602858), which maps to chromosome 11q12-q13.

Smith-Magenis syndrome (SMS) *deletion 17p, interstitial del(17)(p11.2p11.2).* A chromosomal syndrome marked by moderate intellectual disability and characteristic facies: mid-facial hypoplasia (undergrowth) and prognathism (prominent jaw). Also characteristic are short stature, sleep disturbances, orifice stuffing, and pulling out one's nails. The last behavior is almost pathognomonic (indicative) for this syndrome. Characteristic gestures include clasping the hands together in front of the face or putting the arms around the body ("body hugging") when excited. SMS, which is due to a deletion on the proximal short arm of chromosome 17, is clinically difficult to detect early on.

Smith-Riley syndrome *Bannayan-Riley-Ruvalcaba syndrome, Bannayan-Zonana syndrome, Ruvalcaba-Myre syndrome.* A condition whose major features are macrocephaly, polyposis of the intestine, pigmented spots on the penis, and subcutaneous and organ lipomas/hemangiomas. Individuals are characteristically large at birth, but growth slows postnatally to normal levels. Hypotonia, motor delay, frequent seizures, and sometimes intellectual disability can occur. Inheritance is autosomal dominant. This condition is part of the PTEN hamartoma syndromes.

SMR Severe mental retardation. *See* severe intellectual disability.

SMS *See* Smith-Magenis syndrome.

Snellen chart An eye chart with lines of letters of graded sizes to allow translation of successful letter discrimination and/or identification into standardized distance visual acuity designations based on administration at 20 feet. Normal vision is described as 20/20 (in feet) or 6/6 (in meters), meaning that the person can accurately discriminate at 20 feet (or 6 meters) what an individual without visual impairments can discriminate at 20 feet (or 6 meters). A diagnosed visual acuity of 20/200 indicates that what the person can discriminate at 20 feet can be discriminated by a person without visual impairments at 200 feet. This test can be used with children 5–6 years of age and older (as soon as they know the alphabet). Other measures of visual acuity need to be used with children who do not know or cannot consistently discriminate alphabet letters because of age or nonvisual impairments such as intellectual disability or learning disabilities.

SNHI *See* sensorineural hearing impairment.

Snijders-Oomen Nonverbal Intelligence Scale–Revised A Dutch instrument used to measure nonverbal intelligence in children

5;6–17 years of age and in children with hearing and/or speech-language impairments.

Snoezelen   The therapeutic use of controlled sensory stimulation (e.g., sound, smell, touch, or balance) in a special (Snoezelen) room.

snoring   Harsh sounds during breathing while asleep. Snoring may result from an obstruction and can reduce the quality of rest obtained.

snout reflex   An infant reflex in which the stimulus of percussing (tapping) the upper or lower lip produces blinking and lip protrusion. The snout reflex is innervated by the facial nerve (cranial nerve VII); excessive prominence suggests the presence of a degenerative process.

SNR   *See* speech-to-noise ratio.

SOAEs   Spontaneous otoacoustic emissions. *See* otoacoustic emissions.

SOB   *See* shortness of breath.

Social Communication, Emotional Regulation, and Transactional Support (SCERTS®)   A research-based educational approach and multidisciplinary framework that addresses the core problems faced by children and people with autism spectrum disorder (ASD) and related disabilities and their families. SCERTS focuses on building competence in social communication, emotional regulation, and transactional support as the highest priorities and is applicable for individuals of a wide range of abilities and ages across home, school, and community settings.

social competence   The skills of social interaction when communicating with an augmentative and alternative communication system, such as initiating, maintaining, developing, and terminating communication interactions.

social desirability   A frequent source of test bias in which the test taker or research participant responds to questions with answers perceived as socially desirable rather than with responses that truly reflect the individual's thoughts, feelings, and attitudes.

social history   A multidimensional, in-depth social work description and evaluation of a client's biological, psychological, and social history along with current functioning. The social history serves as the basis for service planning by many professionals, including social workers, physicians, lawyers, teachers, and judges.

social intelligence (SI)   The ability to understand and deal effectively with social and interpersonal events.

social learning theory   A theory of development and learning that emphasizes both the principles of behaviorism and the individual's internal attributions and thoughts in determining behavior. Social learning theory includes the concepts of modeling, imitation, and self-efficacy. The likelihood that an individual will imitate the behavior of another is dependent on four factors: 1) The observer is attending to the model, 2) the observer retains the information, 3) the observer can reproduce the modeled behavior, and 4) reinforcement is available for the behavior. Social learning is more likely to occur when the model is attractive, is powerful, or possesses other desirable qualities. Social learning continues to be relevant in debates about the effects of television and video violence on the behavior of children and teens. *See also* modeling.

Social Maturity Scale for Blind Preschool Children   An adaptation of the Vineland Social Maturity Scale for use with preschool children (birth to age 5) with visual impairment. Several categories of social development are assessed: personal-social growth, dressing, eating, communication, socialization, and occupation. The instrument is normed against children who are legally blind and partially sighted.

social promotion Passing a child to a higher grade despite the fact that he or she does not appear to have successfully mastered the prerequisite skills in the current grade. Social promotion is based on the reasoning that it would do more harm to socially separate the child from his or her peers, that his or her self-image would be damaged by the failure, that he or she is growing physically too large to repeat a grade, or some combination of these. Research has shown that social promotion does not succeed but merely delays more appropriate intervention based on a diagnostic assessment that uncovers the treatable reasons for failure.

social reinforcer A reinforcer that is interpersonal in nature (e.g., an interpersonal contact that follows a behavior and increases the future likelihood of the response).

Social Security A group of federally funded social insurance programs that provide a minimum income for people in their old age, for workers with disabilities, and for survivors in case of the death of a worker. The following programs are included in Social Security: Old Age Survivors Insurance (OASI), part of the original Social Security Act of 1935 (PL 74-271) for older adults; Survivors Social Security, added in 1939; Disability Insurance, amendments added in 1956 providing money for workers with disabilities and their families; and Medicare, added in 1965.

Social Security Act of 1935 (PL 74-271) Legislation enacted as part of the New Deal designed to provide security to U.S. workers. The statute created a federal program of old-age retirement benefits as well as a federal–state program for unemployment benefits. *See also* Medicare, Social Security.

social services The range of professional activities and social programs enacted to help people in need. People in need may include troubled families, families that have lost the ability to produce their own income, families with members who have disabilities, children whose families are no longer able to care for them, people with mental illnesses, and others. Social services include the helping relationships provided by social workers and other professionals and the linkage of those services with other direct services and entitlements such as Temporary Assistance for Needy Families (TANF) and Supplemental Security Income (SSI).

Social Skills Improvement System (SSIS) A norm-referenced, multi-rater system designed to enable targeted assessment of social skills, problem behaviors, and academic competence in individuals and small groups ages 3–18. Teacher, parent, and student forms require 10–25 minutes to administer across school, home, and community settings. Respondents rate the frequency and importance of particular skills and behaviors within each setting. The SSIS yields standard scores for social skills, problem behaviors, and academic competence and subscales with behavior levels (below average, average, above average).

Social Skills Rating Scale (SSRS) Norm-referenced questionnaires that obtain information on the social behaviors of children and adolescents from teachers and parents with self-report available for Grades 3–12.

social skills training Specific instruction in the skills necessary for successful interaction with peers and others. Effective social skills training programs involve an assessment of the specific skills that an individual lacks (or does not demonstrate) and teach, coach, and reinforce those skills in context. There are several social skills curricula available, and instruction can occur within a larger individualized program or as part of a targeted intervention for youth at risk for problem behavior.

social smile A milestone in early infant development; the infant's smile should be in response to a social interaction (e.g., being talked to) and not a spontaneous behavior (e.g., burping). The social smile characteristically emerges at 6 weeks of age but will not be noted until later in infants born prematurely. Sometimes referred to as a *communicative smile*.

Social Stories Short stories used to teach social and self-regulation skills. Tailored to the needs of an individual or group, social stories depict commonly encountered challenges, providing positive models and effective solutions. Stories are constructed with salient cues that are likely to be noticed by the individual, and the character engages in desired social behaviors that are the target of intervention.

social welfare A nation's system of laws, programs, benefits, and services in the areas of health; education; and economic, social, and basic human needs. In the United States, there are both federal (nationally mandated and supported) social welfare programs (e.g., Social Security) and state-determined programs (e.g., Medicaid). In state programs, those who are eligible, the range of entitlements, and the level of benefits may vary by state.

social work The professional activity of helping individuals, groups, or communities enhance or restore their capacity for social functioning and creating societal conditions favorable to this goal. Social workers provide clinical services (counseling and psychotherapy), information, and referral and, when necessary, facilitate access to services that individuals may be unable to obtain alone. *See also* master of social work.

socially assistive robotics (SAR) The therapeutic use of robotic playmates.

socioeconomic status (SES) A measure of one's relative standing in society according to a hierarchical grouping of people on a scale of prestige and privilege. Status is determined by such factors as type and amount of income, nature of occupation, location and type of residence, and level of education. SES has implications for educational and economic opportunities, range of experiences and activities, and expectations regarding future achievement.

sociogram A visual representation or map of social relationships among members of a group. Symbols representing each group member are connected by lines that indicate either real or preferred relationships. From this mapping, one can determine leadership, "in" versus "out" groups, cliques, and isolates.

sociopathy *antisocial personality (ASP) disorder.* A possible outcome of inadequately treated conduct disorder, attention-deficit/hyperactivity disorder (ADHD), and learning disabilities.

SOD *See* septo-optic dysplasia.

SODA Acronym for Stop, Observe, Deliberate, and Act—a treatment technique used to deal with stressful social situations.

soft neurological sign A neurological finding that cannot be interpreted as physiological or pathological without taking into account the individual's age. All "abnormal" soft neurological findings are normal at some (usually younger) age. Soft signs do not contribute to the localization of central nervous system (CNS) lesions but rather reflect a more generalized immaturity of the brain, such as occurs in learning disabilities and intellectual disability.

soft spot *See* fontanel.

somatic cells Those cells of the body that are not germ cells.

somatic education A term used in both the Hellerwork and Feldenkrais methods to describe the integration of bodywork and self-awareness, intelligence, and imagination.

somatization disorder Recurrent multiple psychosomatic complaints of several years' duration of sufficient severity for medical consultation to be sought but not due to any underlying physical disorder. Anxiety and depression are frequently seen; diagnosis of this disorder is more likely in females than males.

somatodyspraxia An impairment in learning new motor responses that results in motor clumsiness (dyspraxia). Somatodyspraxia is hypothesized in sensory integration theory to be caused by impaired tactile (touch) discrimination and proprioceptive processing.

somatoform disorder A group of psychiatric disorders characterized by extensive physical symptoms and complaints related to psychological problems rather than to physical illness or disease.

somatosensory Body sensation that does not come from the classic five senses (sight, hearing, taste, touch, and smell) but rather from the skin and internal organs (e.g., pressure).

somatotopy A homunculus (dwarf) projection; the mapping of a human figure on a section of the brain, reflecting either motor or sensory projections.

somatotopy

Son-Rise A program that treats children with autism via intensive stimulation based on an attitude of unconditional love and acceptance. Optiva Dialogue sessions help parent therapists explore the presence of limiting attitudes. The method is offered through The Option Institute and Fellowship.

SORT-R3 *See* Slosson Oral Reading Test–Revised Preschool–Adults.

Sotos syndrome *cerebral gigantism.* A syndrome in which the child has a large body size (birth weight more than 8½ pounds), large hands and feet, poor coordination, and variable intellectual disability. The rapid growth slows down by middle childhood. Because of their large size and motor clumsiness, children with Sotos syndrome often appear slower or to have more severe intellectual disability than is actually the case. They also tend to have macrocephaly (large head), dolichocephaly (prominent forehead), prognathism (protuberant jaw), and an advanced bone age. Sotos syndrome is caused by mutation in the *NSD1* gene. The majority of cases represent fresh mutations. Sotos syndrome is usually detected in early childhood. Treatment involves endocrine management and special education.

sound blending *phonemic synthesis.* The act of synthesizing the individual sound components (i.e., phonemes) of a word, leading to recognition of the word as a whole. This synthesis is an important aspect of word attack skills in reading. However, when sounds are presented in isolation, several forms of distortion are introduced into the speech signal, presenting a challenge to individuals with auditory processing problems.

sound–symbol association The knowledge that specific sounds go with specific visual symbols. This knowledge is important for learning to read, particularly when a phonics approach is used.

Souques finger phenomenon Automatic extension of the fingers when the shoulder is flexed; this phenomenon is common in hemiplegia (paralysis of one side of the body).

Southern blot Electrophoretic gel separation of deoxyribonucleic acid (DNA) fragments that are then absorbed by membrane filters for detection of specific base sequences by radio-labeled complementary probes.

Southern California Postrotary Nystagmus Test (SCPNT)　A test in which the person being tested is spun around 10 times in 20 seconds on a "nystagmus board" and the duration of the resulting nystagmus (involuntary eye movements) is measured with a stopwatch. This is repeated in the opposite direction. Prolonged nystagmus is interpreted as compatible with learning disabilities.

sp　Status post; indicates that the person had a previous condition (disease or operation) that may be relevant to the situation. There is no suggestion of recency, relevance, or sequelae.

Spache Diagnostic Reading Scales　*See* Diagnostic Reading Scales–Revised Edition (DSR).

spasmus nutans　Head rolling or nodding associated with nystagmus (involuntary eye movements) in preschool children who may otherwise be typically developing. Malnutrition, neglect, and intellectual disability may involve a slightly higher frequency of this benign, self-limited condition. Onset is usually before 1 year of age, and it disappears by 3 years. Unlike bobble-head doll syndrome, the bobbing is usually dysrhythmic, intermittent, and inconstant.

spastic cerebral palsy　The most common physiological subtype of cerebral palsy. *Spasticity* refers to an increase in muscle tone that is not the same throughout passive range of motion; rather, the extremity (arm or leg) exhibits a sudden "give" or loss of passive resistance—what is called "clasp-knife" hypertonicity. Strabismus (squint), contractures, and seizures are commonly associated impairments in spastic cerebral palsy. This type of cerebral palsy is further broken down according to a topographical classification into monoplegia (one extremity involvement), hemiplegia (paralysis of one side of the body), triplegia (paralysis of three limbs), diplegia (greater paralysis of

the lower half of the body), quadriplegia (paralysis of all four extremities), and paraplegia (paralysis of the lower half of the body).

spastic dysarthria　A motor speech disorder characterized by the combined effects of weakness, hypertonia, and spasticity in a manner that slows movement and reduces the range of motion.

spasticity　"Clasp-knife" hypertonicity; a velocity-dependent increase in resistance to passive movement that results in increased muscle tone with exaggerated deep-tendon reflexes, clonus, and positive Babinski reflexes. The adjective *spastic* describes tone or a type of cerebral palsy and should never be used to characterize a person.

spatial orientation　The perception of the position and configuration of objects in space from the observer's viewpoint; it is said to involve imagining movement of the entire stimulus without movement of its parts. Orientation enters into tasks that require a geographic sense of direction, such as map reading and piloting a plane through three-dimensional space. *See also* spatial visualization.

spatial relationships　Above/below, right/left, right side up/upside down, inside/outside, near/far, before/behind. *See also* spatial visualization.

spatial visualization　The ability to mentally manipulate a stimulus configuration and the movements of parts within the configuration. This ability enters into the abstract reasoning required in solving math problems. *See also* spatial orientation, spatial relationships.

special　Uncommon or unique. Describes what is different about any person. The term *special* should not be used to categorically describe or specifically characterize people with disabilities; the term can have the patronizing ring of a false compliment or can be interpreted as a euphemism for a more accurate description of a person's needs, limitations, or abilities. Terms such as *special, handicapped,* and *physically challenged* are considered condescending. However, the word *special* is acceptable in reference to the citation of laws and regulations regarding services, rights, and provisions for people with disabilities.

special education Education designed to meet the individual needs of children with disabilities. Children with disabilities are those evaluated as having intellectual disability, deafness, serious emotional disturbances, orthopedic impairments, hearing impairments, visual impairments, specific learning disabilities, speech impairments, deaf-blind multiple disabilities, or other health impairments and who, because of these impairments, need special education and related services. *See also* Education for All Handicapped Children Act of 1975 (PL 94-142).

special education service delivery model A continuum of services required of school districts in order to place students in a least restrictive environment (LRE). Potential placements are classified by the amount of direct intervention provided by someone other than the regular classroom teacher. These may include 1) general class (inclusion) with consultative assistance from special education personnel, 2) general class and consultation plus special materials from special education, 3) general class plus special education itinerant teaching services, 4) general class plus assistance from special education teachers in a resource room, 5) special class in a general school, 6) special class in a special (separate) day school, 7) home or hospital programs (usually temporary), and 8) residential schools.

Special Supplemental Nutrition Program for Women, Infants, and Children (WIC) A program authorized to safeguard the health of low-income, nutritionally at-risk pregnant women (through pregnancy and up to 6 weeks after birth or after pregnancy ends), breast-feeding women (up to the infant's first birthday), non–breast-feeding postpartum women (up to 6 months after the birth of the infant or after pregnancy ends), infants (up to the first birthday), and children (up to the fifth birthday). WIC serves 45% of all infants born in the United States. WIC provides the following benefits to eligible participants: supplemental nutritious foods; nutrition education and counseling at WIC clinics; and screening and referrals to other health, welfare, and social services.

specialist A professional who has taken further training in a specific area of professional competence. A physician (doctor of medicine [M.D.] or doctor of osteopathy [D.O.]) will take further training (usually at least 3 years after the internship) in a specific area of medical practice such as pediatrics, surgery, psychiatry, or neurology. In addition to their state-regulated license to practice medicine, most physician specialists are nationally certified in their specialty area by a national accrediting board. Other disciplines also provide specialty training in the form of postgraduate or postdoctoral fellowships.

specific developmental disorder A subclass of developmental disorders that is characterized by inadequate development of specific academic, language, speech, and motor skills not due to other diagnosed disorders or deficient educational opportunities.

specific language impairment (SLI) An isolated language disorder with no impairment in cognitive, sensorimotor, or emotional areas.

specific learning disability (SLD) *See* learning disability (LD).

specific learning disability in mathematics *See* mathematics disorder.

specificity The true negative rate; co-negativity. A statistic that describes a screening test's ability to successfully identify those tested who do not have the condition for which they are being tested. Specificity is the ratio of true negatives (negative test result, condition absent) to all negative test results (whether the condition is present or not). The closer this ratio is to 1.0, the better the screening test.

SPECT *See* single photon emission computed tomography.

spectrum concept The possibility that several differently classified disorders (e.g., attention-deficit/hyperactivity disorder [ADHD], alcoholism, and antisocial personality disorder) may be the result of the same general genetic pattern. These disorders are then considered to be genetically related.

spectrum of developmental disabilities An approach to classifying neurodevelopmental disorders that focuses on the major category of impairment: cognitive (e.g., intellectual disability), motor (e.g., cerebral palsy), or central processing (e.g., learning disability, language disorder). This concept is complementary to the continuum of developmental disabilities.

speech Oral communication using a system of vocal symbols.

Speech and Language Evaluation Scale (SLES) A teacher rating scale for screening speech and language abilities in the areas of articulation, voice, fluency, form, content, and pragmatics. The scale can be used by the classroom teacher for screening, referral, and follow-up assessment. Administration time is approximately 20 minutes.

speech defect *See* articulation disorder.

speech detection threshold (SDT) The sound level at which speech is heard 50% of the time. The sounds are recognized as speech even though the words may not be decipherable.

speech disorder *See* articulation disorder.

speech reception threshold (SRT) Intelligibility threshold; the faintest intensity (decibel level) at which an individual can identify and repeat 50% of the simple spoken words presented.

speech synthesizer A computerized device that produces audible language when information is inputted.

speech-language impairment (SLI) A communication disorder characterized by speech and/or language difficulties that affect learning and educational performance. SLI involves significant limitations in language functioning that cannot be attributed to impairments in hearing, oral structure and function, or general intelligence.

speech-language pathologist (SLP) An individual with a degree and/or certification in communication disorders who is qualified to make diagnoses, prescribe therapy, and use therapeutic measures for the remediation and amelioration of speech and language problems.

speech-language pathology The study of communication disorders for the purposes of diagnosis and treatment. Communication disorders include disorders of speech, language, and voice.

speech-language sample A sample representative of an individual's naturalistic communication behavior.

speechreading A form of aural rehabilitation (educational methods for people with hearing impairments) that uses visual cues to determine what is being said. People with hearing impairments "read" speech through interpreting the speaker's lips, facial movements, hand

and body expressions, and gestures. Formerly known as *lipreading.*

speech-to-noise ratio (SNR) The relative intensity of information-carrying components of the speech signal to the non–information-carrying signal or noise.

spend down The required reduction of all assets to a minimal level before meeting financial eligibility for federal and state entitlements.

SPH Severe to profound handicap. *See* severe and profound intellectual disability.

spherical grasp The position of the hand for holding a ball the size of a tennis ball in which the fingers and thumb are spread and flexed.

sphingolipidosis A group of hereditary disorders characterized by abnormal metabolism of chemicals called *sphingolipids* in the brain. Although each disorder presents with its own clinical picture, the disorders share the symptoms of progressive loss of vision and intellectual disability. With the exception of those with type E, all affected individuals have a shortened life span. Prenatal diagnosis is available for types A and B in high-risk populations. Type A is more commonly found in people of Ashkenazic Jewish descent. Treatment is supportive.

spica cast A cast that immobilizes an extremity (arm or leg) by incorporating part of the body near that extremity.

spike wave complex Spike and slow wave complex. An electroencephalographic finding in which a spike (a sharp, pointed deviation) is followed by a slow wave (a rounded curve deviation). At the rate of 3 per second, this pattern is associated with absence (petit mal) seizures. At the slower rate of 1–2.5 per second, this pattern

spike wave complex

is associated with severe and intractable epilepsy referred to as *Lennox-Gastaut syndrome.*

spina bifida A neural tube defect. A constellation of malformations of the central nervous system (CNS) that presents with a failure of fusion of the bones in the vertebral column (spine) and with an accompanying herniation (protuberance) of neural components, including meningocele (protuberance of the lining of the spinal cord) and myelomeningocele (protuberance of both the spinal cord and its lining). In addition, there is generally abnormal cellular migration in the brain leading to an Arnold-Chiari malformation and hydrocephalus (excess fluid under pressure in the brain). Syringomyelia (cavitation in the spinal cord) can also be found. Vertebral abnormalities (e.g., misshapen and partial vertebrae) can lead to scoliosis and kyphosis (curvature of the spine). Deformities of the lower extremities (most commonly clubfeet and rocker-bottom feet) may also be present. Other anomalies such as heart defects, kidney agenesis (unformed kidneys), and congenital intestinal obstructions (e.g., duodenal atresia, pyloric stenosis) are present in a greater than normal incidence. Clinically speaking, the peripheral (noncentral) neurological problems depend on the level of the lesion. Low sacral lesions cause bladder and sphincter paralysis but no motor impairment. Lesions in the lumbar region generally result in some degree of flaccid paraplegia with poor function of the anal and bladder sphincters. Higher lesions can result in hypertonic bladders with normal rectal sphincter tone. Treatment of myelomeningocele requires the expertise of pediatric surgical subspecialists, including orthopedic surgeons for lower extremity and back problems; neurosurgeons for initial closure, shunt placement, and monitoring; and urologists for management of incontinence, infection, and reflux of urine into the kidneys, which causes hydronephrosis (kidney enlargement due to obstructed flow). Care should also address managing bowel incontinence, as this contributes to a social disability. About 40% of children with myelomeningocele will have some degree of intellectual disability; however, many children have typical overall cognitive abilities with accompanying learning disabilities. Inheritance is multifactorial.

spina bifida occulta   A failure of fusion of the posterior (back) part of the vertebra without any protuberance of nerve tissue or meninges (brain covering). Although the skin over the spine is generally intact, there may be associated dermal sinuses (deep dimples), nevi (moles), or a hirsute (hairy) patch. A relatively common occurrence (affecting 10% of the general pediatric population), spina bifida occulta may be associated with abnormalities in the formation of the spinal cord, especially in the presence of neurological impairments. Lesions may be present at more than one level of the spinal cord. Surgical repair is indicated in the presence of infection or loss of neurological function.

spinal accessory nerve   The 11th cranial nerve; involvement causes the shoulder to sag and the tongue to deviate to the affected side.

spinal laminectomy   A surgical procedure that involves opening the spinal column to treat nerve compression in the spinal cord.

spinal muscular atrophy (SMA)   A group of neurological conditions of autosomal recessive inheritance that affect the anterior horn cells (motor nerves) but not the sensory nerves. In the infantile form, survival past age 3 years is rare. Children with the intermediate form may survive into adulthood but have weakness in the trunk and extremities; they are often nonambulatory and have orthopedic and cardiopulmonary complications.

spinal muscular atrophy type 1 (SMA1)   *See* Werdnig-Hoffmann syndrome.

spinal tap   A procedure in which a needle with a bore is inserted between the vertebrae of the spinal column into the cerebrospinal fluid (CSF) that surrounds the spinal cord of the lower back. The CSF can be removed and tested for evidence of meningitis (infection) or hemorrhage (a brain bleed); the pressure of the fluid in the CSF system can also be measured. This procedure is performed with the individual in either a lateral reclined position (lying on one side) or a sitting position.

SPLATT   *See* split anterior tibial tendon transfer.

splint   A flexible or rigid appliance for immobilizing broken bones or dislocated joints, for positioning to improve function, for protecting lax or unstable joints, or for reducing the potential for contractures. *See also* braces.

splinter skill   An isolated area of average to far above average skill performance in people with disabilities whose other functional levels remain significantly delayed. Many savant behaviors represent splinter skills.

split anterior tibial tendon transfer (SPLATT)   An orthopedic surgery procedure to treat varus (inward) foot deformity in children with spastic cerebral palsy.

split-half reliability   A measure of the internal consistency of a test.

splitting   The tendency to classify as separate entities items that at first appear to go together. *See also* heterogeneity.

SPMR   Severe and profound mental retardation. *See* severe and profound intellectual disability.

spontaneous miscarriage   *See* fetal wastage.

spontaneous otoacoustic emissions (SOAEs)   *See* otoacoustic emissions (OAEs).

spooning   A hand posture of curved hyperextension. Spooning can be present in a variety of neuromuscular disorders but is most often a sign of minor neurological dysfunction. It is one component of athetoid posturing of the hand in cerebral palsy, and it tends to be exaggerated under stress.

spooning

Sprengel deformity Asymmetry of the scapula, with one shoulder blade being higher than the other, accompanied by some limitation in abducting (turning outward) and elevating the shoulder with the higher scapula.

Sprengel deformity

squeeze machine *squeeze box.* An individually controlled, fully padded, V-shaped device designed to apply pressure over most of the body to reduce nervousness, hyperactivity, anxiety, and tactile defensiveness in people with autism.

squint *See* strabismus.

SRT *See* speech reception threshold.

SS *See* sickle cell anemia.

SSB *See* suck–swallow–breathe sequence.

SSI *See* Supplemental Security Income.

SSIS *See* Social Skills Improvement System.

SSPE *See* subacute sclerosing panencephalitis.

SSQ *See* Barkley's School Situations Questionnaire.

SSQ-R *See* Barkley's School Situations Questionnaire–Revised.

SSRI *See* selective serotonin reuptake inhibitor.

SSRS *See* Social Skills Rating Scale.

stability Maintenance of equilibrium with resistance to a sudden change of position,

achieved through co-contraction of muscle groups so that a joint remains fixed while allowing other muscles to move.

stadiometer One of a number of instruments used to accurately measure height. A stadiometer is usually composed of a measuring strip fixed to a wall and a vertically sliding horizontal headboard.

staffing An interdisciplinary team meeting in which members of a team use their respective expertise to assist in diagnosing and treating a disease or disability. Team members representing several disciplines make recommendations with regard to educational programming, psychological or family intervention, medication, and various ancillary (assistive) therapies. The staffing may include the professionals who performed specific components of the evaluation, teachers, parents or guardians, and other involved professionals. The collaborative effort helps promote a comprehensive and multifaceted view of the individual being evaluated and recognizes the need to consider the condition from several different but related perspectives.

stage A hierarchical level of development, with each level characterized by structural and qualitative changes. There is an implicit but unproven assumption that such stages are invariant and universal. The concept remains heuristic. See the table on page 439.

staggering Reflex foot movements used to maintain upright posture when the body is externally displaced.

stammering *stuttering.* The term *stammering* is used more in Great Britain than in the United States.

stance phase That part of the gait cycle when the index foot is in contact with the ground (from heel strike to toe-off); double stance is that part of the gait cycle in which both feet

Stage theories of development

Age (years)	Sexual (Freud)	Social (Erikson)	Cognitive (Piaget)	Moral (Kohlberg)
0–1	Oral-sensory	Basic trust/ mistrust	Sensorimotor primary circular reaction (1–4.5 months) secondary circular reaction (4.5–9 months)	
1–2	Anal-muscular		Sensorimotor tertiary circular reaction (12–18 months)	
2–3		Autonomy/ shame/doubt	Preoperational preconceptual (2–4 years)	
3–4	Genital-locomotor	Initiative/guilt		
4–7			Preoperational intuitive (4–7 years)	Preconventional punishment reward
7–12	Latency	Industry/ inferiority	Concrete operations (7–11 years)	Conventional social approval respect for authority ("law and order")
12+	Adolescence/ puberty	Identity/ role confusion	Formal operations (11 years+)	Autonomous social contract personal ethics

are in contact with the ground. Stance phase represents 60% of the gait cycle.

standard deviation (SD) A statistic that equals the square root of the variance. SD is a commonly used measure of the extent to which individual scores differ from the mean. A small SD indicates that the group under study is homogeneous with respect to the characteristic in question; a large SD indicates the opposite. Approximately 68% of children fall within 1 SD of the mean. The different Wechsler intelligence scales have a SD of 15 around a mean of 100 for intelligence quotient (IQ) scores and a SD of 3 around a mean of 10 for subtest scores. Thus, approximately 68% of the children achieve IQ scores between 85 and 115 and subtest scores between 7 and 13.

standard error of measurement See error of measurement.

standard score A score that is adjusted to indicate how many standard deviations a score is above or below a given mean.

Commonly used types of standard scores include z-scores, T-scores, deviation intelligence quotient (IQ) scores, and stanines. Standard scores allow for the comparison of performance on one test with a performance on another.

standardization A research process that includes careful selection of test items, administration of the items to a representative sample drawn from a specific population, statistical analysis of results, establishment of age-based norms, and development of instructions and response scoring procedures.

standardization sample Norm group. The group of people whose performance on a specific test becomes the basis of comparison for future individual performances on the same test. The standardization of well-normed tests is based on the performance of a large, representative group of people. Norms are scores (percentile ranks, stanines, standard scores, means, standard deviations) obtained by comparing people's performance with that of the standardization sample. The norm group should be relevant to the examinee.

standardized test　A test with a consistent and uniform procedure for administering, scoring, and interpreting results such that each examinee is assessed in the same manner as was done with the standardization sample or norm group. Deviations from procedure may change the meaning of the resulting test score.

standing height　One's height in the standing position, which is typically 1–2 cm shorter than height (length) in the recumbent, or lying down, position.

Stanford Diagnostic Reading Test–Fourth Edition (SDRT-4)　A group-administered diagnostic reading test for children in kindergarten through Grade 12.

Stanford-Binet Intelligence Scale–Fifth Edition (SB5)　A test of general intelligence for use with people ages 2;0–85+ years that yields verbal, nonverbal, and full-scale intelligence quotients with a mean of 100 and a standard deviation of 15. Its five factors (fluid reasoning, knowledge, quantitative reasoning, visual spatial processing, and working memory) can all be assessed verbally and nonverbally. Subtests have a mean of 10 and a standard deviation of 3.

stanine　A single-digit scoring system with a mean of 5 and a standard deviation of 2. All stanines except 1 and 9 are one half of a standard deviation in width. Stanines differ from standard scores, such as z-scores, T-scores, and deviation intelligence quotient (IQ) scores, in that stanine scores are normalized or forced to fit the normal curve as closely as possible.

staring spells　*See* absence seizure.

startle response　In the newborn, the startle response is very similar to the Moro reflex, with extension of the extremities (arms or legs) followed by flexion; as the Moro fades between 2 and 6 months of age, the initial component of the startle is a protective flexion of the upper extremities. The startle can be part of the alerting response to sound in the first weeks of life.

startle syndrome　*See* hyperexplexia.

STAT　*See* Screening Tool for Autism.

state　A key variable in Prechtl's neurological examination of infants. The depth of sleep, degree of alertness, and presence of crying are scored; the infant's state influences neurological findings and behavioral repertoire.

State Interagency Coordinating Council　Authorized in 1986 through Part C (Program for Infants and Toddlers with Disabilities) of the Individuals with Disabilities Education Act (IDEA, PL 101-456). Each state is required to establish a state interagency coordinating council to advise and assist the state designated lead agency in the development and implementation of the Part C statewide system. The responsibilities of the SICC include 1) Identify program supports and services, 2) promote interagency agreements, 3) transition toddlers with disabilities to preschool, 4) report annually to the Governor and Secretary of Education on the status of early intervention programs for infants and toddlers with disabilities and their families, and 5) advise other appropriate agencies in the state about the integration of services for infants and toddlers and their families.

state management　In infant feeding–swallowing therapy, how an infant responds to sights, sounds, and movements in his environment as well as handling. Infants' appetite and feeding performance can be affected by state.

static augmentative and alternative communication (AAC) display　*See* fixed augmentative and alternative communication (AAC) display.

station   The position or posture assumed in standing (or sitting).

stature   Height.

status epilepticus   A continuous seizure or multiple seizures occurring over a short period of time. Practically speaking, status epilepticus is a seizure that lasts 30 minutes or longer. The term *status epilepticus* does not refer to the type of seizure but only to its continuous and prolonged nature. Thus, one may have tonic-clonic status epilepticus, absence status epilepticus, complex partial (psychomotor) status epilepticus, and so forth. Status epilepticus is a medical emergency that requires treatment to stop the seizure and prevent brain damage that can occur secondary to such a prolonged seizure. Initial management includes the basic principles of cardiopulmonary resuscitation (CPR): maintaining the airway, breathing, and cardiac function. The remainder of the evaluation and treatment is aimed at determining the cause of the seizure activity and using an appropriate (anticonvulsant) medication to stop it. The outcome of status epilepticus depends on the cause and duration of the seizures. Prolonged status epilepticus can lead to brain damage manifested by a decrease in cognitive functioning, motor impairment, movement disorders, or cerebellar dysfunction. Rapid diagnosis and treatment have been shown to decrease the morbidity and mortality of status epilepticus.

status marmoratus   Hypoxic-ischemic encephalopathy (brain damage due to lack of oxygen) that involves the basal ganglia and produces extrapyramidal cerebral palsy. The name derives from the marbled (i.e., marmoratus) appearance of the basal ganglia at autopsy.

steadiness tester   A mechanical device used to measure attention-deficit/hyperactivity

disorders, motor impersistence, hyperactivity, resting tremors, and choreiform (twitching) movements by having the child hold a stylus (pointer) in a hole (sometimes of varying sizes) without touching the sides. "Touch time" relates to age and neurological maturation.

Steinert syndrome   *See* myotonic dystrophy.

stellate iris   An iris pattern with prominent iris stroma radiating out in a star-like fashion from the pupil.

stenosis   Narrowing or constriction of a body passage or opening.

STEP   *See* School Transition to Employment Partnership.

step length   The distance covered in one step.

stepping   A primitive reflex in which a newborn infant held in supported standing appears to "walk." Such newborn walking is readily elicited in the first 6 weeks of life but then rapidly fades. Head extension facilitates the reflex, and practice may prolong it.

stereognosis   Form perception; the ability to identify objects by touch. A component of the neurological assessment, problems with stereognosis are secondary to parietal lobe dysfunction.

stereopsis   Binocular depth perception or three-dimensional vision.

stereotactic neurosurgery   A group of procedures in which brain nuclei (control centers) are destroyed in order to improve movement. Thalamotomy to treat Parkinson's disease in adults provided the paradigm; success in applying this type of procedure to cases of severe cerebral palsy has been limited to those of extrapyramidal type.

stereotypy   Constantly repeated meaningless gestures or movements, such as hand flapping. Stereotypy is common in autism and with severe intellectual disability.

sternum The breastbone.

Stickler syndrome Hereditary progressive arthro-ophthalmopathy. A genetic syndrome characterized by flat facies, progressive myopia (nearsightedness), and arthritis. Infants may present with the Pierre Robin sequence, and a marfanoid habitus (tall, thin appearance) may be noted later; up to half of Pierre Robin anomalies (small jaw, large tongue) may represent cases of Stickler syndrome. Total retinal (inner back wall of the eye) detachment has been noted in more than half of reported cases. Inheritance is autosomal dominant, with a recurrence risk of 50%. Ophthalmological care for the prevention and treatment of eye problems is indicated.

stiff baby syndrome *See* hyperexplexia.

stigmata Signs of a diagnosis or condition, usually physical.

stim Self-stimulatory behavior.

stimulability An individual's responsiveness to trial treatment strategies.

stimulant Psychostimulant medication. A class of drugs used to treat attention-deficit/hyperactivity disorder in children and adults. These drugs include dextroamphetamine (DA; trade name, Dexedrine), and methylphenidate (MPH; trade name, Ritalin). They are less effective in preschool children and people with intellectual disability and autism. The side effects of all of these drugs are similar, with anorexia (loss of appetite) being the primary one.

stimulus Any object, action, or factor that causes an organism to act or that elicits a response; the input to a stimulus–response arc.

stoma A mouth-like opening, especially a drainage opening created as the result of a surgical procedure (e.g., colostomy, ureterostomy).

stop A manner of articulation in which a consonant sound (e.g., /p/, /b/, /d/) is produced by stopping the airflow in the oral cavity and suddenly releasing it.

stopping The phonological process that occurs when a stop is substituted for a non-stop phoneme.

storage disease A subgroup of inborn errors of metabolism that tend to present late in infancy. These disorders are usually genetic in etiology (cause) and are characterized by the inability to break down certain compounds in the body, which then build up in cells and cause damage and poor function of the involved organ system(s). The central nervous system (CNS) is often involved, with a presentation of the loss of developmental milestones or developmental regression. Other organs that can be involved include the liver and the reticuloendothelial system (the organs that make and clear the blood cells). Mucopolysaccharidoses are examples of storage diseases.

STORCH An acronym for the more common congenital or perinatal (near birth) infections that share many clinical similarities and can often be differentiated only by laboratory diagnosis: syphilis, toxoplasmosis, other infections, rubella, cytomegalovirus, and herpes simplex virus. Their common symptomatology includes intrauterine growth retardation (stunting), jaundice (yellowing of the skin) or hepatitis (inflammation of the liver), hepatosplenomegaly (enlargement of the liver and spleen), cataracts (lens) or retinal (eye) involvement, microcephaly (small head), encephalitis (brain infection), and hearing defects. Hepatosplenomegaly and a skin rash are prominent in congenital syphilis; retinopathy and brain calcifications are common with toxoplasmosis;

cataracts and heart disease with rubella; microcephaly, hearing loss, hepatitis, and a bleeding tendency with cytomegalovirus; skin rash, retinopathy, and encephalitis with herpes. All of these infections can contribute to the occurrence of intellectual disability.

stork bite *See* salmon patch.

story grammar Those elements found to be typical (stated or unstated) of stories (e.g., theme, episodes, setting, climax, resolution).

story scripts Actual stories that can be used to teach social skills.

strabismus Crossed eye; wall eye. A condition in which each eye looks at a different object, rather than the norm in which both eyes look at the same object. The causes of strabismus are muscle weakness, central nervous system (CNS) disease (i.e., brain attack [stroke], hemiplegia [paralysis of half the body]), or amblyopi (poorer vision in one eye). The eye deviation may be outward (i.e., exotropia), inward (i.e., esotropia), upward (i.e., hypertropia), or downward (i.e., hypotropia). Strabismus is treated by an ophthalmologist (a medical doctor trained in eye diseases) using glasses, patching, or occasionally surgery. Some forms of strabismus are inherited in an autosomal dominant manner. Strabismus is common in spastic cerebral palsy and myelomeningocele (protuberance of both the spinal cord and its lining).

strabismus

stranger anxiety Childhood anxiety in the presence of unfamiliar people, also known as *8-month anxiety* or *organic bashfulness*. Severity may be muted in households with multiple caregivers. Age-inappropriate lack of wariness of strangers may reflect either cognitive limitations or emotional pathology.

Stransky reflex The stimulus of suddenly releasing the abducted (turned outward) fifth (little) toe to produce the response of dorsiflexion (upgoing movement) of the first (big) toe. A sign of pyramidal tract (motor nerve) dysfunction.

strategic competence The compensatory strategies that people who rely on augmentative and alternative communication (AAC) use to deal with functional limitations associated with AAC use.

strategy training An approach to instruction in which students are taught *how* to learn, not just *what* to learn.

Strattera *See* atomoxetine.

Strauss syndrome *"brain-damaged child syndrome."* The neurobehavioral constellation of distractibility, perseveration, conceptual rigidity, emotional lability (changeability), and difficulty with figure–ground perception that was first reported in children with both intellectual disability and cerebral palsy and was then extended to children without obvious evidence of brain pathology. These symptoms became known as *minimal brain damage/dysfunction* (now an outdated term) and later were subsumed under the terms *attention-deficit/hyperactivity disorder* (ADHD) and *specific learning disability* (SLD).

straw drinking A developmental feeding milestone with a wide range for age of first achievement (12–36 months).

strength Power, force; one measure of the intactness of the neuromotor system.

strephosymbolia Twisted symbols, letter reversals. A sign of reading disorders that was stressed as fundamental by Samuel Orton (1879–1948).

stress fracture A fine hairline fracture difficult to diagnose by x ray. Stress fractures are often seen in young athletes because of repetitive movement trauma (e.g., due to dance, gymnastics, repeated throwing).

stretch reflex The reflex contraction of a muscle when passively stretched; the resistance of the muscle to being longitudinally stretched.

stride length The distance covered in two steps, or one complete gait cycle.

stridency deletion A strident sound is a harsh, somewhat shrill sound produced with intense noise. English includes eight strident sounds, including /s/, /z/, and /f/. Stridency deletion is the phonological process that occurs a strident sound is omitted (usually at the beginning or the end of a word) or a nonstrident sound is substituted for a strident sound (such as /th/ for /f/).

stridor A harsh, high-pitched, shrill sound during inspiration associated with upper airway obstruction. Congenital laryngeal stridor is often associated with weakness in the walls of the windpipe. Such stridor may reflect an isolated airway abnormality that will resolve over time or a congenital defect that is part of a wider syndrome.

stroke *brain attack, cerebrovascular accident (CVA)*. Damage to the brain caused by either a tear in a blood vessel with bleeding (i.e., hemorrhage) in the brain or a blockage in the vessel, both of which would reduce blood flow and oxygen to brain tissue. Strokes can occur at or before birth and at any time during childhood and are sometimes associated with medical conditions such as sickle cell anemia, leukemia, or problems with the heart valves. Strokes can also occur as a result of malformations of the vessels in the brain, such as a berry aneurysm (a small berry-shaped swelling in a cerebral blood vessel). The damage from a stroke is often confined to one side of the brain and thus the person presents with one-sided neurological findings. Resolution of the stroke with healing

usually results in some improvement but not always complete recovery. Motor function is affected on the opposite side of the body from the stroke, whereas cognitive function is affected on the same side. Also called *cerebrovascular accident* (CVA).

Stroop test A neuropsychological measure of ease in shifting perceptual set and suppressing habitual responses in order to conform to changing demands. For example, in one version of the test, the person must name the color ink in which nonmatching color names are printed; any resulting decrease in color-naming speed is referred to as the "color-word interference effect" and can be interpreted as suggesting left frontal lobe damage.

structural analysis A word attack skill that involves the recognition of prefixes and suffixes that may be added to a root word in order to form compound words or to change the meaning of a word in a predictable fashion. Examples are prefixes (*un*happy, *pre*mature), suffixes (runn*ing*, hopp*ed*), and compound words (*raincoat, football*).

structural integration *See* rolfing.

structural theory The psychoanalytic division of mental function into the id, the ego, and the superego.

Student School Records Act *See* Family Educational Rights and Privacy Act (FERPA) of 1974 (PL 93-380).

stupor A state of decreased consciousness from which the individual can only be roused by painful stimuli.

Sturge-Weber syndrome *encephalofacial angiomatosis*. A disorder characterized by unilateral (one-sided) vascular malformations (birthmarks) on the face and eyes and ipsilateral (on the same side) involvement of the meninges (covering of the brain). The vascular (blood vessel) abnormalities are nonraised hemangiomas (similar to a port-wine stain) that can be seen on the face, generally in the distribution of the fifth cranial nerve. The hemangiomas of the meninges are involved, with cerebral calcifications ("railroad track" lines on a skull x ray). Seizures are present in half of all cases, and a third will exhibit hemiplegia (paralysis of one side of the body). Many but not all affected children have intellectual disability. Seizure control is often difficult. Etiology (cause) is unknown, but the clinical picture is consistent with a defect in the cephalic (head) neural crest that migrates to the meninges, the choroid of the eye, and the skin above the eye. Diagnosis can be made in the neonatal period. Treatment involves seizure management and special education.

stuttering A disorder in the rhythm of speech that includes sound, syllable, and word repetitions, prolongations, pauses, and hesitations often accompanied by anxious, tense, and avoidant behaviors. Stuttering is more common in males, with a familial susceptibility but no clearly defined genetic transmission pattern. Stuttering is not indicative of developmental disorders. *See also* fluency disorder.

STYCAR *See* Screening Tests for Young Children and Retardates.

subacute sclerosing panencephalitis (SSPE) A degenerative disease of the central nervous system (CNS) associated with a persistent measles virus infection of the brain. The insidious course of this slow virus infection includes cognitive deterioration, myoclonic seizures, visual impairment, and a variety of movement disorders progressing to opisthotonus (an arching of the back) and decorticate rigidity. The electroencephalogram (EEG) shows suppression bursts.

subarachnoid hemorrhage Bleeding into the subarachnoid space in the head. Usually seen in hypoxic (lowered oxygen to the brain) premature infants, subarachnoid hemorrhage has a good prognosis for recovery,

although hydrocephalus (excess fluid under pressure in the brain) may occur.

subcutaneous Under the skin.

subdural hematoma A collection of blood between the brain and the skull, between the dural and pial layers covering the brain. It is most often the result of injury or abuse.

subluxation Incomplete or partial dislocation of a bone at its joint. *See also* dislocation.

submucous cleft A palpable defect in the hard palate that is not immediately visible because it is covered with normal oral mucosa; it can be suspected in the presence of a bifid (cleft) uvula and a white line running down the middle of the roof of the mouth. Submucous clefts can contribute to severe articulation disorders.

subspecialist A physician (doctor of medicine [M.D.] or doctor of osteopathy [D.O.]) who has completed a fellowship training program (at least 2 years beyond the requirements for specialty certification) in a restricted area of a specialty. A Certificate of Special Qualifications certifies most subspecialty practitioners nationwide.

substance abuse The use of a substance (either legal or illegal) that deviates from accepted social, medical, or legal patterns.

substance dependence Psychological and/or physiological dependence on a drug, either legal or illegal.

subtest scatter The degree of variability of an individual's scores on subtests of a test. The highs and lows compose a profile that indicates strengths and weaknesses in particular areas as defined in specific subtests. The term *scatter* is most commonly used with intellectual assessment, though it may be applied to any multiple subtest battery of basic skills, adaptive behavior, or academic achievement. The precise role that this scatter has in diagnosing and differentiating among populations and conditions has not been definitively determined. Scatter occurs frequently in the general population, so care must be taken when determining if it is rare or different from that in the general population before associating it with significant deviance or abnormality. However, characteristic scatter has been reported consistently for specific groups. Analysis of subtest scatter, although not recommended by itself as a diagnostic standard, is helpful in the diagnostic process and in intervention planning.

subthalamic syndrome A syndrome of chorea and/or ballismus on one side of the body secondary to a lesion in the contralateral (opposite) subthalamic nucleus (corpus Luysii). Characteristics include hemichorea and hemiballismus.

sucking Propulsion of food into the mouth by creating negative pressure in the oral cavity by a complex interaction of the lips, tongue, and cheeks. This phase of oral feeding follows suckling between 6 and 9 months of age and is characterized by vertical (up and down) tongue movements and jaw opening and closing.

suckling An early infantile version of sucking. Suckling is an oral-motor reflex that represents the earliest intake phase for liquids with a definite backward–forward, horizontal (in–out) tongue movement in a rhythmic licking action. Suckling begins in the second to third trimester of gestation and may persist to 12 months of age. It is innervated by cranial nerves V, VII, IX, and XII.

suck–swallow–breathe (SSB) sequence A normal motor pattern exhibited by infants when breast- or bottle feeding. The first phase is voluntary and includes the tongue pushing the bolus to the oropharynx; the second stage is involuntary and requires contraction of the walls of the pharynx, cessation of breathing, elevation of the pharynx, closure of the vocal

folds, and inversion of the epiglottis; the third phase is also reflexive and requires that the upper-esophageal sphincter open so that the bolus can enter the esophagus.

suffix A type of bound morpheme that can be added at the end of a word to change the meaning of the word and the grammatical class to which it belongs.

"sugar baby" See kwashiorkor.

sulcus A groove or furrow, especially one separating the gyri (hills) on the surface of the brain. See also gyrus.

sulcus vocalis A ridge or furrow that runs the entire length of the medial surface of the vocal fold.

sunset sign See setting sun sign.

supernumerary An excess number (e.g., a sixth finger on a hand, a third nipple on the chest).

supersensitivity A hypothetical mechanism of recovery after brain damage in which surviving neurons in the damaged system become increasingly sensitive to neurotransmitter molecules, thus allowing them to function in a deprived state.

super-supraglottic swallow maneuver A swallow technique that aims to tilt the arytenoids (the cartilages to which the vocal cords are attached) forward for stronger closure of the airway by having the person hold his or her breath, bear down, swallow, then release into a cough.

supination The act of assuming the supine position (laying on one's back); applied to the hand, the act of turning the palm upward.

supine An anatomical position in which the individual is lying face upward on the back (the opposite of prone).

Supplemental Security Income (SSI) A federally funded income maintenance program administered through the Social Security Administration that provides people with developmental disabilities as well as those who are blind or have hearing impairments a minimum monthly income. In practice, SSI may be partially supplemented or supplanted by other entitlement programs. Eligibility to receive SSI requires evidence of both disability and low income.

supplemented intelligibility The extent to which a listener can understand an individual's speech when he or she is provided with contextual information (i.e., the topic, first letters of words, and gestures).

support group A self-help group; a voluntary small group formed for mutual help and to accomplish a specific purpose. Although support groups may employ professional facilitators, they are typically composed of peers who have joined together to help and support one another in satisfying a common need, coping with a common problem, or targeting and seeking a desired social change. Such groups use face-to-face interactions and assume personal responsibility by group members. Many parents of children with developmental disabilities find support group input a vital form of education and emotional support for meeting the demands of their children and families.

supported employment On-the-job coaching that supports the worker with intellectual disability (or other developmental disabilities) in a competitive employment situation. The term *supported employment* embraces the processes of job placement, job coaching, and continuous support in and on the job.

supported living A coordinated system of supports clustering around the individual with disabilities and designed to facilitate that person's choices to live, work, learn, and actively participate with people without disabilities in the community. Supported living is based on the philosophy that people with developmental disabilities have a right to make responsible decisions consistent with the choices afforded people without disabilities. The system includes life skills and vocational training, protective oversight, environmental adaptations, and physical assistance. The aim is to include the individual with developmental disabilities in typical society by bringing services to him or her rather than placing the individual in a segregated facility that provides such services. *See also* independent living.

supports Transportation, financial help, support groups, homemaker services, respite services, and other specific services offered to children and families to enable those with disabilities to live as typical a life as possible.

Supports Intensity Scale (SIS) An instrument designed to directly measure the relative intensity of the support needs of an individual with intellectual disabilities. It uses a structured interview to identify the frequency, intensity, and types of supports needed for people with intellectual disability. This information can then be used for planning for services. The SIS assesses 57 life activities related to support needs and protection and advocacy and 27 medical and behavioral areas. Web-based, CD-ROM, and hardcopy versions are available.

suppression burst activity An electroencephalographic pattern with a depressed or flat background accompanied by high-voltage bursts of slow waves with intermingled spikes. This pattern is frequent in comatose people.

suprabulbar paresis *See* pseudobulbar palsy.

supraglottic swallow maneuver A swallow technique that aims to close the vocal folds before and during swallow to rectify reduced or late vocal fold closure when swallowing. The person is asked to hold his or her breath, swallow, then release into a cough.

surfactant A phospholipid (chemical) that contributes to the elasticity of pulmonary tissue (the lungs). Preterm infants have less surfactant, so it is harder for their lungs to breathe. Artificial surfactant replacement therapy is used in the treatment of infant respiratory distress syndrome (RDS).

surfactant deficiency *See* hyaline membrane disease (HMD).

surrender posture *See* tonic labyrinthine response (TLR).

Sutter-Eyberg Student Behavior Inventory–Revised *See* Eyberg Child Behavior Inventory (ECBI) & Sutter-Eyberg Student Behavior Inventory–Revised.

swaddling The practice of wrapping an infant snugly in a blanket. Swaddling can be useful for calming an infant.

swallow therapy techniques Maneuvers that change swallow physiology by improving range of motion, sensory input, and voluntary coordination and timing; they require participation from the individual. *See also* swallowing therapy.

swallowing The neuromuscular process in which liquids and solids move from the mouth into the stomach via the esophagus (throat). Swallowing is both voluntary and involuntary. In newborn infants swallowing automatically follows sucking; later it is dissociated from sucking. This oral-motor reflex is innervated by cranial nerves V, VII, IX, X, and XII.

swallowing therapy Treatment that seeks to 1) improve the oral preparatory and oral stages of swallowing, 2) reduce delay in triggering the pharyngeal swallow, 3) improve pharyngeal transit time, and 4) improve weak and/or mistimed swallows (i.e., swallow initiation).

swan neck deformity An abnormal position of the finger in which the middle (proximal interphalangeal) joint is hyperextended and the fingertip (distal interphalangeal) joint is flexed.

"sway back" *See* lordosis.

"swimmer's ear" *See* otitis externa.

swing phase The part of the gait cycle in which the index foot is not in contact with the ground, from toe-off to heel strike; swing phase represents 40% of the gait cycle.

switch An input mode that interfaces with many devices. It allows a person with a disability to activate and receive feedback from assistive devices.

SWPBS Schoolwide positive behavior support. *See* positive behavioral interventions and supports (PBIS).

Sydenham chorea *chorea minor.* One of five major manifestations of rheumatic fever (arthritis, carditis, subcutaneous [under the skin] nodules, and rash being the other four) after streptococcal infection. The grimacing, wriggling, and writhing can briefly be brought under voluntary control but are exaggerated by excitement. Like most extrapyramidal symptoms, the chorea disappears during sleep. This disorder is transient; is more frequent in girls; and can include emotional lability (changeability), handwriting deterioration, "making faces," "society smile," variable hand grip, and sustained knee-jerks. Thomas Sydenham (1624–1689), the "English Hippocrates," first described this condition in 1686.

Sydney line A palmar crease pattern in which the proximal crease runs completely across the palm. This variant was first identified in rubella embryopathy in Sydney, Australia. It is a minor dysmorphic (atypical) feature Sydney line that may be found as part of other neurodevelopmental disorders.

syllable A part of a word containing a vowel.

syllable reduction A phonological process in which there is deletion of a syllable.

sylvian epilepsy *See* benign childhood epilepsy with centrotemporal spikes (BECTS).

symbol Something that stands for or represents something else. *See* augmentative and alternative communication (AAC) symbol.

Symbol Search A Wechsler (intelligence test) subtest that measures short-term visual memory, visual-motor coordination, cognitive flexibility, visual discrimination, and concentration.

symbolic play Play in which one thing is used to stand in for another, such as a stick for a sword. Such play is intentionally representational.

symmetric tonic neck reflex *"cat posture," "cat reflex."* A primitive reflex in which neck extension produces upper extremity extension and lower extremity flexion ("cat looking up"), and neck flexion produces upper extremity flexion and lower extremity extension ("cat eating"). This reflex pattern is both transient (appearing at 4–6 months of age and integrated by 8–12 months of age) and faint in typically developing infants; exaggeration or persistence of this pattern strongly suggests serious neuromotor impairment such as cerebral palsy.

symmetric tonic neck reflex

sympathetic nervous system *adrenergic system.* That division of the autonomic nervous system that responds to threats or danger by a "fight-or-flight" reaction; this reaction is mediated by a burst or rush of adrenaline. Also known as the *thoracolumbar* or *catabolic system.*

symphysis pubis The most anterior (front) bone of the pelvis just above the genital area.

symptom A subjective concern of a person; the individual's (or parent's) report of pain, discomfort, morbid appearance, or dysfunction; a component of the history. The chief complaint is the symptom that precipitates a diagnostic assessment. Symptoms are subjective; signs are objective.

symptom complex A group of symptoms that tend to occur together.

symptomatology A collection of symptoms; the study of such collections. Some groupings of symptoms suggest specific diagnoses; other groupings do not at first point to a diagnosis but are only coincidentally present in one individual.

synactive theory of development A model for understanding the emerging capabilities of premature infants to organize and control their behavior in response to environmental influences.

synapse The junction between two nerve cells. Chemicals (neurotransmitters) cross the synapse to transmit nerve impulses.

syndactyly Webbing or fusion of fingers or toes; a physical feature found in a number of syndromes. In its mild form, syndactyly is a common nonspecific minor dysmorphic (atypical) feature.

syndactyly

syndrome Literally, "a running together." The term *syndrome* is used to denote a concurrence of signs and symptoms associated with, and together composing, the clinical presentation of a disease or disorder. Syndromes can be genetic, dysmorphic (marked by atypical appearance), behavior, or complaint oriented. Older syndromes were eponymous—named after the person who first described them—such as Down syndrome. There is a tendency to replace eponyms with etiologies (causes); thus, Down syndrome has become trisomy 21. But etiology has multiple layers, so there are translocations and other trisomies. In dysmorphology, a syndrome reflects a greater understanding of pathogenesis (origin) than an association but less understanding than a sequence. Some syndromes are named by a listing of the involved organs (e.g., oto-palato-digital, or ear-palate-finger, syndrome) or by acronyms (e.g., OPD-1 for otopalatodigital syndrome). Loosely speaking, the term *syndrome* can refer to any patterned association; thus, there are, for example, literary and artistic syndromes.

syndromic *dysmorphic.* Pertaining to a syndrome; suggestive of the presence of a specific syndrome or a nonspecific syndrome, the latter because of the presence of dysmorphic (marked by atypical appearance) features.

synergistic movement pattern Simultaneous flexion (or extension) at all joints in an extremity, such as the hip, knee, and ankle.

synergy Cooperation between muscles to perform an action or to pathologically lock the individual into an abnormal pattern of flexion or extension.

synkinesia Associated or overflow movements on the ipsilateral (same) side of the body. Synkinesia suggests central nervous system (CNS) immaturity.

synophrys Eyebrows that meet in the middle; an abnormality of facial hair distribution found in a number of conditions but most characteristic of Cornelia de Lange syndrome.

synophrys

syntax The grammar system of a language by which words are arranged in order into phrases and sentences according to specific rules. These rules may vary by language.

Imperfect understanding of these rules may lead to the misunderstanding of meaning. Difficulty with syntax has been related to sequential processing impairments.

syringoma A small skin-colored or slightly yellow, firm papule (raised skin lesion) that appears in crops in the periorbital (around the eye) area. These benign lesions are common in people with Down syndrome after puberty.

syringomelia A tubular-shaped area in the brainstem or spinal cord. Also termed *hydrosyringomyelia,* syringomelia is often found associated with an Arnold-Chiari malformation, a spinal cord tumor, or a post-traumatic occurrence. The initial symptoms of loss of pain and temperature sensation generally do not occur until adulthood. As the syrinx (tube) enlarges, symptoms progress to include spasticity (increased muscle tone), hyperreflexia (increased reflexes), loss of position and vibratory sense, and rapidly progressing scoliosis (spinal curvature). Diagnosis is made by magnetic resonance imaging (MRI) scan. Treatment includes surgical decompression of the spinal cord.

system advocacy Influencing social and political systems to bring about change for groups of people. Examples of systems change include effecting changes in the law or arranging for the removal of architectural and transportation barriers.

System for Augmenting Language (SAL) An augmentative and alternative communication (AAC) approach in which the child uses both a voice output device and a communication display to send and receive messages.

systematic desensitization *See* desensitization.

systemic Relating to the entire organism; widespread. The opposite of local or localized.

SYSTEMS *See* School-Years Screening Test for the Evaluation of Mental Status.

Tt

TABS *See* Temperament and Atypical Behavior Scale.

tachycardia A rise in heart rate in response to sympathetic stimulation.

tachyphylaxis A rapid onset of resistance to the therapeutic effect of medication. For example, when the antihistamine diphenhydramine (trade name, Benadryl) is used to help get a child to sleep at night, the effect wears off in several weeks.

tachypnea Rapid breathing with an increased respiratory rate. Tachypnea is one of the signs of respiratory distress from a number of causes, including pneumonia.

TACL-3 *See* Test for Auditory Comprehension of Language–Third edition.

tact In operant or Skinnerian conditioning, a verbal operant (statement) that refers to a physical object in the environment but does not signify a request for the item (as does a mand). A tact is essentially a label for an item (indicating a "contact" with that item). When intervention aims to encourage language use, tacts are usually reinforced through general means (such as praise) because they do not specify their own reinforcement in the way that a verbal request does. For example, a child may say "car" as a means to request the car (a mand) or simply to label it or comment on its presence (a tact). Response to the verbal operant (stimulus) is evoked or strengthened by the particular object or some aspect of the object.

tactile Relating to the sense of touch. People who are blind use the tactile sensory modality when learning to read braille. Educators have used this modality as an adjunct to the more traditional visual and auditory modalities with preschoolers and with students experiencing difficulty learning to read. This may include tracing sandpaper letters or drawing shapes in clay. The Fernald Word Learning Technique is a structured method for incorporating both tactile and kinesthetic modalities with auditory and visual modalities in learning to read.

tactile defensiveness Tactile hypersensitivity; a sensory integrative dysfunction characterized by observable aversive or negative behavioral responses to certain types of tactile (touch) stimuli that most people would not find painful, such as stiffening up when hugged. Strong emotional reactions, hyperactivity, and other behavior problems may occur. Sensory integration theory hypothesizes that this affective misinterpretation of tactile experience is the effect of a disorder in the modulation or regulation of tactile sensory input.

Tactile Test of Basic Concepts An adaptation of the Boehm Test of Basic Concepts that substitutes raised figures for pictures to predict success in kindergarten and first grade.

Tadoma A method of teaching speech and speechreading by placing the child's hand on the speaker's face and throat to allow the child to feel the vibrations that are made by sound.

TAG *See* The Association for the Gifted.

Tagamet *See* cimetidine.

TAL *See* tendo Achilles lengthening.

talipes equinovarus *clubfoot.* A (usually congenital) deformity of the foot. The term derives from *talus* (heel/ankle), *pes* (foot), *equinus* (foot extension), and *varus* (inversion/supination of the foot so that only the outer sole touches the ground). This deformity has a polygenic mode of inheritance with a threshold effect; the greater its rate of occurrence in a family, the greater the risk of its recurrence with an increasing severity. Clubfoot is also found in cerebral palsy, spina bifida, arthrogryposis (fixation of the joints), and a variety of genetic syndromes. Orthopedic treatment should take into account etiology (cause). The presence of any otherwise unexplained congenital orthopedic deformity in a newborn should lead to the consideration of a possible neurodevelopmental diagnosis.

TALK *See* Training for Acquisition of Language in Kids.

talus A bone in the foot just below the ankle.

tandem walking Toe–heel gait; walking in a straight line with the toes of one foot and the heel of the other being in contact with each other at the end of every step. Tandem walking is a sensitive indicator of problems with balance.

tangential speech Verbalizations that are overly prone to tangents, with rapid shifts to topics that are only vaguely or loosely associated; flight of ideas; talking about "everything at once" instead of focusing on a topic; "mouth too fast for brain" or "brain too fast for mouth." Tangential speech is a characteristic speech pattern of people with a range of difficulties, including attention-deficit/hyperactivity disorder, traumatic brain injury, and psychotic disorders.

tangible symbols Two- or three-dimensional aided symbols that are permanent, manipulatable with a motor behavior, tactually discriminable, and highly iconic (e.g., real objects, miniature objects, partial objects, artificially associated and textured symbols, and other tangible symbols).

Tanner stages A scoring system for rating the sexual maturation of male genitalia, female pubic hair, and female breast development that is especially useful in the physical examination of adolescents. There is no stage 0; preadolescent/early childhood sexual maturity ratings are all Tanner I. Tanner V and VI represent the mature adult stage. *See* page 453.

TAPS-3 *See* Test of Auditory-Perceptual Skills–Third Edition.

Tardieu Scale A tool for evaluating tone that differentiates contracture from spasticity.

tardive dyskinesia Choreiform (involuntary twitching) movements that can result from the use of neuroleptic medications. These movements occur late (i.e., tardive) in the course of therapy and tend to be limited to stereotypic face, tongue, or mouth activities (e.g., chewing and lip smacking, facial grimacing, tongue thrusting); blinking; and writhing movements of the fingers, hands, and toes. The overall incidence is on the order of 1%, and in children, the tardive dyskinesia tends to resolve when the drugs are discontinued.

tarsi palpebrarum The edges of the eyelid.

tarsus The instep of the foot.

TASH An organization of professionals in partnership with people with disabilities, their families, and others involved in education, research, and advocacy on behalf of individuals with severe intellectual disability and their families. The association publishes a newsletter and a quarterly journal,

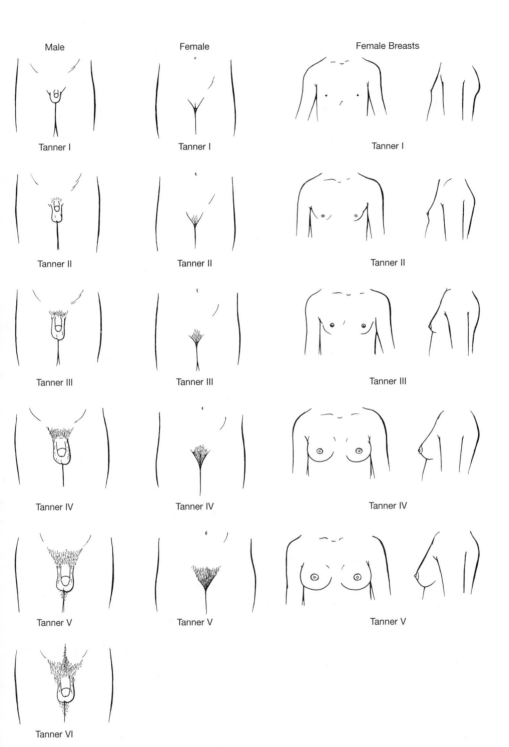

Male

Tanner I

Tanner II

Tanner III

Tanner IV

Tanner V

Tanner VI

Female

Tanner I

Tanner II

Tanner III

Tanner IV

Tanner V

Female Breasts

Tanner I

Tanner II

Tanner III

Tanner IV

Tanner V

Tanner stages

Research and Practice for Individuals with Severe Disabilities. Formerly The Association for Persons with Severe Handicaps.

task analysis *task analysis instruction.* An approach to teaching in which complex behaviors are broken down into their components and taught in an ordered and logical sequence. Prior to instruction, an assessment determines which subskills an individual has and has not mastered. The task analysis refers to the steps required to execute the larger task and does not acknowledge any ability limitations within the learner (other than lack of mastery of specific necessary subskills through lack of practice or experience). Instruction emphasizes teaching those subskills based on an understanding of the individual in the learning context and often involves reinforcement. Steps to this approach include 1) stating objectives to be achieved and skills to be learned; 2) analyzing the skill in terms of specific tasks; 3) listing tasks in a sequential order; 4) determining which tasks are not known by the student; 5) teaching through direct instruction; 6) teaching one task at a time, moving to the next when the previous task has been learned; and 7) evaluating the effectiveness of instruction by whether the skill has been learned.

TAT Thematic Apperception Test. *See also* apperception.

TAWF *See* Test of Adolescent/Adult Word Finding.

taxonomic grid display A type of alternative and augmentative communication visual grid display that groups symbols according to superordinate categories such as people, places, feelings, foods, drinks, and action words.

Tay syndrome *See* IBIDS syndrome.

Tay-Sachs disease An autosomal recessive lipid storage disease characterized by typical development until 4–6 months of age, when a progressive loss of motor and other developmental milestones occurs. Classic features include progressive intellectual disability, hypotonia (decreased muscle tone), loss of interest in surroundings, poor head control, and apathy. Visual acuity decreases, and the retina (light-sensitive inner back wall of the eye) shows a characteristic cherry-red spot on the macula. Seizures may occur, as can macrocephaly (large head) in the final stages. The biochemical defect is a failure to break down a brain chemical (ganglioside) by the enzyme hexosaminidase A. The syndrome causes progressive intellectual and neurological deterioration leading to death. Diagnosis is made by clinical history and measurement of the serum level of the defective enzyme hexosaminidase A. Tay-Sachs disease is found most commonly in Jewish families from Eastern Europe. Although there is a prenatal screening test available, there is to date no effective treatment.

TBI *See* traumatic brain injury.

TC *See* total communication.

TCA *See* tricyclic antidepressant.

TD *See* typically developing.

TDD *See* telecommunications device for the deaf.

TEA *See* term equivalent age.

TEACCH *See* Treatment and Education of Autistic and related Communication Handicapped Children.

Teacher Report Form (TRF) *Achenbach Teacher Report Form.* A 10-minute standardized teacher questionnaire used to assess problem behavior in the classroom.

teaching strategy A series of steps in the thinking process that are applicable to a reading or writing task across the curriculum.

"Tech Act" *See* Assistive Technology Act of 1998 (PL 105-394).

Technology Assisted Waiver (Tech Waiver) A Medicaid program that provides eligible individuals with services in their home and community. Individuals who are dependent on a medical (respiratory or nutritional support) device may qualify for private duty nursing, respite care, assistive technology, and environmental modifications.

Technology-Related Assistance for Individuals with Disabilities Act Amendments of 1994 (PL 103-218) Federal legislation that refunds the Technology-Related Assistance for Individuals with Disabilities Act of 1988 (PL 100-407), allows its extension to states that have not previously enrolled, and strengthens the advocacy and systems change components of the act.

Technology-Related Assistance for Individuals with Disabilities Act of 1988 (PL 100-407) Federal legislation designed to assist states in developing comprehensive and consumer-responsive programs involving technology-related assistance and in expanding the availability of such technology to individuals with disabilities and their families. To give states considerable flexibility in developing and implementing their programs, the act broadly gives a broad definition of *assistive technology device*.

teeth grinding *See* bruxism.

teething Eruption of teeth through the gums, often associated with drooling, mouthing, irritability, and low-grade fever.

TEF *See* tracheoesophageal fistula.

Tegretol *See* carbamazepine.

telangiectasis Prominence of blood vessels on the surface of the skin.

TELD-3 *See* Test of Early Language Development–Third Edition.

telecanthus Lateral displacement of the inner canthi (corners of the eye) that gives rise to an increased inner canthal distance that can contribute to both pseudostrabismus (seemingly crossed eyes) and pseudohypertelorism (seemingly widely spaced eyes).

telecommunications device for the deaf (TDD) A communications apparatus that allows individuals with hearing impairments to receive and send messages via telephone. The sender types in a message that is transmitted via telephone lines to a visual receiver (either a display screen or a receiving typing machine that types the message). TDDs are becoming increasingly available and are routinely used by police and fire departments as well as other public service agencies, including libraries, airlines, utility companies, and schools.

telegraphic speech Highly condensed noun–verb utterances with few to no adjectives, adverbs, prepositions, conjunctions, articles, or auxiliary verbs. Transiently observed in early language development, the presence of telegraphic speech in older children suggests language disorders.

Teller cards A test of visual acuity for use with children from birth to 3 years; it relies on preferential viewing patterns for cards with patterns of black-and-white stripes.

TEMA-3 *See* Test of Early Mathematics Ability–Third Edition.

temperament The constitutional style of an individual, including stable individual differences in emotional reaction, activity level, attention, and self-regulation. Ratings on nine dimensions of temperament are used to classify children as easy, difficult, or slow to warm, though some children present as blends of temperamental characteristics.

Temperament and Atypical Behavior Scale (TABS) A set of two norm-referenced caregiver report instruments used to screen for and assess neurobehavioral markers of regulatory disorders in children ages 11–71 months. The instruments are the TABS Screener, a 15-item form designed to identify children who need more comprehensive assessment; and the TABS Assessment Tool, a 55-item checklist. The latter produces *T*-scores for detached, hypersensitive/hyperactive, underreactive, and dysregulated types and a standard score on the temperament and regulatory index.

temperature A measurement of body heat, often used colloquially but inaccurately as a synonym for fever (e.g., "He has a temperature," meaning "He has an elevated temperature").

temporal cortex The area of the brain responsible for the reception and interpretation of sound, including speech. Damage to this area of the dominant (usually left) hemisphere can contribute to a wide variety of aphasias (loss of language skills; e.g., Wernicke aphasia) and other language disorders. *See also* primary auditory cortex (A1).

temporal lobe The part of the cerebrum located underneath the frontal and parietal lobes. This part of the brain appears to be related to memory and a variety of autonomic (automatic), motor, and sensory responses.

temporal lobe

Temporary Child Care for Handicapped Children and Crises Nurseries Act of 1986 (PL 99-401) An act that provides funding for temporary respite care for children with disabilities or chronic illness who are at risk for abuse or neglect. This act is part of a larger federal law termed the Children's Justice and Assistance Act of 1986.

temporomandibular joint (TMJ) The hinge at which the lower jaw connects to the skull. In addition to causing local pain or tenderness, TMJ problems have been implicated in nonspecific symptoms such as dizziness, headache, backache, and chronic fatigue. No convincing evidence supports a role for TMJ in the etiology (cause) of developmental disabilities.

tendo Achilles lengthening (TAL) Any one of a variety of orthopedic surgery procedures used to lengthen a short, tight, or spastic heel cord. The procedure may be a Z lengthening or a sliding lengthening.

tendon A connective tissue structure that attaches a muscle to a bone.

tendon reflex *See* deep-tendon reflex (DTR).

tendon transfer An orthopedic surgery procedure that realigns abnormal forces at a joint. The procedure corrects posture and improves movement by reinserting a tendon so as to give the contraction of the treated muscle a different impact on posture and movement. The treated muscle need not have initially contributed to the original deformity or disorder.

Tenex *See* guanfacine.

tenotomy A surgical operation in which a tendon is cut. Most tenotomies are orthopedic in nature, however some eye muscle surgeries also involve tenotomy.

TENS *See* transcutaneous electrical nerve stimulation.

tense voice A voice disorder that results from phonation produced with excessive adduction and medial compression of the vocal folds.

TEOAEs *See* transient-evoked otoacoustic emissions.

TEP *See* tracheoesophageal puncture.

TERA-3 *See* Test of Early Reading Ability–Third Edition.

teratogen A chemical or physical agent that causes or increases the incidence of congenital malformations. Teratogens are intrauterine toxins (poisons) to the fetus and generally have their greatest impact early in pregnancy. Human teratogens that produce known syndromes include alcohol, phenytoin (trade name, Dilantin), trimethadione, thalidomide, valproic acid (trade name, Depakene), diethylstilbestrol (DES), warfarin (trade name, Coumadin), aminopterin, and isotretinoin (trade name, Accutane).

teratology of Fallot A group of birth defects of the heart and lung that involve hypoxic episodes of increasing cyanosis (turning blue), crying, and failure to thrive.

terbutaline A beta-sympathomimetic drug used to treat preterm labor and prevent premature birth.

term The period of gestation or length of pregnancy.

term equivalent age (TEA) Chronological age corrected for prematurity or postmaturity.

terminal devices Prostheses.

Terry disease *See* retinopathy of prematurity (ROP).

tertiary prevention Intervention after the problem occurs; attempts to reduce the impact of the problem and prevent secondary complications.

test A historical fact, physical sign, or laboratory value that has diagnostic value.

Test for Auditory Comprehension of Language–Third Edition (TACL-3) A language test for use with children from 3;0 to 9;11 years that can also be administered to adults. The TACL-3 measures receptive spoken grammar, vocabulary, and syntax. It requires 10–20 minutes to administer and yields percentile ranks and age- or grade-based standard scores for vocabulary, grammatical morphemes, and elaborated sentences.

Test of Adolescent and Adult Language–Fourth Edition (TOAL-4) A measure of the spoken and written language abilities of adolescents and young adults 12;0–24;11 years of age. Based on six subtests (Word Opposites, Word Derivations, Spoken Analogies, Word Similarities, Sentence Combining, Orthographic Usage), the TOAL-4 yields composite scores for spoken language, written language, and general language that have a mean of 100 and a standard deviation of 15.

Test of Adolescent/Adult Word Finding (TAWF) A standardized test of word-finding skills for use with people ages 12–80. Naming tasks are organized into five sections: picture naming (nouns), picture naming (verbs), sentence completion naming, description naming, and category naming.

Test of Auditory-Perceptual Skills–Third Edition (TAPS-3) An individualized, norm-referenced test for use with children ages 4–18 years that measures what the person does with what is heard. The TAPS-3 produces one overall score, and individual subtest scores are combined to derive three cluster scores: Basic Auditory Skills (Word Discrimination, Phonological Segmentation, and Phonological Blending subtests), Auditory Memory (Number Memory Forward, Number Memory Reversed, Word Memory, and Sentence Memory subtests), and Auditory Cohesion (Auditory Comprehension and Auditory Reasoning subtests). Administration time is 30–60 minutes.

Test of Early Language Development–Third Edition (TELD-3) An individually administered, norm-referenced measure of spoken language abilities for use with children ages

2;0–7;11 years. The TELD-3 yields an overall Spoken Language score and Receptive Language and Expressive Language subtest scores. It also yields standard scores, percentile ranks, and age equivalents. Administration time is 20 minutes.

Test of Early Mathematics Ability–Third Edition (TEMA-3) A norm-referenced test that measures the mathematics performance of children between the ages of 3;0 and 8;11 years. The TEMA-3 measures numbering skills, number comparison facility, numerical literacy, mastery of number facts, calculation skills, and understanding of concepts.

Test of Early Reading Ability–Third Edition (TERA-3) A direct measure of reading ability in children ages 3;6–8;6 years. The TERA-3 assesses mastery of early-developing reading skills via three subtests: Alphabet, which measures knowledge of the alphabet and its uses; Conventions, which measures knowledge of the conventions of print; and Meaning, which measures the construction of meaning from print. Standard scores are provided for each subtest. An overall Reading Quotient is computed using all three subtest scores.

Test of Early Written Language–Second Edition (TEWL-2) An individually administered test used to assess the strengths and weaknesses of writing ability in children ages 3;0–10;11 years. Two subtests, Basic Writing and Contextual Writing, yield quotients (with a mean of 100 and a standard deviation of 15) and combine to form the Global Writing Quotient. A companion to the Test of Written Language–Fourth Edition (TOWL-4), the TEWL-2 requires 30–45 minutes to administer. Results can be reported in terms of standard scores, percentile ranks, and age equivalents.

Test of Infant Motor Performance (TIMP) A tool used by occupational and physical therapists to examine premature infants from 32 weeks' postconceptual age to 4 months postterm. Intended to predict long-term disability, the TIMP looks at posture and control in supine, prone, and supported upright positions. A total of 28 items are scored pass/fail by observation, and 31 items are administered and scored in a standardized fashion. Administration time is 25–45 minutes.

Test of Language Competence–Expanded Edition (TLC-E) An instrument used to identify language and communication impairments in children ages 5–19 years. The TLC-E includes the following subtests: Ambiguous Sentences, Listening Comprehension, Oral Expression, Figurative Language, and a supplemental memory test, remembering word pairs.

Test of Language Development–Fourth Edition (TOLD-4) A widely used test of spoken language. The primary-level edition (TOLD-P:4) is designed for use with children ages 4;0–8;11 years and has nine subtests that measure different components of spoken language. There is also an intermediate edition (TOLD-I:4) for use with children ages 8;7–12;11 years that has nine subtests. Both forms produce an overall Spoken Language quotient.

Test of Mathematical Abilities–Second Edition (TOMA-2) An instrument designed to identify students who are significantly above or below their peers in 1) attitude toward mathematics, 2) vocabulary, 3) computation, 4) general information, and 5) story problems. Normative tables are provided for ages 8;0–17;11 years.

Test of Motor Impairment An individually administered screening tool of motor function in children 5–12 years of age who also have intellectual disability or learning or behavior difficulties.

Test of Nonverbal Intelligence–Third Edition (TONI-3) A language-free measure of intelligence, aptitude, abstract reasoning, and problem solving that requires no reading, writing, speaking, or listening by the individual being assessed. Instructions can be pantomimed. It includes two forms for use with people ages 6;0–89;11 years and is indicated for use with individuals with speech, hearing, or language impairment; limited English proficiency; as well as those with neurological impairment. The TONI-3 yields standard scores with a mean of 100 and a standard deviation of 15 and requires 15–20 minutes to administer.

Test of Phonological Awareness–Second Edition: PLUS (TOPA-2+) A group of individually administered, norm-referenced tests of phonological awareness. The TOPA-2+ measures a child's ability to isolate individual phonemes in spoken words and understand the relationships between letters and phonemes. Two versions assess children ages 5–8 years: The Kindergarten version requires 30–45 minutes to administer, and the Early Elementary version requires 15–30 minutes to administer. Both yield standard scores and percentiles.

Test of Playfulness A tool designed to capture four elements of playfulness in children: intrinsic motivation, internal control, freedom from some constraints of reality, and framing (the ability to give and read cues).

Test of Practical Knowledge (TPK) A reading level of ninth grade or beyond is required for this test, which assesses knowledge believed to be necessary for daily functioning. The three areas assessed are 1) personal knowledge relating to day-to-day independent living, 2) social knowledge relating to understanding of social interaction and community service, and 3) occupational knowledge relating to job situations. The TPK can be administered individually or in groups via a silent-reading multiple choice format. The test is not suitable for use with students with severe disabilities, non–English-speaking students, or students who lack motivation.

Test of Pragmatic Language–Second Edition (TOPL-2) An individually administered, norm-referenced test for use with children 8–18 years of age that measures the ability to use pragmatic language (i.e., language that is used socially to achieve goals and that emphasizes not only what is said but why and for what purpose). Administered in 45–60 minutes, the TOPL-2 tests subcomponents of pragmatic language through six subtests: Physical Setting, Audience, Topic, Purpose (Speech Acts), Visual-Gestural Cues, and Abstraction. Raw scores, percentiles, standard scores, and age equivalents are provided. The test consists of 43 items in which visuals and expressions must be interpreted by the examinee. The TOPL-2 can be used as a criterion-referenced assessment of older individuals.

Test of Pragmatic Skills–Revised Edition (TOPS-R) A test that uses four guided play interactions to assess the use of language to signify conversational intent by children 3;0–8;11 years of age. The test probes the conversational intentions of requesting information, requesting action, rejection/denial, norming/labeling, answering/responding, informing, reasoning, summoning/calling, greeting, and closing conversation. The TOPS-R is a standardized assessment instrument but is typically administered on the floor in order to create a "nontesting" environment for the child.

Test of Reading Comprehension–Fourth Edition (TORC-4) An individually administered test of silent reading comprehension for use with students 7–17 years. The test is composed of five subtests (Relational Vocabulary, Sentence Completion, Paragraph Construction, Text Comprehension, and Contextual Fluency) that combine to form an overall composite, the Reading Comprehension Index. The test is based on a mean of 100 and a standard deviation of 15. It takes approximately 60 minutes to administer, depending on the speed of the examinee.

Test of Sensory Function in Infants (TSFI) A tool that measures sensory processing and reactivity in infants from birth to 18 months of age. The TSFI identifies infants with sensory integrative dysfunction.

Test of Variables of Attention (TOVA) An objective, standardized, visual continuous performance task used in the diagnosis and medication management of attention-deficit/hyperactivity disorders in children and adults. This is a non–language-based, 22-minute, fixed-interval computerized test with negligible practice effects. Respondents play a "computer game" that requires responses to visual and auditory stimuli. Responses are compared with those of individuals without attention difficulties. Formerly known as the Minnesota Computer Assessment (MCA). *See also* continuous performance task (CPT).

Test of Visual-Motor Skills–Revised (TVMS-R) A 26-item design copying test for use with children ages 2–13 years. The TVMS-R was developed to measure how well the child translates with his or her hand what is visually perceived.

Test of Visual-Perceptual Skills–Third Edition (TVPS-3) A nonmotor multiple choice (by pointing) response measure with seven different subtests.

Test of Word Knowledge (TOWK) An assessment of receptive and expressive vocabulary for use with children 5–17 years of age. Administration time is less than 1 hour.

Test of Written Language–Fourth Edition (TOWL-4) A norm-referenced, comprehensive diagnostic test of written expression for use with students ages 9;0–17;11 years. Seven subtests assess the conventional, linguistic, and conceptual aspects of writing: Vocabulary, Spelling, Punctuation, Logical Sentences, Sentence Combining, Contextual Conventions, and Story Composition, and can be combined into composite scores.

Test of Written Spelling–Fourth Edition (TWS-4) A norm-referenced test of spelling administered using a dictated word format. The TWS-4 has two alternative or equivalent forms (A and B), which makes it more useful in test–teach–test situations. The TWS-4 is appropriate for use with students in Grades 1–12 as well as those in remedial programs. The TWS-4 was developed after a review of 2,000 spelling rules. The words to be spelled are drawn from 10 basal spelling programs and popular graded word lists.

testing of limits Modification or deviation from standard test administration procedures to gain additional information about a child's abilities. Testing of limits techniques include providing additional information, presenting or accepting information in an alternative form, encouraging the child's own problem-solving strategies, eliminating time limits, and asking probing questions. These techniques are used after the entire test has been administered in its standardized form. Successes obtained through testing of limits are not added to the child's score, although the information obtained from testing of limits procedures can often be helpful in clinical and psychoeducational settings. Such testing can affect future test results if retesting is likely to occur within a short time period.

Tests of General Educational Development (GED) A measure used to determine whether an individual meets the requirements for a certificate of high school equivalency. A successfully completed GED is generally accepted as the equivalent of a high school diploma.

tethered cord A condition in which the spinal cord's natural movement upward during the growth of the bony spinal column is impeded. This can occur because of a tumor, scar tissue, or catching of the spinal cord on a bony spur, resulting in traction on the cord and damage to the nerve cells. A tethered cord is suspected when there is loss of motor skills, sensation, or sphincter function. Diagnosis is made by computed tomography (CT) scan or magnetic resonance imaging (MRI). Treatment is generally surgical in nature, with the goal being to loosen the traction on the cord and to restore neurological function.

tetraphocomelia cleft palate syndrome *hypomelia-hypotrichosis-facial hemangioma syndrome, pseudothalidomide syndrome, Roberts–SC phocomelia syndrome, SC syndrome.* An autosomal recessive genetic syndrome characterized by hypomelia (shortness) of all four extremities (arms and legs), cleft lip and palate, and intellectual disability.

tetraplegia An outdated term for *quadriplegia* (paralysis of all four extremities [arms and legs]).

tetrasomy 9p *See* duplication trisomy 9p.

tetrasomy 12p *See* Killian/Teschler-Nicola syndrome.

tetrasomy 15 pter-q12 *bisatellited 15, inverted duplication 15.* A chromosome abnormality seen most often as an extra "marker" chromosome on an otherwise normal karyotype. It is composed of two copies of chromosome 15 from 15pter-q11 or -q12 joined at the breakpoint region. If no or very little long arm material is present, the individual's phenotype may be normal. As the amount of long arm material increases, the phenotype becomes more abnormal. Clinical features include mild growth retardation, severe intellectual disability, low-set ears, high arched palate, almond-shaped and/or mildly downslanted palpebral fissures, telecanthus, and wide-spaced, superiorly placed eyebrows lacking an arch. Behavior problems include hyperactivity, aggression, short attention span, and autistic features.

tetrasomy 22 (pter-q11) *See* cat eye syndrome.

TEWL-2 *See* Test of Early Written Language–Second Edition.

texture A qualitative gradation of food used in assessing and treating feeding disorders; texture involves both viscosity (thickness or thinness) and consistency (smoothness or coarseness).

TFC *See* three-finger crease.

T4 *thyroxine.* A thyroid hormone that is elevated in hyperthyroidism and decreased in hypothyroidism.

thalamotomy A neurosurgical procedure (brain operation) sometimes used in treating dystonia (variable muscle tone) and cerebral palsy.

thalidomide embryopathy *fetal thalidomide syndrome.* Reduction deformities of the limbs, with a shortening or absence of several to all bones in the extremities (arms or legs) that sometimes leads to phocomelia. Many other organ systems can be involved. Etiology (cause) is maternal ingestion of thalidomide early in the first trimester.

The Association for the Gifted (TAG) One of 13 divisions of the Council for Exceptional Children (CEC). Founded in 1958, TAG strives to promote an understanding of gifted and talented students and their educational needs, to disseminate knowledge of the gifted, to expand existing knowledge, and to advocate for policies and legislation on all levels that address the needs of the gifted.

thelarche The onset of breast development in adolescent females.

Thematic Apperception Test (TAT) A projective technique that uses 31 picture cards, some depicting everyday life experiences and others that are more bizarre and ambiguous in form. Different combinations of cards selected for age and sex are used with male and female adults and children. The respondent is asked to tell a story about the picture, indicating what is happening, how the story ends, and what the characters are thinking and feeling. Significant caution is required when administering and interpreting projective tests, particularly with individuals with language and other impairments. *See also* apperception.

thenar   Referring to the fleshy, muscular mass over the ball of the thumb.

thenar longitudinal crease   A crease on the palm of the hand; the "lifeline" of palmistry.

thenar longitudinal crease

theory of mind (ToM)   The ability to think about thoughts and to attribute mental states to others. Impairments in this cognitive ability have been used to explain the impairments found in autism. *See also* false belief paradigm.

therapeutic balls   Adaptive equipment used to promote normal posture and balance responses in children and adults. Balls range in size and density.

therapeutic handling   Optimal techniques for transporting, positioning, and physically interacting with children and adults with motor disorders or hypersensitivity to such handling. Goals include both relaxation and maximizing the individual's independence.

therapeutic horseback riding   *See* hippotherapy.

therapeutic range   In reference to treatment with a drug, the upper and lower blood levels (concentrations generally expressed in micrograms of drug per milliliter of blood) within which a desired effect is achieved without undesirable side effects. These ranges are specific to each drug and are commonly used

with anticonvulsants, antibiotics, and antidepressants. Many medications do not have reliably defined therapeutic ranges, and therefore levels are not routinely determined. Levels can also be used to assess compliance with a medication regimen.

Therapeutic Support Staff (TSS) worker   A person with a bachelor's degree who implements the individual behavior plan for a child or adolescent on a one-to-one basis for a specified number of hours per week in the home, school, or community setting under the supervision of the managing behavior specialist.

therapeutic touch (TT)   Energy healing by the laying on of hands; an unproven alternative treatment modality.

thermal stimulation   A controversial sensory-based swallow treatment that requires application of cold or chilled stimulation to oral cavity structures (e.g., faucial arches/pillars). This technique is believed to increase intra-oral awareness of boli and to "alert" the central nervous system to pending food and liquids.

thermoregulation   The body's ability to control its temperature, a function of the autonomic nervous system. Severe damage to the brain centers involved can produce episodic hyperpyrexia (fever) or poikilothermic behavior (a body temperature that approximates the environmental temperature). Thermoregulatory disorders are common in infants born severely premature and in people with profound intellectual disability.

TheraTogs   Live-in exomuscular systems (body molds) for neuromotor, postural, and sensory treatment. The system has an inner foam layer and an outer Velcro-sensitive layer that applies prolonged, low-load forces to the body. It is used to treat hypotonia (low tone, floppiness), spinal (back) curvature (kyphosis, lordosis [hump]), and joint malalignments.

theta rhythm An electroencephalographic rhythm with a speed of 4–8 per second; theta waves characterize light sleep.

thickener A product added to thin foods to increase their viscosity in order to make it easier for them to be eaten by people with feeding difficulties.

thimerosal A mercury-containing preservative once used in vaccines that was once thought to influence the occurrence of autism in children who received multiple immunizations.

think-aloud A strategy in which one demonstrates a complex thinking process that he or she uses when constructing meaning (e.g., relating information across sentences and paragraphs, deciding on relevant versus irrelevant information, extracting the main idea from text).

thioridazine Trade name, Mellaril. A phenothiazine used to treat hyperactivity and severe behavior disorders in people with intellectual disability. Thioridazine has an appetite-increasing effect and at therapeutic levels may lower intelligence quotient (IQ) scores.

third-degree relative Someone, such as a first cousin, who has one eighth of his or her genes in common with the focal individual.

13q- Deletion of part of the long arm of chromosome 13; a chromosomal condition characterized by intellectual disability, microcephaly (small head), a peculiar facies, eye abnormalities, and hypoplastic (short to absent) thumbs. The deletion is usually sporadic.

thoracic Relating to the thorax (chest). The curve of the thoracic spine is concave forward; when exaggerated, it produces kyphosis ("round shoulders").

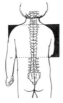

thoracic spine

thoracic insufficiency syndrome (TIS) Impaired and restricted lung growth and function due to chest deformity secondary to scoliosis (curvature of the spine).

thoracolumbosacral orthosis (TLSO) A brace used to treat scoliosis (spinal curvature).

Thorazine *See* chlorpromazine.

three jaw chuck draw A primitive form of grasp similar to the manner in which a drill head holds bits.

3 months' colic *See* colic.

3-day measles *See* rubella.

three-finger crease (TFC) The distal transverse palmar crease.

thrush A yeast infection of the mouth and tongue characterized by the formation of white patches and sometimes ulcers, fever, and gastrointestinal inflammation.

thumb abduction splint A positioning device used to keep the thumb web space expanded to promote improved grasping ability.

thumb web space The space between the thumb and the index finger. A small web space can limit a person's ability to grasp.

thyroxine *See* T4.

TIA *See* transient ischemic attack.

tibia The shin bone; the larger of the two lower leg bones. *See also* fibula.

tibial torsion, internal *See* internal tibial torsion.

tic An involuntary motor movement or repetitive twitching often in the face or upper trunk. Examples include eye blinking, grimacing, and shrugging. There are also vocal tics, such as sniffing, coughing, or clearing of the throat. Tourette syndrome is a disorder characterized by severe motor and vocal tics.

Ticket to Work and Self-Sufficiency Program A program through the Social Security Administration that provides people with disabilities with increased opportunities and choices to obtain employment or vocational rehabilitation services. This program is part of the Ticket to Work and Work Incentives Improvement Act (TWWIIA) of 1999 (PL 106-170), which was designed to remove identified barriers to employment for people with disabilities on Social Security, such as the loss of health insurance coverage.

Ticket to Work and Work Incentives Improvement Act (TWWIIA) of 1999 (PL 106-170) Legislation designed to eliminate barriers to employment for people with disabilities receiving Social Security.

TIE *See* Touch Inventory for Elementary School-Aged Children.

TIME *See* Toddler and Infant Motor Evaluation.

time-out (TO) *time-out from positive reinforcement.* A behavioral procedure in which an individual is temporarily (usually only for minutes) removed from the environment or is otherwise denied pleasant stimuli present in the setting. TO is intended to reduce the occurrence of an undesirable behavior and is used when remaining in the environment encourages the problem behavior. In nonseclusionary TO, the student remains in the environment but may be denied participation in a desired activity. For example, a teacher may assess that peer attention encourages one student's problem behavior, so students may be asked to return to their seats and face forward. In exclusionary or seclusionary TO, an individual is removed from the environment in which problem behavior occurs and temporarily reassigned to an isolating environment (e.g., a hall, seclusion room, or other setting).

time-out from positive reinforcement *See* time-out (TO).

Timothy syndrome A rare autosomal dominant disorder characterized by autism, cardiac anomalies (heart problems) with arrhythmias (irregular heart rates), syndactyly (webbing of the fingers and toes), hypoglycemia (low blood sugar), immunodeficiency (susceptibility to infections), and early death. Timothy syndrome is associated with a *CACNA1C* mutation.

TIMP *See* Test of Infant Motor Performance.

tine test A screening skin test for tuberculosis that involves four small pinpricks that are then observed for a local reaction 2–3 days later. The tine is one of the four prongs used to administer the test.

tinea Ringworm; a fungal infection.

tinnitus Noise in the ears, such as ringing, buzzing, or roaring.

tip Referring to the tongue, the forwardmost portion of the tongue.

tip pinch The position of the hand for holding tiny objects in which the object is held between the thumb and index fingertips, forming an "O."

TIS *See* thoracic insufficiency syndrome.

Title I of the Elementary and Secondary Education Act (ESEA) of 1965 (PL 89-10) The federal government's first effort to provide compensatory education services for educationally disadvantaged and low income students. *See also* Chapter 1 of the Education Consolidation and Improvement Act of 1981 (PL 98-211).

Title I Program *See* Chapter 1 of the Education Consolidation and Improvement Act of 1981 (PL 98-211).

Title V of the Social Security Act of 1935 (PL 74-271) Federal legislation that establishes the Crippled Children's Service (CCS), the first categorical health care program for children, and the Maternal and Child Health Bureau. The Consolidated Omnibus Budget Reconciliation Act of 1985 (PL 99-272) changed the CCS to the Program for Children with Special Health Care Needs.

Title XIX of the Social Security Act of 1935 (PL 74-271) As amended in the Social Security Amendments of 1965 (PL 89-97), established Medicaid, a federally supervised, state-administered medical assistance program. This entitlement has financial (income) qualifications for eligibility.

titubation Head bobbing with a to-and-fro movement of the body that is often due to cerebellar damage or disease in the vermis (the central part of the cerebellum).

TLC-E *See* Test of Language Competence–Expanded Edition.

TLR *See* tonic labyrinthine response.

TLSO *See* thoracolumbosacral orthosis.

TMH Trainable mentally handicapped. *See* trainable mental retardation (TMR).

TMJ *See* temporomandibular joint.

TMR *See* trainable mental retardation.

TO *See* time-out.

TOAL-4 *See* Test of Adolescent and Adult Language–Fourth Edition.

tobacco *See* maternal smoking during pregnancy.

tocolytic Any pharmacological agent used to postpone the process of labor.

Todd paralysis The transient paralysis of a body part involved in a focal seizure; it may

continue for several (always less than 24) hours after the seizure is complete.

Toddler and Infant Motor Evaluation (TIME) A comprehensive assessment of eight subdomains related to the motor abilities of children ages 4–42 months. Subtests include Mobility, Stability, Motor Organization, Social/Emotional Abilities, Functional Performance, Quality Rating, Component Analysis, and Atypical Positions. The assessment is administered using observations of spontaneous and elicited movements, with the examiner prompting the parent or caregiver.

toe walking *equinus gait.* Walking on the balls of the feet with the heels not touching the ground. When associated with spasticity (increased muscle tone), tight calf muscles, shortened heel cords, and brisk deep-tendon reflexes, toe walking is a sign of spastic cerebral palsy, most commonly diplegia (paralysis involving primarily the lower extremities). toe walking Toe walking is frequently seen in children with autism and language disorders. A neurodevelopmental disorder should be suspected when toe walking persists for longer than 3 months.

Tofranil *See* imipramine.

token In behavioral interventions, a reinforcer that can later be exchanged for another reinforcer or reward. For example, a teacher may give a student points, chips, or other items that acquire value through their association with other items that are innately rewarding (e.g., extra time at recess, tangible items such as toys).

token economy A comprehensive behavioral intervention program that involves the use of tokens, such as points, chips, stars, play money, and so forth. The tokens are earned for prespecified behaviors and may be turned in at a later time for tangible items such as food or favored activities.

Token Test for Children–Revised (TTFC-2) A screening test for receptive language in children from 3;0 to 12;5 years of age. The technique of using tokens of different shapes, sizes, and colors to assess receptive language abilities was derived from work with adults who have aphasia (severe loss of language skills).

TOLD-4 *See* Test of Language Development–Fourth Edition.

tolerance A response to a drug or other treatment that necessitates an increase in dosage or intensity to maintain treatment effectiveness.

toluene embryopathy A teratogenic (malformation causing) syndrome that includes low birth weight (LBW), microcephaly (small head), developmental delay, and facial features similar to those of fetal alcohol syndrome (FAS). Etiology (cause) is maternal abuse of the solvent methylbenzene (found in spray paint) during pregnancy.

ToM *See* theory of mind.

TOMA-2 *See* Test of Mathematical Abilities–Second Edition.

Tomitis sound therapy *See* auditory integration training (AIT).

tone reducing ankle foot orthosis (TRAFO) A brace used to treat equinus deformity or posture due to spasticity (increased muscle tone).

tone *tonus.* The degree of involuntary muscle contraction (firmness) or passive resistance to stretch that persists during voluntary relaxation. Tone can be described as normal, hypertonic (increased), hypotonic (decreased), or atonic (absent) and can be scored from 0 (*absent*) to 4 (*severely*

increased). Both the Ashworth Scale and the Tardieu Scales are used for grading tone.

tongue protrusion reflex An oral-motor reflex innervated by cranial nerve XII, in which a tactile (touch) stimulus to the anterior (front) tongue produces the response of tongue protrusion between birth and 6 months of age. Diminution of this reflex permits the introduction of solids.

tongue thrust Forceful, intermittent protrusion of the tongue, often associated with a generalized increase in extensor tone. Tongue thrust is of concern when it interferes with feeding and speech.

tongue-tie *ankyloglossia, hypertrophic lingual frenulum.* A short lingual frenulum that restricts the movement of the tongue, especially at the tip. Except in extreme cases, it rarely affects speech.

TONI-3 *See* Test of Nonverbal Intelligence–Third Edition.

tonic bite An exaggerated version of the bite reflex in which the jaw clamps shut with minimal oral stimulation.

tonic labyrinthine response (TLR) A primitive reflex in which neck extension (stimulus) produces shoulder retraction ("surrender posture," or hands above the shoulders or in the air posture) and lower extremity extension. Presence of this reflex at any age is not normal and reflects serious underlying central nervous system (CNS) injury. In the same infant, response will be extension in supine and flexion in prone.

tonic labyrinthine response (TLR)

tonic seizure A seizure type classified under minor motor seizures or Lennox-Gastaut syndrome. A tonic seizure is characterized by brief spells of muscle tightening. These generally occur during sleep and are resistant to anticonvulsant therapy.

tonic spasms Sudden extension of the entire body, often on the basis of an overactive labyrinthine reflex; this postural extensor thrust is not a true seizure.

tonic-clonic seizure *See* generalized seizure.

tonsil A small oral mass of lymphoid tissue. Two such masses are embedded in the lateral walls of the opening between the mouth and the pharynx. The function of tonsils is uncertain, but they are believed to help protect the body from respiratory infections.

tonsillectomy The surgical removal of the tonsils. Often an adenoidectomy (the surgical removal of the adenoids) is accomplished at the same time in a procedure known as a *T&A*. Indications for T&A have tended to become more restrictive. Recurrent otitis (ear infection) or some degree of cardiac or respiratory compromise should outweigh the risk of severe postoperative bleeding. The fact that tonsillar tissue normally begins to involute (spontaneously grow smaller) by early in the second decade of life should also be taken into account prior to deciding on surgery.

tonsillitis An infection or inflammation of the tonsils (masses of lymphoid tissue in the throat/oropharynx). Tonsillitis is distinct from (although often associated with) pharyngitis (throat infection). The presence of a runny nose (rhinitis) can suggest a viral etiology (cause) to a throat infection that will not benefit from antibiotics.

TOPA-2+ *See* Test of Phonological Awareness–Second Edition: PLUS.

Topamax *See* topiramate.

top-down (conceptually driven) processing Processing that is affected by what an individual brings to a stimulus situation. For example, when a word is unclear or unknown in a sentence, the reader uses expectations based on context and past experience (top-down processing), rather than relying on a detailed analysis of the word (bottom-up processing). In most circumstances, perception involves the interaction of bottom-up and top-down processing. *See also* bottom-up processing, deductive reasoning.

topic *See* domain.

topic-setter cards Simple drawings or symbols on self-adhesive notes or index cards that present topics of interest.

topiramate Trade name, Topamax. An anticonvulsant that is sometimes used to treat challenging behaviors.

TOPL-2 *See* Test of Pragmatic Language–Second Edition.

topographical classification of cerebral palsy Describes which of the four extremities are significantly involved in cerebral palsy. Such a classification is typically used only with spastic cerebral palsy, because most extrapyramidal cerebral palsy involves all four extremities fairly equally. Topographical subtypes include monoplegia, hemiplegia (paralysis of half the body), triplegia (paralysis of three limbs), diplegia (paralysis involving more the lower extremities), quadriplegia (paralysis of all four extremities), and paraplegia (paralysis of the lower extremities).

topographical orientation The ability to determine the location of objects and the route to the location.

topography In psychoanalysis, the division of mental function into three regions: the conscious, the unconscious, and the preconscious.

TOPS-R *See* Test of Pragmatic Skills–Revised Edition.

TORC-4 *See* Test of Reading Comprehension–Fourth Edition.

TORCH *See* STORCH.

torsion dystonia *See* dystonia musculorum deformans.

torticollis *wry neck.* A shortening of the neck muscles; a spasm or tightening of the neck muscles that leads to the head being turned to one side. The sternocleidomastoid muscle is most frequently involved and is responsible for the typical posture of lateral flexion to one side and cervical rotation in the opposite direction. Torticollis results in cranial molding and facial asymmetries in addition to postural asymmetries.

torus palatinus A benign doughnut-shaped bony swelling over the posterior (back) portion of the hard palate. Torus palatinus is a normal anatomical variant without any developmental significance.

torus palatinus

total communication (**TC**) An educational approach used with individuals with speech and hearing impairments in which all communication methods available to the individual are used. Fingerspelling, oral and written language, speechreading, and sign language are among the techniques incorporated to enhance receptive and expressive communication. Synthesizing all sensory modalities and communicative abilities facilitates both the acquisition of language and social development, particularly among children who have congenital or prelingual (occurring before the development of speech) hearing loss.

total parenteral nutrition (**TPN**) *hyperalimentation, total parenteral alimentation (TPA). Parenteral* refers to feeding not through the alimentary canal, typically by the intravenous route. TPN provides all of the nutritional requirements to build and maintain body tissue and expend energy through an intravenous catheter in cases in which the intestine's ability to absorb food has been acutely or chronically impaired.

Touch Inventory for Elementary School-Aged Children (**TIE**) A brief (10-minute) 26-question inventory used to assess tactile (touch) defensiveness. The TIE can be administered alone or as part of a comprehensive sensory integration assessment.

Tourette syndrome *Gilles de la Tourette syndrome.* A condition that starts in childhood, characterized by multifocal (involving several places) motor tics (repeated movements) that progress to vocal tics (most commonly coughing and throat clearing). The tics are performed in response to an urge and can often be held back for only a short time. Occasionally people with Tourette syndrome develop other vocal tics, such as animal noises, echolalia (repetition of what is heard), and, rarely, coprolalia (unprovoked obscene language). Attention-deficit/hyperactivity disorder (ADHD), learning disorders, sleep disturbances, and obsessive compulsive traits such as excessive hand washing are reported. About one third of cases are familial, with an autosomal dominant mode of inheritance. Named after the French neurologist Gilles de la Tourette (1855–1904).

TOVA Test of Variables of Attention. *See also* continuous performance task (CPT).

tower A visual-perceptual motor milestone in infancy and early childhood in which the child is requested to imitate stacking blocks; a tower of 2 blocks can usually be completed by 15 months of age and a tower of 10 blocks by 3 years. The qualitative aspects of the motor grasp and release can also be evaluated during this task. Tower-building block tasks are common components of many infant tests.

TOWK   *See* Test of Word Knowledge.

TOWL-4   *See* Test of Written Language–Fourth Edition.

toxemia of pregnancy   *See* preeclampsia.

toxoplasmosis   A parasitic infection caused by a protozoa that can be transmitted from mother to fetus. Toxoplasmosis is acquired by contact with infected sources, such as raw meat, cat feces, or the eggs of infected animals. Incidence is estimated at 2 in 1,000 live births. Symptoms of the mother range from mild or subclinical to enlarged lymph nodes. It is believed that 40% of children with affected mothers will develop symptoms. Sequelae may include spontaneous abortion, prematurity, hydrocephalus, microcephaly, other central nervous system (CNS) disorders, fever, jaundice, and eye problems.

TPA   Total parenteral alimentation. *See* total parenteral nutrition (TPN).

TPBA   *See* Transdisciplinary Play-Based Assessment.

TPK   *See* Test of Practical Knowledge.

TPN   *See* total parenteral nutrition.

trachea   The windpipe.

tracheoesophageal fistula (TEF)   A congenital malformation in which the esophagus opens into the trachea (windpipe) and leads to aspiration. TEF can be part of the VATER association, Down syndrome, and other malformation syndromes.

tracheoesophageal fistula (TEF)

tracheoesophageal puncture (TEP)   A fistula (connecting hole) created between the esophagus (gullet) and trachea (windpipe) to allow for the placement of a prosthetic (artificial) device to facilitate esophageal speech.

tracheoesophageal speech   Speech that is produced by vibration of the pharyngoesophageal (gullet) segment. A one-way valved prosthesis (artificial device) must be surgically placed in the wall separating the trachea (windpipe) and esophagus to allow lung air to pass into the esophagus.

tracking   Continued visual fixation on a moving object such that the eye continues to follow the object.

tracking   Grouping students on the basis of ability. Being assigned to specific classes at the secondary level based on academic ability influences student friendships, extracurricular activities, and attitudes.

traction response   A test for tone that can be elicited in premature infants at 33 weeks' gestation; the stimulus involves grasping the infant by both hands and pulling to sit. The response includes flexion at the neck, elbows, knees, and ankles. Hypotonia (decreased muscle tone) is suggested by head lag and lack of limb flexion.

trade name   *brand name, proprietary name.* The name of the particular formulation of a drug that is copyrighted or patented by a pharmaceutical manufacturer.

TRAFO   *See* tone reducing ankle foot orthosis.

train   A visual-perceptual motor milestone that requires the child to imitate the construction of a four-block (at 24 months of age) or five-block (at 30 months age) structure.

train

trainable   *See* trainable mental retardation (TMR).

trainable mental retardation (TMR)   Objectionable term once used to describe people with intelligence quotient (IQ) scores between 35 and 50.

trainable mentally handicapped (TMH) *See* trainable mental retardation (TMR).

Training for Acquisition of Language for Kids (TALK) An intensive and highly structured form of behavior analysis for teaching speech and language to young children with autism and other developmental disorders.

trait An inherited or acquired characteristic that is consistent, persistent, and stable.

tranquilizer An antianxiety drug. There are two groupings: major tranquilizers, which include the antipsychotic neuroleptics; and minor tranquilizers, which include the anxiolytic (antianxiety) drugs such as diazepam (trade name, Valium), chlordiazepoxide (trade name, Librium), and meprobamate (trade name, Miltown).

transactional model of development A theoretical model of development based on the assumption that development is facilitated by reciprocal interactions between a child and his or her environment. In this model, developmental outcomes at any time point are seen as resulting from the continuous dynamic interplay between a child's behavior, caregiver responses to that behavior, and environmental variables that influence both the child and the caregiver. This model has been applied specifically to a child's development of communication competency.

transactional support Development and implementation of specific plans to provide educational and emotional support to families to enable them to respond to their child's needs and interests, to appropriately modify and adapt the environment, to provide tools to enhance learning (e.g., picture communication, written schedules, and sensory supports), and to foster teamwork among professionals.

transcutaneous electrical nerve stimulation (TENS) An electrical stimulation technique used for pain relief.

transdisciplinary Describing a team approach to the diagnosis and treatment of neurodevelopmental disabilities. Such a team goes beyond the interdisciplinary model in that one or more of the professionals on the team cross the traditional boundaries of the disciplines. For example, both the pediatrician and the occupational therapist (OT) may assess and comment on a child's cognitive level. Thus, with a transdisciplinary approach, an individual professional can incorporate parts of the interdisciplinary team interaction.

Transdisciplinary Play-Based Assessment (TPBA) A set of criterion-referenced informal assessment scales for use with children whose developmental functioning is between the ages of 6 months and 6 years. A video-recorded play interaction session is scored by multiple professionals who observe four domains: sensorimotor, emotional and social, communication, and cognitive. The outcome focuses on intervention planning. TPBA represents a dynamic, team-based, naturalistic way to assess young children: An arena approach is used in the evaluation session such that an individual clinician or the parent interacts with the child while others observe and glean developmental information. TPBA allows for the simultaneous assessment of several domains and functions along with intervention planning. TPBA contrasts with sequential evaluation models, in which clinicians from various disciplines see children separately, confer regarding their impressions, and produce separate evaluation reports. *See also* play-based assessment.

transduction Reasoning by association. In psychology, reasoning from the particular to the particular, with co-occurrence being taken for a causal relationship.

transfer A modification that occurs in one behavior and that results in changes in a similar behavior (e.g., transfer of learning); a behavior reinforced in the presence of one stimulus event that occurs in the presence of a different stimulus (e.g., transfer of training).

transfer A visual-perceptual motor milestone in which the infant can get both hands to the mid-line and pass a grasped object from one hand to the other; it is typically present by 5 months of age.

transfer In second language learning, an error in a child's second language that is directly produced by the influences of the first or primary language.

transient evoked otoacoustic emissions (TEOAEs) Otoacoustic emissions (sounds generated from the inner ear) that are evoked by transient stimuli such as clicks or tone bursts. *See also* otoacoustic emissions (OAEs).

transient ischemic attack (TIA) A "ministroke"; a stroke in which symptoms resolve within 24 hours.

transient tachypnea of the newborn (TTN) *wet lung.* A self-limited breathing disorder in newborns that typically has no long-term developmental sequelae.

transillumination An older method of examining the head of a newborn or young infant. A very bright light source is placed against the child's head in a darkened room and the amount of surrounding lucency (light transmission) is observed. A marked increase in craniolucency suggests underlying structural impairments such as hydrocephalus (excess fluid under pressure in the brain), subdural effusion (fluid around the brain), cerebral atrophy (wasting), and porencephaly or hydranencephaly (absence of brain tissue).

transition A change from one activity to another. Many children with neurodevelop-mental disabilities have difficulties with transitions.

transition Generically speaking, the process of moving from one service system to another because one "ages out" of the age category served. In education and disabilities, individuals transition from early intervention to preschool service systems, then into kindergarten, with the most significant transition occurring when the individuals approach adulthood.

transition services Programs that help prepare students for adult roles. This might include addressing student needs in terms of skills for continuing their education, job and volunteer skills, skills for living in the community, and relationship skills. The Individuals with Disabilities Education Improvement Act (IDEA) of 2004 (PL 108-446) requires that initial transition planning be included in educational planning at age 16. *See also* Individuals with Disabilities Education Act Amendments (IDEA) of 1997 (PL 105-17), Individuals with Disabilities Education Act (IDEA) of 1990 (PL 101-476), Individuals with Disabilities Education Improvement Act (IDEA) of 2004 (PL 108-446).

transitional feeding A stage of infant feeding when breast milk and/or infant formula no longer adequately meets the child's nutritional needs and must be supplemented by the introduction of smooth or semisolid food.

transitional object An object or action that is transitional between mother and child, such as a security blanket or thumb sucking.

transitional spelling The pattern of spelling behaviors in which one begins to use many of the visual features of standard English spelling but overgeneralizes these features.

translation The linear movement of an object from the finger surface to the palm or from the palm to the fingers using one hand alone. An example is moving a coin from the palm to the fingertips to place it into a vending machine.

translocation A chromosomal abnormality in which a lost or broken part attaches to another chromosome, which may create a trisomy.

translucent symbol A symbol with a referent whose meaning may or may not be obvious. A relationship can be perceived between the symbol and the referent once the meaning is provided.

transparent symbol A symbol with a referent whose shape, motion, or function is depicted to such an extent that the meaning of the symbol can be readily guessed in the absence of the referent.

transverse plane The anatomical plane that divides the body into an upper and a lower half.

transverse tongue reflex An oral-motor reflex innervated by cranial nerve XII, in which a tactile (touch) stimulus to the lateral (outside) surface of the tongue produces the response of tongue movement toward the side of the stimulus. This reflex is present by 7 months of gestation and disappears by 9 months of age.

trauma A wound or injury.

traumatic brain injury (TBI) A closed brain injury in an infant, child, or adult characterized by damage to the brain. TBI may be accidental or caused by child abuse. Long-term outcome is variable and related to the location and severity of the trauma. Not all brain injury produces TBI, but all TBI is secondary to brain injury.

trazodone Trade name, Desyrel. An antidepressant that is structurally unrelated to other antidepressants such as the tricyclics. Trazodone selectively blocks the reuptake of serotonin. A typical indication for use is depression with or without anxiety, but it has also been used to treat aggression and self-injurious behavior (SIB) in children with autism. Common side effects include drowsiness and dizziness.

Treacher Collins syndrome *Franceschetti-Klein syndrome, mandibulofacial dysostosis.* An extremely variable genetic syndrome that involves anomalies (malformations) of structures embryologically derived from the first branchial arch. The dysmorphology (atypical feature) spectrum includes malar hypoplasia (undergrowth of the mid-face with cheekbones flat or depressed), downslanting palpebral fissures (antimongoloid slant), lower lid defects (e.g., absent lower eyelashes), a large fish-like mouth, a receding chin, and malformations of the external pinna (ear). Intellectual disability is present in only 5% of cases, but learning disabilities occur in almost 50%. Neurocognitive impairments are more common in the presence of microcephaly (small head). Plastic surgery is usually indicated. Named after the British ophthalmologist Edward Treacher Collins (1862–1932). Inheritance follows an autosomal dominant pattern, with 100% penetrance; 60% of cases are fresh mutations. Treacher Collins syndrome is caused by mutation in the "treacle" gene (*TCOF1;* 606847).

Treatment and Education of Autistic and related Communication Handicapped Children (TEACCH) An intensive intervention approach in a structured educational environment for use with children with autism. Characterized by significant one-to-one interaction, TEACCH has much overlap with applied behavior analysis (ABA). The approach was developed by Eric Schopler (1927–2006) at the University of North Carolina, and that state has an extensive network of autism-related services that follow this model.

tremor Shaking, trembling. An extrapyramidal type of cerebral palsy whose chief characteristic is involuntary motor oscillations. Tremor is rare as an isolated finding and is often part of a mixed cerebral palsy picture with rigidity.

Trendelenburg gait *gluteus medius gait.* A lurching gait associated with hip abnormalities and weaknesses of the abductor muscles on the involved side. There are two types of Trendelenburg gait: compensated and uncompensated. Both types are associated with weakness of the gluteus medius (hip abductor) musculature. In an uncompensated Trendelenburg gait, the pelvis drops on the unaffected or unsupported side. In a compensated Trendelenburg gait, the trunk lunges to the same side as the weak gluteus medius (thereby preventing the drop of the unsupported hip).

Trendelenburg sign When a child stands on one leg, the pelvis on the opposite side should rise; if it falls, congenital hip dislocation or muscular weakness on the side of the standing leg should be suspected.

TRF *See* Teacher Report Form.

triangular facies A facial appearance associated with a number of different syndromes (e.g., Russell-Silver syndrome); the appearance results from disproportionate rates of growth of the calvarium (upper skull) and facial bones. Hydrocephalus (excess fluid under pressure in the brain) can contribute to a triangular facial appearance.

triangular facies

Tricare A federally funded managed health care system for military personnel and their dependents. Formerly known as the *Civilian Health and Medical Program of the Uniformed Services* (CHAMPUS).

trichobezoar A hairball produced in the stomach or intestinal tract after the ingestion of hair, as is often seen with trichotillomania (hair pulling). *See also* bezoar.

trichoglyphics Patterning of hair follicles, usually expressed as hair whorl patterns. Abnormal trichoglyphics are associated with underlying abnormalities of brain development.

tricho-rhinophalangeal syndrome type II *See* Landouzy-Dejerine dystrophy.

trichorrhexis nodosa Poorly pigmented, brittle hair found in some metabolic disorders.

trichosis An abnormality of hair. *See also* hypertrichosis, hypotrichosis.

trichothiodystrophy Brittle hair and sulfur deficiency seen in BIDS, IBIDS, and PIBIDS syndromes.

tricyclic antidepressant (TCA) A drug that blocks the reuptake of the neurotransmitters norepinephrine and serotonin in the brain and thus alleviates depression in people without organic brain damage. Major side effects include sedation, heart problems, and tardive dyskinesia (slow, rhythmic, automatic movements).

trigeminal nerve The fifth cranial nerve; provides sensation to the face and movement to the jaw for chewing.

trigger The stimulus that initiates a behavioral response. For example, saying "no" to a child may trigger a tantrum.

trigonocephaly A triangular-shaped skull with one of the apexes (extremities) of the triangle being the mid-forehead. Trigonocephaly results from the premature fusion of the metopic (mid-forehead) suture and can contribute to the appearance of hypotelorism (decreased distance between the eyes). A cosmetic deformity, it rarely has developmental consequences. In the presence of a more generalized craniosynostosis (premature fusion of skull sutures) or microcephaly (small head), the risk of developmental disability is increased.

triiodothyronine (T3)   A thyroid hormone that is elevated in hyperthyroidism and decreased in hypothyroidism.

Trileptal   *See* oxcarbazepine.

trimester   A time period of 3 months. The term *trimester* is usually used when describing the thirds of a pregnancy. Common features and certain predictive pathologies (conditions) in the developing fetus are noted by their occurrence in the first, second, or third trimester of a pregnancy.

trimester bleeding   Maternal bleeding during pregnancy that indicates a potential problem with the pregnancy. First trimester bleeding (during the first 3 months of the pregnancy) is related more to problems with the infant (e.g., congenital defects that could lead to a threat of miscarriage), whereas third trimester bleeding (during the last 3 months of the pregnancy) suggests a problem with the placenta (e.g., previa, abruptio).

triphalangeal thumb   A thumb with three phalanges (finger bones).

triple X syndrome   *See* XXX syndrome.

triplegia   Literally, "three paralysis." A topographical subtype of spastic cerebral palsy in which three extremities (arms or legs) are seriously involved and one extremity is relatively spared. Most cases of triplegia represent the overlapping occurrence of a diplegia (paralysis affecting primarily the lower extremities) with a hemiplegia (paralysis of one side of the body).

triploid   A cell or organism with 3 times the haploid chromosomal complement. Unless associated with mosaicism, this condition is lethal in humans.

triploidy   *69, XXX, XXY/69.* In individuals with this disorder, phenotype and growth is normal, motor development is slow, and learning difficulties or intellectual disability occur. Behavior difficulties are frequent, and psychiatric disturbances may occur. Body asymmetry, syndactyly (fused digits) of the third and fourth fingers, clubfoot, abnormal male genitalia, kidney abnormalities, heart defects, dysplastic (deformed) ears, cleft lip and/or palate, and iris/choroid colobomas (eye slits) are common. The most frequent cause is fertilization of the egg by two sperm

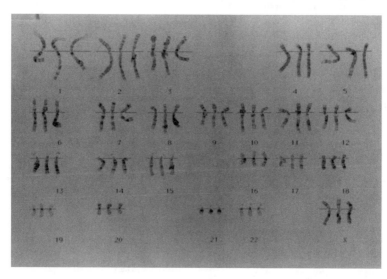

triploidy

(dispermy), resulting in three copies of each chromosome, rather than two.

tripod grasp The position of the hand for holding a pencil in which the thumb is turned toward the index and middle finger and the pencil is held by the pads of those fingers. With a static tripod pencil grasp, writing is accomplished by moving the whole hand or arm rather than the fingers; with a dynamic tripod pencil grasp, writing is accomplished by moving the fingers with the forearm resting on the writing surface.

trisomy The state of having three of a given chromosome instead of the usual pair. Trisomy 21, usually called Down syndrome, is an example. *See* cat eye syndrome.

trisomy 4p A trisomy for all or most of the short arm of chromosome 4. A chromosomal disorder characterized by growth deficiency, severe intellectual disability, a peculiar facies, and seizures. Inheritance patterns are unclear; however, when the disorder is suspected, prenatal diagnosis can be made through chorionic villus sampling, amniocentesis, or percutaneous umbilical blood sampling. Treatment is symptomatic for congenital defects and includes special education.

trisomy 6 long arm *See* duplication 6q dup(6)(q25-qter).

trisomy 8 mosaicism *47,XX or XY, + 8.* The clinical features of trisomy 8 mosaicism may vary depending on the number of cells with trisomy 8 and the specific cell type(s) affected. In general, there is an unusual face with moderately deep-set eyes, hypertelorism (widely spaced eyes), prominent cupped ears, full lips with inverted lower lip, a small jaw, and a cleft palate. There may be camptodactyly (fixed flexion) of the second through fifth fingers, deep creases in the palms and soles, other major joint contractures, vertebral abnormalities, absent patellae (knee caps), conductive deafness, seizures, and mild to severe intellectual disability.

trisomy 9 mosaicism *47,XX or XY, + 9; trisomy 9.* Mosaicism associated with growth failure, multiple anomalies, and severe intellectual disability. Infants with trisomy 9 mosaicism are small at birth and have deep-set eyes, upslanting palpebral fissures (eye slits), a prominent nasal bridge, and small and atypical ears. There are also multiple joint abnormalities with abnormal positioning of the hips, knees, elbows, and fingers. Death usually occurs in infancy.

trisomy 9p A trisomy for all or part of the short arm of chromosome 9. A chromosomal disorder characterized by intellectual disability, growth deficiency, a peculiar facies, and short fingers and/or toes. Although trisomy 9p is rare, if a parent is a carrier of a balanced translocation, recurrence risks are high. When de novo (new) cases occur, there is no apparent recurrence risk. Treatment is symptomatic and includes special education.

trisomy 13 syndrome *D1 trisomy syndrome, Patau syndrome.* A chromosomal disorder secondary to the presence of an extra chromosome 13 (D group). Findings include microcephaly (abnormally small head), incomplete development of the forebrain, severe intellectual disability, clefting, hyperconvex nails, and polydactyly (extra fingers or toes). Fewer than 1 child in 5 with this syndrome survives the first year of life. Advanced maternal age is a contributing factor in the occurrence of this syndrome. Incidence is estimated at 1 in 8,000. Although inheritance patterns are unclear, when the syndrome is suspected, prenatal diagnosis can be made through chorionic villus sampling or amniocentesis. Occasionally, ultrasound indications of a decreased ratio of head-to-trunk circumferences indicate the need for prenatal screening. Treatment is symptomatic.

trisomy 18 syndrome   *E trisomy; Edwards syndrome; 47,+18.* A chromosomal syndrome secondary to the presence of an extra chromosome 18 (E group), usually as a free-lying trisomy. Findings include clenched hands with overlapping fingers, rocker-bottom feet, short sternum, heart disease, severe intellectual disability, and failure to thrive (poor growth). Only 10% of children with this syndrome survive the first year of life. Incidence is noted as 1 in 3,000 births. When the syndrome is suspected, prenatal diagnosis can be made through amniocentesis by the second trimester. Occasionally, ultrasound indicates the need for prenatal screening. Advanced maternal age is a contributory factor in the occurrence of trisomy 18 syndrome. Treatment is symptomatic.

trisomy 21   *See* Down syndrome (DS).

trisomy G   *See* Down syndrome (DS).

trochlear nerve   The fourth cranial nerve, which innervates one of the muscles of the eye. Damage to the trochlear nerve will produce mild convergent strabismus (squint), diplopia (double vision) or downward gaze, and a compensatory head tilt.

truancy   Unjustifiable absence from school without parental knowledge or consent. Unjustifiable absence with parental consent can lead to charges of educational neglect. Truancy and other forms of sociopathic behavior are common outcomes for children with attention-deficit/hyperactivity disorder (ADHD) or learning disabilities that are inadequately treated.

true negative rate   *See* specificity.

true positive rate   *See* sensitivity.

tryptophan   A naturally occurring amino acid that is sometimes used as a supplement to treat autism.

TS   *See* tuberous sclerosis syndrome.

TSC   Tuberous sclerosis complex. *See* tuberous sclerosis (TS) syndrome.

TSC1   Tuberous sclerosis complex 1 (9q34). *See* tuberous sclerosis (TS) syndrome.

TSC2   Tuberous sclerosis complex 2 (16p3). *See* tuberous sclerosis (TS) syndrome.

T-score   A standard score based on a distribution with a mean of 50 and a standard deviation of 10.

TSFI   *See* Test of Sensory Function in Infants.

TSI   *See* DeGangi-Berk Test of Sensory Integration.

TSS   *See* Therapeutic Support Staff worker.

T3   *See* triiodothyronine.

TT   *See* therapeutic touch.

TTFC-2   *See* Token Test for Children–Revised.

TTN   *See* transient tachypnea of the newborn.

TTR   *See* type-token ratio.

tube feeding   *See* enteral feeding.

tuberous sclerosis (TS) syndrome   *adenoma sebaceum, Bourneville-Pringle syndrome, epiloia, tuberous sclerosis complex (TSC), tuberous sclerosis complex 1 (9q34) (TSC1), tuberous sclerosis complex 2 (16p3) (TSC2).* A genetic neurocutaneous (of the nervous system and skin) syndrome of multiple raised skin lesions (predominantly on the face) that may vary in color from white, to yellow, to brown; café au lait spots; renal (kidney) cysts; tooth enamel defects; intellectual disability; and seizures resulting from growths in the cortex and white matter of the brain. Occasionally, malignant brain tumors occur. Between 25% and 50% of individuals with TS have autism. Incidence is estimated at between 1 in 10,000 and 1 in 50,000. Inheritance is autosomal dominant, with most cases (85%) representing de novo (new) mutations. Tuberous sclerosis complex 1 can be caused by a mutation in the *TSC1* gene on chromosome 9q34. Tuberous sclerosis complex 2 can be caused by a mutation in the *TSC2* gene on chromosome 16p13. Treatment includes anticonvulsants for seizures and surgery or plastic surgery for dermatological (skin) involvement.

Turner-like syndrome *See* Noonan syndrome.

Turner syndrome *45,X/46,XX; 45X; 45X/ 46,XY; 46,X,del(Xp); 46Xdel(Xq); 46X,i(Xq).* A syndrome characterized by short stature; pterygium colli (a webbed neck) with a low posterior hairline; widely spaced nipples on a shield-shaped chest; congenital lymphedema with residual puffiness on the tops of the fingers and toes; and ovarian dysgenesis (failure of the ovaries to develop) leading to sexual infantilism with amenorrhea (lack of periods), infertility, and absent secondary sexual characteristics (e.g., lack of breast development). There is also cubitus valgus (an increased carrying angle at the elbows) and occasional other skeletal (50%), cardiac (35%), and renal (kidney; 60%) abnormalities. There is an increased incidence of otitis (ear infections), which contributes to decreased speech and language abilities; however, girls with Turner syndrome have a low prevalence of speech-language disorders compared with the rate of speech language disorders in other sex chromosome anomalies. Turner syndrome is usually identifiable at birth. Incidence is 1 in 5,000 births, or 1 in 2,500 among phenotypic females; it is sporadic, with minimal recurrence risk. Prenatal diagnosis is available. Treatment is symptomatic and focuses on both growth hormone and cyclic estrogen replacement therapy to normalize psychobiology for the affected individuals. Named after the American endocrinologist Henry Turner (1892–1970).

turribrachycephaly *See* acrocephaly.

TVMS-R *See* Test of Visual-Motor Skills–Revised.

TVPS-3 *See* Test of Visual-Perceptual Skills–Third Edition.

22q deletion syndrome *See* velocardiofacial syndrome.

twin Either of two offspring produced from one pregnancy. Two separate conception processes can produce twins. Monozygotic twinning results from a single (*mono*) fertilized egg that splits into two embryos. Although this duplication process occurs in all pregnancies, typically only one of the duplicates survives. The children resulting from this type of process are called *identical twins*. The other type of twinning process, dizygotic twinning, results from the production and fertilization of two (*di*) separate eggs during the conception process. Both fertilized eggs are nurtured during a single pregnancy, resulting in fraternal twins. Fraternal twins can be of either the same or opposite sex. Although most twin births produce typical children, twinning is nonetheless an atypical process in that the uterus of the human female is built for one fetus. Thus, many twin pregnancies are complicated by prematurity; infants smaller than expected for the length of the pregnancy; and an increased number of birth complications, including premature rupture of membranes, preeclampsia, toxicity, hypertension (high blood pressure), and fetal distress. In addition, one twin is usually smaller in utero and postnatally is slower to grow. Twin pregnancies, therefore, are at greater risk for pre- and perinatal birth trauma leading to developmental disabilities. The incidence of twin pregnancies is 1 in 90 births. Monozygotic twins represent one fourth of twin pregnancies, or 1 in 360 births.

two-group approach In the study of intellectual disability, the separation of organic brain damage from cultural familial intellectual disability; the former group fits into a difference approach and the latter into a developmental approach. With the increasing identification of medical etiologies (causes) for mild intellectual disability, this theory may receive increasing support, although with a significant reapportionment between the two groups. *See also* difference approach.

two-point discrimination   A component of the neurological assessment of sensation; difficulty in discriminating whether the skin has been touched at one or two close points is interpreted as a sign of parietal lobe dysfunction.

TWS-4   *See* Test of Written Spelling–Fourth Edition.

Tylenol   *See* acetaminophen.

tympanic membrane   The eardrum; a pearly gray glistening membrane with a triangular area of reflected light. The tympanic membrane is examined visually with an otoscope for signs of otitis media (middle ear infection).

tympanic neurectomy   A surgical procedure that disrupts parasympathetic innervation to the parotid gland as a treatment for drooling. It is usually performed bilaterally and is combined with a chorda tympani section.

tympanometry   A test of the measurement of the mobility of the tympanic membrane and the middle ear that is used to identify conditions such as a perforated eardrum and fluid in the middle ear. The graphic representation of the test results is a tympanogram.

tympanostomy tubes   *See* pressure equalization (PE) tubes.

type-token ratio (TTR)   A measure of the different words that an individual produces. The TTR is calculated by counting each different word in a sample; if a word is repeated in the sample, it is only counted once.

typically developing (TD)   Describing children whose overall development or whose development in specific areas matches the development of most other children without any developmental impairments or diagnoses. Such children were formerly known as *normal.*

typus degenerativus amstelodamensis   *See* Cornelia de Lange syndrome.

tyrosinemia   An inborn error of metabolism in which the defect is in the metabolism of tyrosine. There are two types: 1) type 1, which affects the liver, kidneys, and growth, and 2) type 2, or oculocutaneous tyrosinemia, which causes intellectual disability, microcephaly (small head), and corneal clouding.

Uu

UA *See* urinalysis.

UAF University affiliated facility. *See* University Centers for Excellence in Developmental Disabilities Education, Research, and Service (UCE or UCEDD).

UAP University affiliated program. *See* University Centers for Excellence in Developmental Disabilities Education, Research, and Service (UCE or UCEDD).

UBE3A A gene located on chromosome 15 that provides instructions for producing the enzyme ubiquitin protein ligase. Mutations in this gene are responsible for some cases of Angelman syndrome.

UCBL shoe-insert–type orthosis A corrective appliance named for the original brand, University of California Biomechanics Laboratory.

UCE *See* University Centers for Excellence in Developmental Disabilities Education, Research, and Service.

UCEDD *See* University Centers for Excellence in Developmental Disabilities Education, Research, and Service.

UCP *See* United Cerebral Palsy.

UCPA United Cerebral Palsy Associations. *See* United Cerebral Palsy (UCP).

ulna The thinner of the two bones of the forearm. *See also* radius.

(label: ulna)

ulnar grasp *simian grasp.* An immature grasp pattern in which the object is apprehended (grasped) from the side of the hand farthest from the thumb.

ulnar grasp

ultrasound *ultrasonography.* A radiological technique that uses the echo of sound waves to visualize the deep structures of the body (e.g., heart, kidneys, fetal structures). Because it is not effective for visualizing structures through bone, it is primarily used to visualize the brain in fetuses in utero or infants whose fontanels (soft spots on the skull) are still open.

umbilical hernia A weakening of the abdominal wall that leads to a bulging and a protrusion of the abdominal contents outward at the site of the umbilicus (navel; belly button). The hernia remains well covered with skin, causes no discomfort, and does not usually become incarcerated (trapped) or strangulated (twisted on itself so that it creates an obstruction) as can hernias in other locations (e.g., inguinal [groin] hernias). The hernia usually closes off spontaneously by 2 years of age.

umbilicus Navel; belly button.

unaided augmentative and alternative communication (AAC) A type of AAC that uses the person's body to supplement or enhance speech (e.g., through the use of sign language instead of a communication device).

uncinate fit   Olfactory (related to the sense of smell) hallucinations associated with temporal lobe (a lateral segment of the brain) tumors or seizures. These are described as the perception of unpleasant but usually unidentifiable odors.

unconditioned reflexes   Inborn, biological, permanent reactions of organisms to environmental stimuli, mediated by the nervous system. Such responses (e.g., reflexes such as the eye blink and startle reaction) do not have to be learned.

underresponsiveness   *See* hyporesponsivity.

unfisted   Describing the tendency of infants' hands to remain open at rest for more than half of the time. The unfisted position stands in contrast to the earlier fisting (closed hand position) and typically becomes the preferred hand posture after 3 months of age.

unidisciplinary   Describing an approach to the diagnosis and treatment of developmental disabilities that focuses almost exclusively on the contribution by a single professional discipline or specialty, not a team approach.

unilateral   Pertaining to one side of the body.

unilateral cleft   A cleft that affects only one side (right or left) of the oral cavity.

unilateral upper motor neuron dysarthria A motor speech disorder that results in speech that is unclear or difficult to understand and that is characterized by movements that are slow and reduced in range of motion because of weakness caused by spasticity (increased muscle tone).

uniparental disomy   *genomic imprinting.* The case in which both chromosomes in a pair originate from the same parent (e.g., maternal disomy), in contrast to the usual case in which each pair contains one chromosome from each parent. Disomy pairs can contain identical copies of a chromosome from the same parent (isodisomy) or two different chromosomes from the same parent (heterodisomy). Uniparental disomy has been implicated in certain genetic syndromes in which no genetic material is lost (deleted) or misplaced (translocated) such that lack of contribution of genetic material from both parents is responsible for abnormalities.

UNIT   *See* Universal Nonverbal Intelligence Test.

United Cerebral Palsy (UCP)   A national voluntary association of state and local affiliates along with the national organization, United Cerebral Palsy Associations (UCPA), that provides and coordinates direct services and formulates national policies for providing services for children and adults with cerebral palsy. Standards, advocacy, research, and training represent additional goals and activities.

universal access   The design of environments and facilities to be accessible to everyone regardless of ability or disability.

universal design   A philosophy for designing and delivering services in the educational setting that are usable by students with the widest possible range of functional capabilities. Emerging from the recognition of the broad benefits of "barrier-free" access, universal design applies broadly to the design and construction of buildings, products, and environments to be usable and effective for everyone, not just people with disabilities (e.g., curb cuts that ease access not only for individuals with mobility impairments but also for strollers and bicycles). *See also* barrier-free.

Universal Nonverbal Intelligence Test (UNIT)   An entirely nonverbal (using hand and body gestures and paper and pencil) measure of intelligence for use with people 5;0–17;11 years that takes 10 (Abbreviated Battery) to 45 (Extended Battery) minutes to administer.

university affiliated facility (UAF) *See* University Centers for Excellence in Developmental Disabilities Education, Research, and Service (UCE or UCEDD).

university affiliated program (UAP) *See* University Centers for Excellence in Developmental Disabilities Education, Research, and Service (UCE or UCEDD).

University Centers for Excellence in Developmental Disabilities Education, Research, and Service (UCE or UCEDD) A national network of programs affiliated with universities and teaching hospitals that provides interdisciplinary training for professionals and paraprofessionals in the field of developmental disabilities and offers programs and services for children with disabilities and their families. UCEDDs work to accomplish a shared vision that foresees a nation in which all Americans, including Americans with disabilities, participate fully in their communities. Independence, productivity, and community inclusion are key components of this vision. Some UCEDDs provide direct services; individual centers have staff with expertise in a variety of areas and can furnish information, technical assistance, and in-service training to community agencies, service providers, parent groups, and others. Centers that received building construction monies were originally referred to as university affiliated facilities (UAFs), then as university affiliated programs (UAPs). *See also* Developmental Disabilities Assistance and Bill of Rights Act Amendments of 2000 (PL 106-402).

University Centers on Disabilities *See* University Centers for Excellence in Developmental Disabilities Education, Research, and Service (UCEDD).

untoward reaction A harmful side effect.

upper extremity Arm, forearm, or hand.

upper respiratory infection (URI) A cold, usually caused by a virus.

upper/lower segment ratio The distance from the top of the head to the pubic bone divided by the distance from the pubic bone to the sole of the foot. This number is 1.7 at birth, 1.0 at 10 years of age, and just less than 1.0 in adults. Changes in this ratio are useful to consider in the diagnosis of both endocrine and genetic growth disorders.

upregulation An increase in a cellular component or an increase in the cellular response to an external stimulus, such as an increase in the number of receptors on the surface of cells, resulting in the cells becoming more sensitive to a hormone or another agent. For example, there is an increase in uterine oxytocin receptors in the third trimester of pregnancy, promoting the contraction of the smooth muscle of the uterus.

urea cycle defect One of a group of genetic metabolic diseases, each representing a failure in one of the steps in the conversion of ammonia to urea. Symptoms associated with the resulting hyperammonemia (increased level of ammonia in the blood) include recurrent episodes of lethargy (drowsiness), vomiting, and seizures; repeated episodes lead to increasing intellectual disability. Four of the five enzyme deficits are inherited in an autosomal recessive pattern. Dialysis (the artificial filtering of the blood) is used in the acute stage to reduce the hyperammonemia; drugs, low-protein diets, and amino acid supplements can then be used to regulate the ammonia level depending on the type and severity of the disorder.

Urecholine *See* bethanechol.

URI *See* upper respiratory infection.

urinalysis (UA)　A group of visual, physical, and chemical tests performed on urine specimens.

urinary tract infection (UTI)　A bladder infection; symptoms include urinary frequency (sensation of needing to urinate often) and urgency (sensation of needing to urinate right away), dysuria (pain and discomfort on urination), fever, and malaise (feeling of illness). Recurrent UTIs in children with disability syndromes should raise the suspicion of an underlying genitourinary malformation.

urticaria　Hives. This red, blotchy, and itchy skin reaction can be a reaction to foods or drugs but is most commonly of unknown origin. Urticaria often does not recur.

Usher syndrome　A genetic syndrome characterized by congenital (from birth) nonprogressive sensorineural (auditory nerve) hearing loss of variable severity, retinitis pigmentosa (night blindness and progressively restricted visual field [area of vision]), and loss of olfactory (sense of smell) and vestibular (balance) functions. Neuropsychiatric difficulties occur in 25% of cases. At least 11 loci are involved in causing this syndrome. Inheritance can be autosomal recessive, autosomal dominant, or X-linked. The syndrome accounts for approximately 5% of children with severe hearing loss and half of all adults with deafness and blindness. Named for the Scottish ophthalmologist Charles Usher (1865–1942).

Utah Test of Language Development–Fourth Edition (UTLD-4)　A language test for use with typical children and children with disabilities ages 3;0–9;11 years; it yields subtest standard scores for language comprehension and language expression as well as a language quotient. Administration time is 30–45 minutes.

UTI　*See* urinary tract infection.

UTLD-4　*See* Utah Test of Language Development–Fourth Edition.

Uzgiris-Hunt Ordinal Scales of Psychological Development　*See* Ordinal Scales of Psychological Development.

Vv

VA shunt   *See* ventriculoatrial shunt.

VAB   *See* Vulpe Assessment Battery.

VACTERL   Expansion of VATER (vertebral dysgenesis, anal atresia, tracheoesophageal fistula, esophageal atresia, renal anomalies) to include cardiac and limb anomalies.

VADS   *See* Visual Aural Digit Span Test.

vagal nerve stimulator (VNS)   A surgically implanted device used to treat seizures. The VNS uses a battery to send regular electrical pulses to the vagus nerve and can be activated to send a pulse if a seizure has started.

vagus nerve   The 10th cranial nerve; provides the motor and sensory innervation (supply of nerves) to the pharynx (throat) and the larynx (voicebox), as well as parasympathetic (control of vegetative functions) innervation to the thoracic (heart and lungs) and abdominal (gastrointestinal tract) viscera.

VAKT   Visual, auditory, kinesthetic, tactile. *See* Fernald word learning technique.

valgus   Bent outward, away from the midline (the central line that divides the body in half).

validation   The process of determining a test's validity, or its ability to measure what it claims to measure.

validity   The degree to which an instrument measures what it purports to measure. The extent to which theory and evidence support the use of a tool to measure a trait, skill, or phenomenon. Evidence is collected to support the interpretations of scores for particular applications (e.g., how well a test score predicts later performance or whether its properties hold for special populations; e.g., whether an intelligence quotient [IQ] test is valid for use with individuals with various levels of visual impairment). There are several types of validity: *Content validity* assesses the degree to which the test adequately samples the range of target behaviors (e.g., that a test that claims to measure mathematical ability includes all types of mathematics problems) and all items relate to the subject of the test (e.g., that all the items tap mathematical ability, not some other, irrelevant skill); *face validity* is a subjective impression that the test strongly appears to measure what it claims to measure (e.g., "on its face," the test's contents appear to tap the ability they are designed to assess); *concurrent validity* correlates test scores with performance on another test recognized as a valid measure of the same domain; *construct validity* refers to the ability to explain scores on the test in accordance with a theoretical model of behavior; and *predictive validity* (sometimes called *criterion-related validity*) is a measure of how well test scores predict future behavior (e.g., how they hold up over time and in relation to some external criterion; e.g., Do SAT scores predict success in college?).

Valium *See* diazepam. *See also* Diastat, rectal diazepam.

valproic acid *valproate sodium.* Trade names, Depacon; Depakene; Depakote; Valproate. An anticonvulsant drug used for the treatment of absence seizures (both isolated and when other seizure types are present), generalized tonic-clonic seizures, and partial seizures. Valproic acid is not used in infants, as they are more likely to develop liver damage. It can also produce nausea, weight gain, reversible hair loss, drowsiness, and tremors and rarely can affect blood cells. Usage in pregnancy has been associated with an increased incidence of neural tube defects (e.g., myelomeningocele) as well as a risk of fetal antiepileptic drug syndrome (specific dysmorphic features secondary to intrauterine drug exposure). Valproic acid produces only minimal cognitive impairment; when used concurrently with phenobarbital, it can increase the blood level of that drug and cause sedation (sleepiness). It can also increase the side effects of other anticonvulsants such as carbamazepine (trade name, Tegretol) or phenytoin (trade name, Dilantin). Valproic acid has been used successfully to treat hypomanic states in people with severe intellectual disability.

van Buchem syndrome *hyperostosis corticalis generalisata.* A genetic syndrome characterized by generalized bone overgrowth, most prominent in the skull and jaw, that can compress cranial nerves to produce facial palsy (paralysis of the facial muscles on one side of the face) and vision and hearing loss. Inheritance is autosomal recessive, with an autosomal dominant variant.

van der Woude syndrome *lip pit syndrome.* A genetic syndrome characterized by lower lip pits (indentations), cleft lip with or without cleft palate, and hypodontia (decreased number of teeth). Conductive (middle ear) hearing loss problems are common. Incidence is 1 in 100,000; inheritance is autosomal dominant with variable expression but high penetrance. van der Woude syndrome and the allelic disorder popliteal pterygium syndrome (PPS; 119500) can be caused by mutations in the gene encoding interferon regulatory factor-6 (*IRF6*) on chromosome 1q32-q41.

vancomycin An antibiotic with potentially serious side effects that has been used to treat autism.

Vanderbilt Diagnostic ADHD Parent and Teacher Rating Scales Behavior rating scales to be completed by the parent and teacher to help determine the severity of attention-related problems and how they affect classroom behavior and academic performance. These screening scales provide results that support impressions of attention-deficit/hyperactivity disorder (ADHD)—primarily inattentive type; ADHD—primarily impulsive/hyperactive type; ADHD—combined type; oppositional defiant disorder; conduct disorder; anxiety or depression symptoms; academic performance problems in reading, mathematics, and/or written expression; classroom behavior problems in relationships with peers, assignment completion, following directions or rules, disrupting class, and organizational skills.

vanishing white matter disease (VWM) *childhood ataxia with diffuse central nervous system (CNS) hypomyelination (CACH).* A leukodystrophy (degenerative disease that affects the brain's white matter, or areas of the nerve cells coated with myelin, a fatty insulating material). Symptoms typically start in late infancy or early in childhood; they may worsen with fever or head trauma. VWM results in spasticity (increased muscle tone), ataxia (incoordination), seizures, and often some degree of intellectual disability. It ultimately progresses to death. Magnetic resonance imaging (MRI) of the brain shows abnormal white matter, and follow-up imaging documents its disappearance over time. Inheritance is autosomal dominant.

varicella *chickenpox.* An exanthem (rash) produced by a human herpes virus, varicella-zoster virus (VZV). The disease has a 2-week incubation period and is highly contagious with airborne spread via respiratory secretions from several days prior to the onset of the rash through the first week of the rash. The individual pockmarks are similar to those found in variola (smallpox) but have a different temporal course. An acute cerebellar syndrome with ataxia (unsteady gait), nystagmus (involuntary eye movements), vertigo (dizziness), tremor, slurred speech, and vomiting may persist for several weeks after the rash. A live attenuated (weakened) VZV vaccine was approved for use in the United States by the Food and Drug Administration in 1995.

varix A distended blood or lymph vessel. The term can refer specifically to a distended blood vessel on the superior or free edge of the vocal fold (cord).

varus Bent inward, toward the mid-line.

VATER Acronym for an association of congenital malformations: vertebral anomalies (malformation) and ventricular septal defect (VSD; heart defect), anal atresia (narrowing), tracheoesophageal fistula with esophageal atresia (abnormal connection between the windpipe and esophagus [the passage from the mouth to the stomach], with narrowing of the esophagus), radial (bone of the forearm) and renal (kidney) dysplasia (abnormalities), and single umbilical artery. When VATER is not part of a broader genetic syndrome, such as trisomy 18, people with the condition exhibit typical cognitive functioning.

VC *See* verbal comprehension.

VELBW *See* very extremely low birth weight.

velocardiofacial syndrome *del(22)(q11.21-q11.23), DiGeorge syndrome, Shprintzen syndrome, 22q deletion syndrome.* A genetic syndrome in which affected individuals usually have learning disabilities and mild intellectual disability. Psychiatric disturbances occur in about 10% of cases, particularly in adults. There is wide clinical variability among individuals, even within the same family. Anomalies include cleft palate, which is often submucous (under the surface layer, and so not readily visible); velopharyngeal insufficiency; congenital heart defects; some degree of immune deficiency; and often hypocalcemia (low calcium levels in the blood). Distinctive facial features include prominent long nose, narrow palpebral fissures (short eye slits), small mandible (lower jaw), and flat philtrum (area between the nose and upper lip). Speech problems may be severe, with hypernasality and poor enunciation due to hypotonic pharyngeal musculature. Structural heart defects are present in about 85% of cases.

velopharyngeal closure Sealing off of the nasal cavity by having the soft palate (soft, back part of the roof of the mouth, or velum) move up and backward to come into contact with the posterior pharyngeal wall (back of the throat).

velopharyngeal insufficiency A condition in which it is not possible for complete closure to occur between the oral (mouth) and nasal (nose) cavities because of inadequacies of structure or function. Velopharyngeal insufficiency is common with cleft palate or as a result of paralysis or weakness. Resulting speech has excessive nasal resonance.

velum The soft palate (roof of the mouth).

venipuncture The drawing of blood through a vein via a needle for a laboratory test.

ventilator dependent A person who requires intubation (placement of a breathing tube) and mechanical ventilation (machine breathing) because of an inability to breathe on his or her own over a prolonged period.

ventral Relating to the front; the anterior or belly surface; opposite of dorsal.

ventricle A cavity or chamber, usually in the heart or brain.

ventricular Pertaining to a ventricle.

ventricular septal defect (VSD) A relatively common congenital (from birth) heart defect (structural abnormality) in which an opening between the two ventricles (the large lower chambers) of the heart is sometimes accompanied by a murmur (abnormal heart sound on physical examination), cyanosis (blue color), and other symptoms of heart failure. VSD can be one of a number of organ system malformations included in genetic syndromes associated with intellectual disability and other developmental disabilities. It is possible to outgrow the effect of a small VSD.

ventriculoatrial (VA) shunt A tube used in the neurosurgical treatment for hydrocephalus (excess fluid in the brain). Doctors connect the ventricle of the brain with the right atrium of the heart by means of a tube with a pressure-regulated one-way flow valve. The VA shunt is more prone to infection but less likely to become obstructed (blocked) than the ventriculoperitoneal (VP) shunt (which connects the ventricle of the brain with the abdominal cavity).

ventriculography An outdated radiographic procedure used to visualize (with or without contrast material) the ventricles (fluid-containing spaces) of the brain.

ventriculomegaly Enlargement of the ventricles (fluid-containing spaces) of the brain. Large ventricles seen on computed tomography (CT) scan or ultrasound can be due to hydrocephalus (excess fluid in the brain) or to brain atrophy (wasting or loss of tissue, which creates more space for fluid to occupy).

ventriculoperitoneal (VP) shunt A mechanical pump with a pressure-regulated one-way valve that connects the ventricle of the brain with the peritoneal (abdominal) cavity to relieve the excess fluid (and pressure) in the brain in hydrocephalus. Complications of shunts include infection and meningitis (infection of the brain), blockage, and disconnection of the shunt tubing from the shunt. Shunt infections may contribute to brain injury and an acute decrease in cognitive functioning. The VP shunt is more prone to obstruction (blockage) but less likely to get infected than a ventriculoatrial (VA) shunt (which connects the ventricle of the brain with a chamber of the heart). *See also* shunt.

ventriculoperitoneal (VP) shunt

VEP *See* visual evoked potential.

VER *Visual evoked response. See* visual evoked potential (VEP).

Verbal Comprehension (VC) One of four composite indexes of the Wechsler Intelligence Scale for Children. Verbal Comprehension is comprised of five subtests: Information, Similarities, Vocabulary, Comprehension, and Word Reasoning. As an overall measure of verbal concept formation, verbal comprehension is thought to measure one's ability to listen to a question, draw upon learned information from both formal and informal education, reason through an answer, and express thoughts aloud.

vermilion border   The red-colored edge of the lip where it meets the paler skin of the face.

Versenate   *See* edetate calcium disodium.

versive seizure   One of the more common presentations of a focal seizure, in which the movement of the eyes, head, and extremities (arms or legs) is away from the side of the seizure focus (the area of the brain generating the seizure). Seizure disorders with versive movements and no loss of consciousness often have a frontal lobe focus (i.e., they originate in the front of the brain), whereas those with automatisms (robotic behaviors) and staring have a temporal lobe focus (i.e., they originate on one side of the brain). Electroencephalographic (EEG; brain wave) abnormalities are found anterior to (in front of) the rolandic gyrus (a specific brain area) in either the frontal or temporal lobes and may not be present between seizures. The etiology (cause) of these seizures ranges from underlying structural lesions (e.g., heterotopias [tissue displacement]) to idiopathic (unknown). Treatment is similar to that for other focal seizures.

vertigo   Loss of balance usually accompanied by a sense of dizziness, often attributed to vestibular (balance controlled by the inner ear) dysfunction, as in Ménière disease.

very extremely low birth weight (VELBW)   Relating to an infant with a birth weight less than 750 gm.

very low birth weight (VLBW)   Relating to an infant with a birth weight less than 1,500 grams.

vestibular dysfunction   A hypothetical etiology (cause) for learning disabilities derived from 1) an analogy with the perceptual distortions induced by Ménière disease and 2) the interpretation of mild motor dysfunction as labyrinthine (balance) rather than cortical (cognitive) in origin. Two treatments rely on this hypothesis: 1) the Ayres sensory integration approach and 2) the use of anti–motion sickness drugs (e.g., meclizine) to treat dyslexia.

vestibular processing disorders   A group of disorders thought to reflect a problem in central vestibular (inner ear) processing. The disorders typically involve poor equilibrium (balance) reactions and low muscle tone, particularly of the extensor muscles (those that straighten joints). They are best assessed using formal clinical observations and standardized test scores.

vestibular system   The sense having to do with the ability to detect head position and movement and the awareness of gravity. The source of vestibular function is the semicircular canals and otolith organs in the inner ear.

vestibular-bilateral disorder   A sensory integrative dysfunction characterized by shortened duration of postrotary nystagmus (involuntary eye movements after spinning), poor integration of the two sides of the body and brain, and difficulty learning to read or calculate.

VFSS   *videofluoroscopic swallow study. See* oral-pharyngeal motility study.

vibrotactile hearing aid   A device used to assist individuals with severe hearing impairments to detect sound by converting the sound into vibrations felt by the skin on the chest or arm; the vibrations are spread out in a regional manner, with high frequencies at one end and successively decreasing frequencies at the other end. A vibrotactile hearing aid is often used to supplement an augmentative hearing aid.

vicariation   A hypothetical process of recovery after brain damage that involves the takeover by other parts of the nervous system of functions lost when part of the brain is damaged. This theory is consistent with what is known about plasticity, the brain's capacity to reorganize according to function. The degree of vicariation depends on age; it is more likely to occur in early development.

video modeling   A technique in which an individual learns a new behavior by observing a video demonstration of the skill (a form of observational learning), for example, using videotaped examples of appropriate social interactions to teach social skills. In video modeling, clips of an individual's behavior are edited together to produce an appropriate chain of behaviors that the person is not executing (e.g., social interaction skills, walking a certain distance or around an obstacle). After being exposed to the complete chain via video, the individual is more likely to complete it.

video nasoendoscopy (VNE)   A procedure used to assess speech in which an endoscope (a lighted camera on a flexible base that is used to view inside the body) is used to view the back of the throat during speech.

video swallow study   *See* oral-pharyngeal motility study.

videofluorographic study of speech   An evaluation procedure that uses barium (a liquid that is opaque to x rays) and fluorography (the use of dynamic [moving] x-ray images) to assess velopharyngeal closure, lateral wall movement, and use of the articulators.

videofluoroscopic swallow study (VFSS)   *See* oral-pharyngeal motility study.

vigilance   Conscious mental effort to concentrate on a visual task.

vigilance   Steady-state wakefulness, alertness; the state of being awake, alert, and watchful.

Vineland Adaptive Behavior Scales–Second Edition (Vineland-II)   A structured interview used to measure adaptive behavior in people from birth to 90 years in five separate domains: Communication, Daily Living Skills, Socialization, Motor Skills, and Maladaptive Behaviors. The domains and the adaptive behavior composite can be expressed in a variety of derived scores, including standard scores (with a mean of 100 and a standard deviation of 15), age equivalents, and adaptive levels. Several forms are available: a Survey Interview Form, a Parent/Caregiver Rating Form, an Expanded Interview Form, and a Teacher Rating Form. Extensive standardization, reliability, and validity data are provided in the manuals for the different editions. Impairments in adaptive behavior as measured by this type of instrument are a necessary component in the diagnosis of intellectual disability; the test can be used with people with autism spectrum disorders, attention-deficit/hyperactivity disorder (ADHD), posttraumatic brain injury, hearing impairment, and dementia or Alzheimer's disease.

Vineland Social-Emotional Early Childhood Scales (SEEC)   A parent-report assessment of social-emotional functioning in children from birth to 5;11 years. The SEEC is derived from the socialization domain of the Vineland Adaptive Behavior Scales (VABS) and produces standard scores for the social-emotional composite and three scales: Interpersonal Relationships, Play and Leisure Time, and Coping Skills (ages 2 and older). A program planning profile is intended to assist in the development and monitoring of intervention goals.

virus   A noncellular infectious agent consisting of either deoxyribonucleic acid (DNA) or ribonucleic acid (RNA; both of which are types of genetic material that encode directions to make proteins) surrounded by a protein coat. Viral infections do not respond to antibiotics and are treated preventively by active immunization (vaccination) when available.

viscera The internal organs of the body. The abdominal viscera includes the liver, stomach, and intestines.

viscosity The persistence of traces of earlier structures of thinking into later, more mature levels. For example, children with intellectual disability will remain in a state of transition between two stages of development for a longer time period than children without intellectual disability.

visual acuity Vision. A measure of how well one sees. Most vision screening generates a distance that one eye can see in relation to the distance most people can see. For example, 20/100 vision means that the eye with impaired vision can see at 20 feet what the normal eye can see at 100 feet. More severe visual disturbance is reflected by the inability to detect movement or light. Lack of visual acuity is called *blindness.* Corrective lenses (glasses or contact lenses) attempt to correct vision as closely as possible to 20/20. *Legal blindness* is defined as a visual acuity that can only be corrected to 20/200. Monocular (one eye) poor vision is often asymptomatic (without symptoms) but can result in strabismus (crossed eyes). Visual acuity screening for children is routinely performed in most doctors' offices and schools.

visual, auditory, kinesthetic, tactile (VAKT) *See* Fernald word learning technique.

Visual Aural Digit Span Test (VADS) A refinement of digit span (the repetition of increasingly longer sequences of digits or numbers as a test of auditory sequential memory [memory of what is heard, in a specific order]) used to assess learning style in children from 5;5 to 12;9 years. The number sequences are presented both orally (spoken) and visually (on printed cards), and the responses are both oral and written. The four subtest results are combined to generate six further subscores for aural input, visual input, oral expression, written expression, intrasensory (input and output in the same sensory mode) integration, and intersensory (input and output in different sensory modes) integration. The test is brief and nonthreatening and provides a useful screening or confirmation of more extensive learning disability evaluations.

visual closure Identification of forms or objects from incomplete presentations.

visual discrimination The ability to detect features of visual stimuli for recognition, matching, and categorization.

visual evoked potential (VEP) *visual evoked response (VER).* A quantitative measure of the response of the occiput (the back area of the brain responsible for processing visual information) to a light stimulus as measured on an electroencephalogram (EEG; or a recording of brain wave activity). The VEP provides information about visual activity as well as the integrity of the nerves in the visual system that connect the eye and brain. It is used in the diagnosis of leukodystrophies, lipidoses, demyelinating diseases, and the optic neuritis found in Friedreich ataxia. Values will be abnormal in cortical blindness (loss of sight due to a brain lesion [injury] located specifically in the occipital or visual area of the cerebral cortex) but normal in people with visual-perceptual problems (difficulties interpreting visual information).

visual fields The areas that the eyes can see. The visual fields of the two eyes overlap, but not completely. Damage to the brain or optic nerve can cause a "visual field cut" or deficit ("hole" in the vision). This results in a partial loss of vision in each eye. If the damage is to the right side of the brain, then the vision loss will be to the left side of each eye (i.e., the temporal side of the left eye and the nasal side of the right eye). Visual field cuts are sometimes discovered when the individual neglects or ignores the side of the task that cannot be seen. These are often difficult to diagnose in children but should be suspected in the presence of a hemiplegia (paralysis of one side of the body).

visual fixation   The ability to focus on a stationary object.

visual imagery   The ability to imagine or visualize objects.

visual impairment   Visual acuity worse than 20/70 in the better eye after correction.

visual memory   The ability to retain information presented through visual sensory and perceptual pathways. Visual memory is the capacity to revisualize or retrieve specific images as needed and the ability to recognize previously viewed information on demand. The ability to recognize a face or recall the configuration of a previously viewed word as such are examples of visual memory.

visual perception   The ability to interpret information provided to the brain by the eyes. Determination and discrimination of spatial information (e.g., position in space and relative object size and location) are components of visual perception. Visual perception is not directly related to visual acuity (clearness of vision) or eye movements.

visual scanning   The ability to perceive visual information as the eyes are moving across the visual fields (areas the eyes can see).

visual scene display (VSD)   A picture, photograph, or virtual environment that depicts and represents a situation, place, or experience (e.g., messages such as the names of guests or food items served could be accessed from a photograph of a birthday party).

visual schedule   A system used to represent each activity in an individual's day with symbols or pictures.

visual supports   Visual symbols such as objects, photos, drawings, and text that are used as supplements (aids) to either the acquisition or use of expressive and receptive language. Children with developmental language disorders and those with autism spectrum disorders often benefit from the addition of visual supports to the teaching and use of verbal language. Visual supports are also used to increase understanding of or provide prompts and reminders for environmental expectations (e.g., a pictorial schedule can be used to assist a student with underdeveloped time concepts to be able to adhere to the environmental time structure).

visual threat   Blinking in response to a hand (or other object) moving suddenly toward the eyes. Such a response becomes consistent in infants after 2 months of age.

visual tracking   A perceptual-motor milestone observed in early infancy: At 1 month of age, the infant can consistently follow objects moving in a horizontal direction; by 2 months, in a vertical direction; and by 3 months, in a circle.

visual training   *See* optometric training.

visual-motor   *See* perceptual-motor.

visual-perceptual motor (VPM) function   The ability to interpret and integrate information obtained through the eyes in such a way that a motor act can be performed based upon that information. VPM ability can be tested by having the child copy geometric forms and designs. Tests such as the Beery Developmental Test of Visual Motor Integration (DTVMI) and the Bender Gestalt test are commonly used to assess VPM ability.

vital capacity   The amount of air that can be inhaled or exhaled (breathed in or out) with maximum effort. Vital capacity is an indicator of pulmonary reserve and a measure used to monitor asthma.

vitiligo Depigmentation (loss of pigment or color) of the skin, producing white patches. Acquired and often erratically progressive, vitiligo is a localized albinism. Vitiligo is seen in syndromes (e.g., Waardenburg syndrome), can be an isolated dermatological (skin) disorder, and may be associated genetically with sensorineural (auditory nerve) hearing loss.

VLBW *See* very low birth weight.

VNE *See* video nasoendoscopy.

VNS *See* vagal nerve stimulator.

VOCA *See* voice output communication aid.

vocabulary A lexicon; the words that a person understands (i.e., receptive) and can use (i.e., expressive). Vocabulary generally increases with age so that tests that estimate vocabulary size are used as measures of language function and as components of more generalized cognitive and educational assessments. The term can refer to the number of words (vocabulary size) or to the listing of all the words in a person's dictionary or lexicon.

Vocabulary A Wechsler (intelligence test) subtest that measures a child's word knowledge, learning ability, long-term memory, and degree of language development.

Vocabulary Comprehension Test A criterion-referenced checklist of 95 words and phrases for use with children 2–6 years of age.

vocal abuse Injurious vocal habits or misuse of the voice.

vocal stereotypy Random sounds not associated with speech that may be heard in people with autism. If these are accompanied by body movements, they may represent tics.

vocational rehabilitation The state agency that provides medical, therapeutic, counseling, education, training, assessment, and other services needed to prepare people with disabilities for work.

voice output communication aid (VOCA) A portable augmentative and alternative communication (AAC) device that produces synthetic or digitized (recorded) speech. Different messages can be accessed through visual-graphic symbols, words, or letters.

voiced The classification for consonants produced while the vocal folds are vibrating.

voiceless The classification for consonants produced without vocal fold vibrations.

voicing The phonological process that occurs when a voiced sound is substituted for a voiceless sound.

Vojta Pertaining to a system of physical therapy used to treat cerebral palsy. Developed by the Czech neurologist Václav Vojta (1917–2000), it focuses on reflex creeping patterns.

volitional release The developmental hand skill of dropping an object on purpose (casting, throwing) as opposed to a reflexive (involuntary) hand opening.

von Recklinghausen disease Neurofibromatosis type 1. *See* neurofibromatosis (NF).

V1 *See* primary visual cortex.

vowelization The phonological process that occurs when a vowel is substituted for a liquid phoneme.

voxel A volume element in a three-dimensional (3D) space. The 3D analogue of a two-dimensional (2D) pixel.

VP shunt *See* ventriculoperitoneal shunt.

VPM function *See* visual-perceptual motor function.

VSD *See* ventricular septal defect.

VSD   *See* visual scene display.

vulnerable child syndrome   A behavioral syndrome observed in parents in reaction to the earlier threatened loss of their child. A mother may continue to express and act on (usually in the form of overprotection) unrealistic fears over the health and survival of, for example, a child who had been born premature but is now a healthy preschooler. Illness in the first several months of life is especially liable to engender a continuing parental misperception of childhood vulnerability and deserves firm and caring supportive counseling. Separation anxiety (reluctance to let the child out of the house), infantilization (treating the child as though he or she were much younger and less capable), and hypochondriacal (excessive and unjustified worry about health) concerns are common. Vulnerable child syndrome can be observed in the parents of children with developmental disabilities when the latter were secondary to an early life-threatening event. Vulnerable child syndrome can also occur in the parents of a child who has always been healthy but whose sibling has died.

Vulpe Assessment Battery (VAB)   A comprehensive developmental instrument for use with children from birth through 6 years of age.

VWM   *See* vanishing white matter disease.

VZV   Varicella-zoster virus. *See* varicella.

Ww

Waardenburg syndrome An autosomal dominant genetic condition characterized by lateral displacement of the medial canthi (a wider than usual distance between the inner corners of the eye) and lacrimal punctae (tear duct openings) with a broad nasal root, heterochromia irides (eyes of different colors), patchy hypopigmentation (areas that lack skin color), hyperplasia (overgrowth) of the medial (closest to the nose) portions of the eyebrows, and congenital (from birth) sensorineural (involving damage to the auditory nerve) hearing loss. Named after the Dutch ophthalmologist Petrus Waardenburg (1886–1979). *See also* heterochromia irides.

Wachs Analysis of Cognitive Structures A nonverbal Piagetian scale for use with preschool children from 3 to 6 years of age.

WAGR syndrome *aniridia–Wilms tumor association, del(11)(p13p14), deletion 11p.* The acronym WAGR stands for **W**ilms tumor, **a**niridia, **g**enitourinary problems, and intellectual disability (formerly *retardation*). This interstitial chromosome deletion (missing piece) results in a set of anomalies (abnormalities) that includes the following facial dysmorphisms: prominent lips, small mandible (lower jaw), malformed ears, aniridia (absent iris), cataracts (clouding of the lens of the eye), and ptosis (drooping eyelids). Intellectual disability may be severe and associated with microcephaly (small head). In males, testes may not be descended, and hypospadias (the urethra opening on the underside of the penis) is often found; the genitalia in both sexes may be ambiguous. The risk of Wilms tumor is about 60% in those with clinical features and a visible chromosome deletion.

WAIS-IV *See* Wechsler Adult Intelligence Scale–Fourth Edition.

Waldeyer's ring Rings of lymphatic tissue (that filter the lymph, or the fluid that flows between the body's cells) in the mouth and nasal cavities, including the tonsils and adenoids.

Walker-Warburg syndrome A rare congenital form of severe muscular dystrophy associated with brain abnormalities (lissencephaly [smooth, rather than convoluted, brain surface], hydrocephalus [excess fluid in the brain], cerebellar malformations [abnormalities of brain formation]), and eye abnormalities. Inheritance is autosomal recessive.

wall-eyedness *See* exotropia.

Warburg syndrome *See* Walker-Warburg syndrome.

ward A legal term for a person who has been judged unable to care for or make decisions for himself or herself in one or more areas of his or her life. A person may be declared a ward because of age (e.g., in the case of abandoned children), disability (e.g., intellectual disability), or health (e.g., stroke). After the legal determination of inability to care for oneself has been made, a guardian is assigned, and the person is then declared a ward.

Washer Visual Acuity Screening Technique (WVAST)   A screening test for near and far visual acuity in people with severe disabilities and low cognitive functioning. Intended for use with people with a mental age of 2.5 years and older, the test can be used to screen down to the 18-month level with conditioning (training).

WASI   *See* Wechsler Abbreviated Scale of Intelligence.

"water on the brain"   *See* hydrocephalus.

water protocol   A technique for trial swallowing in which a person's status is assessed after swallowing 3 oz of clear water for signs and symptoms of aspiration (inhaling down the airway) and/or penetration, such as coughing and voice changes.

watershed phenomenon   An analogy used to explain the susceptibility of the parasagittal cortex of the brain to injury when blood perfusion (circulation) is reduced in full-term infants; such parasagittal injury leads to hemiplegia (paralysis of one side of the body), quadriplegia (paralysis of all four extremities), and intellectual disability.

"The Way I Feel About Myself"   *See* Piers-Harris Children's Self Concept Scale–Second Edition.

wayfinding   A means of monitoring one's movement from place to place. *See* topographical orientation.

WCST-R   *See* Wisconsin Card Sorting Test–Revised.

WD   *See* Wilson disease.

weakness   An inability to generate normal voluntary force in a muscle or normal voluntary torque about a joint.

Weaver syndrome   A rare syndrome characterized by macrosomia (large body size)

from birth through adulthood, camptodactyly (permanent flexion of the fingers and toes), a peculiar facies (facial features), developmental delay, and a variety of orthopedic deformities. Some people with Weaver syndrome have a mutation in the *NSD1* gene, which is also mutated in more than three fourths of people with classic Sotos syndrome.

Wechsler Abbreviated Scale of Intelligence (WASI)   A brief measure of intelligence in individuals 6–89 years of age that uses two to four of the Wechsler subtests from a longer intelligence quotient (IQ) test. The WASI was developed independently from the other Wechsler scales and can produce a Full Scale Intelligence Quotient (FSIQ), Verbal IQ (VIQ), and Performance IQ (PIQ) from the four subtests, which require approximately 30 minutes to administer. An estimate of general intellectual ability can be obtained from the two-subtest form, which requires only 15 minutes to administer. The test is useful for estimating IQ when administration of a complete IQ test is not feasible, but it is not used for diagnosis.

Wechsler Adult Intelligence Scale–Fourth Edition (WAIS-IV)   A standardized, individually administered intelligence test for use with individuals ages 16–90 that yields a Full Scale Intelligence Quotient (FSIQ), General Ability Index (GAI), and four index scores (Verbal Comprehension Index [VCI], Perceptual Reasoning Index [PRI], Working Memory Index [WMI], and Processing Speed Index [PSI]), each with a mean of 100 and a standard deviation of 15. The 10 subtests each have a mean of 10 and a standard deviation of 3. Administration time is 60–90 minutes.

Wechsler Individual Achievement Test–Third Edition (WIAT-III)   A standardized, individually administered achievement test composed of 16 subtests and administered to individuals ages 4–19. It produces Fall,

Winter, and Spring grade-based standard scores, age-based standard scores, and age and grade equivalents and composite scores in Oral Language, Total Reading, Basic Reading, Reading Comprehension and Fluency (Grades 2–12), Written Expression, Mathematics, and Math Fluency. Administration time is approximately 1.5 hours with school-age children.

Wechsler Intelligence Scale for Children–Fourth Edition (WISC-IV) An individually administered intelligence scale for use with children 6;0–16;11 years of age. It yields a Full Scale Intelligence Quotient (FSIQ) that is composed of four indexes: Verbal Comprehension, Perceptual Reasoning, Working Memory, and Processing Speed. Five supplemental tests are not included in the indexes or FSIQ score. IQ and index scores have a mean of 100 and a standard deviation of 15, and subtests have a mean of 10 and a standard deviation of 3. The test takes 60–90 minutes to administer and is available in Spanish as well as in an "integrated" version that provides detailed cluster and profile analysis derived from supplementary norms.

Wechsler Nonverbal Scale of Ability (WNV) A nonverbal measure of ability specifically designed for use with linguistically and culturally diverse groups of individuals ages 4;0–21;11 years. It is composed of six nonverbal Wechsler subtests, with a briefer version using two subtests selected by age.

Wechsler Preschool and Primary Scale of Intelligence–Third Edition (WPPSI-III) A 12-subtest standardized measure of intellectual ability in young children 2;6–7;3 years of age. WPPSI-III Verbal, Performance, and Full Scale Intelligence Quotient (FSIQ) scores have a mean of 100 and a standard deviation of 15. The test is divided into 14 subtests that are administered in two age bands: children 2;6–3;11 years are given 4–6 subtests, and children 4;0–7;3 years

are given 7–14 subtests. Administration times are approximately 30 and 50 minutes, respectively.

Wechsler tests A family of tests developed by David Wechsler (1896–1981) to measure intelligence in adults and children. These tests include the Wechsler Adult Intelligence Scale–Fourth Edition (WAIS-IV), the Wechsler Intelligence Scale for Children–Fourth Edition (WISC-IV), and the Wechsler Preschool and Primary Scale of Intelligence–Third Edition (WPPSI-III). Because Wechsler believed that intelligence is an aggregate (collection) of multiple abilities and should be measured as such, his tests are composed of numerous subtests that measure both verbal and nonverbal (performance) aspects of intelligence.

WeeFIM *See* Functional Independence Measure for Children.

weighting The process of mathematically assigning to any given test item that proportion of the total score it will determine.

Weinberg syndrome *See* primary disorder of vigilance (PDV).

Wellbutrin *See* bupropion.

Wender sign *Wender foot sign.* Unilateral (one sided) or bilateral (both sided) foot tapping or crossed-knee foot jiggle as a sign of adult attention-deficit/hyperactivity disorder (ADHD) or alcoholism.

Wender Utah Rating Scale (WURS) A 61-item checklist used to aid in the diagnosis of attention-deficit/hyperactivity disorder (ADHD) in adults. Such a diagnosis in adults requires a childhood history of ADHD in addition to current symptomatology. The WURS checklist is used to rate a variety of childhood behaviors on a 5-point scale (from 0 for *not at all* to 4 for *very much*).

Wepman's Auditory Discrimination Test–Second Edition (ADT-2)   A test of auditory discrimination in which 40 pairs of words (10 identical and 30 differing by only a single phoneme, or sound) are read to the child, who then responds as to whether the words are the same or different. Although this test is supposed to measure auditory processing (how the brain perceives what the ear hears), the results are influenced by hearing acuity, short-term memory, and attention; very inattentive children tend to score quite low on this test.

Werdnig-Hoffmann syndrome   *spinal muscular atrophy type 1 (SMA1)*. A genetic neurological disorder that leads to severe muscle weakness in infancy with fatal respiratory compromise (breathing problems). Inheritance is autosomal recessive. SMA1 is caused by mutation or deletion in the telomeric copy of the *SMN* gene, known as *SMN1* (600354). Changes in expression of the centromeric copy of *SMN*, *SMN2* (601627), are known to modify the phenotype.

Wernicke aphasia   Loss of the ability to find the correct word (i.e., anomia) secondary to damage to a specific area of the temporal lobe (Brodmann area 39, the angular gyrus, Wernicke area, posterior speech cortex), for example due to a stroke.

West syndrome   *Blitz-Nick-Salaam Krämpfe syndrome*. The triad of infantile spasms (a specific seizure type), hypsarrhythmia (a continuous disorganized pattern of high-voltage slow waves and spikes on the electroencephalogram [EEG; brain wave test]), and intellectual disability. Onset is usually between 4 and 7 months of age, and boys are more commonly affected than girls. West syndrome can be separated into a symptomatic group (in which a specific cause is identified or other evidence of brain damage is present) and an idiopathic or cryptogenic (cause unknown) group (in which no evidence of brain damage or other cause is found). Etiological (causal) conditions include phenylketonuria (PKU), maple syrup urine disease (MSUD), leucine-sensitive hypoglycemia (low blood sugar level), porencephaly (holes in the brain), rubella, Sturge-Weber syndrome, and tuberous sclerosis. Signs of brain damage include developmental delay prior to the start of seizures, atypical neurological findings, other types of seizures, and atypical radiographic findings (e.g., on neuroimaging). The prognosis for infants with West syndrome is better for children with cryptogenic infantile spasms than for those with an identified cause. Dr. J. West (1793–1848) wrote a letter to *The Lancet* in 1841 with the first case description of infantile spasms in his son.

Westby Play Scale   A checklist of symbolic play skills often used in play-based assessment of young children ages 9 months to 5 years. The Westby Play Scale is an observational scale and yields language stages and approximate age equivalents.

wet lung   *See* transient tachypnea of the newborn (TTN).

Wharton duct relocation   A surgical procedure that reduces salivary flow from the submandibular gland (a major producer of saliva secreted under the tongue) that is used as a treatment for drooling.

wheelchair bound   An objectionable phrase used to refer to an individual in a wheelchair. The preferable wording is *uses a wheelchair*, which emphasizes function and ability. The wheelchair and other aids are used by individuals to enhance their quality of life by enabling mobility, not by restricting it.

wheezing   Breathing that makes a sound like whistling. Wheezing occurs primarily on exhalation (breathing out) and often indicates constriction (tightening) of the small airways in the lungs. Wheezing is not specific to asthma.

whistling face syndrome *craniocarpotarsal dysplasia, Freeman-Sheldon syndrome (FSS).* A rare genetic syndrome characterized by a distinctive facies (a mask-like face with a small mouth that gives the impression of puckering to whistle), small narrow nostrils, club feet, and flexion contractures (fixed bending) of the fingers. Intellectual disability is an occasional finding. Inheritance is autosomal dominant (rarely, autosomal recessive). It is also called *distal arthrogryposis type 2A (DA2A), craniocarpotarsal syndrome,* and *Windmill-Vane-Hand syndrome.*

white matter Areas of the brain that contain the myelinated nerve axons. These axons are the units that transfer messages quickly from one brain area to another. *See also* white matter disease.

white matter disease *leukodystrophy.* A group of degenerative diseases of the central nervous system (CNS; brain and spinal cord) in which motor signs of pyramidal tract involvement occur early in the course of the disorder, whereas cognitive deterioration and seizures occur late. These conditions are characterized by loss of or abnormalities in the myelinated white matter of the brain (areas of the brain in which cells are coated with fatty insulating myelin to speed the transmission of messages). Examples include adrenoleukodystrophy (ALS), Krabbe disease, and metachromatic leukodystrophy (MLD).

white pupil *leukocoria.* A physical finding on eye exam using a bright light or ophthalmoscope in which the reflection from the back of the eye appears white instead of red (as can sometimes be seen on flash photography). White pupil suggests the possibility of cataract (clouding of the lens of the eye), coloboma (a surface defect), retinoblastoma (a tumor), or retinal detachment.

whole language A theory regarding how children best learn to read and how reading should be taught. Whole language is often discussed in comparison to phonics, because unlike phonics teachers, whole language teachers avoid segmenting language into component parts for specific skill instruction. The whole language approach follows several pedagogical (teaching) principles: 1) Children are always learning; 2) children learn best what is meaningful and relevant to them; 3) students learn most easily when they have some measure of control over decisions that affect learning; 4) children learn to read and write by reading and writing; 5) errors are critical to learning; 6) children's learning should be celebrated, not rewarded; 7) learning is social; and 8) teachers must practice what they teach. Whole language teaching has generally been replaced by phonics instruction in most schools.

whorl A spiral pattern that occurs in nature. Variations from expected whorl patterns in fingerprints and hair can contribute to a dysmorphology (atypical appearance) diagnosis; the depigmented skin lesions (areas of skin that lack normal color) of incontinentia pigmenti may also occur in a whorl pattern.

WIAT-III *See* Wechsler Individual Achievement Test–Third Edition.

WIC *See* Special Supplemental Nutrition Program for Women, Infants, and Children.

Wide Range Achievement Test–Fourth Edition (WRAT-4) A measure of word reading (decoding) and sentence comprehension (combined for a reading composite score), spelling, and mathematics computation. Two equivalent test forms (blue and green) normed by age can be used for pre- and postintervention assessment of people 5–75 years of age and provide standard scores, percentiles, and grade equivalents for each of the three areas of learning. The WRAT-4 is a relatively brief test rather than a comprehensive assessment of academic achievement.

Wide Range Assessment of Memory and Learning–Second Edition (WRAML2) An individually administered test of memory for use with individuals 5–90 years of age. The WRAML2 has eight subtests that yield four indexes, with additional measures of recall and recognition. Administration time is about 1 hour.

widow's peak A downward V-shaped extension of the frontal hairline; a minor variation from normal that can be a component of certain syndromes (e.g., Waardenburg syndrome).

widow's peak

Wiedemann-Rautenstrauch syndrome *congenital pseudohydrocephalic syndrome.* A genetic syndrome that presents at birth with pseudohydrocephalus, a progeric triangular facies (prematurely aged facial features), congenital (present from birth) teeth, deficiency of subcutaneous (under the skin) fat, and, usually, intellectual disability. Inheritance is autosomal recessive.

Wiig Criterion Referenced Inventory of Language (Wiig CRIL or CRIL) A criterion-referenced assessment of language for use with children 4–15 years of age. The Wiig CRIL complements norm-referenced testing and helps experts plan interventions in the areas of semantics (the meaning of words), morphology (word structure), syntax (grammar), and pragmatics.

Wilbarger protocol *brushing, deep pressure proprioception touch technique.* The use of a specially designed brush by an occupational therapist for sensory integration therapy. Joint compression may also be used.

Wildervanck syndrome *See* cervico-oculo-acoustic syndrome.

Wildervanck-Smith syndrome *See* Treacher Collins syndrome.

Williams syndrome *del(7)(q11.23), deletion 7q, elastin deletion, elfin facies syndrome, Fanconi-Schlesinger syndrome, Williams-Beuren syndrome.* A syndrome characterized by short stature, mild microcephaly (small head), and mild to moderate intellectual disability. The person typically has a friendly and talkative personality. Although language ability is higher than overall mental ability (as is musical ability in many cases), the voice sounds hoarse and deep. Those affected show hyperacusis (increased sensitivity to sound), impaired coordination, mild spasticity (increased muscle tone), and hyperactive tendon reflexes. The face has been described as "elfin," with short palpebral fissures (narrow eye slits), epicanthal folds (skin flaps covering the inside [nasal] corner of the eye), and fullness of tissue around the eyes. Eyes are generally blue, with a stellate (starburst) pattern to the iris. The philtrum (upper lip groove) is long, and the mouth is wide with full lips. Joint limitations, scoliosis (curvature of the spine), and renal (kidney) and heart anomalies (supravalvular aortic stenosis and pulmonary stenosis) are frequent. Blood tests may show hypercalcemia (high levels of calcium in the blood). The cause is deletion of the elastin gene; almost all cases are sporadic. The use fluorescent *in situ* hybridization (FISH), a genetic test that probes for specific gene abnormalities, yields positive results in most individuals.

Wilson disease (WD) *hepatolenticular degeneration.* An inborn error of copper metabolism that occurs between 10 and 20 years of age, WD clinically involves primarily the liver and brain (especially the basal ganglia [areas of the brain that help coordinate movement and tone]). It involves the following neurological presentations: dystonia (variable muscle tone), drooling, other bulbar (relating to the medulla oblongata [part of the brainstem]) symptoms, gait (walking) disturbances, and mild intellectual impairment. Learning disabilities and emotional disturbances are occasionally prominent. Physical findings include liver enlargement, Kayser-Fleischer ring (a pigmented ring around the outside of the cornea), and motor dysfunction in the absence of sensory and reflex abnormalities. Diagnosis can be confirmed by serum ceruloplasmin (a copper-binding protein) level and an ophthalmological examination for eye findings. Chelation treatment involves the administration of a copper-binding chemical, such as penicillamine, to help remove the excess copper from the body. Neurological prognosis is variable. Inheritance is autosomal recessive. Named after the British neurologist Samuel A.K. Wilson (1878–1937).

Wilson Reading System A research-based reading and writing program designed for students (in Grades 2–12 and adults) who have difficulty with decoding (reading) and encoding (spelling). This complete curriculum has 12 steps, beginning with phoneme segmentation (breaking up sounds into their components). Its main goal is to teach students language and word structure through a carefully planned program. Although initially designed for older individuals with dyslexia, the Wilson Reading System is appropriate for use with students from kindergarten through high school with decoding or word-level impairments. It provides an organized, sequential approach with extensive controlled text to help teachers implement a multisensory program. Comprehension and fluency are important components of the program.

windswept hip An orthopedic deformity in which both hips and knees are flexed but one hip is abducted and externally rotated and the other is adducted (pulled inward) and internally rotated (and often subluxed [dislocated] also). This deformity pattern occurs in people with severe cerebral palsy

windswept hip deformity

and gives a misleading impression of leg-length discrepancy.

WISC-IV *See* Wechsler Intelligence Scale for Children–Fourth Edition.

Wisconsin Card Sorting Test–Revised (WCST-R) An individually administered neuropsychological test used to assess the ability of children and adults to form abstract concepts and to both shift and maintain the set (i.e., change a strategy that is not working and continue one that is). The person is asked to categorize 64 or 128 cards as belonging to one of four stimulus card groupings; each card has one to four examples of one to four different shapes in one to four different colors (e.g., two red triangles or three blue squares). The ability to detect and shift sets is indicative of cognitive flexibility, executive function, and goal-directed behavior. Perseveration errors (continuing an unsuccessful strategy) are interpreted as indicative of damage to the dorsolateral frontal lobe (a specific brain area) and sometimes chronic alcoholism. Norms are available for ages 6;5–89;0 years.

WJ-III-ACH Woodcock-Johnson III Tests of Achievement. *See* Woodcock-Johnson Battery–Third Edition: Norms Updated (WJ-III-NU).

WJ-III-COG Woodcock-Johnson III Tests of Cognitive Ability. *See* Woodcock-Johnson Battery–Third Edition: Norms Updated (WJ-III-NU).

WJ-III-NU *See* Woodcock-Johnson Battery–Third Edition: Norms Updated.

WLPB-R *See* Woodcock Language Proficiency Battery–Revised.

wnl Medical record abbreviation for "within normal limits" used to characterize both physical examination and laboratory findings. Often used in place of a more detailed description or record of findings.

WNV *See* Wechsler Nonverbal Scale of Ability.

Wolf-Hirschhorn syndrome *critical region 4p16.3, del(4)(q15-pter), deletion 4p.* A chromosome deletion syndrome with easily recognizable features. Growth deficiency is marked; the head is small. There is severe intellectual disability. Movement is weak and slow. The face shows hypertelorism (widely spaced eyes); the bridge of the nose is prominent, forming a straight line from the forehead to the tip of the nose (Greek warrior helmet appearance). Cleft lip and palate and a short philtrum (upper lip groove) are common. The dermal ridges are poorly defined, and clubfeet may be seen. In the male, hypospadias (abnormal position of the urethral opening on the penis) occurs. Cardiac defects are frequent. Skeletal anomalies (abnormalities) are occasionally found. Many children with this syndrome have seizures. The deletion of chromosome 4 is usually a de novo event, but about 13% of cases are the result of a chromosome translocation.

Women, Infants, and Children (Special Supplemental Food Program) *See* Special Supplemental Nutrition Program for Women, Infants, and Children (WIC).

Woodcock Language Proficiency Battery–Revised (WLPB-R) A battery of 13 subtests that measure language in three areas: oral, reading, and written. Different clusters of subtests can be used for different age levels.

Woodcock Reading Mastery Test–Revised (WRMT-R) A test of reading ability used with individuals from kindergarten to 75 years of age. The organization of the WRMT-R is hierarchical and includes five levels: total reading, clusters (readiness, basic skills, reading comprehension), tests,

subtests (and vocabulary), and item error. Readiness is assessed by reading passages made up of newly learned rebus symbol–word associations and by naming upper- and lowercase letters in a variety of type styles. Reading is assessed by reading written words on sight, applying phonic and structural analysis skills to pronounce unfamiliar words, reading a stem aloud and orally providing an antonym or synonym or completing an analogy, and providing a key word missing from a silently read passage. Scoring is tedious, but a computer scoring program is available. Care should be taken when interpreting basic skills and comprehension scores in kindergartners who are at or below average for the group as a whole, because even a raw score of zero can result in an above-average percentile score.

Woodcock-Johnson Battery–Third Edition: Norms Updated (WJ-III-NU) A battery composed of the Woodcock-Johnson III Tests of Cognitive Ability (WJ-III-COG) and the Woodcock-Johnson III Tests of Achievement (WJ-III-ACH). (The norms update occurred in 2007.) Together these tests provide a comprehensive set of individually administered, norm-referenced tests for measuring intellectual ability and academic achievement. By using the cognitive and achievement tests together, one can make comparisons among an individual's cognitive abilities, oral language abilities, and achievement scores. The tests are appropriate for use with individuals ages 2–95. The WJ-III-COG contains 20 tests, each of which uses a standard and extended battery to measure a different aspect of cognitive abilities. The abilities measured by the WJ-III-COG include comprehension/knowledge, long-term retrieval, visuospatial thinking, auditory processing, fluid reasoning, processing, speed, short-term memory, phonemic awareness, working memory, broad attention, cognitive fluency, and executive processes. The WJ-III-ACH has 22 tests that are organized into five areas: reading, mathematics, written language, knowledge, and oral language.

There is a standard and extended battery with two forms: A and B. The WJ-III-NU tests are based on the Cattell-Horn-Carroll (CHC) theory of intelligence. Not all tests must be administered, allowing for a focused approach to testing.

Woodcock-Johnson Tests of Cognitive Ability *See* fluid intelligence.

Wooster-Drought syndrome *See* pseudobulbar palsy.

word association test A projective technique originated by Carl Jung in which an individual is presented with a list of words one at a time and asked to respond with the first word or idea that comes to mind. The examiner interprets aspects such as the length of time required to respond, actual or implied judgments in the person's responses, and the degree of uniqueness or peculiarity of the associations the person makes. The test has some application in neuropsychology in the form of the (normed) Controlled Oral Word Association Test (COWAT), in which responses are examined as part of an assessment battery for brain injury or related impairment.

word attack A group of techniques that enable a child to decode an unknown word, to pronounce it, and to understand it in context. These techniques include phonics analysis (breaking down of sounds), structural analysis, contextual clues, and dictionary skills.

word blindness, congenital *See* congenital word blindness.

word finding The ability to recall a word from memory.

word knowledge A person's understanding of words and symbol definitions.

Word Reasoning A Wechsler (intelligence test) subtest in which the child is asked to identify common concepts from a series of clues. This subtest measures verbal comprehension and the ability to synthesize different types of information.

word recognition The ability to remember and recognize a word that has been known, seen, or experienced before. Word recognition skills are important in building reading fluency skills.

Word Test 2: Adolescent A norm-referenced test of expressive vocabulary and semantic (meaning systems) knowledge for use with children ages 12–17. The test is composed of six subtests: Associations, Synonyms, Semantic Absurdities, Antonyms, Definitions, and Flexible Word Use.

Word Test 2: Elementary A norm-referenced test of expressive language and semantic (meaning systems) knowledge for use with children ages 7–11. The test has six subtests: Associations, Synonyms (different words with the same meaning), Antonyms (words with opposite meanings), Definitions, Semantic Absurdities (recognizing the error in an absurd statement), and Multiple Definitions.

working memory *See* short-term memory.

world knowledge A person's autobiographical and experiential memory along with his or her understanding of particular events.

WPPSI-III *See* Wechsler Preschool and Primary Scale of Intelligence–Third Edition.

WRAML2 *See* Wide Range Assessment of Memory and Learning–Second Edition.

wraparound A care delivery model that relies on therapeutic service coordination to coordinate multiple supports and interventions. Often used for children and teens with complex, intensive needs who are served by multiple providers, wraparound takes an individualized approach and usually involves a team of professionals from different disciplines or systems.

WRAT-4 *See* Wide Range Achievement Test–Fourth Edition.

writing conference A meeting between a writer and someone who is interested in reading and/or listening to the writer's work. The listener offers constructive feedback about content, structure, and language mechanics.

WRMT-R *See* Woodcock Reading Mastery Test–Revised.

wry neck *See* torticollis.

W-sitting A sitting posture with the knees bent and both hips rotated inward with the legs abducted. Although this posture is one of many sitting postures seen in typical children, children with cerebral palsy, acquired brain injury, Down syndrome, and hypotonia often use this position in place of any other sitting position to create a posture of stability. Structural hip damage and shortened muscles may result from prolonged W-sitting. *See* reversed tailor.

WURS *See* Wender Utah Rating Scale.

WVAST *See* Washer Visual Acuity Screening Technique.

xeroderma pigmentosum A genetic syndrome characterized by extreme sensitivity to sunlight leading to progressive disfigurement, skin cancer, and eye problems. There are at least eight subgroups, some of which involve progressive neurological deterioration in both motor and cognitive systems. Inheritance is autosomal recessive, with an incidence of 1 in 100,000. *See also* de Sanctis-Cacchione syndrome.

X-inactivation The process that occurs in the embryo by which the genes on one X chromosome in females are "turned off" in somatic (body) cells.

xiphoid process The bottom of the sternum.

XLID *See* X-linked intellectual disability.

X-linkage Sex-linkage; the characteristics, traits, or disorders carried on genes on the X chromosome. Males more often demonstrate the effects of X-linked traits, as they have only one X chromosome. These traits are never transmitted from father to son, only from (usually clinically unaffected) mother to son.

X-linked Describing genes on the X chromosome, or the traits determined by such genes.

X-linked hydrocephalus syndrome A genetic syndrome characterized by hydrocephalus (excess fluid under pressure in the brain) usually due to aqueductal stenosis (blockage of the aqueduct of Sylvius through which the cerebrospinal fluid [CSF] flows); short, flexed (cortical) thumbs; spasticity (increased muscle tone; usually diplegia [greater paralysis of the lower extremities]); and intellectual disability. Inheritance is X-linked recessive. Ultrasound may be used to attempt prenatal diagnosis in families considered at risk.

X-linked intellectual disability (XLID) Intellectual disability related to the female sex chromosome (the X chromosome). Many genetic disorders and causes of intellectual disability are X-linked. The most common form of XLID is fragile X syndrome, which occurs at a rate of 1 in 4,000 males and 1 in 6,000 females.

X-linked intellectual disability, otherwise undifferentiated *See* Renpenning syndrome.

X-linked myoclonic epilepsy with spasticity and intellectual disability (XMESID) A genetic syndrome in boys (X-linked) that includes myoclonic epilepsy (with seizures characterized by lightning-like muscle jerks), moderate to severe intellectual disability, and late-onset spastic (increased muscle tone) ataxia (uncoordinated gait). The involved site is Xp11.2-22.2.

XO syndrome *See* Turner syndrome.

XXX *See* triploidy.

XXX syndrome *45,X/46,XX/47,XXX; 47, XXX; 46,XX/47,XXX; triple X syndrome.* A syndrome characterized by typical phenotype (physical appearance) and growth, slow motor development, and learning difficulties. Behavior difficulties and psychiatric disturbances may occur. The incidence is about 1 in 1,000 females.

XXY/69 *See* triploidy.

XYY syndrome *47, XYY.* This XYY chromosome constitution is associated with an atypical phenotype (appearance). There is increased height, diminished intelligence, acne, psychosexual problems, and increased behavior difficulties. Fertility is normal, and recurrence risk is very low. The error leading to the extra Y chromosome is most likely a nondisjunction event in the father. The incidence is about 1 in 1,000 live male births.

Yale-Brown Obsessive Compulsive Scale (Y-BOC) A 10-question scale (5 items for obsessions and 5 for compulsions) used in research and clinical practice to assess the severity of obsessive-compulsive disorder (OCD) and to monitor improvement with treatment. The person earns from 0 to 4 points for each of the 10 questions, and the total score can be used for diagnosis and treatment.

Yale Children's Inventory (YCI) A 63-item parent questionnaire that assesses attention, behavior, and cognitive problems in children. The YCI is part of the Yale Neuropsychological Assessment Scales (YNPAS), which also includes a Child's Personal Data Inventory (CPDI) and a Teacher's Behavior Rating Scale (TBRS).

Yale Global Tic Severity Scale (YGTSS) A checklist developed at the Yale Child Study Center to measure the severity of six areas of motor and vocal tics in children with tic disorders. A parent and child interview is used to complete the checklist. Severity scores range from 0 to 50 for each type of tic, and a total score is determined. The YGTSS is used both clinically and in research studies, as it has good reliability and validity in the assessment of pediatric Tourette syndrome.

Yale Special Interests Survey An assessment of the circumscribed interests of a factual nature found in people with autism spectrum disorders, their all-absorbing quality and their deleterious impact on reciprocal conversation.

Y-BOC *See* Yale-Brown Obsessive Compulsive Scale.

YCAT *See* Young Children's Achievement Test.

YCI *See* Yale Children's Inventory.

yeast *See Candida albicans.*

YGTSS *See* Yale Global Tic Severity Scale.

Y-linked Describing genes on the Y chromosome (the male chromosome), or traits determined by such genes.

Young Children's Achievement Test (YCAT) An individually administered test for use with children ages 4;0–7;11 years that results in standard scores, percentiles, and age-equivalent scores for each subtest and for overall achievement. The YCAT is used to identify children at an early age who may be at risk for later school failure. It measures early achievement using five subtests: General Information, Reading, Writing, Mathematics, and Spoken Language. These skills have been shown to be predictive of later academic achievement. The YCAT can be completed in 25–45 minutes.

Yutopar *See* ritodrine hydrochloride.

Zz

Zantac *See* ranitidine.

Zarontin *See* ethosuximide.

zebra A rare disease or condition. The aphorism "Uncommon presentations of common diseases are more common than common presentations of uncommon diseases" is an anti-zebra statement. It suggests that more time, effort, and energy should be expended pursuing statistically more probable conditions than expensive explorations of possible zebras (e.g., obtaining magnetic resonance imaging [MRI] in the workup of a tension headache).

Zellweger syndrome *cerebrohepatorenal syndrome.* A syndrome caused by alterations in peroxisomal biogenesis (peroxisomes are cell organelles ["little organs"] that break down cell wastes) and manifested by atypical brain structures, hypotonia (decreased muscle tone), enlarged liver, large fontanels (soft spots), heart disease, and kidney cysts. Most infants with this syndrome are born breech (delivered feet first) and live only a few months. The hypotonia and atypical brain structures are associated with severe developmental delay. Inheritance is autosomal recessive. Decreased enzyme and altered fatty acid levels in amniotic fluid cells allow for prenatal diagnosis.

zero reject The provision of the Individuals with Disabilities Education Act (IDEA) of 1990 (PL 101-476) that states that all students, regardless of the nature or severity of their disabilities, are entitled to a free appropriate public education (FAPE). In short, the provision states that no student can be denied access to education (rejected) because of his or her disability status.

zero to three A generic term used to describe many state early intervention (birth-to-3) programs.

ZERO TO THREE: National Center for Infants, Toddlers, and Families A nonprofit national organization that informs, trains, and supports professionals, policy makers, and parents in their efforts to improve the lives of infants and toddlers. It publishes the journal *Zero to Three* as well as the *Diagnostic Classification of Mental Health and Developmental Disorders of Infancy and Early Childhood–Revised (DC:0-3R),* a downward extension of the *Diagnostic and Statistical Manual of Mental Disorders, Fourth Edition, Text Revision (DSM-IV-TR).*

zero tolerance A policy of automatic punishment for rule infraction that does not allow any discretion in allowing for circumstances. The term usually refers to severe school conduct policies.

Zoloft *See* sertraline.

zone of proximal development (ZPD) A term that reflects the learning potential of a child at a given moment in time. ZPD describes the difference between the child's independent problem solving or mastery and what the child can achieve with assistance from peers or adults. Ascertaining the ZPD is useful for instruction.

Z-plasty A tendon-lengthening procedure that involves sectioning half of the tendon (e.g., the tibialis posterior) lower down and the contralateral (opposite) half of the tendon higher up and then suturing the overlapped ends with the extremity (e.g., the foot) in a neutral position.

z-score A standard score with a mean of zero and a standard deviation of 1. If a test has a mean of 63 and a standard deviation of 9, a raw score of 72 would be equivalent to a *z*-score of +1. The *z*-score is the number of standard deviations a given value is from the test mean.

zygomatic bone *zygoma.* The cheekbone.

Bibliography

Aase, J.M. (1990). *Diagnostic dysmorphology.* New York: Plenum Medical Book Co.

Accardo, P.J. (Ed.). (2008). *Capute and Accardo's neurodevelopmental disabilities in infancy and childhood* (3rd ed., Vols. I–II). Baltimore: Paul H. Brookes Publishing Co.

Accardo, P.J., Blondis, T.A., Whitman, B.Y., & Stein, M.A. (Eds.). (2000). *Attention deficits and hyperactivity in children and adults.* New York: Marcel Dekker.

Aicardi, J. (2009). *Diseases of the nervous system in childhood* (3rd ed.). London: MacKeith Press.

Alberto, P.A., & Troutman, A.C. (2006). *Applied behavior analysis for teachers* (7th ed.). Upper Saddle River, NJ: Pearson.

American Psychiatric Association. (1987). *Diagnostic and statistical manual of mental disorders* (3rd ed., rev.). Washington, DC: Author.

American Psychiatric Association. (1994). *Diagnostic and statistical manual of mental disorders* (4th ed.). Washington, DC: Author.

American Psychiatric Association. (2000). *Diagnostic and statistical manual of mental disorders* (4th ed., text rev.). Washington, DC: Author.

American Psychological Association. (2009). *Publication manual of the American Psychological Association* (6th ed.). Washington, DC: Author.

American School Health Association. (2010). *Mission/goals.* Retrieved from http://www.ashaweb.org/i4a/pages/index.cfm?pageid=3280

American Speech-Language-Hearing Association. (1993). Definitions of communication disorders and variations. *ASHA, 35*(Suppl. 10), 40, 41.

American Speech-Language-Hearing Association. (1997). *Preferred practice patterns for the profession of speech-language pathology.* Rockville, MD: Author.

American Speech-Language-Hearing Association Special Interest Division 4: Fluency and Fluency Disorders. (1999, March). Terminology pertaining to fluency and fluency disorders: Guidelines. *ASHA, 41*(Suppl. 9), 30–31, 35.

Ayd, F.J., Jr. (2000). *Lexicon of psychiatry, neurology, and the neurosciences* (2nd ed.). Philadelphia: Lippincott Williams & Wilkins.

Barker, R.L. (1999). *The social work dictionary.* Washington, DC: National Association of Social Workers Press.

Barness, L.A. (1981). *Manual of pediatric physical diagnosis.* Chicago: Year Book Medical Publishers.

Batshaw, M.L. (2007). *Children with disabilities* (6th ed.). Baltimore: Paul H. Brookes Publishing Co.

Beighton, P., & Beighton, G. (1997). *The person behind the syndrome.* New York: Springer-Verlag.

Bergsma, D. (Ed.). (1979). *Birth defects compendium* (2nd ed.). New York: Alan R. Liss.

Blauvelt, C.T., & Nelson, F.R. (1998). *A manual of orthopaedic terminology.* St. Louis: Mosby.

Brown, I., & Percy, M. (Eds.). (2007). *A comprehensive guide to intellectual and developmental disabilities.* Baltimore: Paul H. Brookes Publishing Co.

Bry, A. (1975). *A primer of behavioral psychology.* New York: New American Library.

Buros, O.K. (Ed.). (1965). *The sixth mental measurement yearbook.* Highland Park, NJ: Gryphon Press.

Buros, O.K. (Ed.). (1972). *The seventh mental measurement yearbook.* Highland Park, NJ: Gryphon Press.

Buros, O.K. (Ed.). (1978). *The eighth mental measurement yearbook.* Highland Park, NJ: Gryphon Press.

Bush, C.L., & Andrews, R.C. (1980). *Dictionary of reading and learning disability.* Los Angeles: Western Psychological Services.

Carter, C.H. (1975). *Handbook of mental retardation syndromes.* Springfield, IL: Charles C Thomas.

Case-Smith, J. (Ed.). (2001). *Occupational therapy for children* (4th ed.). St. Louis: Mosby.

Case-Smith, J., Allen, A.S., & Pratt, P.N. (Eds.). (1996). *Occupational therapy for children* (3rd ed.). St. Louis: Mosby.

Chamberlin, S.L., & Narins, B. (Eds.). (2005). *The Gale encyclopedia of neurological disorders* (Vols. 1–2). Farmington Hills, MI: Thomson Gale.

Chaplin, J.P. (1985). *Dictionary of psychology.* New York: Laurel.

Cohen, P., Cohen, J., Kasen, S., Velez, C., Hartmark, C., Johnson, J., et al. (1993). An epidemiological study of disorders in late childhood and adolescence: I. Age- and gender-specific prevalence. *Journal of Child Psychiatry, 34,* 869–877.

The compact edition of the Oxford English Dictionary (Vols. 1–3). (1971–1987). Oxford, England: Oxford University Press.

Cooke, R.E. (Ed.). (1968). *The biological basis of pediatric practice.* New York: McGraw-Hill.

D'Avanzo, C.E. (2008). *Cultural health assessment.* St. Louis: Mosby.

David, R.B. (Ed.). (2005). *Child and adolescent neurology.* Malden: Blackwell.

Dorland's illustrated medical dictionary. (1981). Philadelphia: W.B. Saunders.

Fink, C., & Kraynak, J. (2005). *Bipolar disorder for dummies.* Hoboken, NJ: Wiley.

Firkin, B.G., & Whitworth, J.A. (1987). *Dictionary of medical eponyms.* Park Ridge, NJ: Parthenon.

Frankenburg, W.K., & Camp, B.W. (Eds.). (1975). *Pediatric screening tests.* Springfield, IL: Charles C Thomas.

Fraser, B.A., Hensinger, R.N., & Phelps, J.A. (1990). *Physical management of multiple handicaps: A professional's guide* (2nd ed.). Baltimore: Paul H. Brookes Publishing Co.

Fritsch, M.H., & Sommer, A. (1991). *Handbook of congenital and early onset hearing loss.* New York: Igaku-Shoin.

Gazzaniga, M.S., Irvy, R.B., & Mangun, G.R. (2009). *Cognitive neuroscience.* New York: W.W. Norton.

Gellis, S.S., Feingold, M., & Rutman, J.Y. (1968). *Atlas of mental retardation syndromes: Visual diagnosis of facies and physical findings.* Washington, DC: U.S. Government Printing Office.

Gillam, R., Marquardt, T., & Martin, F. (Eds.). (2000). *Communication sciences and disorders from science to clinical practice.* San Diego: Singular Thomson Learning.

Goldenson, R.M. (Ed.). (1970). *The encyclopedia of human behavior: Psychology, psychiatry, and mental health* (Vols. 1–2). New York: Doubleday.

Goldenson, R.M. (Ed.). (1978). *Disability and rehabilitation handbook.* New York: McGraw-Hill.

Gorlin, R.J., Cohen, M.M., & Levin, L.S. (1990). *Syndromes of the head and neck* (Oxford Monographs on Medical Genetics No. 19). New York: Oxford University Press.

Grossman, H.J. (Ed.). (1983). *Classification in mental retardation.* Washington, DC: American Association on Mental Deficiency.

Gurman, A.S., & Kniskern, D.P. (Eds.). (1981). *Handbook of family therapy.* New York: Brunner/Mazel.

Hall, J.G., Froster-Iskenius, U.G., & Allanson, J.E. (1989). *Handbook of normal physical measurements.* London: Oxford University Press.

Harré, R., & Lamb, R. (Eds.). (1983). *The encyclopedic dictionary of psychology.* Cambridge, MA: The MIT Press.

Harré, R., & Lamb, R. (Eds.). (1986). *The dictionary of ethology and animal learning.* Cambridge, MA: The MIT Press.

Hartl, D.L., & Jones, E.W. (2009). *Genetics.* Boston: Jones & Bartlett.

Haslam, R.H.A. & Valletutti, P.J. (Eds.). (2004). *Medical problems in the classroom* (4th ed.). Austin, TX: PRO-ED.

Henderson, A., & Pehoski, C. (1995). *Hand function in the child.* St. Louis: Mosby.

Hopkins, H.L., & Smith, H.D. (Eds.). (1988). *Willard and Spackman's occupational therapy.* Philadelphia: W.B. Saunders.

Jacobs, K. (Ed.). (1999). *Quick reference dictionary for occupational therapy* (2nd ed.). Thorofare, NJ: Slack.

Jones, K.L. (1988). *Smith's recognizable patterns of human malformation.* Philadelphia: W.B. Saunders.

Jung, J.H. (1989). *Genetic syndromes in communication disorders.* Boston: College Hill.

Kaplan, H.I., & Sadock, B.J. (1991). *Comprehensive glossary of psychiatry and psychology.* Baltimore: Lippincott Williams & Wilkins.

Kaplan, H.I., & Sadock, B.J. (Eds.). (1997). *Kaplan and Sadock's synopsis of psychiatry.* Baltimore: Lippincott Williams & Wilkins.

King, R.C., & Stansfield, W.D. (1990). *A dictionary of genetics.* New York: Oxford University Press.

Konigsmark, B.W., & Gorlin, R.J. (1976). *Genetic and metabolic deafness.* Philadelphia: W.B. Saunders.

Kuper, A., & Kuper, J. (Eds.). (1999). *The social science encyclopedia.* New York: Routledge.

Landau, S.I. (Ed.). (1986). *International dictionary of medicine and biology* (Vols. 1–2). New York: Wiley.

Lynch, E.W., & Hanson, M.J. (2004). *Developing cross-cultural competence: A guide for working with children and their families* (3rd ed.). Baltimore: Paul H. Brookes Publishing Co.

McKusick, V.A. (1998). *Mendelian inheritance in man: A catalog of human genes and genetic disorders* (12th ed.). Baltimore: The Johns Hopkins University Press.

Menkes, J.H. (1990). *Textbook of child neurology.* Philadelphia: Lea & Febiger.

Merin, S. (1991). *Inherited eye diseases: Diagnosis and clinical management.* New York: Dekker.

Mervyn, L. (1984). *The dictionary of vitamins: The complete guide to vitamins and vitamin therapy.* New York: Thorsons.

Miller, B.F., & Keane, C.B. (1997). *Miller-Keane encyclopedia and dictionary of medicine, nursing, and allied health* (6th ed.). Philadelphia: W.B. Saunders.

Millington, T.A., & Millington, W. (1971). *Dictionary of mathematics*. New York: Barnes & Noble.

Moore, B.E., & Fine, B.D. (Eds.). (1967). *A glossary of psychoanalytic terms and concepts*. New York: American Psychoanalytic Association.

Mussen, P.H. (Ed.). (1983). *Handbook of child psychology* (Vols. 1–4). New York: Wiley.

Neisworth, J.T., & Wolfe, P.S. (Eds.). (2004). *The autism encyclopedia*. Baltimore: Paul H. Brookes Publishing Co.

Nelson, L.B., Brown, G.C., & Arentsen, J.J. (1985). *Recognizing patterns of ocular childhood disease*. Thorofare, NJ: Slack.

Nicolosi, L., Harryman, E., & Kresheck, J. (1996). *Terminology of communication disorders: Speech-language-hearing* (4th ed.). Baltimore: Lippincott Williams & Wilkins.

Noshpitz, J.D. (Ed.). (1979–1987). *Basic handbook of child psychiatry* (Vols. 1–5). New York: Basic Books.

Online Mendelian Inheritance in Man at http://www.ncbi.nlm.nih.gov/omim

Oski, F.A., DeAngelis, C.D., Feigin, R.D., & Warshaw, J.B. (Eds.). (1994). *Principles and practice of pediatrics*. Philadelphia: Lippincott Williams & Wilkins.

Pinney, E.L., Jr., & Slipp, S. (1982). *Glossary of group and family therapy*. New York: Brunner/Mazel.

Porr, S.M., & Rainville, E.B. (1999). *Pediatric therapy: A systems approach*. Philadelphia: F.A. Davis.

Quinn, L., & Gordon, J. (2010). *Functional outcomes: Documentation for rehabilitation*. New York: W.B. Saunders.

Reynolds, C.R., & Mann, L. (Eds.). (2000). *Encyclopedia of special education: A reference for the education of the handicapped and other exceptional children and adults* (2nd ed., Vols. 1–3). New York: Wiley.

Reynolds, C.R., & Fletcher-Janzen, E.F. (Eds.). (2002). *Concise encyclopedia of special education: A reference for the education of the handicapped and other exceptional children and adults* (2nd ed.). Hoboken, NJ: Wiley.

Rubin, I.L., & Crocker, A.C. (Eds.). (2006). *Medical care for children and adults with developmental disabilities* (2nd ed.). Baltimore: Paul H. Brookes Publishing Co.

Sapira, J.D. (1990). *The art and science of bedside diagnosis*. Baltimore: Urban & Schwarzenberg.

Schalock, R.L., Borthwick-Duffy, S.A., Bradley, V.J., Buntinx, W.H.E., Coulter, D.L., Craig, E.M., et al. (2010). *Intellectual disability: Definition, classification, and systems of supports* (11th ed.). Washington, DC: American Association on Intellectual and Developmental Disabilities.

Singh, S., & Kent, R.D. (2000). *Singular's illustrated dictionary of speech-language pathology*. San Diego: Singular.

Smith, D.W. (1981). *Recognizable patterns of human deformation: Identification and management of mechanical effects on morphogenesis*. Philadelphia: W.B. Saunders.

Smith, S.D. (Ed.). (1986). *Genetics and learning disabilities*. San Diego: College Hill.

Spreen, O., & Strauss, E. (1991). *Compendium of neuropsychological tests*. New York: Oxford University Press.

Stanaszek, M.J., Stanaszek, W.F., Carlstedt, B.C., & Strauss, S. (1991). *The inverted medical dictionary* (2nd ed.). Lancaster, PA: Technomic.

Stedman's medical dictionary (28th ed.). (2006). Baltimore: Lippincott Williams & Wilkins.

Subcommittee of the Committee on Public Information. (1975). *A psychiatric glossary: The meaning of terms frequently used in psychiatry*. Washington, DC: American Psychiatric Association.

Taybi, H., & Lachman, R.S. (1990). *Radiology of syndromes, metabolic disorders, and skeletal dysplasias*. Chicago: Year Book Medical Publishers.

Tecklin, J.S. (1999). *Pediatric physical therapy*. Philadelphia: Lippincott Williams & Wilkins.

Tymchuk, A.J. (1973). *The mental retardation dic·tion·ar·y*. Los Angeles: Western Psychological Services.

Walker, B. (1978). *Encyclopedia of metaphysical medicine*. London: Routledge & Kegan Paul.

Wallach, J. (1983). *Interpretation of pediatric tests: A handbook synopsis of pediatric, fetal, and obstetrical laboratory medicine*. Boston: Little, Brown.

Warkany, J. (1971). *Congenital malformations*. Chicago: Year Book Medical Publishers.

Warkany, J., Lemire, R.J., & Cohen, M.M., Jr. (1981). *Mental retardation and congenital malformations of the central nervous system*. Chicago: Year Book Medical Publishers.

Watson, L., Crais, E., & Layton, T. (Eds.). (2000). *Handbook of early language impairment in children: Assessment and treatment*. Albany, NY: Delmar Thompson.

Wiedemann, H.R., Grosse, F.R., & Dibbern, H. (1985). *Atlas of characteristic syndromes*. Chicago: Year Book Medical Publishers.

Wolf, L.S., & Glass, R.P. (1992). *Feeding and swallowing disorders in infancy*. Tucson, AZ: Therapy Skill Builders.

Wolman, B.B. (1978). *Dictionary of behavioral sciences*. New York: Van Nostrand Reinhold.

Wolman, B.B. (Ed.). (1982). *Handbook of developmental psychology*. Upper Saddle River, NJ: Prentice Hall.

L